The Tomes of Delphi 3:
Win32 Graphical API

**by John Ayres, David Bowden, Larry Diehl,
Phil Dorcas, Kenneth Harrison, Rod Mathes,
Ovais Reza, and Mike Tobin**

Wordware Publishing, Inc.

Library of Congress Cataloging-in-Publication Data

Ayres, John.
The tomes of Delphi 3 : Win32 graphical API / by John Ayres . . . [et al.]
  p. cm.
Includes index.
ISBN 1-55622-610-1 (pbk)
1. Computer software—Development. 2. Delphi (Computer file)
3. Microsoft Win32. I. Ayers, John
QA76.76.D47T65   1997   97-49186
005.26'8--dc21   CIP

ISBN 1-55622-610-1
10 9 8 7 6 5 4 3 2 1
9801

The Ventilate font used in some Text Output Functions examples is copyright © 1997 by Brian J. Bonislawsky - Astigmatic One Eye.

All inquiries for volume purchases of this book should be addressed to Wordware Publishing, Inc., at the above address. Telephone inquiries may be made by calling:

(972) 423-0090

Dedication

John Ayres

I would like to dedicate this book to the following people and/or deities who have had a profound influence in my life: First, to God, whom I've been growing much closer to these last few years, for giving me the intelligence to wade through the confusing and sometimes maddening sea of Windows API documentation and make sense of it all; second, to my family, for putting up with my lack of participation in family activities during this project; and finally, but most of all, to my wife and soulmate, Marci, who made sure I had clothes to wear in the morning, food in the evening, fixed my lunches, and generally took up all of my housework responsibilities so I could concentrate on the book. She encouraged me and prodded me along when the weight of this project became unbearable, and because of this she is directly responsible for this work being completed. She is a very inspiring task master; cracking the whip to bring me in line when I would have rather been playing X-Wing Vs. Tie Fighter, she earned the nick-name "Dragon Lady" from the guys on the writing staff when she used the same tactics to motivate them. I am unworthy of such a devoted and loving wife, and I thank God every day for providing me with such a perfect companion. Baby, this one's for you.

David Bowden

The people listed below have left a very profound mark on my life. I have been taught, pushed, encouraged, and challenged by all of them. I can honestly say that I would have never accomplished anything had it not been for the impact and influence they have made on my life. For that I will be eternally grateful: Don and Ethel Allred, Richard and Susie Azar, Ken Blystone, Lori Bruns, Larry Bujanda, E. Davis Chauviere AIA, Sandra Crow, Alfonso Diaz, Larry F. Diehl III, Wade Driver AIA, Charles Evans, Jerry W. Francis II, Glen Hill, Patrick Smith, Ann Stewart, Dan Stiles, Volker Thein, Ryan, and Desi. Finally, and most importantly, Henry J. Dipietro PE, Intergraph Corporation. Had it not been for your insight and willingness to give me a chance, I would not be where I am today. Words cannot express my gratitude for the opportunity, encouragement, and guidance you gave me. I will never forget what you did for my career. Thanks, Hank, you da man!

Larry Diehl

I dedicate my work on this book to the past and to the future. From the bottom of my soul, I thank my wife, parents, and brother for their unwavering support through the years. That support has allowed me to reach a point in my life where I am as happy as any man could ever wish to be. In regards to the future, I only hope that our work here will in some way contribute to a better world, into which my first child shall soon be born. As for the present, it is what you make of it . . .

Phil Dorcas

To my daughters, Jennifer and Amanda, who are the joy of my life.

Kenneth Harrison

I would like to dedicate this book to my parents, Melvin and Judith Harrison, for all the sacrifices they made to provide myself and my siblings a safe, nurturing environment to grow up in, and the continuous belief that we could do anything we set our minds to. I would also like to thank Daniel Roberts and Stethman Grayson for all the fundamental knowledge of Windows and for being such good friends.

Rod Mathes

I would like to thank all of the co-authors for giving me this opportunity to be a part of such a great masterpiece. A very special thanks to John Ayres for allowing me to live even though some things were a little late at times. I would also like to give a really big thanks to my wife, Sherry, and three children, Keith, Kimberly, and Amber, who for nights on end had to live without me, but through it all we made it—we do have a life, wow!

Ovais Reza

This book is dedicated to my family and friends.

Mike Tobin

To my wife, Lisa, for putting up with my late hours on the book so close to our wedding and to my four cats for the company during those late hours.

Contents

About the Authors

John Ayres

John Ayres developed his love of programming using early home PC predecessors such as the Texas Instruments TI 99/4A and the Commodore 64. He got his start in the real world by taking classes in C and Pascal at the University of North Texas, where he participated in an advanced experimental course in computer game programming started by Dr. Ian Parberry. After college, he worked as a developer support technician at Stream International, where he authored numerous technical training manuals, and along with Kenneth Harrison produced his first professional application using Delphi 1, a call tracking database program. He moved on to become the lead developer for Puzzled Software, using Delphi 2, and also worked as a software engineer for 7th Level, where he worked on the Li'l Howie series of children's educational games. Currently, John works in Dallas at Ensemble, Inc., using Delphi 3 to create high-end client-server applications for Fortune 500 clients. He also serves on the board of directors for the Delphi Developers of Dallas users group as the director of vendor relations, contributing regularly to the group's newsletter. He has developed numerous Delphi components and shareware utilities, and has written articles for the *Delphi Informant*, including the cover article of the February 1997 issue.

David Bowden

Dave Bowden began writing programs in 1982 on a Timex Sinclair computer. This was at a time when computers were virtually unusable unless you could program them. After completing his degree in architecture from Texas Tech University, he went on to practice the profession and began developing Computer Aided Drafting (CAD) tools on the side. Eventually, he decided to leave the architecture profession and focus on what he loved the most, CAD and software development. This led to accepting a position with Intergraph Corporation where he specialized in 3D modeling, architectural workflow tools, and digital video production. As a professional developer, he got his start by creating Puzzled Software. Puzzled Software existed to develop architectural related workflow automation tools addressing the medium end CAD market. The company started out as just Dave and grew to find venture capital and become a major player in the medium level CAD market. With software for three different CAD engines and users around the world, Puzzled Software continued to grow until it eventually shut its doors after six years of development. From there he went on to become the general manager of DemoShield Corporation (a division of InstallShield), where he managed the design, development, planning, and business development for the company.

Bowden has over 10 years of experience in coding professionally and 12 years of experience in computer graphics, software development, and user interface design. Having used several different languages over the years, Delphi is now the only language he uses for development.

Larry Diehl

Larry Diehl has recently moved into a position as a Web engineer with American Airlines, where he will be part of a highly skilled team of developers using Delphi to produce applications that will be used all over the world. Prior to that, he was a quality assurance engineer with InstallShield Corporation. Over the course of nearly 15 years, Diehl has used various programming languages but currently uses Borland's Delphi exclusively for work related utilities as well as shareware applications he produces in his spare time.

Phil Dorcas

Phil Dorcas received his degree in physics from Texas Tech in 1969, and has done graduate work in physics, electrical engineering, and computer science. He was co-owner and manager of the second computer store in Texas. He has worked as consultant and designer on numerous hardware and software projects. As an author he has contributed to computer coursework for junior colleges and trade schools and written computer columns for industry magazines. Phil has used Turbo Pascal since the first version for CP/M, and now enjoys Delphi as his development tool of choice.

Kenneth Harrison

Kenneth Harrison is a certified Delphi 3 client-server developer working for Rent Roll as an Advanced Technology Group team member designing and developing Rent Roll's Portfolio, Accounting, and Screening products. Rent Roll offers management and accounting software that addresses the unique needs of property management, as well as applicant screening services. Kenneth has worked with a wide range of programs including dBASE, Pascal, Delphi, Visual Basic, and SQL. Kenneth has also worked with a wide range of hardware from the old TI 99-4As to the latest Pentium systems. He is also the Webmaster for the Delphi Developers of Dallas.

Rod Mathes

Rod Mathes has been programming for the past 12 years in several different languages. He is currently a Delphi developer for The Thomas Group Interactive Technologies, developing a wide range of software products. He has been a member of the Delphi Developers of Dallas for the past two years. He came to Delphi with a Cobol, RPGII, dBASE, RBase, Pascal, and C++ background.

Ovais Reza

Ovais Reza is a programmer/analyst working for First American. He is an experienced programmer in C/C++ and Delphi. He did his undergraduate work at Western Michigan University and is an active member of the Delphi Developers of Dallas users group. Ovais has seven years of PC- and UNIX-related experience. Currently, he is living in the Dallas area. Besides programming and pondering on the philosophies of the East, he likes to watch "The Simpsons" and old episodes of "Star Trek." His future goal is to receive his doctorate in neural networks.

Mike Tobin

Mike Tobin has been working with Delphi since version 1.0. Mike began his career in criminal justice but after realizing his purpose as a hacker, he left to join the software industry. He is currently a senior systems engineer for American General in Dallas and plays an active role in the Delphi Developers of Dallas users group as the director of communication. He enjoys spending time with his new bride, Lisa, and their four cats, Elisabeth, Alexander, Einstein, and Copernicus.

Acknowledgments

Teamwork. This abstract concept leads one to think of other abstract concepts such as victory, accomplishment, and conquest. Teamwork is the secret ingredient behind innumerable triumphs throughout history, and so it was with this book. The eight of us on the writing staff put in many long, hard hours, but this project would not have been completed without the help of so many generous, caring people. In an effort to give credit to those who deserve so much more, the writers would like to collectively thank the following people, in no particular order, for their contributions to the book:

Marian Broussard, who was our front-line proofreader. She ruthlessly pointed out all of our grammar mistakes and spelling errors, and helped correct a lot of inconsistencies in the book. She selflessly volunteered her time to help a group of new writers accurately and clearly transcribe their thoughts to paper.

Joe Hecht, our mentor and idol. Joe was always eager to answer any questions we had, looked at our code and pointed out our mistakes when we were having problems, and pointed us in the right direction when Microsoft's API documentation became a little confusing.

Jim Hill and all the good people down at Wordware Publishing, who took a chance on a bunch of eager, enthusiastic, greenhorn writers. He kept us in line, on track, and even took us all out for dinner once in a while.

DemoShield Consulting Services' Cuauhtemoc Chamorro, Henry Chung, and Dana Kovanic, for donating their time and efforts in creating the CD browser and the spectacular art for both the cover and the CD.

Our friends Jan and Jillian of Skyline tools for donating their entire evaluation line of image processing tools for the CD.

Marci Ayres, who performed a lot of code testing, grayscale image conversion, document formatting, and other support functions.

Lisa Tobin, for performing additional proofreading duties.

A very special thank you goes to Viresh Bhatia, president and CEO of InstallShield Corporation, for allowing the inclusion of both the retail version of PackageForTheWeb and the entire line of evaluation products from InstallShield.

Damon Tomlinson, who served as a backboard from which we bounced many ideas, and as a quick proofreader when no one else was available.

Marco Cocco, of D3K Artisan of Ware whose brilliant insight and help on the arcane GetGlyphOutline function led to its inclusion in the Text Output Functions chapter. Check out Artisan of Ware's website at free.websight.com/Cocco2.

Special thanks to Astigmatic One Eye for their generous donation of shareware and freeware fonts, some of which appear in the examples in the Text Output Functions chapter. Check out their impressive array of freeware and shareware fonts at www.comptechdev.com/cavop/aoe.

Of course, no acknowledgment would be complete without thanking the Delphi development staff at Borland for giving all of us such an awesome development tool.

Additionally, John Ayres would like to thank all of the writing staff for pulling together, making the sacrifices, and helping produce a product that we can all be proud of; Rusty Cornet, for introducing me to this new development environment called Delphi; Debbie Vilbig and Darla Corley, for giving me the time to learn Delphi and write a call tracking application when I should have been doing real work; Sarah Miles, for providing me with a short-term loan that allowed me to buy the machine that this book was written on; and Suzy Weaver and Brian Donahoo for trusting a former employee and providing a nice, quiet place to work on the weekends.

Foreword

The Windows API is the foundation upon which most contemporary programs are built. It is the heart and soul of database applications, multimedia applications, even many network based applications. Every Windows application relies on the Windows API to perform everything from the most mundane to the most esoteric task.

All of the good programmers I know have a solid foundation in the Windows API. It is the language in which the architecture of the Windows operating system is most eloquently expressed, and it holds the secrets programmers need to know if they want to develop powerful, well tuned applications.

There are at least three reasons why most serious programmers need to know the Windows API:

1. It is occasionally possible to write strong, robust applications without having a good understanding of the Windows API. However, there comes a time in the course of most application development projects when you simply have to turn to the Windows API in order to solve a particular problem. Usually this happens because a tool you are using does not have a feature you need, or because the feature is not implemented properly. In such cases, you have to turn to the Windows API in order to implement the feature yourself.

2. Another reason to use the Windows API surfaces when you want to create a component or utility that others can use. If you want to build a component, ActiveX control, or simple utility that will perform a useful function needed by other developers or power users, then you probably will need to turn to the Windows API. Without recourse to the Windows API, such projects are usually not feasible.

3. The final and best reason for learning the Windows API is that it helps you see how you should architect your application. We have many high-level tools these days that let us build projects at a very remote, and powerful, level of abstraction. However, each of these tools is built on top of the Windows API, and it is difficult, if not impossible, to understand how to use them without understanding the architecture on which they are founded. If you understand the Windows API, then you know what the operating system can do for you and how it goes about providing that service. With this knowledge under your belt, you can use high-level tools in an intelligent and thoughtful manner.

I am particularly pleased to see the publication of Wordware's books on the Windows API because they are built around the world's greatest development tool: Delphi. Delphi gives you full access to the entire Windows API. It is a tool designed to let you plumb the depths of the operating system, to best utilize the features that have made Windows the preeminent operating system in the world today.

Armed with these books on the Windows API, and a copy of Delphi, you can build any type of application you desire, and can be sure that it is being constructed in the optimal possible manner. No other compiler can bring you closer to the operating system, nor can any other compiler let you take better advantage of the operating system's features. These books are the Rosetta stone which forms the link between Delphi and the Windows API. Readers will be able to use them to create the most powerful applications supported by the operating system. My hat is off to the authors for providing these books as a service to the programming community.

Charles Calvert
Borland Developer Relations Manager

Introduction

The Windows programming environment. No other operating system in history has caused so much controversy or confusion among the programming industry. Of course, no other operating system in history has made so many millionaires either. Like it or not, Windows is here to stay. It's hard to ignore such a large user base, and there are few job opportunities anymore that do not require the programmer to have knowledge of the Windows environment.

In the beginning, a programmer's only choice of tools for creating Windows applications was C/C++. The age of this language has resulted in a wealth of Windows API documentation, filled with abstract and incomplete information, and examples that are as esoteric and arcane as the C language itself. Then along came Delphi. A new era in Windows programming was born, with the ability to easily create complex and advanced Windows applications with a turnaround time unheard of previously. Although Delphi tries its best to insulate the programmer from the underlying Windows architecture, Delphi programmers have found that some programming obstacles simply cannot be overcome without using low-level Windows API functions. Although there have been a few books that touched on the subject of using Windows API functions in Delphi, none have ever tackled the issue in depth. There are numerous magazine articles that describe very specific subsets of the API, but unless the Delphi programmer has a background in C, and the time to convert a C example into Delphi, there was simply no recourse of action. Thus, this book was born.

This book is a reference manual for using Windows 32-bit API functions in the Delphi environment. As such, it is not a Windows or Delphi programming tutorial, nor is it a collection of Delphi tricks that solve specific problems. To date, this book is the most complete and accurate reference to the Windows API for the Delphi programmer. It is not a complete reference, as the Windows API includes thousands upon thousands of functions that would fill many volumes much larger than the one you are holding. However, this book covers the most common and important cross section of the Windows API. Additionally, every function in this book is available under both Windows 95 and Windows NT 4.0. Most of these functions will also work under Windows NT prior to the new version.

The Featured Chapters

Chapter 1: Delphi and the Windows API

This chapter introduces the reader to *The Tomes of Delphi 3: Win32 Graphical API*. It covers general Windows programming concerns and techniques, and explains various nuances of programming with the Win32 API in the Delphi environment.

Chapter 2: Graphical Device Interface Functions

The basic Graphical Device Interface functions are integral to any graphics programming in Windows. This chapter covers functions used to manipulate and create device contexts. Examples include creating various types of device contexts, retrieving device capabilities, and changing the display mode.

Chapter 3: Painting and Drawing Functions

Basic graphical output starts with drawing lines, circles, squares, and other geometrical primitives. This chapter covers functions for all types of geometrical drawing and painting. Examples include drawing lines and shapes, creating brushes and pens, and a quick and dirty bitmap fade technique.

Chapter 4: Region and Path Functions

Region and path functions are almost ignored by most graphical programming references, yet these functions allow the developer to perform some amazing special effects. This chapter covers the functions used to create and manipulate regions and paths. Examples include clipping graphical output to a region or path, and using paths to produce special text effects.

Chapter 5: Bitmap and Metafile Functions

Bitmaps and metafiles are the two graphics formats that are natively supported by Windows. The bitmap functions are essential to almost any graphics programming in Windows, and this chapter covers the functions used to create and manipulate bitmap and metafile graphics. Examples include creating device-dependent and device-independent bitmaps, creating metafiles, and parsing metafile records.

Chapter 6: Icon, Cursor, and Caret Functions

Icons, carets, and cursors are also fundamental graphics objects. This chapter describes the functions used to create and manipulate icons, cursors, and carets. Examples include extracting icons from external files, manipulating the caret, and creating new cursors.

Chapter 7: Palette Functions

Under 256-color display drivers, palettes control the colors available to an application. This chapter covers the functions used to create new palettes, manipulate the system palette, and manipulate the palettes stored in bitmap and metafile files. Examples include extracting and setting the palette in a bitmap, creating a new palette, and palette animation.

Chapter 8: Text Output Functions

Outputting text to the screen is the most commonly performed graphical operation in almost any Windows application. No program can get by very well without displaying some kind of text, and this chapter covers those functions used to manipulate fonts and display text on the screen. Examples include enumerating fonts, retrieving font information, font embedding, and various methods of text output.

Chapter 9: Resource Functions

Although Delphi makes the need for most types of resources obsolete, a Delphi developer can still take advantage of binding such things as graphics and user-defined information to the executable. This chapter covers functions used to load and use various resource types. Examples include loading a 256-color bitmap without losing its palette information and how to use various types of user-defined resources.

Chapter 10: Window Movement Functions

Controlling a window's position can be an important part of a complex user interface. This chapter covers those functions used to control a window's position and size. Examples include moving multiple windows simultaneously and retrieving window positioning and size information.

Chapter 11: Shell Functions

The Windows environment provides many system level functions that can be very useful when manipulating files. This chapter covers those functions used to copy and move files and retrieve file information. Examples include creating an appbar application, copying and moving files, and querying file information.

Chapter 12: Menu Functions

Menus are a very common user interface navigational tool. Although Delphi wraps the menu API functions nicely, these functions can be used by the Delphi developer to perform some pretty amazing special effects with menus. This chapter covers functions used to create and manipulate menus. Examples include adding menu items to the system menu, creating bitmap menus, specifying new menu checkmark bitmaps, and using owner-drawn menus.

Appendix A: Messages

Messages are the lifeblood of Windows, and the messaging architecture allows the event-driven programming techniques used today. Although knowledge of various Windows messages is not a requirement for learning Delphi programming, it is hard to perform many complicated tasks without knowing at least some of the Windows messages. This appendix documents many of the Windows messages for which Delphi provides a message data structure.

Appendix B: Tertiary Raster Operation Codes

A chart listing all 256 tertiary raster operation codes used when performing raster operations with bitmaps and pens.

Appendix C: ASCII Character Set

A chart displaying the codes and their printable characters for the ASCII character set.

Appendix D: Virtual Key Code Chart

A chart listing the values for the Windows virtual keys.

Conventions

Certain writing conventions have been used throughout this book to convey specific meanings. All example code throughout each chapter appears in a monospace font, such as:

```
function HelloThere(Info: string): Integer;
begin
  ShowMessage(Info);
end;
```

In order to be consistent with other works on Delphi programming, the example code uses Borland's coding conventions, which includes using mixed case for variable names and identifiers, lowercase for reserved words, and nested code indented two spaces per level. Any constants used in the code will appear in all capitals, such as TRUE and FALSE. Also, notice that the name of the unit that contains an individual function is located on the same line as the function name. This unit must be included in the Uses clause of any unit in which this function is used. However, most of the functions covered in this series are located in the Windows.Pas file, which is automatically added to the Uses clause by Delphi. In addition, when the text refers to a window, as in a visual object on the screen, the word "window" will begin with a lowercase letter. When the text refers to Windows, as in the operating system, the word "Windows" will be capitalized.

Function Descriptions

The Windows API function descriptions have been laid out in a format that provides an increasing amount of detail to the reader. This should allow the reader to quickly glance at a function description for a simple reminder of required parameters, or to read further for a detailed explanation of the function, an example of its use, and any acceptable constant values used in a parameter.

Each function description includes the exact syntax found in the Delphi source code, a description of what the function does, a detailed list and description of the function's parameters, the value returned from the function, a list of related functions, and an example of its use. Any defined constants used in a function parameter are found in tables that follow the example, so that the descriptive text of the function is not broken by a distraction, and all of the constants are available in one place for easy perusal.

Sample Programs

Although every book reaches a point where the authors are frantically hacking away at the text trying to meet deadlines, the authors did not want the example code to suffer due to time restraints. Unlike some other books, we wanted to make sure that our example code worked in every case. Therefore, the writers have taken every effort to ensure that the source code on the CD works as expected and that the code in the book is the exact code on the CD. This should guarantee that code entered straight from the text will work as described. However, most of the code examples rely on buttons, edit boxes, or other components residing on the form, which may not be apparent from the code listing. When in doubt, always look at the source code included on the CD.

The CD-ROM

The companion CD-ROM that accompanies this book is a multimedia experience containing all of the source code from the book, a complete Delphi syntax-compliant help file, shareware, freeware, and an assortment of third-party development and evaluation tools. Using the CD Browser you can navigate through the CD and choose which applications and chapter code to install with a single mouse click. Using the CD Browser is simple; on a Windows 95 or Windows NT system, simply insert the CD and the browser will begin automatically.

The third-party development and evaluation tools include:

Eagle Software:

reAct

reAct version 2.0 is the ultimate component test file generator for Delphi 2.0. With it, you can quickly generate test programs for components, view and change properties at run-time with the built-in Component Inspector, monitor events in real-time (as events are triggered, LED lights flash), set breakpoints, and log events visually and dynamically. You can find elusive bugs, evaluate third-party components, and learn how poorly documented components really work. If you build or purchase components, you need this tool. It's totally integrated with Delphi 2.0 and the CDK 2.0.

InstallShield Software Corporation:

PackageForTheWeb: FREE Retail version

Rapidly deploy your applications and ActiveX controls on the Internet with Package-ForTheWeb. Create self-extracting EXEs or CAB files to distribute your applications and components. PackageForTheWeb requests all the information needed in a simple wizard and immediately builds the file to your specifications. PackageForTheWeb will also digitally sign files so your customers know they are getting authentic software. This is a complete FREE version of this program courtesy of InstallShield Corporation.

DemoShield 5.3 Evaluation Edition

DemoShield is a demo creation tool that lets even nontechnical Windows users design interactive software demos, tutorials, and CD browsers. Multimedia demos are a snap with DemoShield's SmartTemplates and wizards that automate demo creation, software simulation, and distribution by floppy disk, CD, intranet, or the Internet. Use our point-and-click designer and prebuilt templates to create fully interactive demonstrations easily. When you finish designing, our Setup Wizard walks you through the steps to create a custom installation that sets up your demo on any Windows PC.

InstallShield5.1 Evaluation Edition

InstallShield5.1 Evaluation Edition will forever change the way commercial developers create world-class bulletproof installation systems for Windows applications. InstallShield5.1 features an installation integrated development environment (IDE) with integrated visual file layout and media-building tools. A Microsoft Visual C++-like IDE offers developers unprecedented levels of productivity for application installation design, development, and deployment. The new multiple-document interface eliminates multiple steps in the installation development process. A color syntax highlighted editor allows you to build and manage large-scale scripts.

Nevrona:

ReportPrinter Pro 2.0 Demo

ReportPrinter Pro provides a powerful and flexible suite of reporting components and classes. It contains 13 components with over 400 methods, properties, and events and compiles into your application with no external files. A few of its features are word wrapped memos, full graphics, justification, precise page positioning, real world measurements, printer configuration, font control, full-featured print preview, and it works both with or without a database. ReportPrinter Pro 2.0 can easily handle banded style reports (with master-detail to unlimited levels), cross tabs, form letters, invoices, snaking columns, preprinted forms, and any other report you will want to create.

Propel 2.0 Demo

Propel helps you reuse your code and components better by combining the flexibility of cut and paste, the reusability of components and the power of form inheritance into a single package called a feature. Features allow you to connect any component's behavior to other components, even of completely different types. As much as components have changed the way you program, features will enhance your development process and must be seen to be believed.

AdHocery 1.1 Demo

AdHocery is a set of visual components that can be used to create completely custom ad hoc query interfaces. A variety of designs includes grid based, list based, outline based, or a unique tree view to allow the best designs for your application. AdHocery even includes a custom TDataSource component that can be linked with any data control component for powerful form based queries. If you have been searching for a good SQL based query tool that your users can understand, AdHocery is the answer.

Oops Software:

Sifter

Sifter is a new type of image management utility. With Sifter, you will find it exceedingly easy to view, convert, sort, and delete all common image formats. This software was written in response to a need that arose with the introduction of applications specifically designed to automatically download images from the Internet. After letting one of these applications run for several hours, I find myself with a directory full of images and no convenient way of sorting through them. Other image viewing applications are written to view, edit, and save images. They are not designed to view and delete. Sifter is.

AfterImage

AfterImage is a powerful batch image translation and manipulation tool. If you use, collect, or need to manipulate several images at one time, download a copy of AfterImage today. A must for serious collectors, art directors, graphic artists, web developers, or anyone who works with digital images. With AfterImage, you can process thousands of images automatically without ever having to use other drawing or image programs again. AfterImage is an easy-to-use utility that gives you powerful image editing and processing functions.

Digital Metaphors:

Piparti Pro 3.0

Piparti Pro 3.0 is a native Delphi reporting tool featuring an interactive report designer and previewer, standard components (text, shapes, lines), advanced components (regions, rich text, memos), subreports (multiple master-detail, side-by-side), full printer and page setup control, report templates, precision (to thousandths of mm), open data access, international support (11 languages), end-user report designer, end-user application framework, and report wizard. Piparti 3.0 and Piparti Pro 3.0 include versions for Delphi 1, 2, and 3, and ship with full source code. Demo copies are available at http://www.digital-metaphors.com.

Skyline:

Corporate Suite

The ImageLib Corporate Suite Document Imaging package is the first Delphi and C++Builder VCL package to add "reading and writing" of TIFF3/CITT, TIFF4/CITT, Multipage TIFF, Packbits, and LZW to its already robust imaging package.

The Edge

This great add-on package of special effects allows users of ImageLib to add these features to their programs.

Gif Shaker

Using Gif Shaker, web designers can create, open, save, scan, and edit 256-color images with a powerful built-in visual editor—giving them unprecedented control over their web animations. And with Gif Shaker's time-saving collection of 34 plug-n-play filters, web designers will now be able to effortlessly add professional special effects to their animated GIFs—right out of the box.

ImageLib

ImageLib allows programmers to implement BMP, CMS, GIF, ICO, JPG, PCX, PNG, SCM, TIF, and WMF images into their applications. In addition, AVI, MOV, MID, WAV, and RMI multimedia formats are supported. These image and multimedia formats can be implemented to/from a file or database BLOB field. This Twain-compliant release of ImageLib is available in a combo package (includes both 16- and 32-bit versions) with source code examples and online documentation.

Turbo Power:

Abbrevia

Add a little ZIP to your Delphi and C++Builder programs. Finally, it's easy to add industry standard, PKZIP-compatible archiving features to your Delphi and C++Builder applications: Just drop in Abbrevia components from Turbo Power Software Company. Abbrevia components deliver the full power of PKZIP in native VCL components that compile right into your program. There are no DLLs to distribute and install. Just drop in Abbrevia components and compile in real ZIP power!

Async Professional

To add high-powered serial communications and fax support to your Delphi and C++Builder programs, there's simply no better choice then Async Professional. No other product delivers this kind of flexibility and capability in native VCL components.

Essentials, Volume I

You see them everywhere, the cool controls that make programs really shine. Now it's easy to add those same controls to your programs. Essentials has 13 absolutely must-have components you'll use in virtually every app you write. Use them right out of the box or customize them anyway you like. Just like the components in Delphi itself, Essentials are native VCL controls so there's nothing extra to distribute and install. Essentials components compile right in. And Essentials work equally well in all versions of Delphi and C++Builder.

OnGuard

Every day thousands of 'net surfers download programs from the Internet, AOL, CompuServe, and electronic bulletin boards. Sometimes they pay for what they use. Often they don't. That's the reality of the new medium for software distribution. It's easy to get software into the hands of your potential customers, but it can be hard to convert those users into paying customers. But OnGuard can help. OnGuard lets you take advantage of world-wide software distribution via the Internet while protecting your intellectual property.

Orpheus

With over 50 components, 100 classes, and nearly 100,000 lines of code, Orpheus is the powerhouse toolset that's a natural companion to Delphi and C++Builder. Orpheus components expand the VCL tool palette with capabilities Delphi and C++Builder just don't provide, like scrolling checkbox lists, incremental search fields, and data-entry fields editors for every native data type. Then Orpheus extends some of the existing VCL components to give them professional power.

Memory Sleuth

Like the very best detectives, Memory Sleuth doesn't just warn you about problems, it reports back to you with details. With Memory Sleuth at your side, finding memory and resource leaks is a snap. Never before have Delphi developers had this kind of power at their fingertips. Memory Sleuth's streamlined interface identifies problems and puts them right in front of you so you can make the necessary changes and move on. Allocation errors are identified with the exact line number in your source code where the allocation took place. Don't bother translating hexadecimal addresses to seek out problem code; Memory Sleuth does the dirty work for you.

SysTools

Stop wasting time recoding the same routines, and leverage the power of SysTools in your next Delphi project. SysTools brings together over 600 popular routines for string manipulation, date and time arithmetic, high-precision mathematics, sorting, and much more.

Additional Tools:

Astigmatic One Eye Fonts

Freeware, Shareware, and Purchasable Fonts Galore © 1997 by Astigmatic One Eye Fonts. The freeware fonts included in this pack were created by Astigmatic One Eye

Font Foundry. Since November of 1997, I have been striving to create as many high quality fonts as I can, sometimes serious, sometimes bizarre, always interesting, and at least one new FREEWARE font EVERY MONTH! Available for Macintosh and Windows PC in TrueType format, (in the pack also available in PostScript Type 1 format with .AFM and .PFM files). There are currently over 50 fonts available online for viewing and download or purchase. If you download our Freeware fonts don't forget to check out what's available for purchase; after all, without your support we will be unable to offer you FREE fonts EVERY MONTH. Any $10 or more font purchase will get the full version of that particular font in whatever format best suits your needs (PostScript or TrueType), and also a full copy of one of our special freebie with purchase fonts, some of our freeware fonts, and trial versions of some of our latest releases. Be sure to check out our full variety of fonts, always growing. Visit A.O.E. at: http://www.comptechdev.com/cavop/aoe or send e-mail to: astigma@comptechdev.com

Complete chapter code from the book along with examples ready to compile.

A comprehensive help file that can be added to and used from Delphi.

Who This Book is For

Due to the nature of reference manuals, and the lack of any involved explanations into general Windows or Delphi programming, this book is intended for use by experienced Delphi programmers with a working knowledge of Windows programming. This is not to say that intermediate or beginning Delphi programmers will not benefit from this book; in fact, there are quite a few example programs included that solve a number of everyday programming conundrums. The heavily documented examples should provide enough explanation for even the most neophyte Delphi programmer. As a reference manual, the book is not intended to be read sequentially. However, the chapters have been laid out in a logical order of progression, starting with the most fundamental Windows API functions and working towards the more specialized functions.

If you are looking for an introduction to Delphi programming, or a step-by-step Windows programming tutorial, there are plenty of other fine books out there to get you started. However, if you've got a nasty problem whose only hope of salvation is using the Windows API, if you want to extend the functionality of Delphi components and objects, or if you want a down-and-dirty, no-holds-barred collection of Delphi Win32 API programming examples, then this book is for you. You will not find a more complete and accurate guide to the Win32 API for the Delphi programmer.

Chapter 1

Delphi and the Windows API

Delphi has brought a new era to Windows programming. Never before has it been so easy to create robust, full-featured applications for the Windows environment with such short development times. Now in its third incarnation, Delphi is known worldwide as the de facto visual Windows programming environment. No other visual programming tool even comes close to matching Delphi's power, ease of use, or quality of executables.

One of Delphi's strengths is the Visual Component Library, Borland's new object model. This object model has allowed the Delphi development team to encapsulate the vast majority of Windows programming tedium into easy to use components. Earlier Windows programming languages required the developer to write large amounts of code just to squeeze a minimal amount of functionality out of Windows. The mere act of creating a window and accepting menu selections could take pages of code to create. Delphi's excellent encapsulation of this dreary requirement of Windows programming has turned what once was a chore into a fun, exciting experience.

The Windows API Versus the VCL

The Delphi development team did a world-class job of encapsulating that vast majority of important Windows API functionality into the VCL. However, due to the vastness of the Windows API, it would be impossible and impractical to wrap every API function in an Object Pascal object. To achieve certain goals or solve specific problems, a developer may be forced to use lower-level Windows API functions that are simply not encapsulated by a Delphi object. It may also be necessary to extend the functionality of a Delphi object, and if this object encapsulates some part of the Windows API, it will be the API that the developer will likely have to use to extend the functionality by any great amount.

Windows Data Types

Windows API functions use a number of data types that may be unfamiliar to the casual Delphi programmer. These data types are all taken from the original C header files that define the Windows API function syntax. For the most part, these new data types are simply Pascal data types that have been renamed to make them similar to the original data types used in legacy Windows programming languages. This was done so that experienced Windows programmers would understand the parameter types and function return values, and the function prototypes would match the syntax shown in existing Windows API documentation to avoid confusion. The following table outlines the most common Windows data types and their correlating Object Pascal data type.

Table 1-1: Windows Data Types

Windows Data Type	Object Pascal Data Type	Description
LPSTR	PAnsiChar;	String pointer
LPCSTR	PAnsiChar;	String pointer
DWORD	Integer;	Whole numbers
BOOL	LongBool;	Boolean values
PBOOL	^BOOL;	Pointer to a Boolean value
Pbyte	^Byte;	Pointer to a byte value
PINT	^Integer;	Pointer to an integer value
Psingle	^Single;	Pointer to a single (floating point) value
PWORD	^Word;	Pointer to a 16-bit value
PDWORD	^DWORD;	Pointer to a 32-bit value
LPDWORD	PDWORD;	Pointer to a 32-bit value
UCHAR	Byte;	8-bit values (can represent characters)
PUCHAR	^Byte;	Pointer to 8-bit values
SHORT	Smallint;	16-bit whole numbers
UINT	Integer;	32-bit whole numbers. Traditionally, this was used to represent unsigned integers, but Object Pascal does not have a true unsigned integer data type.
PUINT	^UINT;	Pointer to 32-bit whole numbers
ULONG	Longint;	32-bit whole numbers. Traditionally, this was used to represent unsigned integers, but Object Pascal does not have a true unsigned integer data type.
PULONG	^ULONG;	Pointer to 32-bit whole numbers
PLongint	^Longint;	Pointer to 32-bit values
PInteger	^Integer;	Pointer to 32-bit values
PSmallInt	^Smallint;	Pointer to 16-bit values
PDouble	^Double;	Pointer to double (floating point) values
LCID	DWORD;	A local identifier
LANGID	Word;	A language identifier
THandle	Integer;	An object handle. Many Windows API functions return a value of type THandle, which identifies that object within Windows' internal object tracking tables.
PHandle	^THandle;	A pointer to a handle

Windows Data Type	Object Pascal Data Type	Description
WPARAM	Longint;	A 32-bit message parameter. Under earlier versions of Windows, this was a 16-bit data type.
LPARAM	Longint;	A 32-bit message parameter
LRESULT	Longint;	A 32-bit function return value
HWND	Integer;	A handle to a window. All windowed controls, child windows, main windows, etc., have a corresponding window handle that identifies them within Windows' internal tracking tables.
HHOOK	Integer;	A handle to an installed Windows system hook
ATOM	Word;	An index into the local or global atom table for a string
HGLOBAL	THandle;	A handle identifying a globally allocated dynamic memory object. Under 32-bit Windows, there is no distinction between globally and locally allocated memory.
HLOCAL	THandle;	A handle identifying a locally allocated dynamic memory object. Under 32-bit Windows, there is no distinction between globally and locally allocated memory.
FARPROC	Pointer;	A pointer to a procedure, usually used as a parameter type in functions that require a callback function
HGDIOBJ	Integer;	A handle to a GDI object. Pens, device contexts, brushes, etc., all have a handle of this type that identifies them within Windows' internal tracking tables.
HBITMAP	Integer;	A handle to a Windows bitmap object
HBRUSH	Integer;	A handle to a Windows brush object
HDC	Integer;	A handle to a device context
HENHMETAFILE	Integer;	A handle to a Windows enhanced metafile object
HFONT	Integer;	A handle to a Windows logical font object
HICON	Integer;	A handle to a Windows icon object
HMENU	Integer;	A handle to a Windows menu object
HMETAFILE	Integer;	A handle to a Windows metafile object
HINST	Integer;	A handle to an instance object
HMODULE	HINST;	A handle to a module
HPALETTE	Integer;	A handle to a Windows color palette
HPEN	Integer;	A handle to a Windows pen object
HRGN	Integer;	A handle to a Windows region object
HRSRC	Integer;	A handle to a Windows resource object
HKL	Integer;	A handle to a keyboard layout
HFILE	Integer;	A handle to an open file
HCURSOR	HICON;	A handle to a Windows mouse cursor object
COLORREF	DWORD;	A Windows color reference value, containing values for the red, green, and blue components of a color

Handles

An important concept in Windows programming is the concept of an object handle. Many functions return a handle to an object that the function created or loaded from a resource. Functions like CreateWindow and CreateWindowEx return a window handle. Other functions return a handle to an open file, like CreateFile, or return a handle to a newly allocated heap, like HeapCreate. Internally, Windows keeps track of all of these handles, and the handle serves as the link through the operating system between the object and the application. It is this mechanism that allows an application to communicate so seamlessly with the operating system. Using these handles, an application can easily refer to any of these objects and the operating system instantly knows which object a piece of code wants to manipulate.

Constants

The Windows API functions declare literally thousands upon thousands of different constants to be used as parameter values. Constants for everything from color values to return values have been defined in the Windows.Pas file. The constants that are defined for each API function are listed with that function within the text. However, the Windows.Pas file may yield more information concerning the constants for any particular function, and it is a good rule of thumb to check this Delphi source code file when using complicated functions.

Strings

All Windows API functions that use strings require a pointer to a null-terminated string type. Windows is written in C, which does not have the Pascal string type. Earlier versions of Delphi required the application to allocate a string buffer and convert the String type to a PChar. However, Delphi 3's new string conversion mechanism allows a string to be used as a PChar by simply typecasting it (i.e., PChar(MyString), where MyString is declared as MyString: string). For the most part, this conversion will work with almost all Windows API functions that require a string parameter.

Importing Windows Functions

The Windows API is huge. It defines functions for almost every kind of utility or comparison or action that a programmer could think of. Due to the sheer volume of Windows API functions, some functions simply fell through the cracks and were not imported by the Delphi source code. Since all Windows API functions are simply functions exported from a DLL, importing a new Windows API function is a relatively simple process, if the function parameters are known.

Importing a new Windows API function is exactly like importing any other function from a DLL. For example, the BroadcastSystemMessage function described in the Message Processing Functions chapter of *The Tomes of Delphi 3: Win32 Core API* is not imported by the Delphi source code. In order to import this function for use within an application, it is simply declared as a function from within a DLL as:

```
function BroadcastSystemMessage(Flags: DWORD; Recipients: PDWORD;
    uiMessage: UINT; wParam: WPARAM; lParam: LPARAM): Longint; stdcall;

implementation

function BroadcastSystemMessage; external user32 name 'BroadcastSystemMessage';
```

As long as the parameters required by the function and the DLL containing the function are known, any Windows API function can be imported and used by a Delphi application. It is important to note that the stdcall directive must be appended to the prototype for the function, as this defines the standard mechanism by which Windows passes parameters to a function on the stack.

Incorrectly Imported Functions

Some functions have been incorrectly imported by the Delphi source code. These exceptions are noted in the individual function descriptions. For the most part, the functions that have been imported incorrectly deal with the ability to pass NIL as a value to a pointer parameter, usually to retrieve the required size of a buffer so the buffer can be dynamically allocated to the exact length before calling the function to retrieve the real data. In Delphi, some of these functions have been imported with parameters defined as VAR or CONST. These types of parameters can accept a pointer to a buffer but can never be set to NIL, thus limiting the use of the function within the Delphi environment. As is the case with almost anything in Delphi, it is a simple matter to fix. Simply reimport the function as if it did not exist, as outlined above. Functions that have been imported incorrectly are identified in their individual function descriptions throughout the book.

Callback Functions

Another very important concept in Windows programming is that of a callback function. A callback function is a function within the developer's application that is never called directly by any other function or procedure within that application but is instead called by the Windows operating system. This allows Windows to communicate directly with the application, passing it various parameters as defined by the individual callback function. Most of the enumeration functions require some form of application-defined callback function that receives the enumerated information.

Individual callback functions have specific parameters that must be declared exactly by the application. This is required so that Windows passes the correct information to the application in the correct order. A good example of a function that uses a callback function is EnumWindows. The EnumWindows function parses through all top-level windows on the screen, passing the handle of each window to an application-defined callback function. This continues until all top-level windows have been enumerated or the callback function returns FALSE. The callback function used by EnumWindows is defined as:

EnumWindowsProc(
hWnd: HWND;   {a handle to a top-level window}
lParam: LPARAM   {the application-defined data}
): BOOL;   {returns TRUE or FALSE}

A function matching this function prototype is created within the application, and a pointer to the function is passed as one of the parameters to the EnumWindows function. The Windows operating system calls this callback function for each top-level window, passing the window's handle in one of the callback function's parameters. It is important to note that the stdcall directive must be appended to the prototype for the callback function, as this defines the standard mechanism by which Windows passes parameters to a function on the stack. For example, the above callback function would be prototyped as:

```
EnumWindowsProc(hWnd: HWND; lParam: LPARAM); stdcall;
```

Without the stdcall directive, Windows will not be able to access the callback function. This powerful software mechanism, in many cases, allows an application to retrieve information about the system that is only stored internally by Windows and would otherwise be unreachable. For a complete example of callback function usage, see the EnumWindows function, and many other functions throughout the book.

Function Parameters

The vast majority of Windows API functions simply take the static parameters handed to them and perform some function based on the value of the parameters. However, certain functions return values that must be stored in a buffer, and that buffer is passed to the function in the form of a pointer. In most cases, when the function description specifies that it returns some value in a buffer, null-terminated string buffer, or a pointer to a data structure, these buffers and data structures must be allocated by the application before the function is called.

In many cases, a parameter may state that it can contain one or more values from some table. These values are defined as constants, and they are combined using the Boolean OR operator. The actual value passed to the function usually identifies a bitmask, where the state of each bit has some significance to the function. This is why the constants can be combined using Boolean operations. For example, the CreateWindow function has a parameter called dwStyle which can accept a number of constants combined with the Boolean OR operator. To pass more than one constant to the function, the parameter would be set to something like "WS_CAPTION or WS_CHILD or WS_CLIPCHILDREN". This would create a child window that includes a caption bar and would clip around its child windows during painting.

Conversely, when a function states that it returns one or more values that are defined as specific constants, the return value can be combined with one of the constants using the

Boolean AND operator to determine if that constant is contained within the return value. If the result of the combination is equal to the constant (i.e., if(Result and WS_CHILD)=WS_CHILD then …), the constant is included in the return value.

Unicode

Originally, software only needed a single byte to define a character within a character set. This allowed for up to 256 characters, which was more than plenty for the entire alphabet, numbers, punctuation symbols, and common mathematical symbols. However, due to the shrinking of the global community and the subsequent internationalization of Windows and Windows software, a new method of identifying characters was needed. Many languages have well over 256 characters used for writing, much more than a single byte can describe. Therefore, Unicode was invented. A Unicode character is 16 bits long, and can therefore identify 65,535 characters within a language's alphabet. To accommodate the new character set type, many Windows API functions come in two flavors: ANSI and Unicode. When browsing the Windows.Pas source code, many functions are defined with an A or W appended to the end of the function name, identifying them as an ANSI function or Wide character (Unicode) function. The functions within this book cover only the ANSI functions. However, the Unicode functions usually differ only in the type of string information passed to a function, and if the string is in Unicode format, the text within this book should adequately describe the Unicode function's behavior.

Chapter 2

Graphical Device Interface Functions

The Windows Graphical Device Interface (GDI) functions form the heart of the display system for Windows 95 and Windows NT. This graphical system provides access to the display, printer, and plotter devices through a rich set of API functions.

Software which interacts with an output device must go through two major levels of abstraction: the Windows GDI kernel and the manufacturer's device driver. The device driver is a specific software interface for a hardware device, and the GDI provides the interface to the device driver for Windows applications. The GDI is capable of connecting to a variety of devices, even those which do not provide the sophisticated routines available in more advanced devices. In some areas the GDI must take up the slack when the device driver does not provide high-level support.

The GDI is capable of supporting several kinds of devices simultaneously while maintaining a consistent interface to the application's program. The GDI must therefore be able to manage a collection of device drivers with varying capabilities and relate to them according to their functionality. It must do this while presenting to the application a consistent set of API functions which allow the programmer freedom from dealing with the devices directly.

The GDI functions operate at various levels depending on how specific the application needs to be with graphical output. At a low level, an application can manipulate an image on a pixel-by-pixel basis. At a higher level, an application can issue commands such as drawing ellipses or other device-independent graphical primitives. The GDI commands are processed by the GDI.EXE kernel in the Windows operating system and then passed to the device driver for that graphical output device according to the capabilities of the driver. Delphi encapsulates the majority of GDI functions through the TCanvas object. However, it is sometimes necessary to use lower level GDI functions to perform such tasks as drawing in nonclient areas of windows or changing the window mapping mode. This chapter covers those functions used to manipulate device contexts and modify coordinate systems.

Device Independence

Windows supports a wide variety of output devices with varying capabilities. It is the task of the GDI to be able to understand the level of support that a particular device driver can provide, and issue commands to that driver based on that driver's individual capability.

If an application issues a command to draw an ellipse on a device, the GDI will determine whether that device is sophisticated enough to handle a high-level command for drawing an ellipse. If so, it will provide the most efficient set of commands to that device driver so that the image may be drawn under control of the driver. However, if the device has no such capability, the GDI must assume the drawing responsibility and issue lower level commands, perhaps on a pixel-by-pixel basis, to achieve the same results.

Regardless of the device driver that is supporting the output device, the GDI gives the high-level capability to the application. The programmer is generally not burdened with the task of knowing how to write code for formatting an image on a variety of output devices. That is the task of the GDI. There is a rich mixture of both high-level and low-level commands for presenting output from the Win32 API.

The programmer can generally choose how device independent the application will be. The API functions which reference hardware pixels will not be device independent, because devices of differing resolutions will show the images with their own capabilities. There would be no automatic scaling to account for the different resolutions. The functions which are given in terms of logical measurements instead of pixels are more device independent. The Win32 GDI system performs many internal tasks which map the API requests into device specific commands, thereby giving the application a level of separation from the hardware.

Device Contexts

Windows contains an internal structure for images which are displayable or printable. These internal structures are known as device contexts, and contain information about how the image is to be presented. GDI functions need this handle because the device context structure contains information about presentation attributes, the coordinate system, clipping, graphics objects, and display modes. The graphics objects can include pens, brushes, bitmaps, palettes, regions, and paths. An application will not access a device context structure's information directly. The information in a device context is obtained and manipulated by using API calls. There are functions to get or create a device context, set or obtain device context attributes, and to release a device context.

The GetDC and GetWindowDC functions will obtain device context handles representing the displayable surface of a window. These device contexts can be used in subsequent drawing functions to produce output directly on the window or form. A memory-based device context can be created with the CreateCompatibleDC function.

This allows an application to prepare images offscreen that will later be copied to the surface of the window.

Device Context Types

A device context may be one of three types: common, class, or private. When the device context refers to a display, it may be called a display context and refer to a specific area on the screen, such as a window, the client area of a window, or the entire display.

Display context types are created based on the class options for the window when the window is registered. The following table describes the display context type retrieved by a call to the GetDC function as a result of the applicable class styles registered by the window.

Table 2-1: Class Flags and Display Contexts

Value	Description
none	A new device context must be obtained for each occurrence where one is needed. It is created with default values. The default clipping region is the client area. This is a common device context, and it is allocated from the application's heap space. There is no practical limit to the number of common device contexts that can be created other than memory limitations, but it is good practice to return the memory associated with a common device context by calling the ReleaseDC function when it is no longer needed.
CS_CLASSDC	A single display context is shared for all windows of the same class. Changes made to a display context will affect all other windows created from the same class. The use of class device contexts is not recommended.
CS_OWNDC	A private device context is created for the window. Each window will have its own device context, and the attributes of the device context are persistent. After the GetDC function is called the first time, any changes to the device context will be present when it is next retrieved. It is unnecessary to call the ReleaseDC function for private device contexts. This provides a boost in performance at the cost of approximately 800 additional bytes of memory per window.

In general, if the application will be performing few graphical output operations, common device contexts will provide all the functionality necessary. However, for graphically intense applications that will be drawing to the screen continuously, it is advisable to create a window with a private device context. The following example illustrates how to use the CS_OWNDC class style to create a window with a private device context.

2

Chapter

Listing 2-I: Creating a Window with a Private Device Context

```
var
  Form1: TForm1;
  NewBrush,                    // a handle to a new brush
  OldBrush: HBRUSH;            // holds the old brush

implementation

{$R *.DFM}

procedure TForm1.CreateParams(var Params: TCreateParams);
begin
  {initialize the parameters with default values}
  inherited CreateParams(Params);

  {indicate that this window should have its own device context. comment
   this line out to see the effects}
  Params.WindowClass.style := Params.WindowClass.Style or CS_OWNDC;
end;

procedure TForm1.FormActivate(Sender: TObject);
var
  TempDC: HDC;             // a temporary device context handle
begin
  {retrieve a handle to the private device context for this window}
  TempDC := GetDC(Form1.Handle);

  {create a new brush and select it into this device context}
  NewBrush := CreateHatchBrush(HS_DIAGCROSS, clRed);
  OldBrush := SelectObject(TempDC, NewBrush);

  {release the device context. note that since we are dealing with a private
   device context, the new brush will remain within the device context.}
  ReleaseDC(Form1.Handle, TempDC);
end;

procedure TForm1.FormPaint(Sender: TObject);
var
  TempDC: HDC;               // a temporary device context handle
begin
  {retrieve a handle to the private device context}
  TempDC := GetDC(Form1.Handle);

  {draw a rectangle. note that we are not creating a new brush, so the
   rectangle should be filled with the default brush selected in a device
   context.  since this is a private device context, it will use the brush
   previously selected to fill the rectangle}
  Rectangle(TempDC, 0, 0, ClientWidth, ClientHeight);

  {release the device context}
  ReleaseDC(Form1.Handle, TempDC);
end;
```

```
procedure TForm1.FormDestroy(Sender: TObject);
begin
  {delete the brush}
  SelectObject(GetDC(Form1.Handle), OldBrush);
  DeleteObject(NewBrush);
end;
```

Screen, Window, and Client Area Device Contexts

By default, display contexts relate to a window client area. This is where drawing is normally performed. It is also possible to obtain a device context for the entire window or for the display.

A device context for a window is obtained by using the GetWindowDC function. It obtains a device context for the window that includes the nonclient area (borders, title bar, etc). The device context is always a common device context and shares no properties with other device contexts regardless of type. Any changes to a device context retrieved from the GetWindowDC function will not affect private device contexts.

A device context for the entire screen is obtained by calling the GetDC function with zero as a window handle. This allows an application to perform drawing operations directly on the screen surface, drawing over windows or any other graphics. Drawing to the screen in this manner violates general Windows programming rules, however, and is not recommended.

Coordinate Systems

Windows provides several different coordinate systems for producing graphical output on display or print devices. The coordinate system can be based on device units, such as pixels, or it can be a logical measurement system, where one logical unit might translate into one or more pixels based on the method in which the logical units are mapped. A relative or logical coordinate system will allow an application to have a common set of commands which produce similar effects on different devices even when those devices have different display properties.

Graphical output is performed on a display or printing device which has its own units of measurement. The output device performs operations in pixels. The pixel is the single unit point of output on the device. It is sometimes called the device unit. The coordinate system at the device performs measurements in pixels (device units). Many of the graphical API functions use device units as a reference.

Location of pixels on a screen or printer is generally relative to an origin at the upper left corner of the paper, screen, window, or client area of a window. In most cases the measurement values increase as the pixel point moves down or to the right of the origin. Device coordinate systems make the measurements in actual pixels, so that if the device has 100 pixels to the inch, then a point one inch down from the origin would have a vertical coordinate of 100.

The GDI provides some high-level functions which use logical coordinate systems. Such a system can provide the application with a logical representation of the drawing canvas which has measurements which are independent of that device's pixel resolution. The GDI functions which use logical coordinates will perform a translation on the coordinates and then issue commands to the device driver in its device coordinate system. This translation of measurements between logical and device coordinates is supported by a rich set of API function calls.

Some GDI functions support the higher level logical coordinates, and some functions apply only to pixel operations. The GDI functions which apply to logical coordinates are generally the drawing commands, which by default provide no mapping and seem, in effect, to be applied directly to pixel measurements. To obtain device-independent mapping of logical coordinates, an application must set a mapping mode and use the offset and scaling capabilities described below.

Each device context maintains a structure containing information needed to map logical coordinates to device coordinates. The device context for a display knows the hardware characteristics well enough to support the GDI calls which perform the coordinate mappings. The translations are performed at the device context level, and each creation of a device context needs its mapping mode set if it is to be able to convert from logical to display coordinates.

Mapping Logical Coordinates into Device Coordinates

The mapping of logical coordinates to display coordinates involves several possible GDI functions. There is an origin offset that can be applied to the logical coordinate reference, which is called the *window*, and an offset that can be applied to the device coordinate reference, which is called the *viewport*. Similarly, there are scaling factors which can be applied to the window and to the viewport. The point that is given in logical coordinates may make a mathematical transformation if it is allowed to do so by the mapping mode that is in effect for the display context. The MM_TEXT mode is the default mapping mode, which provides for a 1:1 mapping from logical to display coordinates.

The calculations for coordinate transformations take place for the horizontal and vertical components independently, and consist of the following mathematical operations:

xViewport = (xWindow - xWindowOrg) * (xViewportExt/xWindowExt) + xViewportOrg.

yViewport = (yWindow - yWindowOrg) * (yViewportExt/yWindowExt) + yViewportOrg.

The logical coordinate has the logical offset applied to it, then is multiplied by the scaling factor between the logical and device extents, and then has the device offset applied to it. It would be simpler to apply the scaling factor and offset to only the logical system or to the device system, but these are whole numbers, not floating point values. Also, the transformation can be designed with several devices in mind, where the applications of offset and scaling for logical ("window") coordinates apply to all devices.

Applications to the device ("viewport") might be programmed to apply to different devices in a custom manner.

The "org" functions are concerned with a quantity being added or subtracted to a coordinate as it is changed from logical to device environments. The "ext" functions are concerned with the coordinate being scaled, made larger or smaller, as it is changed from logical to device environments. Each of these concepts has a property in both the logical and the device environment. The SetWindowOrgEx function, for example, sets the value for how much is subtracted from a coordinate as it leaves the logical coordinate system. The SetViewportOrgEx sets the value that is added to the coordinate as it reaches the device coordinate system. SetWindowExtEx sets a factor that is divided out of the coordinate as it leaves the logical coordinate system, and SetViewportExtEx sets a factor that is multiplied by the coordinate as it arrives at the device coordinate system. This is the behavior that is expressed in the mathematical formulas above.

Mapping Modes

The default mapping mode in a device context is MM_TEXT, which is a 1:1 translation and therefore no transformations take place. GDI functions which are specified to be in "logical units" are really also in device units when the MM_TEXT mode is in effect. For an application to use true logical coordinates, the mapping mode must be changed. The SetMapMode function is used for this purpose. The MM_ANISOTROPIC mode allows for complete flexibility in programming origin offsets and scaling. With this mode (and others except for MM_TEXT and MM_ISOTROPIC) it is possible to scale horizontal and vertical factors differently, resulting in skewed images. The basic unit of measurement stems from the pixel at the device level, with scaling and offsets applied as per settings by the programmer. MM_ISOTROPIC is similar to MM_ANISOTROPIC except that horizontal and vertical scaling are ensured to be maintained the same. The other mapping modes have built-in initial scaling factors based on the resolution of the device. They are initialized for specific units of measurement for logical coordinates. An application can place coordinates on a canvas based on actual physical measurements, while letting the GDI figure out how many pixels it takes to produce that measured coordinate.

Listing 2-2 illustrates how to move the origin and to apply a scaling factor to coordinate transformations. It allows the user to select a mapping mode, apply offsets to the logical (window) and device (viewport) systems, and apply scaling factors to the logical and device systems. The example displays the "org" and "ext" values currently in effect. The org values may be modified with the SetWindowOrgEx, SetViewportOrgEx, OffsetWindowOrgEx, and OffsetViewportOrgEx functions. The scaling or "ext" extents may be modified with the SetWindowExtEx, SetViewportExtEx, ScaleWindowExtEx, and ScaleViewportExtEx functions.

Listing 2-2: Modifying the Viewport and Window Extents and Origins

```
var
  Form1: TForm1;
  WOrigin: TPoint;          // holds the window origin
  VOrigin: TPoint;          // holds the viewport origin
  WExt: TPoint;             // holds the window extent
  VExt: TPoint;             // holds the viewport extent
  MyDisplayDC: HDC;         // holds the device context
  MyMapMode: Integer;       // holds the mapping mode

implementation

{$R *.DFM}

procedure TForm1.FormCreate(Sender: TObject);
begin
  {set the scale of the origin trackbars}
  TrackbarSWOX.Max := Panel1.Width;
  TrackbarSWOY.Max := Panel1.Height;
  TrackbarSVOX.Max := Panel1.Width;
  TrackbarSVOY.Max := Panel1.Height;

  {initialize the trackbars to their midpoints}
  TrackbarSWOX.Position := TrackbarSWOY.Max div 2;
  TrackbarSWOY.Position := TrackbarSWOX.Max div 2;
  TrackbarSVOX.Position := TrackbarSVOY.Max div 2;
  TrackbarSVOY.Position := TrackbarSVOX.Max div 2;
  TrackbarSWEX.Position := TrackbarSWEY.Max div 2;
  TrackbarSWEY.Position := TrackbarSWEX.Max div 2;
  TrackbarSVEX.Position := TrackbarSVEY.Max div 2;
  TrackbarSVEY.Position := TrackbarSVEX.Max div 2;
end;

procedure TForm1.ReportPosition;
var
  ReturnValue: TPoint;      // holds the window and viewport origins
  ReturnSize: TSize;        // holds the window and viewport extents
  ReadMapMode: Integer;     // holds the mapping mode
  ReadFinalOrigin: TPoint;  // holds the device origin
begin
  {display the window origin}
  GetWindowOrgEx(MyDisplayDC,ReturnValue);
  Label9.Caption := IntToStr(ReturnValue.x)
        + ', ' + IntToStr(ReturnValue.y);

  {display the viewport origin}
  GetViewportOrgEx(MyDisplayDC,ReturnValue);
  Label10.Caption := IntToStr(ReturnValue.x)
        + ', ' + IntToStr(ReturnValue.y);
```

```
  {display the window extents}
  GetWindowExtEx(MyDisplayDC,ReturnSize);
  Label11.Caption := IntToStr(ReturnSize.cx)
       + ', ' + IntToStr(ReturnSize.cy);

  {display the viewport extents}
  GetViewportExtEx(MyDisplayDC,ReturnSize);
  Label12.Caption := IntToStr(ReturnSize.cx)
       + ', ' + IntToStr(ReturnSize.cy);

  {display the current mapping mode}
  ReadMapMode := GetMapMode(MyDisplayDC);
  case ReadMapMode of
    MM_TEXT:         LabelGMMresult.Caption := 'MM_TEXT';
    MM_ANISOTROPIC:LabelGMMresult.Caption := 'MM_ANISOTROPIC';
    MM_ISOTROPIC:  LabelGMMresult.Caption := 'MM_ISOTROPIC';
    MM_HIENGLISH:  LabelGMMresult.Caption := 'MM_HIENGLISH';
    MM_HIMETRIC:   LabelGMMresult.Caption := 'MM_HIMETRIC';
    MM_LOENGLISH:  LabelGMMresult.Caption := 'MM_LOENGLISH';
    MM_LOMETRIC:   LabelGMMresult.Caption := 'MM_LOMETRIC';
    MM_TWIPS:      LabelGMMresult.Caption := 'MM_TWIPS';
  end;

  {display the final translation origin for the device context}
  GetDCOrgEx(MyDisplayDC, ReadFinalOrigin);
  LabelGetDCOrgExResult.Caption := IntToStr(ReadFinalOrigin.X) + ', ' +
                                   IntToStr(ReadFinalOrigin.Y);
end;

procedure TForm1.ReadUserRequest;
begin
  {retrieve the selected mapping mode}
  case RadioGroup1.ItemIndex of
    0: MyMapMode := MM_TEXT;
    1: MyMapMode := MM_ANISOTROPIC;
    2: MyMapMode := MM_ISOTROPIC;
    3: MyMapMode := MM_HIENGLISH;
    4: MyMapMode := MM_HIMETRIC;
    5: MyMapMode := MM_LOENGLISH;
    6: MyMapMode := MM_LOMETRIC;
    7: MyMapMode := MM_TWIPS;
  end;

  {set the origin and extent values according to the trackbar positions}
  WOrigin.x := TrackBarSWOX.Position;
  WOrigin.y := TrackBarSWOY.Position;
  VOrigin.x := TrackBarSVOX.Position;
  VOrigin.y := TrackBarSVOY.Position;
  WExt.x    := TrackBarSWEX.Position;
  WExt.y    := TrackBarSWEY.Position;
  VExt.x    := TrackBarSVEX.Position;
  VExt.y    := TrackBarSVEY.Position;
end;
```

2

Chapter

```
procedure TForm1.PaintImage;
begin
  {retrieve a device context for the panel}
  MyDisplayDC := GetDC(Panel1.Handle);

  {erase the current image}
  Panel1.Repaint;

  {retrieve the user defined values}
  ReadUserRequest;

  {set the mapping mode to the selected value}
  SetMapMode(MyDisplayDC, MyMapMode);
  if Checkbox1.Checked
    then SetWindowOrgEx(MyDisplayDC, WOrigin.x, WOrigin.y, nil);
  if Checkbox2.Checked
    then SetViewportOrgEx(MyDisplayDC, VOrigin.x, VOrigin.y, nil);
  if Checkbox3.Checked
    then SetWindowExtEx(MyDisplayDC, WExt.x, WExt.y, nil);
  if Checkbox4.Checked
    then SetViewportExtEx(MyDisplayDC, VExt.x, VExt.y, nil);

  {draw the image. note that the image is drawn to the same, hard-coded
   coordinates. this demonstrates how changing the viewport and window
   origin and extents can affect drawn objects}
  Windows.Rectangle(MyDisplayDC,0,0,50,50);
  Windows.Rectangle(MyDisplayDC,-25,24,75,26);
  Windows.Rectangle(MyDisplayDC,24,-25,26,75);

  {display the current settings}
  ReportPosition;

  {release the device context}
  ReleaseDC(Panel1.Handle, MyDisplayDC);
end;

procedure TForm1.FormPaint(Sender: TObject);
begin
  {display the image}
  PaintImage;
end;
```

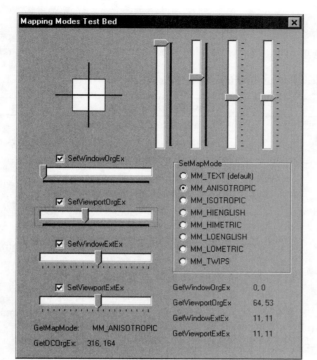

*Figure 2-1:
The Viewport
and Window
Extent and
Origin test
bed in action*

Problems with Logical Coordinate Mapping

An application which is not performing its translation of logical coordinates to device coordinates in the expected manner may have one of the following problems:

1. The device context may have a mapping mode which does not support the translation as expected. The mapping mode must be changed from the default value of MM_TEXT if any transformation is to take place.

2. The coordinates may be out of range. When possible, keep device and logical coordinates within 16-bit values. The transformations support up to 27 bits in size, but some display functions only support 16-bit coordinate sizes.

3. The image might be clipped (off the display area), or too small or large to be visible.

4. The scaling might not be as expected because the application is really placing the same number for the window and viewport extent, which produces a scaling factor of one (no effect).

5. The scaling factor might be producing no effect because the application is multiplying and dividing by the same number. To zoom the effective scaling factor, try setting only the multiplication or the division parameter, or be sure they are different factors.

6. The device context might be invalid. Test for errors when returning from GDI functions.

Graphical Device Interface Functions

The following graphical device interface functions are covered in this chapter:

Table 2-2: Graphical Device Interface Functions

Function	Description
ChangeDisplaySettings	Changes the display mode.
ClientToScreen	Converts client coordinates to screen coordinates.
CreateCompatibleDC	Creates a memory device context.
DeleteDC	Deletes a device context.
DPtoLP	Converts device points to logical points.
EnumDisplaySettings	Enumerates available display modes.
GetDC	Retrieves a handle to a device context.
GetDCOrgEx	Retrieves the final translation origin from the specified device context.
GetDeviceCaps	Retrieves device capabilities.
GetMapMode	Retrieves the current mapping mode.
GetSystemMetrics	Retrieves system element measurements.
GetViewportExtEx	Retrieves the viewport extents.
GetViewportOrgEx	Retrieves the viewport origin.
GetWindowDC	Retrieves a handle to a window device context.
GetWindowExtEx	Retrieves the window extents.
GetWindowOrgEx	Retrieves the window origin.
LPtoDP	Converts logical points to device points.
MapWindowPoints	Converts multiple coordinates from one window coordinate system to another.
OffsetViewportOrgEx	Offsets the viewport origin.
OffsetWindowOrgEx	Offsets the window origin.
ReleaseDC	Releases a device context.
RestoreDC	Restores a saved device context state.
SaveDC	Saves the state of a device context.
ScaleViewportExtEx	Scales the viewport extents.
ScaleWindowExtEx	Scales the window extents.
ScreenToClient	Converts screen coordinates to client coordinates.
ScrollDC	Scrolls an area of a device context.
SetMapMode	Sets the mapping mode.
SetViewportExtEx	Sets the viewport extents.
SetViewportOrgEx	Sets the viewport origin.
SetWindowExtEx	Sets the window extents.
SetWindowOrgEx	Sets the window origin.

ChangeDisplaySettings   Windows.Pas

Syntax

```
ChangeDisplaySettings(
lpDevMode: PDeviceMode;        {points to TDeviceMode structure}
dwFlags: DWORD                 {display change options}
): Longint;                    {returns a result code}
```

Description

This function changes the graphics mode of the system display. The new device settings are contained in the TDeviceMode structure passed as the first parameter. It is common to place a call to EnumDisplaySettings prior to calling ChangeDisplaySettings to get a valid TDeviceMode structure. This helps to ensure that the ChangeDisplaySettings function gets parameters that are compatible with the currently installed display driver.

A WM_DISPLAYCHANGE message is sent to all applications as notification that the display settings were changed. This is performed by Windows automatically and does not have to be explicitly performed by the caller.

Parameters

lpDevMode: A pointer to a TDeviceMode structure containing the information used to initialize the new graphics mode. If this parameter is set to NIL, the display mode values currently stored in the registry are used for the new display mode. Of the members in the TDeviceMode structure, only the dmSize, dmBitsPerPel, dmFields, dmPelsWidth, dmPelsHeight, dmDisplayFlags, and dmDisplayFrequency members are used by this function. The TDeviceMode structure is defined as:

```
TDeviceMode = packed record
     dmDeviceName: array[0..CCHDEVICENAME - 1]
     of AnsiChar;                                       {not used}
     dmSpecVersion: Word;                               {not used}
     dmDriverVersion: Word;                             {not used}
     dmSize: Word;                                      {structure size}
     dmDriverExtra: Word;                               {not used}
     dmFields: DWORD;                                   {valid fields}
     dmOrientation: SHORT;                              {not used}
     dmPaperSize: SHORT;                                {not used}
     dmPaperLength: SHORT;                              {not used}
     dmPaperWidth: SHORT;                               {not used}
     dmScale: SHORT;                                    {not used}
     dmCopies: SHORT;                                   {not used}
     dmDefaultSource: SHORT;                            {not used}
     dmPrintQuality: SHORT;                             {not used}
     dmColor: SHORT;                                    {not used}
     dmDuplex: SHORT;                                   {not used}
```

dmYResolution: SHORT;	{not used}
dmTTOption: SHORT;	{not used}
dmCollate: SHORT;	{not used}
dmFormName: array[0..CCHFORMNAME - 1]	
of AnsiChar;	{not used}
dmLogPixels: Word;	{not used}
dmBitsPerPel: DWORD;	{color depth}
dmPelsWidth: DWORD;	{screen width}
dmPelsHeight: DWORD;	{screen height}
dmDisplayFlags: DWORD;	{display mode}
dmDisplayFrequency: DWORD;	{frequency}
dmICMMethod: DWORD;	{not used}
dmICMIntent: DWORD;	{not used}
dmMediaType: DWORD;	{not used}
dmDitherType: DWORD;	{not used}
dmICCManufacturer: DWORD;	{not used}
dmICCModel: DWORD;	{not used}
dmPanningWidth: DWORD;	{not used}
dmPanningHeight: DWORD;	{not used}

end;

Only the following members are used by this function:

dmSize: Specifies the size of the TDeviceMode structure. This member must be set to SizeOf(TDeviceMode).

dmFields: A series of flags indicating which other members of the structure contain valid information. This member may be set to one or more values from Table 2-3.

dmBitsPerPel: Indicates the number of bits required to describe the color of one pixel (i.e., 4 bits for 16-color displays, 8 bits for 256-color displays, etc.).

dmPelsWidth: Specifies the width of the screen, in pixels.

dmPelsHeight: Specifies the height of the screen, in pixels.

dmDisplayFlags: A flag indicating the display mode. This member can be set to one value from Table 2-4.

dmDisplayFrequency: Specifies the vertical display refresh rate, in hertz. A value of zero or one represents the hardware's default refresh rate.

dwFlags: A flag specifying how the graphics mode is to be changed. This parameter may be set to one value from Table 2-5. If the CDS_UPDATEREGISTRY flag is specified, the system attempts to make a dynamic graphics mode change and update the registry without a reboot. If a reboot is required, the DISP_CHANGE_RESTART return value is set and the application is responsible for rebooting Windows. The CDS_TEST mode can be used to see which graphics modes are available without performing the actual change.

Return Value

This function returns a flag indicating success or failure, and may be one value from Table 2-6.

See Also

EnumDisplaySettings, WM_DISPLAYCHANGE

Example

Listing 2-3: Changing the Display Mode

```
{Whoops! Delphi imports this function incorrectly, so we must manually
 import it}
function ChangeDisplaySettings(lpDevMode: PDeviceMode;
                              dwFlags: DWORD): Longint; stdcall;
var
  Form1: TForm1;
  DevModeArray: TList;     // holds a list of device mode information structures

implementation

uses Math;

{$R *.DFM}

{import the function}
function ChangeDisplaySettings; external user32 name 'ChangeDisplaySettingsA';

procedure TForm1.FormCreate(Sender: TObject);
var
  DevModeCount: Integer;            // tracks the number of display modes
  DevModeInfo: ^TDevMode;           // a pointer to display mode information
begin
  {create the list to hold display mode information structures}
  DevModeArray := TList.Create;

  {initialize the counter}
  DevModeCount := 0;

  {dynamically allocate memory to hold display mode information}
  GetMem(DevModeInfo, SizeOf(TDevMode));

  {begin enumerating display modes}
  while EnumDisplaySettings(NIL, DevModeCount, DevModeInfo^) do
  begin
    {add the information to the list}
    DevModeArray.Add(DevModeInfo);

    {increment the counter}
    Inc(DevModeCount);

    {display the resolution of the enumerated display mode}
    ListBox1.Items.Add(IntToStr(DevModeInfo^.dmPelsWidth)+'x'+
```

```
                              IntToStr(DevModeInfo^.dmPelsHeight)+', '+
                              IntToStr(Trunc(IntPower(2, DevModeInfo^.dmBitsPerPel)))+
                              ' colors');

    {allocate another slot for device mode information}
    GetMem(DevModeInfo, SizeOf(TDevMode));
  end;

  {the above loop always exits with one extra, unused block of memory,
   so delete it}
  FreeMem(DevModeInfo, SizeOf(TDevMode));

  {select the first item in the list box}
  ListBox1.ItemIndex := 0;
end;

procedure TForm1.FormDestroy(Sender: TObject);
var
  iCount: Integer;          // a general loop counter
begin
  {free all memory pointed to by each item in the list}
  for iCount := 0 to DevModeArray.Count-1 do
    FreeMem(DevModeArray.Items[iCount], SizeOf(TDevMode));

  {free the list}
  DevModeArray.Free;
end;

procedure TForm1.Button1Click(Sender: TObject);
var
  ModeChange: Longint;          // indicates if a Windows reboot is necessary
begin
  {change the display mode}
  ModeChange:=ChangeDisplaySettings(DevModeArray[ListBox1.ItemIndex],
                                    CDS_UPDATEREGISTRY);

  {indicate if a dynamic change was successful or if Windows must be rebooted}
  if ModeChange=DISP_CHANGE_SUCCESSFUL then
    ShowMessage('Dynamic display mode change successful.');
  if ModeChange=DISP_CHANGE_RESTART then
    ShowMessage('Change successful; Windows must be restarted for the changes '+
                'to take effect');
end;
```

Table 2-3: ChangeDisplaySettings lpDevMode.dmFields Values

Value	Description
DM_BITSPERPEL	The dmBitsPerPel member contains new data.
DM_PELSWIDTH	The dmPelsWidth member contains new data.
DM_PELSHEIGHT	The dmPelsHeight member contains new data.
DM_DISPLAYFLAGS	The dmDisplayFlags member contains new data.
DM_DISPLAYFREQENCY	The dmDisplayFrequency member contains new data.

Table 2-4: ChangeDisplaySettings lpDevMode.dmDisplayFlags Values

Value	Description
DM_GRAYSCALE	Indicates a noncolor display.
DM_INTERLACED	Indicates an interlaced display.

Table 2-5: ChangeDisplaySettings dwFlags Values

Value	Description
0	The change will be made dynamically.
CDS_UPDATEREGISTRY	The change is made dynamically, and the registry will be updated to reflect the new graphics mode under the USER key.
CDS_TEST	The change is not made, but the system is tested to see if it could be made. The function sets the same return values as if the change had been made.

Table 2-6: ChangeDisplaySettings Return Values

Value	Description
DISP_CHANGE_SUCCESSFUL	The function was successful.
DISP_CHANGE_RESTART	Windows must be restarted for the changes to take effect.
DISP_CHANGE_BADFLAGS	The caller passed invalid flags to the function.
DISP_CHANGE_FAILED	The display driver did not accept the newly specified graphics mode.
DISP_CHANGE_BADMODE	The specified graphics mode is not supported.
DISP_CHANGE_NOTUPDATED	Windows NT only: Unable to write the new settings to the registry.

ClientToScreen   **Windows.Pas**

Syntax

```
ClientToScreen(
hWnd: HWND;                {the handle of a window}
var lpPoint: TPoint        {a pointer to a TPoint structure}
): BOOL;                   {returns TRUE or FALSE}
```

Description

This function changes the coordinates of a point from client coordinates to screen coordinates. The point to be translated is in a TPoint structure pointed to by the lpPoint parameter. The function takes the coordinates pointed to by the lpPoint parameter and converts them into coordinates relative to the screen. The results are placed back into this TPoint structure. The coordinates of the point being passed use the top left corner of the client area of the specified window as the origin. The coordinates of the result use the top left corner of the screen as the origin.

Parameters

hWnd: The handle to the window that contains the point. The top left corner of the client area of this window is the origin of the coordinate system that defines the coordinates of the point being converted.

lpPoint: A pointer to a TPoint structure that contains the point to be converted. This TPoint structure receives the converted point when the function returns.

Return Value

If the function succeeds, it returns TRUE; otherwise it returns FALSE. To get extended error information, call GetLastError.

See Also

MapWindowPoints, ScreenToClient

Example

Listing 2-4: Converting Coordinates Between Coordinate Systems

```
procedure TForm1.Memo1MouseDown(Sender: TObject; Button: TMouseButton;
  Shift: TShiftState; X, Y: Integer);
var
  Coords: TPoint;     // holds the point being converted
begin
  {indicate the clicked coordinates relative to the child window}
  Label1.Caption := 'Memo Coordinates: '+IntToStr(X)+', '+IntToStr(Y);

  {convert these coordinates into screen coordinates}
  Coords := Point(X, Y);
  Windows.ClientToScreen(Memo1.Handle, Coords);

  {display the clicked coordinates relative to the screen}
  Label2.Caption := 'Screen Coordinates: '+IntToStr(Coords.X)+', '+
                    IntToStr(Coords.Y);

  {convert the coordinates into window client coordinates}
  Windows.ScreenToClient(Form1.Handle, Coords);

  {display the clicked coordinates relative to the client area of the window}
  Label3.Caption := 'Form Coordinates: '+IntToStr(Coords.X)+', '+
                    IntToStr(Coords.Y);
end;
```

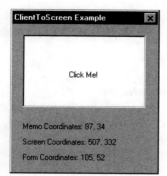

Figure 2-2:
The converted
coordinates

CreateCompatibleDC   Windows.Pas

Syntax

CreateCompatibleDC(
DC: HDC   {the handle to a device context}
): HDC;   {returns a handle to a memory device context}

Description

This function creates a memory device context that is compatible with the specified device context. This is used with images that will be copied to the screen or to a printer. A bitmap must be selected into the device context returned by this function before the device context can be used with drawing operations. When an application is finished with the memory device context, it should be deleted by calling the DeleteDC function.

Parameters

DC: Specifies a handle to a device context for which the new device context will be compatible. This must be a device context that supports raster operations. The application can call the GetDeviceCaps function to determine if the device context meets this requirement. If this parameter is set to zero, the function creates a device context compatible with the screen.

Return Value

If the function succeeds, it returns a handle to the new memory device context. If it fails, it returns zero.

See Also

CreateCompatibleBitmap, DeleteDC, GetDeviceCaps

Example

Listing 2-5: Using Memory Device Contexts for Animation

```
var
  Form1: TForm1;
  OffscreenDC: HDC;          // an offscreen device context
  ANDMaskBitmap,             // used for holding the different parts of the
  ORMaskBitmap,              // circle graphic
  BackgroundBitmap,
  OldBitmap: HBITMAP;
  BallXCoord: Integer;       // the current horizontal coordinates of the circle

implementation

{$R *.DFM}

procedure TForm1.Timer1Timer(Sender: TObject);
var
  ScreenDC,                  // a handle to the screen device context
  WorkDC: HDC;               // a handle to a temporary device context
  OldBitmap: HBITMAP;        // holds the previous bitmap
begin
  {retrieve a handle to the device context for the screen}
  ScreenDC := GetDC(0);

  {create a memory device context}
  WorkDC := CreateCompatibleDC(Canvas.Handle);

  {restore the previous background to the screen}
  BitBlt(ScreenDC, BallXCoord, Form1.Top, 40, 40, OffscreenDC, 0, 0, SRCCOPY);

  {increment the horizontal coordinate of the circle}
  Inc(BallXCoord);

  {wrap the circle around the screen if it has gone beyond the edges}
  if BallXCoord>GetSystemMetrics(SM_CXSCREEN) then
    BallXCoord := -40;

  {save the background at the current location of the circle}
  BitBlt(OffscreenDC, 0, 0, 40, 40, ScreenDC, BallXCoord, Form1.Top, SRCCOPY);

  {select the AND mask of the circle into the memory device context, and
   copy it to the screen}
  OldBitmap := SelectObject(WorkDC, ANDMaskBitmap);
  BitBlt(ScreenDC, BallXCoord, Form1.Top, 40, 40, WorkDC, 0, 0, SRCAND);

  {select the OR mask of the circle into the memory device context, and
   copy it to the screen}
```

```
  SelectObject(WorkDC, ORMaskBitmap);
  BitBlt(ScreenDC, BallXCoord, Form1.Top, 40, 40, WorkDC, 0, 0, SRCPAINT);

  {select the old bitmap back into the memory device context, and delete or
   release all unneeded objects}
  SelectObject(WorkDC, OldBitmap);
  ReleaseDC(0, ScreenDC);
  DeleteDC(WorkDC);
end;

procedure TForm1.FormCreate(Sender: TObject);
var
  TempBrush: HBRUSH;      // a handle to a brush
begin
  {create a memory device context}
  OffscreenDC   := CreateCompatibleDC(Canvas.Handle);

  {a lot of attributes of the device context will change, so save its original
   state so we don't have to reselect the original objects back into the
   device context}
  SaveDC(OffscreenDC);

  {create the bitmap for the circle's AND mask}
  AndMaskBitmap := CreateCompatibleBitmap(Canvas.Handle, 40, 40);

  {select the bitmap into the memory device context and draw a black circle
   on a white background}
  SelectObject(OffscreenDC, AndMaskBitmap);
  SelectObject(OffscreenDC, GetStockObject(WHITE_BRUSH));
  SelectObject(OffscreenDC, GetStockObject(NULL_PEN));
  Rectangle(OffscreenDC, 0, 0, 41, 41);
  SelectObject(OffscreenDC, GetStockObject(BLACK_BRUSH));
  Ellipse(OffscreenDC, 0, 0, 40, 40);

  {create the bitmap for the circle's OR mask}
  ORMaskBitmap := CreateCompatibleBitmap(Canvas.Handle, 40, 40);

  {select the bitmap into the memory device context and draw a hatched circle
   on a black background}
  SelectObject(OffscreenDC, ORMaskBitmap);
  SelectObject(OffscreenDC, GetStockObject(BLACK_BRUSH));
  Rectangle(OffscreenDC, 0, 0, 41, 41);
  TempBrush := CreateHatchBrush(HS_DIAGCROSS, clRed);
  SelectObject(OffscreenDC, GetStockObject(BLACK_PEN));
  SelectObject(OffscreenDC, TempBrush);
  Ellipse(OffscreenDC, 0, 0, 40, 40);

  {restore the device context's original settings. this eliminates the need to
   reselect all of the original objects back into the device context when we
   are through}
  RestoreDC(OffscreenDC, -1);
```

2

Chapter

```
    {delete the brush}
    DeleteObject(TempBrush);

    {finally create a bitmap to hold the background of the screen. this keeps
     the animated circle from leaving a trail behind it}
    BackgroundBitmap := CreateCompatibleBitmap(Canvas.Handle, 40, 40);

    {select the background bitmap into the memory device context}
    SelectObject(OffscreenDC, BackgroundBitmap);

    {initialize the coordinates of the circle so it will begin off screen
     to the left}
    BallXCoord := -40;
end;

procedure TForm1.FormDestroy(Sender: TObject);
begin
    {delete all unneeded bitmaps and device contexts}
    SelectObject(OffscreenDC, OldBitmap);
    DeleteObject(BackgroundBitmap);
    DeleteObject(ANDMaskBitmap);
    DeleteObject(ORMaskBitmap);
    DeleteDC(OffscreenDC);
end;
```

Figure 2-3:
The animated
circle

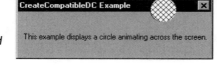

DeleteDC   Windows.Pas

Syntax

> DeleteDC(
> DC: HDC   {the handle of a device context}
>): BOOL;   {returns TRUE or FALSE}

Description

The DeleteDC function deletes the specified device context. When an application uses CreateCompatibleDC, it should also call DeleteDC when finished with the handle.

Parameters

DC: The handle to the device context to be deleted.

Return Value

If the function succeeds, it returns TRUE; otherwise it returns FALSE.

See Also

CreateCompatibleDC, GetDC, ReleaseDC

Example

Please see Listing 2-5 under CreateCompatibleDC.

DPtoLP   *Windows.Pas*

Syntax

```
DPtoLP(
DC: HDC;              {the handle of a device context}
var Points;           {a pointer to an array of TPoint structures}
Count: Integer        {the number of entries in the array}
): BOOL;              {returns TRUE or FALSE}
```

Description

The DPtoLP function converts points from device coordinates to logical coordinates. The Points parameter points to an array of TPoint structures containing the coordinates to be translated. These TPoint structures will receive the translated coordinates when the function returns. The coordinate transformation is performed based on the values set by the SetWindowOrgEx, SetViewportOrgEx, SetWindowExtEx, and SetViewportExtEx functions. The DPtoLP function will fail if any of the points in the TPoint structures specify a value greater in size than 27 bits. It will also fail if any of the transformed points are greater in size than 32 bits. In the event of failure, the values in the entire Points array are undefined.

Parameters

DC: A handle to the device context for which the coordinate transformations will be made.

Points: A pointer to an array of TPoint structures containing the coordinates to be converted.

Count: Specifies the number of entries in the array pointed to by the Points parameter.

Return Value

If the function succeeds, it returns TRUE; otherwise it returns FALSE.

See Also

LPtoDP, SetWindowOrgEx, SetViewportOrgEx, SetWindowExtEx, SetViewportExtEx

Example

Please see Listing 2-12 under ScaleViewportExtEx.

EnumDisplaySettings   *Windows.Pas*

Syntax

```
EnumDisplaySettings(
lpszDeviceName: PChar;              {the display device}
iModeNum: DWORD;                    {the graphics mode}
var lpDevMode: TDeviceMode          {a pointer to a structure to receive device settings}
): BOOL;                            {returns TRUE or FALSE}
```

Description

The EnumDisplaySettings function retrieves information from the specified display device about the specified graphics mode. To retrieve all display modes available for the specified device, start by setting the iModeNum to zero and incrementing it by one for each subsequent call to the function. This should continue until the function returns FALSE.

Parameters

lpszDeviceName: The name of the device for which information is to be retrieved. If this parameter is set to NIL, the function enumerates display modes for the current display device. The string pointed to by this parameter must be in the form of \\.\Display1, \\.\Display2, or \\.\Display3. Under Windows 95, this parameter must always be set to NIL.

iModeNum: The index value for the graphics mode for which information is to be retrieved. This value must be less than the index of the display's last graphics mode. If the iModeNum parameter is out of range, the function will return an error.

var lpDevMode: A pointer to a TDeviceMode structure that receives information about the specified display mode. Of the members in the TDeviceMode structure, only the dmSize, dmBitsPerPel, dmPelsWidth, dmPelsHeight, dmDisplayFlags, and dmDisplay-Frequency members are used by this function. The TDeviceMode structure is defined as:

```
TDeviceMode = packed record
     dmDeviceName: array[0..CCHDEVICENAME - 1]
     of AnsiChar;                                           {not used}
     dmSpecVersion: Word;                                   {not used}
     dmDriverVersion: Word;                                 {not used}
     dmSize: Word;                                          {structure size}
     dmDriverExtra: Word;                                   {not used}
     dmFields: DWORD;                                       {not used}
     dmOrientation: SHORT;                                  {not used}
     dmPaperSize: SHORT;                                    {not used}
     dmPaperLength: SHORT;                                  {not used}
     dmPaperWidth: SHORT;                                   {not used}
```

dmScale: SHORT;	{not used}
dmCopies: SHORT;	{not used}
dmDefaultSource: SHORT;	{not used}
dmPrintQuality: SHORT;	{not used}
dmColor: SHORT;	{not used}
dmDuplex: SHORT;	{not used}
dmYResolution: SHORT;	{not used}
dmTTOption: SHORT;	{not used}
dmCollate: SHORT;	{not used}
dmFormName: array[0..CCHFORMNAME - 1]	
of AnsiChar;	{not used}
dmLogPixels: Word;	{not used}
dmBitsPerPel: DWORD;	{color depth}
dmPelsWidth: DWORD;	{screen width}
dmPelsHeight: DWORD;	{screen height}
dmDisplayFlags: DWORD;	{display mode}
dmDisplayFrequency: DWORD;	{frequency}
dmICMMethod: DWORD;	{not used}
dmICMIntent: DWORD;	{not used}
dmMediaType: DWORD;	{not used}
dmDitherType: DWORD;	{not used}
dmICCManufacturer: DWORD;	{not used}
dmICCModel: DWORD;	{not used}
dmPanningWidth: DWORD;	{not used}
dmPanningHeight: DWORD;	{not used}

end;

Please see the ChangeDisplaySettings function for a description of this data structure.

Return Value

If the function succeeds, it returns TRUE; otherwise it returns FALSE.

See Also

ChangeDisplaySettings

Example

Listing 2-6: Enumerating All Available Display Modes for the Current Display

```
procedure TForm1.Button1Click(Sender: TObject);
var
  DeviceInfo: TDevMode;      // holds device information
  DeviceCount: Integer;      // tracks the number of display modes
begin
  {initialize the tracking variable}
  DeviceCount := 0;
```

```
{enumerate all display modes for the current display device}
while EnumDisplaySettings(NIL, DeviceCount, DeviceInfo) do
begin
  {display the relevent information for the display mode}
  ListBox1.Items.Add('Device '+IntToStr(DeviceCount)+' -');
  ListBox1.Items.Add('Pixels/Inch: '+IntToSTr(DeviceInfo.dmLogPixels));
  ListBox1.Items.Add('Bits/Pixel: '+IntToStr(DeviceInfo.dmBitsPerPel));
  ListBox1.Items.Add('Pixel Width: '+IntToStr(DeviceInfo.dmPelsWidth));
  ListBox1.Items.Add('Pixel Height: '+IntToStr(DeviceInfo.dmPelsHeight));

  {indicate the display mode type}
  case DeviceInfo.dmDisplayFlags of
    DM_GRAYSCALE:  ListBox1.Items.Add('Display Mode: Grayscale');
    DM_INTERLACED: ListBox1.Items.Add('Display Mode: Interlaced');
  end;

  {indicate the refresh rate}
  if (DeviceInfo.dmDisplayFrequency=0)or(DeviceInfo.dmDisplayFrequency=1) then
    ListBox1.Items.Add('Refresh Rate: Hardware Default')
  else
    ListBox1.Items.Add('Refresh Rate: '+IntToStr(DeviceInfo.dmDisplayFrequency)+'
hrz');

  {add a blank line and increment the tracking variable}
  ListBox1.Items.Add('');
  Inc(DeviceCount);
  end;
end;
```

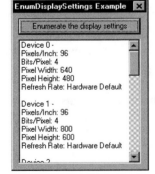

Figure 2-4:
The available
display mode
information

GetDC   Windows.Pas

Syntax

```
GetDC(
hWnd: HWND                 {the handle of a window}
): HDC;                    {returns a device context}
```

Description

The GetDC function retrieves a device context for the client area of the window specified by the hWnd parameter. The device context retrieved will be a common, class, or private device context as determined by the class styles of the specified window. For common device contexts, the GetDC function initializes the device context with default attributes each time it is retrieved. Class and private device contexts retrieved by this function will retain their last settings. When the device context is no longer needed, it should be released by calling the ReleaseDC function.

Parameters

hWnd: A handle to the window for which a device context is retrieved. If this parameter is set to zero, the function retrieves a device context for the screen.

Return Value

If the function succeeds, it returns a device context for the client area of the specified window. If the function fails, it returns a zero.

See Also

ReleaseDC, GetWindowDC

Example

Listing 2-7: Retrieving a Common Device Context for a Window

```
procedure TForm1.FormPaint(Sender: TObject);
var
  FormDC: HDC;        // holds the device context
  OldFont: HFONT;     // holds the original font
begin
  {retrieve a common device context for the form}
  FormDC := GetDC(Form1.Handle);

  {select the form's font into the device context}
  OldFont := SelectObject(FormDC, Form1.Font.Handle);

  {output some text onto the device context}
  SetBkMode(FormDC, TRANSPARENT);
  TextOut(FormDC, 10, 10, 'Delphi Rocks!', Length('Delphi Rocks!'));

  {reselect the original font and release the device context}
  SelectObject(FormDC, OldFont);
  ReleaseDC(Form1.Handle, FormDC);
end;
```

2

Chapter

*Figure 2-5:
Drawing on
the device*

GetDCOrgEx   Windows.Pas

Syntax

GetDCOrgEx(
DC: HDC;   {the handle of a device context}
var Origin: TPoint   {a pointer to a TPoint structure}
): BOOL;   {returns TRUE or FALSE}

Description

The GetDCOrgEx function retrieves final translation origin from the specified device context. This location is the final offset that Windows will use when translating device coordinates into client coordinates.

Parameters

DC: A handle to the device context whose origin is being retrieved.

Origin: A pointer to a TPoint structure that will receive the origin coordinates. The coordinates are relative to the physical origin of the screen, and is given in device units.

Return Value

If the function succeeds, it returns TRUE; otherwise it returns FALSE.

See Also

GetWindowOrgEx, GetViewportOrgEx

Example

Please see Listing 2-2 in the introduction.

GetDeviceCaps   Windows.Pas

Syntax

GetDeviceCaps(
DC: HDC;   {the handle of a device context
Index: Integer   {the capability index}
): Integer;   {returns the capability value}

Description

The GetDeviceCaps function gets device information about a particular capability from the specified device context. A wide variety of capabilities can be queried as shown in Table 2-7.

Parameters

DC: The handle of the device context for which the capability is being queried.

Index: A flag indicating the specific capability being queried. This parameter may be set to one value from Table 2-7.

Return Value

If the function succeeds, it returns a value specific to the queried capability. This function does not indicate an error condition.

See Also

CreateEnhMetaFile, GetDIBits, GetObjectType, GetSystemMetrics, SetDIBits, SetDIBitsToDevice, StretchBlt, StretchDIBits

Example

Listing 2-8: Retrieving Device Capabilities

```
procedure TForm1.Button1Click(Sender: TObject);
begin
  with ListBox1.Items do
  begin
    {display the driver version}
    Add('Display Driver Version: '+IntToStr(GetDeviceCaps(Canvas.Handle,
        DRIVERVERSION)));

    {display the technology}
    case GetDeviceCaps(Canvas.Handle, TECHNOLOGY) of
      DT_PLOTTER:    Add('Driver Type: Vector Plotter');
      DT_RASDISPLAY: Add('Driver Type: Raster Display');
      DT_RASPRINTER: Add('Driver Type: Raster Printer');
      DT_RASCAMERA:  Add('Driver Type: Raster Camera');
      DT_CHARSTREAM: Add('Driver Type: Character Stream');
      DT_METAFILE:   Add('Driver Type: Metafile');
      DT_DISPFILE:   Add('Driver Type: Display File');
    end;

    {display the screen size}
    Add('Screen Size: '+IntToStr(GetDeviceCaps(Canvas.Handle, HORZSIZE))+' X '+
        IntToStr(GetDeviceCaps(Canvas.Handle, VERTSIZE))+' millimeters');
    Add('Screen Resolution: '+IntToStr(GetDeviceCaps(Canvas.Handle, HORZRES))+
        ' X '+IntToStr(GetDeviceCaps(Canvas.Handle, VERTRES))+' pixels');

    {display the pixels per logical inch}
    Add('Pixels/Logical Inch - Horizontal: '+IntToStr(GetDeviceCaps(
        Canvas.Handle, LOGPIXELSX)));
    Add('Pixels/Logical Inch - Vertical: '+IntToStr(GetDeviceCaps(
        Canvas.Handle, LOGPIXELSY)));
```

2

Chapter

```
{display the color depth and number of common graphical objects}
Add('Bits/Pixel: '+IntToStr(GetDeviceCaps(Canvas.Handle, BITSPIXEL)));
Add('Brushes: '+IntToStr(GetDeviceCaps(Canvas.Handle, NUMBRUSHES)));
Add('Pens: '+IntToStr(GetDeviceCaps(Canvas.Handle, NUMPENS)));
Add('Fonts: '+IntToStr(GetDeviceCaps(Canvas.Handle, NUMFONTS)));

{display the number of entries in the color table}
if GetDeviceCaps(Canvas.Handle, NUMCOLORS)>-1 then
  Add('Entries in color table: '+IntToStr(GetDeviceCaps(
      Canvas.Handle, NUMCOLORS)));

{display pixel dimensions}
Add('Pixel Width: '+IntToStr(GetDeviceCaps(Canvas.Handle, ASPECTX)));
Add('Pixel Height: '+IntToStr(GetDeviceCaps(Canvas.Handle, ASPECTY)));
Add('Pixel Diagonal: '+IntToStr(GetDeviceCaps(Canvas.Handle, ASPECTXY)));

{indicate if the device can clip to a rectangle}
if GetDeviceCaps(Canvas.Handle, CLIPCAPS)=1 then
  Add('Device can clip to a rectangle')
else
  Add('Device cannot clip to a rectangle');

{display the palette size, reserved colors, and color depth}
Add('Palette Size: '+IntToStr(GetDeviceCaps(Canvas.Handle, SIZEPALETTE)));
Add('Number of Reserved Colors: '+IntToStr(GetDeviceCaps(
    Canvas.Handle, NUMRESERVED)));
Add('Color Resolution: '+IntToStr(Trunc(IntPower(2, GetDeviceCaps(
    Canvas.Handle, COLORRES))))+' colors');

{display the raster capabilities}
Add('Raster Capabilities -');
if (GetDeviceCaps(Canvas.Handle, RASTERCAPS) and
    RC_BANDING)=RC_BANDING then
      Add('     Requires Banding');
if (GetDeviceCaps(Canvas.Handle, RASTERCAPS) and
    RC_BITBLT)=RC_BITBLT then
      Add('     Can Transfer Bitmaps');
if (GetDeviceCaps(Canvas.Handle, RASTERCAPS) and
    RC_BITMAP64)=RC_BITMAP64 then
      Add('     Supports Bitmaps > 64K');
if (GetDeviceCaps(Canvas.Handle, RASTERCAPS) and
    RC_DI_BITMAP)=RC_DI_BITMAP then
      Add('     Supports SetDIBits and GetDIBits');
if (GetDeviceCaps(Canvas.Handle, RASTERCAPS) and
    RC_DIBTODEV)=RC_DIBTODEV then
      Add('     Supports SetDIBitsToDevice');
if (GetDeviceCaps(Canvas.Handle, RASTERCAPS) and
    RC_FLOODFILL)=RC_FLOODFILL then
      Add('     Can Perform Floodfills');
if (GetDeviceCaps(Canvas.Handle, RASTERCAPS) and
    RC_GDI20_OUTPUT)=RC_GDI20_OUTPUT then
      Add('     Supports Windows 2.0 Features');
if (GetDeviceCaps(Canvas.Handle, RASTERCAPS) and
    RC_PALETTE)=RC_PALETTE then
      Add('     Palette Based');
```

```
    if (GetDeviceCaps(Canvas.Handle, RASTERCAPS) and
        RC_SCALING)=RC_SCALING then
          Add('      Supports Scaling');
    if (GetDeviceCaps(Canvas.Handle, RASTERCAPS) and
        RC_STRETCHBLT)=RC_STRETCHBLT then
          Add('      Supports StretchBlt');
    if (GetDeviceCaps(Canvas.Handle, RASTERCAPS) and
        RC_STRETCHDIB)=RC_STRETCHDIB then
          Add('      Supports StretchDIBits');

  {display curve capabilities}
  Add('Curve Capabilities -');
  if GetDeviceCaps(Canvas.Handle, CURVECAPS)=CC_NONE then
    Add('      Device Does Not Support Curves')
  else
  begin
    if (GetDeviceCaps(Canvas.Handle, CURVECAPS) and
        CC_CIRCLES)=CC_CIRCLES then
          Add('      Supports Circles');
    if (GetDeviceCaps(Canvas.Handle, CURVECAPS) and
        CC_PIE)=CC_PIE then
          Add('      Supports Pie Wedges');
    if (GetDeviceCaps(Canvas.Handle, CURVECAPS) and
        CC_CHORD)=CC_CHORD then
          Add('      Supports Chords');
    if (GetDeviceCaps(Canvas.Handle, CURVECAPS) and
        CC_ELLIPSES)=CC_ELLIPSES then
          Add('      Supports Ellipses');
    if (GetDeviceCaps(Canvas.Handle, CURVECAPS) and
        CC_WIDE)=CC_WIDE then
          Add('      Supports Wide Borders');
    if (GetDeviceCaps(Canvas.Handle, CURVECAPS) and
        CC_STYLED)=CC_STYLED then
          Add('      Supports Styled Borders');
    if (GetDeviceCaps(Canvas.Handle, CURVECAPS) and
        CC_WIDESTYLED)=CC_WIDESTYLED then
          Add('      Supports Wide And Styled Borders');
    if (GetDeviceCaps(Canvas.Handle, CURVECAPS) and
        CC_INTERIORS)=CC_INTERIORS then
          Add('      Supports Interiors');
    if (GetDeviceCaps(Canvas.Handle, CURVECAPS) and
        CC_ROUNDRECT)=CC_ROUNDRECT then
          Add('      Supports Rounded Rectangles');
  end;

  {display line capabilities}
  Add('Line Capabilities -');
  if GetDeviceCaps(Canvas.Handle, LINECAPS)=LC_NONE then
    Add('      Device Does Not Support Lines')
  else
  begin
    if (GetDeviceCaps(Canvas.Handle, LINECAPS) and
        LC_POLYLINE)=LC_POLYLINE then
          Add('      Supports Polylines');
    if (GetDeviceCaps(Canvas.Handle, LINECAPS) and
```

```
                    LC_MARKER)=LC_MARKER then
              Add('    Supports Markers');
      if (GetDeviceCaps(Canvas.Handle, LINECAPS) and
          LC_POLYMARKER)=LC_POLYMARKER then
              Add('    Supports Multiple Markers');
      if (GetDeviceCaps(Canvas.Handle, LINECAPS) and
          LC_WIDE)=LC_WIDE then
              Add('    Supports Wide Lines');
      if (GetDeviceCaps(Canvas.Handle, LINECAPS) and
          LC_STYLED)=LC_STYLED then
              Add('    Supports Styled Lines');
      if (GetDeviceCaps(Canvas.Handle, LINECAPS) and
          LC_WIDESTYLED)=LC_WIDESTYLED then
              Add('    Supports Wide And Styled Lines');
      if (GetDeviceCaps(Canvas.Handle, LINECAPS) and
          LC_INTERIORS)=LC_INTERIORS then
              Add('    Supports Interiors');
  end;

  {display polygonal capabilities}
  Add('Polygonal Capabilities -');
  if GetDeviceCaps(Canvas.Handle, POLYGONALCAPS)=PC_NONE then
    Add('    Device Does Not Support Polygons')
  else
  begin
      if (GetDeviceCaps(Canvas.Handle, POLYGONALCAPS) and
          PC_POLYGON)=PC_POLYGON then
              Add('    Supports Alternate Fill Polygons');
      if (GetDeviceCaps(Canvas.Handle, POLYGONALCAPS) and
          PC_RECTANGLE)=PC_RECTANGLE then
              Add('    Supports Rectangles');
      if (GetDeviceCaps(Canvas.Handle, POLYGONALCAPS) and
          PC_WINDPOLYGON)=PC_WINDPOLYGON then
              Add('    Supports Winding Fill Polygons');
      if (GetDeviceCaps(Canvas.Handle, POLYGONALCAPS) and
          PC_SCANLINE)=PC_SCANLINE then
              Add('    Supports Single Scanlines');
      if (GetDeviceCaps(Canvas.Handle, POLYGONALCAPS) and
          PC_WIDE)=PC_WIDE then
              Add('    Supports Wide Borders');
      if (GetDeviceCaps(Canvas.Handle, POLYGONALCAPS) and
          PC_STYLED)=PC_STYLED then
              Add('    Supports Styled Borders');
      if (GetDeviceCaps(Canvas.Handle, POLYGONALCAPS) and
          PC_WIDESTYLED)=PC_WIDESTYLED then
              Add('    Supports Wide And Styled Borders');
      if (GetDeviceCaps(Canvas.Handle, POLYGONALCAPS) and
          PC_INTERIORS)=PC_INTERIORS then
              Add('    Supports Interiors');
  end;
```

```
      {display text capabilities}
      Add('Text Capabilities -');
      if (GetDeviceCaps(Canvas.Handle, TEXTCAPS) and
          TC_OP_CHARACTER)=TC_OP_CHARACTER then
            Add('      Capable of Character Output Precision');
      if (GetDeviceCaps(Canvas.Handle, TEXTCAPS) and
          TC_OP_STROKE)=TC_OP_STROKE then
            Add('      Capable of Stroke Output Precision');
      if (GetDeviceCaps(Canvas.Handle, TEXTCAPS) and
          TC_CP_STROKE)=TC_CP_STROKE then
            Add('      Capable of Stroke Clip Precision');
      if (GetDeviceCaps(Canvas.Handle, TEXTCAPS) and
          TC_CR_90)=TC_CR_90 then
            Add('      Supports 90 Degree Character Rotation');
      if (GetDeviceCaps(Canvas.Handle, TEXTCAPS) and
          TC_CR_ANY)=TC_CR_ANY then
            Add('      Supports Character Rotation to Any Angle');
      if (GetDeviceCaps(Canvas.Handle, TEXTCAPS) and
          TC_SF_X_YINDEP)=TC_SF_X_YINDEP then
            Add('      X And Y Scale Independent');
      if (GetDeviceCaps(Canvas.Handle, TEXTCAPS) and
          TC_SA_DOUBLE)=TC_SA_DOUBLE then
            Add('      Supports Doubled Character Scaling');
      if (GetDeviceCaps(Canvas.Handle, TEXTCAPS) and
          TC_SA_INTEGER)=TC_SA_INTEGER then
            Add('      Supports Integer Multiples Only When Scaling');
      if (GetDeviceCaps(Canvas.Handle, TEXTCAPS) and
          TC_SA_CONTIN)=TC_SA_CONTIN then
            Add('      Supports Any Multiples For Exact Character Scaling');
      if (GetDeviceCaps(Canvas.Handle, TEXTCAPS) and
          TC_EA_DOUBLE)=TC_EA_DOUBLE then
            Add('      Supports Double Weight Characters');
      if (GetDeviceCaps(Canvas.Handle, TEXTCAPS) and
          TC_IA_ABLE)=TC_IA_ABLE then
            Add('      Supports Italics');
      if (GetDeviceCaps(Canvas.Handle, TEXTCAPS) and
          TC_UA_ABLE)=TC_UA_ABLE then
            Add('      Supports Underlines');
      if (GetDeviceCaps(Canvas.Handle, TEXTCAPS) and
          TC_SO_ABLE)=TC_SO_ABLE then
            Add('      Supports Strikeouts');
      if (GetDeviceCaps(Canvas.Handle, TEXTCAPS) and
          TC_RA_ABLE)=TC_RA_ABLE then
            Add('      Supports Raster Fonts');
      if (GetDeviceCaps(Canvas.Handle, TEXTCAPS) and
          TC_VA_ABLE)=TC_VA_ABLE then
            Add('      Supports Vector Fonts');
      if (GetDeviceCaps(Canvas.Handle, TEXTCAPS) and
          TC_SCROLLBLT)=TC_SCROLLBLT then
            Add('      Cannot Scroll Using Blts');
  end;
end;
```

2

Chapter

Figure 2-6:
The device
capabilities

Table 2-7: GetDeviceCaps Index Values

Value	Description
DRIVERVERSION	The device driver version.
TECHNOLOGY	Device technology type. This flag returns one value from Table 2-8. The DC parameter can refer to an enhanced metafile, in which case the device technology returned is that of the device referenced in the metafile. Use the GetObjectType function to determine whether the device context refers to a device in an enhanced metafile.
HORZSIZE	Physical screen width in millimeters.
VERTSIZE	Physical screen height in millimeters.
HORZRES	Screen width in pixels.
VERTRES	Screen height in raster lines.
LOGPIXELSX	The number of horizontal pixels per logical inch.
LOGPIXELSY	The number of vertical pixels per logical inch.
BITSPIXEL	The number of adjacent color bits per pixel.
PLANES	The number of color planes.
NUMBRUSHES	The number of device-specific brushes.
NUMPENS	The number of device-specific pens.
NUMFONTS	The number of device-specific fonts.
NUMCOLORS	The number of entries in the device's color table, if the device has a color depth of 8 bits per pixel or less. It returns -1 for greater color depths.
ASPECTX	Relative width of a device pixel used for line drawing.
ASPECTY	Relative height of a device pixel used for line drawing.
ASPECTXY	Diagonal width of the device pixel used for line drawing.
CLIPCAPS	Clipping capability indicator of the device. If the device can clip to a rectangle, this value is 1; otherwise it is 0.
SIZEPALETTE	The number of system palette entries. This result is valid only for Windows 3.0 or later drivers, and only if the device driver sets the RC_PALETTE bit in the RASTERCAPS index.

Value	Description
NUMRESERVED	Number of reserved entries in the system palette. This index is valid only for Windows 3.0 or later drivers, and only if the device driver sets the RC_PALETTE bit in the RASTERCAPS index.
COLORRES	Device color resolution in bits per pixel. This index is valid only for Windows 3.0 or later drivers, and only if the device driver sets the RC_PALETTE bit in the RASTERCAPS index.
PHYSICALWIDTH	Physical width of a printed page for printing devices, in device units. This is generally a larger number than the printable pixel width of the page because of nonprintable margins.
PHYSICALHEIGHT	Physical height of a printed page for printing devices, in device units. This is generally a larger number than the printable pixel height of the page because of nonprintable margins.
PHYSICALOFFSETX	Left printer margin. This is the distance from the left edge of the physical page to the left edge of the printable area in device units.
PHYSICALOFFSETY	Top printer margin. This is the distance from the top edge of the physical page to the top edge of the printable area in device units.
VREFRESH	Windows NT only: The current vertical refresh rate for display devices in hertz. A value of 0 or 1 represents the display hardware's default refresh rate, generally settable by switches on a display card or computer motherboard, or by a configuration program that is not compatible with Win32 display functions such as ChangeDisplaySettings.
DESKTOPHORZRES	Windows NT only: Virtual desktop width in pixels. This value may be larger than HORZRES if the device supports a virtual desktop or multiple displays.
DESKTOPVERTRES	Windows NT only: Virtual desktop height in pixels. This value may be larger than VERTRES if the device supports a virtual desktop or multiple displays.
BLTALIGNMENT	Windows NT only: Preferred horizontal drawing alignment, expressed as a multiple of pixels. For best drawing performance, windows should be horizontally aligned to a multiple of this value. A value of zero indicates that the device is accelerated, and any alignment may be used.
RASTERCAPS	Indicates the raster capabilities of the device. It returns one or more flags from Table 2-9.
CURVECAPS	Indicates the curve capabilities of the device. It returns one or more flags from Table 2-10.
LINECAPS	Indicates the line capabilities of the device. It returns one or more flags from Table 2-11.

2

Chapter

Value	Description
POLYGONALCAPS	Indicates the polygon capabilities of the device. It returns one or more flags from Table 2-12.
TEXTCAPS	Indicates the text capabilities of the device. It returns one or more flags from Table 2-13.

Table 2-8: GetDeviceCaps Index TECHNOLOGY Return Values

Value	Description
DT_PLOTTER	A vector plotter.
DT_RASDISPLAY	A raster display.
DT_RASPRINTER	A raster printer.
DT_RASCAMERA	A raster camera.
DT_CHARSTREAM	A character stream.
DT_METAFILE	A metafile.
DT_DISPFILE	A display file.

Table 2-9: GetDeviceCaps Index RASTERCAPS Return Values

Value	Description
RC_BANDING	The device requires banding support.
RC_BITBLT	Device can transfer bitmaps.
RC_BITMAP64	Device can support bitmaps larger than 64K.
RC_DI_BITMAP	Device can support the SetDIBits and GetDIBits functions.
RC_DIBTODEV	Device can support the SetDIBitsToDevice function.
RC_FLOODFILL	Device can perform flood fills.
RC_GDI20_OUTPUT	Device can support the features of Windows 2.0.
RC_PALETTE	Device is a palette-based device.
RC_SCALING	Device can scale.
RC_STRETCHBLT	Device can support the StretchBlt function.
RC_STRETCHDIB	Device can support the StretchDIBits function.

Table 2-10: GetDeviceCaps Index CURVECAPS Return Values

Value	Description
CC_NONE	Device is not capable of supporting curves.
CC_CIRCLES	Device is capable of drawing circles.
CC_PIE	Device is capable of drawing pie wedges.
CC_CHORD	Device is capable of drawing chord arcs.
CC_ELLIPSES	Device is capable of drawing ellipses.
CC_WIDE	Device is capable of drawing wide borders.
CC_STYLED	Device is capable of drawing styled borders.

Value	Description
CC_WIDESTYLED	Device is capable of drawing borders that are wide and styled.
CC_INTERIORS	Device is capable of drawing interiors.
CC_ROUNDRECT	Device is capable of drawing rounded rectangles.

Table 2-11: GetDeviceCaps Index LINECAPS Return Values

Value	Description
LC_NONE	Device is not capable of supporting lines.
LC_POLYLINE	Device is capable of drawing a polyline.
LC_MARKER	Device is capable of drawing a marker.
LC_POLYMARKER	Device is capable of drawing multiple markers.
LC_WIDE	Device is capable of drawing wide lines.
LC_STYLED	Device is capable of drawing styled lines.
LC_WIDESTYLED	Device is capable of drawing lines that are wide and styled.
LC_INTERIORS	Device is capable of drawing interiors.

Table 2-12: GetDeviceCaps Index POLYGONALCAPS Return Values

Value	Description
PC_NONE	Device is not capable of supporting polygons.
PC_POLYGON	Device is capable of drawing alternate-fill polygons.
PC_RECTANGLE	Device is capable of drawing rectangles.
PC_WINDPOLYGON	Device is capable of drawing winding-fill polygons.
PC_SCANLINE	Device is capable of drawing a single scan line.
PC_WIDE	Device is capable of drawing wide borders.
PC_STYLED	Device is capable of drawing styled borders.
PC_WIDESTYLED	Device is capable of drawing borders that are wide and styled.
PC_INTERIORS	Device is capable of drawing interiors.

Table 2-13: GetDeviceCaps Index TEXTCAPS Return Values

Value	Description
TC_OP_CHARACTER	Device has capability of character output precision.
TC_OP_STROKE	Device has capability of stroke output precision.
TC_CP_STROKE	Device has capability of stroke clip precision.
TC_CR_90	Device has capability of 90-degree character rotation.
TC_CR_ANY	Device has capability of any character rotation.
TC_SF_X_YINDEP	Device has capability to scale independently in the x- and y-directions.

2

Chapter

Value	Description
TC_SA_DOUBLE	Device has capability of doubled character for scaling.
TC_SA_INTEGER	Device uses only integer multiples for character scaling.
TC_SA_CONTIN	Device uses any multiples for exact character scaling.
TC_EA_DOUBLE	Device is capable of drawing double-weight characters.
TC_IA_ABLE	Device is capable of italicizing.
TC_UA_ABLE	Device is capable of underlining.
TC_SO_ABLE	Device is capable of drawing strikeouts.
TC_RA_ABLE	Device is capable of drawing raster fonts.
TC_VA_ABLE	Device is capable of drawing vector fonts.
TC_SCROLLBLT	The device cannot scroll using a bit block transfer.

GetMapMode   *Windows.Pas*

Syntax

```
GetMapMode(
DC: HDC                {the handle of a device context}
): Integer;            {returns the mapping mode}
```

Description

The GetMapMode function retrieves the current mapping mode of the specified device context.

Parameters

DC: The handle of the device context whose current mapping mode is retrieved.

Return Value

If the function succeeds, it returns a flag indicating the current mapping mode, and may be one value from Table 2-14. If the function fails, it returns a zero.

See Also

SetMapMode, SetWindowExtEx, SetViewportExtEx

Example

Please see Listing 2-2 in the introduction.

Table 2-14: GetMapMode Return Values

Value	Description
MM_ANISOTROPIC	The units, scaling, and orientation are set by SetWindowExtEx and SetViewportExtEx. The x and y axis scaling are set independently and are not required to be the same.
MM_HIENGLISH	High-resolution mapping in English units. Each unit is 0.001 inch with x being positive to the right and y being positive in the upward direction.
MM_HIMETRIC	High-resolution mapping in metric units. Each unit is 0.01 millimeter with x being positive to the right and y being positive in the upward direction.
MM_ISOTROPIC	The units, scaling, and orientation are set by SetWindowExtEx and SetViewportExtEx with the horizontal and vertical units set as equal. The units and orientation are settable, but the units for the x and y axes are forced to be the same by the GDI. This mode ensures a 1:1 aspect ratio.
MM_LOENGLISH	Low-resolution mapping in English units. Each unit is 0.01 inch with x being positive to the right and y being positive in the upward direction.
MM_LOMETRIC	Low-resolution mapping in metric units. Each unit is 0.1 inch with x being positive to the right and y being positive in the upward direction.
MM_TEXT	Each unit is mapped to one device pixel. This is not a device-independent setting. Devices with different resolutions or scalings will have different results from graphical functions. X is positive to the right and y is positive in the downward direction. This is the default setting.
MM_TWIPS	Each unit is mapped to 1/1440 inch, which is one-twentieth of a printer's point. Coordinates are oriented with x being positive to the right and y being positive in the upward direction.

GetSystemMetrics   Windows.Pas

Syntax

```
GetSystemMetrics(
nIndex: Integer        {the item index}
): Integer;            {returns the item measurement}
```

Description

The GetSystemMetrics function retrieves the dimensions, in pixels, of a specific Windows display element. A variety of items may be queried based on the value of the nIndex parameter. All measured results are provided in numerical values or pixels except for the SM_ARRANGE flag, which returns a combination of values from Table 2-15.

Parameters

nIndex: A flag indicating the Windows display element for which a measurement is to be retrieved. This parameter may be set to one value from Table 2-16.

Return Value

If the function succeeds, it returns the measurement of the queried item. If the function fails, it returns a zero.

See Also

GetDeviceCaps

Example

Listing 2-9: Retrieving Specific Item Dimensions

```
procedure TForm1.Button1Click(Sender: TObject);
begin
  with ListBox1.Items do
  begin
    {display the minimized window arrangement}
    Add('Minimized Window Arrangement -');
    if (GetSystemMetrics(SM_ARRANGE) and ARW_BOTTOMLEFT)=ARW_BOTTOMLEFT then
      Add('      Starts in the lower left corner');
    if (GetSystemMetrics(SM_ARRANGE) and ARW_BOTTOMRIGHT)=ARW_BOTTOMRIGHT then
      Add('      Starts in the lower right corner');
    if (GetSystemMetrics(SM_ARRANGE) and ARW_HIDE)=ARW_HIDE then
      Add('      Minimized windows are hidden');
    if (GetSystemMetrics(SM_ARRANGE) and ARW_TOPLEFT)=ARW_TOPLEFT then
      Add('      Starts in the top left corner');
    if (GetSystemMetrics(SM_ARRANGE) and ARW_TOPRIGHT)=ARW_TOPRIGHT then
      Add('      Starts in the top right corner');

    if (GetSystemMetrics(SM_ARRANGE) and ARW_DOWN)=ARW_DOWN then
      Add('      Arranged vertically, top to bottom');
    if (GetSystemMetrics(SM_ARRANGE) and ARW_LEFT)=ARW_LEFT then
      Add('      Arranged horizontally, left to right');
    if (GetSystemMetrics(SM_ARRANGE) and ARW_RIGHT)=ARW_RIGHT then
      Add('      Arranged horizontally, right to left');
    if (GetSystemMetrics(SM_ARRANGE) and ARW_UP)=ARW_UP then
      Add('      Arrange vertically, bottom to top');

    {display window border dimensions}
    Add('Window border width: '+IntToStr(GetSystemMetrics(SM_CXEDGE)));
```

```
    Add('Window border height: '+IntToStr(GetSystemMetrics(SM_CYEDGE)));

    {display cursor dimensions}
    Add('Cursor width: '+IntToStr(GetSystemMetrics(SM_CXCURSOR)));
    Add('Cursor height: '+IntToStr(GetSystemMetrics(SM_CYCURSOR)));

    {display icon dimensions}
    Add('Icon width: '+IntToStr(GetSystemMetrics(SM_CXICON)));
    Add('Icon height: '+IntToStr(GetSystemMetrics(SM_CYICON)));

    {display maximized window dimensions}
    Add('Maximized window width: '+IntToStr(GetSystemMetrics(SM_CXMAXIMIZED)));
    Add('Maximized window height: '+IntToStr(GetSystemMetrics(SM_CYMAXIMIZED)));

    {display screen dimensions}
    Add('Screen width: '+IntToStr(GetSystemMetrics(SM_CXSCREEN)));
    Add('Screen height: '+IntToStr(GetSystemMetrics(SM_CYSCREEN)));

    {display the caption height}
    Add('Caption height: '+IntToStr(GetSystemMetrics(SM_CYCAPTION)));
  end;
end;
```

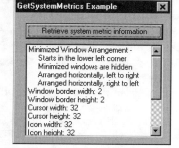

Figure 2-7: Specific system item dimensions

Table 2-15: GetSystemMetrics SM_ARRANGE Values

Value	Description
ARW_BOTTOMLEFT	The default position for starting placement of minimized windows in the lower left corner.
ARW_BOTTOMRIGHT	Begin minimized window placement in bottom right of the screen.
ARW_HIDE	Place minimized windows off the screen in a nonvisible area.
ARW_TOPLEFT	Place minimized windows in the upper left corner of the screen.
ARW_TOPRIGHT	Place minimized windows in the upper right corner of the screen.
ARW_DOWN	Position minimized windows vertically, top to bottom.

Value	Description
ARW_LEFT	Position minimized windows horizontally, left to right.
ARW_RIGHT	Position minimized windows horizontally, right to left.
ARW_UP	Position minimized windows vertically, bottom to top.

Table 2-16: GetSystemMetrics nIndex Values

Value	Description
SM_ARRANGE	Returns a combination of values from Table 2-15 which specify how the system arranges minimized windows.
SM_CLEANBOOT	Returns a value that specifies how the system booted up: 0 = Normal boot 1 = Safe Mode boot 2 = Safe Mode boot with network support.
SM_CMOUSEBUTTONS	Returns the number of buttons on the mouse, or zero if no mouse is installed.
SM_CXBORDER, SM_CYBORDER	The width and height of a window border. These are the same as the SM_CXEDGE and SM_CYEDGE values for windows with the 3-D look.
SM_CXCURSOR, SM_CYCURSOR	Width and height of a cursor. These are the dimensions supported by the current display driver. Because of the requirements of the display driver, the system cannot create cursors of other sizes.
SM_CXDOUBLECLK, SM_CYDOUBLECLK	Width and height of the rectangle around the location of a first click in a double-click operation. The second click must occur within this rectangle for the system to consider the two clicks a double-click. For a double-click to be generated, the second click must occur within a specified time frame, and within this specified rectangle.
SM_CXDRAG, SM_CYDRAG	Width and height of a rectangle centered on a drag point to allow for limited movement of the mouse pointer before a drag operation begins. This gives the user some allowance for mouse movement without inadvertently beginning a drag operation.
SM_CXEDGE, SM_CYEDGE	Dimensions of a 3-D border. These are the 3-D equivalents to SM_CXBORDER and SM_CYBORDER.
SM_CXFIXEDFRAME, SM_CYFIXEDFRAME	Thickness of the frame around a window that has a caption but is not sizable. SM_CXFIXEDFRAME is the horizontal border width and SM_CYFIXEDFRAME is the vertical border height.

Value	Description
SM_CXFULLSCREEN, SM_CYFULLSCREEN	Width and height of a full-screen window client area. The size of the window not obscured by the tray is available by calling the SystemParametersInfo function with the SPI_GETWORKAREA value.
SM_CXHSCROLL, SM_CYHSCROLL	Width of the arrow bitmap on a horizontal scroll bar; and height of a horizontal scroll bar.
SM_CXHTHUMB	Width of the thumb box in a horizontal scroll bar.
SM_CXICON, SM_CYICON	The default width and height of an icon. This is normally 32x32, but can depend on the installed display hardware. The LoadIcon function is restricted to loading only icons of these dimensions.
SM_CXICONSPACING, SM_CYICONSPACING	Dimensions of a grid cell for items in large icon view. The screen is mapped into rectangles of this size, with each item fitting into one of the rectangles when arranged. These values are always greater than or equal to SM_CXICON and SM_CYICON.
SM_CXMAXIMIZED, SM_CYMAXIMIZED	Default size of a maximized top-level window.
SM_CXMAXTRACK, SM_CYMAXTRACK	Default maximum size of a window that has a caption and sizing borders. The system will not allow the user to drag the window frame to a size larger. An application can override these values by processing the WM_GETMINMAXINFO message.
SM_CXMENUCHECK, SM_CYMENUCHECK	Size of the default menu check-mark bitmap.
SM_CXMENUSIZE, SM_CYMENUSIZE	Size of menu bar buttons.
SM_CXMIN, SM_CYMIN	Minimum width and height of a window.
SM_CXMINIMIZED, SM_CYMINIMIZED	Size of a normal minimized window.
SM_CXMINSPACING, SM_CYMINSPACING	Size of a grid cell for minimized windows. See SM_CXICONSPACING, SM_CYICONSPACING. Minimized windows are arranged into rectangles of this size. These values are always greater than or equal to SM_CXMINIMIZED and SM_CYMINIMIZED.
SM_CXMINTRACK, SM_CYMINTRACK	Minimum tracking width and height of a window. The system will not allow a user to drag the window frame to a size smaller than these dimensions. An application can override these values by processing the WM_GETMINMAXINFO message.
SM_CXSCREEN, SM_CYSCREEN	Width and height of the screen.
SM_CXSIZE, SM_CYSIZE	Width and height of a button in a window's caption or title bar.

2

Chapter

Value	Description
SM_CXSIZEFRAME, SM_CYSIZEFRAME	Thickness of the sizing border around a window that can be resized. SM_CXSIZEFRAME is the horizontal border width and SM_CYSIZEFRAME is the vertical border height. Same as SM_CXFRAME and SM_CYFRAME.
SM_CXSMICON, SM_CYSMICON	Recommended size of a small icon. Small icons would normally appear in window captions and in small icon view.
SM_CXSMSIZE, SM_CYSMSIZE	Size of small caption buttons.
SM_CXVSCROLL, SM_CYVSCROLL	Width of a vertical scroll bar; and height of the arrow bitmap on a vertical scroll bar.
SM_CYCAPTION	Height of normal caption area.
SM_CYKANJIWINDOW	For systems using double-byte character sets, the height of the Kanji window at the bottom of the screen.
SM_CYMENU	Height of a single-line menu bar.
SM_CYSMCAPTION	Height of a small caption.
SM_CYVTHUMB	Height of the thumb box in a vertical scroll bar.
SM_DBCSENABLED	Nonzero if the double-byte character set version of USER.EXE is installed; zero if DBCS is not installed.
SM_DEBUG	Nonzero if the debug USER.EXE is installed; zero if it is not.
SM_MENUDROPALIGNMENT	Nonzero if drop-down menus are right-aligned relative to the corresponding menu-bar item; zero if they are left-aligned.
SM_MIDEASTENABLED	Nonzero if the system is enabled for Hebrew/Arabic languages; zero if it is not.
SM_MOUSEPRESENT	Nonzero if a mouse is installed; zero if it is not.
SM_MOUSEWHEELPRESENT	Windows NT only: Nonzero if a mouse with a wheel is installed; zero if it is not.
SM_NETWORK	The least significant bit is set if a network is present; otherwise, it is cleared. The other bits are reserved.
SM_PENWINDOWS	Nonzero if the Microsoft Windows for Pen computing extensions are installed; zero if it is not.
SM_SECURE	Nonzero if security is present; zero if it is not present.
SM_SHOWSOUNDS	Nonzero if the user specifies that audible-only presentations also have a visual representation; zero if visual displays are not required for audible-only software.
SM_SLOWMACHINE	Nonzero if the computer has a low-end processor; zero otherwise.
SM_SWAPBUTTON	Nonzero if the left and right mouse buttons have been configured to be swapped; zero if they have not been so configured.

GetViewportExtEx   ***Windows.Pas***

Syntax

GetViewportExtEx(
DC: HDC;   {the handle of a device context}
var Size: TSize   {the x and y extents of the viewport}
): BOOL;   {returns TRUE or FALSE}

Description

The GetViewportExtEx function retrieves the horizontal and vertical extents of the viewport associated with the device context handle.

Parameters

DC: The handle of the device context whose viewport extents are to be retrieved.

Size: A pointer to a TSize structure that receives the horizontal and vertical extents of the viewport associated with the specified device context.

Return Value

If the function succeeds, it returns TRUE; otherwise it returns FALSE.

See Also

GetViewportOrgEx, GetWindowExtEx, GetWindowOrgEx, SetViewportExtEx, SetViewportOrgEx, SetWindowExtEx, SetWindowOrgEx

Example

Please see Listing 2-2 in the introduction.

GetViewportOrgEx   ***Windows.Pas***

Syntax

GetViewportOrgEx(
DC: HDC;   {the handle of a device context}
var Point: TPoint   {the origin of the viewport coordinates}
): BOOL;   {returns TRUE or FALSE}

Description

The GetViewportOrgEx function retrieves the origin of the coordinate system of the viewport associated with the specified device context.

Parameters

DC: The handle of the device context whose associated viewport's coordinate system origin is to be retrieved.

Point: A pointer to a TPoint structure that receives the x and y values of the origin of the viewport's coordinate system.

2

Chapter

Return Value

If the function succeeds, it returns TRUE; otherwise it returns FALSE.

See Also

GetViewportExtEx, GetWindowExtEx, GetWindowOrgEx, SetViewportExtEx, SetViewportOrgEx, SetWindowExtEx, SetWindowOrgEx

Example

Please see Listing 2-2 in the introduction.

GetWindowDC   Windows.Pas

Syntax

```
GetWindowDC(
hWnd: HWND              {the handle of a window}
): HDC;                 {returns the window's device context}
```

Description

The GetWindowDC function returns a device context for the window specified by the hWnd parameter. The retrieved device context refers to the entire specified window, including the nonclient area such as the title bar, menu, scroll bars, and frame. This allows an application to implement custom graphics in the nonclient areas, such as a custom title bar or border. When the device context is no longer needed, it should be released by calling the ReleaseDC function. Note that this function retrieves only a common device context, and any attributes modified in this device context will not be reflected in the window's private or class device context, if it has one.

Parameters

hWnd: The handle of the window for which a device context is retrieved.

Return Value

If the function succeeds, it returns a handle to the device context for the selected window. If the function fails, it returns zero.

See Also

BeginPaint, GetDC, GetSystemMetrics, ReleaseDC

Example

Listing 2-10: Painting a Custom Caption Bar

```
procedure TForm1.WMNCPaint(var Msg: TMessage);
var
  WinDC: HDC;        // holds the window device context
  OldFont: HFONT;    // holds the previous font
begin
```

```
    {call the inherited paint handler}
    inherited;

    {retrieve a handle to the window device context}
    WinDC := GetWindowDC(Form1.Handle);

    {initialize the font}
    Canvas.Font.Height := GetSystemMetrics(SM_CYCAPTION)-4;
    Canvas.Font.Name := 'Times New Roman';
    Canvas.Font.Style := [fsBold, fsItalic];

    {select the font into the window device context}
    OldFont := SelectObject(WinDC, Canvas.Font.Handle);

    {if the window is active}
    if GetActiveWindow=0 then
    begin
      {draw active colors}
      SetBkColor(WinDC, GetSysColor(COLOR_INACTIVECAPTION));
      SetTextColor(WinDC, GetSysColor(COLOR_INACTIVECAPTIONTEXT));
    end
    else
    begin
      {otherwise draw inactive colors}
      SetBkColor(WinDC, GetSysColor(COLOR_ACTIVECAPTION));
      SetTextColor(WinDC, GetSysColor(COLOR_CAPTIONTEXT));
    end;

    {draw the text of the caption in a bold, italic style}
    SetBkMode(WinDC, OPAQUE);

    TextOut(WinDC, GetSystemMetrics(SM_CXEDGE)+GetSystemMetrics(SM_CXSMICON)+6,
            GetSystemMetrics(SM_CYEDGE)+3, 'GetWindowDC Example',
            Length('GetWindowDC Example'));

    {replace the original font and release the window device context}
    SelectObject(WinDC, OldFont);
    ReleaseDC(Form1.Handle, WinDC);
end;

procedure TForm1.WMActivate(var Msg: TWMActivate);
begin
  {call the inherited message handle and repaint the caption bar}
  inherited;
  PostMessage(Form1.Handle, WM_NCPAINT, 0, 0);
end;
```

2

Chapter

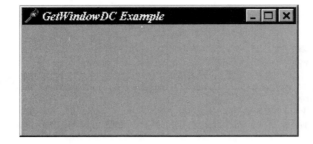

Figure 2-8:
The custom
caption bar

GetWindowExtEx   *Windows.Pas*

Syntax

```
GetWindowExtEx(
DC: HDC;                {the handle of a device context}
var Size: TSize         {the x and y extents of window}
): BOOL;                {returns TRUE or FALSE}
```

Description

The GetWindowExtEx function retrieves the horizontal and vertical extents of the window associated with the specified device context.

Parameters

DC: The handle of the device context for which the horizontal and vertical window extents are retrieved.

Size: A pointer to a TSize structure that receives the horizontal and vertical extents of the window associated with the specified device context.

Return Value

If the function succeeds, it returns TRUE; otherwise it returns FALSE.

See Also

GetViewportExtEx, GetViewportOrgEx, GetWindowOrgEx, SetViewportExtEx, SetViewportOrgEx, SetWindowExtEx, SetWindowOrgEx

Example

Please see Listing 2-2 in the introduction.

GetWindowOrgEx   *Windows.Pas*

Syntax

```
GetWindowOrgEx(
DC: HDC;                {the handle of a device context}
```

var Point: TPoint	{the origin of the window coordinates}
): BOOL;	{returns TRUE or FALSE}

Description

The GetWindowOrgEx function retrieves the origin of the window associated with the specified device context.

Parameters

DC: The handle of the device context whose associated window's coordinate system origin is to be retrieved.

Point: A pointer to a TPoint structure that receives the x and y values of the origin of the window's coordinate system.

Return Value

If the function succeeds, it returns TRUE; otherwise it returns FALSE.

See Also

GetViewportExtEx, GetViewportOrgEx, GetWindowExtEx, SetViewportExtEx, SetViewportOrgEx, SetWindowExtEx, SetWindowOrgEx

Example

Please see Listing 2-2 in the introduction.

LPtoDP   *Windows.Pas*

Syntax

LPtoDP(	
DC: HDC;	{the handle of a device context}
var Points;	{a pointer to an array of TPoint structures}
Count: Integer	{the number of entries in the array}
): BOOL;	{returns TRUE or FALSE}

Description

The LPtoDP function converts points from logical coordinates to device coordinates. The Points parameter points to an array of TPoint structures containing the coordinates to be translated. These TPoint structures will receive the translated coordinates when the function returns. The coordinate transformation is performed based on the values set by the SetWindowOrgEx, SetViewportOrgEx, SetWindowExtEx, and SetViewportExtEx functions. The LPtoDP function will fail if any of the points in the TPoint structures specify a value greater in size than 27 bits. It will also fail if any of the transformed points are greater in size than 32 bits. In the event of failure, the values in the entire Points array are undefined.

Parameters

DC: The device context for which the coordinate transformations will be made.

Points: A pointer to an array of TPoint structures containing the coordinates to be converted.

Count: Specifies the number of entries in the array pointed to by the Points parameter.

Return Value

If the function succeeds, it returns TRUE; otherwise it returns FALSE.

See Also

DPtoLP, SetWindowOrgEx, SetViewportOrgEx, SetWindowExtEx, SetViewportExtEx

Example

Please see Listing 2-12 under ScaleViewportExtEx.

MapWindowPoints   *Windows.Pas*

Syntax

```
MapWindowPoints(
hWndFrom: HWND;              {the handle of the source window}
hWndTo: HWND;               {the handle of the destination window}
var lpPoints:UINT;          {a pointer to an array of points}
cPoints: UINT               {the size of the array}
): Integer;                 {returns pixel offsets}
```

Description

The MapWindowPoints function converts a set of points from a coordinate system relative to one window to the coordinate system of another window. Any number of points can be transformed with a single function call.

Parameters

hWndFrom: The handle of the window from which the points are to be translated. The points listed in the lpPoints parameter have dimensions relative to this window. If this parameter is set to NIL or HWND_DESKTOP, the points are relative to the screen.

hWndTo: The handle of the window to which the points are to be translated. If this parameter is set to NIL or HWND_DESKTOP, the points are relative to the screen.

lpPoints: A pointer to an array of TPoint structures containing the coordinates to be translated. These TPoint structures receive the translated coordinates when the function returns.

cPoints: Specifies the number of elements in the array pointed to by the lpPoints parameter.

Return Value

If the function succeeds, the low-order word of the return value specifies the number of pixels that are added to the horizontal dimension of the coordinates, and the high-order word of the return value specifies the number of pixels added to the vertical dimension of the coordinates. If the function fails, it returns a zero.

See Also

ClientToScreen, ScreenToClient

Example

Listing 2-11: Translating Multiple Coordinates from One Coordinate System to Another

```
var
  Form1: TForm1;
  DrawnRect: TRect;        // holds the rectangular coordinates
  Drawing: Boolean;        // indicates if a rectangle is being drawn

implementation

{$R *.DFM}

procedure TForm1.PaintBox1MouseDown(Sender: TObject; Button: TMouseButton;
  Shift: TShiftState; X, Y: Integer);
begin
  {indicate that a drawing operation has commenced, and initialize the
   rectangular coordinates}
  Drawing := TRUE;
  DrawnRect := Rect(X, Y, X, Y);
end;

procedure TForm1.PaintBox1MouseMove(Sender: TObject; Shift: TShiftState; X,
  Y: Integer);
begin
  {if we are redrawing...}
  if Drawing then
  with PaintBox1.Canvas do
  begin
    {initialize the canvas's pen and brush}
    Pen.Mode := pmNot;
    Pen.Width := 2;
    Brush.Style := bsClear;

    {draw a rectangle over the previous one to erase it}
    Rectangle(DrawnRect.Left, DrawnRect.Top, DrawnRect.Right, DrawnRect.Bottom);

    {set the rectangle to the current coordinates}
    DrawnRect := Rect(DrawnRect.Left, DrawnRect.Top, X, Y);

    {draw the new rectangle}
    Rectangle(DrawnRect.Left, DrawnRect.Top, DrawnRect.Right, DrawnRect.Bottom);
```

```
   end;
end;

procedure TForm1.PaintBox1MouseUp(Sender: TObject; Button: TMouseButton;
  Shift: TShiftState; X, Y: Integer);
begin
  {we are no longer drawing}
  Drawing := FALSE;

  {display the coordinates relative to the panel}
  Label2.Caption := 'Panel coordinates - L:'+IntToStr(DrawnRect.Left)+', T: '+
                     IntToStr(DrawnRect.Top)+', R: '+IntToStr(DrawnRect.Right)+
                     ', B: '+IntToStr(DrawnRect.Bottom);

  {translate the rectangular coordinates relative to the form}
  MapWindowPoints(Panel1.Handle, Form1.Handle, DrawnRect, 2);

  {display the coordinates relative to the form}
  Label3.Caption := 'Form coordinates - L:'+IntToStr(DrawnRect.Left)+', T: '+
                     IntToStr(DrawnRect.Top)+', R: '+IntToStr(DrawnRect.Right)+
                     ', B: '+IntToStr(DrawnRect.Bottom);
end;
```

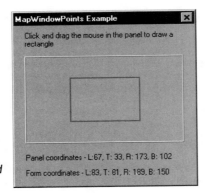

Figure 2-9:
The translated
points

OffsetViewportOrgEx   Windows.Pas

Syntax

```
OffsetViewportOrgEx(
DC: HDC;              {the handle of a device context}
X: Integer;           {the horizontal offset}
Y: Integer;           {the vertical offset}
Points: Pointer       {the previous origin}
): BOOL;              {returns TRUE or FALSE}
```

Description

The OffsetViewportOrgEx function modifies the existing origin of the viewport by adding a value to the current origin's location. The parameters can specify positive or negative offsets in the horizontal and vertical directions. The location of the previous origin is passed back in the Points parameter. OffsetViewportOrgEx moves the viewport origin to a new location relative to its existing coordinates. To place the origin at an absolute position regardless of the current position, use SetViewportOrgEx instead.

Parameters

DC: The handle of the device context whose viewport origin is to be modified.

X: The horizontal offset to add to or subtract from the current x value of the origin.

Y: The vertical offset to add to or subtract from the current y value of the origin.

Points: A pointer to a TPoint structure which receives the original location of the origin. This parameter can be set to NIL if the original coordinates are not needed.

Return Value

If the function succeeds, it returns TRUE; otherwise it returns FALSE.

See Also

GetViewportOrgEx, OffsetWindowOrgEx, ScaleViewportExtEx, SetViewportOrgEx

Example

Please see Listing 2-12 under ScaleViewportExtEx.

OffsetWindowOrgEx   Windows.Pas

Syntax

```
OffsetWindowOrgEx(
DC: HDC;                    {the handle of a device context}
X: Integer;                 {the horizontal offset}
Y: Integer;                 {the vertical offset}
Points: Pointer             {the previous origin}
): BOOL;                    {returns TRUE or FALSE}
```

Description

The OffsetWindowOrgEx function modifies the existing origin of the window by adding a value to the current origin's location. The parameters can specify positive or negative offsets in the horizontal and vertical directions. The location of the previous origin is passed back in the Points parameter. OffsetWindowOrgEx moves the window origin to a new value relative to its existing coordinates. To place the origin at an absolute position regardless of the current position, use SetWindowOrgEx instead.

Chapter **2**

Parameters

DC: The handle of the device context whose associated window's origin is to be modified.

X: The horizontal offset to add to or subtract from the current x value of the origin.

Y: The vertical offset to add to or subtract from the current y value of the origin.

Points: A pointer to a TPoint structure which receives the original location of the origin. This parameter can be set to NIL if the original coordinates are not needed.

Return Value

If the function succeeds, it returns TRUE; otherwise it returns FALSE.

See Also

GetViewportOrgEx, OffsetViewportOrgEx, ScaleWindowExtEx, SetViewportOrgEx

Example

Please see Listing 2-12 under ScaleViewportExtEx.

ReleaseDC   *Windows.Pas*

Syntax

```
ReleaseDC(
hWnd: HWND;              {the handle of a window}
hDC: HDC                 {the device context}
): Integer;              {returns zero or one}
```

Description

The ReleaseDC function releases a device context retrieved by the GetDC or GetWindowDC functions, returning its resources to Windows. The ReleaseDC function affects only common device contexts. ReleaseDC has no effect on class or private device contexts.

Parameters

hWnd: The handle of the window whose associated device context is to be released.

hDC: The handle of the device context to be released.

Return Value

If the function succeeds, it returns a one; otherwise it returns a zero.

See Also

CreateCompatibleDC, DeleteDC, GetDC, GetWindowDC

Example

Please see Listing 2-5 under CreateCompatibleDC and other functions throughout this chapter.

RestoreDC   Windows.Pas

Syntax

```
RestoreDC(
DC: HDC;                    {the handle of a device context}
SavedDC: Integer           {the state to be restored}
): BOOL;                    {returns TRUE or FALSE}
```

Description

The RestoreDC function restores the state of a previously saved device context. The state of a device context can be saved by calling the SaveDC function. The SaveDC function returns a value identifying the saved device context, which should be used in the SavedDC parameter to restore an explicit state.

Parameters

DC: The handle of the device context whose state is to be restored. The device context should already exist and have states that were previously saved with the SaveDC function.

SavedDC: Specifies the instance number of the state to be restored. This value is returned by the SaveDC function when the state was originally saved. A negative value can be specified to restore a state relative to the current state (i.e., -1 restores the most recently saved state). If the restored state is not the most recently saved state, all other states between the most recently saved state and the specified state are disposed.

Return Value

If the function succeeds, it returns TRUE; otherwise it returns FALSE.

See Also

CreateCompatibleDC, GetDC, GetWindowDC, SaveDC

Example

Please see Listing 2-5 under CreateCompatibleDC.

SaveDC   Windows.Pas

Syntax

```
SaveDC(
DC: HDC                    {the handle of a device context}
): Integer;                {returns a saved state index}
```

Chapter **2**

Description

This function saves the state of the specified device context into an internal stack maintained by Windows. This state includes the information and graphical objects associated with the device context such as bitmaps, brushes, palettes, fonts, the drawing mode, the mapping mode, etc. The state can be recalled with the RestoreDC function.

Parameters

DC: The handle of the device context for which state information is to be saved.

Return Value

If the function succeeds, it returns a value identifying the saved state, which can be used in subsequent calls to the RestoreDC function. If the function fails, it returns a zero.

See Also

CreateCompatibleDC, GetDC, GetWindowDC, RestoreDC

Example

Please see Listing 2-5 under CreateCompatibleDC.

ScaleViewportExtEx   Windows.Pas

Syntax

```
ScaleViewportExtEx(
DC: HDC;                    {the handle of a device context}
XM: Integer;                {the horizontal multiplier}
XD: Integer;                {the horizontal divisor}
YM: Integer;                {the vertical multiplier}
YD: Integer;                {the vertical divisor}
Size: PSize                 {a pointer to the previous extents}
): BOOL;                    {returns TRUE or FALSE}
```

Description

The ScaleViewportExtEx function modifies the existing extents of the viewport associated with the specified device context, according to the specified scaling factors. For horizontal and vertical extents, a multiplier and divisor parameter is available for making the extent in that direction larger or smaller. Parameters not used should be supplied with a value of 1. For example, making the horizontal extent half of the current value would require the XD parameter to be set to 2. All other parameters would be 1. Making the horizontal extent three-fourths of its current value could be accomplished by setting the XM parameter to 3 and the XD parameter to 4.

Parameters

DC: The handle of the device context whose viewport extents are to be scaled.

XM: The horizontal extent multiplier.

XD: The horizontal extent divisor.

YM: The vertical extent multiplier.

YD: The vertical extent divisor.

Size: A pointer to a TSize structure that receives the previous extent values.

Return Value

If the function succeeds, it returns TRUE; otherwise it returns FALSE.

See Also

GetViewportExtEx, ScaleWindowExtEx

Example

Listing 2-12: Scaling Viewports and Windows

```
{Whoops!  Delphi incorrectly imports this function, so we must reimport it
 manually}
function OffsetViewportOrgEx(DC: HDC; X, Y: Integer;
                            Points: Pointer): BOOL; stdcall;

{Whoops!  Delphi incorrectly imports this function, so we must reimport it
 manually}
function OffsetWindowOrgEx(DC: HDC; X, Y: Integer;
                           Points: Pointer): BOOL; stdcall;

var
  Form1: TForm1;
  MyDisplayDC: HDC;                // a handle to the device context
  MyMapMode: Integer;             // holds the mapping mode
  PrevWindowSize: TSize;          // holds the previous window size
  PrevViewportSize: TSize;        // holds the previous viewport size
  PrevWindowPoint: TPoint;        // holds the previous window origin
  PrevViewportPoint: TPoint;      // holds the previous viewport origin

implementation

{$R *.DFM}

{re-import the corrected functions}
function OffsetViewportOrgEx; external gdi32 name 'OffsetViewportOrgEx';
function OffsetWindowOrgEx; external gdi32 name 'OffsetWindowOrgEx';

procedure TForm1.ReportPosition;
var
  ReturnValue: TPoint;            // holds the window and viewport origin
  ReturnSize: TSize;              // holds the window and viewport extents
begin
  {display the window origin}
  GetWindowOrgEx(MyDisplayDC,ReturnValue);
```

Chapter **2**

```
    Label9.Caption := IntToStr(ReturnValue.x)
         + ', ' + IntToStr(ReturnValue.y);

    {display the viewport origin}
    GetViewportOrgEx(MyDisplayDC,ReturnValue);
    Label10.Caption := IntToStr(ReturnValue.x)
         + ', ' + IntToStr(ReturnValue.y);

    {display the window extents}
    GetWindowExtEx(MyDisplayDC,ReturnSize);
    Label11.Caption := IntToStr(ReturnSize.cx)
         + ', ' + IntToStr(ReturnSize.cy);

    {display the viewport extents}
    GetViewportExtEx(MyDisplayDC,ReturnSize);
    Label12.Caption := IntToStr(ReturnSize.cx)
         + ', ' + IntToStr(ReturnSize.cy);
end;

procedure TForm1.ReadUserRequest;
begin
  {retrieve the selected mapping mode}
  case RadioGroup1.ItemIndex of
    0: MyMapMode := MM_TEXT;
    1: MyMapMode := MM_ANISOTROPIC;
    2: MyMapMode := MM_ISOTROPIC;
    3: MyMapMode := MM_HIENGLISH;
    4: MyMapMode := MM_HIMETRIC;
    5: MyMapMode := MM_LOENGLISH;
    6: MyMapMode := MM_LOMETRIC;
    7: MyMapMode := MM_TWIPS;
  end;
end;

procedure TForm1.PaintImage;
begin
  {erase the previous image}
  Panel1.Repaint;

  {get the values of the user controls}
  ReadUserRequest;

  {set the Map Mode according to the radiogroup}
  SetMapMode(MyDisplayDC,MyMapMode);

  {offset the window origin by the specified amount}
  OffsetWindowOrgEx(MyDisplayDC,
    StrToInt(EditOWX.text),StrToInt(EditOWY.text),
    @PrevWindowPoint);

  {offset the viewport origin by the specified amount}
  OffSetViewportOrgEx(MyDisplayDC,
    StrToInt(EditOVX.text),StrToInt(EditOVY.text),
    @PrevViewportPoint);
```

```
  {scale the window extents by the specified amount}
  ScaleWindowExtEx(MyDisplayDC,
    StrToInt(EditSWEXM.text),StrToInt(EditSWEXD.text),
    StrToInt(EditSWEYM.text),StrToInt(EditSWEYD.text),
    @PrevWindowSize);

  {scale the viewport extents by the specified amount}
  ScaleViewportExtEx(MyDisplayDC,
    StrToInt(EditSVEXM.text),StrToInt(EditSVEXD.text),
    StrToInt(EditSVEYM.text),StrToInt(EditSVEYD.text),
    @PrevViewportSize);

  {draw the image. note that the coordinates used are hard-coded and do not
   change, demonstrating how the window origin and extents affect drawing
   operations}
  Windows.Rectangle(MyDisplayDC, 0, 0, 50, 50);
  Windows.Rectangle(MyDisplayDC, -25, 24, 75, 26);
  Windows.Rectangle(MyDisplayDC, 24, -25, 26, 75);

  {display the new origin and extent values}
  ReportPosition;
end;

procedure TForm1.FormPaint(Sender: TObject);
begin
  {paint the image}
  PaintImage;
end;

procedure TForm1.FormCreate(Sender: TObject);
begin
  {retrieve a handle to the panel's device context}
  MyDisplayDC := GetDC(Panel1.handle);
end;

procedure TForm1.FormDestroy(Sender: TObject);
begin
  {release the device context}
  ReleaseDC(Panel1.handle,MyDisplayDC);
end;

procedure TForm1.BitBtn1Click(Sender: TObject);
var
  MyPoint: TPoint;    // holds converted points
begin
  {convert device units to logical units with DPtoLP}
  MyPoint.X := StrToInt(EditDevX.text);
  MyPoint.Y := StrToInt(EditDevY.text);

  {check for errors}
  if not DPtoLP(MyDisplayDC,MyPoint,1) then
    ShowMessage('Error in device coordinates')
  else
  begin
    {MyPoint now contains converted logical coordinates}
```

```
      EditLogX.text := IntToStr(MyPoint.X);
      EditLogY.text := IntToStr(MyPoint.Y);
  end;
end;

procedure TForm1.BitBtn2Click(Sender: TObject);
var
  MyPoint: TPoint;     // holds converted points
begin
  {convert device units to logical units with DPtoLP}
  MyPoint.X := StrToInt(EditLogX.Text);
  MyPoint.Y := StrToInt(EditLogY.Text);

  {check for errors}
  if not LPtoDP(MyDisplayDC,MyPoint,1) then
    ShowMessage('Error in logical coordinates')
  else
  begin
    {MyPoint now contains converted device coordinates}
    EditDevX.Text := IntToStr(MyPoint.X);
    EditDevY.Text := IntToStr(MyPoint.Y);
  end;
end;
```

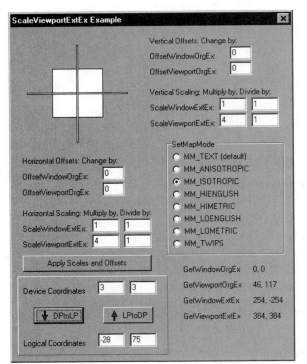

Figure 2-10:
The scaled
image

2

ScaleWindowExtEx   *Windows.Pas*

Syntax

```
ScaleWindowExtEx(
DC: HDC;                      {the handle of a device context}
XM: Integer;                  {the horizontal multiplier}
XD: Integer;                  {the horizontal divisor}
YM: Integer;                  {the vertical multiplier}
YD: Integer;                  {the vertical divisor}
Size: PSize                   {a pointer to the previous extents}
): BOOL;                      {returns TRUE or FALSE}
```

Description

The ScaleWindowExtEx function modifies the existing extents of the window associated with the specified device context, according to the specified scaling factors. For horizontal and vertical extents, a multiplier and divisor parameter is available for making the extent in that direction larger or smaller. Parameters not used should be supplied with a value of 1. For example, making the horizontal extent half of the current value would require the XD parameter to be set to 2. All other parameters would be 1. Making the horizontal extent three-fourths of its current value could be accomplished by setting the XM parameter to 3 and the XD parameter to 4.

Parameters

DC: The handle of the device context whose associated window extents are to be scaled.

XM: The horizontal extent multiplier.

XD: The horizontal extent divisor.

YM: The vertical extent multiplier.

YD: The vertical extent divisor.

Size: A pointer to a TSize structure that receives the previous extent values.

Return Value

If the function succeeds, it returns TRUE; otherwise it returns FALSE.

See Also

GetWindowExtEx, ScaleViewportExtEx

Example

Please see Listing 2-12 under ScaleViewportExtEx.

ScreenToClient   *Windows.Pas*

Syntax

```
ScreenToClient(
hWnd: HWND;              {the handle of a window}
var lpPoint: TPoint      {a pointer to a TPoint structure}
): BOOL;                 {returns TRUE or FALSE}
```

Description

This function changes the coordinates of a point from screen coordinates to client coordinates. The point to be translated is in a TPoint structure pointed to by the lpPoint parameter. The function takes the coordinates pointed to by the lpPoint parameter and converts them into coordinates relative to the client area of the specified window. The results are placed back into this TPoint structure. The coordinates of the point being passed use the top left corner of the screen as the origin. The coordinates of the result use the top left corner of the client area of the specified window as the origin.

Parameters

hWnd: The handle to the window to which the point is converted. When the function returns, the point will be relative to the top left corner of the client area of this window.

lpPoint: A pointer to a TPoint structure that contains the point to be converted. This TPoint structure receives the converted point when the function returns.

Return Value

If the function succeeds, it returns TRUE; otherwise it returns FALSE.

See Also

ClientToScreen, MapWindowPoints

Example

Please see Listing 2-4 under ClientToScreen.

ScrollDC   *Windows.Pas*

Syntax

```
ScrollDC(
DC: HDC;                 {the handle of a device context}
DX: Integer;             {the horizontal scroll increment}
DY: Integer;             {the vertical scroll increment}
var Scroll: TRect;       {the scrolling rectangle}
Clip: TRect;             {the clipping rectangle}
Rgn: HRGN;               {the exposed region}
Update: PRect            {the exposed rectangle}
): BOOL;                 {returns TRUE or FALSE}
```

Description

The ScrollDC function scrolls a rectangle of bits horizontally and vertically. The amount of scrolling is given in device units.

Parameters

DC: The handle to the device context which contains the rectangle where the bits are to be scrolled.

DX: The number of horizontal device units to scroll by. This value is positive for scrolling to the right, and negative for scrolling to the left.

DY: The number of vertical device units to scroll by. This value is positive for scrolling down, and negative for scrolling up.

Scroll: Specifies a TRect structure which contains the location of the rectangle to be scrolled.

Clip: Specifies a TRect structure which contains the location of the clipping rectangle.

Rgn: Specifies the handle of the region which the scrolling process uncovers. This region is not limited to being a rectangle. This parameter may be set to zero if the update region is not needed.

Update: A pointer to a TRect structure that receives the location of the rectangle uncovered by the scrolled area. The coordinates of this rectangle are given in client coordinates regardless of the current mapping mode of the specified device context. This parameter can be set to NIL if the update rectangle is not needed

Return Value

If the function succeeds, it returns TRUE; otherwise it returns FALSE.

See Also

InvalidateRect, InvalidateRgn, BitBlt

Example

Listing 2-13: Scrolling an Image Inside of a Viewing Area

```
var
  Form1: TForm1;
  PreviousX, PreviousY: Integer;      // tracks the previous scroll offset

implementation

{$R *.DFM}

procedure TForm1.FormCreate(Sender: TObject);
begin
  {initialize the scroll bars}
  ScrollBar1.Max := Image1.Picture.Bitmap.Width-Image1.Width;
```

```
      ScrollBar2.Max := Image1.Picture.Bitmap.Height-Image1.Height;

   {initialize the offset tracking variables}
   PreviousX := 0;
   PreviousY := 0;
end;

procedure TForm1.ScrollBar1Change(Sender: TObject);
var
   ScrollRect,            // the rectangular area to be scrolled
   ClipRect,              // the clipping rectangle of the scrolled area
   UpdateRect: TRect;     // the area uncovered by scrolling
begin
   {initialize the scrolling and clipping rectangles to the entire area
    of the image}
   ScrollRect := Image1.BoundsRect;
   ClipRect := Image1.BoundsRect;

   {scroll the area horizontally by the specified amount}
   ScrollDC(Canvas.Handle, PreviousX-ScrollBar1.Position, 0, ScrollRect,
            ClipRect, 0, @UpdateRect);

   {copy the appropriate area of the original bitmap into the newly uncovered
    area}
   Canvas.CopyRect(UpdateRect, Image1.Picture.Bitmap.Canvas,
                   Rect((UpdateRect.Left-Image1.Left)+ScrollBar1.Position,
                   ScrollBar2.Position, (UpdateRect.Left-Image1.Left)+
                   ScrollBar1.Position+(UpdateRect.Right-UpdateRect.Left),
                   Image1.Height+ScrollBar2.Position));

   {record the current position}
   PreviousX := ScrollBar1.Position;
end;

procedure TForm1.ScrollBar2Change(Sender: TObject);
var
   ScrollRect,            // the rectangular area to be scrolled
   ClipRect,              // the clipping rectangle of the scrolled area
   UpdateRect: TRect;     // the area uncovered by scrolling
begin
   {initialize the scrolling and clipping rectangles to the entire area
    of the image}
   ScrollRect := Image1.BoundsRect;
   ClipRect := Image1.BoundsRect;

   {scroll the area vertically by the specified amount}
   ScrollDC(Canvas.Handle, 0, PreviousY-ScrollBar2.Position, ScrollRect,
            ClipRect, 0, @UpdateRect);

   {copy the appropriate area of the original bitmap into the newly uncovered
    area}
   Canvas.CopyRect(UpdateRect, Image1.Picture.Bitmap.Canvas,
                   Rect(ScrollBar1.Position, (UpdateRect.Top-Image1.Top)+
                   ScrollBar2.Position, Image1.Width+ScrollBar1.Position,
                   (UpdateRect.Top-Image1.Top)+ScrollBar2.Position+
```

```
                            (UpdateRect.Bottom-UpdateRect.Top)));

      {record the current position}
      PreviousY := ScrollBar2.Position;
    end;
```

Figure 2-11:
The scrolled
image

SetMapMode   *Windows.Pas*

Syntax

SetMapMode(
DC: HDC;   {the handle of a device context}
p2: Integer   {the mapping mode}
): Integer;   {returns the previous mapping mode}

Description

This function sets a new method for mapping graphical units on the specified device context. The units may be measured in terms of pixels, inches, millimeters, or printer's points. The orientation of the x and y axes may also be set. This function is used to determine how software-defined measurements are mapped to the physical graphical devices.

Parameters

DC: A handle to the device context whose mapping mode is to be set.

p2: A flag indicating the new mapping mode. This parameter can be set to one value from Table 2-17.

Return Value

If the function succeeds, it returns the value of the previous mapping mode, and will be one value from Table 2-17. If the function fails, it returns a zero.

See Also

GetMapMode, SetViewportExtEx, SetViewportOrgEx, SetWindowExtEx, SetWindowOrgEx

Example

Please see Listing 2-2 in the introduction.

Table 2-17: SetMapMode p2 Values

Value	Description
MM_ANISOTROPIC	The units, scaling, and orientation are set by SetWindowExtEx and SetViewportExtEx. The x and y axis scaling are set independently and are not required to be the same.
MM_HIENGLISH	High-resolution mapping in English units. Each unit is 0.001 inch with x being positive to the right and y being positive in the upward direction.
MM_HIMETRIC	High-resolution mapping in metric units. Each unit is 0.01 millimeter with x being positive to the right and y being positive in the upward direction.
MM_ISOTROPIC	The units, scaling, and orientation are set by SetWindowExtEx and SetViewportExtEx with the horizontal and vertical units set as equal. The units and orientation are settable, but the units for the x and y axes are forced to be the same by the GDI. This mode ensures a 1:1 aspect ratio.
MM_LOENGLISH	Low-resolution mapping in English units. Each unit is 0.01 inch with x being positive to the right and y being positive in the upward direction.
MM_LOMETRIC	Low-resolution mapping in metric units. Each unit is 0.1 inch with x being positive to the right and y being positive in the upward direction.
MM_TEXT	Each unit is mapped to one device pixel. This is not a device-independent setting. Devices with different resolutions or scalings will have different results from graphical functions. X is positive to the right and y is positive in the downward direction. This is the default setting.
MM_TWIPS	Each unit is mapped to 1/1440 inch, which is one-twentieth of a printer's point. Coordinates are oriented with x being positive to the right and y being positive in the upward direction.

SetViewportExtEx   *Windows.Pas*

Syntax

```
SetViewportExtEx(
DC: HDC;                    {the handle of a device context}
XExt: Integer;             {the new horizontal extent}
YExt: Integer;             {the new vertical extent}
Size: PSize                {a pointer to the original extent}
): BOOL;                   {returns TRUE or FALSE}
```

Description

This function establishes a new size for the viewport associated with the specified device context. Calls to this function are only valid when the SetMapMode function has set the mapping mode of the specified device context to MM_ANISOTROPIC or MM_ISOTROPIC. Calls to SetViewportExtEx are ignored for any other map modes. In the case of MM_ISOTROPIC, a call to the SetWindowExtEx function must be made before the SetViewportExtEx function is used.

Parameters

DC: A handle to the device context whose associated viewport's size is being modified.

XExt: The new horizontal size of the viewport, in device units.

YExt: The new vertical size of the viewport, in device units.

Size: A pointer to a TSize structure that receives the previous size of the viewport. If this parameter is set to NIL, the previous size is not returned.

Return Value

If the function succeeds, it returns TRUE; otherwise it returns FALSE.

See Also

GetMapMode, GetViewportExtEx, SetMapMode, SetWindowExtEx

Example

Please see Listing 2-2 in the introduction.

SetViewportOrgEx   Windows.Pas

Syntax

```
SetViewportOrgEx(
DC: HDC;                  {the handle of a device context}
X: Integer;               {the new x value of origin}
Y: Integer;               {the new y value of origin}
Point: PPoint             {a pointer to the original origin values}
): BOOL;                  {returns TRUE or FALSE}
```

Description

This function establishes a new coordinate system origin for the specified device context. Devices normally set their origin in the upper left-hand corner of their displayed or printed image. The SetViewportOrgEx function may be useful when plotting functions which will display negative values. By locating the origin of the device context where the origin of a graph is located (traditionally in the lower left-hand corner), an application can avoid performing a coordinate transform for every point that is plotted. Due to a small amount of overhead incurred by the GDI in accepting a new coordinate system origin, an application should be tested for speed when deciding to use this

Chapter **2**

function. An application which already performs a calculation to plot points on a device context might run faster if the device origin is left at the default location while the application performs calculations which account for that location of the device origin.

Parameters

DC: The handle of the device context whose viewport origin is to be modified.

X: The horizontal location of the new origin, in device units.

Y: The vertical location of the new origin, in device units.

Point: A pointer to a TPoint structure which receives the location of the previous origin location, in device units. If this parameter is set to NIL, the previous origin location is not returned.

Return Value

If the function succeeds, it returns TRUE; otherwise it returns FALSE.

See Also

GetViewportOrgEx, SetWindowOrgEx

Example

Please see Listing 2-2 in the introduction.

SetWindowExtEx   **Windows.Pas**

Syntax

```
SetWindowExtEx(
DC: HDC;                {the handle of a device context}
XExt: Integer;         {the new horizontal extent}
YExt: Integer;         {the new vertical extent}
Size: PSize            {a pointer to the original extent}
): BOOL;               {returns TRUE or FALSE}
```

Description

This function establishes a new size for the window associated with the specified device context. Calls to this function are only valid when the SetMapMode function has set the mapping mode of the specified device context to MM_ANISOTROPIC or MM_ISOTROPIC. Calls to the SetWindowExtEx function are ignored with other mapping modes. In the case of MM_ISOTROPIC, a call to the SetWindowExtEx function must be made before the SetViewportExtEx function is used.

Parameters

DC: The handle of the device context whose associated window size is to be modified.

XExt: The new horizontal size of the window, in device units.

YExt: The new vertical size of the window, in device units.

Size: A pointer to a TSize structure that receives the previous size of the window. If this parameter is set to NIL, the previous size is not returned.

Return Value

If the function succeeds, it returns TRUE; otherwise it returns FALSE.

See Also

GetViewportExtEx, GetViewportOrgEx, GetWindowExtEx, GetWindowOrgEx, Set-ViewportExtEx, SetViewportOrgEx, SetWindowOrgEx

Example

Please see Listing 2-2 in the introduction.

SetWindowOrgEx   *Windows.Pas*

Syntax

```
SetWindowOrgEx(
DC: HDC;                    {the handle of a device context}
X: Integer;                 {the new horizontal location of the origin}
Y: Integer;                 {the new vertical location of the origin}
Point: PPoint               {a pointer to the original origin values}
): BOOL;                    {returns TRUE or FALSE}
```

Description

SetWindowOrgEx establishes a new coordinate system origin for the window associated with the specified device context. A window will normally have its origin in its upper left-hand corner. The SetWindowOrgEx function may be useful when plotting functions which will display negative values. By making the origin of the window and the origin of a graph coincide at the same point, an application can avoid performing a coordinate transform for every point that is plotted. Due to a small amount of overhead incurred by the GDI in accepting a new coordinate system origin, an application should be tested for speed when deciding to use this function. An application which already performs a calculation to plot points on a device context might run faster if the window origin is left at the default location while the application performs calculations which account for that location of the window origin.

Parameters

DC: The handle of the device context whose associated window's origin is to be modified.

X: The horizontal location of the new origin, in device units.

Y: The vertical location of the new origin, in device units.

Point: A pointer to a TPoint structure which receives the location of the previous origin, in device units. If this parameter is set to NIL, the previous origin location is not returned.

Return Value

If the function succeeds, it returns TRUE; otherwise it returns FALSE.

See Also

GetViewportOrgEx, GetWindowOrgEx, SetViewportOrgEx

Example

Please see Listing 2-2 in the introduction.

Chapter 3

Painting and Drawing Functions

Windows provides a plethora of functions for drawing simple graphics and graphics primitives. Windows is quite capable of performing high-end graphics manipulation, as is evident by the amount of digital image manipulation software on the market. However, drawing a simple graphic is sometimes the most efficient means of communicating with the user. For example, a simple rectangle can be drawn around a portion of an image to indicate it has been selected. Windows itself makes heavy use of the functions in this chapter for drawing standard user interface elements and common controls. Delphi encapsulates a large portion of the functions presented in this chapter as methods and properties of the TCanvas object. However, the complexity of the VCL sometimes gets in the way, and dropping down to the Windows API level is the only way to go. This chapter describes the most common functions used to draw simple graphics onto a device context.

Graphical Objects

In order to draw onto a device context, Windows needs some method of knowing exactly what it is supposed to draw—what color the object should be, how wide it is, etc. These attributes are encapsulated in a graphical object. All of the CreateXXX functions, such as CreateBrush, CreateBitmap, or CreatePen, return a handle to a graphical object. Internally, this handle references data that contains all of the attribute's defining object.

In order to use most graphical objects, they need to be selected into a device context by using the SelectObject function. Once an object is selected into a device context it is automatically used by those functions that need the specific object. For example, a new pen can be created with the CreatePen object and selected into a device context. From then on, any drawing functions that require a pen will use the specific pen selected into the device context automatically. Only one object of a given type can be selected into a device context at any given time.

It is important to delete a graphical object when it is no longer needed. Each graphical object handle represents a certain amount of memory and resources, taking away from the overall resources available to the system. Although low resources is less of a problem with Windows 95 and NT than it was with previous Windows versions, memory leaks can occur if graphical objects are not deleted properly. To delete a graphical object, it must first be unselected from its device context. This is done by saving a handle to the original object when the new object was selected, and then reselecting the original object when the new one is to be disposed. Once the object is no longer selected into any device context, it can be deleted by calling the DeleteObject function.

Pens and Brushes

Perhaps the most commonly used graphical objects in Windows drawing functions are the pen and the brush. A brush defines a color and pattern used to fill the interiors of closed figures, such as polygons, rectangles, paths, and regions. A pen defines a color and pattern used to outline figures, both closed and open. These two graphical objects are encapsulated by Delphi as the Pen and Brush properties of a TCanvas object. Delphi fully encompasses all functionality offered by the Windows brush functions. However, Windows offers two styles of pens, cosmetic and geometric, and Delphi currently does not encapsulate all of the functionality offered by these objects.

Cosmetic Pens   A cosmetic pen is measured in device units and cannot be scaled. Currently, Windows supports a cosmetic pen of only 1 pixel in width. The pen style can be set to various patterns ranging from solid to a variety of different dash and dot combinations. Drawing with cosmetic pens is much faster than geometric pens.

Geometric Pens   A geometric pen is measured in logical units and will scale accordingly. They support the same pen styles available for cosmetic pens, but they also support user-defined styles and styles normally available only to brushes. Additionally, geometric pens can apply an end cap style to the endpoints of lines, and a join style where two lines meet. The end cap and join styles are illustrated in the following figures. Note that under Windows 95, geometric pens do not support user-defined pen styles, cannot use most of the cosmetic pen styles, and can only be used when drawing paths.

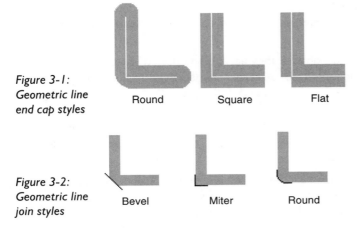

Figure 3-1:
Geometric line
end cap styles

Round   Square   Flat

Figure 3-2:
Geometric line
join styles

Bevel   Miter   Round

Painting and Drawing Functions

The following painting and drawing functions are covered in this chapter:

Table 3-1: Painting and Drawing Functions

Function	Description
Arc	Draws an arc.
BeginPaint	Begins a painting operation.
Chord	Draws a chord.
CreateBrushIndirect	Creates a brush from a data structure.
CreateHatchBrush	Creates a hatch pattern brush.
CreatePatternBrush	Creates a pattern brush.
CreatePen	Creates a pen.
CreatePenIndirect	Creates a pen from a data structure.
CreateSolidBrush	Creates a brush of a solid color.
DeleteObject	Deletes a graphical object.
DrawCaption	Draws a window caption bar.
DrawEdge	Draws three-dimensional lines.
DrawFocusRect	Draws a focus rectangle.
DrawFrameControl	Draws standard user interface buttons
DrawState	Draws disabled text or graphics.
Ellipse	Draws an ellipse.
EndPaint	Ends a painting operation.
EnumObjects	Enumerates graphical objects.
ExtCreatePen	Creates cosmetic or geometric pens.
ExtFloodFill	Fills an area with a color.
FillPath	Fills a path with a color.
FillRect	Fills a rectangle with a color.
FillRgn	Fills a region with a color.
FrameRect	Draws the perimeter of a rectangle.
FrameRgn	Draws the perimeter of a region.
GetBkColor	Retrieves the background color of a device context.
GetBkMode	Retrieves the background mode of a device context.
GetBoundsRect	Retrieves the accumulated bounding rectangle of a device context.
GetBrushOrgEx	Retrieves the origin of a brush pattern.
GetCurrentObject	Retrieves the currently select object in a device context.
GetCurrentPositionEx	Retrieves the current position from a device context.
GetMiterLimit	Retrieves the miter limit of miter joined lines.
GetObject	Retrieves information about a graphical object.
GetObjectType	Determines the type of a graphical object.

3

Chapter

Function	Description
GetPixel	Retrieves a pixel color.
GetPolyFillMode	Retrieves the current polygon fill mode.
GetROP2	Retrieves the foreground mix mode of a device context.
GetStockObject	Retrieves a handle to a predefined graphical object.
GetUpdateRect	Retrieves the bounding rectangle of the current update region.
GetUpdateRgn	Retrieves the update region.
GrayString	Draws a color converted string.
InvalidateRect	Invalidates a rectangular area.
InvalidateRgn	Invalidates a region.
LineDDA	Draws a custom line.
LineTo	Draws a line.
LockWindowUpdate	Disables window painting.
MoveToEx	Moves the current position of a device context.
PaintDesktop	Paints the desktop wallpaper onto a device context.
PaintRgn	Fills a region with the current brush.
Pie	Draws a pie wedge.
PolyBezier	Draws a bézier curve.
PolyBezierTo	Draws multiple bézier curves.
Polygon	Draws a filled polygon.
Polyline	Draws a polygon outline.
PolylineTo	Draws a polygon outline, updating the current position.
PolyPolygon	Draws multiple filled polygons.
PolyPolyline	Draws multiple polygon outlines.
Rectangle	Draws a rectangle.
RoundRect	Draws a rounded rectangle.
SelectObject	Selects a graphical object into a device context.
SetBkColor	Sets the background color of a device context.
SetBkMode	Sets the background mode of a device context.
SetBoundsRect	Sets the bounding rectangle accumulation behavior.
SetBrushOrgEx	Sets the origin of a brush pattern.
SetMiterLimit	Sets the miter limit of miter joined lines.
SetPixel	Sets the color of a pixel in a device context.
SetPixelV	Sets the color of a pixel in a device context (generally faster than SetPixel).
SetPolyFillMode	Sets the polygon filling mode.
SetROP2	Sets the foreground mix mode of the device context.
StrokeAndFillPath	Outlines and fills a path.
StrokePath	Outlines a path.

Arc   *Windows.Pas*

Syntax

```
Arc(
hDC: HDC;                {the handle of a device context}
left: Integer;           {x coordinate of the upper left corner}
top: Integer;            {y coordinate of the upper left corner}
right: Integer;          {x coordinate of the lower right corner}
bottom: Integer;         {y coordinate of the lower right corner}
startX: Integer;         {x coordinate of the first radial ending point}
startY: Integer;         {y coordinate of the first radial ending point}
endX: Integer;           {x coordinate of the second radial ending point}
endY: Integer            {y coordinate of the second radial ending point}
): BOOL;                 {returns TRUE or FALSE}
```

Description

This function draws an elliptical arc. The arc will be drawn with the current pen, and will not use or update the current position. The bounding rectangle defined by the left, top, right, and bottom parameters defines the curve of the arc. The startX and startY parameters define the endpoints of a line starting from the center of the bounding rectangle and identify the starting location of the arc. The endX and endY parameters define the endpoints of a line starting from the center of the bounding rectangle and identify the ending location of the arc.

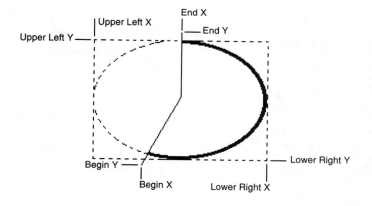

Figure 3-3:
Arc
coordinates

Parameters

hDC: Specifies the device context upon which the arc is drawn.

left: Specifies the horizontal coordinate of the upper left corner of the bounding rectangle, in logical units. Under Windows 95, the sum of the Left and Right parameters must be less than 32,767.

top: Specifies the vertical coordinate of the upper left corner of the bounding rectangle, in logical units. Under Windows 95, the sum of the Top and Bottom parameters must be less than 32,767.

right: Specifies the horizontal coordinate of the lower right corner of the bounding rectangle, in logical units.

bottom: Specifies the vertical coordinate of the lower right corner of the bounding rectangle, in logical units.

startX: Specifies the horizontal coordinate, in logical units, of the ending point of the radial line that defines the starting point of the arc.

startY: Specifies the vertical coordinate, in logical units, of the ending point of the radial line that defines the starting point of the arc.

endX: Specifies the horizontal coordinate, in logical units, of the ending point of the radial line that defines the ending point of the arc.

endY: Specifies the vertical coordinate, in logical units, of the ending point of the radial line that defines the ending point of the arc.

Return Value

If this function succeeds, it returns TRUE; otherwise it returns FALSE.

See Also

Chord, Ellipse, Pie

Example

Listing 3-1: Drawing a Rainbow

```
procedure TForm1.Button1Click(Sender: TObject);
var
  iCount: Integer;    // a general loop control variable
  ArcBounds: TRect;   // the bounding rectangle of the arc
begin
  {initialize the bounding rectangle}
  ArcBounds := PaintBox1.BoundsRect;

  {initialize the pen used to draw the arcs}
  PaintBox1.Canvas.Pen.Width := 2;

  {draw 5 arcs}
  for iCount := 1 to 5 do
  begin
    {Draw the arc}
    Arc(PaintBox1.Canvas.Handle, ArcBounds.Left, ArcBounds.Top, ArcBounds.Right,
        ArcBounds.Bottom,ArcBounds.Right, (ArcBounds.Bottom-ArcBounds.Top)div 2,
        ArcBounds.Left, (ArcBounds.Bottom-ArcBounds.Top)div 2);
```

```
{reduce the size of the bounding rectangle for the next arc}
InflateRect(ArcBounds, -2, -2);

{change the color of the pen used to draw the next arc}
PaintBox1.Canvas.Pen.Color := PaletteIndex(iCount+10);
    end;
  end;
```

*Figure 3-4:
A rainbow
drawn with
arcs*

3

Chapter

BeginPaint   Windows.Pas

Syntax

BeginPaint(
hWnd: HWND;   {the handle of a window}
var lpPaint: TPaintStruct   {a pointer to a TPaintStruct structure}
): HDC   {returns a device context handle}

Description

This function prepares the specified window for painting and fills the TPaintStruct structure pointed to by the lpPaint parameter with information concerning the painting operation. The BeginPaint function excludes any area outside of the update region by setting the clipping region of the device context. The update region is set by calling the InvalidateRect or InvalidateRgn functions, or by any action that affects the client area of the window, such as sizing, moving, scrolling, etc. BeginPaint sends a WM_ERASEBKGND message to the window if the update region is marked for erasing. The BeginPaint function should be called in conjunction with EndPaint and only in response to a WM_PAINT message.

Parameters

hWnd: Specifies the handle of the window to be painted.

lpPaint: Specifies a pointer to a TPaintStruct structure that receives painting information. The TPaintStruct structure is defined as:

```
TPaintStruct = packed record
        hdc: HDC;                        {a handle to a device context}
        fErase: BOOL;                    {erase background flag}
        rcPaint: TRect;                  {painting rectangle coordinates}
        fRestore: BOOL;                  {reserved}
        fIncUpdate: BOOL;                {reserved}
        rgbReserved: array[0..31] of Byte; {reserved}
end;
```

hdc: Specifies the device context upon which painting operations should occur.

fErase: A flag indicating if the background should be erased. If this member is set to TRUE, the background of the device context should be erased before other drawing operations are performed. The application must handle erasing the background if the window class does not have a background brush.

rcPaint: A TRect structure defining the rectangular area within the device context where painting operations should occur.

fRestore: This member is reserved for internal use and should be ignored.

fIncUpdate: This member is reserved for internal use and should be ignored.

rgbReserved: This member is reserved for internal use and should be ignored.

Return Value

If this function succeeds, it returns a handle to the device context for the specified window; otherwise it returns zero.

See Also

EndPaint, InvalidateRect, InvalidateRgn

Example

Please see Listing 3-29 under InvalidateRect and Listing 3-30 under InvalidateRgn.

Chord   Windows.Pas

Syntax

```
Chord(
DC: HDC;            {the handle of a device context}
X1: Integer;        {x coordinate of the upper left corner}
Y1: Integer;        {y coordinate of the upper left corner}
X2: Integer;        {x coordinate of the lower right corner}
Y2: Integer;        {y coordinate of the lower right corner}
X3: Integer;        {x coordinate of the first radial ending point}
Y3: Integer;        {y coordinate of the first radial ending point}
X4: Integer;        {x coordinate of the second radial ending point}
Y4: Integer         {y coordinate of the second radial ending point}
): BOOL;            {returns TRUE or FALSE}
```

Description

This function draws a chord with the current pen and fills the chord with the current brush. A chord is a region bounded by an ellipse and a line segment. The extent of the chord is defined by the bounding rectangle. The curve is defined by a line identified by the X3, Y3, X4, and Y4 parameters. It will extend counterclockwise from the line's first intersection point on the bounding rectangle to the line's second intersection point on the bounding rectangle. If these two points are the same, a complete ellipse is drawn. This function will not affect the current position.

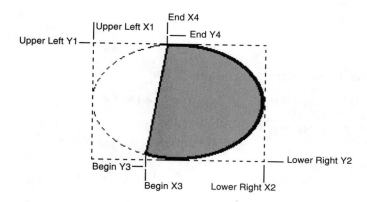

Figure 3-5:
Chord
coordinates

Parameters

DC: Specifies the device context upon which the chord is drawn.

X1: Specifies the horizontal coordinate of the upper left corner of the bounding rectangle, in logical units. Under Windows 95, the sum of the X1 and X2 parameters must be less than 32,767.

Y1: Specifies the vertical coordinate of the upper left corner of the bounding rectangle, in logical units. Under Windows 95, the sum of the Y1 and Y2 parameters must be less than 32,767.

X2: Specifies the horizontal coordinate of the lower right corner of the bounding rectangle, in logical units.

Y2: Specifies the vertical coordinate of the lower right corner of the bounding rectangle, in logical units.

X3: Specifies the horizontal coordinate, in logical units, of the ending point of the line that defines the starting point of the chord.

Y3: Specifies the vertical coordinate, in logical units, of the ending point of the line that defines the starting point of the chord.

X4: Specifies the horizontal coordinate, in logical units, of the ending point of the line that defines the ending point of the chord.

Y4: Specifies the vertical coordinate, in logical units, of the ending point of the line that defines the ending point of the chord.

Return Value

If this function succeeds, it returns TRUE; otherwise it returns FALSE. To get extended error information, call the GetLastError function.

See Also

Arc, Ellipse, Pie

Example

Listing 3-2: Drawing a Chord

```
procedure TForm1.Button1Click(Sender: TObject);
begin
  {initialize the brush and pen used to draw the chord}
  Canvas.Brush.Color := clLime;
  Canvas.Brush.Style := bsCross;
  Canvas.Pen.Color := clRed;

  {draw a chord}
  Chord(Canvas.Handle, 10, 10, 110, 110, 110, 85, 10, 85);
end;
```

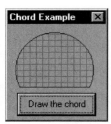

Figure 3-6:
The chord

CreateBrushIndirect   Windows.Pas

Syntax

```
CreateBrushIndirect(
const p1: TLogBrush          {a pointer to a TLogBrush structure}
): HBRUSH;                    {returns a handle to a brush}
```

Description

This function creates a new brush based on the settings in the TLogBrush structure pointed to by the p1 parameter. If the brush's pattern is a monochrome bitmap, black pixels are drawn using the current text color and white pixels are drawn using the current background color. When the brush is no longer needed, it should be deleted by calling the DeleteObject function.

Parameters

p1: A pointer to a TLogBrush structure that defines the new brush. The TLogBrush structure is defined as:

TLogBrush = packed record
        lbStyle: UINT;   {brush style flag}
        lbColor: COLORREF;   {a color specifier}
        lbHatch: Longint;   {hatch style flag}
end;

lbStyle: A flag indicating the brush style. This member can contain one value from Table 3-2.

lbColor: Specifies a color specifier defining the color of the brush. This member is ignored if the lbStyle member is set to BS_HOLLOW or BS_PATTERN. If the lbStyle member is set to BS_DIBPATTERN or BS_DIBPATTERNBT, the low-order word of this member will contain a flag indicating the type of color palette used by the DIB. This flag can be either DIB_PAL_COLORS, indicating that the DIB's palette is an array of indices into the currently realized logical palette, or DIB_RGB_COLORS, indicating that the DIB's palette is an array of literal RGB values.

lbHatch: Specifies a flag indicating the type of hatch style used by the brush. If the lbStyle member is set to BS_HATCHED, this member contains one flag from Table 3-3 specifying the orientation of the lines used to draw the hatch. If the lbStyle member is set to BS_DIBPATTERN, this member contains a handle to a packed DIB. If the lbStyle member is set to BS_DIBPATTERNPT, this member contains a pointer to a packed DIB. If the lbStyle member is set to BS_PATTERN, this member contains a handle to a bitmap. This bitmap handle cannot be a handle to a DIB. If the lbStyle member is set to BS_SOLID or BS_HOLLOW, this member is ignored.

Return Value

If the function succeeds, it returns the handle to a new brush; otherwise it returns zero.

See Also

CreateDIBSection, CreateHatchBrush, CreatePatternBrush, CreateSolidBrush, DeleteObject, GetBrushOrgEx, SelectObject, SetBrushOrgEx

Example

Listing 3-3: Creating and Using a New Brush

```
procedure TForm1.Button1Click(Sender: TObject);
var
  Region: HRGN;              // a handle to a region
  LogBrush: TLogBrush;       // holds logical brush information
  NewBrush: HBrush;          // a handle to the new brush
begin
  {define the attributes of the new brush}
```

```
with LogBrush do
begin
  lbStyle := BS_HATCHED;
  lbColor := clBlue;
  lbHatch := HS_CROSS;
end;

{create the brush}
NewBrush := CreateBrushIndirect(LogBrush);

{create a region to fill}
Region := CreateEllipticRgnIndirect(PaintBox1.BoundsRect);

{fill the region with the new brush}
FillRgn(PaintBox1.Canvas.Handle, Region, NewBrush);

{delete the region and brush}
DeleteObject(NewBrush);
DeleteObject(Region);
end;
```

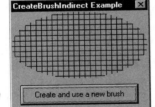

Figure 3-7:
The new brush
pattern

Table 3-2: CreateBrushIndirect pl.lbStyle Values

Value	Description
BS_DIBPATTERN	Indicates that the brush pattern is defined by a device-independent bitmap. The lbHatch member will contain a handle to the packed DIB used as the brush pattern. Under Windows 95, a DIB brush pattern can be no larger than eight pixels square. If a DIB larger than this is specified as the pattern, only an eight-pixel-square portion of the bitmap will be used.
BS_DIBPATTERNPT	Indicates that the brush pattern is defined by a device-independent bitmap. The lbHatch member will contain a pointer to the packed DIB used as the brush pattern. Under Windows 95, a DIB brush pattern can be no larger than eight pixels square. If a DIB larger than this is specified as the pattern, only an eight-pixel-square portion of the bitmap will be used.

Value	Description
BS_HATCHED	Indicates a hatched brush.
BS_HOLLOW	Indicates a hollow brush.
BS_PATTERN	Indicates that the brush pattern is defined by a device-dependent bitmap. The lbHatch member will contain a handle to the bitmap used as the brush pattern. Under Windows 95, a bitmap brush pattern can be no larger than eight pixels square. If a bitmap larger than this is specified as the pattern, only an eight-pixel-square portion of the bitmap will be used.
BS_SOLID	Indicates a solid brush.

Table 3-3: CreateBrushIndirect pl.lbHatch Values

Value	Description
HS_BDIAGONAL	A hatch composed of 45 degree upward, left to right lines.
HS_CROSS	A hatch composed of horizontal and vertical lines.
HS_DIAGCROSS	Same as the HS_CROSS flag, rotated 45 degrees.
HS_FDIAGONAL	A hatch composed of 45-degree downward, left to right lines.
HS_HORIZONTAL	A hatch composed of horizontal lines.
HS_VERTICAL	A hatch composed of vertical lines.

CreateHatchBrush   Windows.Pas

Syntax

```
CreateHatchBrush(
p1: Integer;            {the hatch style}
p2: COLORREF            {the color specifier}
): HBRUSH;             {returns a handle to a brush}
```

Description

This function creates a new brush with the specified color and hatch pattern. The patterns available for use by this function are illustrated in the following figure. If a hatch brush with the same pattern and color is used to paint the background of both a child window and its parent, it may be necessary to call the SetBrushOrgEx function to align the brush pattern before painting the background of the child window. When the brush is no longer needed, it should be deleted by calling the DeleteObject function.

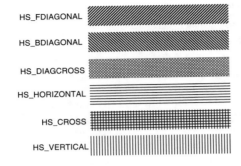

Figure 3-8:
Hatch
patterns

Parameters

p1: A flag specifying the hatch pattern of the brush. This parameter can be set to one value from Table 3-4.

p2: A color specifier indicating the foreground color used when drawing the hatch lines.

Return Value

If the function succeeds, it returns a handle to a new brush; otherwise it returns zero.

See Also

CreateBrushIndirect, CreatePatternBrush, CreateSolidBrush, DeleteObject, GetBrushOrgEx, SelectObject, SetBrushOrgEx

Example

Listing 3-4: Creating a Hatched Brush

```
procedure TForm1.Button1Click(Sender: TObject);
var
   TheBrush: HBRUSH;      // holds the new brush
   HandleRgn: THandle;    // a region handle
begin
  {create the hatch brush}
  TheBrush := CreateHatchBrush(HS_DIAGCROSS, clRed);

  {create a region}
  HandleRgn := CreateEllipticRgnIndirect(ClientRect);

  {fill the region with the brush}
  FillRgn(Canvas.Handle, HandleRgn, TheBrush);

{delete the brush and region}
  DeleteObject(TheBrush);
  DeleteObject(HandleRgn);end;
```

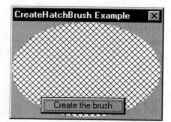

Figure 3-9:
The hatch
brush

Table 3-4: CreateHatchBrush pl Values

Value	Description
HS_BDIAGONAL	A hatch composed of 45 degree upward, left to right lines.
HS_CROSS	A hatch composed of horizontal and vertical lines.
HS_DIAGCROSS	Same as the HS_CROSS flag, rotated 45 degrees.
HS_FDIAGONAL	A hatch composed of 45-degree downward, left to right lines.
HS_HORIZONTAL	A hatch composed of horizontal lines.
HS_VERTICAL	A hatch composed of vertical lines.

CreatePatternBrush   Windows.Pas

Syntax

```
CreatePatternBrush(
Bitmap: HBITMAP          {the handle of the bitmap}
): HBRUSH;               {returns a handle to the new brush}
```

Description

This function creates a new brush with the specified bitmap pattern. If the brush's pattern is a monochrome bitmap, black pixels are drawn using the current text color and white pixels are drawn using the current background color. When the brush is no longer needed, it should be deleted by calling the DeleteObject function. Note that deleting the brush does not delete the bitmap defining the brush's pattern.

Parameters

Bitmap: Specifies the handle of the bitmap used to define the brush pattern. This cannot be a handle to a DIB created by a call to the CreateDIBSection function. Under Windows 95, a bitmap brush pattern can be no larger than eight pixels square. If a bitmap larger than this is specified as the pattern, only an eight-pixel-square portion of the bitmap will be used.

Return Value

If the function succeeds, it returns a handle to the new brush; otherwise it returns zero.

See Also

CreateBitmap, CreateBitmapIndirect, CreateCompatibleBitmap, CreateDIBSection, CreateHatchBrush, DeleteObject, GetBrushOrgEx, LoadBitmap, SelectObject, SetBrushOrgEx

Example

Listing 3-5: Using a Bitmap as a Brush Pattern

```
implementation

{$R *.DFM}
{$R BrushPatterns.Res}

procedure TForm1.Button1Click(Sender: TObject);
var
  NewBrush: HBrush;        // brush handle
  BitmapHandle: THandle;   // handle to a bitmap
begin
  {get a bitmap that is stored in the exe}
  BitmapHandle := LoadBitmap(Hinstance, 'BrushPattern');

  {Create the pattern brush with the bitmap as the pattern}
  NewBrush := CreatePatternBrush(BitmapHandle);

  {fill the region with the pattern using the brush}
  FillRect(Canvas.Handle, ClientRect, NewBrush);

  {clean up the memory}
  DeleteObject(NewBrush);
  DeleteObject(BitmapHandle);
end;
```

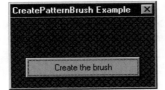

*Figure 3-10:
The pattern
brush*

CreatePen   Windows.Pas

Syntax

CreatePen(
Style: Integer;   {the pen style flag}
Width: Integer;   {the pen width}
Color: COLORREF   {the pen color}
): HPEN;   {returns the handle of a new pen}

Description

This function creates a new pen in the specified style, width, and color. When the pen is no longer needed, it should be deleted by calling the DeleteObject function.

Parameters

Style: A flag indicating the pen style. This parameter can be set to one value from Table 3-5.

Width: Specifies the width of the pen in logical units. A width of zero will create a pen exactly one pixel wide regardless of any current transformations. If this parameter is set to a value greater than one, the Style parameter must be set to the flags PS_NULL, PS_SOLID, or PS_INSIDEFRAME. If this parameter is greater than one and the Style parameter is set to PS_INSIDEFRAME, the line drawn with this pen will be inside the frame of all graphics primitives except those drawn with the polygon and polyline functions.

Color: A color specifier indicating the color of the pen.

Return Value

If the function succeeds, it returns a handle to the new pen; otherwise it returns zero.

See Also

CreatePenIndirect, DeleteObject, ExtCreatePen, GetObject, SelectObject

Example

Listing 3-6: Creating a New Pen

```
procedure TForm1.Button1Click(Sender: TObject);
var
  Style: Integer;      // holds the pen styles
  PenHandle: HPen;     // the handle of the pen
begin
  {erase any previous image}
  Canvas.Brush.Color := clBtnFace;
  Canvas.FillRect(Rect(10, 10, 111, 111));

  {determine the pen style}
  case RadioGroup1.ItemIndex of
    0: Style := PS_SOLID;
    1: Style := PS_DASH;
    2: Style := PS_DOT;
    3: Style := PS_DASHDOT;
    4: Style := PS_DASHDOTDOT;
    5: Style := PS_NULL;
    6: Style := PS_INSIDEFRAME;
  end;

  {create the pen}
  PenHandle := CreatePen(Style, 1, 0);
```

3

Chapter

```
{instruct the canvas to use the new pen}
Canvas.Pen.Handle := PenHandle;

{draw a square with the pen}
Canvas.MoveTo(10, 10);
Canvas.LineTo(110, 10);
Canvas.LineTo(110, 110);
Canvas.LineTo(10, 110);
Canvas.LineTo(10, 10);

{delete the pen}
DeleteObject(PenHandle);
end;
```

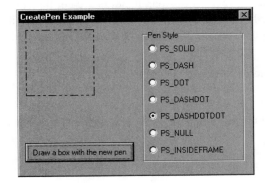

Figure 3-11:
The new pen

Table 3-5: CreatePen Style Values

Value	Description
PS_SOLID	Specifies a solid pen.
PS_DASH	Specifies a dashed pen. This flag can be used only when the pen width is one or less.
PS_DOT	Specifies a dot pen. This flag can be used only when the pen width is one or less.
PS_DASHDOT	Specifies an alternating dash and dot pen. This flag can be used only when the pen width is one or less.
PS_DASHDOTDOT	Specifies an alternating dash dot dot pen. This flag can be used only when the pen width is one or less.
PS_NULL	Specifies an invisible pen.
PS_INSIDEFRAME	Specifies a solid pen. When this pen is used with drawing functions that require a bounding rectangle, the dimensions of the figure are shrunk to fit within the bounding rectangle with respect to the width of the pen.

CreatePenIndirect   *Windows.Pas*

Syntax

```
CreatePenIndirect(
const LogPen: TLogPen          {a pointer to a TLogPen structure}
): HPEN;                       {returns the handle of a new pen}
```

Description

This function creates a new pen in the style, width, and color specified by the TLogPen structure pointed to by the LogPen parameter. When the pen is no longer needed, it should be deleted by calling the DeleteObject function.

Parameters

LogPen: A pointer to a TLogPen structure defining the attributes of the new pen. The TLogPen structure is defined as:

```
TLogPen = packed record
     lopnStyle: UINT;          {the pen style}
     lopnWidth: TPoint;        {the pen width}
     lopnColor: COLORREF;      {the pen color}
end;
```

lopnStyle: A flag indicating the pen style. This member can be set to one value from Table 3-6.

lopnWidth: The X member of this TPoint structure specifies the width of the pen in logical units. The Y member is not used. A width of zero will create a pen exactly one pixel wide regardless of any current transformations. If this member is set to a value greater than one, the lopnStyle member must be set to the flags PS_NULL, PS_SOLID, or PS_INSIDEFRAME. If this member is greater than one and the lopnStyle member is set to PS_INSIDEFRAME, the line drawn with this pen will be inside the frame of all graphics primitives except those drawn with the polygon and polyline functions.

lopnColor: A color specifier indicating the color of the pen.

Return Value

If the function succeeds, it returns a handle to the new pen; otherwise it returns zero.

See Also

CreatePen, DeleteObject, ExtCreatePen, GetObject, SelectObject

Example

Listing 3-7: Creating a Pen Indirectly

```
procedure TForm1.Button1Click(Sender: TObject);
var
  Pen: TLogPen;        // the logical pen record
```

3

Chapter

```
      PenHandle: HPen;    // the handle of a pen
begin
  {erase any previous image}
  Canvas.Brush.Color := clBtnFace;
  Canvas.FillRect(Rect(10, 10, 111, 111));

  {initialize the logical pen structure}
  with Pen do
  begin
    {determine the pen style}
    Case RadioGroup1.ItemIndex of
      0: lopnStyle := PS_SOLID;
      1: lopnStyle := PS_DASH;
      2: lopnStyle := PS_DOT;
      3: lopnStyle := PS_DASHDOT;
      4: lopnStyle := PS_DASHDOTDOT;
      5: lopnStyle := PS_NULL;
      6: lopnStyle := PS_INSIDEFRAME;
    end;

    {set the pen width and color}
    lopnWidth.X := 1;
    lopnColor   := clRed;
  end;

  {create the new pen}
  PenHandle := CreatePenIndirect(Pen);

  {draw a square with the new pen}
  Canvas.Pen.Handle := PenHandle;
  Canvas.MoveTo(10, 10);
  Canvas.LineTo(110, 10);
  Canvas.LineTo(110, 110);
  Canvas.LineTo(10, 110);
  Canvas.LineTo(10, 10);

  {delete the new pen}
  DeleteObject(PenHandle);
end;
```

Table 3-6: CreatePenIndirect LogPen.lopnStyle Values

Value	Description
PS_SOLID	Specifies a solid pen.
PS_DASH	Specifies a dashed pen. This flag can be used only when the pen width is one or less.
PS_DOT	Specifies a dot pen. This flag can be used only when the pen width is one or less.
PS_DASHDOT	Specifies an alternating dash and dot pen. This flag can be used only when the pen width is one or less.
PS_DASHDOTDOT	Specifies an alternating dash dot dot pen. This flag can be used only when the pen width is one or less.

Value	Description
PS_NULL	Specifies an invisible pen.
PS_INSIDEFRAME	Specifies a solid pen. When this pen is used with drawing functions that require a bounding rectangle, the dimensions of the figure are shrunk to fit within the bounding rectangle with respect to the width of the pen.

CreateSolidBrush   *Windows.Pas*

Syntax

```
CreateSolidBrush(
p1: COLORREF          {the brush color}
): HBRUSH;            {returns the handle of a new brush}
```

Description

This function creates a new solid brush in the specified color. Once the brush is no longer needed, it should be deleted by calling the DeleteObject function.

Parameters

P1: A color specifier indicating the color of the brush.

Return Value

If the function succeeds, it returns a handle to a new brush; otherwise it returns zero.

See Also

CreateHatchBrush, CreatePatternBrush, DeleteObject, SelectObject

Example

Listing 3-8: Creating a Solid Brush

```
procedure TForm1.Button1Click(Sender: TObject);
var
  NewBrush: HBrush;    // the handle of the brush
  OldBrush: HBrush;    // the handle of the device context's original brush
  FormDC: HDC;         // the handle of the form device context
begin
  {create the brush}
  NewBrush := CreateSolidBrush(clGreen);

  {Get the form's device context}
  FormDC := GetDC(Form1.Handle);

  {Select the brush handle into the form's device context}
  OldBrush := SelectObject(FormDC, NewBrush);

  {fill a rectangle with the brush}
```

```
    FillRect(FormDC, Rect(10, 10, 170, 110), NewBrush);

    {clean up the memory}
    SelectObject(FormDC, OldBrush);
    DeleteObject(NewBrush);
  end;
```

Figure 3-12:
The solid
brush

DeleteObject   Windows.Pas

Syntax

```
DeleteObject(
p1: HGDIOBJ              {a handle to a GDI object}
): BOOL;                 {returns TRUE or FALSE}
```

Description

This function will delete a logical pen, brush, font, bitmap, region, or palette, freeing its associated resources. The object's handle is invalidated when this function returns. This function will fail if it attempts to delete an object while it is selected into a device context. Note: Deleting a pattern brush does not affect its bitmap. The brush's bitmap must by independently deleted.

Parameters

P1: Specifies the handle of the object to be deleted.

Return Value

If the function succeeds, it returns TRUE. If the function fails, the specified handle is invalid, or the object is currently selected into a device context, it returns FALSE.

See Also

GetObject, SelectObject

Example

Please see Listing 3-3 under CreateBrushIndirect and other examples throughout the book.

DrawCaption   Windows.Pas

Syntax

```
DrawCaption(
p1: HWND;                {a handle to a window}
p2: HDC;                 {a handle to a device context}
const p3: TRect;         {the rectangular coordinates}
p4: UINT                 {drawing flags}
): BOOL;                 {returns TRUE or FALSE}
```

Description

This function draws a caption bar in the rectangular area identified by the p3 parameter. The caption bar retrieves its text and icon from the window identified by the p1 parameter.

Parameters

p1: A handle to the window containing the text and icon used in drawing the caption bar.

p2: A handle to the device context upon which the caption bar is drawn.

p3: Specifies the rectangular coordinates within which the caption bar is drawn.

p4: Specifies a series of flags defining drawing options. This parameter may be set to a combination of values from Table 3-7.

Return Value

If the function succeeds, it returns TRUE; otherwise it returns FALSE.

See Also

DrawEdge, DrawFocusRect, DrawFrameControl, DrawState, SetWindowRgn

Example

Listing 3-9: Programmatically Drawing a Caption Bar

```
procedure TForm1.FormPaint(Sender: TObject);
begin
  DrawCaption(Handle, Canvas.Handle, Rect(16, 40, 288, 60),
          DC_ACTIVE or DC_ICON or DC_TEXT);
end;
```

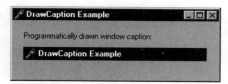

Figure 3-13: The Caption bar

Table 3-7: DrawCaption p4 Values

Value	Description
DC_ACTIVE	The caption is drawn in the active caption color.
DC_ICON	The window icon is drawn in the caption.
DC_INBUTTON	The caption is drawn in a "pushed" state.
DC_SMALLCAP	The text of the caption is drawn using the current small caption font.
DC_TEXT	The window text is drawn in the caption.

DrawEdge   *Windows.Pas*

Syntax

```
DrawEdge(
hdc: HDC;            {the device context}
var qrc: TRect;      {the rectangular coordinates}
edge: UINT;          {edge type flags}
grfFlags: UINT       {border type flags}
): BOOL;             {returns TRUE or FALSE}
```

Description

This function draws a line or rectangle using the specified three-dimensional edge effect.

Parameters

hdc: Specifies the handle of the device context upon which the edge is drawn.

qrc: A pointer to a TRect structure containing the rectangular coordinates, in logical units, defining the edge.

edge: A series of flags specifying the type of edge to draw. This parameter must be set to a combination of one value from the inner border flags table (Table 3-8) and one value from the outer border flags table (Table 3-9). A single value from the border combination flags table (Table 3-10) can be used in place of the combined values.

grfFlags: A series of flags specifying the type of border to draw. This parameter can be set to a combination of flags from Table 3-11.

Return Value

If this function succeeds, it returns TRUE; otherwise it returns FALSE. To get extended error information, call the GetLastError function.

See Also

MoveToEx, LineDDA, LineTo, Rectangle

Example

Listing 3-10: Drawing 3-Dimensional Edges

```
type
  TFlagsArray = array[0..18] of UINT;   // holds an array of border type flags

const
  {initialize the border flags array}
  BorderFlags: TFlagsArray = (BF_ADJUST, BF_BOTTOM, BF_BOTTOMLEFT,
                              BF_BOTTOMRIGHT, BF_DIAGONAL,
                              BF_DIAGONAL_ENDBOTTOMLEFT,
                              BF_DIAGONAL_ENDBOTTOMRIGHT,
                              BF_DIAGONAL_ENDTOPLEFT, BF_DIAGONAL_ENDTOPRIGHT,
                              BF_FLAT, BF_LEFT, BF_MIDDLE, BF_MONO, BF_RECT,
                              BF_RIGHT, BF_SOFT, BF_TOP, BF_TOPLEFT,
                              BF_TOPRIGHT);

procedure TForm1.Button1Click(Sender: TObject);
var
  TheRect: TRect;            // defines the edge rectangle
  Edge, Border: UINT;        // holds the edge flag values
  iCount: Integer;           // a general loop counter
begin
  {define the rectangle for the edge}
  TheRect := Rect(21, 200, 216, 300);

  {erase the last drawn edge}
  Canvas.Brush.Color := clBtnFace;
  Canvas.FillRect(TheRect);

  {define the kind of edge}
  case RadioGroup_Additional.ItemIndex of
   0: Edge := EDGE_BUMP;    //Combination BDR_RAISEDOUTER and BDR_SUNKENINNER
   1: Edge := EDGE_ETCHED;  //Combination BDR_SUNKENOUTER and BDR_RAISEDINNER
   2: Edge := EDGE_RAISED;  //Combination BDR_RAISEDOUTER and BDR_RAISEDINNER
   3: Edge := EDGE_SUNKEN;  //Combination BDR_SUNKENOUTER and BDR_SUNKENINNER
  end;

  {initialize the border flags}
  Border := 0;

  {determine the selected border type flags}
  for iCount := 0 to 18 do
    if CheckListBox2.Checked[iCount] then Border:=Border or BorderFlags[iCount];

  {draw the edge}
  DrawEdge(Canvas.Handle, TheRect, Edge, Border);
end;
```

3

Chapter

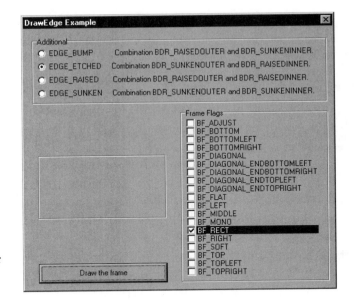

Figure 3-14:
An etched
rectangle

Table 3-8: DrawEdge edge Inner Border Flags Values

Value	Description
BDR_RAISEDINNER	Indicates a raised inner edge.
BDR_SUNKENINNER	Indicates a sunken inner edge.

Table 3-9: DrawEdge edge Outer Border Flags Values

Value	Description
BDR_RAISEDOUTER	Indicates a raised outer edge.
BDR_SUNKENOUTER	Indicates a sunken outer edge.

Table 3-10: DrawEdge edge Border Combination Flags Values

Value	Description
EDGE_BUMP	Combination of BDR_RAISEDOUTER and BDR_SUNKENINNER.
EDGE_ETCHED	Combination of BDR_SUNKENOUTER and BDR_RAISEDINNER.
EDGE_RAISED	Combination of BDR_RAISEDOUTER and BDR_RAISEDINNER.
EDGE_SUNKEN	Combination of BDR_SUNKENOUTER and BDR_SUNKENINNER.

Table 3-11: DrawEdge grfFlags Values

Value	Description
BF_ADJUST	The rectangular coordinates are decreased to account for the width of the edge lines.
BF_BOTTOM	Draws the bottom border of the rectangle.
BF_BOTTOMLEFT	Draws the bottom and left borders of the rectangle.
BF_BOTTOMRIGHT	Draws the bottom and right borders of the rectangle.
BF_DIAGONAL	Draws a diagonal border.
BF_DIAGONAL_ENDBOTTOMLEFT	Draws a diagonal border starting at the top right corner and ending at the bottom left.
BF_DIAGONAL_ENDBOTTOMRIGHT	Draws a diagonal border starting at the top left corner and ending at the bottom right.
BF_DIAGONAL_ENDTOPLEFT	Draws a diagonal border starting at the bottom right corner and ending at the top left.
BF_DIAGONAL_ENDTOPRIGHT	Draws a diagonal border starting at the bottom left corner and ending at the top right.
BF_FLAT	Draws a flat border.
BF_LEFT	Draws the left border of the rectangle.
BF_MIDDLE	Fills the interior of the rectangle.
BF_MONO	Draws a one-dimensional border.
BF_RECT	Draws a border around the entire rectangle.
BF_RIGHT	Draws the right border of the rectangle.
BF_SOFT	Draws the border in a soft style.
BF_TOP	Draws the top border of the rectangle.
BF_TOPLEFT	Draws the top and left borders of the rectangle.
BF_TOPRIGHT	Draws the top and right borders of the rectangle.

3

Chapter

DrawFocusRect   Windows.Pas

Syntax

```
DrawFocusRect(
hDC: HDC;                {the device context}
const lprc: TRect        {the rectangular coordinates}
): BOOL;                 {returns TRUE or FALSE}
```

Description

This function draws a rectangle in a style that denotes focus. The rectangle is drawn using an XOR Boolean operation. Therefore, calling this function a second time with the same coordinates will erase the rectangle.

Parameters

hDC: A handle to the device context upon which the rectangle is drawn.

lprc: Specifies the rectangular coordinates defining the borders of the drawn rectangle.

Return Value

If the function succeeds, it returns TRUE; otherwise it returns FALSE. To get extended error information, call the GetLastError function.

See Also

DrawCaption, DrawEdge, DrawFrameControl, FrameRect, Rectangle, RoundRect

Example

Listing 3-11: Drawing a Focus Rectangle

```
procedure TForm1.Button1Click(Sender: TObject);
var
  MyRect: TRect; // the focus rectangle coordinates
begin
  {set up the rectangle}
  MyRect := Rect(14, 10, 151, 90);

  {draw the focus rectangle}
  if not(DrawFocusRect(Canvas.Handle, MyRect)) then
    ShowMessage('DrawFocusRect not working');
end;
```

Figure 3-15:
The focus
rectangle

DrawFrameControl   Windows.Pas

Syntax

```
DrawFrameControl(
DC: HDC;                              {a handle to a device context}
const Rect: TRect;                   {the rectangular coordinates}
```

uType: UINT;	{frame control type flags}
uState: UINT	{frame control state flags}
): BOOL;	{returns TRUE or FALSE}

Description

This function draws various system-defined buttons in the specified style and state.

Parameters

DC: The handle of the device context upon which the frame control is drawn.

Rect: Specifies the rectangular coordinates defining the size of the frame control.

uType: A series of flags indicating the type of frame control to be drawn. This parameter can be set to one value from Table 3-12.

uState: A series of flags indicating the state of the frame control to be drawn. This parameter can be a combination of flags from Tables 3-13 to 3-16, and is dependent upon the value of the uType parameter. A separate table is listed for each uType parameter value. One value may be taken from the table appropriate for the uType value, and can be combined with one or more values from the general state flags table (Table 3-17).

Return Value

If the function succeeds, it returns TRUE; otherwise it returns FALSE. To get extended error information, call the GetLastError function.

See Also

DrawCaption, DrawEdge, DrawFocusRect, DrawState

Example

Listing 3-12: Drawing Various Frame Controls

```
procedure TForm1.Button1Click(Sender: TObject);
var
  TheRect: TRect;    // the bounding rectangle for the control image
  TheType: UINT;     // holds the type of control
  TheState: UINT;    // holds the state of the control
begin
  {initialize the type and state flags}
  TheType := 0;
  TheState := 0;

  {define the bounding rectangle}
  TheRect := Rect(10, 10, 50, 50);

  {choose the type of frame control}
  case RadioGroup_ButtonType.ItemIndex of
    0:
```

```
      begin
        {indicate we are drawing a button}
        TheType := DFC_BUTTON;

        {chose the state of the control}
        case RadioGroup1.ItemIndex of
          0:  TheState := DFCS_BUTTON3STATE;
          1:  TheState := DFCS_BUTTONCHECK;
          2:  TheState := DFCS_BUTTONPUSH;
          3:  TheState := DFCS_BUTTONRADIO;
          4:  TheState := DFCS_BUTTONRADIOIMAGE;
          5:  TheState := DFCS_BUTTONRADIOMASK;
        end;
    end;
    1:
    begin
      {indicate we are drawing a caption bar button}
      TheType := DFC_CAPTION;

      {chose the state of the control}
      case RadioGroup2.ItemIndex of
        0: TheState := DFCS_CAPTIONCLOSE;
        1: TheState := DFCS_CAPTIONHELP;
        2: TheState := DFCS_CAPTIONMAX;
        3: TheState := DFCS_CAPTIONMIN;
        4: TheState := DFCS_CAPTIONRESTORE;
      end;
    end;
    2:
    begin
      {indicate we are drawing a menu item bitmap}
      TheType := DFC_MENU;

      {chose the state of the control}
      case RadioGroup3.ItemIndex of
        0: TheState := DFCS_MENUARROW;
        1: TheState := DFCS_MENUBULLET;
        2: TheState := DFCS_MENUCHECK;
      end;
    end;
    3:
    begin
      {indicate we are drawing a scroll bar button}
      TheType := DFC_SCROLL;

      {chose the TheState of the control}
      case RadioGroup4.ItemIndex of
        0: TheState := DFCS_SCROLLCOMBOBOX;
        1: TheState := DFCS_SCROLLDOWN;
        2: TheState := DFCS_SCROLLLEFT;
        3: TheState := DFCS_SCROLLRIGHT;
        4: TheState := DFCS_SCROLLSIZEGRIP;
        5: TheState := DFCS_SCROLLUP;
      end;
    end;
```

```
end;

{identify the state of the button}
case RadioGroup5.ItemIndex of
  0:  TheState := TheState or DFCS_CHECKED;
  1:  TheState := TheState or DFCS_FLAT;
  2:  TheState := TheState or DFCS_INACTIVE;
  3:  TheState := TheState or DFCS_MONO;
  4:  TheState := TheState or DFCS_PUSHED;
end;

{erase any previous image}
Canvas.Brush.Color := clBtnFace;
Canvas.FillRect(TheRect);

{draw the frame control}
DrawFrameControl(Canvas.Handle, TheRect, TheType, TheState);
end;
```

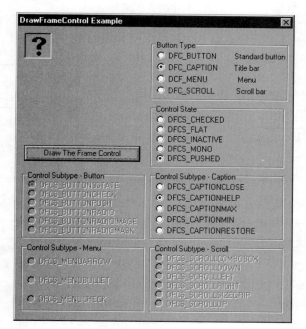

Figure 3-16: The Frame Control test bed example program

3

Chapter

Table 3-12: DrawFrameControl uType Values

Value	Description
DFC_BUTTON	Draws a standard button.
DFC_CAPTION	Draws caption bar buttons.
DCF_MENU	Draws images used in menus.
DFC_SCROLL	Draws scroll bar buttons.

Table 3-13: DrawFrameControl uState Values (for DFC_BUTTON)

Value	Description
DFCS_BUTTON3STATE	Draws a three-state button.
DFCS_BUTTONCHECK	Draws a check box.
DFCS_BUTTONPUSH	Draws a normal push button.
DFCS_BUTTONRADIO	Draws a radio button.
DFCS_BUTTONRADIOIMAGE	Draws the radio button XOR mask.
DFCS_BUTTONRADIOMASK	Draws the radio button AND mask.

Table 3-14: DrawFrameControl uState Values (for DFC_CAPTION)

Value	Description
DFCS_CAPTIONCLOSE	Draws a close button.
DFCS_CAPTIONHELP	Draws a help button.
DFCS_CAPTIONMAX	Draws a maximize button.
DFCS_CAPTIONMIN	Draws a minimize button.
DFCS_CAPTIONRESTORE	Draws a restore button.

Table 3-15: DrawFrameControl uState Values (for DFC_MENU)

Value	Description
DFCS_MENUARROW	Draws a submenu arrow.
DFCS_MENUBULLET	Draws a bullet.
DFCS_MENUCHECK	Draws a check mark.

Table 3-16: DrawFrameControl uState Values (for DFC_SCROLL)

Value	Description
DFCS_SCROLLCOMBOBOX	Draws a combo box drop-down button.
DFCS_SCROLLDOWN	Draws a scroll bar down button.
DFCS_SCROLLLEFT	Draws a scroll bar left button.
DFCS_SCROLLRIGHT	Draws a scroll bar right button.
DFCS_SCROLLSIZEGRIP	Draws a size grip.
DFCS_SCROLLUP	Draws a scroll bar up button.

Table 3-17: DrawFrameControl uState General State Flags Values

Value	Description
DFCS_ADJUSTRECT	The specified rectangle is reduced to exclude the surrounding edge of the control.
DFCS_CHECKED	Indicates that the button is pressed or checked.
DFCS_FLAT	Draws the button with a flat border.

Value	Description
DFCS_INACTIVE	Draws the button as inactive (grayed).
DFCS_MONO	Draws the button with a monochrome border.
DFCS_PUSHED	Indicates that the button is pushed.

DrawState   *Windows.Pas*

Syntax

```
DrawState(
DC: HDC;                  {a handle to a device context}
p2: HBRUSH;               {the handle of a brush}
p3: TFNDrawStateProc;     {the address of the callback function (optional)}
p4: LPARAM;               {bitmap or icon handle or string pointer}
p5: WPARAM;               {string length}
p6: Integer;              {the horizontal coordinate of the image location}
p7: Integer;              {the vertical coordinate of the image location}
p8: Integer;              {the image width}
p9: Integer;              {the image height}
p10: UINT                 {image type and state flags}
): BOOL;                  {returns TRUE or FALSE}
```

Description

This function displays an icon, bitmap, or text string, applying a visual effect to indicate its state. It can apply various state effects as determined by the flags specified in the p10 parameter, or it can call an application-defined callback function to draw complex, application-defined state effects.

Parameters

DC: A handle to the device context upon which the image is drawn.

p2: Specifies the handle of a brush. This brush will be used if the p10 parameter contains the DSS_MONO flag. If the p10 parameter does not contain this flag, this parameter is ignored.

p3: Specifies a pointer to an application-defined callback function. This function is called to draw the image in the specified state when the p10 parameter contains the DST_COMPLEX flag. If the p10 parameter does not contain this flag, this parameter is ignored.

p4: If the p10 parameter contains the DST_BITMAP flag, this parameter contains the handle to the bitmap to be drawn. If the p10 parameter contains the DST_ICON flag, this parameter contains the handle to the icon to be drawn. If the p10 parameter contains the DST_PREFIXTEXT or the DST_TEXT flags, this parameter contains a pointer to the string to be drawn. Otherwise, this parameter may be set to an application-defined value.

p5: Contains the length of the string to be drawn if the p10 parameter contains the DST_PREFIXTEXT or the DST_TEXT flags. This parameter may be set to zero if the strings are null terminated. Otherwise, this parameter may be set to an application-defined value.

p6: Specifies the horizontal coordinate at which the image is drawn.

p7: Specifies the vertical coordinate at which the image is drawn.

p8: Specifies the width of the image, in device units. If the p10 parameter contains the DST_COMPLEX flag, this parameter is required. Otherwise, it can be set to zero, forcing the system to calculate the width of the image.

p9: Specifies the height of the image, in device units. If the p10 parameter contains the DST_COMPLEX flag, this parameter is required. Otherwise, it can be set to zero, forcing the system to calculate the height of the image.

p10: A series of flags indicating the image type and state. This parameter is set to a combination of one flag from Table 3-18 and one flag from Table 3-19.

Return Value

If the function succeeds, it returns TRUE; otherwise it returns FALSE.

Callback Function Syntax

```
DrawStateProc(
  hDC: HDC;            {a handle to a device context}
  lData: LPARAM;       {application-defined data}
  wData: WPARAM;       {application-defined data}
  cx: Integer;         {the image width}
  cy: Integer          {the image height}
  ): BOOL;             {returns TRUE or FALSE}
```

Description

This callback is used when the p10 parameter contains the DST_COMPLEX flag. Its purpose is to render the complex image in whatever manner desired. This callback function can perform any desired action.

Parameters

hDC: A handle to the device context upon which the image is drawn.

lData: Specifies application specific data as passed to the DrawState function in the p4 parameter.

wData: Specifies application specific data as passed to the DrawState function in the p5 parameter.

cx: Specifies the width of the image, in device units, as passed to the DrawState function in the p8 parameter.

cy: Specifies the width of the image, in device units, as passed to the DrawState function in the p9 parameter.

Return Value

The callback function should return TRUE to indicate that the function succeeded, or FALSE to indicate that it failed.

See Also

DrawFocusRect, DrawText, TextOut, SetTextColor

Example

Listing 3-13: Drawing Images in a Disabled State

```
procedure TForm1.FormPaint(Sender: TObject);
var
  Text: PChar;          // holds a string of text
begin
  {initialize the text string}
  Text := 'A DISABLED ICON';

  {draw the text to the screen in a disabled state}
  DrawState(Canvas.Handle, 0, nil, Integer(Text), 0, 20, 20, 0, 0,
          DST_TEXT or DSS_DISABLED);

  {draw the application's icon in a disabled state}
  DrawState(Canvas.Handle, 0, nil, Application.Icon.Handle, 0, 50, 50, 0, 0,
          DST_ICON or DSS_DISABLED);
end;
```

*Figure 3-17:
The disabled
images*

Table 3-18: DrawState p10 Image Type Values

Value	Description
DST_BITMAP	Indicates a bitmap image. The low-order word of the p4 parameter contains the bitmap handle.
DST_COMPLEX	Indicates an application-defined, complex image. The callback function identified by the p3 parameter is called to render the image.

Value	Description
DST_ICON	Indicates an icon image. The low-order word of p4 parameter contains the icon handle.
DST_PREFIXTEXT	Indicates that the image is text that may contain an accelerator mnemonic. Any ampersand (&) characters are translated into an underscore on the following character. The p4 parameter contains a pointer to the string, and the p5 parameter contains the string's length.
DST_TEXT	Indicates that the image is text. The p4 parameter contains a pointer to the string, and the p5 parameter contains the string's length.

Table 3-19: DrawState p10 Image State Values

Value	Description
DSS_NORMAL	Draws the image in its original form.
DSS_UNION	Draws the image in a dithered form.
DSS_DISABLED	Draws the image in an embossed form.
DSS_MONO	Draws the image using the brush specified by the p2 parameter.

Ellipse   Windows.Pas

Syntax

```
Ellipse(
DC: HDC;            {the handle of the device context}
X1: Integer;        {the horizontal coordinate of the upper left corner}
Y1: Integer;        {the vertical coordinate of the upper left corner}
X2: Integer;        {the horizontal coordinate of the lower right corner}
Y2: Integer         {the vertical coordinate of the lower right corner}
): BOOL;            {returns TRUE or FALSE}
```

Description

This function draws an ellipse within the bounding rectangle defined by the X1, Y1, X2, and Y2 parameters. The center of the bounding rectangle defines the center of the ellipse. The ellipse is filled with the current brush and drawn with the current pen. The current position is neither used nor updated by this function.

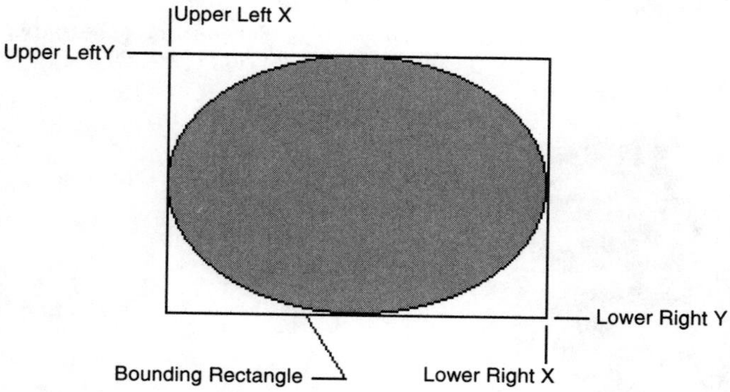

Figure 3-18:
Ellipse
coordinates

Parameters

DC: A handle to the device context upon which the ellipse is drawn.

X1: Specifies the horizontal coordinate of the upper left corner of the bounding rectangle defining the shape of the ellipse. Under Windows 95, the sum of the X1 and X2 parameters must be less than 32,767.

Y1: Specifies the vertical coordinate of the upper left corner of the bounding rectangle defining the shape of the ellipse. Under Windows 95, the sum of the Y1 and Y2 parameters must be less than 32,767.

X2: Specifies the horizontal coordinate of the lower right corner of the bounding rectangle defining the shape of the ellipse.

Y2: Specifies the vertical coordinate of the lower right corner of the bounding rectangle defining the shape of the ellipse.

Return Value

If the function succeeds, it returns TRUE; otherwise it returns FALSE. To get extended error information, call the GetLastError function.

See Also

Arc, Chord, CreateEllipticRgn, CreateEllipticRgnIndirect

Example

Listing 3-14: Drawing Ellipses

```
procedure TForm1.Timer1Timer(Sender: TObject);
begin
  {set the canvas's brush to a random color}
  Canvas.Brush.Color := $01000000 or Random(10);
```

```
{draw a random ellipse}
Ellipse(Canvas.Handle, Random(ClientWidth), Random(ClientHeight),
        Random(ClientWidth), Random(ClientHeight))
end;
```

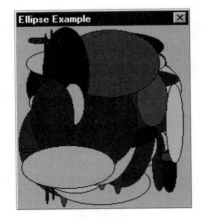

Figure 3-19: Random ellipses

EndPaint   Windows.Pas

Syntax

EndPaint(
hWnd: HWND;   {the handle of a window}
const lpPaint: TPaintStruct   {a pointer to a TPaintStruct structure}
): BOOL;   {this function always returns TRUE}

Description

This function is used with the BeginPaint function to mark the end of painting operations in the specified window. Any caret hidden by the BeginPaint function will be restored.

Parameters

hWnd: Specifies the handle of the window being painted.

lpPaint: Specifies a pointer to a TPaintStruct structure containing painting information. The TPaintStruct structure is defined as:

TPaintStruct = packed record
      hdc: HDC;   {a handle to a device context}
      fErase: BOOL;   {erase background flag}
      rcPaint: TRect;   {painting rectangle coordinates}
      fRestore: BOOL;   {reserved}
      fIncUpdate: BOOL;   {reserved}
      rgbReserved: array[0..31] of Byte; {reserved}
end;

Please see the BeginPaint function for a description of this data structure.

Return Value

This function always returns TRUE.

See Also

BeginPaint

Example

Please see Listing 3-29 under InvalidateRect and Listing 3-30 under InvalidateRgn.

EnumObjects   Windows.Pas

Syntax

```
EnumObjects(
DC: HDC;                     {a handle to a device context}
p2: Integer;                 {object type flag}
p3: TFNGObjEnumProc;         {the application-defined callback function}
p4: LPARAM                   {application-defined data}
): Integer;                  {returns a success code}
```

Description

This function enumerates all pens or brushes available in the specified device context. Information for each brush or pen is passed to the application-defined callback pointed to by the p3 parameter. This continues until all objects have been enumerated or the callback function returns zero.

Parameters

DC: A handle to the device context containing the objects to be enumerated.

p2: A flag indicating what type of object to enumerate. If this parameter is set to OBJ_BRUSH, all brushes are enumerated. If this parameter is set to OBJ_PEN, all pens are enumerated.

p3: A pointer to the application-defined callback function.

p4: Specifies a 32-bit application-defined value that is passed to the callback function.

Return Value

This function returns the last value returned by the callback function. If there are too many objects to enumerate, the function returns -1. This function does not indicate an error condition.

Callback Function Syntax

```
EnumObjectsProc(
lpLogObject: Pointer;              {a pointer to an object data structure}
```

lpData: LPARAM   {application-defined data}
): Integer;   {returns zero or one}

Description

This function is called once for each type of object enumerated in the specified device context. It may perform any desired action.

Parameters

lpLogObject: A pointer to a TLogPen structure if the p2 parameter of the EnumObjects function contains the OBJ_PEN flag, or a pointer to a TLogBrush structure if the p2 parameter contains the OBJ_BRUSH flag. Please see the CreatePenIndirect function for a description of the TLogPen structure, and the CreateBrushIndirect function for a description of the TLogBrush parameter.

lpData: Specifies the 32-bit application-defined value passed to the p4 parameter of the EnumObjects function. This value is intended for application specific use.

Return Value

This function should return a one to continue enumeration, or zero to discontinue enumeration.

See Also

GetObject, GetObjectType

Example

Listing 3-15: Enumerating All Pens in a Device Context

```
{the callback function prototype}
  function EnumObjProc(ObjType: PLogPen; lData: lParam): Integer; stdcall;

var
  Form1: TForm1;

implementation

{$R *.DFM}

function EnumObjProc(ObjType: PLogPen; lData: lParam): Integer;
var
  LocalObjType: TLogPen;     // holds logical pen information
  PenDescription: String;    // holds a pen description
begin
  {get the pen information}
  LocalObjType := ObjType^;
```

```
{determine the type of pen being enumerated}
case LocalObjType.lopnStyle of
   PS_SOLID:         PenDescription := 'PS_SOLID';
   PS_DASH:          PenDescription := 'PS_DASH';
   PS_DOT:           PenDescription := 'PS_DOT';
   PS_DASHDOT:       PenDescription := 'PS_DASHDOT';
   PS_DASHDOTDOT:    PenDescription := 'PS_DASHDOTDOT';
   PS_NULL:          PenDescription := 'PS_NULL';
   PS_INSIDEFRAME:   PenDescription := 'PS_INSIDEFRAME';
end;

{determine the color of the pen being enumerated}
case LocalObjType.lopnColor of
   clBlack:    PenDescription := PenDescription+' Color: clBlack';
   clMaroon:   PenDescription := PenDescription+' Color: clMaroon';
   clGreen:    PenDescription := PenDescription+' Color: clGreen';
   clOlive:    PenDescription := PenDescription+' Color: clOlive';
   clNavy:     PenDescription := PenDescription+' Color: clNavy';
   clPurple:   PenDescription := PenDescription+' Color: clPurple';
   clTeal:     PenDescription := PenDescription+' Color: clTeal';
   clGray:     PenDescription := PenDescription+' Color: clGray';
   clSilver:   PenDescription := PenDescription+' Color: clSilver';
   clRed:      PenDescription := PenDescription+' Color: clRed';
   clLime:     PenDescription := PenDescription+' Color: clLime';
   clYellow:   PenDescription := PenDescription+' Color: clYellow';
   clBlue:     PenDescription := PenDescription+' Color: clBlue';
   clFuchsia:  PenDescription := PenDescription+' Color: clFuchsia';
   clAqua:     PenDescription := PenDescription+' Color: clAqua';
   clWhite:    PenDescription := PenDescription+' Color: clWhite';
end;

{indicate the pen's width}
PenDescription:=PenDescription+' Width: '+IntToStr(LocalObjType.lopnWidth.X);

{add the description to the list box}
Form1.ListBox.Items.Add(PenDescription);

{indicate that enumeration should continue}
Result := 1;
end;


procedure TForm1.Button1Click(Sender: TObject);
begin
   {enumerate all pens in the form's device context}
   EnumObjects(Canvas.Handle, OBJ_PEN, @EnumObjProc, 0);
end;
```

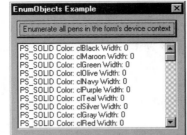

*Figure 3-20:
Listing every
pen in the
device context*

ExtCreatePen   Windows.Pas

Syntax

ExtCreatePen(
PenStyle: DWORD;   {pen type, style, end cap, and join flags}
Width: DWORD;   {the pen width}
const Brush: TLogBrush;   {a pointer to a TLogBrush structure}
StyleCount: DWORD;   {the number of entries in the custom style array}
Style: Pointer   {a pointer to an array of dash and space length values}

): HPEN;   {returns the handle to a pen}

Description

This function creates a new cosmetic or geometric pen with the specified attributes. Geometric pens can be any width, and have the same attributes as a brush. Cosmetic pens must always be one pixel in size, but perform faster than geometric pens. Additionally, under Windows NT, this function can create a pen with a user-defined style pattern. When the application no longer needs the pen, it should be deleted by calling the DeleteObject function.

Parameters

PenStyle: A series of flags defining the pen's type, style, end caps, and joins. This parameter may contain a combination of one value from the Table 3-20 and one value from Table 3-21. If this parameter contains the PS_GEOMETRIC style flag, it can contain an additional combination of one value from Table 3-22 and one value from Table 3-23. Note: Under Windows 95, the end cap and join styles are supported only for geometric pens when used to draw a path.

Width: Specifies the width of the pen, in logical units. If the PenStyle parameter contains the PS_COSMETIC flag, this parameter must be set to one.

Brush: A pointer to a TLogBrush structure defining additional pen attributes. If the PenStyle parameter contains the PS_COSMETIC flag, the lbColor member of this structure specifies the color of the pen, and the lbStyle member must be set to BS_SOLID. If the PenStyle parameter contains the PS_GEOMETRIC flag, all members of this structure are used to specify the pen attributes. The TLogBrush structure is defined as:

TLogBrush = packed record
      lbStyle: UINT;   {brush style flag}
      lbColor: COLORREF;   {a color specifier}
      lbHatch: Longint;   {hatch style flag}
end;

Note that if the lbHatch member points to a bitmap, it cannot be a bitmap created by the CreateDIBSection function. Please see the CreateBrushIndirect function for a description of this data structure.

StyleCount: Specifies the number of entries in the user-defined pen style array pointed to by the Style parameter. If the PenStyle parameter does not contain the PS_USERSTYLE flag, this parameter is ignored.

Style: A pointer to an array of DWORD values defining the pattern of dashes and spaces for a user-defined pen style. The first entry in the array specifies the length of the first dash, in logical units. The second entry specifies the length of the first space, in logical units. This continues until the line is fully defined. The pattern will be repeated as necessary when drawing a line created with the pen. If the PenStyle parameter does not contain the PS_USERSTYLE flag, this parameter is ignored.

Return Value

If the function succeeds, it returns the handle to a new pen; otherwise it returns zero.

See Also

CreateBrushIndirect, CreatePen, CreatePenIndirect, DeleteObject, GetObject, SelectObject, SetMiterLimit

Example

Listing 3-16: Drawing Paths with Geometric Pens

```
procedure TForm1.Button1Click(Sender: TObject);
var
  NewPen, OldPen: HPen;      // holds the old and new pens
  FormDC: HDC;               // holds a handle to the form's device context
  BrushInfo: TLogBrush;      // the logical brush structure
  MiterLimit: Single;        // the miter limit
begin
  {get the form's device context}
  FormDC := GetDC(Form1.Handle);

  {define the brush}
  with BrushInfo do
  begin
    lbStyle := BS_SOLID;
    lbColor := clBlue;
    lbHatch := 0;
```

3

Chapter

```
end;

{create a geometric pen with square end caps and mitered joins, 20 units wide}
NewPen := ExtCreatePen(PS_GEOMETRIC or PS_ENDCAP_SQUARE or PS_JOIN_MITER, 20,
                       BrushInfo, 0, nil);

{select the pen into the form's device context}
OldPen := SelectObject(FormDC, NewPen);

{begin a path bracket}
BeginPath(FormDC);

{define a closed triangle path}
MoveToEx(FormDC, ClientWidth div 2, 20, nil);
LineTo(FormDC, ClientWidth-20, 90);
LineTo(FormDC, 20, 90);
CloseFigure(FormDC);

{end the path bracket}
EndPath(FormDC);

{ensure that the miter limit is 2 units}
GetMiterLimit(FormDC, MiterLimit);
if MiterLimit>2 then
  SetMiterLimit(FormDC, 2, NIL);

{draw the path with the geometric pen}
StrokePath(FormDC);

{delete the pen and the device context}
SelectObject(FormDC, OldPen);
ReleaseDC(Form1.Handle, FormDC);
DeleteObject(NewPen);
end;
```

*Figure 3-21:
The geometric
pen in action*

Table 3-20: ExtCreatePen PenStyle Pen Type Values

Value	Description
PS_GEOMETRIC	Indicates a geometric pen.
PS_COSMETIC	Indicates a cosmetic pen.

Table 3-21: ExtCreatePen PenStyle Pen Style Values

Value	Description
PS_ALTERNATE	Windows NT only: Sets every other pixel when drawing a line (cosmetic pens only).
PS_SOLID	Creates a solid pen.
PS_DASH	Creates a dashed pen. Windows 95 only: This style is not supported for geometric pens.
PS_DOT	Creates a dotted pen. Windows 95 only: This style is not supported for geometric pens.
PS_DASHDOT	Creates an alternating dash and dot pen. Windows 95 only: This style is not supported for geometric pens.
PS_DASHDOTDOT	Creates an alternating dash and double dot pen. Windows 95 only: This style is not supported for geometric pens.
PS_NULL	Creates an invisible pen.
PS_USERSTYLE	Windows NT only: Creates a user-defined style pen. The Style parameter points to an array of DWORD values that specify the dashes and spaces of the pen.
PS_INSIDEFRAME	Creates a solid pen. When this pen is used in any function that specifies a bounding rectangle, the dimensions of the figure are reduced so that the entire figure, when drawn with the pen, will fit within the bounding rectangle (geometric pens only).

Table 3-22: ExtCreatePen PenStyle End Cap Values (geometric pens only)

Value	Description
PS_ENDCAP_ROUND	Line ends are round.
PS_ENDCAP_SQUARE	Line ends are square.
PS_ENDCAP_FLAT	Line ends are flat.

Table 3-23: ExtCreatePen PenStyle Join Values (geometric pens only)

Value	Description
PS_JOIN_BEVEL	Line joins are beveled.
PS_JOIN_MITER	Line joins are mitered when they are within the current limit set by the SetMiterLimit function. If it exceeds this limit, the join is beveled.
PS_JOIN_ROUND	Line joins are round.

3

Chapter

| *ExtFloodFill* | *Windows.Pas* |

Syntax

```
ExtFloodFill(
DC: HDC;                {the handle of a device context}
X: Integer;             {horizontal coordinate of fill origin}
Y: Integer;             {vertical coordinate of fill origin}
Color: COLORREF;        {the fill color}
FillType: UINT          {fill type flags}
): BOOL;                {returns TRUE or FALSE}
```

Description

This function fills an area of the specified device context with the current brush.

Parameters

DC: A handle to the device context upon which the fill is drawn.

X: Specifies the horizontal coordinate, in logical units, of the origin of the fill.

Y: Specifies the vertical coordinate, in logical units, of the origin of the fill.

Color: A color specifier indicating the color of the border or area to be filled. The meaning of this parameter is dependent on the value of the FillType parameter.

FillType: A flag indicating the type of fill to perform. This parameter may be set to one value from Table 3-24.

Return Value

If the function succeeds, it returns TRUE; otherwise it returns FALSE. To get extended error information, call the GetLastError function.

See Also

FillPath, FillRect, FillRgn, GetDeviceCaps

Example

Listing 3-17: Filling an Area

```
procedure TForm1.Button1Click(Sender: TObject);
begin
  {set the color of the brush used for the flood fill}
  Canvas.Brush.Color := clLime;

  {fill the red square with the new brush color}
  ExtFloodFill(Canvas.Handle, 20, 20, clRed, FLOODFILLSURFACE);
end;
```

Table 3-24: ExtFloodFill FillType Values

Value	Description
FLOODFILLBORDER	Indicates that the area to be filled is bounded by pixels of the color specified in the Color parameter. The function fills pixels in all directions from the origin with the color of the brush until the color specified by the Color parameter is encountered.
FLOODFILLSURFACE	Indicates that the area to be filled is defined by a solid color. The function fills pixels in all directions from the origin with the color of the brush while the color specified by the Color parameter is encountered.

FillPath   *Windows.Pas*

Syntax

```
FillPath(
DC: HDC              {the handle of a device context}
): BOOL;             {returns TRUE or FALSE}
```

Description

This function closes any open paths in the device context, filling the path's interior with the current brush. The path is filled according to the current polygon filling mode. Note that after this function returns, the path is discarded from the device context.

Parameters

DC: A handle to a device context containing the valid path to be filled.

Return Value

If the function succeeds, it returns TRUE; otherwise it returns FALSE. To get extended error information, call the GetLastError function.

See Also

BeginPath, ExtFloodFill, FillRgn, SetPolyFillMode, StrokeAndFillPath, StrokePath

Example

Listing 3-18: Filling a Path

```
procedure TForm1.FormPaint(Sender: TObject);
begin
  {open a path bracket}
  BeginPath(Canvas.Handle);

  {draw text into the path, indicating that the path consists of the
   text interior}
  SetBkMode(Canvas.Handle, TRANSPARENT);
```

```
  Canvas.TextOut(10, 10, 'DELPHI ROCKS!');

  {end the path bracket}
  EndPath(Canvas.Handle);

  {initialize the canvas's brush}
  Canvas.Brush.Color := clBlue;
  Canvas.Brush.Style := bsDiagCross;

  {fill the path with the current brush}
  FillPath(Canvas.Handle);
end;
```

Figure 3-22:
The filled path

FillRect   **Windows.Pas**

Syntax

```
FillRect(
hDC: HDC;                {the handle of a device context}
const lprc: TRect;       {the rectangular coordinates}
hbr: HBRUSH              {the handle of the brush}
): Integer;              {returns zero or one}
```

Description

This function fills the specified rectangular area in the device context with the indicated brush. The top and left borders of the rectangle are included in the fill, but the bottom and right borders are excluded.

Parameters

hDC: The handle of the device context upon which the filled rectangle is drawn.

lprc: A pointer to a TRect structure defining the rectangular coordinates, in logical units, of the area to be filled.

hbr: Specifies the handle of the brush used to fill the rectangle. Optionally, a system color can be used to fill the rectangle by setting this parameter to one value from Table 3-25. Note that when using a system color, a one must be added to the value (i.e., COLOR_ACTIVEBORDER+1).

Return Value

If the function succeeds, it returns one; otherwise it returns zero. To get extended error information, call the GetLastError function.

See Also

CreateHatchBrush, CreatePatternBrush, CreateSolidBrush, GetStockObject, ExtFloodFill, FrameRect, FillPath, FillRgn

Example

Please see Listing 3-5 under CreatePatternBrush.

Table 3-25: FillRect hbr System Color Values

Value	Description
COLOR_3DDKSHADOW	The dark shadow color for three-dimensional display elements.
COLOR_3DLIGHT	The lighted edge color for three-dimensional display elements.
COLOR_ACTIVEBORDER	The active window border color.
COLOR_ACTIVECAPTION	The active window caption color.
COLOR_APPWORKSPACE	The background color used in multiple document interface applications.
COLOR_BACKGROUND	The desktop color.
COLOR_BTNFACE	The color of pushbutton faces.
COLOR_BTNHIGHLIGHT	The color of a highlighted pushbutton.
COLOR_BTNSHADOW	The shaded edge color on pushbuttons.
COLOR_BTNTEXT	The text color on pushbuttons.
COLOR_CAPTIONTEXT	The text color used in caption, size box, and scroll bar arrow box controls.
COLOR_GRAYTEXT	The color of disabled text. This will be set to zero if the display driver cannot support solid gray.
COLOR_HIGHLIGHT	The color used for selected items in a control.
COLOR_HIGHLIGHTTEXT	The color used for the text of selected items in a control.
COLOR_INACTIVEBORDER	The inactive window border color.
COLOR_INACTIVECAPTION	The inactive window caption color.
COLOR_INACTIVECAPTIONTEXT	The text color in an inactive caption bar.
COLOR_INFOBK	The background color for tooltip controls.
COLOR_INFOTEXT	The text color for tooltip controls.
COLOR_MENU	The menu background color.
COLOR_MENUTEXT	The text color used in menus.
COLOR_SCROLLBAR	The scroll bar "gray" area color.
COLOR_WINDOW	The window background color.
COLOR_WINDOWFRAME	The window frame color.
COLOR_WINDOWTEXT	The color of text used in a window.

3

Chapter

FillRgn   **Windows.Pas**

Syntax

```
FillRgn(
DC: HDC;              {the handle of a device context}
p2: HRGN;            {the handle of the region}
p3: HBRUSH          {the handle of the brush}
): BOOL;             {returns TRUE or FALSE}
```

Description

This function fills the specified region with the brush identified by the p3 parameter.

Parameters

DC: A handle to the device context upon which the filled region is drawn.

p2: Specifies a handle to the region to be filled.

p3: Specifies a handle to the brush used to fill the region.

Return Value

If the function succeeds, it returns TRUE; otherwise it returns FALSE.

See Also

CreateBrushIndirect, CreateHatchBrush, CreatePatternBrush, CreateSolidBrush, FrameRgn, FillPath, FillRect, PaintRgn

Example

Please see Listing 3-3 under CreateBrushIndirect.

FrameRect   **Windows.Pas**

Syntax

```
FrameRect(
hDC: HDC;            {the handle of a device context}
const lprc: TRect;   {the rectangular coordinates}
hbr: HBRUSH         {the handle of the brush}
): Integer;          {returns zero or one}
```

Description

This function draws a border around the specified rectangle on the device context using the brush identified by the hbr parameter. This border is always one logical unit in width.

Parameters

hDC: A handle to the device context upon which the rectangular frame is drawn.

lprc: A pointer to a TRect structure containing the rectangular coordinates defining the frame.

hbr: Specifies a handle to the brush used to draw the rectangular frame.

Return Value

If the function succeeds, it returns one; otherwise it returns zero. To get extended error information, call the GetLastError function.

See Also

CreateHatchBrush, CreatePatternBrush, CreateSolidBrush, FillRect, FrameRgn, GetStockObject, Rectangle

Example

Listing 3-19: Drawing a Rectangular Frame

```
procedure TForm1.Button1Click(Sender: TObject);
var
  TheRect: TRect;      // the rectangular coordinates
begin
  {define the rectangle}
  TheRect := Rect(10, 10, 110, 110);

  {initialize the brush}
  Canvas.Brush.Color := clRed;
  Canvas.Brush.Style := bsCross;

  {frame the rectangle}
  FrameRect(Canvas.Handle, TheRect, Canvas.Brush.Handle);
end;
```

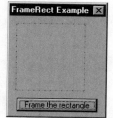

Figure 3-23: The framed rectangle

FrameRgn   Windows.Pas

Syntax

```
FrameRgn(
DC: HDC;              {the handle of a device context}
p2: HRGN;             {the handle of the region}
p3: HBRUSH;           {the handle of the brush}
```

p4: Integer;   {the width of vertical brush strokes}
p5: Integer   {the height of horizontal brush strokes}
): BOOL;   {returns TRUE or FALSE}

Description

This function draws the perimeter of the specified region with the brush identified by the p3 parameter.

Parameters

DC: A handle to the device context upon which the framed region is drawn.

p2: A handle to the region whose perimeter is being drawn.

p3: Specifies the handle of the brush used to draw the frame.

p4: Specifies the width of vertical brush strokes when drawing the frame, in logical units.

p5: Specifies the height of horizontal brush strokes when drawing the frame, in logical units.

Return Value

If the function succeeds, it returns TRUE; otherwise it returns FALSE.

See Also

CreateHatchBrush, CreatePatternBrush, CreateSolidBrush, FrameRect, FillRgn, PaintRgn

Example

Listing 3-20: Framing a Region

```
procedure TForm1.Button1Click(Sender: TObject);
var
  RegionHandle: HRGN;                  // the region handle
  PointsArray: array[0..5] of TPoint; // points defining the region
begin
  {define the region}
  PointsArray[0].X := 50;
  PointsArray[0].y := 50;
  PointsArray[1].x := 100;
  PointsArray[1].y := 50;
  PointsArray[2].x := 125;
  PointsArray[2].y := 75;
  PointsArray[3].x := 100;
  PointsArray[3].y := 100;
  PointsArray[4].x := 50;
  PointsArray[4].y := 100;
  PointsArray[5].x := 25;
  PointsArray[5].y := 75;

  {create the polygonal region}
```

```
RegionHandle := CreatePolygonRgn(PointsArray, 6, ALTERNATE);

{frame the region in black}
Canvas.Brush.Color := clBlack;
FrameRgn(Canvas.Handle, RegionHandle, Canvas.Brush.Handle, 2, 2);
end;
```

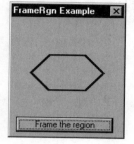

*Figure 3-24:
The framed
region*

GetBkColor   ### Windows.Pas

Syntax

```
GetBkColor(
hDC: HDC                         {the handle of a device context}
): COLORREF;                     {returns the background color}
```

Description

This function retrieves the background color for the specified device context.

Parameters

hDC: A handle to the device context from which the background color is to be retrieved.

Return Value

If the function succeeds, it returns a color specifier describing the background color; otherwise it returns CLR_INVALID.

See Also

GetBkMode, SetBkColor

Example

Listing 3-21: Drawing Text With and Without the Background Color

```
procedure TForm1.Button1Click(Sender: TObject);
begin
  {if the background color is not red, make it so}
  if GetBkColor(Canvas.Handle)<>clRed then
    SetBkColor(Canvas.Handle, clRed);
```

```
{output some text; the background color will be used}
Canvas.TextOut(20, 20, 'Text with a background color');

{if the background mode is not transparent, make it so}
if GetBkMode(Canvas.Handle)<>TRANSPARENT then
  SetBkMode(Canvas.Handle, TRANSPARENT);

{draw some text; the background color will not be used}
Canvas.TextOut(20, 40, 'Text drawn with a transparent background');
end;
```

Figure 3-25:
Text with and
without a
background
color

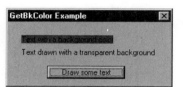

GetBkMode   Windows.Pas

Syntax

```
GetBkMode(
hDC: HDC                    {the handle of a device context}
): Integer;                 {returns the current background mode}
```

Description

This function retrieves the current background mix mode for the specified device context.

Parameters

hDC: A handle to the device context from which the background mix mode is to be retrieved.

Return Value

If the function succeeds, it returns a flag indicating the current background mix mode of the specified device context. This flag can be either OPAQUE or TRANSPARENT. Please see the SetBkMode function for a description of these flags. If the function fails, it returns zero.

See Also

GetBkColor, SetBkMode

Example

Please see Listing 3-21 under GetBkColor.

| *GetBoundsRect* | *Windows.Pas* |

Syntax

```
GetBoundsRect(
DC: HDC;                {handle of the device context}
var p2: TRect;          {a pointer to a TRect structure}
p3: UINT                {operation flags}
): UINT;                {returns the accumulated bounding rectangle state}
```

Description

This function retrieves the current bounding rectangle for the specified device context. Windows maintains an accumulated bounding rectangle for each device context that identifies the extent of output from drawing functions. When a drawing function reaches beyond this boundary, the rectangle is extended. Thus, the bounding rectangle is the smallest rectangle that can be drawn around the area affected by all drawing operations in the device context.

Parameters

DC: A handle to the device context from which the accumulated bounding rectangle is to be retrieved.

p2: A pointer to a TRect structure that receives the coordinates of the device context's bounding rectangle.

p3: A flag indicating if the bounding rectangle will be cleared. If this parameter is set to zero, the bounding rectangle will not be modified. If this parameter is set to DCB_RESET, the bounding rectangle is cleared when the function returns.

Return Value

This function returns a code indicating the state of the bounding rectangle or an error condition, and will be one or more values from Table 3-26.

See Also

GetUpdateRect, SetBoundsRect

Example

Listing 3-22: Setting and Retrieving the Device Context's Bounding Rectangle

```
procedure TForm1.Button1Click(Sender: TObject);
var
  TheRect: TRect;         // receives the bounding rectangle
  FormDC: HDC;            // a handle to the form's device context
  BoundRectState: UINT;   // holds the bounding rectangle state
begin
  {get the device context of the form}
  FormDC := GetDC(Form1.Handle);
```

3

Chapter

```
{initialize and set the bounds rectangle}
TheRect := Rect(10, 10, 110, 110);
SetBoundsRect(FormDC, @TheRect, DCB_ENABLE);

{retrieve the bounds rectangle}
BoundRectState := GetBoundsRect(FormDC, TheRect, 0);

{release the device context}
ReleaseDC(Form1.Handle, FormDC);

{display the bounds rectangle coordinates}
with TheRect do
begin
  Label1.Caption := 'Top: '+IntToStr(Top) +' Left: '+IntToStr(Left)+
                    ' Bottom: '+IntToStr(Bottom)+' Right: '+IntToStr(Right);
end;

{display the bounds rectangle state}
case BoundRectState of
  DCB_DISABLE:  Label2.Caption := 'State: DCB_DISABLE';
  DCB_ENABLE:   Label2.Caption := 'State: DCB_ENABLE';
  DCB_RESET:    Label2.Caption := 'State: DCB_RESET';
  DCB_SET:      Label2.Caption := 'State: DCB_SET';
end;
end;
```

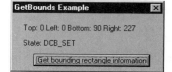

Figure 3-26:
The current
BoundsRect

Table 3-26: GetBoundsRect Return Values

Value	Description
0	Indicates that an error occurred.
DCB_DISABLE	Boundary accumulation is off.
DCB_ENABLE	Boundary accumulation is on.
DCB_RESET	The bounding rectangle is empty.
DCB_SET	The bounding rectangle is not empty.

GetBrushOrgEx   Windows.Pas

Syntax

```
GetBrushOrgEx(
DC: HDC;                    {the handle of a device context}
var p2: TPoint             {a pointer to a TPoint structure}
): BOOL;                    {returns TRUE or FALSE}
```

Description

This function retrieves the origin of the brush for the specified device context. The brush origin is relative to the hatch or bitmap defining the brush's pattern. The default brush origin is at 0,0. A brush pattern can be no more than eight pixels square. Thus, the origin can range from 0-7 vertically and horizontally. As the origin is moved, the brush pattern is offset by the specified amount. If an application is using a pattern brush to draw the backgrounds of child windows and parent windows, the brush origin may need to be moved to align the patterns. Note that under Windows NT, the system automatically tracks the brush origin so that patterns will be aligned.

Parameters

DC: A handle to the device context from which the brush origin is to be retrieved.

p2: A pointer to a TPoint structure that receives the coordinates of the brush origin, in device units.

Return Value

If the function succeeds, it returns TRUE; otherwise it returns FALSE. To get extended error information, call the GetLastError function.

See Also

CreateBrushIndirect, CreateHatchBrush, CreatePatternBrush, FillRect, FillRgn, SelectObject, SetBrushOrgEx

Example

Please see Listing 3-42 under Rectangle.

GetCurrentObject   Windows.Pas

Syntax

```
GetCurrentObject(
DC: HDC;                    {the handle of a device context}
p2: UINT                    {the object type flag}
): HGDIOBJ;                 {returns the handle to a GDI object}
```

Description

This function returns a handle to the specified object currently selected into the device context identified by the DC parameter.

Parameters

DC: A handle to the device context from which the currently selected object is to be retrieved.

p2: A flag specifying what type of object to retrieve. This parameter can be set to one value from Table 3-27.

Return Value

If the function succeeds, it returns a handle to the currently selected object of the specified type. If the function fails, it returns zero.

See Also

DeleteObject, GetObject, GetObjectType, SelectObject

Example

Please see Listing 3-24 under GetObject.

Table 3-27: GetCurrentObject p2 Values

Value	Description
OBJ_PEN	Retrieves the handle of the currently selected pen.
OBJ_BRUSH	Retrieves the handle of the currently selected brush.
OBJ_PAL	Retrieves the handle of the currently selected palette.
OBJ_FONT	Retrieves the handle of the currently selected font.
OBJ_BITMAP	Retrieves the handle of the currently selected bitmap if the DC parameter identifies a memory device context.

GetCurrentPositionEx **Windows.Pas**

Syntax

```
GetCurrentPositionEx(
DC: HDC;              {the handle of a device context}
Point: PPoint         {a pointer to a TPoint structure}
): BOOL;              {returns TRUE or FALSE}
```

Description

This function retrieves the coordinates of the current position in logical units.

Parameters

DC: A handle to the device context from which the current position is to be retrieved.

Point: A pointer to a TPoint structure that receives the coordinates of the current position, in logical units.

Return Value

If the function succeeds, it returns TRUE; otherwise it returns FALSE.

See Also

LineTo, MoveToEx, PolyBezierTo, PolylineTo

Example

Listing 3-23: Displaying the Current Position

```
procedure TForm1.Button1Click(Sender: TObject);
var
  CurPosPt: TPoint;           // holds the current position
begin
  {set the background mode to transparent}
  SetBkMode(Canvas.Handle, TRANSPARENT);

  {display the first point}
  MoveToEx(Canvas.Handle, 60, 20, NIL);
  GetCurrentPositionEx(Canvas.Handle, @CurPosPt);
  TextOut(Canvas.Handle, CurPosPt.x-55, CurPosPt.y, PChar('X:
'+IntToStr(CurPosPt.X)+
          ' Y: '+IntToStr(CurPosPt.Y)), Length('X: '+IntToStr(CurPosPt.X)+
          ' Y: '+IntToStr(CurPosPt.Y)));

  {display the second point}
  LineTo(Canvas.Handle, 160, 20);
  GetCurrentPositionEx(Canvas.Handle, @CurPosPt);
  TextOut(Canvas.Handle, CurPosPt.x+2, CurPosPt.y, PChar('X:
'+IntToStr(CurPosPt.X)+
          ' Y: '+IntToStr(CurPosPt.Y)), Length('X: '+IntToStr(CurPosPt.X)+
          ' Y: '+IntToStr(CurPosPt.Y)));

  {display the third point}
  LineTo(Canvas.Handle, 160, 120);
  GetCurrentPositionEx(Canvas.Handle, @CurPosPt);
  TextOut(Canvas.Handle, CurPosPt.x+2, CurPosPt.y, PChar('X:
'+IntToStr(CurPosPt.X)+
          ' Y: '+IntToStr(CurPosPt.Y)), Length('X: '+IntToStr(CurPosPt.X)+
          ' Y: '+IntToStr(CurPosPt.Y)));

  {display the fourth point}
  LineTo(Canvas.Handle, 60, 120);
  GetCurrentPositionEx(Canvas.Handle, @CurPosPt);
  TextOut(Canvas.Handle, CurPosPt.x-55, CurPosPt.y, PChar('X:
'+IntToStr(CurPosPt.X)+
          ' Y: '+IntToStr(CurPosPt.Y)), Length('X: '+IntToStr(CurPosPt.X)+
          ' Y: '+IntToStr(CurPosPt.Y)));

  {close the figure}
  LineTo(Canvas.Handle, 60, 20);
end;
```

3

Chapter

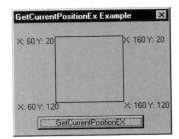

Figure 3-27:
Tracking the
current
position

GetMiterLimit *Windows.Pas*

Syntax

```
GetMiterLimit(
DC: HDC;                {the handle of a device context}
var Limit: Single       {a pointer to a variable receiving the miter limit}
): BOOL;                {returns TRUE or FALSE}
```

Description

This function retrieves the miter limit for the specified device context. The miter limit is used for geometric lines that have miter joins, and is the maximum ratio of the miter length to the line width. The miter length is the distance from the intersection of the inner wall to the intersection of the outer wall.

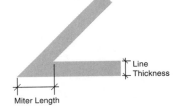

Figure 3-28:
Miter limit
dimensions

Parameters

DC: A handle to the device context from which the miter limit is to be retrieved.

Limit: A pointer to a variable of type Single that receives the device context's miter limit.

Return Value

If the function succeeds, it returns TRUE; otherwise it returns FALSE. To get extended error information, call the GetLastError function.

See Also

ExtCreatePen, SetMiterLimit

Example

Please see Listing 3-16 under ExtCreatePen.

GetObject   Windows.Pas

Syntax

```
GetObject(
p1: HGDIOBJ;          {a handle to a graphics object}
p2: Integer;          {the size of the buffer pointed to by the p3 parameter}
p3: Pointer           {a pointer to a buffer receiving object information}
): Integer;           {returns the number of bytes written to the buffer}
```

Description

This function retrieves information about the graphical object identified by the p1 parameter. Depending on the object type, the p3 parameter should point to a buffer that receives a TBitmap, TDIBSection, TExtLogPen, TLogBrush, TLogFont, or TLogPen structure containing information about the specified object. Note: If the p1 parameter contains a handle to a bitmap created with any function other than CreateDIBSection, the data structure returned in the buffer contains only the bitmap's width, height, and color format.

Parameters

p1: Specifies a handle to the graphical object whose information is to be retrieved. This can be a handle to a bitmap, DIB section, brush, font, pen, or palette.

p2: Specifies the size of the buffer pointed to by the p3 parameter.

p3: A pointer to a buffer that receives a data structure containing information about the specified graphical object. The type of data structure received is dependent on the type of object specified in the p1 parameter. If this parameter is set to NIL, the function returns the required size of the buffer to hold the retrieved information. If the p1 parameter contains a handle to a palette, the buffer pointed to by this parameter receives a 16-bit value indicating the number of entries in the palette. If the p1 parameter contains a handle to a bitmap, pen, brush, or font, the buffer pointed to by this parameter receives a TBitmap, TLogPen, TLogBrush, or TLogFont data structure, respectively. Please see the CreateBitmapIndirect, CreatePenIndirect, CreateBrushIndirect, or CreateFontIndirect functions for descriptions of these data structures. If the p1 parameter contains a handle to a bitmap returned by the CreateDIBSection function, the buffer pointed to by this parameter receives a TDIBSection structure. If the p1 parameter contains a handle to a pen returned by the ExtCreatePen function, the buffer pointed to by this parameter receives a TExtLogPen structure.

3

Chapter

The TDIBSection data structure is defined as:

```
TDIBSection = packed record
      dsBm: TBitmap;                        {a TBitmap structure}
      dsBmih: TBitmapInfoHeader;            {a TBitmapInfoHeader structure}
      dsBitfields: array[0..2] of DWORD;   {color masks}
      dshSection: THandle;                  {a handle to a file mapping object}
      dsOffset: DWORD;                      {bit values offset}
end;
```

dsBm: Specifies a TBitmap structure containing information about the bitmap's type, dimensions, and a pointer to its bits. Please see the CreateBitmapIndirect function for a description of this data structure.

dsBmih: Specifies a TBitmapInfoHeader structure containing information about the bitmap's color format. Please see the CreateDIBSection function for a description of this data structure.

dsBitfields: An array containing the three color masks, if the bitmap has a color depth greater than eight bits per pixel.

dshSection: Specifies a handle to the file mapping object passed to the Create-DIBSection when the bitmap was created. If a file mapping object was not used to create the bitmap, this member will contain zero.

dsOffset: Specifies the offset within the file mapping object to the start of the bitmap bits. If a file mapping object was not used to create the bitmap, this member will contain zero.

The TExtLogPen data structure is defined as:

```
TExtLogPen = packed record
      elpPenStyle: DWORD;                   {type, style, end cap, and join flags}
      elpWidth: DWORD;                      {the pen width}
      elpBrushStyle: UINT;                  {the brush style}
      elpColor: COLORREF;                   {the pen color}
      elpHatch: Longint;                    {the hatch style}
      elpNumEntries: DWORD;                 {the number of entries in the array}
      elpStyleEntry: array[0..0] of DWORD;  {specifies a user-defined style}
end;
```

elpPenStyle: A series of flags defining the pen's type, style, end caps, and joins. Please see the ExtCreatePen function for a list of available flags.

elpWidth: Specifies the width of the pen, in logical units. If the PenStyle parameter contains the PS_COSMETIC flag, this parameter must be set to one.

elpBrushStyle: A flag indicating the brush style of the pen. Please see the Create-BrushIndirect function for a list of available styles.

elpColor: Specifies the color of the pen.

elpHatch: Specifies the hatch pattern of the pen. Please see the CreateHatchBrush function for a list of available flags.

elpNumEntries: Specifies the number of entries in the user-defined pen style array pointed to by the elpStyleEntry member. If the elpPenStyle member does not contain the PS_USERSTYLE flag, this member is ignored.

elpStyleEntry: A pointer to an array of DWORD values defining the pattern of dashes and spaces for a user-defined pen style. The first entry in the array specifies the length of the first dash, in logical units. The second entry specifies the length of the first space, in logical units. This continues until the line is fully defined. The pattern will be repeated as necessary when drawing a line created with the pen. If the elpPenStyle member does not contain the PS_USERSTYLE flag, this member is ignored.

Return Value

If the function succeeds, it returns the number of bytes written to the buffer pointed to by the p3 parameter; otherwise it returns zero. To get extended error information, call the GetLastError function.

See Also

CreateBitmapIndirect, CreateBrushIndirect, CreateDIBSection, CreateFontIndirect, CreatePenIndirect, ExtCreatePen, GetBitmapBits, GetDIBits, GetCurrentObject, GetObjectType, GetPaletteEntries, GetRegionData, GetStockObject

Example

Listing 3-24: Retrieving Information About an Object

```
function GetStyle(Style: Integer): string;
begin
  {display the brush style}
  case Style of
    BS_DIBPATTERN:    Result := 'BS_DIBPATTERN';
    BS_DIBPATTERN8X8: Result := 'BS_DIBPATTERN8X8';
    BS_DIBPATTERNPT:  Result := 'BS_DIBPATTERNPT';
    BS_HATCHED:       Result := 'BS_HATCHED';
    BS_HOLLOW:        Result := 'BS_HOLLOW';
    BS_PATTERN:       Result := 'BS_PATTERN';
    BS_PATTERN8X8:    Result := 'BS_PATTERN8X8';
    BS_SOLID:         Result := 'BS_SOLID';
  end;
end;

function GetHatch(Hatch: Integer): string;
begin
  {display the hatch style}
  case Hatch of
    HS_BDIAGONAL:  Result := 'HS_BDIAGONAL';
    HS_CROSS:      Result := 'HS_CROSS';
    HS_DIAGCROSS:  Result := 'HS_DIAGCROSS';
    HS_FDIAGONAL:  Result := 'HS_FDIAGONAL';
    HS_HORIZONTAL: Result := 'HS_HORIZONTAL';
    HS_VERTICAL:   Result := 'HS_VERTICAL';
  end;
```

3

Chapter

```
    end;

procedure TForm1.Button1Click(Sender: TObject);
var
  hObject: HGDIOBJ;      // holds the handle to a brush object
  LogBrush: TLogBrush;   // holds brush information
  FormDC: HDC;           // a handle to the form's device context
begin
  {retrieve the form's device context}
  FormDC := GetDC(Form1.Handle);

  {initialize the form's brush, and then retrieve a handle to it}
  Canvas.Brush.Color := clRed;
  Canvas.Brush.Style := bsDiagCross;
  hObject := GetCurrentObject(Canvas.Handle, OBJ_BRUSH);

  {retrieve information about the object}
  GetObject(hObject, SizeOf(TLogBrush), @LogBrush);

  {indicate the type of object retrieved}
  case GetObjectType(hObject) of
    OBJ_BITMAP:        Edit4.Text := 'Bitmap';
    OBJ_BRUSH:         Edit4.Text := 'Brush';
    OBJ_FONT:          Edit4.Text := 'Font';
    OBJ_PAL:           Edit4.Text := 'Palette';
    OBJ_PEN:           Edit4.Text := 'Pen';
    OBJ_EXTPEN:        Edit4.Text := 'Extended Pen';
    OBJ_REGION:        Edit4.Text := 'Region';
    OBJ_DC:            Edit4.Text := 'Device Context';
    OBJ_MEMDC:         Edit4.Text := 'Memory Device Context';
    OBJ_METAFILE:      Edit4.Text := 'Metafile';
    OBJ_METADC:        Edit4.Text := 'Metafile Device Context';
    OBJ_ENHMETAFILE:   Edit4.Text := 'Enhanced Metafile';
    OBJ_ENHMETADC:     Edit4.Text := 'Enhanced Metafile Device Context';
  end;

  {display the object's information}
  with LogBrush do
  begin
    Edit1.Text := GetStyle(lbStyle);
    Edit2.Text := IntToHex(lbColor, 8);
    Edit3.Text := GetHatch(lbHatch);
  end;

  {select the brush into the form's device context}
  SelectObject(FormDC, hObject);

  {draw an ellipse with the brush}
  Ellipse(FormDC, 50, 10, 150, 110);

  {delete the device context}
  ReleaseDC(Form1.Handle, FormDC);
end;
```

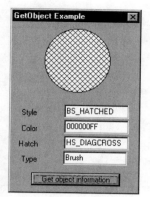

Figure 3-29:
The object
information

GetObjectType   Windows.Pas

Syntax

GetObjectType(
h: HGDIOBJ   {a handle to a graphic object}
): DWORD;   {returns an object type flag}

Description

This function returns a flag indicating what type of object is referenced by the h parameter.

Parameters

h: A handle to a graphical object whose type is to be retrieved.

Return Value

If the function succeeds, it returns a flag indicating the object type, and it can be one value from Table 3-28. If the function fails, it returns zero.

See Also

DeleteObject, GetCurrentObject, GetObject, GetStockObject, SelectObject

Example

Please see Listing 3-24 under GetObject.

Table 3-28: GetObjectType Return Values

Value	Description
OBJ_BITMAP	Bitmap
OBJ_BRUSH	Brush
OBJ_FONT	Font
OBJ_PAL	Palette

Value	Description
OBJ_PEN	Pen
OBJ_EXTPEN	Extended pen
OBJ_REGION	Region
OBJ_DC	Device context
OBJ_MEMDC	Memory device context
OBJ_METAFILE	Metafile
OBJ_METADC	Metafile device context
OBJ_ENHMETAFILE	Enhanced metafile
OBJ_ENHMETADC	Enhanced metafile device context

GetPixel *Windows.Pas*

Syntax

```
GetPixel(
DC: HDC;                {the handle of a device context}
X: Integer;             {the horizontal pixel coordinate}
Y: Integer              {the vertical pixel coordinate}
): COLORREF;            {returns a color specifier}
```

Description

This function retrieves the color of the pixel at the specified coordinates in the indicated device context. The coordinates must be within the boundaries of the current clipping region.

Parameters

DC: A handle to the device context from which the pixel color is retrieved.

X: The horizontal coordinate of the pixel within the device context, in logical units.

Y: The vertical coordinate of the pixel within the device context, in logical units.

Return Value

If the function succeeds, it returns the color specifier of the pixel at the indicated coordinates. If the function fails, it returns CLR_INVALID.

See Also

SetPixel, SetPixelV

Example

Please see Listing 3-44 under SetPixel.

GetPolyFillMode

Syntax

```
GetPolyFillMode(
DC: HDC                    {the handle of a device context}
): Integer;                {returns the polygon fill mode}
```

Description

This function retrieves the current polygon fill mode for the given device context.

Parameters

DC: A handle to the device context from which the current polygon fill mode is to be retrieved.

Return Value

If the function succeeds, it returns a flag indicating the polygon fill mode of the specified device context, and may be one value from Table 3-29. If the function fails, it returns zero. Please see the SetPolyFillMode for a description of these flags.

See Also

FillPath, Polygon, PolyPolygon, SetPolyFillMode

Example

Listing 3-25: Setting and Retrieving the Polygon Fill Mode

```
procedure TForm1.FormPaint(Sender: TObject);
var
  PointsArray: Array[0..10] of TPoint;  // holds the polygon definition
  FillMode: Integer;                     // holds the fill mode
begin
  {define the polygon}
  PointsArray[0].X := 145;
  PointsArray[0].Y := 220;
  PointsArray[1].X := 145;
  PointsArray[1].Y := 20;
  PointsArray[2].X := 310;
  PointsArray[2].Y := 20;
  PointsArray[3].X := 310;
  PointsArray[3].Y := 135;
  PointsArray[4].X := 105;
  PointsArray[4].Y := 135;
  PointsArray[5].X := 105;
  PointsArray[5].Y := 105;
  PointsArray[6].X := 280;
  PointsArray[6].Y := 105;
  PointsArray[7].X := 280;
  PointsArray[7].Y := 50;
  PointsArray[8].X := 175;
  PointsArray[8].Y := 50;
```

3

Chapter

```
PointsArray[9].X := 175;
PointsArray[9].Y := 220;

{set the polygon fill mode to the selected value}
if RadioGroup1.ItemIndex = 0 then
  SetPolyFillMode(Canvas.Handle, ALTERNATE)
else
  SetPolyFillMode(Canvas.Handle, WINDING);

{display the device context's polygon fill mode}
FillMode := GetPolyFillMode(Canvas.Handle);
if FillMode = Alternate then
  Caption := 'GetPolyFillMode Example - Alternate'
else
  Caption := 'GetPolyFillMode Example - Winding';

{set the brush to red and draw a filled polygon}
Canvas.Brush.Color := clRed;
Polygon(Canvas.Handle, PointsArray, 10);
end;
```

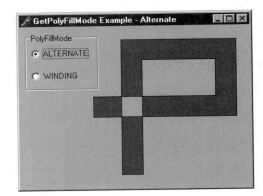

Figure 3-30:
A specific
polygon fill
mode

Table 3-29: GetPolyFillMode Return Values

Value	Description
ALTERNATE	Fills the polygon using the Alternate method.
WINDING	Fills the polygon using the Winding method.

GetROP2   *Windows.Pas*

Syntax

```
GetROP2(
DC: HDC                  {the handle of a device context}
): Integer;              {returns the foreground mix mode}
```

Description

This function retrieves the foreground mix mode for the specified device context. The foreground mix mode determines how the color of the pen used in drawing operations is combined with the color of pixels on the specified device context.

Parameters

DC: A handle to the device context from which the foreground mix mode is to be retrieved.

Return Value

If the function succeeds, it returns a flag indicating the device context's foreground mix mode, and can be one flag from Table 3-30. If the function fails, it returns zero.

See Also

LineTo, PolyBezier, Polyline, Rectangle, SetROP2

Example

Listing 3-26: Using the Foreground Mix Mode to Draw a Draggable Rectangle

```
var
  Form1: TForm1;
  RectDragging: Boolean;    // indicates if a dragging operation has begun
  OldRect: TRect;           // holds the old rectangular coordinates

implementation

{$R *.DFM}

procedure TForm1.FormMouseDown(Sender: TObject; Button: TMouseButton;
  Shift: TShiftState; X, Y: Integer);
begin
  {indicate that a dragging operation has begun}
  RectDragging := TRUE;
end;

procedure TForm1.FormMouseMove(Sender: TObject; Shift: TShiftState; X,
  Y: Integer);
begin
  {if we are dragging a rectangle...}
  if RectDragging then
  begin
    {initialize the canvas's pen}
    Canvas.Pen.Width := 5;

    {if the foreground mix mode is not R2_NOT, make it so}
    if GetRop2(Canvas.Handle)<>R2_NOT then
      SetRop2(Canvas.Handle, R2_NOT);
```

```
      {set the brush to be clear so only the lines show}
      Canvas.Brush.Style := bsClear;

      {draw a rectangle over the previous one to erase it}
      Canvas.Rectangle(OldRect.Left, OldRect.Top, OldRect.Right, OldRect.Bottom);

      {draw a rectangle at the new position}
      Canvas.Rectangle(X-20, Y-20, X+20, Y+20);

      {store the current rectangle coordinates for next time}
      OldRect := Rect(X-20, Y-20, X+20, Y+20);
    end;
  end;

procedure TForm1.FormMouseUp(Sender: TObject; Button: TMouseButton;
  Shift: TShiftState; X, Y: Integer);
begin
  {dragging has stopped}
  RectDragging := FALSE;
end;
```

*Figure 3-31:
Drawing the
draggable
rectangle*

Table 3-30: GetROP2 Return Values

Value	Description
R2_BLACK	The destination pixel is always black.
R2_COPYPEN	The destination pixel is set to the pen color.
R2_MASKNOTPEN	The destination pixel is a combination of the colors common to the screen and the inverse of the pen.
R2_MASKPEN	The destination pixel is a combination of the colors common to the screen and the pen.
R2_MASKPENNOT	The destination pixel is a combination of the colors common to the pen and the inverse of the screen.
R2_MERGENOTPEN	The destination pixel is a combination of the screen and the inverse of the pen.
R2_MERGEPEN	The destination pixel is a combination of the pen and the screen.

Value	Description
R2_MERGEPENNOT	The destination pixel is a combination of the pen and the inverse of the screen.
R2_NOP	The destination pixel is not modified.
R2_NOT	The destination pixel is the inverse of the screen.
R2_NOTCOPYPEN	The destination pixel is the inverse of the pen.
R2_NOTMASKPEN	The destination pixel is the inverse of the R2_MASKPEN flag.
R2_NOTMERGEPEN	The destination pixel is the inverse of the R2_MERGEPEN flag.
R2_NOTXORPEN	The destination pixel is the inverse of the R2_XORPEN flag.
R2_WHITE	The destination pixel is always white.
R2_XORPEN	The destination pixel is a combination of the colors in the pen and in the screen, but not in both.

GetStockObject   Windows.Pas

Syntax

```
GetStockObject(
Index: Integer                       {the stock object type flag}
): HGDIOBJ;                          {returns a handle to the graphical object}
```

Description

This function retrieves a handle to a predefined pen, brush, font, or palette. When the application no longer needs the object, it is not necessary to delete it by calling the DeleteObject function.

Note: Use the DKGRAY_BRUSH, GRAY_BRUSH, and LTGRAY_BRUSH stock brushes only in windows with the CS_HREDRAW and CS_VREDRAW class styles, or misalignment of brush patterns may occur if the window is moved or sized. The origin of stock brushes cannot be modified.

Parameters

Index: A flag indicating the type of stock object to retrieve. This parameter may be set to one value from Table 3-31.

Return Value

If the function succeeds, it returns a handle to the predefined graphical object; otherwise it returns zero.

See Also

DeleteObject, GetObject, GetObjectType, SelectObject

Example

Listing 3-27: Using a Stock Object

```
procedure TForm1.Button1Click(Sender: TObject);
var
  ARegion: HRGN;      // holds a region
begin
  {create a region to be filled}
  ARegion := CreateRectRgn(20, 20, 190, 110);

  {fill the region with a stock brush}
  FillRgn(Canvas.Handle, ARegion, GetStockObject(BLACK_BRUSH));
end;
```

Table 3-31: GetStockObject Index Values

Value	Description
BLACK_BRUSH	Retrieves a handle to a black brush.
DKGRAY_BRUSH	Retrieves a handle to a dark gray brush.
GRAY_BRUSH	Retrieves a handle to a gray brush.
HOLLOW_BRUSH	Retrieves a handle to a hollow brush.
LTGRAY_BRUSH	Retrieves a handle to a light gray brush.
WHITE_BRUSH	Retrieves a handle to a white brush.
BLACK_PEN	Retrieves a handle to a black pen.
NULL_PEN	Retrieves a handle to a null pen.
WHITE_PEN	Retrieves a handle to a white pen.
ANSI_FIXED_FONT	Retrieves a handle to a Windows fixed-pitch (monospace) system font.
ANSI_VAR_FONT	Retrieves a handle to a Windows variable-pitch (proportional space) system font.
DEVICE_DEFAULT_FONT	Windows NT only: Retrieves a handle to a device-dependent font.
DEFAULT_GUI_FONT	Windows 95 only: Retrieves a handle to the default font used in user interface objects.
OEM_FIXED_FONT	Retrieves a handle to an original equipment manufacturer dependent fixed-pitch (monospace) font.
SYSTEM_FONT	Retrieves a handle to the system font.
SYSTEM_FIXED_FONT	Retrieves a handle to the fixed-pitch (monospace) system font used in Windows versions earlier than 3.0.
DEFAULT_PALETTE	Retrieves a handle to the default palette containing the static colors in the system palette.

GetUpdateRect   *Windows.Pas*

Syntax

GetUpdateRect(
hWnd: HWND;   {the handle to a window}
var lpRect: TRect;   {a pointer to a TRect structure}
bErase: BOOL   {background erasure flag}
): BOOL;   {returns TRUE or FALSE}

Description

This function retrieves the coordinates of the smallest rectangle that can be drawn around the invalid region in the specified window. The rectangle will be in terms of client coordinates unless the window was created with the CS_OWNDC class style and its mapping mode is not MM_TEXT. In this case, the rectangle will be in terms of logical coordinates. Note that this function must be used before the BeginPaint function is called, as BeginPaint validates the update region, causing this function to return an empty rectangle.

Parameters

hWnd: A handle to the window whose update region's bounding rectangle is to be retrieved.

lpRect: A pointer to a TRect structure that receives the coordinates of the bounding rectangle.

bErase: A flag indicating if the background in the invalid region should be erased. If this parameter is set to TRUE and the region is not empty, the WM_ERASEBKGND message is sent to the specified window.

Return Value

If the function succeeds, it returns TRUE; otherwise it returns FALSE.

See Also

BeginPaint, GetUpdateRgn, InvalidateRect

Example

Please see Listing 3-29 under InvalidateRect.

GetUpdateRgn   *Windows.Pas*

Syntax

GetUpdateRgn(
hWnd: HWND;   {the handle to a window}
hRgn: HRGN;   {a region handle}
bErase: BOOL   {background erasure flag}
): Integer;   {returns the type of invalid region}

3

Chapter

Description

This function retrieves the handle of the invalid region in the specified window. The region is relative to the window's client area. Note that this function must be used before the BeginPaint function is called, as BeginPaint validates the update region, causing this function to return an empty region.

Parameters

hWnd: A handle to the window from which the update region is to be retrieved.

hRgn: A handle to a preexisting region. This handle will be reset to point to the invalid region when the function returns.

bErase: A flag indicating if the background in the invalid region should be erased and the nonclient areas of child windows redrawn. If this parameter is set to TRUE and the region is not empty, the WM_ERASEBKGND message is sent to the specified window and nonclient areas of child windows are redrawn.

Return Value

This function returns a result indicating the type of region retrieved or an error condition, and may be one value from Table 3-32.

See Also

GetUpdateRect, InvalidateRgn

Example

Please see Listing 3-30 under InvalidateRgn.

Table 3-32: GetUpdateRgn Return Values

Value	Description
NULLREGION	Indicates an empty region.
SIMPLEREGION	Indicates a single rectangular region.
COMPLEXREGION	Indicates a region consisting of more than one rectangle.
ERROR	Indicates an error occurred.

GrayString   Windows.Pas

Syntax

```
GrayString(
  hDC: HDC;                            {the handle of a device context}
  hBrush: HBRUSH;                      {the brush handle}
  lpOutputFunc: TFNGrayStringProc;     {a pointer to the callback function}
  lpData: LPARAM;                      {a pointer to the string}
  nCount: Integer;                     {the length of the string}
```

X: Integer;	{the horizontal output coordinate}
Y: Integer;	{the vertical output coordinate}
nWidth: Integer;	{the width of the offscreen bitmap}
nHeight: Integer	{the height of the offscreen bitmap}
): BOOL;	{returns TRUE or FALSE}

Description

This function draws text at the specified location on the indicated device context. The text is drawn by creating an offscreen bitmap, drawing the text into the bitmap, converting the color of the text using the specified brush or a default brush, and finally copying the bitmap onto the specified canvas at the indicated coordinates. The font currently selected into the specified device context is used to draw the text. If the lpOutputFunc parameter is set to NIL, the lpData parameter must contain a pointer to a string and the TextOut function is used to draw the string into the offscreen bitmap. Otherwise, the lpData parameter can point to any type of user-defined data, such as a bitmap, and the callback function pointed to by the lpOutputFunc parameter must draw the data into the offscreen bitmap.

Parameters:

hDC: A handle to the device context upon which the string is drawn.

hBrush: A handle to a brush used to convert the color of the text. If this parameter is set to zero, this function uses the default brush used to draw window text.

lpOutputFunc: A pointer to a callback function that will handle the output of the text. If this parameter is set to NIL, the function uses the TextOut function to draw the text onto the offscreen bitmap.

lpData: If the lpOutputFunc parameter contains NIL, this parameter specifies a pointer to the string to be drawn. This must be a null-terminated string if the nCount parameter is set to zero. Otherwise, this parameter contains a pointer to data that will be passed to the callback function.

nCount: Specifies the length of the string pointed to by the lpData parameter, in characters. If this parameter is set to zero, the function will calculate the length of the string if it is null terminated. If this parameter is set to -1 and the callback function pointed to by the lpOutputFunc parameter returns FALSE, the string will be displayed in its original form.

X: Specifies the horizontal coordinate at which to display the string, in device units.

Y: Specifies the vertical coordinate at which to display the string, in device units.

nWidth: Specifies the width, in device units, of the offscreen bitmap into which the string is drawn. If this parameter is set to zero, the function will calculate the width of the offscreen bitmap if the lpData parameter contains a pointer to a string.

nHeight: Specifies the height, in device units, of the offscreen bitmap into which the string is drawn. If this parameter is set to zero, the function will calculate the height of the offscreen bitmap if the lpData parameter contains a pointer to a string.

Return Value

If the function succeeds, it returns TRUE; otherwise it returns FALSE.

Callback Function Syntax

```
GrayStringOutputProc(
    hdc: HDC;                {the handle of the offscreen bitmap device context}
    lpData: LPARAM;          {a pointer to the data to be drawn}
    cchData: Integer         {the length of the string}
    ): BOOL;                 {returns TRUE or FALSE}
```

Description

This callback function is used to draw the specified string or user-defined data in an application specific manner. The hdc parameter specifies a handle to a device context representing the offscreen bitmap created by the GrayString function. The callback function must draw the data in whatever manner desired onto this device context, which will be copied onto the device context specified by the hDC parameter of the GrayString function when the callback function returns. This callback function can perform any desired action.

Parameters

hdc: A handle to the device context of the offscreen bitmap upon which the data or string must be drawn. The device context will have the same width and height as specified by the nWidth and nHeight parameters of the GrayString function.

lpData: A pointer to the data to be drawn, as specified by the lpData parameter of the GrayString function.

cchData: Specifies the length of the string, in characters, as passed to the GrayString function in the nCount parameter.

Return Value

The callback function should return TRUE to indicate it was successful; it should return FALSE otherwise.

See Also

DrawText, GetSysColor, SetTextColor, TabbedTextOut, TextOut

Example

Listing 3-28: Drawing Grayed Text

```
procedure TForm1.FormPaint(Sender: TObject);
var
  Str: PChar;         // points to the string to be drawn
begin
  {initialize the string pointer}
  Str := 'Delphi Rocks!';

  {initialize the brush used to draw the string}
  Canvas.Brush.Color := clRed;

  {draw the string}
  GrayString(Canvas.Handle, Canvas.Brush.Handle, NIL, LPARAM(Str), Length(Str),
          10, 10, 0, 0);
end;
```

Figure 3-32:
The grayed
text

3

Chapter

InvalidateRect   Windows.Pas

Syntax

InvalidateRect(
hWnd: HWND;   {the handle of a window}
lpRect: PRect;   {a pointer to the rectangular coordinates}
bErase: BOOL;   {background erasure flag}
): BOOL;   {returns TRUE or FALSE}

Description

This function adds the specified rectangle to the invalid region of the indicated window, causing it to receive a WM_PAINT message.

Parameters

hWnd: A handle to the window containing the invalid region to which the specified rectangle is added. If this parameter is set to zero, all windows are invalidated and will receive the WM_ERASEBKGND and WM_NCPAINT messages before the function returns.

lpRect: A pointer to a TRect structure containing the rectangular coordinates of the area to be added to the invalid region. If this parameter is set to NIL, the entire client area is added to the invalid region.

bErase: A flag indicating if the background in the invalid region should be erased. If this parameter is set to TRUE and the region is not empty, the background of the entire invalid region is erased when the BeginPaint function is called.

Return Value

If the function succeeds, it returns TRUE; otherwise it returns FALSE.

See Also

BeginPaint, GetUpdateRect, InvalidateRgn

Example

Listing 3-29: Drawing Only the Invalid Rectangle of a Canvas

```
procedure TForm1.Button2Click(Sender: TObject);
var
  InvalidRectangle: TRect; //rectangle to invalidate
begin
  {define the rectangle}
  InvalidRectangle := Rect(10, 10, 110, 110);

  {erase only the rectangular area}
  InvalidateRect(Form1.Handle, @InvalidRectangle, TRUE);
end;

procedure TForm1.WMPaint(var Msg: TWMPaint);
var
  InvalidRect: TRect;            // holds the invalid rectangular area
  PaintStruct: TPaintStruct;     // holds painting information
begin
  {retrieve the invalid rectangle}
  GetUpdateRect(Handle, InvalidRect, TRUE);

  {begin the painting process; this validates the invalid region}
  BeginPaint(Handle, PaintStruct);

  {if the entire client area is invalid...}
  if EqualRect(InvalidRect, ClientRect) then
    {...redraw the bitmap in Image1 to the canvas}
    Canvas.Draw(0, 0, Image1.Picture.Bitmap)
  else
  begin
    {...otherwise, draw a red rectangle in the entire invalid rectangular
     area, and label it as a previously invalid area}
    Canvas.Brush.Color := clRed;
    Canvas.Rectangle(InvalidRect.Left, InvalidRect.Top, InvalidRect.Right,
                     InvalidRect.Bottom);
    Canvas.TextOut(InvalidRect.Left+10, InvalidRect.Top+10, 'Invalid Rect');
  end;

  {end the painting operation}
  EndPaint(Handle, PaintStruct);
end;
```

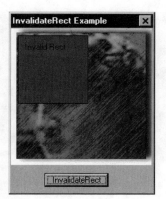

Figure 3-33:
The invalid
rectangle

InvalidateRgn   Windows.Pas

Syntax

```
InvalidateRgn(
hWnd: HWND;               {the handle of a window}
hRgn: HRGN;               {the handle of a region}
bErase: BOOL              {background erasure flag}
): BOOL;                  {always returns TRUE}
```

Description

This function adds the given region to the invalid region of the specified window, causing it to receive a WM_PAINT message.

Parameters

hWnd: A handle to the window containing the invalid region to which the specified region is added.

hRgn: A handle to the region defining the area to be added to the invalid region. The region is assumed to be in client coordinates. If this parameter is set to zero, the entire client area is added to the invalid region.

bErase: A flag indicating if the background in the invalid region should be erased. If this parameter is set to TRUE and the region is not empty, the background of the entire invalid region is erased when the BeginPaint function is called.

Return Value

This function always returns TRUE.

See Also

BeginPaint, GetUpdateRgn, InvalidateRect

3

Chapter

Example

Listing 3-30: Drawing Only the Invalid Region of a Canvas

```
procedure TForm1.Button2Click(Sender: TObject);
var
  PointsArray: array[0..2] of TPoint; // an array of points defining the region
  RegionHandle: HRGN;                 // a handle to the region
begin
  {define the region}
  PointsArray[0].X := 20;
  PointsArray[0].y := 20;
  PointsArray[1].x := 100;
  PointsArray[1].y := 65;
  PointsArray[2].x := 20;
  PointsArray[2].y := 120;

  {create the region}
  RegionHandle := CreatePolygonRgn(PointsArray, 3, ALTERNATE);

  {invalidate the region}
  InvalidateRgn(Form1.Handle, RegionHandle, TRUE);

  {the region is no longer needed, so delete it}
  DeleteObject(RegionHandle);
end;

procedure TForm1.WMPaint(var Msg: TWMPaint);
var
  InvalidRgn: HRGN;           // a handle to the invalid region
  PaintStruct: TPaintStruct; // holds painting information
begin
  {GetUpdateRgn requires a handle to a pre-existing region, so create one}
  InvalidRgn := CreateRectRgn(0, 0, 1, 1);

  {retrieve the handle to the update region}
  GetUpdateRgn(Handle, InvalidRgn, FALSE);

  {begin the painting operation}
  BeginPaint(Handle, PaintStruct);

  {if the region is equal to the entire client area...}
  if EqualRgn(InvalidRgn, CreateRectRgnIndirect(ClientRect)) then
    {...draw the bitmap in Image1 to the form's canvas}
    Canvas.Draw(0, 0, Image1.Picture.Bitmap)
  else
  begin
    {...otherwise draw the invalid region in red}
    Canvas.Brush.Color := clRed;
    FillRgn(Canvas.Handle, InvalidRgn, Canvas.Brush.Handle);
  end;

  {end the painting operation}
  EndPaint(Handle, PaintStruct);
```

```
   {delete the region object, as it is no longer needed}
   DeleteObject(InvalidRgn);
end;
```

Figure 3-34:
The invalid
region

LineDDA   Windows.Pas

Syntax

LineDDA(

p1: Integer;	{the horizontal coordinate of the starting point}
p2: Integer;	{the vertical coordinate of the starting point}
p3: Integer;	{the horizontal coordinate of the ending point}
p4: Integer;	{the vertical coordinate of the ending point}
p5: TFNLineDDAProc;	{a pointer to the callback function}
p6: LPARAM	{application-defined data}
): BOOL;	{returns TRUE or FALSE}

Description

This function draws a line by passing the coordinates for each point on the line, except the endpoint, to the application-defined callback function. The callback function determines how the line will actually be drawn. If the default mapping modes and transformations are in effect, the coordinates passed to the callback function match the pixels on the video display.

Parameters

p1: Specifies the horizontal coordinate of the line's starting point.

p2: Specifies the vertical coordinate of the line's starting point.

p3: Specifies the horizontal coordinate of the line's ending point.

p4: Specifies the vertical coordinate of the line's ending point.

p5: A pointer to the application-defined callback function.

p6: Specifies an application-defined value.

Return Value

If the function succeeds, it returns TRUE; otherwise it returns FALSE.

Callback Function Syntax

```
LineDDAProc(
  X: Integer;              {the horizontal line coordinate}
  Y: Integer;              {the vertical line coordinate}
  lpData: LPARAM           {application-defined data}
  );                       {this procedure does not return a value}
```

Description

This procedure is called for each pixel in the line defined by the LineDDA function. The callback function can perform any desired drawing action based on these coordinates, such as placing a pixel, copying a bitmap, etc.

Parameters

X: The current horizontal coordinate along the line.

Y: The current vertical coordinate along the line.

lpData: Specifies a 32-bit application-defined data as passed to the LineDDA function in the p6 parameter. This value is intended for application specific purposes.

Return Value

This procedure does not return a value.

See Also

ExtCreatePen, LineTo

Example

Listing 3-31: Drawing an Animated Selection Rectangle

```
{the callback function prototype}
  procedure AnimLines(X, Y: Integer; lpData: lParam); stdcall;

var
  Form1: TForm1;
  Offset: Integer;

const
  AL_HORIZONTAL = 1;    // indicates if the line to be drawn is
  AL_VERTICAL = 2;      // horizontal or vertical
```

```
implementation

{$R *.DFM}

procedure AnimLines(X, Y: Integer; lpData: lParam);
var
  Coord: Integer;        // holds the coordinate used in the calculation
begin
  {if the line is horizontal, use the X coordinate, otherwise use Y}
  if lpData=AL_HORIZONTAL then
    Coord := X
  else
    Coord := Y;

  {determine if the pixel at this point should be black or white}
  if (Coord mod 5=Offset) then
    SetPixelV(Form1.Canvas.Handle, X, Y, clBlack)
  else
    SetPixelV(Form1.Canvas.Handle, X, Y, clWhite);
end;

procedure TForm1.Timer1Timer(Sender: TObject);
begin
  {increment the offset}
  Inc(Offset);

  {if the offset has gone too far, reset it}
  if Offset>4 then Offset := 0;

  {draw a rectangle with animated lines}
  LineDDA(20, 20, 120, 20, @AnimLines, AL_HORIZONTAL);
  LineDDA(120, 20, 120, 120, @AnimLines, AL_VERTICAL);
  LineDDA(20, 20, 20, 120, @AnimLines, AL_VERTICAL);
  LineDDA(20, 120, 120, 120, @AnimLines, AL_HORIZONTAL);
end;
```

*Figure 3-35:
The animated
rectangle*

LineTo   *Windows.Pas*

Syntax

```
LineTo(
DC: HDC;              {the handle of a device context}
X: Integer;           {the horizontal coordinate of the line destination}
Y: Integer            {the vertical coordinate of the line destination}
): BOOL;              {returns TRUE or FALSE}
```

Description

This function draws a line using the current pen selected into the specified device context. The line is drawn from the current position to the specified coordinates. The point at the specified coordinates is excluded from the actual drawn pixels of the line. The current position will be updated to the specified coordinates when the function returns.

Parameters

DC: A handle to the device context upon which the line is drawn.

X: Specifies the horizontal coordinate of the endpoint of the line, in logical units.

Y: Specifies the vertical coordinate of the endpoint of the line, in logical units.

Return Value

If the function succeeds, it returns TRUE; otherwise it returns FALSE.

See Also

LineDDA, MoveToEx, PolyBezier, PolyBezierTo, Polyline, PolylineTo, PolyPolyline

Example

Please see Listing 3-23 under GetCurrentPositionEx.

LockWindowUpdate   *Windows.Pas*

Syntax

```
LockWindowUpdate(
hWndLock: HWND        {the handle of a window}
): BOOL;              {returns TRUE or FALSE}
```

Description

This function disables or reenables all painting and drawing operations within the specified window. A locked window cannot be moved, and only one window may be locked at a time. Windows records the areas in which any painting or drawing operations are attempted in the locked window. When the window is unlocked, the area affected by these drawing operations is invalidated, causing a WM_PAINT message to be sent to the window. If the GetDC or BeginPaint functions are used on a locked window, the returned device context will contain an empty visible region.

Parameters

hWndLock: A handle to the window for which drawing operations are to be disabled. If this parameter is set to zero, the currently locked window is reenabled.

Return Value

If the function succeeds, it returns TRUE; otherwise it returns FALSE.

See Also

BeginPaint, GetDC

Example

Listing 3-32: Enabling and Disabling Window Updating

```
procedure TForm1.Button1Click(Sender: TObject);
begin
 {disable window painting}
 LockWindowUpdate(Form1.Handle);
end;

procedure TForm1.Button2Click(Sender: TObject);
begin
  {enable window painting}
  LockWindowUpdate(0);
end;
```

MoveToEx   Windows.Pas

Syntax

```
MoveToEx(
DC: HDC;           {the handle of a device context}
p2: Integer;       {the horizontal coordinate}
p3: Integer;       {the vertical coordinate}
p4: PPoint         {a pointer to a TPoint structure}
): BOOL;           {TRUE if successful}
```

Description

This function moves the current position of the indicated device context to the specified coordinates, returning the old position. This affects all drawing functions that use the current position as a starting point.

Parameters

DC: A handle to the device context whose current position is to be set.

p2: Specifies the horizontal coordinate of the new current position, in logical units.

p3: Specifies the vertical coordinate of the new current position, in logical units.

3

Chapter

p4: A pointer to a TPoint structure that receives the coordinates of the old current position. This parameter may be set to NIL if the old current position coordinates are not needed.

Return Value

If the function succeeds, it returns TRUE; otherwise it returns FALSE.

See Also

LineTo, PolyBezierTo, PolylineTo

Example

Please see Listing 3-23 under GetCurrentPositionEx.

PaintDesktop   Windows.Pas

Syntax

```
PaintDesktop(
hdc: HDC                {the handle of a device context}
): BOOL;                {returns TRUE or FALSE}
```

Description

This function paints the clipping region in the given device context with the desktop wallpaper bitmap or pattern.

Parameters

hdc: A handle to the device context upon which the desktop wallpaper or pattern is drawn.

Return Value

If the function succeeds, it returns TRUE; otherwise it returns FALSE.

See also

BitBlt, GetDC, SystemParametersInfo

Example

Listing 3-33: Drawing the Desktop onto a Form

```
procedure TForm1.FormPaint(Sender: TObject);
begin
  {display the desktop wallpaper}
  PaintDesktop(Canvas.Handle);
end;

procedure TForm1.WMMoving(var Msg: TMessage);
begin
  {display the desktop wallpaper when moving}
```

```
        PaintDesktop(Canvas.Handle);
      end;
```

PaintRgn   *Windows.Pas*

Syntax

```
PaintRgn(
DC: HDC;              {the handle of a device context}
RGN: HRGN            {the handle of a region}
): BOOL;             {returns TRUE or FALSE}
```

Description

This function paints the specified region onto the device context using its currently selected brush.

Parameters

DC: A handle to the device context upon which the region is drawn.

RGN: A handle to the region to be drawn.

Return Value

If the function succeeds, it returns TRUE; otherwise it returns FALSE.

See Also

ExtFloodFill, FillPath, FillRect, FillRgn, FrameRect, FrameRgn

Example

Listing 3-34: Filling a Region with the Current Brush

```
procedure TForm1.FormPaint(Sender: TObject);
var
  PointsArray: Array[0..5] of TPoint;      // points defining a region
  RegionHandle: HRgn;                      // the handle of the region
begin
  {define the region}
  PointsArray[0].X := 50;
  PointsArray[0].y := 50;
  PointsArray[1].x := 100;
  PointsArray[1].y := 50;
  PointsArray[2].x := 125;
  PointsArray[2].y := 75;
  PointsArray[3].x := 100;
  PointsArray[3].y := 100;
  PointsArray[4].x := 50;
  PointsArray[4].y := 100;
  PointsArray[5].x := 25;
  PointsArray[5].y := 75;
```

3

Chapter

```
{create the region}
RegionHandle := CreatePolygonRgn(PointsArray, 6, ALTERNATE);

{paint the region using the canvas's brush}
Canvas.Brush.Color := clGreen;
Canvas.Brush.Style := bsBDiagonal;
PaintRgn(Canvas.Handle, RegionHandle);
end;
```

Figure 3-36:
The painted
region

Pie   Windows.Pas

Syntax

Pie(	
DC: HDC;	{the handle of a device context}
X1: Integer;	{x coordinate of the upper left corner}
Y1: Integer;	{y coordinate of the upper left corner}
X2: Integer;	{x coordinate of the lower right corner}
Y2: Integer;	{y coordinate of the lower right corner}
X3: Integer;	{x coordinate of the first radial ending point}
Y3: Integer;	{y coordinate of the first radial ending point}
X4: Integer;	{x coordinate of the second radial ending point}
Y4: Integer	{y coordinate of the second radial ending point}
): BOOL;	{returns TRUE or FALSE}

Description

This function draws a pie-shaped wedge with the current pen and fills the wedge with the current brush. A pie is a region bounded by an ellipse and two radial line segments. The extent of the pie-shaped wedge is defined by the bounding rectangle. The X3 and Y3 parameters define the endpoints of a radial line starting from the center of the bounding rectangle and identify the starting location of the wedge area. The X4 and Y4 parameters define the endpoints of a radial line starting from the center of the bounding rectangle and identify the ending location of the wedge area. The wedge is drawn in a counterclockwise direction, and will not affect the current position.

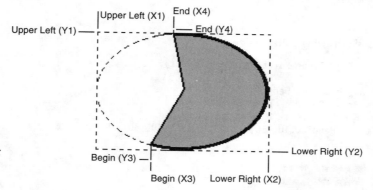

Figure 3-37: Pie coordinates

Parameters

DC: Specifies the device context upon which the pie is drawn.

X1: Specifies the horizontal coordinate of the upper left corner of the bounding rectangle, in logical units. Under Windows 95, the sum of the X1 and X2 parameters must be less than 32,767.

Y1: Specifies the vertical coordinate of the upper left corner of the bounding rectangle, in logical units. Under Windows 95, the sum of the Y1 and Y2 parameters must be less than 32,767.

X2: Specifies the horizontal coordinate of the lower right corner of the bounding rectangle, in logical units.

Y2: Specifies the vertical coordinate of the lower right corner of the bounding rectangle, in logical units.

X3: Specifies the horizontal coordinate, in logical units, of the ending point of the radial line that defines the starting point of the pie.

Y3: Specifies the vertical coordinate, in logical units, of the ending point of the radial line that defines the starting point of the pie.

X4: Specifies the horizontal coordinate, in logical units, of the ending point of the radial line that defines the ending point of the pie.

Y4: Specifies the vertical coordinate, in logical units, of the ending point of the radial line that defines the ending point of the pie.

Return Value

If this function succeeds, it returns TRUE; otherwise it returns FALSE. To get extended error information, call the GetLastError function.

See Also

Arc, Chord, Ellipse

Example

Listing 3-35: Drawing a Pie Wedge

```
procedure TForm1.FormPaint(Sender: TObject);
begin
  {draw a pie shaped wedge}
  Canvas.Brush.Color := clRed;
  Canvas.Brush.Style := bsDiagCross;
  Pie(Canvas.Handle, 10, 10, 110, 110, 10, 60, 60, 10);
end;
```

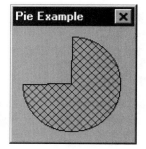

Figure 3-38:
The pie wedge

PolyBezier　　　***Windows.Pas***

Syntax

PolyBezier(	
DC: HDC;	{the handle of a device context}
const Points;	{a pointer to an array of coordinates}
Count: DWORD	{the number of entries in the array}
): BOOL;	{returns TRUE or FALSE}

Description

This function draws one or more cubic bézier curves on the specified device context using its current pen. The Points parameter points to an array of TPoint structures containing the start point, control points, and endpoint of the bézier curves. The first point in the array defines the starting point of the curve. The next two points are used as the control points, and the fourth point defines the ending point. Every three points after that define the two control points and the endpoint of another bézier curve, using the endpoint of the previous curve as its starting point. This function does not affect the current position.

Parameters

DC: A handle to the device context upon which the bézier curve is drawn.

Points: A pointer to an array of TPoint structures containing the control points and endpoints of the bézier curves.

Count: Specifies the number of entries in the array pointed to by the Points parameter.

Return Value

If the function succeeds, it returns TRUE; otherwise it returns FALSE.

See Also

MoveToEx, PolyBezierTo

Example

Listing 3-36: Drawing a Bézier Curve

```
procedure TForm1.FormPaint(Sender: TObject);
var
  Points: array[0..6] of TPoint; // points defining the bezier curve
begin
  {define the bezier curve}
  Points[0].X := 10;
  Points[0].Y := 50;
  Points[1].X := 40;
  Points[1].Y := 90;
  Points[2].X := 80;
  Points[2].Y := 10;
  Points[3].X := 110;
  Points[3].Y := 50;
  Points[4].X := 140;
  Points[4].Y := 10;
  Points[5].X := 180;
  Points[5].Y := 90;
  Points[6].X := 210;
  Points[6].Y := 50;

  {draw the bezier curve}
  PolyBezier(Canvas.Handle, Points, 7);
end;
```

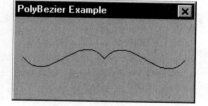

Figure 3-39:
The bézier
curve

PolyBezierTo   *Windows.Pas*

Syntax

PolyBezierTo(
DC: HDC;   {the handle of a device context}

const Points;   {a pointer to an array of coordinates}
Count: DWORD   {the number of entries in the array}
): BOOL;   {returns TRUE or FALSE}

Description

This function draws one or more cubic bézier curves on the specified device context using its current pen. The Points parameter points to an array of TPoint structures containing the start point, control points, and endpoint of the bézier curves. The first point in the array defines the starting point of the curve. The next two points are used as the control points, and the fourth point defines the ending point. Every three points after that define the two control points and the endpoint of another bézier curve, using the endpoint of the previous curve as its starting point. The current position will be updated to the last point in the Points array.

Parameters

DC: A handle to the device context upon which the bézier curve is drawn.

Points: A pointer to an array of TPoint structures containing the control points and endpoints of the bézier curves.

Count: Specifies the number of entries in the array pointed to by the Points parameter.

Return Value

If the function succeeds, it returns TRUE; otherwise it returns FALSE.

See Also

MoveToEx, PolyBezier

Example

Listing 3-37: Drawing a Bézier Curve and Updating the Current Position

```
procedure TForm1.FormPaint(Sender: TObject);
var
  Points: array[0..2] of TPoint;  // the points defining the bezier curve
begin
  {define the bezier curve}
  Points[0].X := 40;
  Points[0].Y := 110;
  Points[1].X := 80;
  Points[1].Y := 30;
  Points[2].X := 110;
  Points[2].Y := 70;

  {move the current position to the correct starting point}
  MoveToEx(Canvas.Handle, 10, 70, NIL);

  {draw the bezier curve}
  PolyBezierTo(Canvas.Handle, Points, 3);
```

```
{the current position was updated, so we can use this to continue
  drawing an image}
LineTo(Canvas.Handle, 110, 10);
LineTo(Canvas.Handle, 10, 10);
LineTo(Canvas.Handle, 10, 70);
end;
```

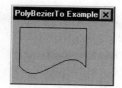

Figure 3-40:
The bézier
curve

Polygon   Windows.Pas

Syntax

Polygon(
DC: HDC;   {the handle of a device context}
const Points;   {a pointer to an array of coordinates}
Count: DWORD   {the number of entries in the array}
): BOOL;   {returns TRUE or FALSE}

Description

This function draws a polygon on the specified device context using its current pen, and fills the polygon using the device context's current brush and polygon fill mode. The Points parameter points to an array of TPoint structures defining the vertices of the polygon. The polygon will automatically be closed by drawing a line from the last vertex in the array to the first vertex in the array. This function does not affect the current position.

Parameters

DC: A handle to the device context upon which the polygon is drawn.

Points: A pointer to an array of TPoint structures containing the vertices of the polygon. This array must contain at least two vertices or the function will fail.

Count: Specifies the number of entries in the array pointed to by the Points parameter.

Return Value

If the function succeeds, it returns TRUE; otherwise it returns FALSE. To get extended error information, call the GetLastError function.

See Also

GetPolyFillMode, Polyline, PolylineTo, PolyPolygon, PolyPolyline, SetPolyFillMode

3

Chapter

Example

Please see Listing 3-25 under GetPolyFillMode.

Polyline   *Windows.Pas*

Syntax

Polyline(
DC: HDC;   {the handle of a device context}
const Points;   {a pointer to an array of coordinates}
Count: DWORD   {the number of entries in the array}
): BOOL;   {returns TRUE or FALSE}

Description

This function draws a polygon on the specified device context using its current pen. The Points parameter points to an array of TPoint structures defining the vertices of the polygon. The polygon is drawn by connecting the points in the array with line segments. This function does not affect the current position.

Parameters

DC: A handle to the device context upon which the polygon is drawn.

Points: A pointer to an array of TPoint structures containing the vertices of the polygon.

Count: Specifies the number of entries in the array pointed to by the Points parameter.

Return Value

If the function succeeds, it returns TRUE; otherwise it returns FALSE.

See Also

LineTo, MoveToEx, PolylineTo, PolyPolyline

Example

Listing 3-38: Drawing a Polygon Outline

```
procedure TForm1.FormPaint(Sender: TObject);
var
  PointsArray: array[0..6] of TPoint;        // points defining the polygon
begin
  {define the vertices of the polygon}
  PointsArray[0].X := 50;
  PointsArray[0].y := 50;
  PointsArray[1].x := 100;
  PointsArray[1].y := 50;
  PointsArray[2].x := 125;
  PointsArray[2].y := 75;
  PointsArray[3].x := 100;
  PointsArray[3].y := 100;
```

```
     PointsArray[4].x := 50;
     PointsArray[4].y := 100;
     PointsArray[5].x := 25;
     PointsArray[5].y := 75;
     PointsArray[6].X := 50;
     PointsArray[6].Y := 50;

     {draw the polygon}
     Polyline(Canvas.Handle, PointsArray, 7);
   end;
```

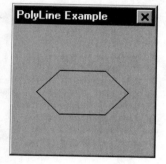

Figure 3-41:
The unfilled
polygon

PolylineTo   Windows.Pas

Syntax

```
PolylineTo(
DC: HDC;                {the handle of a device context}
const Points;           {a pointer to an array of coordinates}
Count: DWORD            {the number of entries in the array}
): BOOL;                {returns TRUE or FALSE}
```

Description

This function draws a polygon on the specified device context using its current pen. The Points parameter points to an array of TPoint structures defining the vertices of the polygon. The polygon is drawn by connecting the points in the array with line segments, starting from the current position. The current position is updated to the last coordinate in the array of vertices when the function returns.

Parameters

DC: A handle to the device context upon which the polygon is drawn.

Points: A pointer to an array of TPoint structures containing the vertices of the polygon.

Count: Specifies the number of entries in the array pointed to by the Points parameter.

Return Value

If the function succeeds, it returns TRUE; otherwise it returns FALSE.

See Also

LineTo, MoveToEx, Polyline, PolyPolyline

Example

Listing 3-39: Drawing an Unfilled Polygon Starting from the Current Position

```
procedure TForm1.FormPaint(Sender: TObject);
var
  PointsArray: array[0..5] of TPoint; // the points defining the polygon
begin
  {move the current position to where the polygon will start}
  MoveToEx(Canvas.Handle, 50, 50, nil);

  {define the polygon}
  PointsArray[0].x := 100;
  PointsArray[0].y := 50;
  PointsArray[1].x := 125;
  PointsArray[1].y := 75;
  PointsArray[2].x := 100;
  PointsArray[2].y := 100;
  PointsArray[3].x := 50;
  PointsArray[3].y := 100;
  PointsArray[4].x := 25;
  PointsArray[4].y := 75;
  PointsArray[5].X := 50;
  PointsArray[5].Y := 50;

  {draw the polygon, starting at the current position}
  PolylineTo(Canvas.Handle, PointsArray, 6);
end;
```

PolyPolygon   *Windows.Pas*

Syntax

```
PolyPolygon(
DC: HDC;              {the handle of a device context}
var Points;           {a pointer to an array of coordinates}
var nPoints;          {a pointer to an array of vertex counts}
p4: Integer           {the number of polygons}
): BOOL;              {returns TRUE or FALSE}
```

Description

This function draws a series of closed polygons on the specified device context using its current pen, and fills the polygons using the device context's current brush and polygon fill mode. The Points parameter points to an array of TPoint structures defining the vertices of each polygon. The nPoints parameter points to an array of integers, where each integer specifies the number of entries in the Points array that define one polygon. The polygon will automatically be closed by drawing a line from the last vertex defining the polygon to the first vertex defining the polygon. This function does not affect the current position.

Parameters

DC: A handle to the device context upon which the polygons are drawn.

Points: A pointer to an array of TPoint structures containing the vertices of each polygon. The vertices are arranged in consecutive order, and should only be specified once. The polygons defined by this array can overlap.

nPoints: A pointer to an array of integers, where each integer specifies the number of entries in the array pointed to by the Points parameter that define an individual polygon.

p4: Indicates the total number of polygons that will be drawn.

Return Value

If the function succeeds, it returns TRUE; otherwise it returns FALSE. To get extended error information, call the GetLastError function.

See Also

GetPolyFillMode, Polygon, Polyline, PolylineTo, PolyPolyline, SetPolyFillMode

Example

Listing 3-40: Drawing Multiple Polygons

```
procedure TForm1.FormPaint(Sender: TObject);
var
  PointsArray: array[0..9] of TPoint;   // holds the vertices of the polygons
  NPoints: array[0..1] of Integer;      // the number of vertices in each polygon
begin
  {define the polygons -}
  {first polygon}
  PointsArray[0].X := 50;
  PointsArray[0].y := 50;
  PointsArray[1].x := 100;
  PointsArray[1].y := 50;
  PointsArray[2].x := 125;
  PointsArray[2].y := 75;
  PointsArray[3].x := 100;
  PointsArray[3].y := 100;
  PointsArray[4].x := 50;
  PointsArray[4].y := 100;
  PointsArray[5].x := 25;
  PointsArray[5].y := 75;
  {second polygon}
  PointsArray[6].X := 200;
  PointsArray[6].y := 25;
  PointsArray[7].X := 300;
  PointsArray[7].Y := 25;
  PointsArray[8].X := 300;
```

```
PointsArray[8].Y := 125;
PointsArray[9].X := 200;
PointsArray[9].Y := 125;

{indicate how many vertices are in each polygon}
NPoints[0] := 6;
NPoints[1] := 4;

{draw the polygons}
PolyPolygon(Canvas.Handle, PointsArray, NPoints, 2);
end;
```

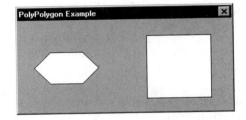

Figure 3-42: Multiple polygons

PolyPolyline   Windows.Pas

Syntax

PolyPolyline(
DC: HDC;	{the handle of a device context}
const PointStructs;	{a pointer to an array of coordinates}
const Points;	{a pointer to an array of vertex counts}
p4: DWORD	{the number of polygons}
): BOOL;	{returns TRUE or FALSE}

Description

This function draws a series of polygons on the specified device context using its current pen. The PointStructs parameter points to an array of TPoint structures defining the vertices of each polygon. The Points parameter points to an array of integers, where each integer specifies the number of entries in the PointStructs array that define one polygon. The polygon is drawn by connecting the points in the array with line segments. This function does not affect the current position.

Parameters

DC: A handle to the device context upon which the polygons are drawn.

PointStructs: A pointer to an array of TPoint structures containing the vertices of each polygon. The vertices are arranged in consecutive order, and should only be specified once.

Points: A pointer to an array of integers, where each integer specifies the number of entries in the array pointed to by the PointStructs parameter that define an individual polygon.

p4: Indicates the total number of polygons that will be drawn.

Return Value

If the function succeeds, it returns TRUE; otherwise it returns FALSE.

See Also

Polygon, Polyline, PolylineTo, PolyPolygon

Example

Listing 3-4l: Drawing Multiple Unfilled Polygons

```
procedure TForm1.FormPaint(Sender: TObject);
var
  PointsArray: array[0..11] of TPoint; // the vertices defining the polygons
  NPoints: array[0..1] of Integer;      // the number of vertices in each polygon
begin
  {define the polygons -}
  {first polygon}
  PointsArray[0].X := 50;
  PointsArray[0].y := 50;
  PointsArray[1].x := 100;
  PointsArray[1].y := 50;
  PointsArray[2].x := 125;
  PointsArray[2].y := 75;
  PointsArray[3].x := 100;
  PointsArray[3].y := 100;
  PointsArray[4].x := 50;
  PointsArray[4].y := 100;
  PointsArray[5].x := 25;
  PointsArray[5].y := 75;
  PointsArray[6].X := 50;
  PointsArray[6].Y := 50;
  {second polygon}
  PointsArray[7].X := 200;
  PointsArray[7].y := 25;
  PointsArray[8].X := 300;
  PointsArray[8].Y := 25;
  PointsArray[9].X := 300;
  PointsArray[9].Y := 125;
  PointsArray[10].X := 200;
  PointsArray[10].Y := 125;
  PointsArray[11].X := 200;
  PointsArray[11].Y := 25;

  {indicate how many vertices are in each polygon}
  NPoints[0] := 7;
  NPoints[1] := 5;
```

3

Chapter

```
{draw the unfilled polygons}
PolyPolyline(Canvas.Handle, PointsArray, NPoints, 2);
end;
```

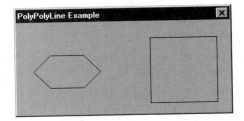

Figure 3-43: Multiple unfilled polygons

Rectangle   Windows.Pas

Syntax

```
Rectangle(
DC: HDC;            {the handle of a device context}
X1: Integer;        {the horizontal coordinate of the upper left corner}
Y1: Integer;        {the vertical coordinate of the upper left corner}
X2: Integer;        {the horizontal coordinate of the lower right corner}
Y2: Integer         {the vertical coordinate of the lower right corner}
): BOOL;            {returns TRUE or FALSE}
```

Description

This function draws a rectangle on the specified device context at the indicated coordinates using the current pen and fills it with the current brush. This function does not affect the current position.

Parameters

DC: A handle to the device context upon which the rectangle is drawn.

X1: Specifies the horizontal coordinate of the upper left corner of the rectangle, in logical units.

Y1: Specifies the vertical coordinate of the upper left corner of the rectangle, in logical units.

X2: Specifies the horizontal coordinate of the lower right corner of the rectangle, in logical units.

Y2: Specifies the vertical coordinate of the lower right corner of the rectangle, in logical units.

Return Value

If the function succeeds, it returns TRUE; otherwise it returns FALSE. To get extended error information, call the GetLastError function.

See Also

CreateRectRgn, CreateRectRgnIndirect, FillRect, FrameRect, Polygon, Polyline, RoundRect

Example

Listing 3-42: Drawing a Rectangle with an Animated Fill

```
var
  Form1: TForm1;
  BrushOffset: Integer;        // holds the current brush offset

implementation

{$R *.DFM}

procedure TForm1.Timer1Timer(Sender: TObject);
var
  BrushPt: TPoint;                       // holds the current brush origin
  BrushHndl, OldBrush: HBRUSH;           // handles to brushes
  FormDC: HDC;                           // the form's device context
begin
  {retrieve the form's device context}
  FormDC := GetDC(Form1.Handle);

  {increment the brush offset}
  Inc(BrushOffset);

  {create a hatched brush}
  BrushHndl := CreateHatchBrush(HS_DIAGCROSS, clRed);

  {set the brushes origin}
  SetBrushOrgEx(FormDC, BrushOffset, BrushOffset, nil);

  {select the brush into the device context}
  OldBrush := SelectObject(FormDC, BrushHndl);

  {retrieve the current brush origin}
  GetBrushOrgEx(FormDC, BrushPt);

  {if the brush origin is beyond the limit, reset it}
  if BrushPt.X>7 then
  begin
    BrushOffset := 0;
    SetBrushOrgEx(FormDC, BrushOffset, BrushOffset, nil);
  end;

  {draw the rectangle}
  Rectangle(FormDC, 10, 10, 110, 110);

  {delete the new brush}
  SelectObject(FormDC, OldBrush);
  DeleteObject(BrushHndl);
```

Chapter **3**

```
{release the form's device context}
ReleaseDC(Form1.Handle, FormDC);
end;
```

Figure 3-44:
The animated
rectangle

RoundRect   **Windows.Pas**

Syntax

RoundRect(
DC: HDC;   {the handle of a device context}
X1: Integer;   {the horizontal coordinate of the upper left corner}
Y1: Integer;   {the vertical coordinate of the upper left corner}
X2: Integer;   {the horizontal coordinate of the lower right corner}
Y2: Integer;   {the vertical coordinate of the lower right corner}
X3: Integer;   {the width of the corner ellipse}
Y3: Integer   {the height of the corner ellipse}
): BOOL;   {returns TRUE or FALSE}

Description

This function draws a rectangle on the specified device context at the indicated coordinates using the current pen and fills it with the current brush. The corners of the rectangle will be rounded according to the ellipse formed by the X3 and Y3 parameters. This function does not affect the current position.

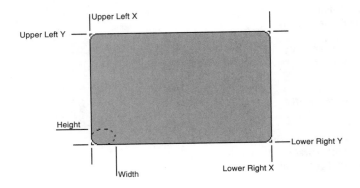

Figure 3-45:
RoundRect
coordinates

Parameters

DC: A handle to the device context upon which the rounded rectangle is drawn.

X1: Specifies the horizontal coordinate of the upper left corner of the rounded rectangle, in logical units.

Y1: Specifies the vertical coordinate of the upper left corner of the rounded rectangle, in logical units.

X2: Specifies the horizontal coordinate of the lower right corner of the rounded rectangle, in logical units.

Y2: Specifies the vertical coordinate of the lower right corner of the rounded rectangle, in logical units.

X3: Indicates the width of the ellipse used to draw the corners.

Y3: Indicates the height of the ellipse used to draw the corners.

Return Value

If the function succeeds, it returns TRUE; otherwise it returns FALSE. To get extended error information, call the GetLastError function.

See Also

CreateRoundRectRgn, FillRect, FrameRect, Polygon, Polyline, Rectangle

Example

Listing 3-43: Drawing a Rounded Rectangle

```
procedure TForm1.FormPaint(Sender: TObject);
begin
  {create a rounded rectangle}
  RoundRect(Canvas.Handle, 10, 10, 110, 110, 20, 20);
end;
```

Figure 3-46:
The rounded
rectangle

SelectObject   Windows.Pas

Syntax

SelectObject(

DC: HDC;	{the handle to a device context}
p2: HGDIOBJ	{the handle to a graphical object}
): HGDIOBJ;	{returns a handle to the previously selected object}

Description

This function selects the specified graphical object into the indicated device context for use. Most graphical objects must be selected into a device context before they can be used in drawing functions. The newly selected object replaces the previously selected object of the same type. The application should reselect the previously selected object back into the device context when the new object is no longer needed. A graphical object must not be destroyed while it is selected into a device context.

Parameters

DC: A handle to the device context into which the object is selected.

p2: Specifies a handle to the graphical object to be selected into the device context, such as a brush, pen, bitmap, region, or font. Note that bitmaps can only be selected into one device context at a time.

Return Value

If the selected object is not a region and the function succeeds, it returns a handle to the previously selected object of the same type. If the function succeeds and the selected object is a region, it returns one value from Table 3-33. If the function fails and the selected object is not a region, it returns zero; otherwise it returns GDI_ERROR.

See Also

CombineRgn, CreateBitmap, CreateBitmapIndirect, CreateBrushIndirect, CreateCompatibleBitmap, CreateDIBitmap, CreateEllipticRgn, CreateEllipticRgnIndirect, CreateFont, CreateFontIndirect, CreateHatchBrush, CreatePatternBrush, CreatePen, CreatePenIndirect, CreatePolygonRgn, CreateRectRgn, CreateRectRgnIndirect, CreateSolidBrush, DeleteObject, SelectClipRgn, SelectPalette

Example

Please see Listing 3-8 under CreateSolidBrush and other examples throughout this book.

Table 3-33: SelectObject Return Values

Value	Description
SIMPLEREGION	The region is a single rectangle.
COMPLEXREGION	The region consists of multiple rectangles.
NULLREGION	The region is empty.

SetBkColor   *Windows.Pas*

Syntax

SetBkColor(
DC: HDC;   {the handle of a device context}
Color: COLORREF   {the new background color}
): COLORREF;   {returns the previous background color}

Description

This function sets the background color for the specified device context. If the device cannot represent the specified color, the nearest physical color is used.

Parameters

DC: A handle to the device context whose background color is being set.

Color: A color specifier identifying the new color.

Return Value

If the function succeeds, it returns the previous background color; otherwise it returns CLR_INVALID.

See Also

CreatePen, ExtCreatePen, GetBkColor, GetBkMode, SetBkMode

Example

Please see Listing 3-21 under GetBkColor.

SetBkMode   *Windows.Pas*

Syntax

SetBkMode(
DC: HDC;   {the handle of a device context}
BkMode: Integer   {a background mode flag}
): Integer;   {returns the previous background mode}

Description

This function sets the background mix mode of the given device context.

Parameters

DC: A handle to the device context whose background mix mode is to be set.

BkMode: A flag indicating the new background mix mode. This parameter can be set to one value from Table 3-34.

3

Chapter

Return Value

If the function succeeds, it returns the previous background mix mode; otherwise it returns zero.

See Also

CreatePen, ExtCreatePen, GetBkColor, GetBkMode, SetBkColor

Example

Please see Listing 3-21 under GetBkColor.

Table 3-34: SetBkMode BkMode Values

Value	Description
OPAQUE	The background color is used to fill the gaps in text, hatched brushes, and pen patterns.
TRANSPARENT	The color of the device context shows through the gaps in text, hatched brushes, and pen patterns.

SetBoundsRect	***Windows.Pas***

Syntax

```
SetBoundsRect(
DC: HDC;                {handle of the device context}
p2: TRect;              {a pointer to a TRect structure}
p3: UINT                {operation flags}
): UINT;                {returns the previous bounding rectangle state}
```

Description

This function modifies the bounding rectangle accumulation behavior of the given device context. Windows maintains an accumulated bounding rectangle for each device context that identifies the extent of output from drawing functions. When a drawing function reaches beyond this boundary, the rectangle is extended. Thus, the bounding rectangle is the smallest rectangle that can be drawn around the area affected by all drawing operations in the device context.

Parameters

DC: A handle to the device context whose bounding rectangle accumulation behavior is to be modified.

p2: A pointer to a TRect structure containing the rectangular coordinates, in logical units, of the new bounding rectangle. This parameter can be set to NIL if the bounding rectangle does not need to be set.

p3: A series of flags indicating how the specified rectangle is to be combined with the current bounding rectangle, and whether bounding rectangle accumulation is enabled. This parameter may be set to a combination of values from Table 3-35.

Return Value

This function returns a code indicating the state of the bounding rectangle or an error condition, and will be one or more values from Table 3-36.

See Also

GetBoundsRect, GetUpdateRect

Example

Please see Listing 3-22 under GetBoundsRect.

Table 3-35: SetBoundsRect p3 Values

Value	Description
DCB_ACCUMULATE	Adds the rectangle specified by the p2 parameter to the current bounding rectangle by performing a union. If both the DCB_RESET and DCB_ACCUMULATE flags are specified, the bounding rectangle is set to the exact rectangle specified by the p2 parameter.
DCB_DISABLE	Turns bounding rectangle accumulation off. This is the default state.
DCB_ENABLE	Turns bounding rectangle accumulation on.
DCB_RESET	Clears the bounding rectangle.

Table 3-36: SetBoundsRect Return Values

Value	Description
0	Indicates that an error occurred.
DCB_DISABLE	Boundary accumulation is off.
DCB_ENABLE	Boundary accumulation is on.
DCB_RESET	The bounding rectangle is empty.
DCB_SET	The bounding rectangle is not empty.

SetBrushOrgEx   Windows.Pas

Syntax

```
SetBrushOrgEx(
DC: HDC;          {the handle of a device context}
X: Integer;       {the horizontal coordinate of the origin}
Y: Integer;       {the vertical coordinate of the origin}
```

PrevPt: PPoint	{a pointer to a TPoint structure}
): BOOL;	{returns TRUE or FALSE}

Description

This function sets the origin of the next brush selected into the specified device context. The brush origin is relative to the hatch or bitmap defining the brush's pattern. The default brush origin is at 0,0. A brush pattern can be no more than eight pixels square. Thus, the origin can range from 0-7 vertically and horizontally. As the origin is moved, the brush pattern is offset by the specified amount. If an application is using a pattern brush to draw the backgrounds of child windows and parent windows, the brush origin may need to be moved to align the patterns. Note that under Windows NT, the system automatically tracks the brush origin so that patterns will be aligned.

Parameters

DC: A handle to the device context whose brush origin is to be set.

X: Specifies the horizontal coordinate of the brush origin, in device units.

Y: Specifies the vertical coordinate of the brush origin, in device units.

PrevPt: A pointer to a TPoint structure that receives the coordinates of the previous brush origin. This parameter can be set to NIL if the previous coordinates are not needed.

Return Value

If the function succeeds, it returns TRUE; otherwise it returns FALSE. To get extended error information, call the GetLastError function.

See Also

CreateBrushIndirect, CreateHatchBrush, CreatePatternBrush, FillRect, FillRgn, GetBrushOrgEx, SelectObject

Example

Please see Listing 3-42 under Rectangle.

SetMiterLimit	**Windows.Pas**

Syntax

SetMiterLimit(	
DC: HDC;	{the handle of a device context}
NewLimit: Single;	{the new miter limit}
OldLimit: PSingle	{receives the old miter limit}
): BOOL;	{returns TRUE or FALSE}

Description

This function sets the miter limit for the specified device context. The miter limit is used for geometric lines that have miter joins, and is the maximum ratio of the miter length to the line width. The miter length is the distance from the intersection of the inner wall to the intersection of the outer wall. The default miter limit is 10.0.

Parameters

DC: A handle to the device context whose miter limit is to be set.

NewLimit: Specifies the new miter limit for the given device context.

OldLimit: A pointer to a variable that receives the old miter limit. This parameter can be set to NIL if the old miter limit is not needed.

Return Value

If the function succeeds, it returns TRUE; otherwise it returns FALSE. To get extended error information, call the GetLastError function.

See Also

ExtCreatePen, GetMiterLimit

Example

Please see Listing 3-16 under ExtCreatePen.

SetPixel   Windows.Pas

Syntax

```
SetPixel(
DC: HDC;                {the handle of a device context}
X: Integer;             {the horizontal pixel coordinate}
Y: Integer;             {the vertical pixel coordinate}
Color: COLORREF         {the new pixel color}
): COLORREF;            {returns a color specifier}
```

Description

This function sets the color of the pixel at the specified coordinates in the indicated device context. The coordinates must be within the boundaries of the current clipping region.

Parameters

DC: A handle to the device context in which the new pixel color is set.

X: The horizontal coordinate of the pixel within the device context, in logical units.

Y: The vertical coordinate of the pixel within the device context, in logical units.

Color: Specifies the color of the pixel.

Return

If the function succeeds, it returns the color to which the pixel was set. This may be different from the specified color if an exact color match could not be found. If the function fails, it returns CLR_INVALID.

See also

GetPixel, SetPixelV

Example

Listing 3-44: Implementing a Cheap Bitmap Fade-in Effect

```
procedure TForm1.Button1Click(Sender: TObject);
begin
  {erase the current image}
  Canvas.Brush.Color := Color;
  Canvas.FillRect(ClientRect);

  {begin the effect}
  Timer1.Enabled := TRUE;
end;

procedure TForm1.Timer1Timer(Sender: TObject);
var
  X, Y: Integer;        // tracks pixel coordinates
  iCount: Integer;      // a general loop counter
begin
  {begin the cheap fade effect}
  for iCount := 0 to 20000 do
  begin
    {retrieve a random coordinate}
    X := Random(Image1.Width-1);
    Y := Random(Image1.Height-1);

    {in a 4x4 pixel square at this coordinate, retrieve the pixels in the
     source image, and set them in the form's canvas}
    SetPixel(Canvas.Handle, X+Image1.Left, Y+Image1.Top,
             GetPixel(Image1.Picture.Bitmap.Canvas.Handle, X, Y));
    SetPixel(Canvas.Handle, X+1+Image1.Left, Y+Image1.Top,
             GetPixel(Image1.Picture.Bitmap.Canvas.Handle, X+1, Y));
    SetPixel(Canvas.Handle, X+Image1.Left, Y+1+Image1.Top,
             GetPixel(Image1.Picture.Bitmap.Canvas.Handle, X, Y+1));
    SetPixel(Canvas.Handle, X+1+Image1.Left, Y+1+Image1.Top,
             GetPixel(Image1.Picture.Bitmap.Canvas.Handle, X+1, Y+1));
  end;

  {draw the finished image so that there are no holes left}
  Canvas.Draw(Image1.Left, Image1.Top, Image1.Picture.Bitmap);

  {disable the timer}
  Timer1.Enabled := FALSE;
end;
```

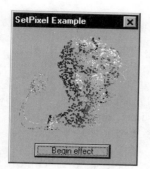

Figure 3-47:
The bitmap
fade-in effect
in progress

SetPixelV   **Windows.Pas**

Syntax

SetPixelV(
DC: HDC;   {the handle of a device context}
X: Integer;   {the horizontal pixel coordinate}
Y: Integer;   {the vertical pixel coordinate}
Color: COLORREF   {the new pixel color}
): BOOL;   {returns TRUE or FALSE}

Description

This function sets the color of the pixel at the specified coordinates in the indicated device context. It is generally faster than SetPixel because it does not have to return a color. The coordinates must be within the boundaries of the current clipping region.

Parameters

DC: A handle to the device context in which the new pixel color is set.

X: The horizontal coordinate of the pixel within the device context, in logical units.

Y: The vertical coordinate of the pixel within the device context, in logical units.

Color: Specifies the color of the pixel.

Return Value

If the function succeeds, it returns TRUE; otherwise it returns FALSE. To get extended error information, call the GetLastError function.

See Also

GetPixel, SetPixel

Example

Please see Listing 3-31 under LineDDA.

SetPolyFillMode   *Windows.Pas*

Syntax

```
SetPolyFillMode(
DC: HDC;                      {the handle of a device context}
PolyFillMode: Integer        {the polygon fill mode flag}
): Integer;                   {returns the previous polygon fill mode}
```

Description

This function sets the polygon fill mode of the specified device context. The polygon fill mode determines how complex polygons and regions are to be filled. To determine what pixels will be filled when using the ALTERNATE mode, select any pixel within the polygon's interior and draw an imaginary line in the positive X direction out to infinity. For each line in the polygon crossed by the imaginary line, a value is incremented. The pixel will be highlighted if this value is an odd number. To determine what pixels will be filled when using the WINDING mode, select any pixel within the polygon's interior and draw an imaginary line in the positive X direction out to infinity. For each line in the polygon crossed by the imaginary line, if the polygon line was drawn in a positive Y direction, a value is incremented; if the polygon line was drawn in a negative Y direction, a value is decremented. The pixel will be highlighted if this value is nonzero.

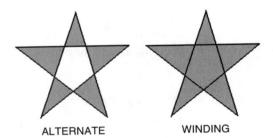

Figure 3-48: Polygon fill mode results

ALTERNATE   WINDING

Parameters

DC: A handle to the device context whose current polygon fill mode is to be set.

PolyFillMode: A flag indicating the new polygon fill mode. This parameter may be set to one value from Table 3-37.

Return Value

If the function succeeds, it returns a value from Table 3-37 indicating the previous polygon fill mode. If the function fails, it returns zero.

See Also

FillPath, GetPolyFillMode, Polygon, PolyPolygon

Example

Please see Listing 3-25 under GetPolyFillMode.

Table 3-37: SetPolyFillMode PolyFillMode and Return Values

Value	Description
ALTERNATE	Fills the polygon using the Alternate method.
WINDING	Fills the polygon using the Winding method.

SetROP2   *Windows.Pas*

Syntax

```
SetROP2(
DC: HDC;           {the handle of a device context}
p2: Integer        {the foreground mix mode flag}
): Integer;        {returns the previous foreground mix mode}
```

Description

This function sets the foreground mix mode for the specified device context. The foreground mix mode determines how the color of the pen used in drawing operations is combined with the color of pixels on the specified device context.

Parameters

DC: A handle to the device context whose foreground mix mode is to be set.

p2: A flag specifying the new foreground mix mode. This parameter can be set to one value from Table 3-38.

Return Value

If the function succeeds, it returns a value from Table 3-38 indicating the previous foreground mix mode. If the function fails, it returns zero.

See Also

GetROP2, LineTo, PolyBezier, Polyline, Rectangle

Example

Please see Listing 3-26 under GetROP2.

Table 3-38: SetROP2 p2 and Return Values

Value	Description
R2_BLACK	The destination pixel is always black.
R2_COPYPEN	The destination pixel is set to the pen color.

3

Chapter

Value	Description
R2_MASKNOTPEN	The destination pixel is a combination of the colors common to the screen and the inverse of the pen.
R2_MASKPEN	The destination pixel is a combination of the colors common to the screen and the pen.
R2_MASKPENNOT	The destination pixel is a combination of the colors common to the pen and the inverse of the screen.
R2_MERGENOTPEN	The destination pixel is a combination of the screen and the inverse of the pen.
R2_MERGEPEN	The destination pixel is a combination of the pen and the screen.
R2_MERGEPENNOT	The destination pixel is a combination of the pen and the inverse of the screen.
R2_NOP	The destination pixel is not modified.
R2_NOT	The destination pixel is the inverse of the screen.
R2_NOTCOPYPEN	The destination pixel is the inverse of the pen.
R2_NOTMASKPEN	The destination pixel is the inverse of the R2_MASKPEN flag.
R2_NOTMERGEPEN	The destination pixel is the inverse of the R2_MERGEPEN flag.
R2_NOTXORPEN	The destination pixel is the inverse of the R2_XORPEN flag.
R2_WHITE	The destination pixel is always white.
R2_XORPEN	The destination pixel is a combination of the colors in the pen and in the screen, but not in both.

StrokeAndFillPath   *Windows.Pas*

Syntax

```
StrokeAndFillPath(
DC: HDC                    {the handle of a device context}
): BOOL;                   {returns TRUE or FALSE}
```

Description

This function closes any open figures in the path in the specified device context, and outlines and fills the path with the device context's currently selected pen and brush, respectively. The path is filled according to the current polygon filling mode. Note that after this function returns, the path is discarded from the device context.

Parameters

DC: A handle to the device context containing the path to be outlined and filled.

Return Value

If the function succeeds, it returns TRUE; otherwise it returns FALSE. To get extended error information, call the GetLastError function.

See Also

BeginPath, FillPath, SetPolyFillMode, StrokePath

Example

Listing 3-45: Outlining and Filling a Path Simultaneously

```
procedure TForm1.FormPaint(Sender: TObject);
begin
  {begin a path bracket}
  BeginPath(Canvas.Handle);

  {draw some cool text}
  SetBkMode(Canvas.Handle, TRANSPARENT);
  Canvas.TextOut(10, 10, 'DELPHI ROCKS!');

  {end the path bracket}
  EndPath(Canvas.Handle);

  {initialize the pen and brush to be used in filling and outlining the path}
  Canvas.Pen.Color := clRed;
  Canvas.Pen.Style := psSolid;
  Canvas.Brush.Color := clBlue;
  Canvas.Brush.Style := bsDiagCross;

  {fill and outline the path}
  StrokeAndFillPath(Canvas.Handle);
end;
```

Figure 3-49:
The outlined
and filled path

StrokePath   **Windows.Pas**

Syntax

```
StrokePath(
DC: HDC          {the handle of a device context}
): BOOL;         {returns TRUE or FALSE}
```

Description

This function outlines the path contained in the specified device context with the currently selected pen. Note that after this function returns, the path is discarded from the device context.

Parameters

DC: A handle to the device context containing the path to be outlined.

Return Value

If the function succeeds, it returns TRUE; otherwise it returns FALSE. To get extended error information, call the GetLastError function.

See Also

BeginPath, EndPath, FillPath, ExtCreatePen, StrokeAndFillPath

Example

Listing 3-46: Outlining a Path

```
procedure TForm1.FormPaint(Sender: TObject);
begin
  {begin a path bracket}
  BeginPath(Canvas.Handle);

  {draw some cool text}
  SetBkMode(Canvas.Handle, TRANSPARENT);
  Canvas.TextOut(10, 10, 'DELPHI ROCKS!');

  {end the path bracket}
  EndPath(Canvas.Handle);

  {initialize the pen to be used in outlining the path}
  Canvas.Pen.Color := clRed;
  Canvas.Pen.Style := psSolid;

  {outline the path}
  StrokePath(Canvas.Handle);
end;
```

Figure 3-50: The outlined path

Chapter 4

Region and Path Functions

When producing graphical output on a device context, it is often necessary to confine the output to an area smaller than the client area, or to a nonrectangular area. Monochrome masks, offscreen buffers, and raster operations could be combined to produce the desired effect, resulting in a rather complicated method of graphical output. Alternatively, the developer can take advantage of a special Windows feature known as regions and paths. The region and path functions are not encapsulated by the Delphi VCL, and are therefore almost undocumented in most Delphi literature. These functions can be used to create startling effects, and can provide elegant solutions that might otherwise involve the complicated series of steps suggested above. This chapter discusses the region and path functions available in the Win32 API.

Regions and Paths

At first, a region and a path may appear to be very similar. They both define a shape. They can be filled or outlined with user-defined brushes and pens as desired. Upon further inspection, however, the differences between regions and paths become apparent.

Regions

A region is a closed, polygonal shape. It is not a shape in the visual sense; it acts as a shape definition that can be rendered with various techniques. Generally, a region is constructed with specific functions that create a shape definition in the form of a polygonal primitive, such as a rectangle or ellipse. As such, regions tend to be simpler in shape than paths. However, regions can be combined with other regions in various ways to produce more complex shapes. The CombineRgn function performs this service, using various flags representing Boolean operations to combine regions in different ways, as illustrated below.

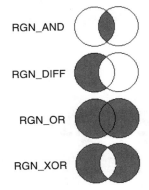

RGN_AND

RGN_DIFF

RGN_OR

RGN_XOR

*Figure 4-1:
CombineRgn
region
combination
methods*

Unlike a path, a region can be used for hit testing. Hit testing is the act of determining where the mouse cursor is relative to a given area, usually in response to a mouse click. By using the PtInRect or PtInRegion functions combined with rectangles or regions, the developer can create "hot spots" of very complex shapes. For example, an application could define fifty different regions in the form of the fifty states. Using these regions as hot spots on a map of the United States, a particular state could be highlighted when the mouse cursor enters its perimeter, or information could be displayed when it is clicked upon. This could easily be accomplished in the OnMouseDown event of a TImage or the form itself, using the PtInRegion function to compare the clicked coordinates with each region until the correct region is found. Also different from paths, a region can be moved relative to its original coordinates, and can be compared to other regions for equality.

If more detailed information on a region is required, an application can use the GetRegionData function to retrieve the various attributes of a region. In particular, a region is internally defined as a series of rectangles, sorted in top to bottom, left to right order. The GetRegionData function can be used to retrieve the individual rectangles that define a region, as illustrated in the following example.

Listing 4-1: Retrieving Region Information

```
procedure TForm1.Button1Click(Sender: TObject);
var
  TheRegion: HRGN;           // holds the region
  RegionDataSize: DWORD;     // holds the size of region information
  RegionData: Pointer;       // a pointer to the region information
  iCount: Integer;           // general loop control variable
  RectPointer: ^TRect;       // a pointer used to extract rectangle coordinates
begin
  {create a round rectangular region}
  TheRegion := CreateRoundRectRgn(10, 10, 110, 110, 30, 30);

  {initialize the canvas's brush and draw the region}
  Canvas.Brush.Color := clRed;
  FillRgn(Canvas.Handle, TheRegion, Canvas.Brush.Handle);
```

```
{retrieve the size of the buffer required to hold the region data,
 and allocate the specified memory}
RegionDataSize := GetRegionData(TheRegion, 0, NIL);
GetMem(RegionData, RegionDataSize);

{retrieve the information about the round rectangular region}
GetRegionData(TheRegion, RegionDataSize, RegionData);

{display the information}
with ListBox1.Items do
begin
  {display the number of rectangles in the region, and the size of
   the region's bounding rectangle}
  Add('Number of rectangles: '+IntToStr(TRgnData(RegionData^).rdh.nCount));
  Add('Region bounding rectangle -');
  Add('Left: '+IntToStr(TRgnData(RegionData^).rdh.rcBound.Left)+
      ' Top: '+IntToStr(TRgnData(RegionData^).rdh.rcBound.Top)+
      ' Right: '+IntToStr(TRgnData(RegionData^).rdh.rcBound.Right)+
      ' Bottom: '+IntToStr(TRgnData(RegionData^).rdh.rcBound.Bottom));
  Add('');

  {initialize a pointer to the address of the buffer containing the
   coordinates of the rectangles defining the region}
  RectPointer := @TRgnData(RegionData^).Buffer;

  {set the canvas's pen to a different color so the rectangles will show}
  Canvas.Pen.Color := clBlack;

  {loop through the indicated number of rectangles}
  for iCount := 0 to TRgnData(RegionData^).rdh.nCount-1 do
  begin
    {the RectPointer pointer by definition will typecast the values in the
     Buffer array as a TRect, thereby allowing the application to extract
     the necessary members}
    Add('Rect: '+IntToStr(iCount)+
        ' - L: '+IntToStr(RectPointer^.Left)+
        ', T: '+IntToStr(RectPointer^.Top)+
        ', R: '+IntToStr(RectPointer^.Right)+
        ', B: '+IntToStr(RectPointer^.Bottom));

    {draw this specific rectangle over the region}
    Canvas.Rectangle(RectPointer^.Left, RectPointer^.Top, RectPointer^.Right,
                     RectPointer^.Bottom);

    {since the pointer is a pointer to a TRect, incrementing its value will
     move it forward by the size of a TRect structure. Thus, it will be
     pointing to the next rectangle in the series}
    Inc(RectPointer);
  end;
end;

{delete the region and free the allocated memory}
FreeMem(RegionData);
DeleteObject(TheRegion);
end;
```

4

Chapter

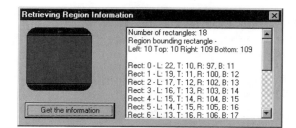

*Figure 4-2:
The region
information*

Paths

Like a region, a path is a shape definition. However, paths do not need to form a closed polygonal shape. A path can be anything from a rectangle to a complex series of lines and bézier curves. A path is created by using a series of GDI drawing functions in what is known as a path bracket. A path bracket is a section of code that starts with the BeginPath function and ends with the EndPath function. Specific drawing functions used between these two functions will not produce output to the screen. They will instead define the shape of a path. As such, paths are generally much more complex in shape than regions. Please see the BeginPath function for a list of drawing functions that can be used in a path bracket.

Unlike regions, any number of which can be created, a path is associated with the device context in which it was defined. Only one path can exist in a device context at a time, and when another path bracket is started or the device context is destroyed, the current path is destroyed. However, a path can be converted into a region by using the PathToRegion function. This allows the developer to create incredibly complex region shapes. The points defining the path can be retrieved by calling the GetPath function. This function returns an array of TPoint structures containing the coordinates of the points defining the region, in logical units. A common use for this function is in algorithms that fit text to a path or shape, such as a curve.

Special Effects

Perhaps the most common use of a region or path is to define a clipping region. When a clipping region is defined and selected into a device context, any graphical output to the device context is confined within the boundaries of the region. Any output that would appear outside of the region is discarded, or "clipped." Combining the functionality of regions with paths and using the result as a clipping region can produce some astonishing special effects. For example, a path can be created by using the TextOut function to define a word or sentence. This path can then be converted into a region, and used in conjunction with bitmap functions and some animation techniques to produce a truly unique splash screen. The following example demonstrates this technique. Note that the bitmap used inside of the text is moving from right to left.

Listing 4-2: Cool Special Effects Produced with Regions and Paths

```
var
  Form1: TForm1;
  Offset: Integer;              // bitmap offset counter
  Buffer, TileBitmap: TBitmap;  // offscreen and texture bitmaps

implementation

{$R *.DFM}

procedure TForm1.FormPaint(Sender: TObject);
begin
  {draw a frame of the effect}
  DrawEffect;
end;

procedure TForm1.FormCreate(Sender: TObject);
begin
  {initialize the offset counter}
  Offset := 0;

  {create an offscreen buffer the size of the form's client area}
  Buffer := TBitmap.Create;
  Buffer.Width  := ClientWidth;
  Buffer.Height := ClientHeight;

  {create and load the texture bitmap used in the letters}
  TileBitmap := TBitmap.Create;
  TileBitmap.LoadFromFile(ExtractFilePath(ParamStr(0))+'Tile.bmp');
end;

procedure TForm1.FormDestroy(Sender: TObject);
begin
  {free the offscreen and texture bitmaps}
  Buffer.Free;
  TileBitmap.Free;
end;

procedure TForm1.Timer1Timer(Sender: TObject);
begin
  {increment the offset counter}
  Inc(Offset);

  {if the offset is larger than the texture bitmap (64 pixels), reset it}
  if Offset>63 then
    Offset := 0;

  {draw a frame of the effect}
  DrawEffect;
end;

procedure TForm1.DrawEffect;
var
  iCount: Integer;              // a general loop counter
```

```
    ClipRgn: HRGN;                  // holds the region
begin
  {begin a path bracket}
  BeginPath(Canvas.Handle);

  {output some text, defining the path as the interior of the text}
  SetBkMode(Canvas.Handle, TRANSPARENT);
  TextOut(Canvas.Handle, 10, 60, 'DELPHI', 6);

  {end the path bracket}
  EndPath(Canvas.Handle);

  {convert the path into a region, and select this region as the offscreen
   buffer's clipping region}
  ClipRgn := PathToRegion(Canvas.Handle);
  SelectClipRgn(Buffer.Canvas.Handle, ClipRgn);

  {draw the texture bitmap into the area defined by the region. it will get
   clipped to the interior of the letters}
  for iCount := 0 to 4 do
    Buffer.Canvas.Draw(iCount*64-Offset, 60, TileBitmap);

  {delete the clipping region of the offscreen buffer}
  SelectClipRgn(Buffer.Canvas.Handle, 0);

  {reset the clipping region of the offscreen buffer, this time defining the
   clipping region as the area outside of the letters}
  ExtSelectClipRgn(Buffer.Canvas.Handle, ClipRgn, RGN_DIFF);

  {draw the image of the Earth onto the offscreen buffer. the previously drawn
   letters will not be obscured by the bitmap, as they are protected by the
   current clipping region}
  Buffer.Canvas.Draw(0, 0, Image1.Picture.Bitmap);

  {draw the offscreen buffer to the form. this eliminates flicker and is an
   animation technique known as double buffering}
  Canvas.Draw(0, 0, Buffer);
end;
```

Figure 4-3:
A cool new
splash screen

Region and Path Functions

The following region and path functions are covered in this chapter:

Table 4-1: Region and Path Functions

Function	Description
AbortPath	Discards a path and closes an open path bracket.
BeginPath	Starts a path bracket.
CloseFigure	Closes an open figure in a path bracket.
CombineRgn	Combines two regions using a Boolean operation.
CopyRect	Copies one rectangle's coordinates into another.
CreateEllipticRgn	Creates an elliptical region.
CreateEllipticRgnIndirect	Creates an elliptical region based on properties defined in a data structure.
CreatePolygonRgn	Creates a polygonal region.
CreatePolyPolygonRgn	Creates a region consisting of multiple polygons.
CreateRectRgn	Creates a rectangular region.
CreateRectRgnIndirect	Creates a rectangular region based on properties defined in a data structure.
CreateRoundRectRgn	Creates a rounded rectangular region.
EndPath	Ends an open path bracket.
EqualRect	Determines if the coordinates of two rectangles are equal.
EqualRgn	Determines if the size and shape of two regions are equal.
ExcludeClipRect	Creates a new clipping region minus the specified region.
ExtCreateRegion	Transforms an existing region.
ExtSelectClipRgn	Selects a clipping region, combining it with the existing clipping region using Boolean operations.
FlattenPath	Converts curves in a path into flat line segments.
GetClipBox	Retrieves the bounding box of the clipping region.
GetClipRgn	Retrieves a handle to the current clipping region.
GetPath	Retrieves the points that define a path.
GetRegionData	Retrieves information about a region.
GetRgnBox	Retrieves the bounding box of a region.
InflateRect	Modifies the size of a rectangle.
IntersectRect	Creates a rectangle from the intersection of two rectangles.
InvertRect	Inverts the colors of the pixels within the area defined by a rectangle.
InvertRgn	Inverts the colors of the pixels within the area defined by a region.
IsRectEmpty	Determines if a rectangle is empty.
OffsetClipRgn	Moves a clipping region.
OffsetRect	Moves a rectangle.
OffsetRgn	Moves a region.

4

Chapter

Function	Description
PathToRegion	Converts a path into a region.
PtInRect	Determines if a specific coordinate falls within a rectangle.
PtInRegion	Determines if a specific coordinate falls within a region.
PtVisible	Determines if a specific coordinate falls within the clipping region.
RectInRegion	Determines if a rectangle falls within a region.
RectVisible	Determines if a rectangle falls within the clipping region.
SelectClipPath	Selects the current path as the clipping region.
SelectClipRgn	Selects a region as the clipping region.
SetRect	Initializes a rectangle.
SetRectEmpty	Empties a rectangle.
SetRectRgn	Converts a region into a rectangular region.
SetWindowRgn	Sets the window region to the specific region.
SubtractRect	Subtracts one rectangle from another.
UnionRect	Creates a rectangle from the sum of two rectangles.
WidenPath	Redefines a path shape with respect to the current pen.

AbortPath   Windows.Pas

Syntax

```
AbortPath(
DC: HDC              {a handle to a device context}
): BOOL;             {returns TRUE or FALSE}
```

Description

This function discards any path in the device context identified by the DC parameter. If the function is called inside an open path bracket, the path bracket is closed and the path is discarded.

Parameters

DC: A handle to a device context containing the path to be eliminated.

Return Value

If the function succeeds, it returns TRUE; otherwise it returns FALSE. To get extended error information, call the GetLastError function.

See Also

BeginPath, CloseFigure, EndPath

Example

Please see Listing 4-3 under CloseFigure.

BeginPath   *Windows.Pas*

Syntax

```
BeginPath(
DC: HDC            {a handle to a device context}
): BOOL;           {returns TRUE or FALSE}
```

Description

This function opens a path bracket for the specified device context. Any previously existing paths in the specified device context are discarded. Use the EndPath function to close a path bracket. Once a path bracket has been started, certain drawing functions used with the specified device context will be translated into path information and will not display any visible output. Once the path bracket is closed, the path is associated with the specified device context. It can be converted into a region by calling the PathToRegion function.

Under Windows NT, the following functions can be used inside a path bracket: Angle-Arc, Arc, ArcTo, Chord, CloseFigure, Ellipse, ExtTextOut, LineTo, MoveToEx, Pie, PolyBezier, PolyBezierTo, PolyDraw, Polygon, Polyline, PolylineTo, PolyPolygon, PolyPolyline, Rectangle, RoundRect, and TextOut.

Under Windows 95, the following functions can be used inside a path bracket: Close-Figure, ExtTextOut, LineTo, MoveToEx, PolyBezier, PolyBezierTo, Polygon, Polyline, PolylineTo, PolyPolygon, PolyPolyline, and TextOut.

Parameters

DC: A handle to the device context in which certain drawing functions will be translated into path information.

Return Value

If the function succeeds, it returns TRUE; otherwise it returns FALSE. To get extended error information, call the GetLastError function.

See Also

CloseFigure, EndPath, ExtTextOut, FillPath, LineTo, MoveToEx, PathToRegion, PolyBezier, PolyBezierTo, Polygon, Polyline, PolylineTo, PolyPolygon, PolyPolyline, SelectClipPath, StrokeAndFillPath, StrokePath, TextOut, WidenPath

Example

Please see Listing 4-19 under SelectClipPath, and other examples throughout this chapter.

CloseFigure   *Windows.Pas*

Syntax

```
CloseFigure(
```

4

Chapter

DC: HDC	{a handle to a device context}
): BOOL;	{returns TRUE or FALSE}

Description

This function closes the figure created in a path bracket in the specified device context. The figure is closed by performing a LineTo operation from the current point to the point specified in the most recent call to the MoveToEx function. The lines will be connected by using the line join style identified by the currently selected geometric pen. If the LineTo function is called to close the figure before calling the CloseFigure function, the end cap style of the currently selected geometric pen is used to draw the ends of the lines. This function is useful only when called within an open path bracket. A figure in a path bracket is open unless explicitly closed by calling this function. After this function is called, any other drawing functions used in the path will start a new figure.

Parameters

DC: Specifies the device context containing the path whose current figure will be closed.

Return Value

If the function succeeds, it returns TRUE; otherwise it returns FALSE. To get extended error information, call the GetLastError function.

See Also

BeginPath, EndPath, ExtCreatePen, LineTo, MoveToEx

Example

Listing 4-3: Closing an Open Figure in a Path Bracket

```
procedure TForm1.Button1Click(Sender: TObject);
begin
  {start a path bracket.  all subsequent drawing functions will define a
   path and will not produce visible output}
  BeginPath(Canvas.Handle);

  {start drawing a path}
  Canvas.MoveTo(65, 15);
  Canvas.LineTo(25, 234);
  Canvas.MoveTo(78, 111);
  Canvas.LineTo(98, 79);

  {if the path is incorrect, there was a mistake, or for any reason desired,
   the current path can be abandoned}
  AbortPath(Canvas.Handle);

  {the path was closed and abandoned, so we must start a new path bracket}
  BeginPath(Canvas.Handle);
```

```
{draw three lines into the path}
Canvas.MoveTo(25, 10);
Canvas.LineTo(125, 10);
Canvas.LineTo(125, 110);
Canvas.LineTo(25, 110);

{close the current figure. this should create a square path}
CloseFigure(Canvas.Handle);

{end the path bracket.  the path will now be associated with
 the device context}
EndPath(Canvas.Handle);

{initialize the device context's pen and brush as desired}
Canvas.Pen.Width :=3;
Canvas.Pen.Color := clRed;
Canvas.Brush.Color := clLime;

{render the path onto the device context}
StrokeAndFillPath(Canvas.Handle);
end;
```

Figure 4-4:
The closed
figure

CombineRgn   Windows.Pas

Syntax

```
CombineRgn(
p1: HRGN;                    {a handle to the combined region}
p2: HRGN;                    {a handle to the first region}
p3: HRGN;                    {a handle to the second region}
p4: Integer                  {region combination flag}
): Integer;                  {returns the type of the combined region}
```

Description

This function combines the regions identified by the p2 and p3 parameters according to the flag indicated in the p4 parameter. The region identified by the p1 parameter is reset to point to the resulting region. The regions identified by the p1, p2, and p3 parameters do not need to be unique (i.e., the result region identified by the p1 parameter can be the same region identified by the p2 or p3 parameters). When the combined region is no longer needed, it should be deleted by calling the DeleteObject function.

Parameters

p1: A handle to a region that will receive a handle to the combined region. This parameter must specify a handle to an existing region.

p2: A handle to the first region to be combined.

p3: A handle to the second region to be combined.

p4: A flag indicating how the regions identified by the p2 and p3 parameters are to be combined. This parameter can contain one value from Table 4-2.

Return Value

This function returns a result indicating the type of region created or an error condition, and may be one value from Table 4-3.

See Also

CreateEllipticRgn, CreateEllipticRgnIndirect, CreatePolygonRgn, CreatePolyPolygonRgn, CreateRectRgn, CreateRectRgnIndirect, CreateRoundRectRgn, DeleteObject

Example

Listing 4-4: Combining Two Regions to Create a Special Effect

```
var
  Form1: TForm1;
  BinocularRgn: HRGN;    // a handle to the combined region

implementation

{$R *.DFM}

procedure TForm1.FormCreate(Sender: TObject);
var
  Circle1, Circle2: HRGN;  // holds two circular regions
begin
  {the handle to the combined region must identify a pre-existing region, so
   create a bogus region}
  BinocularRgn := CreateEllipticRgnIndirect(BoundsRect);

  {create two circular regions, the first taking up 3/4 of the left side
   of the area covered by Image1, and the second taking up 3/4 of the right
   side of the area covered by Image1}
  Circle1 := CreateEllipticRgn(Image1.Left, Image1.Top,
                               Image1.Left+MulDiv(Image1.Width,3,4),
                               Image1.Top+Image1.Height);
  Circle2 := CreateEllipticRgn(Image1.Left +(Image1.Width div 4),
                               Image1.Top, Image1.Left+Image1.Width,
                               Image1.Top+Image1.Height);

  {combine the two regions, creating a region reminiscent of a view through
   a pair of binoculars}
  CombineRgn(BinocularRgn, Circle1, Circle2, RGN_OR);
```

```
      {delete the two circular regions as they are no longer needed}
      DeleteObject(Circle1);
      DeleteObject(Circle2);
   end;

   procedure TForm1.FormPaint(Sender: TObject);
   var
      ClipRect: TRect;      // holds the current clipping region coordinates
   begin
      {select the combined region into the device context as a clipping region}
      SelectClipRgn(Canvas.Handle, BinocularRgn);

      {draw the contents of the image (which is invisible) onto the surface of the
       form.  it will be clipped to the current clipping region, resulting in what
       looks like the view of a ship through a pair of binoculars}
      Canvas.Draw(Image1.Left, Image1.Top, Image1.Picture.Bitmap);

      {draw the perimeter of the region in red to make it stand out}
      Canvas.Brush.Color := clRed;
      FrameRgn(Canvas.Handle, BinocularRgn, Canvas.Brush.Handle, 2, 2);

      {retrieve the smallest rectangle that will fit around the currently visible
       portion of the device context}
      GetClipBox(Canvas.Handle, ClipRect);

      {delete the clipping region so that drawing can be performed on the entire
       device context surface}
      SelectClipRgn(Canvas.Handle, 0);

      {draw the extents of the previously selected clipping region}
      Canvas.Brush.Style := bsClear;
      Canvas.Pen.Color := clBlack;
      Rectangle(Canvas.Handle, ClipRect.Left, ClipRect.Top, ClipRect.Right,
                ClipRect.Bottom);
   end;

   procedure TForm1.FormDestroy(Sender: TObject);
   begin
      {delete the combined region}
      DeleteObject(BinocularRgn);
   end;
```

Figure 4-5:
The combined
region used as
a clipping
region

4

Chapter

Table 4-2: CombineRgn p4 Values

Value	Description
RGN_AND	The resulting region is the intersection of the two specified regions.
RGN_COPY	The resulting region is a copy of the region identified by the p2 parameter.
RGN_DIFF	The resulting region is the area of the region identified by the p2 parameter that is not in the area of the region identified by the p3 parameter.
RGN_OR	The resulting region is the union of the two specified regions.
RGN_XOR	The resulting region is the union of the two specified regions excluding any overlapping areas.

Table 4-3: CombineRgn Return Values

Value	Description
NULLREGION	Indicates an empty region.
SIMPLEREGION	Indicates a single rectangular region.
COMPLEXREGION	Indicates a region consisting of more than one rectangle.
ERROR	Indicates an error occurred and no region was created.

CopyRect   Windows.Pas

Syntax

```
CopyRect(
var lprcDst: TRect;        {a pointer to the destination rectangle}
const lprcSrc: TRect       {a pointer to the source rectangle}
): BOOL;                   {returns TRUE or FALSE}
```

Description

This function copies the coordinates in the rectangle pointed to by the lprcSrc parameter into the coordinates of the rectangle pointed to by the lprcDst parameter.

Parameters

lprcDst: A pointer to a TRect structure that receives the coordinates of the rectangle pointed to by the lprcSrc parameter.

lprcSrc: A pointer to a TRect structure containing the coordinates to be copied to the rectangle pointed to by the lprcDst parameter.

Return Value

If the function succeeds, it returns TRUE; otherwise it returns FALSE. To get extended error information, call the GetLastError function.

See Also

IsRectEmpty, SetRect, SetRectEmpty, SetRectRgn

Example

Please see Listing 4-16 under OffsetRect.

CreateEllipticRgn   Windows.Pas

Syntax

```
CreateEllipticRgn(
p1: Integer;          {the upper left bounding box horizontal coordinate}
p2: Integer;          {the upper left bounding box vertical coordinate}
p3:Integer;           {the lower right bounding box horizontal coordinate}
p4: Integer           {the lower right bounding box vertical coordinate}
): HRGN;              {returns a handle to a region}
```

Description

This function creates an elliptical region. The specified coordinates represent the smallest rectangle that can be drawn around the resulting ellipse. When the region is no longer needed, it should be deleted by calling the DeleteObject function.

Parameters

p1: Specifies the horizontal coordinate of the upper left corner of the rectangle bounding the ellipse, in logical units.

p2: Specifies the vertical coordinate of the upper left corner of the rectangle bounding the ellipse, in logical units.

p3: Specifies the horizontal coordinate of the lower right corner of the rectangle bounding the ellipse, in logical units.

p4: Specifies the vertical coordinate of the lower right corner of the rectangle bounding the ellipse, in logical units.

Return Value

If the function succeeds, it returns a handle to an elliptic region; otherwise it returns zero.

See Also

CreateEllipticRgnIndirect, DeleteObject

4

Chapter

Example

Please see Listing 4-4 under CombineRgn.

CreateEllipticRgnIndirect   *Windows.Pas*

Syntax

```
CreateEllipticRgnIndirect(
const p1: TRect          {a pointer to rectangular coordinates}
): HRGN;                 {returns a handle to a region}
```

Description

This function creates an elliptical region based on the rectangular coordinates pointed to by the p1 parameter. The specified coordinates represent the smallest rectangle that can be drawn around the resulting ellipse. When the region is no longer needed, it should be deleted by calling the DeleteObject function.

Parameters

p1: A pointer to a TRect structure containing coordinates, in logical units, that define the smallest rectangle that can be drawn around the resulting ellipse.

Return Value

If the function succeeds, it returns a handle to an elliptic region; otherwise it returns zero.

See Also

CreateEllipticRgn, DeleteObject

Example

Listing 4-5: Dynamically Creating an Elliptical Region Based on the Form Size

```
var
  Form1: TForm1;
  TheRegion: HRGN;        // holds the elliptic region

implementation

{$R *.DFM}

procedure TForm1.FormPaint(Sender: TObject);
begin
  {erase the current image on the form}
  Canvas.Brush.Color := clBtnFace;
  Canvas.FillRect(BoundsRect);

  {outline the elliptic region in red}
  Canvas.Brush.Color := clRed;
  FrameRgn(Canvas.Handle, TheRegion, Canvas.Brush.Handle, 2, 2);
end;
```

```
procedure TForm1.FormResize(Sender: TObject);
begin
  {delete the current region, if it exists}
  if TheRegion<>0 then
    DeleteObject(TheRegion);

  {create a new elliptical region based on the boundaries of the client area}
  TheRegion := CreateEllipticRgnIndirect(ClientRect);

  {repaint the form}
  Repaint;
end;

procedure TForm1.FormDestroy(Sender: TObject);
begin
  {delete the elliptic region}
  DeleteObject(TheRegion);
end;
```

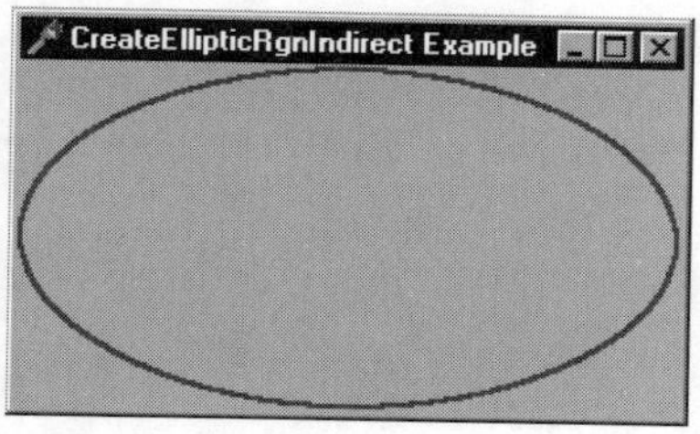

Figure 4-6:
The
dynamically
created region

CreatePolygonRgn   Windows.Pas

Syntax

```
CreatePolygonRgn(
const Points;                {the array of points}
Count: Integer;              {the number of points in the array}
FillMode: Integer            {the fill mode flag}
): HRGN;                     {returns a handle to a region}
```

Description

This function creates a polygonal region in the shape described by the array of vertices pointed to by the Points parameter. When the region is no longer needed, it should be deleted by calling the DeleteObject function.

Parameters

Points: A pointer to an array of TPoint structures describing the vertices of the polygon, in device units. The polygon is assumed to be closed, and each vertex can be specified only once.

Count: Specifies the number of TPoint entries in the array pointed to by the Points parameter.

FillMode: A flag specifying the fill mode used when determining which pixels are included in the region. If this parameter is set to ALTERNATE, the region is filled between odd-numbered and even-numbered sides of the specified polygon. If this parameter is set to WINDING, any part of the region with a nonzero winding value is filled. Please see the SetPolyFillMode function for more information on these flags.

Return Value

If the function succeeds, it returns a handle to the polygonal region; otherwise it returns zero.

See Also

CreatePolyPolygonRgn, DeleteObject, SetPolyFillMode

Example

Listing 4-6: Creating a Star-Shaped Region

```
var
  Form1: TForm1;
  PolygonRgn, ScaledRgn: HRGN;  // holds the original and scaled regions

implementation

{$R *.DFM}

procedure TForm1.FormCreate(Sender: TObject);
var
  Vertices: array[0..9] of TPoint;  // holds the vertices of the polygon region
  RegionData: Pointer;              // a pointer to region data
  RgnDataSize: DWORD;               // the size of the region data
  Transform: TXForm;                // the scaling transformation matrix
begin
  {specify a polygon in the shape of a star}
  Vertices[0] := Point(120, 5);
  Vertices[1] := Point(140, 70);
  Vertices[2] := Point(210, 70);
  Vertices[3] := Point(150, 100);
  Vertices[4] := Point(180, 175);
  Vertices[5] := Point(120, 120);
  Vertices[6] := Point(60, 175);
  Vertices[7] := Point(90, 100);
  Vertices[8] := Point(30, 70);
  Vertices[9] := Point(100, 70);

  {create a star shaped polygonal region}
  PolygonRgn := CreatePolygonRgn(Vertices, 10, WINDING);

  {retrieve the size of the region's data}
  RgnDataSize := GetRegionData(PolygonRgn, 0, NIL);

  {allocate enough memory to hold the region data}
  GetMem(RegionData, RgnDataSize);
```

```
      {retrieve the region data for the star-shaped region}
      GetRegionData(PolygonRgn, RgnDataSize, RegionData);

      {initialize a transformation matrix to indicate a slight increase in size
        and a translation in position}
      with Transform do
      begin
        eM11 := 1.35;
        eM12 := 0;
        eM21 := 0;
        eM22 := 1.35;
        eDx  := -42;
        eDy  := -35;
      end;

      {create a new, scaled region based on the original star-shaped region}
      ScaledRgn := ExtCreateRegion(@Transform, RgnDataSize, TRgnData(RegionData^));

      {free the region data as it is no longer needed}
      FreeMem(RegionData, RgnDataSize);
    end;

procedure TForm1.FormPaint(Sender: TObject);
var
    TempRgn: HRGN;     // holds a retrieved region handle
begin
    {select the scaled star-shaped region as a clipping region}
    SelectClipRgn(Canvas.Handle, ScaledRgn);

    {draw the cityscape image onto the form. it will be clipped to the boundaries
      of the star-shaped region}
    Canvas.Draw(0, 0, Image1.Picture.Bitmap);

    {even though we explicitly know what the clipping region is, we can retrieve
      it from the device context, using the retrieved region in any region
      functions. the GetClipRgn function requires the specified region handle
      to identify an existing region, so set it to the original star-shaped
      region.  this will retrieve the current clipping region, which is the
      scaled region}
    TempRgn := PolygonRgn;
    GetClipRgn(Canvas.Handle, TempRgn);

    {draw the edges of the region to make it stand out}
    Canvas.Brush.Color := clRed;
    FrameRgn(Canvas.Handle, TempRgn, Canvas.Brush.Handle, 2, 2);
end;

procedure TForm1.FormMouseDown(Sender: TObject; Button: TMouseButton;
    Shift: TShiftState; X, Y: Integer);
begin
    {select the scaled star-shaped region as a clipping region}
    SelectClipRgn(Canvas.Handle, ScaledRgn);

    {indicate if the clicked area of the canvas is visible within
      the current clipping region (the scaled star-shaped region)}
```

```
    if PtVisible(Canvas.Handle, X, Y) then
      Caption := 'CreatePolygonRgn Example - Visible'
    else
      Caption := 'CreatePolygonRgn Example - Invisible';
end;

procedure TForm1.FormDestroy(Sender: TObject);
begin
  {free all resources associated with both regions}
  DeleteObject(PolygonRgn);
  DeleteObject(ScaledRgn);
end;
```

Figure 4-7:
The
star-shaped
region

CreatePolyPolygonRgn   Windows.Pas

Syntax

```
CreatePolyPolygonRgn(
const pPtStructs;          {the array of points}
const pIntArray;           {the array of vertex counts}
p3: Integer;               {the number of entries in the vertex count array}
p4: Integer                {the fill mode flag}
): HRGN;                   {returns a handle to a region}
```

Description

This function creates a region defined from multiple polygons. The vertices of each polygon are specified consecutively in the array of TPoint structures pointed to by the pPtStructs parameter. Each entry in the array pointed to by the pIntArray parameter indicates the number of points in the array of TPoint structures that define the vertices of each polygon. The polygons defined by this array are allowed to overlap. When the region is no longer needed, it should be deleted by calling the DeleteObject function.

Parameters

pPtStructs: A pointer to an array of TPoint structures describing the vertices of each polygon, in device units. Each polygon is described consecutively and is assumed to be closed. Each vertex can be specified only once.

pIntArray: A pointer to an array of integers. Each integer specifies the number of points in the array pointed to by the pPtStructs parameter that define one polygon.

p3: Specifies the number of entries in the array pointed to by the pIntArray parameter.

p4: A flag specifying the fill mode used when determining which pixels are included in the region. If this parameter is set to ALTERNATE, the region is filled between odd-numbered and even-numbered sides of the specified polygon. If this parameter is set to WINDING, any part of the region with a nonzero winding value is filled. Please see the SetPolyFillMode function for more information on these flags.

Return Value

If the function succeeds, it returns a handle to the polygonal region; otherwise it returns zero.

See Also

CreatePolygonRgn, DeleteObject, SetPolyFillMode

Example

Listing 4-7: Creating a Multiple Polygon Region

```
var
  Form1: TForm1;
  HotSpotRgn: HRGN;        // holds the multiple polygon region

implementation

{$R *.DFM}

procedure TForm1.FormCreate(Sender: TObject);
var
  PolyPoints: array[0..11] of TPoint;    // holds the points of the polygons
  VertexCounts: array[0..1] of Integer;  // holds the vertex counts
begin
  {define one polygon in the region}
  PolyPoints[0] := Point(68, 80);
  PolyPoints[1] := Point(76, 72);
  PolyPoints[2] := Point(87, 80);
  PolyPoints[3] := Point(86, 96);
  PolyPoints[4] := Point(100, 96);
  PolyPoints[5] := Point(100, 160);
  PolyPoints[6] := Point(68, 160);

  {define another polygon in the region}
  PolyPoints[7] := Point(173, 53);
  PolyPoints[8] := Point(184, 66);
  PolyPoints[9] := Point(184, 146);
  PolyPoints[10] := Point(160, 146);
  PolyPoints[11] := Point(160, 66);

  {indicate that the first polygon consists of 7 points, and the second
   consists of 5 points}
```

4

Chapter

```
    VertexCounts[0] := 7;
    VertexCounts[1] := 5;

    {create the multiple polygon region}
    HotSpotRgn := CreatePolyPolygonRgn(PolyPoints, VertexCounts, 2, WINDING);
end;

procedure TForm1.Button1Click(Sender: TObject);
begin
    {invert the area defined by the multiple polygon region}
    InvertRgn(Canvas.Handle, HotSpotRgn);
end;

procedure TForm1.Image1MouseDown(Sender: TObject; Button: TMouseButton;
  Shift: TShiftState; X, Y: Integer);
var
    TranslatedPt: TPoint;     // holds a form specific coordinate
begin
    {since the region is defined in logical coordinates relative to the form,
     the indicated location of the mouse click must be translated appropriately}
    TranslatedPt := Image1.ClientToScreen(Point(X,Y));
    TranslatedPt := Form1.ScreenToClient(TranslatedPt);

    {indicate if the point is within the 'hotspot' area defined by the
     multiple polygon region}
    if PtInRegion(HotSpotRgn, TranslatedPt.X, TranslatedPt.Y) then
      Caption := 'Clicked on a hotspot'
    else
      Caption := 'No hot spot clicked';
end;

procedure TForm1.FormDestroy(Sender: TObject);
begin
    {delete the region}
    DeleteObject(HotSpotRgn);
end;
```

Figure 4-8:
Using the
multiple
polygon region
as a hot spot

CreateRectRgn   Windows.Pas

Syntax

```
CreateRectRgn(
p1: Integer;              {the upper left horizontal coordinate}
p2: Integer;              {the upper left vertical coordinate}
p3: Integer;              {the lower right horizontal coordinate}
p4: Integer               {the lower right vertical coordinate}
): HRGN;                  {returns a handle to a region}
```

Description

This function creates a rectangular region based on the specified coordinates. When the region is no longer needed, it should be deleted by calling the DeleteObject function.

Parameters

p1: Specifies the horizontal coordinate of the upper left corner of the rectangle, in device units.

p2: Specifies the vertical coordinate of the upper left corner of the rectangle, in device units.

p3: Specifies the horizontal coordinate of the lower right corner of the rectangle, in device units.

p4: Specifies the vertical coordinate of the lower right corner of the rectangle, in device units.

Return Value

If the function succeeds, it returns a handle to the region; otherwise it returns zero.

See Also

CreateRectRgnIndirect, CreateRoundRectRgn, DeleteObject

Example

Listing 4-8: Creating a Rectangular Region

```
procedure TForm1.Button1Click(Sender: TObject);
var
  RegionHandle: HRGN;        // holds the rectangular region
begin
  {initialize the canvas's brush}
  Canvas.Brush.Style := bsCross;
  Canvas.Brush.Color := clRed;

  {create a rectangular region}
  RegionHandle := CreateRectRgn(10, 40, 175, 175);
```

4

Chapter

```
{paint the region}
FillRgn(Canvas.Handle, RegionHandle, Canvas.Brush.Handle);

{delete the region}
DeleteObject(RegionHandle);
end;
```

*Figure 4-9:
The
rectangular
region*

CreateRectRgnIndirect   Windows.Pas

Syntax

```
CreateRectRgnIndirect(
const p1: TRect          {the rectangular region coordinates}
): HRGN;                 {returns a handle to a region}
```

Description

This function creates a rectangular region based on the coordinates in the rectangle identified by the p1 parameter. When the region is no longer needed, it should be deleted by calling the DeleteObject function.

Parameters

p1: A TRect structure containing the rectangular coordinates defining the region, in device units.

Return Value

If the function succeeds, it returns a handle to the region; otherwise it returns zero.

See Also

CreateRectRgn, CreateRoundRectRgn, DeleteObject

Example

Listing 4-9: Indirectly Creating a Rectangular Region

```
procedure TForm1.Button1Click(Sender: TObject);
var
```

```
    RegionHandle: HRGN;     // a handle to the region
  begin
    {create a rectangular region the size of the form's client area}
    RegionHandle := CreateRectRgnIndirect(Form1.ClientRect);

    {initialize the brush}
    Canvas.Brush.Style := bsDiagCross;
    Canvas.Brush.Color := clRed;

    {fill the rectangular region}
    FillRgn(Canvas.Handle, RegionHandle, Canvas.Brush.Handle);

    {we no longer need the region, so delete it}
    DeleteObject(RegionHandle);
  end;
```

Figure 4-10: The rectangular region

CreateRoundRectRgn   **Windows.Pas**

Syntax

CreateRoundRectRgn(
p1: Integer;	{the upper left horizontal coordinate}
p2: Integer;	{the upper left vertical coordinate}
p3: Integer;	{the lower right horizontal coordinate}
p4: Integer;	{the lower right vertical coordinate}
p5: Integer;	{the width of the rounded corner ellipse}
p6: Integer	{the height of the rounded corner ellipse}
): HRGN;	{returns a handle to a region}

Description

This function creates a rectangular region with rounded corners, based on the specified coordinates. When the region is no longer needed, it should be deleted by calling the DeleteObject function.

Parameters

p1: Specifies the horizontal coordinate of the upper left corner of the rectangle, in device units.

p2: Specifies the vertical coordinate of the upper left corner of the rectangle, in device units.

p3: Specifies the horizontal coordinate of the lower right corner of the rectangle, in device units.

p4: Specifies the vertical coordinate of the lower right corner of the rectangle, in device units.

p5: Specifies the width of the ellipse used to define the rounded corners of the rectangle, in device units.

p6: Specifies the height of the ellipse used to define the rounded corners of the rectangle, in device units.

Return Value

If the function succeeds, it returns a handle to the region; otherwise it returns zero.

See Also

CreateRectRgn, CreateRectRgnIndirect, CreateRoundRectRgn, DeleteObject

Example

Listing 4-10: Creating a Rounded Rectangular Region

```
procedure TForm1.Button1Click(Sender: TObject);
var
  RegionHandle: HRGN;    // holds the region
begin
  {create a rounded rectangular region}
  RegionHandle := CreateRoundRectRgn(10, 40, 217, 175, 80, 80);

  {initialize the brush}
  Canvas.Brush.Style := bsDiagCross;
  Canvas.Brush.Color := clBlue;

  {draw the perimeter of the region}
  FrameRgn(Canvas.Handle, RegionHandle, Canvas.Brush.Handle, 8, 8);

  {delete the region}
  DeleteObject(RegionHandle);
end;
```

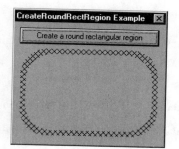

Figure 4-11:
The rounded
rectangular
region

EndPath   Windows.Pas

Syntax

```
EndPath(
DC: HDC              {a handle to a device context}
): BOOL;             {returns TRUE or FALSE}
```

Description

This function closes an open path bracket. The resulting path is associated with the device context identified by the DC parameter.

Parameters

DC: Specifies the device context which will contain the resulting path.

Return Value

If the function succeeds, it returns TRUE; otherwise it returns FALSE. To get extended error information, call the GetLastError function.

See Also

BeginPath

Example

Please see Listing 4-19 under SelectClipPath, and other examples throughout this chapter.

EqualRect   Windows.Pas

Syntax

```
EqualRect(
const lprc1: TRect;      {the first rectangle to compare}
const lprc2: TRect       {the second rectangle to compare}
): BOOL;                 {returns TRUE or FALSE}
```

4

Chapter

Description

This function determines if the coordinates identified by the two rectangles are identical.

Parameters

lprc1: A pointer to a TRect structure containing coordinates to be compared.

lprc2: A pointer to a TRect structure containing coordinates to be compared.

Return Value

If the function succeeds and the coordinates of the rectangle identified by the lprc1 parameter are identical to the coordinates of the rectangle identified by the lprc2 parameter, it returns TRUE. If the function fails or the coordinates are not identical, it returns FALSE. To get extended error information, call the GetLastError function.

See Also

EqualRgn, IsRectEmpty, PtInRect

Example

Please see Listing 4-16 under OffsetRect.

EqualRgn   Windows.Pas

Syntax

```
EqualRgn(
p1: HRGN;            {a handle to the first region to compare}
p2: HRGN             {a handle to the second region to compare}
): BOOL;             {returns TRUE or FALSE}
```

Description

This function determines if the two regions are identical in size and shape and occupy the same coordinates.

Parameters

p1: A handle to a region to be compared.

p2: A handle to a region to be compared.

Return Value

If the two regions are identical in size and shape and reside at the same coordinates, the function returns TRUE; otherwise it returns FALSE. A return value of ERROR indicates that at least one of the specified region handles is invalid.

See Also

CreateEllipticRgn, CreateEllipticRgnIndirect, CreatePolygonRgn, CreatePolyPolygonRgn, CreateRectRgn, CreateRectRgnIndirect, CreateRoundRectRgn

Example

Listing 4-II: Comparing Two Regions

```
procedure TForm1.FormPaint(Sender: TObject);
var
  Region1, Region2: HRGN;  // holds the regions to be compared
begin
  {create an elliptical region}
  Region1 := CreateEllipticRgn(50, 50, 150, 150);

  {transform the region into a rectangular region. this function can be
   performed on any pre-existing region}
  SetRectRgn(Region1, 50, 50, 150, 150);

  {create a rectangular region identical to Region1}
  Region2 := CreateRectRgn(50, 50, 150, 150);

  {paint both regions red}
  Canvas.Brush.Color := clRed;
  PaintRgn(Canvas.Handle, Region1);
  PaintRgn(Canvas.Handle, Region2);

  {indicate if the regions are identical}
  if EqualRgn(Region1, Region2) then
    Label1.Caption := 'Regions Equal'
  else
    Label1.Caption := 'Regions Not Equal';

  {delete both regions as they are no longer needed}
  DeleteObject(Region1);
  DeleteObject(Region2);
end;
```

4

Chapter

ExcludeClipRect   Windows.Pas

Syntax

```
ExcludeClipRect(
DC: HDC;              {a handle to a device context}
p2: Integer;          {the upper left horizontal coordinate}
p3: Integer;          {the upper left vertical coordinate}
p4: Integer;          {the lower right horizontal coordinate}
p5: Integer           {the lower right vertical coordinate}
): Integer;           {returns the type of clipping region}
```

Description

This function excludes the rectangle defined by the given coordinates from the clipping region of the specified device context. The upper and left edges of the defined rectangle are excluded from the clipping region, but not the lower and right edges.

Parameters

DC: A handle to the device context containing the clipping region to be modified.

p2: Specifies the horizontal coordinate of the upper left corner of the rectangle, in logical units.

p3: Specifies the vertical coordinate of the upper left corner of the rectangle, in logical units.

p4: Specifies the horizontal coordinate of the lower right corner of the rectangle, in logical units.

p5: Specifies the vertical coordinate of the lower right corner of the rectangle, in logical units.

Return Value

This function returns a result indicating the type of region created or an error condition, and may be one value from Table 4-4.

See Also

OffsetClipRgn, SetRect, SetRectRgn

Example

Listing 4-12: Drawing a Foreground Image Only Once

```
{the record structure defining a moving dot}
TDot = record
  Pos: TPoint;
  Vel: TPoint;
end;

var
  Form1: TForm1;
  Dots: array[0..9] of TDot;   // the array of moving dots
  Offscreen: TBitmap;          // the offscreen double buffer

implementation

{$R *.DFM}

procedure TForm1.FormPaint(Sender: TObject);
begin
  {draw the foreground image.  this will be drawn only once}
  Canvas.Draw(Image2.Left, Image2.Top, Image2.Picture.Bitmap);
end;
```

```
procedure TForm1.FormCreate(Sender: TObject);
var
  iCount: Integer;    // a general loop control variable
begin
  {create and initialize the offscreen bitmap}
  OffScreen := TBitmap.Create;
  OffScreen.Width  := Form1.ClientWidth;
  OffScreen.Height := Form1.ClientHeight;

  {create and initialize the array of moving dots}
  for iCount := 0 to 9 do
  begin
    Dots[iCount].Pos.X := Random(ClientWidth);
    Dots[iCount].Pos.Y := Random(ClientHeight);
    if Random(2)=0 then Dots[iCount].Vel.X := -1 else Dots[iCount].Vel.X := 1;
    if Random(2)=0 then Dots[iCount].Vel.Y := -1 else Dots[iCount].Vel.Y := 1;
  end;
end;

procedure TForm1.FormDestroy(Sender: TObject);
begin
  {the offscreen bitmap is no longer needed, so free it}
  Offscreen.Free;
end;

procedure TForm1.Timer1Timer(Sender: TObject);
var
  iCount: Integer;        // a general loop counter
begin
  {erase the last frame of animation in the offscreen bitmap}
  Offscreen.Canvas.Brush.Color := clBlack;
  Offscreen.Canvas.FillRect(Offscreen.Canvas.ClipRect);

  {loop through all 10 moving dots}
  for iCount := 0 to 9 do
  begin
    {change the dot's position according to velocity}
    Dots[iCount].Pos.X := Dots[iCount].Pos.X+Dots[iCount].Vel.X;
    Dots[iCount].Pos.Y := Dots[iCount].Pos.Y+Dots[iCount].Vel.Y;

    {reverse the dot's velocity if it has reached the edge of the screen}
    if (Dots[iCount].Pos.X<0) or (Dots[iCount].Pos.X>ClientWidth) then
      Dots[iCount].Vel.X := 0-Dots[iCount].Vel.X;
    if (Dots[iCount].Pos.Y<0) or (Dots[iCount].Pos.Y>ClientHeight) then
      Dots[iCount].Vel.Y := 0-Dots[iCount].Vel.Y;

    {draw a red dot on the offscreen bitmap (2X2 pixels)}
    Offscreen.Canvas.Pixels[Dots[iCount].Pos.X,Dots[iCount].Pos.Y] := clRed;
    Offscreen.Canvas.Pixels[Dots[iCount].Pos.X+1,Dots[iCount].Pos.Y] := clRed;
    Offscreen.Canvas.Pixels[Dots[iCount].Pos.X,Dots[iCount].Pos.Y+1] := clRed;
    Offscreen.Canvas.Pixels[Dots[iCount].Pos.X+1,Dots[iCount].Pos.Y+1] := clRed;
  end;
```

{the bitmap stored in Image1 has already been drawn to the form. this happens
only once, when the Paint event fires, which happens only when the form is

4

Chapter

displayed the first time or after it has been uncovered by a top-level
window. since we don't want to destroy this "foreground" image, we exclude
its rectangular area from the clipping region. this will effectively cut a
hole in the clipping region, and any drawing attempted in this area will be
denied}
```
ExcludeClipRect(Canvas.Handle, Image2.Left, Image2.Top,
                Image2.Left+Image2.Width, Image2.Top+Image2.Height);

{draw the offscreen bitmap to the screen. the 'hole' in the clipping region
 prevents the bitmap from being drawn over the foreground bitmap}
Canvas.Draw(0, 0, Offscreen);
end;
```

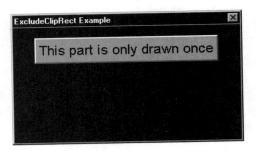

Figure 4-12:
The
foreground
image is
unaffected
during
continuous
animation

Table 4-4: ExcludeClipRect Return Values

Value	Description
NULLREGION	Indicates an empty region.
SIMPLEREGION	Indicates a single rectangular region.
COMPLEXREGION	Indicates a region consisting of more than one rectangle.
ERROR	Indicates an error occurred.

ExtCreateRegion *Windows.Pas*

Syntax

```
ExtCreateRegion(
p1: PXForm;          {a pointer to a TXForm structure}
p2: DWORD;           {the size of the region data structure}
const p3: TRgnData   {a pointer to a TRgnData structure}
): HRGN;             {returns a handle to a region}
```

Description

This function creates a new region by applying the transformation matrix identified by
the p1 parameter to the region data specified by the p3 parameter. Note that under Windows 95, shearing and rotation transformations are not supported and the function will

fail if the structure identified by the p1 parameter contains anything other than scaling or translation values.

Parameters

p1: A pointer to a TXForm structure containing a transformation matrix that is applied to the region identified by the p3 parameter. If this parameter is NIL, the region is not transformed in any way. Please see Table 4-5 describing how the members of this structure are used for various transformations. The TXForm data structure is defined as:

```
TXForm = packed record
      eM11: Single;           {rotation, scaling, or reflection value}
      eM12: Single;           {rotation or shearing value}
      eM21: Single;           {rotation or shearing value}
      eM22: Single;           {rotation, scaling, or reflection value}
      eDx: Single;            {the horizontal translation}
      eDy: Single;            {the vertical translation}
end;
```

eM11: Specifies the horizontal scaling value, the cosine of the rotation angle, or the horizontal reflection value.

eM12: Specifies the horizontal proportionality constant for shearing or the sine of the rotation angle.

eM21: Specifies the vertical proportionality constant for shearing or the negative sine of the rotation angle.

eM22: Specifies the vertical scaling value, the cosine of the rotation angle, or the vertical reflection value.

eDx: Specifies the horizontal translation value.

eDy: Specifies the vertical translation value.

p2: Specifies the size of the region data pointed to by the p3 parameter, in bytes.

p3: A pointer to a TRgnData structure containing information on the region to be transformed. This is a variable length data structure that must be initialized by a previous call to the GetRegionData function. The TRgnData structure is defined as:

```
TRgnData = record
      rdh: TRgnDataHeader;        {region data information}
      Buffer: array[0..0] of CHAR;   {an array of rectangles}
end;
```

rdh: Specifies a TRgnDataHeader structure containing information about the definition of the region. The TRgnDataHeader structure is defined as:

```
TRgnDataHeader = packed record
      dwSize: DWORD;        {the size of the structure}
      iType: DWORD;         {a region type flag}
      nCount: DWORD;        {the number of rectangles}
      nRgnSize: DWORD;      {the size of the rectangular coordinate buffer}
```

        rcBound: TRect;   {the bounding rectangle coordinates}

    end;

dwSize: Specifies the size of the TRgnDataHeader structure, in bytes. This member should be set to SizeOf(TRgnDataHeader).

iType: Specifies a flag indicating the type of region. Currently, this member can only contain the value RDH_RECTANGLES.

nCount: Specifies the number of rectangles defining the region.

nRgnSize: Specifies the size of buffer required to receive the coordinates of the rectangles defining the region. This is the size of the buffer identified by the Buffer member of the TRgnData structure.

rcBound: Specifies a TRect structure containing the coordinates of the bounding rectangle for the region, in logical units.

Buffer: Specifies a variable length buffer containing the coordinates that make up the rectangles defining the region.

Return Value

If the function succeeds, it returns a handle to the new, transformed region; otherwise it returns zero.

See Also

CreateEllipticRgn, CreateEllipticRgnIndirect, CreatePolygonRgn, CreatePolyPolygonRgn, CreateRectRgn, CreateRectRgnIndirect, CreateRoundRectRgn, GetRegionData

Example

Please see Listing 4-6 under CreatePolygonRgn.

Table 4-5: ExtCreateRegion pl Transformation Values

Transformation	*eM11 Value*	*eM12 Value*	*eM21 Value*	*eM22 Value*
Rotation	Cosine of the rotation angle	Sine of the rotation angle	Negative Sine of the rotation angle	Cosine of the rotation angle
Scaling	Horizontal scaling value	Zero	Zero	Vertical scaling value
Shearing	Zero	Horizontal proportionality value	Vertical proportionality value	Zero
Reflection	Horizontal reflection value	Zero	Zero	Vertical reflection value

ExtSelectClipRgn Windows.Pas

Syntax

```
ExtSelectClipRgn(
DC: HDC;                    {a handle to a device context}
p2: HRGN;                   {a handle to a region}
p3: Integer                 {region combination flags}
): Integer;                 {returns the type of the combined region}
```

Description

This function combines the clipping region of the device context identified by the DC parameter with the region identified by the p2 parameter according to the flag specified in the p3 parameter. The coordinates of the region identified by the p2 parameter are assumed to be in device units. This function uses a copy of the region identified by the p2 parameter; the original region is unaffected and can be used in other functions.

Parameters

DC: A handle to the device context containing the clipping region to be combined with the specified region.

p2: A handle to the region to be combined with the specified device context's clipping region.

p3: A flag indicating how the device context's clipping region and the specified region are to be combined. This parameter can contain one value from Table 4-6.

Return Value

This function returns a result indicating the type of region created or an error condition, and may be one value from Table 4-7. If an error occurs, the clipping region of the specified device context is unaffected.

See Also

GetClipBox, GetClipRgn, OffsetClipRgn, SelectClipPath, SelectClipRgn

Example

Please see Listing 4-15 under OffsetClipRgn.

Table 4-6: ExtSelectClipRgn p3 Values

Value	Description
RGN_AND	The resulting region is the intersection of the two specified regions.
RGN_COPY	The resulting region is a copy of the region identified by the p2 parameter. This functionality is identical to the SelectClipRgn function. If this flag is specified and the p2 parameter contains zero, the current clipping region is reset to the default clipping region for the specified device context.

4

Chapter

Value	Description
RGN_DIFF	The resulting region is the area of the region identified by the p2 parameter that is not in the area of the current clipping region.
RGN_OR	The resulting region is the union of the two specified regions.
RGN_XOR	The resulting region is the union of the two specified regions excluding any overlapping areas.

Table 4-7: ExtSelectClipRgn Return Values

Value	Description
NULLREGION	Indicates an empty region.
SIMPLEREGION	Indicates a single rectangular region.
COMPLEXREGION	Indicates a region consisting of more than one rectangle.
ERROR	Indicates an error occurred.

FlattenPath   Windows.Pas

Syntax

```
FlattenPath(
DC: HDC          {a handle to a device context}
): BOOL;         {returns TRUE or FALSE}
```

Description

This function converts any curves located in the path selected into the specified device context into a series of straight line segments.

Parameters

DC: A handle to the device context containing the path to be converted into line segments.

Return Value

If the function succeeds, it returns TRUE; otherwise it returns FALSE. To get extended error information, call the GetLastError function.

See Also

GetPath, PathToRegion, WidenPath

Example

Please see Listing 4-13 under GetPath.

GetClipBox   *Windows.Pas*

Syntax

GetClipBox(
DC: HDC;   {a handle to a device context}
var Rect: TRect   {a pointer to a TRect structure}
): Integer;   {returns the type of clipping region}

Description

This function retrieves the coordinates of the smallest rectangle that can be drawn around the currently visible area in the device context identified by the DC parameter.

Parameters

DC: A handle to the device context from which the visible area bounding rectangle is to be retrieved.

Rect: A pointer to a TRect structure that receives the coordinates of the smallest rectangle encompassing the visible area of the specified device context, in logical units.

Return Value

This function returns a result indicating the type of region created or an error condition, and may be one value from Table 4-8.

See Also

ExtSelectClipRgn, GetClipRgn, GetRgnBox, OffsetClipRgn, SelectClipPath, SelectClipRgn

Example

Please see Listing 4-4 under CombineRgn.

Table 4-8: GetClipBox Return Values

Value	Description
NULLREGION	Indicates an empty region.
SIMPLEREGION	Indicates a single rectangular region.
COMPLEXREGION	Indicates a region consisting of more than one rectangle.
ERROR	Indicates an error occurred.

GetClipRgn   *Windows.Pas*

Syntax

GetClipRgn(
DC: HDC;   {a handle to a device context}

4

Chapter

rgn: HRGN   {a handle to a pre-existing region}
): Integer;   {returns an error code}

Description

This function retrieves a handle to the application-defined clipping region set by the last call to the SelectClipRgn function. The region identified by the rgn parameter must be a pre-existing region.

Parameters

DC: Specifies a handle to the device context containing the application-defined clipping region to be retrieved.

rgn: Specifies a handle to a preexisting region. This handle will identify a copy of the application-defined clipping region when the function returns. Any changes to this copied region will not affect the actual clipping region.

Return Value

If the function succeeds and the device context does not contain a clipping region, it returns 0. If the function succeeds and the device context does contain a clipping region, it returns 1. If the function fails, it returns -1.

See Also

GetClipBox, GetRgnBox, SelectClipRgn

Example

Please see Listing 4-6 under CreatePolygonRgn.

GetPath   Windows.Pas

Syntax

GetPath(
DC: HDC;   {a handle to a device context}
var Points;   {a pointer to an array of TPoint structures}
var Types;   {a pointer to an array of bytes}
nSize: Integer   {the number of entries in the arrays}
): Integer;   {returns the number of points retrieved}

Description

This function retrieves the coordinates and vertex types of the line segment endpoints and bézier curve control points defining the path in the specified device context. The endpoints and control points of the path are stored in the array of TPoint structures pointed to by the Points parameter, and the vertex types are stored in the array of bytes pointed to by the Types parameter.

Parameters

DC: A handle to the device context containing the path from which points and vertex types are to be retrieved.

Points: A pointer to an application allocated array of TPoint structures that receives the endpoints of lines and control points of curves in the path. These coordinates are specified in logical units.

Types: A pointer to an application allocated array of bytes, where each entry receives a flag indicating the type of vertex retrieved. There will be one entry in this array corresponding to each entry in the array pointed to by the Points parameter. The value of entries in this array may be one value from Table 4-9.

nSize: Specifies the total number of entries in the arrays pointed to by the Points and Types parameters. If this parameter is set to zero, the function returns the total number of entries required to hold all points defining the path.

Return Value

If the function succeeds, it returns the total number of points retrieved from the path. If the function fails, the nSize parameter specifies an amount less than the actual number of points in the path, or there are not enough entries in the arrays pointed to by the Points and Types parameters, the function returns -1. To get extended error information, call the GetLastError function.

See Also

BeginPath, EndPath, FlattenPath, PathToRegion, WidenPath

Example

Listing 4-13: Retrieving the Points Defining a Flattened Curve

```
procedure TForm1.Button1Click(Sender: TObject);
type
  TPointsArray = array[0..0] of TPoint;   // array of TPoints storing vertices
  TTypesArray = array[0..0] of Byte;      // array of bytes storing vertex types
var
  CurvePts: array[0..3] of TPoint;        // array of points defining the curve
  Points: ^TPointsArray;                  // pointer to array of points
  Types: ^TTypesArray;                    // pointer to array of bytes
  PtCount: Integer;                       // the number of points in the path
  iCount: Integer;                        // general loop control variable
  FormDC: HDC;                            // a handle to the form's DC
  ThePen, OldPen: HPEN;                   // pen handles
  InfoString: String;                     // a string describing a point
begin
  {define points used to draw a bézier curve}
  CurvePts[0] := Point(30, 80);
  CurvePts[1] := Point(55, 30);
  CurvePts[2] := Point(105, 30);
  CurvePts[3] := Point(130, 80);
```

```
{retrieve a handle to the form's device context}
FormDC := GetDC(Form1.Handle);

{begin a path bracket}
BeginPath(FormDC);

{draw a bézier curve}
PolyBezier(FormDC, CurvePts, 4);

{end the path bracket}
EndPath(FormDC);

{convert the path into a series of line segments}
FlattenPath(FormDC);

{retrieve the number of points defining the path}
PtCount := GetPath(FormDC, Points^, Types^, 0);

{allocate enough memory to store the points and their type flags}
GetMem(Points, SizeOf(TPoint)*PtCount);
GetMem(Types, PtCount);

{retrieve the points and vertex types of the path}
GetPath(FormDC, Points^, Types^, PtCount);

{for each point in the path...}
for iCount := 0 to PtCount-1 do
begin
  {record the point's coordinates}
  InfoString := 'X: '+IntToStr(Points[iCount].X)+
                ' Y: '+IntToStr(Points[iCount].Y);

  {record the type of point}
  case (Types[iCount] and not PT_CLOSEFIGURE) of
    PT_MOVETO:   InfoString := InfoString+' Type: MoveTo';
    PT_LINETO:   InfoString := InfoString+' Type: LineTo';
    PT_BEZIERTO: InfoString := InfoString+' Type: BezierTo';
  end;

  {since the PT_CLOSEFIGURE flag can be combined with the other flags, check
   it separately and record if the figure in the path is closed}
  if (Types[iCount] and PT_CLOSEFIGURE)=PT_CLOSEFIGURE then
    InfoString := InfoString+', Close Figure';

  {display the information about this point in the path}
  ListBox1.Items.Add(InfoString);
end;

{create and select a pen into the device context}
ThePen := CreatePen(PS_SOLID, 1, clBlack);
OldPen := SelectObject(FormDC, ThePen);

{draw the path}
StrokePath(FormDC);
```

```
{the pen is no longer needed, so delete it}
SelectObject(FormDC, OldPen);
DeleteObject(ThePen);

{free the memory used to store the points and vertex types}
FreeMem(Points);
FreeMem(Types);
end;
```

*Figure 4-13:
The line
segment
endpoints of a
flattened
curve*

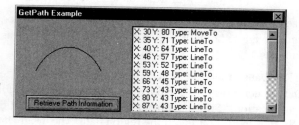

Table 4-9: GetPath Types Values

Value	Description
PT_MOVETO	The associated point begins a new figure.
PT_LINETO	The associated point and the previous point form a line segment.
PT_BEZIERTO	The associated point is a control point or endpoint for a bézier curve. The point preceding the first PT_BEZIERTO point is the starting point for the bézier curve. The following two PT_BEZIERTO points are the control points for the curve. These will be followed by another PT_BEZIERTO point identifying the endpoint of the bézier curve if one was specified.
PT_CLOSEFIGURE	This value may be combined with the PT_LINETO or PT_BEZIERTO flags using the Boolean OR operator, and signifies the last point in a closed figure.

GetRegionData   *Windows.Pas*

Syntax

```
GetRegionData(
RGN: HRGN;              {a handle of a region}
p2: DWORD;              {the size of the region data buffer}
p3: PRgnData            {a pointer to a TRgnData structure}
): DWORD;               {returns a 1 if successful}
```

Description

This function retrieves information about the region identified by the RGN parameter, primarily information concerning the rectangles that define the region. This information is stored in the variable length data structure pointed to by the p3 parameter.

Parameters

RGN: A handle to the region for which information is to be retrieved.

p2: Specifies the size of the data structure pointed to by the p3 parameter, in bytes. If this value is not large enough to hold the region data, the function returns the required size of the buffer, in bytes.

p3: A pointer to a TRgnData structure that receives information about the specified region. The TRgnData structure is a variable length structure, memory for which must be allocated by the application. If this parameter is set to NIL, the function returns the required size of the buffer, in bytes, to hold the region data. The TRgnData structure is defined as:

```
TRgnData = record
    rdh: TRgnDataHeader;            {region data information}
    Buffer: array[0..0] of CHAR;    {an array of rectangles}
end;
```

Please see the ExtCreateRegion function for a description of this data structure.

Return Value

If the function succeeds, it returns one; otherwise it returns zero.

See Also

ExtCreateRegion, GetClipRgn

Example

Please see Listing 4-6 under CreatePolygonRgn.

GetRgnBox   Windows.Pas

Syntax

```
GetRgnBox(
RGN: HRGN;              {a handle to a region}
var p2: TRect           {a pointer to a TRect structure}
): Integer;             {returns the type of region}
```

Description

This function retrieves the coordinates of the smallest rectangle that can be drawn around the specified region.

Parameters

RGN: A handle to the region for which a bounding rectangle is to be retrieved.

p2: A pointer to a TRect structure that receives the coordinates of the smallest rectangle encompassing the specified region, in logical units.

Return Value

This function returns a result indicating the type of region for which the bounding box was retrieved or an error condition, and may be one value from Table 4-10.

See Also

GetClipBox, GetClipRgn, GetRegionData

Example

Please see Listing 4-17 under OffsetRgn and Listing 4-18 under PathToRegion.

Table 4-10: GetRgnBox Return Values

Value	Description
NULLREGION	Indicates an empty region.
SIMPLEREGION	Indicates a single rectangular region.
COMPLEXREGION	Indicates a region consisting of more than one rectangle.
ERROR	Indicates an error occurred.

InflateRect   Windows.Pas

Syntax

```
InflateRect(
var lprc: TRect;        {a pointer to a TRect structure}
dx: Integer;            {the horizontal increase or decrease value}
dy: Integer;            {the vertical increase or decrease value}
): BOOL;                {returns TRUE or FALSE}
```

Description

This function modifies the size of the rectangle identified by the lprc parameter by adding the value in the dx parameter to the rectangle's left and right sides and the value in the dy parameter to the rectangle's top and bottom sides.

Parameters

lprc: A pointer to a TRect structure containing the rectangle to be increased or decreased in size.

dx: Specifies the amount by which to increase or decrease the width of the rectangle. A positive value increases the width; a negative value decreases it.

4

Chapter

dy: Specifies the amount by which to increase or decrease the height of the rectangle. A positive value increases the height; a negative value decreases it.

Return Value

If the function succeeds, it returns TRUE; otherwise it returns FALSE. To get extended error information, call the GetLastError function.

See Also

CopyRect, IntersectRect, OffsetRect, PtInRect, SetRect, UnionRect

Example

Please see Listing 4-16 under OffsetRect.

IntersectRect   Windows.Pas

Syntax

```
IntersectRect(
var lprcDst: TRect;          {the rectangle receiving the intersection coordinates}
const lprcSrc1: TRect;       {the first rectangle}
const lprcSrc2: TRect        {the second rectangle}
): BOOL;                     {returns TRUE or FALSE}
```

Description

This function determines the intersection between the rectangles identified by the lprcSrc1 and lprcSrc2 parameters. The coordinates of the intersection rectangle are stored in the TRect structure pointed to by the lprcDst parameter. If there is no intersection, the coordinates of the lprcDst rectangle will all be set to zero.

Parameters

lprcDst: A pointer to a TRect structure that receives the coordinates of the intersection between the rectangles identified by the lprcSrc1 and lprcSrc2 parameters.

lprcSrc1: A pointer to a TRect structure containing the coordinates of the first rectangle.

lprcSrc2: A pointer to a TRect structure containing the coordinates of the second rectangle.

Return Value

If the function succeeds and the rectangles intersect, it returns TRUE. If the function fails or the rectangles do not intersect, it returns FALSE. To get extended error information, call the GetLastError function.

See Also

InflateRect, OffsetRect, PtInRect, SetRect, UnionRect

Example

Please see Listing 4-16 under OffsetRect.

InvertRect   *Windows.Pas*

Syntax

```
InvertRect(
hDC: HDC;                {a handle to a device context}
const lprc: TRect        {a pointer to a TRect structure}
): BOOL;                 {returns TRUE or FALSE}
```

Description

This function performs a Boolean NOT operation on the color value of every pixel in the specified device context that falls within the rectangular area defined by the rectangle pointed to by the lprc parameter.

Parameters

hDC: A handle to the device context containing the color pixels to be inverted.

lprc: A pointer to a TRect structure containing the coordinates of the rectangular area to invert, in logical units.

Return Value

If the function succeeds, it returns TRUE; otherwise it returns FALSE. To get extended error information, call the GetLastError function.

See Also

FillRect, InvertRgn, SetRect

Example

Listing 4-14: Inverting a Rectangular Portion of an Image

```
procedure TForm1.Button1Click(Sender: TObject);
var
  TheRect: TRect;      // holds the rectangular coordinates
begin
  {create a rectangle}
  SetRect(TheRect, 46, 40, 106, 100);

  {invert the pixels inside the rectangle}
  InvertRect(Image1.Canvas.Handle, TheRect);

  {repaint the new image}
  Image1.Refresh;
end;
```

Chapter 4

Figure 4-14:
The inverted
rectangular
area

InvertRgn   *Windows.Pas*

Syntax

```
InvertRgn(
DC: HDC;              {a handle to a device context}
p2: HRGN             {a handle to a region}
): BOOL;             {returns TRUE or FALSE}
```

Description

This function performs a Boolean NOT operation on the color value of every pixel in the specified device context that falls within the region identified by the p2 parameter.

Parameters

DC: A handle to the device context containing the color pixels to be inverted.

p2: A handle to the region defining the area to invert. The coordinates of this region are assumed to be in logical units.

Return Value

If the function succeeds, it returns TRUE; otherwise it returns FALSE.

See Also

FillRgn, InvertRect, PaintRgn

Example

Please see Listing 4-7 under CreatePolyPolygonRgn.

IsRectEmpty   *Windows.Pas*

Syntax

```
IsRectEmpty(
const lprc: TRect    {a pointer to a TRect structure}
): BOOL;             {returns TRUE or FALSE}
```

Description

This function determines if the specified rectangle is empty. A rectangle is considered empty if its bottom side is less than or equal to its top side or its right side is less than or equal to its left side.

Parameters

lprc: A pointer to the TRect structure to be tested. The coordinates of this rectangle are in logical units.

Return Value

If the function succeeds and the rectangle is empty, it returns TRUE. If the function fails or the rectangle is not empty, it returns FALSE. To get extended error information, call the GetLastError function.

See Also

EqualRect, PtInRect, SetRect, SetRectEmpty, SetRectRgn

Example

Please see Listing 4-21 under SetRectEmpty.

OffsetClipRgn   Windows.Pas

Syntax

```
OffsetClipRgn(
DC: HDC;              {a handle to a device context}
p2: Integer;         {the horizontal offset}
p3: Integer          {the vertical offset}
): Integer;          {returns the type of region}
```

Description

This function moves the clipping region of the specified device context by the horizontal and vertical amounts identified by the p2 and p3 parameters.

Parameters

DC: A handle to the device context containing the clipping region to move.

p2: Specifies the horizontal offset by which to move the clipping region, in logical units.

p3: Specifies the vertical offset by which to move the clipping region, in logical units.

Return Value

This function returns a result indicating the type of clipping region resulting from the movement or an error condition, and may be one value from Table 4-11.

4

Chapter

See Also

OffsetRgn, SelectClipRgn

Example

Listing 4-15: Performing Special Animation Effects By Moving the Clipping Region

```
var
  Form1: TForm1;
  MovingRgn: HRGN;               // holds a region
  XPos, YPos, XVel, YVel: Integer;  // holds the region's velocity and position

implementation

{$R *.DFM}

procedure TForm1.FormCreate(Sender: TObject);
begin
  {create a small circular region to be used as the clipping region}
  MovingRgn := CreateEllipticRgn(0, 0, 75, 75);

  {initialize the region's position and velocity}
  XPos := 1;
  YPos := 1;
  XVel := 1;
  YVel := 1;
end;

procedure TForm1.Timer1Timer(Sender: TObject);
var
  TempBitmap: TBitmap;    // holds an offscreen bitmap
begin
  {create the offscreen bitmap and initialize its size to that of the
   invisible TImage. this offscreen bitmap is used to eliminate flicker}
  TempBitmap := TBitmap.Create;
  TempBitmap.Width := Image1.Width;
  TempBitmap.Height := Image1.Height;

  {increase the region's position by its velocity}
  Inc(XPos, XVel);
  Inc(YPos, YVel);

  {if the region has reached the edge of the screen, reverse its velocity}
  if (XPos<0) or (XPos>ClientRect.Right-75) then
    XVel := 0-XVel;
  if (YPos<0) or (YPos>ClientRect.Bottom-75) then
    YVel := 0-YVel;

  {select the circular region into the device context of the offscreen bitmap,
   indicating that it should be logically ANDed with the bitmap's current
   clipping region}
  ExtSelectClipRgn(TempBitmap.Canvas.Handle, MovingRgn, RGN_AND);

  {move the clipping region to the position being tracked}
```

```
OffsetClipRgn(TempBitmap.Canvas.Handle, XPos, YPos);

{draw the picture stored in Image1 into the bitmap. the clipping region will
  only allow the bitmap to be drawn within the small circular area of the
  region}
TempBitmap.Canvas.Draw(0, 0, Image1.Picture.Bitmap);

{draw the offscreen bitmap to the form. this will result in an animation of
  a small, bouncing circle}
Canvas.Draw(Image1.Left, Image1.Top, TempBitmap);

{free the offscreen bitmap}
TempBitmap.Free;
end;

procedure TForm1.FormDestroy(Sender: TObject);
begin
  {we no longer need the region, so delete it}
  DeleteObject(MovingRgn);
end;
```

Figure 4-15:
The offset
clipping region

Table 4-11: OffsetClipRgn Return Values

Value	Description
NULLREGION	Indicates an empty region.
SIMPLEREGION	Indicates a single rectangular region.
COMPLEXREGION	Indicates a region consisting of more than one rectangle.
ERROR	Indicates an error occurred.

OffsetRect Windows.Pas

Syntax

```
OffsetRect(
var lprc: TRect;        {a pointer to a TRect structure}
dx: Integer;            {the horizontal offset}
```

dy: Integer   {the vertical offset}
): BOOL;   {returns TRUE or FALSE}

Description

This function moves the specified rectangle by the horizontal and vertical amounts specified by the dx and dy parameters.

Parameters

lprc: A pointer to a TRect structure containing the rectangular coordinates to be moved, in logical units.

dx: Specifies the horizontal offset by which to move the rectangle, in logical units.

dy: Specifies the vertical offset by which to move the rectangle, in logical units.

Return Value

If the function succeeds, it returns TRUE; otherwise it returns FALSE. To get extended error information, call the GetLastError function.

See Also

CopyRect, InflateRect, IntersectRect, OffsetRgn, SubtractRect, UnionRect

Example

Listing 4-16: A Demonstration of Various Rectangle Manipulation Functions

```
var
  Form1: TForm1;
  Rect1, Rect2: TRect;                  // the two test rectangles
  DragRect: PRect;                      // points to the rectangle being dragged
  DraggingRect: Boolean;                // indicates if a drag is occurring
  MouseOffsetX, MouseOffsetY: Integer;  // used to offset the dragged rectangle

implementation

{$R *.DFM}

procedure TForm1.FormCreate(Sender: TObject);
begin
  {initialize the two test rectangles}
  SetRect(Rect1, 10, 30, 110, 130);
  SetRect(Rect2, 60, 80, 160, 180);

  {initialize the drag flag to indicate that dragging is not occurring}
  DraggingRect := FALSE;
end;

procedure TForm1.FormPaint(Sender: TObject);
var
  Intersection, Union: TRect;  // shows the union and intersection
begin
  {retrieve the union of the two test rectangles}
```

```
    UnionRect(Union, Rect1, Rect2);

    {draw this union rectangle in green}
    Form1.Canvas.Brush.Color := clGreen;
    Form1.Canvas.FillRect(Union);

    {draw the two test rectangles in red}
    Form1.Canvas.Brush.Color := clRed;
    Form1.Canvas.FillRect(Rect1);
    Form1.Canvas.FillRect(Rect2);

    {retrieve the intersection of the two test rectangles}
    IntersectRect(Intersection, Rect1, Rect2);

    {draw this intersection in blue}
    Form1.Canvas.Brush.Color := clBlue;
    Form1.Canvas.FillRect(Intersection);

    {indicate if the two rectangles are at exactly the same coordinates}
    if EqualRect(Rect1, Rect2) then
      Form1.Caption := 'OffsetRectExample - Rectangles are equal'
    else
      Form1.Caption := 'OffsetRectExample - Rectangles are not equal';
end;

procedure TForm1.FormMouseDown(Sender: TObject; Button: TMouseButton;
  Shift: TShiftState; X, Y: Integer);
begin
  {if the mouse was clicked inside of the first rectangle...}
  if PtInRect(Rect1, Point(X, Y)) then
  begin
    {indicate that dragging has commenced}
    DraggingRect := TRUE;

    {indicate that we are dragging rectangle 1}
    DragRect := @Rect1;
  end;

  {if the mouse was clicked inside of the second rectangle...}
  if PtInRect(Rect2, Point(X, Y)) then
  begin
    {indicate that dragging has commenced}
    DraggingRect := TRUE;

    {indicate that we are dragging rectangle 2}
    DragRect := @Rect2;
  end;

  {if a dragging operation has started...}
  if DraggingRect then
  begin
    {retrieve the offset of the current mouse coordinate within the
     dragged rectangle.  this is used when moving the rectangle so that the
     original spot where the mouse was clicked inside of the rectangle is
     preserved.  otherwise, when the rectangle is moved the upper left-hand
```

4

Chapter

```
                        corner of the rectangle will be positioned at the mouse cursor position.}
          MouseOffsetX := X-DragRect^.Left;
          MouseOffsetY := Y-DragRect^.Top;
     end;
end;

procedure TForm1.FormMouseMove(Sender: TObject; Shift: TShiftState; X,
  Y: Integer);
begin
  {if a dragging operation is occurring...}
  if DraggingRect then
  begin
    {erase the form}
    Form1.Canvas.Brush.Color := clBtnFace;
    Form1.Canvas.FillRect(DragRect^);

    {move the dragged rectangle, offsetting it from the current mouse position
     so that the original clicked location within the rectangle is preserved}
    OffsetRect(DragRect^, X-DragRect^.Left-MouseOffsetX,
              Y-DragRect^.Top-MouseOffsetY);

    {repaint the form}
    Form1.Repaint;
  end;
end;

procedure TForm1.FormMouseUp(Sender: TObject; Button: TMouseButton;
  Shift: TShiftState; X, Y: Integer);
begin
  {indicate that dragging has stopped}
  DraggingRect := FALSE;
end;

procedure TForm1.SpeedButton1Click(Sender: TObject);
begin
  {increase or decrease the size of the last dragged rectangle. the amount by
   which to increase or decrease the size is stored in the Tag property of
   the speed buttons on the toolbar}
  if DragRect<>NIL then
    InflateRect(DragRect^, TSpeedButton(Sender).Tag, TSpeedButton(Sender).Tag);

  {repaint the form to show the results}
  Form1.Repaint;
end;

procedure TForm1.Button1Click(Sender: TObject);
begin
  {force rectangle 2 to become an exact duplicate of rectangle 1}
  CopyRect(Rect2, Rect1);

  {repaint the form to show the results}
  Form1.Repaint;
end;
```

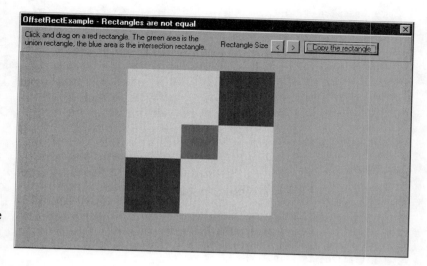

Figure 4-16:
The Rectangle
function test
bed

OffsetRgn   Windows.Pas

Syntax

```
OffsetRgn(
RGN: HRGN;          {a handle to a region}
p2: Integer;        {the horizontal offset}
p3: Integer         {the vertical offset}
): Integer;         {returns the type of region}
```

Description

This function moves the specified region by the horizontal and vertical amounts specified by the p2 and p3 parameters.

Parameters

RGN: A handle to the region to be moved.

p2: Specifies the horizontal offset by which to move the region, in logical units.

p3: Specifies the vertical offset by which to move the region, in logical units.

Return Value

This function returns a result indicating the type of region resulting from the movement or an error condition, and may be one value from Table 4-12.

See Also

EqualRgn, OffsetClipRgn, OffsetRect

4

Chapter

Example

Listing 4-17: Moving a Region to Produce Special Animation Effects

```
var
  Form1: TForm1;
  MovingRgn: HRGN;        // a handle to the moving region
  XVel, YVel: Integer;    // the region's velocity

implementation

{$R *.DFM}

procedure TForm1.FormCreate(Sender: TObject);
begin
  {create an elliptical region}
  MovingRgn := CreateEllipticRgn(0, 0, 75, 75);

  {initialize its velocity}
  XVel := 1;
  YVel := 1;
end;

procedure TForm1.FormPaint(Sender: TObject);
begin
  {select the circular region as a clipping region for the form}
  SelectClipRgn(Canvas.Handle, MovingRgn);

  {draw the image in the invisible TImage onto the form. the circular
   clipping region prevents any drawing outside of the circular region}
  Canvas.Draw(Image1.Left, Image1.Top, Image1.Picture.Bitmap);
end;

procedure TForm1.Timer1Timer(Sender: TObject);
var
  RegionBounds: TRect;    // holds the bounding rectangle of the region
begin
  {retrieve the smallest rectangle that can be drawn around the circular region}
  GetRgnBox(MovingRgn, RegionBounds);

  {the bounding rectangle is used to determine if the circular region has
   reached the edges of the screen. if so, reverse the velocity}
  if (RegionBounds.Left<0) or (RegionBounds.Left>ClientRect.Right-75) then
    XVel := 0-XVel;
  if (RegionBounds.Top<0) or (RegionBounds.Top>ClientRect.Bottom-75) then
    YVel := 0-YVel;

  {move the region by its current velocity}
  OffsetRgn(MovingRgn, XVel, YVel);

  {repaint the form to show the results}
  Repaint;
end;

procedure TForm1.FormDestroy(Sender: TObject);
```

```
begin
  {the region is no longer needed, so destroy it}
  DeleteObject(MovingRgn);
end;
```

Figure 4-17:
The moving
region

Table 4-12: OffsetRgn Return Values

Value	Description
NULLREGION	Indicates an empty region.
SIMPLEREGION	Indicates a single rectangular region.
COMPLEXREGION	Indicates a region consisting of more than one rectangle.
ERROR	Indicates an error occurred.

PathToRegion   *Windows.Pas*

Syntax

```
PathToRegion(
  DC: HDC                {a handle to a device context}
): HRGN;                 {returns a handle to a region}
```

Description

This function converts the path in the specified device context into a region. The path must be closed, and it is discarded from the device context when the function returns. When the region is no longer needed, it should be deleted by calling the DeleteObject function.

Parameters

DC: A handle to the device context containing the closed path to be converted into a region.

Return Value

If the function succeeds, it returns a handle to a new region; otherwise it returns zero. To get extended error information, call the GetLastError function.

4

Chapter

See Also

BeginPath, EndPath, GetPath

Example

Listing 4-18: Converting a Path Into a Region

```
var
  Form1: TForm1;
  TextRgn: HRGN;        // holds the text region
  YVel: Integer;        // the region's vertical velocity
  TempBitmap: TBitmap;  // an offscreen bitmap used to eliminate flicker

implementation

{$R *.DFM}

procedure TForm1.FormCreate(Sender: TObject);
begin
  {begin a path bracket for the form's device context}
  BeginPath(Canvas.Handle);

  {set the background mode to transparent. this is necessary so that the path
   will consist of the area inside of the text. without this, the path is
   defined as the area outside of the text}
  SetBkMode(Canvas.Handle, TRANSPARENT);

  {Output a word to the form. this is captured as part of the path. note that
   the form's font is set to size 48 Arial}
  TextOut(Canvas.Handle, 1, 1, 'DELPHI', Length('DELPHI'));

  {end the path bracket}
  EndPath(Canvas.Handle);

  {convert the path into a region. note that this discards the path in the
   device context}
  TextRgn := PathToRegion(Canvas.Handle);

  {create the offscreen bitmap and initialize it to the size of the
   invisible TImage}
  TempBitmap := TBitmap.Create;
  TempBitmap.Width := Image1.Width;
  TempBitmap.Height := Image1.Height;

  {initialize the vertical velocity}
  YVel := 1;
end;

procedure TForm1.Timer1Timer(Sender: TObject);
var
  RegionBounds: TRect;    // holds the bounding rectangle of the region
begin
  {retrieve the bounding rectangle of the region}
```

```
        GetRgnBox(TextRgn, RegionBounds);

        {if the region is at the top or bottom edge of the form, reverse its velocity}
        if (RegionBounds.Top<0) or (RegionBounds.Top>ClientRect.Bottom-
                                    (RegionBounds.Bottom-RegionBounds.Top)) then
          YVel := 0-YVel;

        {offset the region vertically by its velocity}
        OffsetRgn(TextRgn, 0, YVel);

        {draw the graphic in the invisible TImage to the offscreen bitmap}
        TempBitmap.Canvas.Draw(0, 0, Image1.Picture.Bitmap);

        {invert the area inside of the text region}
        InvertRgn(TempBitmap.Canvas.Handle, TextRgn);

        {copy the offscreen bitmap to the form, eliminating flicker}
        Canvas.Draw(0, 0, TempBitmap);
      end;

      procedure TForm1.FormDestroy(Sender: TObject);
      begin
        {the region is no longer needed, so destroy it}
        DeleteObject(TextRgn);
      end;
```

Figure 4-18:
The converted
path

PtInRect   Windows.Pas

Syntax

PtInRect(

const lprc: TRect;   {a pointer to a TRect structure}

pt: TPoint   {a pointer to a TPoint structure}

): BOOL;   {returns TRUE or FALSE}

Description

This function determines if the point identified by the pt parameter lies inside of the rectangle pointed to by the lprc parameter. The point is considered to be outside of the rectangle if it lies exactly on the bottom or right edges of the rectangle.

Parameters

lprc: A pointer to a TRect structure containing the coordinates within which the point is to be tested.

pt: A pointer to a TPoint structure containing the point to be tested.

Return Value

If the function succeeds and the point lies within the rectangle, it returns TRUE. If the function fails or the point is not located within the rectangle, it returns FALSE. To get extended error information, call the GetLastError function.

See Also

EqualRect, IsRectEmpty, PtInRegion, PtVisible, RectInRegion, SetRect

Example

Please see Listing 4-16 under OffsetRect.

PtInRegion   **Windows.Pas**

Syntax

```
PtInRegion(
RGN: HRGN;          {a handle to a region}
p2: Integer;        {a horizontal coordinate}
p3: Integer         {a vertical coordinate}
): BOOL;            {returns TRUE or FALSE}
```

Description

This function determines if the point identified by the p2 and p3 parameters lies inside of the region specified by the RGN parameter.

Parameters

RGN: A handle to the region within which the point is to be tested.

p2: Specifies the horizontal coordinate of the point to test.

p3: Specifies the vertical coordinate of the point to test.

Return Value

If the function succeeds and the point lies within the region, it returns TRUE. If the function fails or the point is not located within the region, it returns FALSE.

See Also

PtInRect, PtVisible, RectInRegion

Example

Please see Listing 4-7 under CreatePolyPolygonRgn.

PtVisible   Windows.Pas

Syntax

PtVisible(
DC: HDC;   {a handle to a device context}
p2: Integer;   {a horizontal coordinate}
p3: Integer   {a vertical coordinate}
): BOOL;   {returns TRUE or FALSE}

Description

This function determines if the point identified by the p2 and p3 parameters lies inside of the clipping region of the specified device context.

Parameters

DC: A handle to the device context containing the clipping region within which the point is to be tested.

p2: Specifies the horizontal coordinate of the point to test.

p3: Specifies the vertical coordinate of the point to test.

Return Value

If the function succeeds and the point lies within the clipping region, it returns TRUE. If the function fails or the point is not located within the clipping region, it returns FALSE.

See Also

PtInRect, PtInRegion, RectInRegion, RectVisible

Example

Please see Listing 4-6 under CreatePolygonRgn.

RectInRegion   Windows.Pas

Syntax

RectInRegion(
RGN: HRGN;   {a handle to a region}
const p2: TRect   {a pointer to a TRect structure}
): BOOL;   {returns TRUE or FALSE}

Description

This function determines if any portion of the rectangle pointed to by the p2 parameter lies within the region identified by the RGN parameter. Note that the bottom and right sides of the rectangle are excluded from the comparison.

4

Chapter

Parameters

RGN: A handle to the region within which the rectangle is tested.

p2:A pointer to a TRect structure containing the rectangular coordinates to test.

Return Value

If the function succeeds and some portion of the rectangle lies within the region, it returns TRUE. If the function fails, or no part of the rectangle lies within the region, it returns FALSE.

See Also

PtInRect, PtInRegion, PtVisible, RectVisible, SelectClipRegion

Example

Please see Listing 4-20 under SelectClipRgn.

RectVisible   *Windows.Pas*

Syntax

```
RectVisible(
DC: HDC;                    {a handle to a device context}
const Rect: TRect          {a pointer to a TRect structure}
): BOOL;                    {returns TRUE or FALSE}
```

Description

This function determines if any portion of the rectangle pointed to by the Rect parameter lies within the clipping region of the device context identified by the DC parameter.

Parameters

DC: A handle to the device context containing the clipping region within which the rectangle is tested.

Rect: A pointer to a TRect structure containing the rectangular coordinates to test.

Return Value

If the function succeeds and some portion of the rectangle lies within the clipping region, it returns TRUE. If the function fails or no part of the rectangle lies within the clipping region, it returns FALSE.

See Also

GetClipRgn, PtInRegion, PtVisible, RectInRegion, SelectClipRgn

Example

Please see Listing 4-20 under SelectClipRgn.

SelectClipPath   *Windows.Pas*

Syntax

```
SelectClipPath(
DC: HDC;                    {a handle to a device context}
Mode: Integer              {region combination flag}
): BOOL;                    {returns TRUE or FALSE}
```

Description

This function selects the current path in the specified device context as the device context's clipping region, combining it with the current clipping region according to the flag specified in the Mode parameter.

Parameters

DC: A handle to the device context containing the path to be used as a clipping region. This must be a closed path.

Mode: A flag indicating how the clipping region formed from the path is to be combined with the device context's current clipping region. This parameter can contain one value from Table 4-13.

Return Value

If the function succeeds, it returns TRUE; otherwise it returns FALSE. To get extended error information, call the GetLastError function.

See Also

BeginPath, EndPath, PathToRegion, SelectClipRgn

Example

Listing 4-19: Creating Special Text Effects

```
var
  Form1: TForm1;
  ThePalette: HPalette;    // a handle to the application-defined palette

implementation

{$R *.DFM}

procedure TForm1.FormCreate(Sender: TObject);
var
  NewPalette: PLogPalette;    // a pointer to logical palette information
  iCount: Integer;            // a general loop counter
begin
  {initialize the form's font}
  Font.Name := 'Arial';
  Font.Size := 48;
```

```
    {retrieve enough memory to create a 75-entry palette}
    GetMem(NewPalette, SizeOf(TLogPalette)+75*SizeOf(TPaletteEntry));

    {initialize specific palette information}
    NewPalette^.palVersion := $300;
    NewPalette^.palNumEntries := 75;

    {retrieve the first 10 system palette entries}
    GetSystemPaletteEntries(Form1.Canvas.Handle, 0, 10, NewPalette^.palPalEntry);

    {create a gradient palette for the remaining entries}
    for iCount := 10 to 74 do
    begin
      NewPalette^.palPalEntry[iCount].peRed   := 255;
      NewPalette^.palPalEntry[iCount].peGreen := ((256 div 64)*(iCount-10));
      NewPalette^.palPalEntry[iCount].peBlue  := 0;
      NewPalette^.palPalEntry[iCount].peFlags := PC_NOCOLLAPSE;
    end;

    {create a new palette}
    ThePalette := CreatePalette(NewPalette^);

    {free the memory allocated for the logical palette information}
    FreeMem(NewPalette);
end;

{this draws gradient, radial lines originating from the center of the text}
procedure TForm1.DrawRadial;
var
  iCount: Integer;         // a general loop counter variable
  RayOrigin: TPoint;       // the origin of the radial lines
  Radius: Integer;         // the radius within which to draw the lines
  NewPen, OldPen: HPen;    // holds a new and old pen
begin
  {begin a path bracket within the form's device context}
  BeginPath(Canvas.Handle);

  {set the background mode to transparent. this is necessary so that the path
   will consist of the area inside of the text. without this, the path is
   defined as the area outside of the text}
  SetBkMode(Canvas.Handle, TRANSPARENT);

  {output a word onto the form. this is captured as part of the path}
  TextOut(Canvas.Handle, 50, 50, 'Delphi Rocks!', Length('Delphi Rocks!'));

  {end the path bracket}
  EndPath(Canvas.Handle);

  {select this path as a clipping region for the form's device context}
  SelectClipPath(Canvas.Handle, RGN_COPY);

  {the radial lines should originate from the center of the text}
  RayOrigin.X := (Canvas.TextWidth('Delphi Rocks!') div 2)+50;
  RayOrigin.Y := (Canvas.TextHeight('Delphi Rocks!') div 2)+50;
```

```
{the radius of the circle within which the lines are drawn will be
  equal to the length of the text}
Radius := Canvas.TextWidth('Delphi Rocks!');

{draw lines in a 90 degree arc}
for iCount := 0 to 89 do
begin
  {create a new pen, specifying a color from the new palette}
  NewPen := CreatePen(PS_SOLID, 1, PaletteIndex(75-Trunc(iCount*(64/90)+10)));

  {select this pen into the device context}
  OldPen := SelectObject(Canvas.Handle, NewPen);

  {draw a line starting at the center of the text. these lines will radiate
   outwards in a circular fashion. the following code draws a line in the
   first quadrant of a circular area within the text, and then reflects that
   line to the other 3 quadrants}
  MoveToEx(Canvas.Handle, RayOrigin.X, RayOrigin.Y, NIL);
  LineTo(Canvas.Handle, RayOrigin.X+Trunc(Radius*cos(iCount/(180/PI))),
         RayOrigin.Y+Trunc(Radius*sin(iCount/(180/PI))));
  MoveToEx(Canvas.Handle, RayOrigin.X, RayOrigin.Y, NIL);
  LineTo(Canvas.Handle, RayOrigin.X+Trunc(Radius*cos(iCount/(180/PI))),
         RayOrigin.Y-Trunc(Radius*sin(iCount/(180/PI))));
  MoveToEx(Canvas.Handle, RayOrigin.X, RayOrigin.Y, NIL);
  LineTo(Canvas.Handle, RayOrigin.X-Trunc(Radius*cos(iCount/(180/PI))),
         RayOrigin.Y-Trunc(Radius*sin(iCount/(180/PI))));
  MoveToEx(Canvas.Handle, RayOrigin.X, RayOrigin.Y, NIL);
  LineTo(Canvas.Handle, RayOrigin.X-Trunc(Radius*cos(iCount/(180/PI))),
         RayOrigin.Y+Trunc(Radius*sin(iCount/(180/PI))));

  {delete the new pen}
  SelectObject(Canvas.Handle, OldPen);
  DeleteObject(NewPen);
end;
end;

{this function draws gradient filled text}
procedure TForm1.DrawGradient;
var
  iCount: Integer;               // a general loop counter
  TempRect: TRect;               // holds a temporary rectangle
  NewBrush, OldBrush: HBrush;    // holds an old and new brush
begin
  {begin a path bracket within the form's device context}
  BeginPath(Canvas.Handle);

  {set the background mode to transparent. this is necessary so that the path
   will consist of the area inside of the text. without this, the path is
   defined as the area outside of the text}
  SetBkMode(Canvas.Handle, TRANSPARENT);

  {output a word onto the form. this is captured as part of the path}
  TextOut(Canvas.Handle, 50, 150, 'Delphi Rocks!', Length('Delphi Rocks!'));

  {end the path bracket}
```

```
    EndPath(Canvas.Handle);

    {select this path as a clipping region for the form's device context}
    SelectClipPath(Canvas.Handle, RGN_COPY);

    {draw a series of rectangles within the text, resulting in a gradient fill}
    for iCount := 0 to 64 do
    begin
      {create a new brush, specifying a color from the new palette}
      NewBrush := CreateSolidBrush(PaletteIndex(iCount+10));

      {select the brush into the device context}
      OldBrush := SelectObject(Form1.Canvas.Handle, NewBrush);

      {create a rectangle, incremented from the left side of the text}
      TempRect := Rect(Trunc(50+iCount*Canvas.TextWidth('Delphi Rocks!')/64), 150,
                  Trunc(50+(iCount*Canvas.TextWidth('Delphi Rocks!')/64)+
                  (Canvas.TextWidth('Delphi Rocks!')/64)),
                  150+Canvas.TextHeight('Delphi Rocks!'));

      {fill the rectangle with the brush. the final product will be the illusion
       of gradient filled text}
      FillRect(Canvas.Handle, TempRect, NewBrush);

      {delete the new brush}
      SelectObject(Form1.Canvas.Handle, OldBrush);
      DeleteObject(NewBrush);
    end;
end;

procedure TForm1.FormPaint(Sender: TObject);
begin
  {select and realize the new palette into the form's device context}
  SelectPalette(Form1.Canvas.Handle, ThePalette, FALSE);
  RealizePalette(Form1.Canvas.Handle);

  {draw radially filled text}
  DrawRadial;

  {draw gradient filled text}
  DrawGradient;
end;

procedure TForm1.FormDestroy(Sender: TObject);
begin
  {the palette is no longer needed, so delete it}
  DeleteObject(ThePalette);
end;
```

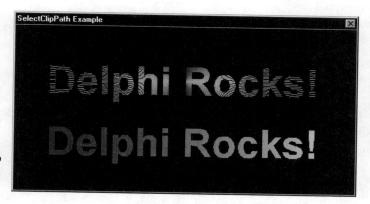

*Figure 4-19:
Using paths to
create special
text effects*

Table 4-13: SelectClipPath Mode Values

Value	Description
RGN_AND	The resulting region is the intersection of the current clipping region and the path.
RGN_COPY	The resulting region is the path.
RGN_DIFF	The resulting region is the area of the current clipping region that is not in the area of the path.
RGN_OR	The resulting region is the union of the current clipping region and the path.
RGN_XOR	The resulting region is the union of the current clipping region and the path excluding any overlapping areas.

SelectClipRgn   Windows.Pas

Syntax

```
SelectClipRgn(
DC: HDC;              {a handle to a device context}
p2: HRGN              {a handle to a region}
): Integer;           {returns the type of region}
```

Description

This function selects the region identified by the p2 parameter as the clipping region for the specified device context.

Parameters

DC: A handle to the device context whose clipping region is to be set.

p2: A handle to the region to be selected as the specified device context's clipping region. This function uses a copy of the region; the original region is unaffected and can be used in other functions. The coordinates of the region are assumed to be in

4

Chapter

device units. If this parameter is set to zero, the device context's current clipping region is removed.

Return Value

This function returns a result indicating the type of clipping region set or an error condition, and may be one value from Table 4-14.

See Also

ExtSelectClipRgn, GetClipRgn, OffsetClipRgn, SelectClipPath

Example

Listing 4-20: Clipping Drawing to a Defined Region

```
var
  Form1: TForm1;
  ClippingRegion: HRGN;        // a handle to the clipping region
  DraggingRect: Boolean;       // indicates that a drag operation is occurring
  TheRect: TRect;              // the dragged rectangle
  MouseOffsetX,                // used to offset the dragged rectangle
  MouseOffsetY: Integer;

implementation

{$R *.DFM}

procedure TForm1.FormCreate(Sender: TObject);
begin
  {create an elliptical region to be used for clipping}
  ClippingRegion := CreateEllipticRgn(40, 40, ClientWidth-50, ClientHeight-50);

  {create a rectangle}
  SetRect(TheRect, (ClientWidth div 2)-30, (ClientHeight div 2)-30,
          (ClientWidth div 2)+30, (ClientHeight div 2)+30);

  {initialize the dragging flag}
  DraggingRect := FALSE;
end;

procedure TForm1.FormPaint(Sender: TObject);
begin
  {select the elliptical region as the clipping region}
  SelectClipRgn(Canvas.Handle, ClippingRegion);

  {indicate if the dragged rectangle is visible within the clipping region}
  if RectVisible(Canvas.Handle, TheRect) then
    Caption := Caption+'Rect Visible'
  else
    Caption := Caption+'Rect Not Visible';

  {draw the perimeter of the clipping region in red}
  Canvas.Brush.Color := clRed;
```

```
    FrameRgn(Canvas.Handle, ClippingRegion, Canvas.Brush.Handle, 4, 4);

    {draw the draggable rectangle in blue}
    Canvas.Brush.Color := clBlue;
    Canvas.FillRect(TheRect);
  end;

procedure TForm1.FormMouseDown(Sender: TObject; Button: TMouseButton;
  Shift: TShiftState; X, Y: Integer);
begin
  {if the mouse was clicked within the draggable rectangle}
  if PtInRect(TheRect, Point(X, Y)) then
  begin
    {indicate that a drag operation has commenced}
    DraggingRect := TRUE;

    {retrieve the offset of the current mouse coordinate within the
     dragged rectangle.  this is used when moving the rectangle so that the
     original spot where the mouse was clicked inside of the rectangle is
     preserved.  otherwise, when the rectangle is moved the upper left-hand
     corner of the rectangle will be positioned at the mouse cursor position}
    MouseOffsetX := X-TheRect.Left;
    MouseOffsetY := Y-TheRect.Top;
  end;

end;

procedure TForm1.FormMouseMove(Sender: TObject; Shift: TShiftState; X,
  Y: Integer);
begin
  {if a drag operation is occurring...}
  if DraggingRect then
  begin
    {erase the form's canvas}
    Form1.Canvas.Brush.Color := clBtnFace;
    Form1.Canvas.FillRect(TheRect);

    {move the dragged rectangle, offsetting it from the current mouse position
     so that the original clicked location within the rectangle is preserved}
    OffsetRect(TheRect, X-TheRect.Left-MouseOffsetX,
               Y-TheRect.Top-MouseOffsetY);

    {initialize the form's caption}
    Caption := 'SelectClipRgn Example - ';

    {indicate if the rectangle is within the elliptical region}
    if RectInRegion(ClippingRegion, TheRect) then
      Caption := Caption+'Rect In Region - '
    else
      Caption := Caption+'Rect Not In Region - ';

    {repaint the form to display the changes}
    Form1.Repaint;
  end;
```

```
end;

procedure TForm1.FormMouseUp(Sender: TObject; Button: TMouseButton;
  Shift: TShiftState; X, Y: Integer);
begin
  {indicate that the drag operation has stopped}
  DraggingRect := FALSE;
end;

procedure TForm1.FormDestroy(Sender: TObject);
begin
  {the region is no longer needed, so delete it}
  DeleteObject(ClippingRegion);
end;
```

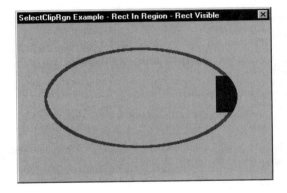

Figure 4-20:
The clipping
region

Table 4-14: SelectClipRgn Return Values

Value	Description
NULLREGION	Indicates an empty region.
SIMPLEREGION	Indicates a single rectangular region.
COMPLEXREGION	Indicates a region consisting of more than one rectangle.
ERROR	Indicates an error occurred.

SetRect   **Windows.Pas**

Syntax

```
SetRect(
var lprc: TRect;        {a pointer to a TRect structure}
xLeft: Integer;         {the upper left horizontal coordinate}
yTop: Integer;          {the upper left vertical coordinate}
xRight: Integer;        {the lower right horizontal coordinate}
```

yBottom: Integer   {the lower right vertical coordinate}
): BOOL;   {returns TRUE or FALSE}

Description

This function sets the coordinates of the rectangle pointed to by the lprc parameter to the specified coordinates.

Parameters

lprc: A pointer to a TRect structure whose coordinates are to be set.

xLeft: Specifies the upper left horizontal coordinate of the rectangle.

yTop: Specifies the upper left vertical coordinate of the rectangle.

xRight: Specifies the lower right horizontal coordinate of the rectangle.

yBottom: Specifies the lower right vertical coordinate of the rectangle.

Return Value

If the function succeeds, it returns TRUE; otherwise it returns FALSE. To get extended error information, call the GetLastError function.

See Also

CopyRect, IntersectRect, SetRectEmpty, SetRectRgn, SubtractRect, UnionRect

Example

Please see Listing 4-20 under SelectClipRgn, and other examples throughout this chapter.

SetRectEmpty   Windows.Pas

Syntax

SetRectEmpty(
var lprc: TRect   {a pointer to a TRect structure}
): BOOL;   {returns TRUE or FALSE}

Description

This function sets all coordinates of the specified rectangle to zero.

Parameters

lprc: A pointer to a TRect structure whose coordinates are to be set to zero.

Return Value

If the function succeeds, it returns TRUE; otherwise it returns FALSE. To get extended error information, call the GetLastError function.

See Also

CopyRect, IntersectRect, SetRect, SetRectRgn, SubtractRect, UnionRect

Example

Listing 4-21: Emptying Out a Rectangle

```
var
  Form1: TForm1;
  TheRect: TRect;     // holds the rectangle

implementation

{$R *.DFM}

procedure TForm1.FormActivate(Sender: TObject);
begin
  {create a new rectangle}
  SetRect(TheRect, 8, 40, 169, 160);
end;

procedure TForm1.FormPaint(Sender: TObject);
begin
  {display the rectangle}
  Form1.Canvas.Brush.Color := clRed;
  Form1.Canvas.FillRect(TheRect);
end;

procedure TForm1.Button1Click(Sender: TObject);
begin
  {empty the rectangle}
  SetRectEmpty(TheRect);

  {indicate if the rectangle is empty}
  if IsRectEmpty(TheRect) then
    Button1.Caption := 'Rectangle is empty'
  else
    Button1.Caption := 'Rectangle is not empty';

  {repaint the form to show the changes}
  Form1.Repaint;
end;
```

SetRectRgn   Windows.Pas

Syntax

```
SetRectRgn(
  Rgn: HRgn;              {a handle to a pre-existing region}
  X1: Integer;           {the upper left horizontal coordinate}
  Y1: Integer;           {the upper left vertical coordinate}
  X2: Integer;           {the lower right horizontal coordinate}
```

```
Y2: Integer              {the lower right vertical coordinate}
): BOOL;                 {returns TRUE or FALSE}
```

Description

This function converts the region identified by the Rgn parameter into a rectangular region at the specified coordinates. Note that the bottom and right edges of the rectangle are excluded from the region.

Parameters

Rgn: Specifies a handle to the region to be converted into a rectangular region.

X1: Specifies the upper left horizontal coordinate of the rectangular region, in logical units.

Y1: Specifies the upper left vertical coordinate of the rectangular region, in logical units.

X2: Specifies the lower right horizontal coordinate of the rectangular region, in logical units.

Y2: Specifies the lower right vertical coordinate of the rectangular region, in logical units.

Return Value

If the function succeeds, it returns TRUE; otherwise it returns FALSE.

See Also

CreateRectRgn, CreateRectRgnIndirect, CreateRoundRectRgn, SetRect

Example

Please see Listing 4-11 under EqualRgn.

SetWindowRgn   **Windows.Pas**

Syntax

```
SetWindowRgn(
hWnd: HWND;              {a handle to a window}
hRgn: HRGN;              {a handle to a region}
bRedraw: BOOL            {window redraw flag}
): BOOL;                 {returns TRUE or FALSE}
```

Description

This function sets the specified window's region to the region identified by the hRgn parameter. The window region determines the area within the window where drawing is permitted, and Windows will not allow any drawing to succeed outside of the window region. When this function returns, the operating system is responsible for the specified region, and it should not be used in any subsequent functions. This function is typically used to create windows with a nonrectangular shape.

Parameters

hWnd: A handle to the window whose region is to be set.

hRgn: A handle to the region to be used as the window region. The coordinates of this region are relative to the window, not the client area. If this parameter is set to zero, the window region is reset to the default region.

bRedraw: Indicates if the window should be redrawn when the region is set. If this value is set to TRUE, the window is redrawn and the WM_WINDOWPOSCHANGING and WM_WINDOWPOSCHANGED messages are sent to the window. If this value is set to FALSE, the window is not redrawn.

Return Value

If the function succeeds, it returns TRUE; otherwise it returns FALSE.

See Also

CreateEllipticRgn, CreateEllipticRgnIndirect, CreatePolygonRgn, CreatePolyPolygonRgn, CreateRectRgn, CreateRectRgnIndirect, CreateRoundRectRgn, ExtCreateRegion, ExtSelectClipRgn, SelectClipRgn

Example

Listing 4-22: Creating a Round Window for an Analog Clock Application

```
var
  Form1: TForm1;
  OriginX, OriginY: Integer;     // holds the center coordinates of the window

implementation

uses Math;

{$R *.DFM}

procedure TForm1.FormCreate(Sender: TObject);
var
  NewShape: HRGN;     // holds the region
begin
  {create a circular region}
  NewShape := CreateEllipticRgn(GetSystemMetrics(SM_CXBORDER)+3,
                                GetSystemMetrics(SM_CYCAPTION)+3,
                                GetSystemMetrics(SM_CXBORDER)+103,
                                GetSystemMetrics(SM_CYCAPTION)+103);

  {determine the center of the circle. this is used when drawing the numbers
   of the clock}
  OriginX := (GetSystemMetrics(SM_CXBORDER)+90) div 2;
```

```
    OriginY := ((GetSystemMetrics(SM_CXBORDER)+90) div 2)-3;

    {set the window region to the circular region. this will create
     a round window}
    SetWindowRgn(Handle, NewShape, TRUE);
end;

procedure TForm1.FormPaint(Sender: TObject);
var
  iCount: Integer;                       // a general loop control variable
  Hour, Minute, Second, MilSec: Word;    // used to decode the time
begin
  {set the background mode to transparent for drawing text}
  SetBkMode(Canvas.Handle, TRANSPARENT);

  {draw a highlighted bevel}
  Canvas.Pen.Color := clWhite;
  Canvas.Pen.Width := 2;
  Arc(Canvas.Handle, 1, 1, 98, 98, 98, 1, 1, 98);

  {draw a shadowed bevel}
  Canvas.Pen.Color := clBtnShadow;
  Arc(Canvas.Handle, 1, 1, 98, 98, 1, 98, 98, 1);

  {for every hour of the day...}
  for iCount := 1 to 12 do
  begin
    {...draw an hour measurement in a circular form around the window}
    Canvas.TextOut(Trunc(Sin(((360/12)*iCount)*(PI/180))*40)+OriginX,
                   Trunc(-Cos(-((360/12)*iCount)*(PI/180))*40)+OriginY,
                   IntToStr(iCount));
  end;

  {retrieve the current time in a useable format}
  DecodeTime(Now, Hour, Minute, Second, MilSec);

  {translate military hours to civilian hours}
  if Hour>12 then Hour := Hour-12;

  {draw the hour hand}
  Canvas.Pen.Color := clBlack;
  Canvas.MoveTo(50, 50);
  Canvas.LineTo(Trunc(Sin(((360/12)*Hour)*(PI/180))*30)+50,
                Trunc(-Cos(-((360/12)*Hour)*(PI/180))*30)+50);

  {draw the minutes hand}
  Canvas.MoveTo(50, 50);
  Canvas.LineTo(Trunc(Sin(((360/60)*Minute)*(PI/180))*40)+50,
                Trunc(-Cos(-((360/60)*Minute)*(PI/180))*40)+50);

  {draw the seconds hand}
  Canvas.Pen.Color := clRed;
  Canvas.MoveTo(50, 50);
  Canvas.LineTo(Trunc(Sin(((360/60)*Second)*(PI/180))*40)+50,
                Trunc(-Cos(-((360/60)*Second)*(PI/180))*40)+50);
```

4

Chapter

```
end;

procedure TForm1.Timer1Timer(Sender: TObject);
begin
  {repaint the form once per second}
  Repaint;
end;

procedure TForm1.WMNCHitTest(var Msg: TWMNCHitTest);
begin
  {this allows the user to drag the window by clicking anywhere on the form}
  inherited;
  Msg.Result := HTCAPTION;
end;
```

Figure 4-21:
The analog
clock

SubtractRect   Windows.Pas

Syntax

```
SubtractRect(
var lprcDst: TRect;          {a pointer to the destination TRect structure}
const lprcSrc1: TRect;       {a pointer to the first rectangle}
const lprcSrc2: TRect        {a pointer to the second rectangle}
): BOOL;                     {returns TRUE or FALSE}
```

Description

This function subtracts the rectangular coordinates pointed to by the lprcSrc2 parameter from the rectangular coordinates pointed to by the lprcSrc1 parameter. Note that this function succeeds only when the two rectangles intersect completely in either the horizontal or vertical axis.

Parameters

lprcDst: A pointer to a TRect structure that receives the resulting coordinates from subtracting the rectangle pointed to by the lprcSrc2 parameter from the rectangle pointed to by the lprcSrc1 parameter.

lprcSrc1: A pointer to a TRect structure from which the rectangle pointed to by the lprcSrc2 parameter is subtracted.

lprcSrc2: A pointer to a TRect structure containing the rectangle to be subtracted from the rectangle pointed to by the lprcSrc1 parameter.

Return Value

If the function succeeds, it returns TRUE; otherwise it returns FALSE.

See Also

EqualRect, IntersectRect, SetRect, UnionRect

Example

Listing 4-23: Subtracting One Rectangle from Another

```
procedure TForm1.FormPaint(Sender: TObject);
var
  Rect1, Rect2, Subtract: TRect;    // holds the rectangles
begin
  {set the coordinates of the two test rectangles}
  SetRect(Rect1, 10, 10, 110, 110);
  SetRect(Rect2, 60, 10, 160, 160);

  {subtract rectangle 2 from rectangle 1}
  SubtractRect(Subtract, Rect1, Rect2);

  with Form1.Canvas do
  begin
    {initialize canvas objects to draw outlines}
    Brush.Style := bsClear;
    Pen.Style := psSolid;

    {draw the outlines of rectangle 1 and 2}
    Rectangle(Rect1.Left, Rect1.Top, Rect1.Right, Rect1.Bottom);
    Rectangle(Rect2.Left, Rect2.Top, Rect2.Right, Rect2.Bottom);

    {initialize canvas objects to draw the result}
    Brush.Style := bsSolid;
    Brush.Color := clRed;

    {fill the resulting rectangle with red}
    FillRect(Subtract);
  end;
end;
```

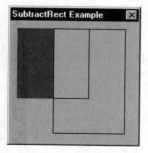

*Figure 4-22:
The resulting
rectangle*

4

Chapter

UnionRect   Windows.Pas

Syntax

```
UnionRect(
var lprcDst: TRect;          {a pointer to the destination TRect structure}
const lprcSrc1: TRect;       {a pointer to the first rectangle}
const lprcSrc2: TRect        {a pointer to the second rectangle}
): BOOL;                     {returns TRUE or FALSE}
```

Description

This function creates a rectangle that is the union of the rectangles pointed to by the lprcSrc1 and lprcSrc2 parameters.

Parameters

lprcDst: A pointer to a TRect structure that receives the resulting coordinates from the union of the rectangles pointed to by the lprcSrc1 and lprcSrc2 parameters.

lprcSrc1: A pointer to a TRect structure containing a rectangle to be joined.

lprcSrc2: A pointer to a TRect structure containing a rectangle to be joined.

Return Value

If the function succeeds and the rectangle pointed to by the lprcDst parameter is not empty, it returns TRUE. If the function fails or the rectangle pointed to by the lprcDst parameter is empty, it returns FALSE. To get extended error information, call the Get-LastError function.

See Also

EqualRect, InflateRect, IntersectRect, IsRectEmpty, SetRect, SetRectEmpty, SubtractRect

Example

Please see Listing 4-16 under OffsetRect.

WidenPath   Windows.Pas

Syntax

```
WidenPath(
DC: HDC           {a handle to a device context}
): BOOL;          {returns TRUE or FALSE}
```

Description

This function widens the path contained in the specified device context. The new path is defined as the area that would be painted if the StrokePath function were called using the currently selected pen. Any bézier curves defining a part of the path are converted into line segments.

Parameters

DC: A handle to the device context containing the path to be widened.

Return Value

If the function succeeds, it returns TRUE; otherwise it returns FALSE. To get extended error information, call the GetLastError function.

See Also

BeginPath, CreatePen, EndPath, ExtCreatePen, FlattenPath, GetPath, PathToRegion, SetMiterLimit

Example

Listing 4-24: Drawing the Outline of Text

```
procedure TForm1.FormPaint(Sender: TObject);
begin
  {begin a path bracket}
  BeginPath(Canvas.Handle);

  {set the background mode to TRANSPARENT so that the path will be defined as
   the area inside of the text}
  SetBkMode(Canvas.Handle, TRANSPARENT);

  {draw some text. note that the form's font is set to size 48 Arial, bold}
  TextOut(Canvas.Handle, 20, 20, 'Delphi Rocks!', Length('Delphi Rocks!'));

  {end the path bracket}
  EndPath(Canvas.Handle);;

  {modify the pen so that it is 4 pixels wide}
  Canvas.Pen.Width := 4;

  {widen the path defined by the text. due to the pen width, above, the new
   path is a 4 pixel wide outline of the letters}
  WidenPath(Canvas.Handle);

  {reset the pen width and brush color for drawing the path}
  Canvas.Pen.Width := 1;
  Canvas.Brush.Color := clRed;

  {set the fill mode so that the path will be drawn correctly}
  SetPolyFillMode(Canvas.Handle, WINDING);

  {fill the path with the red brush}
  FillPath(Canvas.Handle);
end;
```

4

Chapter

Figure 4-23:
The text
outline

Chapter 5

Bitmap and Metafile Functions

It's hard to imagine writing a Windows application without performing some sort of image manipulation. Graphical images can be classified in two categories: bitmapped and vector based. The Win32 API provides the developer with a wide variety of functions with which to manipulate these types of graphical images. Windows natively supports bitmap images and a vector-based image format known as a metafile. This chapter describes the Win32 API functions available for handling these types of graphics.

Note that the example programs in this chapter assume that the video driver has been set to 256 colors. Some examples may not work properly if the color depth is different.

Bitmaps

A bitmap is an array of bytes that store the color information of image elements known as pixels. A pixel is a small square of color that, when viewed together as a whole, form the bitmapped image, as illustrated in Figure 5-1.

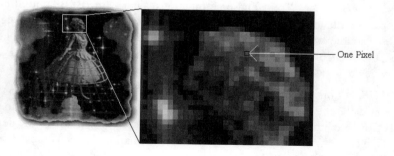

One Pixel

Figure 5-1:
A pixel is the
smallest
element of an
image.

5

Chapter

The number of bits that are used to describe one individual pixel varies widely according to the color depth of the image. The pixels of a 16-color image can be described with 4 bits per pixel; thus, a single byte can contain 2 pixels of the image. A 256-color image uses 1 byte for each pixel, whereas a true-color (16.7 million color) image uses 3 bytes for an individual pixel. See Table 5-6 under CreateDIBSection for a thorough description of bitmap color depths.

Device-Dependent Bitmaps

Device-dependent bitmaps are so named because they are very dependent on the device upon which they are displayed for certain information. DDBs only store information on their width and height, their color format, and the array of pixels describing the image. They do not contain any information concerning the color palette of the image they contain or their original resolution. This bitmap type was the only one available to early Windows programmers, and still exists only for backward compatibility. Win32 developers should use device-independent bitmaps.

Device-Independent Bitmaps

Device-independent bitmaps contain more information about their image than device-dependent bitmaps. For example, device-independent bitmaps contain the color palette for the image, the resolution of the device upon which the bitmap was originally created, and a data compression flag. Perhaps the biggest advantage of device-independent bitmaps is that the developer has direct access to the bytes making up the pixels of the bitmap. This allows a developer to modify the image directly, as opposed to device-dependent bitmaps which require the developer to use GDI functions to manipulate the bitmap image.

By default, device-independent bitmaps are oriented in a "bottom-up" fashion, meaning that the origin of the bitmap pixels starts in the lower left-hand corner of the image. However, a device-independent bitmap can be oriented in a "top-down" fashion like device-dependent bitmaps by providing a negative value for their height.

Bitmap Operations

Numerous functions exist for displaying bitmap images on the screen. The action of copying the pixels of a bitmap to the screen is known as a Blt (pronounced "blit"), meaning Bit bLock Transfer. Some functions, such as the BitBlt and StretchBlt functions, are intended for use with device-dependent bitmaps, and require device contexts as the source and destination of the pixel transfer action. Device-independent bitmaps use the SetDIBitsToDevice and StretchDIBits functions to copy the DIB directly to a device context.

Some functions, such as StretchBlt and StretchDIBits, allow the bitmap to be drawn at a size different from its original dimensions. Windows will add pixels to or remove pixels from the bitmap as needed according to the stretching mode of the destination device context. The stretching mode of the destination device context can be set by calling the SetStretchBltMode function.

Scaling A bitmap can be stretched and still retain its original aspect ratio by finding the smallest side of the rectangular area defining the new bitmap size and determining the ratio of this new dimension versus the original size of the same side of the bitmap. For example, if a 5 X 10 pixel bitmap were to be stretched into a 10 X 20 pixel area, the smallest side of this new area is 10 (the height). The height of the original bitmap is

5, and 10 ÷ 5 is 2, for a 200 percent increase in size. Multiplying all sides of the original bitmap's dimensions by 2 results in a new bitmap size of 10 X 20 pixels, thus retaining its original aspect ratio. The following example demonstrates using this formula to allow the user to scale a bitmap to any size while retaining the bitmap's original aspect ratio.

Listing 5-I: Scaling a Bitmap and Retaining the Original Aspect Ratio

```
var
  Form1: TForm1;
  ScaleRect: TRect;          // holds the user-drawn rectangle coordinates
  IsDragging: Boolean;       // indicates if the user is drawing a rectangle
  ScaledImage: TBitmap;      // holds the image to be scaled

implementation

{$R *.DFM}

procedure TForm1.FormMouseDown(Sender: TObject; Button: TMouseButton;
  Shift: TShiftState; X, Y: Integer);
begin
  {indicate that the user is dragging a rectangle}
  IsDragging := TRUE;

  {initialize the rectangle}
  ScaleRect := Rect(X, Y, X, Y);
end;

procedure TForm1.FormMouseMove(Sender: TObject; Shift: TShiftState; X,
  Y: Integer);
begin
  {if we are dragging a rectangle}
  if IsDragging then
  begin
    {draw over the current rectangle to erase it}
    Canvas.Pen.Style := psSolid;
    Canvas.Pen.Color := clBlack;
    Canvas.Pen.Mode := pmNot;
    Canvas.Brush.Style := bsClear;
    Canvas.Rectangle(ScaleRect.Left, ScaleRect.Top, ScaleRect.Right,
                     ScaleRect.Bottom);

    {modify the user-drawn rectangle coordinates to the new coordinates}
    ScaleRect := Rect(ScaleRect.Left, ScaleRect.Top, X, Y);

    {draw a new rectangle}
    Canvas.Rectangle(ScaleRect.Left, ScaleRect.Top, ScaleRect.Right,
                     ScaleRect.Bottom);
  end;
end;

procedure TForm1.FormMouseUp(Sender: TObject; Button: TMouseButton;
  Shift: TShiftState; X, Y: Integer);
var
```

5

Chapter

```
    Ratio: Real;        // holds the scaling ratio
begin
  {indicate that the user is no longer dragging a rectangle}
  IsDragging := FALSE;

  {clear the entire window}
  Canvas.Brush.Color := clBtnFace;
  Canvas.Brush.Style := bsSolid;
  Canvas.FillRect(Form1.ClientRect);

  {redraw a new, empty rectangle at the current rectangle coordinates}
  Canvas.Brush.Style := bsClear;
  Canvas.Rectangle(ScaleRect.Left, ScaleRect.Top, ScaleRect.Right,
                   ScaleRect.Bottom);

  {select the image's palette into the form's canvas and realize it}
  SelectPalette(Canvas.Handle, ScaledImage.Palette, FALSE);
  RealizePalette(Canvas.Handle);

  {determine the appropriate scaling ratio}
  if ScaleRect.Right-ScaleRect.Left<ScaleRect.Bottom-ScaleRect.Top then
    Ratio := (ScaleRect.Right-ScaleRect.Left)/ScaledImage.Width
  else
    Ratio := (ScaleRect.Bottom-ScaleRect.Top)/ScaledImage.Height;

  {copy the image to the canvas, centered in the rectangle and scaled so that
   the aspect ratio of the original image is retained}
  StretchBlt(Canvas.Handle, ScaleRect.Left+(((ScaleRect.Right-ScaleRect.Left)
             div 2)-(Trunc(ScaledImage.Width*Ratio) div 2)), ScaleRect.Top+
             (((ScaleRect.Bottom-ScaleRect.Top) div 2)-(Trunc(ScaledImage.Height
             *Ratio) div 2)), Trunc(ScaledImage.Width*Ratio),
             Trunc(ScaledImage.Height*Ratio), ScaledImage.Canvas.Handle, 0, 0,
             ScaledImage.Width, ScaledImage.Height, SRCCOPY);
end;

procedure TForm1.FormCreate(Sender: TObject);
begin
  {create and load the image to be scaled}
  ScaledImage := TBitmap.Create;
  ScaledImage.LoadFromFile('Image9.bmp');
end;

procedure TForm1.FormDestroy(Sender: TObject);
begin
  {free the image bitmap}
  ScaledImage.Free;
end;
```

*Figure 5-2:
The scaled,
aspect ratio
corrected
bitmap*

Raster Operations   In addition to simply copying the pixels from a bitmap to the screen, certain functions can perform raster operations on the pixels. A raster operation determines how the pixels from the source, the destination, and the destination device context's selected brush are combined. The most commonly used raster operations are listed in the functions throughout this chapter. However, there are 256 total raster operations, although some may not be applicable to all functions. Please see Appendix B for a full description of all available raster operations.

Certain raster operations can be used to produce special effects, such as the illusion of transparency. To copy a bitmap to a destination using raster operations to simulate the effect of transparent pixels, the application must have two versions of the bitmap to be copied, known as an AND mask and an OR mask. The AND mask image is a monochrome silhouette of the original bitmap. The white pixels indicate where the background will show through (the transparent pixels), and the black pixels indicate where the actual image of the bitmap will appear. The OR mask contains the real image of the bitmap to be copied, where the black pixels of the image indicate transparency. First, the application copies the AND mask to the destination using the SRCAND raster operation. This combines the pixels of the source and destination using a Boolean AND operation. The white pixels of the AND mask will preserve the original pixels of the background image, where the black pixels will turn the pixels in the background image black, resulting in a "carved out" area for the final bitmap image. Once this is complete, the application copies the OR mask to the destination using the SRCPAINT raster operation. This combines the pixels of the source and destination using a Boolean OR operation. The black pixels of the OR mask will preserve the original pixels of the bitmap, where the actual pixels of the image should fall into the black pixels in the background produced by the first step. The result is the illusion of a transparent copy operation. The following example demonstrates the technique of using masks to produce transparency with bitmaps.

5

Chapter

Listing 5-2: Displaying a Bitmap with Transparent Pixels

```
procedure TForm1.FormCreate(Sender: TObject);
begin
  {copy the background image to the destination}
  Image3.Canvas.Draw(0, 0, Image1.Picture.Bitmap);

  {combine the AND mask image with the background image in the destination
   using a Boolean AND operation. this carves out an area for the final
   foreground image}
  BitBlt(Image3.Canvas.Handle, (Image3.Width div 2)-(Image2.Width div 2),
         (Image3.Height div 2)-(Image2.Height div 2), Image2.Width,
         Image2.Height, Image2.Canvas.Handle, 0, 0, SRCAND);

  {copy the result of step one into the 'background' image used for step 2}
  Image4.Canvas.Draw(0, 0, Image3.Picture.Bitmap);

  {copy the "background" image resulting from step 1 into the destination}
  Image6.Canvas.Draw(0, 0, Image4.Picture.Bitmap);

  {combine the OR mask image with the result from step 1 in the destination
   using a Boolean OR operation.  this copies the foreground image into the
   area carved out by step 1 while preserving the pixels around it, thereby
   creating the illusion of transparency.}
  BitBlt(Image6.Canvas.Handle, (Image6.Width div 2)-(Image5.Width div 2),
         (Image6.Height div 2)-(Image5.Height div 2), Image5.Width,
         Image5.Height, Image5.Canvas.Handle, 0, 0, SRCPAINT);
end;
```

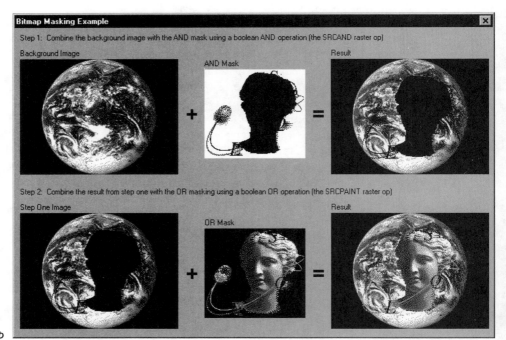

Figure 5-3: The transparently copied bitmap

DIBs and the GDI Although a device-independent bitmap differs from a device-dependent bitmap in many ways, a DIB can still be selected into a device context and modified using GDI functions like a regular device-dependent bitmap. This gives the developer a tremendous amount of flexibility when dealing with bitmaps, as custom drawing functions can be utilized alongside regular GDI drawing functions to manipulate the bitmap image. The following example demonstrates selecting a DIB into a device context and drawing on the bitmap using GDI drawing functions.

Listing 5-3: Manipulating a DIB Using GDI Drawing Functions

```
procedure TForm1.Button1Click(Sender: TObject);
var
  Dib: HBITMAP;            // holds a handle to the DIB
  DibInfo: PBitmapInfo;    // a pointer to the bitmap information data structure
  BitsPtr: PByte;          // holds a pointer to the bitmap bits
  ReferenceDC: HDC;        // a handle to the reference device context
  iCount: Integer;         // general loop counter
  OldBitmap: HBITMAP;      // holds a handle to the old DC bitmap
  ScratchCanvas: TCanvas;  // holds a temporary canvas for drawing

  APolygon: array[0..2] of TPoint;                  // holds a polygon

  SystemPalette: array[0..255] of TPaletteEntry;    // required for converting the
                                                    // system palette into a DIB
                                                    // compatible palette
begin
  {get the memory needed for the bitmap information data structure}
  GetMem(DibInfo, SizeOf(TBitmapInfo)+256*SizeOf(TRGBQuad));

  {initialize the bitmap information}
  DibInfo^.bmiHeader.biWidth         := 64;       // create a 64 X 64 pixel DIB,
  DibInfo^.bmiHeader.biHeight        := -64;      // oriented top-down
  DibInfo^.bmiHeader.biPlanes        := 1;
  DibInfo^.bmiHeader.biBitCount      := 8;        // 256 colors
  DibInfo^.bmiHeader.biCompression   := BI_RGB;   // no compression
  DibInfo^.bmiHeader.biSizeImage     := 0;        // let Windows determine size
  DibInfo^.bmiHeader.biXPelsPerMeter := 0;
  DibInfo^.bmiHeader.biYPelsPerMeter := 0;
  DibInfo^.bmiHeader.biClrUsed       := 0;
  DibInfo^.bmiHeader.biClrImportant  := 0;
  DibInfo^.bmiHeader.biSize          := SizeOf(TBitmapInfoHeader);

  {retrieve the current system palette}
  GetSystemPaletteEntries(Form1.Canvas.Handle, 0, 256, SystemPalette);

  {the system palette is returned as an array of TPaletteEntry structures,
   which store the palette colors in the form of Red, Green, and Blue.  however,
   the TBitmapInfo structure's bmiColors member takes an array of TRGBQuad
   structures, which store the palette colors in the form of Blue, Green, and
   Red.  therefore, we must translate the TPaletteEntry structures into the
   appropriate TRGBQuad structures to get the correct color entries.}
  for iCount := 0 to 255 do
  begin
```

```
      DibInfo^.bmiColors[iCount].rgbBlue      := SystemPalette[iCount].peBlue;
      DibInfo^.bmiColors[iCount].rgbRed       := SystemPalette[iCount].peRed;
      DibInfo^.bmiColors[iCount].rgbGreen     := SystemPalette[iCount].peGreen;
      DibInfo^.bmiColors[iCount].rgbReserved := 0;
    end;

    {create a memory-based device context}
    ReferenceDC := CreateCompatibleDC(0);

    {create the DIB based on the memory device context and the
     initialized bitmap information}
    Dib := CreateDIBSection(ReferenceDC, DibInfo^, DIB_RGB_COLORS,
                            Pointer(BitsPtr), 0, 0);

    {select the DIB into the device context}
    OldBitmap := SelectObject(ReferenceDC, Dib);

    {create a canvas and set its handle to the created device context}
    ScratchCanvas := TCanvas.Create;
    ScratchCanvas.Handle := ReferenceDC;

    {fill the canvas with red}
    ScratchCanvas.Brush.Color := clRed;
    ScratchCanvas.FillRect(ScratchCanvas.ClipRect);

    {draw a green circle}
    ScratchCanvas.Brush.Color := clLime;
    ScratchCanvas.Ellipse(0, 0, 32, 32);

    {draw a triangle}
    ScratchCanvas.Brush.Color := clBlue;
    APolygon[0] := Point(63, 63);
    APolygon[1] := Point(32, 63);
    APolygon[2] := Point(48, 32);
    ScratchCanvas.Polygon(APolygon);

    {the above functions have drawn IB functions}
    SetDIBitsToDevice(Form1.Canvas.Handle, 30, 5, 64, 64, 0, 0, 0, 64, BitsPtr,
                      DibInfo^, DIB_RGB_COLORS);

    {draw the DIB again, but this time let's stretch it to twice its size}
    StretchDIBits(Form1.Canvas.Handle, 105, 5, 128, 128, 0, 0, 64, 64, BitsPtr,
                  DibInfo^, DIB_RGB_COLORS, SRCCOPY);

    {we no longer need the DIB, so delete it, the canvas, and the
     allocated memory for the information data structure}
    SelectObject(ReferenceDC, OldBitmap);
    ScratchCanvas.Free;
    DeleteObject(Dib);
    DeleteDC(ReferenceDC);
    FreeMem(DibInfo, SizeOf(TBitmapInfo)+256*SizeOf(TRGBQuad));
  end;
```

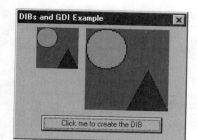

*Figure 5-4:
The modified
device-
independent
bitmap*

Metafiles

A metafile is a vector-based graphic format for storing images. The image is stored as a series of instructions that describe how to draw the image, rather than an array of pixels that explicitly describe the image like a bitmap. This affords metafiles a certain amount of device independence in that a metafile can be displayed in its original size and resolution on a printing device or on the screen.

Specifically, a metafile is a collection of metafile records that correspond to GDI function calls for drawing lines and shapes, and filling regions, etc. When a metafile is displayed, it "replays" these GDI functions in sequence upon a specified device context, drawing the image as if the specific GDI drawing functions had been called programmatically.

The method by which a metafile stores its image allows it to be scaled to almost any size with little to no loss of resolution. Thus, metafile graphics are commonly used for clip art or to store technical drawings such as CAD designs or architectural plans. In addition, since metafile records only describe the image and do not store each individual pixel, metafiles are usually much smaller than a bitmap would be for the same image. However, since the GDI functions used to describe the image are replayed each time the metafile is drawn to the screen, metafiles are drawn much slower than bitmaps.

Enhanced Metafiles

Win32 applications should use the enhanced metafile format instead of the Win16 metafile format. The enhanced metafile format contains a header describing the original resolution and dimensions for which the metafile was created. It also stores a palette for the metafile image. The Win16 metafile format contains neither. Note that enhanced metafiles are subject to the limitations of the Windows 95 GDI. Specifically, the Windows 95 GDI only supports 16-bit signed coordinates. Therefore, any enhanced metafile records with coordinates outside of the range -32,768 to 32,767 will fail to display. Delphi's TMetafile object encapsulates both the Win16 and the enhanced metafile formats.

Bitmap and Metafile Functions

The following bitmap and metafile functions are covered in this chapter:

Table 5-1: Bitmap and Metafile Functions

Function	Description
BitBlt	Copies bits from one device context to another.
CloseEnhMetaFile	Closes an enhanced metafile device context and returns a handle to the metafile.
CopyEnhMetaFile	Creates a duplicate of an enhanced metafile.
CopyImage	Creates a duplicate of an icon, bitmap, or cursor.
CreateBitmap	Creates a device-dependent bitmap.
CreateBitmapIndirect	Creates a device-dependent bitmap from information in a data structure.
CreateCompatibleBitmap	Creates a device-dependent bitmap compatible with a specified device context.
CreateDIBitmap	Creates a device-dependent bitmap from a device-independent bitmap.
CreateDIBSection	Creates a device-independent bitmap.
CreateEnhMetaFile	Creates an enhanced metafile.
DeleteEnhMetaFile	Deletes an enhanced metafile.
EnumEnhMetaFile	Enumerates the metafile records in an enhanced metafile.
GetBitmapBits	Retrieves pixels from a bitmap into an array.
GetBitmapDimensionEx	Retrieves the preferred bitmap dimensions.
GetDIBits	Creates a device-independent bitmap from a device-dependent bitmap.
GetEnhMetaFile	Opens an enhanced metafile.
GetEnhMetaFileDescription	Retrieves the enhanced metafile description string.
GetEnhMetaFileHeader	Retrieves the enhanced metafile header.
GetStretchBltMode	Retrieves the current bitmap stretching mode.
LoadBitmap	Loads a bitmap resource.
LoadImage	Loads an icon, cursor, or bitmap from a resource or a file.
PatBlt	Fills a specified rectangle with the brush of the destination DC, and can perform certain raster operations.
PlayEnhMetaFile	Draws a metafile onto a device context.
PlayEnhMetaFileRecord	Draws a single metafile record onto a device context.
SetBitmapBits	Sets the pixels of a device-dependent bitmap.
SetBitmapDimensionEx	Sets the preferred bitmap dimensions.

Function	Description
SetDIBits	Sets the pixels in a device-dependent bitmap to the pixel values of a device-independent bitmap.
SetDIBitsToDevice	Draws a device-independent bitmap to a device context.
SetStretchBltMode	Sets the bitmap stretching mode.
StretchBlt	Draws and scales pixels from one device context to another.
StretchDIBits	Draws and scales a device-independent bitmap onto a device context.

BitBlt   Windows.Pas

Syntax

```
BitBlt(
DestDC: HDC;          {a handle to the destination device context}
X: Integer;           {the horizontal coordinate of the destination rectangle}
Y: Integer;           {the vertical coordinate of the destination rectangle}
Width: Integer;       {the width of the source and destination rectangle}
Height: Integer;      {the height of the source and destination rectangle}
SrcDC: HDC;           {a handle to the source device context}
XSrc: Integer;        {the horizontal coordinate of the source rectangle}
YSrc: Integer;        {the vertical coordinate of the source rectangle}
Rop: DWORD            {the raster operation code}
): BOOL;              {returns TRUE or FALSE}
```

Description

This function copies a rectangle of pixels from the bitmap in the specified source device context into the bitmap in the specified destination device context. The width and height of the destination rectangle determine the width and height of the source rectangle. If the color formats of the source and destination device contexts differ, this function converts the color format of the source into the color format of the destination.

Parameters

DestDC: A handle to the device context to which the pixels are copied.

X: The horizontal coordinate of the upper left corner of the destination rectangle in the destination device context, measured in logical units.

Y: The vertical coordinate of the upper left corner of the destination rectangle in the destination device context, measured in logical units.

Width: The width of the source and destination rectangles, measured in logical units.

Height: The height of the source and destination rectangles, measured in logical units.

SrcDC: A handle to the device context from which the pixels are copied. This cannot be the handle to a metafile device context.

XSrc: The horizontal coordinate of the upper left corner of the source rectangle in the source device context, measured in logical units.

YSrc: The vertical coordinate of the upper left corner of the source rectangle in the source device context, measured in logical units.

Rop: A raster operation code that determines how the colors of the pixels in the source are combined with the colors of the pixels in the destination. This parameter can be one value from Table 5-2.

Return Value

If the function succeeds, it returns TRUE; otherwise it returns FALSE. To get extended error information, call the GetLastError function.

See Also

GetDC, CreateCompatibleDC, CreateBitmap, LoadBitmap, StretchBlt

Example

Please see Listing 5-16 under LoadImage, and other examples throughout this chapter.

Table 5-2: BitBlt Rop Values

Value	Description
BLACKNESS	Fills the pixels in the specified rectangle in the destination with the color in index 0 of the physical palette. By default, this color is black.
DSTINVERT	Inverts the colors of the pixels in the specified rectangle in the destination.
MERGECOPY	Combines the pixel colors of the source rectangle with the pixel colors of the pattern contained in the brush selected into the destination device context using the Boolean AND operator.
MERGEPAINT	Inverts the pixel colors of the source rectangle and combines them with the pixel colors of the destination rectangle using the Boolean OR operator.
NOTSRCCOPY	Inverts the pixel colors of the source rectangle and copies them into the destination rectangle.
NOTSRCERASE	Combines the pixel colors of the source and destination rectangles using the Boolean OR operator, then inverts the resulting color.
PATCOPY	Copies the pattern contained in the brush selected into the destination device context directly into the destination.

Value	Description
PATINVERT	Combines the pixel colors of the pattern contained in the brush selected into the destination device context with the colors of the pixels in the destination using the Boolean XOR operator.
PATPAINT	Combines the colors of the pattern contained in the brush selected into the destination device context with the inverted pixel colors of the source rectangle using the Boolean OR operator, then combines the result with the pixel colors of the destination rectangle using the Boolean OR operator.
SRCAND	Combines the pixel colors of the source and destination rectangles using the Boolean AND operator.
SRCCOPY	Copies the pixel colors of the source rectangle directly into the destination rectangle.
SRCERASE	Combines the pixel colors of the source rectangle with the inverted colors of the destination rectangle using the Boolean AND operator.
SRCINVERT	Combines the pixel colors of the source and destination rectangles using the Boolean XOR operator.
SRCPAINT	Combines the pixel colors of the source and destination rectangles using the Boolean OR operator.
WHITENESS	Fills the pixels in the specified rectangle in the destination with the color in index 255 of the physical palette. By default, this color is white.

CloseEnhMetaFile   Windows.Pas

Syntax

```
CloseEnhMetaFile(
DC: HDC              {a handle to a metafile device context}
): HENHMETAFILE;     {returns a handle to an enhanced metafile}
```

Description

This function closes the specified enhanced metafile device context and returns a handle to the new enhanced metafile. This handle can be used in all functions requiring a handle to an enhanced metafile. When the metafile is no longer needed, it should be removed by calling DeleteEnhMetaFile.

Parameters

DC: A handle to an enhanced metafile device context.

Return Value

If the function succeeds, it returns a handle to an enhanced metafile; otherwise it returns zero.

5

Chapter

See Also

CopyEnhMetaFile, CreateEnhMetaFile, DeleteEnhMetaFile, GetEnhMetaFileDescription, GetEnhMetaFileHeader, PlayEnhMetaFile

Example

Please see Listing 5-10 under CreateEnhMetaFile.

CopyEnhMetaFile Windows.Pas

Syntax

```
CopyEnhMetaFile(
p1: HENHMETAFILE;        {a handle to an enhanced metafile}
p2: PChar                {a string specifying a filename}
): HENHMETAFILE;         {returns a handle to an enhanced metafile}
```

Description

This function copies the specified enhanced metafile to a file or memory, returning a handle to the copied enhanced metafile. When the metafile is no longer needed, it should be removed by calling DeleteEnhMetaFile.

Parameters

p1: A handle to the enhanced metafile to be copied.

p2: A null-terminated string specifying the destination filename. If this parameter is NIL, the function simply copies the enhanced metafile to memory.

Return Value

If the function succeeds, it returns a handle to the copied enhanced metafile; otherwise it returns zero. To get extended error information, call the GetLastError function.

See Also

CreateEnhMetaFile, DeleteEnhMetaFile, GetEnhMetaFileDescription, GetEnhMetaFileHeader, PlayEnhMetaFile

Example

Please see Listing 5-14 under GetEnhMetaFile.

CopyImage   Windows.Pas

Syntax

```
CopyImage(
hImage: THandle;         {a handle to an image}
ImageType: UINT;         {the image type flag}
X: Integer;              {width of new image}
Y: Integer;              {height of new image}
```

```
Flags: UINT              {the copy operation flags}
): THandle;              {returns a handle to the copied image}
```

Description

This function makes a duplicate of the specified image (bitmap, icon, or cursor). The new image can be expanded or compressed as desired, and can be converted to a monochrome color format.

Parameters

hImage: A handle to the image being copied.

ImageType: A flag indicating the type of image to be copied. This parameter can be one value from Table 5-3.

X: Indicates the desired width of the copied image in pixels.

Y: Indicates the desired height of the copied image in pixels.

Flags: A value indicating how the image should be copied. This parameter can be one or more values from Table 5-4.

Return Value

If the function succeeds, it returns a handle to the copied image; otherwise it returns zero. To get extended error information, call the GetLastError function.

See Also

LoadBitmap, LoadCursor, LoadCursorFromFile, LoadIcon, LoadImage

Example

Listing 5-4: Creating a Monochrome Image to Perform a Transparent Copy

```
var
ForegroundImage: TBitmap;     // holds the foreground image

implementation

procedure TForm1.FormCreate(Sender: TObject);
begin
  {create the foreground bitmap and load it}
  ForegroundImage := TBitmap.Create;
  ForegroundImage.LoadFromFile('Foreground.bmp');
end;

procedure TForm1.FormDestroy(Sender: TObject);
begin
  {free the foreground bitmap}
  ForegroundImage.Free;
end;

procedure TForm1.FormPaint(Sender: TObject);
var
```

5

Chapter

```
TempBitmap: HBITMAP;      // a handle to the copied image
OldBitmap: HBITMAP;       // holds the old bitmap from the DC
OffscreenDC: HDC;         // a handle to an offscreen device context
begin
  {make a monochrome mask of the foreground image}
  TempBitmap := CopyImage(ForegroundImage.Handle, IMAGE_BITMAP,
                          ForegroundImage.Width, ForegroundImage.Height,
                          LR_MONOCHROME);

  {create a memory device context}
  OffscreenDC := CreateCompatibleDC(0);

  {select the monochrome mask image into the memory device context}
  OldBitmap := SelectObject(OffscreenDC, TempBitmap);

  {blit the monochrome mask onto the background image.  $00220326 is a raster
   operation that inverts the pixels of the source rectangle and then combines
   these pixels with those of the destination bitmap using the Boolean AND
   operator. this carves out an area for the regular foreground bitmap}
  BitBlt(Image1.Picture.Bitmap.Canvas.Handle, 150, 50, 100, 100, OffscreenDC,
         0, 0, $00220326);

  {blit the foreground bitmap onto the background by combining the foreground
   and background pixels with the Boolean OR operator.  the result is the
   foreground orb being copied onto the background while the edges of the
   orb image appear transparent}
  BitBlt(Image1.Picture.Bitmap.Canvas.Handle, 150, 50, 100, 100,
         ForegroundImage.Canvas.Handle, 0, 0, SRCPAINT);

  {select the previous bitmap back into the memory device context}
  SelectObject(OffscreenDC, OldBitmap);

  {delete the mask bitmap and the memory device context}
  DeleteObject(TempBitmap);
  DeleteDC(OffscreenDC);
end;
```

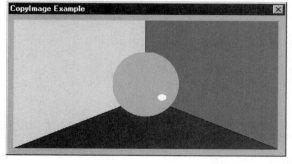

Figure 5-5:
The
transparently
copied image

Table 5-3: CopyImage ImageType Values

Value	Description
IMAGE_BITMAP	The image is a bitmap.
IMAGE_CURSOR	The image is a cursor.
IMAGE_ENHMETAFILE	The image is an enhanced metafile.
IMAGE_ICON	The image is an icon.

Table 5-4: CopyImage Flags Values

Value	Description
LR_COPYDELETEORG	The original image is deleted after the copy is made.
LR_COPYFROMRESOURCE	The function tries to reload an icon or cursor resource from the resource file instead of making a copy. The image retrieved from the resource file is the image closest to the desired size; it does not stretch the image to the indicated width and height. If the image was not loaded with the LoadIcon or LoadCursor functions or by the LoadImage function with the LR_SHARED flag set, this function fails.
LR_COPYRETURNORG	Creates an exact duplicate of the original image. The X and Y parameters are ignored.
LR_MONOCHROME	Creates a black and white version of the original image.

CreateBitmap   Windows.Pas

Syntax

```
CreateBitmap(
Width: Integer;          {width of bitmap in pixels}
Height: Integer;         {height of bitmap in pixels}
Planes: Longint;         {number of color planes}
BitCount: Longint;       {number of bits required to identify a color}
Bits: Pointer            {a pointer to an array of color data}
): HBITMAP;              {returns a handle to a bitmap}
```

Description

This function creates a new bitmap with the specified width, height, and color depth. An array of pixel information can be specified to create a bitmap with an initial image. If the Width and Height parameters are set to zero, this function returns a handle to a 1-pixel-by-1 pixel monochrome bitmap. Once the bitmap is created, it can be selected into a device context with the SelectObject function. When the bitmap is no longer needed, it should be deleted with the DeleteObject function.

Although this function can be used to create color bitmaps, for performance reasons applications should use CreateBitmap to create monochrome bitmaps and CreateCompatibleBitmap to create color bitmaps. CreateCompatibleBitmap requires a device context, returning a bitmap that has the same color format as the given device. For this reason, SelectObject calls are faster with a color bitmap returned from CreateCompatibleBitmap.

Parameters

Width: The width of the bitmap in pixels.

Height: The height of the bitmap in pixels.

Planes: The number of color planes used by the device.

BitCount: The number of bits required to describe the color of one pixel (i.e., 8 bits for 256-color images, 24 bits for 16.7 million-color images, etc.).

Bits: A pointer to an array of bytes that contain the color data describing the image of the bitmap. This array specifies the color of the pixels in a rectangular area. Each horizontal row of pixels in the rectangle is known as a scan line. Each scan line must be word aligned, meaning that its width must be a multiple of 2. A scan line can be padded with zeroes to facilitate the word alignment. If this parameter is NIL, the new bitmap is not defined and does not contain an image.

Return Value

If the function succeeds, it returns a handle to a bitmap; otherwise it returns zero.

See Also

CreateBitmapIndirect, CreateCompatibleBitmap, CreateDIBitmap, DeleteObject, GetBitmapBits, GetBitmapDimensionEx, SelectObject, SetBitmapBits, SetBitmapDimensionEx

Example

Listing 5-5: Creating a Bitmap

```
procedure TForm1.Button1Click(Sender: TObject);
var
  TheBitmap: HBitmap;             // a handle for the new bitmap
  TheBits: array[0..4095] of Byte;    // an array of original bitmap bits
  GotBits: array[0..4095] of Byte;    // an array to retrieve the bitmap bits
  LoopX,                          // general loop counter variables
  LoopY: Integer;
  OffScreen: HDC;                 // an offscreen device context
  TheSize: TSize;                 // holds the bitmap size dimensions
begin
  {set every bit in the new bitmap to the color stored
   in the system palette slot 3}
  FillMemory(@TheBits, 4096, 3);

  {set a 10 X 10 pixel square in the middle of the
```

```
      image to the color in system palette slot 1}
    for LoopX:=27 to 37 do
    begin
        TheBits[LoopX*64+27]:=1;
        TheBits[LoopX*64+28]:=1;
        TheBits[LoopX*64+29]:=1;
        TheBits[LoopX*64+30]:=1;
        TheBits[LoopX*64+31]:=1;
        TheBits[LoopX*64+32]:=1;
        TheBits[LoopX*64+33]:=1;
        TheBits[LoopX*64+34]:=1;
        TheBits[LoopX*64+35]:=1;
        TheBits[LoopX*64+36]:=1;
    end;

    {create a 64 X 64 pixel bitmap, using the information
     in the array TheBits}
    TheBitmap:=CreateBitmap(64,64,1,8,@thebits);

    {set the prefered bitmap dimensions. this is not used
     by Windows; it simply sets some user-defined information}
    SetBitmapDimensionEx(TheBitmap,100,100,nil);

    {create an offscreen device context that is
     compatible with the screen}
    OffScreen:=CreateCompatibleDC(0);

    {select the new bitmap into the offscreen device context}
    SelectObject(OffScreen, TheBitmap);

    {copy the bitmap from the offscreen device context
     onto the canvas of the form. this will display the bitmap}
    BitBlt(Form1.Canvas.Handle,162,16,64,64,OffScreen,0,0,SRCCOPY);

    {retrieve the bits that make up the bitmap image}
    GetBitmapBits(TheBitmap, 4096,@GotBits);

    {display the bits in the string grid}
    for LoopX:=0 to 63 do
      for LoopY:=0 to 63 do
        StringGrid1.Cells[LoopX,LoopY]:=IntToStr(GotBits[LoopX*64+LoopY]);

    {retrieve the user-defined, preferred bitmap dimensions}
    GetBitmapDimensionEx(TheBitmap,TheSize);

    {Display these dimensions}
    Label1.Caption:='Preferred bitmap dimensions - Width: '+IntToStr(TheSize.CX)+
                    ' Height: '+IntToStr(TheSize.CY);

    {delete the offscreen device context}
    DeleteDC(OffScreen);

    {delete the new bitmap}
    DeleteObject(TheBitmap);
end;
```

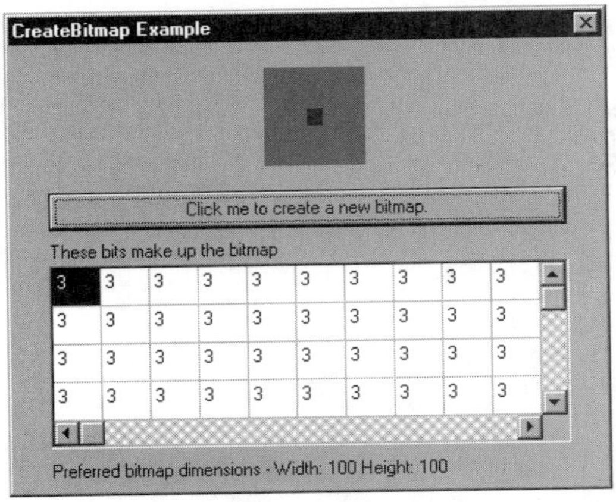

Figure 5-6:
The new
bitmap

CreateBitmapIndirect   Windows.Pas

Syntax

```
CreateBitmapIndirect(
const p1: TBitmap          {a pointer to a bitmap information structure}
): HBITMAP;                {returns a handle to a bitmap}
```

Description

This function creates a new bitmap with the specified width, height, and color depth. An array of pixel information can be specified to create a bitmap with an initial image. If the Width and Height parameters are set to zero, this function returns a handle to a 1-pixel-by-1-pixel monochrome bitmap. Once the bitmap is created, it can be selected into a device context with the SelectObject function. When the bitmap is no longer needed, it should be deleted with the DeleteObject function.

Although this function can be used to create color bitmaps, for performance reasons applications should use CreateBitmapIndirect to create monochrome bitmaps and CreateCompatibleBitmap to create color bitmaps. CreateCompatibleBitmap requires a device context, returning a bitmap that has the same color format as the given device. For this reason, SelectObject calls are faster with a color bitmap returned from CreateCompatibleBitmap.

Parameters

p1: Identifies a TBitmap data structure containing information about the bitmap image being created. The TBitmap data structure is defined as:

```
TBitmap = packed record
    bmType: Longint;           {the bitmap type}
    bmWidth: Longint;          {the width of the bitmap in pixels}
    bmHeight: Longint;         {the height of the bitmap in pixels}
    bmWidthBytes: Longint;     {the number of bytes in a scan line}
```

```
bmPlanes: Word;        {the number of color planes}
bmBitsPixel: Word;     {the number of bits describing one pixel}
bmBits: Pointer;       {a pointer to a bitmap image}
end;
```

bmType: Indicates the type of bitmap. As of this writing, this member must be set to zero.

bmWidth: The width of the bitmap in pixels.

bmHeight: The height of the bitmap in pixels.

bmWidthBytes: The number of bytes in each scan line of the array pointed to by the bmBits parameter. The scan lines formed by this array must be word aligned, so the value of this member must be a multiple of 2.

bmPlanes: The number of color planes used by the device.

bmBitsPixel: The number of bits required to describe the color of one pixel (i.e., 8 bits for 256-color images, 24 bits for 16.7 million-color images, etc.).

bmBits: A pointer to an array of bytes that contain the color data describing the image of the bitmap. This array specifies the color of the pixels in a rectangular area. Each horizontal row of pixels in the rectangle is known as a scan line. Each scan line must be word aligned, meaning that its width must be a multiple of 2. A scan line can be padded with zeroes to facilitate the word alignment. If this parameter is NIL, the new bitmap is not defined and does not contain an image.

Return Value

If the function succeeds, it returns a handle to the new bitmap; otherwise it returns zero.

See Also

BitBlt, CreateBitmap, CreateCompatibleBitmap, CreateDIBitmap, DeleteObject, SelectObject

Example

Listing 5-6: Indirectly Creating a Bitmap

```
procedure TForm1.Button1Click(Sender: TObject);
var
  TheBitmap: HBITMAP;               // a handle to the new bitmap
  BitmapInfo: Windows.TBitmap;      // the bitmap information structure
  OffscreenDC: HDC;                 // a handle to a memory device context
  BitmapBits: array[0..4095] of byte; // holds the bitmap image
begin
  {initialize the bitmap image to the color in palette slot 5}
  FillMemory(@BitmapBits, 4096, 5);

  {define the new bitmap}
  BitmapInfo.bmType    := 0;
  BitmapInfo.bmWidth   := 64;
  BitmapInfo.bmHeight  := 64;
```

5

Chapter

```
BitmapInfo.bmWidthBytes := 64;
BitmapInfo.bmPlanes     := 1;
BitmapInfo.bmBitsPixel  := 8;              // 8 bits/pixel, a 256-color bitmap
BitmapInfo.bmBits       := @BitmapBits;

{create the bitmap based on the bitmap information}
TheBitmap := CreateBitmapIndirect(BitmapInfo);

{create a memory device context compatible with the screen}
OffscreenDC := CreateCompatibleDC(0);

{select the new bitmap and a stock pen into the memory device context}
SelectObject(OffscreenDC, TheBitmap);
SelectObject(OffscreenDC, GetStockObject(WHITE_PEN));

{draw a single line on the bitmap}
MoveToEx(OffscreenDC, 0, 0, nil);
LineTo(OffscreenDC, 64, 64);

{display the bitmap}
BitBlt(PaintBox1.Canvas.Handle, (PaintBox1.Width div 2)-32,
       (PaintBox1.Height div 2)-32, 64, 64, OffscreenDC, 0, 0, SRCCOPY);

{we are done with the memory device context and bitmap, so delete them}
DeleteDC(OffscreenDC);
DeleteObject(TheBitmap);
end;
```

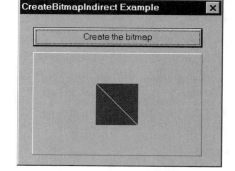

*Figure 5-7:
The new
bitmap
created
indirectly*

CreateCompatibleBitmap   Windows.Pas

Syntax

```
CreateCompatibleBitmap(
DC: HDC;                    {a handle to a device context}
Width: Integer;            {the width of the bitmap in pixels}
Height: Integer            {the height of the bitmap in pixels}
): HBITMAP;                {returns a handle to the bitmap}
```

Description

This function creates a bitmap whose color format (i.e., 8 bits per pixel, 24 bits per pixel, etc.) and palette matches the color format and palette of the display device associated with the specified device context. If a DIB section bitmap created with the CreateDIBSection function is selected into the specified device context, this function creates a DIB bitmap. Use the DeleteObject function to delete the bitmap when it is no longer needed. If the Width and Height parameters are set to zero, this function returns a handle to a 1-pixel-by-1-pixel monochrome bitmap.

Parameters

DC: A handle to the device context from which the bitmap retrieves its color format.

Width: The width of the bitmap in pixels.

Height: The height of the bitmap in pixels.

Return Value

If the function succeeds, it returns a handle to the new bitmap; otherwise it returns zero.

See Also

CreateBitmap, CreateBitmapIndirect, CreateDIBSection, DeleteObject, SelectObject

Example

Listing 5-7: Creating a Bitmap Compatible with the Current Display Device

```
procedure TForm1.Button1Click(Sender: TObject);
var
  TheBitmap: HBitmap;              // a handle for the new bitmap
  TheBits: array[0..4095] of Byte; // an array of original bitmap bits
  LoopX: Integer;                  // general loop counter variables
  OffScreen: HDC;                  // an offscreen device context
  ScreenDC: HDC;                   // a handle to a temporary device context
begin
  {set every bit in the new bitmap to the color stored
   in the system palette slot 3}
  FillMemory(@TheBits, 4095, 3);

  {set a 10 X 10 pixel square in the middle of the
   image to the color in system palette slot 1}
  for LoopX:=27 to 37 do
  begin
    TheBits[LoopX*64+27]:=1;
    TheBits[LoopX*64+28]:=1;
    TheBits[LoopX*64+29]:=1;
    TheBits[LoopX*64+30]:=1;
    TheBits[LoopX*64+31]:=1;
    TheBits[LoopX*64+32]:=1;
    TheBits[LoopX*64+33]:=1;
    TheBits[LoopX*64+34]:=1;
```

```
      TheBits[LoopX*64+35]:=1;
      TheBits[LoopX*64+36]:=1;
   end;

   {retrieve a device context for the desktop}
   ScreenDC := GetDC(0);

   {create a 64 X 64 pixel bitmap that is
    color compatible with the current display device}
   TheBitmap := CreateCompatibleBitmap(ScreenDC, 64, 64);

   {release the desktop device context}
   ReleaseDC(0,ScreenDC);

   {set the bitmap image}
   SetBitmapBits(TheBitmap, 64*64, @TheBits);

   {create an offscreen device context that is
    compatible with the screen}
   OffScreen := CreateCompatibleDC(0);

   {select the new bitmap into the offscreen device context}
   SelectObject(OffScreen, TheBitmap);

   {copy the bitmap from the offscreen device context
    onto the canvas of the form. this will display the bitmap}
   BitBlt(Form1.Canvas.Handle,(Width div 2)-32,16,64,64,OffScreen,0,0,SRCCOPY);

   {delete the offscreen device context}
   DeleteDC(OffScreen);

   {delete the new bitmap}
   DeleteObject(TheBitmap);
end;
```

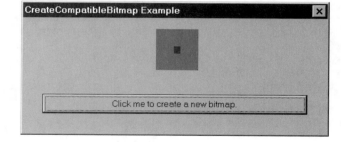

Figure 5-8:
The
compatible
bitmap

CreateDIBitmap   *Windows.Pas*

Syntax

```
CreateDIBitmap(
DC: HDC;                                {a handle to a reference device context}
```

var InfoHeader: TBitmapInfoHeader;	{a pointer to a TBitmapInfoHeader data structure}
dwUsage: DWORD;	{bitmap initialization flags}
InitBits: PChar;	{a pointer to the DIB bitmap bit values}
var InitInfo: TBitmapInfo;	{a pointer to a TBitmapInfo data structure}
wUsage: UINT	{color type flags}
): HBITMAP;	{returns a handle to a device-dependent bitmap}

Description

This function creates a device-dependent bitmap based on the attributes and image of the specified device-independent bitmap. When the new bitmap is no longer needed, it should be deleted using the DeleteObject function.

Parameters

DC: A handle to a device context. The format of the new device-dependent bitmap is based on this device context. Therefore, it must not be a memory device context. This parameter can be set to the value returned from either GetDC or CreateDC.

InfoHeader: A handle to a TBitmapInfoHeader data structure. CreateDIBitmap uses the information in this structure to set the attributes of the new device-dependent bitmap, such as its width and height. The TBitmapInfoHeader data structure is defined as:

TBitmapInfoHeader = packed record	
biSize: DWORD;	{the size of the structure in bytes}
biWidth: Longint;	{the width of the bitmap in pixels}
biHeight: Longint;	{the height of the bitmap in pixels}
biPlanes: Word;	{the number of color planes}
biBitCount: Word;	{the bits per pixel required to describe a color}
biCompression: DWORD;	{compression flags}
biSizeImage: DWORD;	{the size of the image in bytes}
biXPelsPerMeter: Longint;	{horizontal pixels per meter of the target device}
biYPelsPerMeter: Longint;	{vertical pixels per meter of the target device}
biClrUsed: DWORD;	{the number of color indices used}
biClrImportant: DWORD;	{the number of important color indices}
end;	

Please see the CreateDIBSection function for a description of this data structure.

dwUsage: A flag specifying how the new device-dependent bitmap is to be initialized. If this parameter is set to zero, the bits of the new bitmap's image will not be initialized. If this parameter is set to CBM_INIT, Windows uses the information pointed to by the InitBits and InitInfo parameters to set the bits of the new device-dependent bitmap to match those in the device-independent bitmap.

InitBits: A pointer to the image representing the DIB, in the form of an array of bytes. If the dwUsage parameter is set to zero, this parameter is ignored.

InitInfo: A pointer to a TBitmapInfo data structure describing the dimensions and color format of the DIB image pointed to by the InitBits parameter. If the dwUsage parameter is set to zero, this parameter is ignored. The TBitmapInfo data structure is defined as:

```
TBitmapInfo = packed record
      bmiHeader: TBitmapInfoHeader;        {bitmap header information}
      bmiColors: array[0..0] of TRGBQuad;  {the color table used by the
                                            bitmap}
end;
```

Please see the CreateDIBSection function for a description of this data structure.

wUsage: A flag indicating the type of color information stored in the bmiColors member of the TBitmapInfo data structure pointed to by the InitInfo parameter. This parameter can be one value from Table 5-5.

Return Value

If the function succeeds, it returns a handle to a device-dependent bitmap; otherwise it returns zero.

See Also

CreateBitmap, CreateBitmapIndirect, CreateDIBSection, DeleteObject

Example

Listing 5-8: Creating a Device-dependent Bitmap from a Device-independent Bitmap

```
procedure TForm1.Button1Click(Sender: TObject);
var
  Dib: HBITMAP;             // holds a handle to a new device-independent bitmap
  DDB: HBITMAP;             // holds a handle to a new device-dependent bitmap
  DibInfo: PBitmapInfo;     // a pointer to a bitmap information structure
  BitsPtr: PByte;           // a pointer to the DIB bitmap bits
  ReferenceDC: HDC;         // holds a handle to a reference device context
  ScreenDC: HDC;            // holds a handle to a screen device context
  iCount: Integer;          // general loop counter

  SystemPalette: array[0..255] of TPaletteEntry;  // required for converting the
                                                  // system palette into a DIB-
                                                  // compatible palette
begin
  {allocate memory for the DIB}
  GetMem(DibInfo, SizeOf(TBitmapInfo)+256*SizeOf(TRGBQuad));

  {initialize the DIB information}
  DibInfo^.bmiHeader.biWidth       := 64;    // create a 64 X 64 pixel DIB,
  DibInfo^.bmiHeader.biHeight      := -64;   // oriented top-down
  DibInfo^.bmiHeader.biPlanes      := 1;
```

```
DibInfo^.bmiHeader.biBitCount      := 8;      // 256 colors
DibInfo^.bmiHeader.biCompression   := BI_RGB; // no compression
DibInfo^.bmiHeader.biSizeImage     := 0;      // let Windows determine size
DibInfo^.bmiHeader.biXPelsPerMeter := 0;
DibInfo^.bmiHeader.biYPelsPerMeter := 0;
DibInfo^.bmiHeader.biClrUsed       := 0;
DibInfo^.bmiHeader.biClrImportant  := 0;
DibInfo^.bmiHeader.biSize          := SizeOf(TBitmapInfoHeader);

{retrieve the current system palette}
GetSystemPaletteEntries(Form1.Canvas.Handle, 0, 256, SystemPalette);

{the system palette is returned as an array of TPaletteEntry structures,
 which store the palette colors in the form of Red, Green, and Blue. however,
 the TBitmapInfo structure's bmiColors member takes an array of TRGBQuad
 structures, which store the palette colors in the form of Blue, Green, and
 Red. therefore, we must translate the TPaletteEntry structures into the
 appropriate TRGBQuad structures to get the correct color entries.}
for iCount := 0 to 255 do
begin
  DibInfo^.bmiColors[iCount].rgbBlue     := SystemPalette[iCount].peBlue;
  DibInfo^.bmiColors[iCount].rgbRed      := SystemPalette[iCount].peRed;
  DibInfo^.bmiColors[iCount].rgbGreen    := SystemPalette[iCount].peGreen;
  DibInfo^.bmiColors[iCount].rgbReserved := 0;
end;

{create a memory-based device context}
ReferenceDC := CreateCompatibleDC(0);

{create the DIB based on the memory device context and the
 initialized bitmap information}
Dib := CreateDIBSection(ReferenceDC, DibInfo^, DIB_RGB_COLORS,
                        Pointer(BitsPtr), 0, 0);

{draw bands of color into the DIB}
FillMemory(BitsPtr, 8*64, $03);
FillMemory(Pointer(LongInt(BitsPtr)+8*64), 8*64, $05);
FillMemory(Pointer(LongInt(BitsPtr)+2*(8*64)), 8*64, $03);
FillMemory(Pointer(LongInt(BitsPtr)+3*(8*64)), 8*64, $05);
FillMemory(Pointer(LongInt(BitsPtr)+4*(8*64)), 8*64, $03);
FillMemory(Pointer(LongInt(BitsPtr)+5*(8*64)), 8*64, $05);
FillMemory(Pointer(LongInt(BitsPtr)+6*(8*64)), 8*64, $03);
FillMemory(Pointer(LongInt(BitsPtr)+7*(8*64)), 8*64, $05);

{get a screen-based DC which is used as a reference point
 when creating the device-dependent bitmap}
ScreenDC := GetDC(0);

{create a device-dependent bitmap from the DIB}
DDB := CreateDIBitmap(ScreenDC, DibInfo^.bmiHeader, CBM_INIT, PChar(BitsPtr),
                      DibInfo^, DIB_RGB_COLORS);

{delete the screen-based device context}
ReleaseDC(0, ScreenDC);
```

5

Chapter

```
{select the device-dependent bitmap into the offscreen DC}
SelectObject(ReferenceDC, DDB);

{copy the device-independent bitmap to the form}
SetDIBitsToDevice(Form1.Canvas.Handle, 50, 5, 64, 64, 0, 0, 0, 64, BitsPtr,
                  DibInfo^, DIB_RGB_COLORS);

{copy the device-dependent bitmap to the form}
BitBlt(Form1.Canvas.Handle, 166, 5, 64, 64, ReferenceDC, 0, 0, SRCCOPY);

{we no longer need the bitmaps or the device context, so free everything}
DeleteDC(ReferenceDC);
DeleteObject(Dib);
DeleteObject(DDB);
FreeMem(DibInfo, SizeOf(TBitmapInfo)+256*SizeOf(TRGBQuad));
end;
```

Figure 5-9:
The new
device-
dependent
bitmap

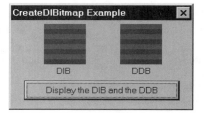

Table 5-5: CreateDIBitmap wUsage Values

Value	Description
DIB_PAL_COLORS	The bmiColors member of the TBitmapInfo structure is an array of 16-bit indices into the currently realized logical palette of the specified device context. This value should not be used if the bitmap will be saved to disk.
DIB_RGB_COLORS	The bmiColors member of the TBitmapInfo structure is an array of literal RGB color values.

CreateDIBSection   Windows.Pas

Syntax

```
CreateDIBSection(
DC: HDC;                      {a handle to a device context}
const p2: TBitmapInfo;        {a pointer to a TBitmapInfo data structure}
p3: UINT;                     {color type flags}
var p4: Pointer;              {a variable that receives a pointer to the bitmap bits}
p5: THandle;                  {a handle to a file mapping object}
p6: DWORD                     {an offset to the bitmap bit values}
): HBITMAP;                   {returns a handle to a DIB}
```

Description

This function creates a device-independent bitmap based on the specified bitmap attributes. It returns a handle to this new bitmap, and a pointer to the bit values that make up the bitmap image. The developer can specify a file mapping object to store the bitmap image bits, or let Windows automatically allocate the memory. When the bitmap is no longer needed, it should be deleted with a call to DeleteObject.

Parameters

DC: A handle to a device context. If the p3 parameter contains the DIB_PAL_COLORS flag, the new DIB's color palette will match the logical palette of the device context identified by this parameter.

p2: A pointer to a TBitmapInfo data structure. This data structure contains information describing the type of DIB to create, such as its dimensions, color format, and compression. The TBitmapInfo data structure is defined as:

```
TBitmapInfo = packed record
      bmiHeader: TBitmapInfoHeader;        {bitmap header information}
      bmiColors: array[0..0] of TRGBQuad;  {the color table used by the bitmap}
end;
```

bmiHeader: A TBitmapInfoHeader data structure containing information about the dimensions and color format of the DIB. The TBitmapInfoHeader data structure is defined as:

```
TBitmapInfoHeader = packed record
      biSize: DWORD;                {the size of the structure in bytes}
      biWidth: Longint;             {the width of the bitmap in pixels}
      biHeight: Longint;            {the height of the bitmap in pixels}
      biPlanes: Word;               {the number of color planes}
      biBitCount: Word;             {the bits per pixel required to describe a
                                     color}
      biCompression: DWORD;         {compression flags}
      biSizeImage: DWORD;           {the size of the image in bytes}
      biXPelsPerMeter: Longint;     {horizontal pixels per meter of the target
                                     device}
      biYPelsPerMeter: Longint;     {vertical pixels per meter of the target device}
      biClrUsed: DWORD;             {the number of color indices used}
      biClrImportant: DWORD;        {the number of important color indices}
end;
```

biSize: The size of the TBitmapInfoHeader in bytes. This member should be set to SizeOf(TBitmapInfoHeader).

biWidth: Specifies the width of the bitmap in pixels.

biHeight: Specifies the height of the bitmap in pixels. If this value is positive, the DIB is oriented in a bottom-up fashion, with its origin in the lower left-hand corner. If this value is negative, the DIB is oriented in a top-down fashion, with its origin in the upper left-hand corner like a regular bitmap.

biPlanes: Specifies the number of color planes in use.

biBitCount: The number of bits required to describe the color of one pixel (i.e., 8 bits for 256-color images, 24 bits for 16.7 million-color images, etc.). This member can be one value from Table 5-6.

biCompression: A flag indicating the type of compression used for bottom-up oriented DIBs (top-down oriented DIBs cannot use compression). This member can be one value from Table 5-7.

biSizeImage: Specifies the size of the image in bytes. This member may be set to 0 for DIBs using the BI_RGB flag in the biCompression member. Although the biWidth member can be set to any value, each scan line of a DIB must be double word aligned. To find the correct value for this member that will cause the scan lines of the DIB to be double word aligned, use the following formula:

$$(((((biBitCount * biWidth) + 31) \text{ div } 32) * 4) * ABS(biHeight))$$

Any extra bits will be padded with zeroes and will not be used.

biXPelsPerMeter: Specifies the horizontal pixels per meter resolution of the target display device indicated by the DC parameter. This value may be used to select a bitmap from the application's resources that best matches the characteristics of the current display device.

biYPelsPerMeter: Specifies the vertical pixels per meter resolution of the target display device indicated by the DC parameter.

biClrUsed: Specifies the number of color indices from the color table that are in use by the bitmap. If this member is zero, the bitmap uses the maximum number of colors indicated by the biBitCount member for the compression mode indicated by the biCompression member. If the DIB is a packed bitmap, meaning that the array of bits describing the image directly follows the TBitmapInfo structure and the entire contiguous chunk of data is referenced by one pointer, then this member must be set to either zero or the actual size of the color table. If the p3 parameter is set to DIB_PAL_COLORS and the DIB is a packed bitmap, this member must be set to an even number so that the DIB bitmap values will start on a double word boundary.

biClrImportant: Specifies the number of slots in the color table that are considered important for displaying the bitmap correctly. The colors in the bmiColors array should be arranged in the order of importance, with the most important colors going into the first entries of the array. This member may be set to zero, in which case all colors are considered important.

bmiColors: An array of either TRGBQuad records or double word values that define the color table of the bitmap. The TRGBQuad data structure is defined as:

```
TRGBQuad = packed record
      rgbBlue: Byte;                {blue color intensity}
      rgbGreen: Byte;               {green color intensity}
      rgbRed: Byte;                 {red color intensity}
      rgbReserved: Byte;            {reserved value}
end;
```

rgbBlue: Specifies the blue color intensity.

rgbGreen: Specifies the green color intensity.

rgbRed: Specifies the red color intensity.

rgbReserved: This member is reserved and must be set to zero.

p3: A flag indicating the type of color information stored in the bmiColors member of the TBitmapInfo data structure pointed to by the p2 parameter. This parameter can be one value from Table 5-8.

p4: A pointer to a variable that receives a pointer to the DIB's bitmap bit values.

p5: An optional handle to a file mapping object created from a call to the CreateFile-Mapping function. This file mapping object is used to create the DIB bitmap. The DIB's bit values will be located at the offset indicated by the p6 parameter into the file mapping object. This file mapping object can be retrieved at a later time by a call to the GetObject function using the HBITMAP handle returned by CreateDIBSection. The developer must manually close the file mapping object once the bitmap is deleted. If this parameter is zero, Windows allocates the memory for the DIB, the p6 parameter is ignored, and the file mapping handle returned from GetObject will be zero.

p6: Specifies the offset from the beginning of the file mapping object referred to by the p5 parameter to the DIB's bitmap bit values. The bitmap bit values are double word aligned, so this parameter must be a multiple of 4. If the p5 parameter is zero, this parameter is ignored.

Return Value

If the function succeeds, it returns a handle to a new device-independent bitmap, and the variable indicated by the p4 parameter contains a pointer to the bitmap's bit values. If the function fails, it returns zero, and the variable indicated by the p4 parameter contains NIL. To get extended error information, call the GetLastError function.

See Also

CreateFileMapping, DeleteObject, GetDIBColorTable, GetObject, SetDIBits, SetDIBitsTo-Device, SetDIBColorTable, StretchDIBits

5

Chapter

Example

Listing 5-9: Creating a Device-independent Bitmap

```
procedure TForm1.Button1Click(Sender: TObject);
var
  Dib: HBITMAP;              // holds a handle to the DIB
  DibInfo: PBitmapInfo;      // a pointer to the bitmap information data structure
  BitsPtr: PByte;            // holds a pointer to the bitmap bits
  ReferenceDC: HDC;          // a handle to the reference device context
  iCount: Integer;           // general loop counter

  SystemPalette: array[0..255] of TPaletteEntry;  // required for converting the
                                                  // system palette into a DIB-
                                                  // compatible palette
begin
  {get the memory needed for the bitmap information data structure}
  GetMem(DibInfo, SizeOf(TBitmapInfo)+256*SizeOf(TRGBQuad));

  {initialize the bitmap information}
  DibInfo^.bmiHeader.biWidth         := 64;    // create a 64 X 64 pixel DIB,
  DibInfo^.bmiHeader.biHeight        := -64;   // oriented top-down
  DibInfo^.bmiHeader.biPlanes        := 1;
  DibInfo^.bmiHeader.biBitCount      := 8;     // 256 colors
  DibInfo^.bmiHeader.biCompression   := BI_RGB; // no compression
  DibInfo^.bmiHeader.biSizeImage     := 0;     // let Windows determine size
  DibInfo^.bmiHeader.biXPelsPerMeter := 0;
  DibInfo^.bmiHeader.biYPelsPerMeter := 0;
  DibInfo^.bmiHeader.biClrUsed       := 0;
  DibInfo^.bmiHeader.biClrImportant  := 0;
  DibInfo^.bmiHeader.biSize          := SizeOf(TBitmapInfoHeader);

  {retrieve the current system palette}
  GetSystemPaletteEntries(Form1.Canvas.Handle, 0, 256, SystemPalette);

  {the system palette is returned as an array of TPaletteEntry structures,
   which store the palette colors in the form of Red, Green, and Blue. however,
   the TBitmapInfo structure's bmiColors member takes an array of TRGBQuad
   structures, which store the palette colors in the form of Blue, Green, and
   Red. therefore, we must translate the TPaletteEntry structures into the
   appropriate TRGBQuad structures to get the correct color entries.}
  for iCount := 0 to 255 do
  begin
    DibInfo^.bmiColors[iCount].rgbBlue     := SystemPalette[iCount].peBlue;
    DibInfo^.bmiColors[iCount].rgbRed      := SystemPalette[iCount].peRed;
    DibInfo^.bmiColors[iCount].rgbGreen    := SystemPalette[iCount].peGreen;
    DibInfo^.bmiColors[iCount].rgbReserved := 0;
  end;

  {create a memory-based device context}
  ReferenceDC := CreateCompatibleDC(0);

  {create the DIB based on the memory device context and the
   initialized bitmap information}
  Dib := CreateDIBSection(ReferenceDC, DibInfo^, DIB_RGB_COLORS,
```

```
                        Pointer(BitsPtr), 0, 0);

{delete the reference device context}
DeleteDC(ReferenceDC);

{fill the DIB image bits with alternating bands of color}
FillMemory(BitsPtr, 8*64, $03);
FillMemory(Pointer(LongInt(BitsPtr)+8*64), 8*64, $05);
FillMemory(Pointer(LongInt(BitsPtr)+2*(8*64)), 8*64, $03);
FillMemory(Pointer(LongInt(BitsPtr)+3*(8*64)), 8*64, $05);
FillMemory(Pointer(LongInt(BitsPtr)+4*(8*64)), 8*64, $03);
FillMemory(Pointer(LongInt(BitsPtr)+5*(8*64)), 8*64, $05);
FillMemory(Pointer(LongInt(BitsPtr)+6*(8*64)), 8*64, $03);
FillMemory(Pointer(LongInt(BitsPtr)+7*(8*64)), 8*64, $05);

{draw the DIB onto the form surface}
SetDIBitsToDevice(Form1.Canvas.Handle, 30, 5, 64, 64, 0, 0, 0, 64, BitsPtr,
                  DibInfo^, DIB_RGB_COLORS);

{draw the DIB again, but this time let's stretch it to twice its size}
StretchDIBits(Form1.Canvas.Handle, 105, 5, 128, 128, 0, 0, 64, 64, BitsPtr,
              DibInfo^, DIB_RGB_COLORS, SRCCOPY);

{we no longer need the DIB, so delete it and the
 allocated memory for the information data structure}
DeleteObject(Dib);
FreeMem(DibInfo, SizeOf(TBitmapInfo)+256*SizeOf(TRGBQuad));
end;
```

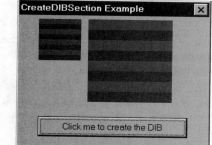

*Figure 5-10:
The DIB,
original size
and double
sized*

5

Chapter

Table 5-6: CreateDIBSection p2.bmiHeader.biBitCount Values

Value	Description
I	This bitmap has a maximum of two colors, and the bmiColors array contains only two entries. Each pixel in the bitmap image is represented by a single bit. If the bit is off, that pixel is drawn using the color in the first slot of the bmiColors array. If the bit is on, that pixel is drawn using the color in the second slot of the bmiColors array.

Value	Description
4	This bitmap has a maximum of 16 colors, and the bmiColors array can contain up to 16 entries. Each byte in the bitmap bit values represents two pixels. The first 4 bits in the byte represent the index into the color palette for the first pixel, and the last 4 bits represent the index for the second pixel.
8	This bitmap has a maximum of 256 colors, and the bmiColors array can contain up to 256 entries. Each byte in the bitmap bit values represents one pixel, specifying that pixel's index into the 256-entry bmiColors array.
16	This bitmap has a maximum of 65,536 colors. If the biCompression member of the TBitmapInfoHeader structure is set to BI_RGB, the bmiColors member is set to NIL. In this case, each word in the bitmap bit values represents one pixel. Moving from the least significant bit to the most significant, the last 5 bits of the word specify the pixel's blue intensity, the next 5 bits specify the green intensity, and the next 5 bits specify the red intensity. The most significant bit of the word is not used. If the biCompression member of the TBitmapInfoHeader structure is set to BI_BITFIELDS, the bmiColors member contains three double word values that represent a bitmask. These bitmasks are applied to the word value for each pixel using the Boolean AND operator to retrieve the red, green, and blue color intensities, respectively, for that pixel. Under Windows NT, the bits set in each double word mask must be contiguous and should not overlap the bits of another mask. In this case, the developer does not have to use all of the bits describing the pixel. Under Windows 95, only the following double word bitmask values are allowed: a 5-5-5 format, where the blue mask is $00000001F$, green is $000003E0$, and red is $00007C00$, or a 5-6-5 format, where the blue mask is $00000001F$, green is $000007E0$, and red is $0000F800$.
24	This bitmap has a maximum of 16.7 million colors, and the bmiColors member is set to NIL. Each pixel in the bitmap image is represented by 3 bytes. These 3 bytes indicate the relative intensities of the blue, green, and red colors, respectively, of the pixel.
32	This bitmap has a maximum of approximately 4.3 billion colors. If the biCompression member of the TBitmapInfoHeader structure is set to BI_RGB, the bmiColors member is set to NIL. In this case, each double word in the bitmap bit values represents one pixel. Moving from the least significant bit to the most significant, the last byte of the double word specifies the pixel's blue intensity, the next byte specifies the green intensity, and the next byte specifies the red intensity. The most significant byte of the double word is not used. If the biCompression member of the TBitmapInfoHeader structure is set to BI_BITFIELDS, the bmiColors member contains three double word values that represent a bitmask. These bitmasks are applied to the double word value for each pixel using the Boolean AND operator to retrieve the red, green, and blue color intensities, respectively, for that pixel. Under Windows NT, the bits set in each double word mask must be contiguous and should not overlap the bits of another mask. In this case, the developer does not have to use all of the bits describing the pixel. Under Windows 95, only a blue mask of $000000FF$, green mask of $0000FF00$, and red mask of $00FF0000$ are allowed.

Table 5-7: CreateDIBSection p2.bmiHeader.biCompression Values

Value	Description
BI_RGB	No compression.
BI_RLE8	A run-length encoded format for 256-color bitmaps (color format is 8 bits per pixel). This compression format consists of two byte pairs. The first byte in a pair is a count byte, specifying how many times to repeat the following byte when drawing the image. The second byte is an index into the color table.
BI_RLE4	A run-length encoded format for 16-color bitmaps (color format is 4 bits per pixel). This compression format consists of two byte pairs. The first byte in a pair is a count byte, specifying how many times to repeat the following byte when drawing the image. The second byte specifies two indices into the color table, the first index in the high-order 4 bits, the second in the low-order 4 bits.
BI_BITFIELDS	This format is valid only for 16 and 32 bits per pixel color bitmaps. The bitmap is not compressed, and the color table consists of three double word color masks, one each for the red, blue, and green intensities. These color masks, when combined with the bits describing each individual pixel using the Boolean AND operator, specify the red, green, and blue intensities, respectively, of each pixel.

Table 5-8: CreateDIBSection p3 Values

Value	Description
DIB_PAL_COLORS	The bmiColors member of the TBitmapInfo structure is an array of 16-bit indices into the currently realized logical palette of the specified device context. This value should not be used if the bitmap will be saved to disk.
DIB_RGB_COLORS	The bmiColors member of the TBitmapInfo structure is an array of literal RGB color values.

CreateEnhMetaFile   Windows.Pas

Syntax

```
CreateEnhMetaFile(
DC: HDC;                {a handle to a reference device context}
p2: PChar;              {a pointer to a filename}
p3: PRect;              {a pointer to a bounding rectangle}
p4: PChar;              {a pointer to a description string}
): HDC;                 {returns a handle to a metafile device context}
```

Description

This function creates an enhanced metafile device context. This device context can be used with any GDI function to draw into the enhanced metafile. A handle to the metafile is obtained by calling the CloseEnhMetaFile function, and the subsequent metafile is drawn by using the PlayEnhMetaFile function.

Parameters

DC: A handle to a device context used as a reference for the new enhanced metafile device context. This reference device context is used to record the resolution and units of the device on which the metafile originally appeared. If this parameter is zero, the current display device is used as the reference. This information is used to scale the metafile when it is drawn.

p2: A pointer to a null-terminated string describing a filename in which to store the enhanced metafile. The extension of this filename is typically .EMF. If this parameter is NIL, the enhanced metafile will only exist in memory and is deleted upon the call to the DeleteEnhMetaFile function.

p3: A pointer to a rectangle describing the dimensions of the picture stored in the enhanced metafile. These dimensions are in terms of .01 millimeter units (i.e., a value of 3 equals .03 millimeters). If this parameter is NIL, the dimensions of the smallest rectangle surrounding the metafile picture will automatically be calculated. This information is used to scale the metafile when it is drawn.

p4: A pointer to a null-terminated string containing a description of the metafile and its contents. Typically, this consists of the application name followed by a null character, followed by the title of the metafile, terminating with two null characters (i.e., "CreateEnhMetaFile Example Program"+Chr(0)+ "Example Metafile"+Chr(0)+Chr(0)). This parameter can be NIL, in which case there will be no description string stored in the metafile. Under Windows 95, the maximum length for the enhanced metafile description is 16,384 bytes.

Return Value

If the function succeeds, it returns a handle to an enhanced metafile device context, which can be used in any GDI function call. Otherwise, it returns zero.

See Also

CloseEnhMetaFile, CopyEnhMetaFile, DeleteEnhMetaFile, GetEnhMetaFileDescription, GetEnhMetaFileHeader, PlayEnhMetaFile

Example

Listing 5-10: Creating an Enhanced Metafile

```
procedure TForm1.Button1Click(Sender: TObject);
var
   {these hold important screen dimension information used when creating
```

```
        the reference rectangle}
      WidthInMM,
      HeightInMM,
      WidthInPixels,
      HeightInPixels: Integer;

      {holds millimeter per pixel ratios}
      MMPerPixelHorz,
      MMPerPixelVer: Integer;

      {the reference rectangle}
      ReferenceRect: TRect;

      {a handle to the metafile device context}
      MetafileDC: HDC;

      {the handle to a metafile}
      TheMetafile: HENHMETAFILE;

      {a handle to a brush used in drawing on the metafile}
      TheBrush: HBRUSH;
      OldBrush: HBRUSH;
begin
      {the CreateEnhMetaFile function assumes that the dimensions in the reference
      rectangle are in terms of .01 millimeter units (i.e., a 1 equals .01
      millimeters, 2 equals .02 millimeters, etc.).  therefore, the following
      lines are required to obtain a millimeters per pixel ratio. this can then
      be used to create a reference rectangle with the appropriate dimensions.}

      {retrieve the size of the screen in millimeters}
      WidthInMM:=GetDeviceCaps(Form1.Canvas.Handle, HORZSIZE);
      HeightInMM:=GetDeviceCaps(Form1.Canvas.Handle, VERTSIZE);

      {retrieve the size of the screen in pixels}
      WidthInPixels:=GetDeviceCaps(Form1.Canvas.Handle, HORZRES);
      HeightInPixels:=GetDeviceCaps(Form1.Canvas.Handle, VERTRES);

      {compute a millimeter per pixel ratio. the millimeter measurements must be
      multiplied by 100 to get the appropriate unit measurement that the
      CreateEnhMetaFile is expecting (where a 1 equals .01 millimeters)}
      MMPerPixelHorz:=(WidthInMM * 100) div WidthInPixels;
      MMPerPixelVer:=(HeightInMM * 100) div HeightInPixels;

      {create our reference rectangle for the metafile}
      ReferenceRect.Top:=0;
      ReferenceRect.Left:=0;
      ReferenceRect.Right:=Image1.Width * MMPerPixelHorz;
      ReferenceRect.Bottom:=Image1.Height * MMPerPixelVer;

      {create a metafile that will be saved to disk}
      MetafileDC:=CreateEnhMetaFile(Form1.Canvas.Handle, 'Example.emf',
                          @ReferenceRect,
                          'CreateEnhMetaFile Example Program'+Chr(0)+
                          'Example Metafile'+Chr(0)+Chr(0));
```

5

Chapter

```
{display some text in the metafile}
TextOut(MetafileDC,15,15,'This is an enhanced metafile.',29);

{create a diagonal hatched brush and select it into the metafile}
TheBrush:=CreateHatchBrush(HS_DIAGCROSS, clRed);
OldBrush:=SelectObject(MetafileDC, TheBrush);

{draw a filled rectangle}
Rectangle(MetafileDC, 15, 50, 250, 250);

{delete the current brush}
SelectObject(MetafileDC, OldBrush);
DeleteObject(TheBrush);

{create a horizontal hatched brush and select it into the metafile}
TheBrush:=CreateHatchBrush(HS_CROSS, clBlue);
OldBrush:=SelectObject(MetafileDC, TheBrush);

{draw a filled ellipse}
Ellipse(MetafileDC, 15, 50, 250, 250);

{delete the current brush}
SelectObject(MetafileDC, OldBrush);
DeleteObject(TheBrush);

{close the metafile, saving it to disk and retrieving a handle}
TheMetafile:=CloseEnhMetaFile(MetafileDC);

{draw the metafile into the Image1 canvas}
PlayEnhMetaFile(Image1.Canvas.Handle, TheMetafile, Image1.Canvas.Cliprect);

{we are done with the metafile, so delete its handle}
DeleteEnhMetaFile(TheMetafile);
end;
```

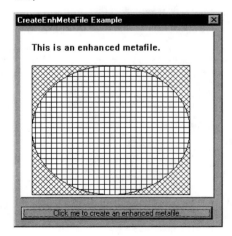

Figure 5-11:
The new
metafile

DeleteEnhMetaFile   *Windows.Pas*

Syntax

```
DeleteEnhMetaFile(
p1: HENHMETAFILE          {a handle to an enhanced metafile}
): BOOL;                  {returns TRUE or FALSE}
```

Description

This function deletes the metafile associated with the given handle. If this metafile is stored in memory, it deletes the metafile and frees the associated memory. If this handle identifies a metafile stored in a file on disk, the handle and associated memory is freed but the file is not destroyed.

Parameters

p1: A handle to the enhanced metafile to be deleted.

Return Value

If the function succeeds, it returns TRUE; otherwise it returns FALSE.

See Also

CopyEnhMetaFile, CreateEnhMetaFile, GetEnhMetaFile

Example

Please see Listing 5-10 under CreateEnhMetaFile.

EnumEnhMetaFile   *Windows.Pas*

Syntax

```
EnumEnhMetaFile(
DC: HDC;                  {a handle to a device context}
p2: HENHMETAFILE;         {a handle to the enhanced metafile being enumerated}
p3: TFNEnhMFEnumProc;     {a pointer to an application-defined callback function}
p4: Pointer;              {a pointer to application-defined data}
const p5: TRect           {a pointer to a TRect structure}
): BOOL;                  {returns TRUE or FALSE}
```

Description

This function iterates through all of the metafile records stored in the specified enhanced metafile, passing each one to an application-defined callback function. This callback function processes the record as needed, and enumeration continues until all records have been processed or the callback function returns zero.

Parameters

DC: A handle to the device context into which the metafile can be played. This parameter is passed directly to the callback function, and can be set to zero if the callback will not play the metafile records.

p2: A handle to the enhanced metafile whose records are to be enumerated

p3: The address of the application-defined callback function.

p4: A pointer to application-defined data. This data is intended for application specific purposes only, and is passed directly to the application-defined callback function.

p5: A pointer to a TRect data structure containing the upper left and lower right coordinates of the rectangle containing the metafile picture, measured in logical units. Points along the edge of this rectangle are included in the picture. If the DC parameter contains zero, this parameter is ignored.

Return Value

If the function succeeds and the callback function enumerated all enhanced metafile records, it returns TRUE. If the function fails, or the callback function did not enumerate all enhanced metafile records, it returns FALSE.

Callback Syntax

```
EnumerateEnhMetafileProc(
DisplaySurface: HDC;                    {a handle to a device context}
var MetafileTable: THandleTable;        {a pointer to a metafile handle table}
var MetafileRecord: TEnhMetaRecord;     {a pointer to a metafile record}
ObjectCount: Integer;                   {the number of objects with handles}
var Data: Longint                       {a pointer to application-defined data}
): Integer;                             {returns an integer value}
```

Description

This function receives a pointer to a metafile record for every record stored in the enhanced metafile being enumerated. It can perform any desired task.

Parameters

DisplaySurface: A handle to the device context into which the metafile record can be played. If metafile records are not going to be played by the callback function, this parameter can be zero.

MetafileTable: A pointer to an array of type HGDIOBJ. This array contains handles to graphics objects, such as pens and brushes, in the metafile. The first entry in this array is a handle to the enhanced metafile itself.

MetafileRecord: A pointer to a TEnhMetaRecord structure. This data structure defines the current metafile record being enumerated. The TEnhMetaRecord structure is defined as:

TEnhMetaRecord = packed record
    iType: DWORD;   {the record type}
    nSize: DWORD;   {the record size}
    dParm: array[0..0] of DWORD;   {an array of parameters}
end;

iType: Indicates the record type and indirectly the GDI function that created the record. This is a constant of the form EMR_XXX, and all record types are listed in the Windows.Pas file.

nSize: The size of the record in bytes.

dParm: An array of parameters used by the GDI function identified by the iType member.

ObjectCount: An integer indicating the number of GDI graphics objects with handles in the handle table pointed to by the MetafileTable parameter.

Data: A pointer to application-defined data. This data is intended for application specific purposes only.

Return Value

The callback function should return a nonzero value to continue enumeration; otherwise it should return zero.

See Also

GetEnhMetaFile, PlayEnhMetaFile, PlayEnhMetaFileRecord

Example

Listing 5-11: Changing the Brushes in an Enhanced Metafile

```
{the callback function for enumerating enhanced metafile records}
function EnumerateEnhMetafile(DisplaySurface: HDC;
                             var MetafileTable: THandleTable;
                             var MetafileRecord: TEnhMetaRecord;
                             ObjectCount: Integer;
                             var Data: Longint): Integer; stdcall;

implementation

procedure TForm1.FileListBox1Click(Sender: TObject);
var
  TheMetafile: HENHMETAFILE;     // holds an enhanced metafile
begin
  {open and retrieve a handle to the selected metafile}
  TheMetafile:=GetEnhMetaFile(PChar(FileListBox1.FileName));

  {erase the last image}
  Image1.Canvas.FillRect(Image1.Canvas.ClipRect);

  {enumerate the records in the metafile}
  EnumEnhMetaFile(Image1.Canvas.Handle, TheMetafile, @EnumerateEnhMetafile,
```

5

Chapter

```
                                 nil, Image1.BoundsRect);
          end;

          {this function will fire for every record stored in the metafile}
          function EnumerateEnhMetafile(DisplaySurface: HDC;
                                        var MetafileTable: THandleTable;
                                        var MetafileRecord: TEnhMetaRecord;
                                        ObjectCount: Integer;
                                        var Data: Longint): Integer;
          var
            NewBrush: HBRUSH;         // holds a new brush
            BrushInfo: TLogBrush;     // defines a new brush
          begin
            {if the metafile is trying to create a brush...}
            if MetafileRecord.iType=EMR_CREATEBRUSHINDIRECT then
            begin
              {...intercept it and create our own brush}
              BrushInfo.lbStyle := BS_SOLID;
              BrushInfo.lbColor := clRed;
              BrushInfo.lbHatch := 0;
              NewBrush := CreateBrushIndirect(BrushInfo);

              {select this brush into the device context where the
               metafile is being played. this will replace all brushes
               in the metafile with a red, solid brush}
              SelectObject(DisplaySurface,NewBrush);
            end
            else
              {if it's not a create brush record, play it}
              PlayEnhMetaFileRecord(DisplaySurface, MetafileTable, MetafileRecord,
                                    ObjectCount);

            Result:=1;   // continue enumeration
          end;
```

*Figure 5-12:
All brushes in
the enhanced
metafile were
changed.*

GetBitmapBits   *Windows.Pas*

Syntax

```
GetBitmapBits(
Bitmap: HBITMAP;          {a handle to a bitmap}
Count: Longint;           {the number of bytes in the Bits array}
Bits: Pointer             {a pointer to an array of bytes}
): Longint;               {returns the number of bytes retrieved from the bitmap}
```

Description

This function copies the color information from the specified bitmap into a buffer. The GetBitmapBits function is included for compatibility purposes. Win32-based applications should use the GetDIBits function.

Parameters

Bitmap: A handle to the bitmap from which color information is retrieved.

Count: Indicates the number of bytes pointed to by the Bits parameter.

Bits: A pointer to an array of bytes which receives the color information from the bitmap.

Return Value

If the function succeeds, it returns the number of bytes retrieved from the bitmap; otherwise it returns zero.

See Also

CreateBitmap, GetDIBits, SetBitmapBits, SetDIBits

Example

Listing 5-12: Retrieving Bitmap Color Data

```
procedure TForm1.Button1Click(Sender: TObject);
type
  TBitmapBits = array[0..0] of Byte;
var
  BitmapBits: ^TBitmapBits;           // holds the bytes from the bitmap
  LoopRow, LoopCol: Integer;          // loop control variables
begin
  {set the string grid to the dimensions of the bitmap}
  StringGrid1.ColCount:=Image1.Picture.Bitmap.Width;
  StringGrid1.RowCount:=Image1.Picture.Bitmap.Height;

  {dynamically allocate the needed space for the bitmap color data}
  GetMem(BitmapBits,StringGrid1.RowCount*StringGrid1.ColCount);
```

5

Chapter

```
{retrieve the color data from the bitmap}
GetBitmapBits(Image1.Picture.Bitmap.Handle, StringGrid1.RowCount*
             StringGrid1.ColCount, BitmapBits);

{display the values that define the bitmap in the string grid. since this
 is a 256-color bitmap, these values represent indexes into the bitmap's
 color palette.}
for LoopRow:=0 to Image1.Height-1 do
  for LoopCol:=0 to Image1.Width-1 do
    StringGrid1.Cells[LoopCol,
LoopRow]:=IntToStr(BitmapBits[LoopRow*Image1.Width+LoopCol]);

{free the allocated memory}
FreeMem(BitmapBits);
end;
```

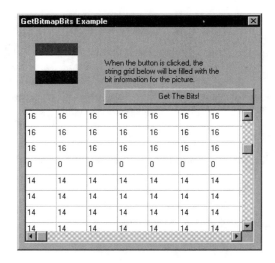

Figure 5-13:
The bitmap
bits

GetBitmapDimensionEx   Windows.Pas

Syntax

```
GetBitmapDimensionEx(
p1: HBITMAP;              {a handle to a bitmap}
var p2: TSize             {the address of a TSize structure}
): BOOL;                  {returns TRUE or FALSE}
```

Description

This function retrieves the preferred bitmap dimensions set by the call to SetBitmapDimensionEx. If this function has not been called, the TSize structure returned by GetBitmapDimensionEx will contain zero in every field.

Parameters

p1: A handle to the bitmap whose preferred dimensions are to be retrieved.

p2: A pointer to a TSize structure. The TSize structure describes the width and height of a rectangle, and is defined as:

```
TSize = record
      cx: Longint;                    {the preferred width}
      cy: Longint;                    {the preferred height}
end;
```

      cx: The bitmap's preferred width. Each unit represents 0.1 millimeters.

      cy: The bitmap's preferred height. Each unit represents 0.1 millimeters.

Return Value

If the function succeeds, it returns TRUE; otherwise it returns FALSE. To get extended error information, call the GetLastError function.

See Also

SetBitmapDimensionEx

Example

Please see Listing 5-5 under CreateBitmap.

GetDIBits Windows.Pas

Syntax

```
GetDIBits(
DC: HDC;                     {a handle to a device context}
Bitmap: HBITMAP;             {a handle to a regular bitmap}
StartScan: UINT;             {the starting scan line}
NumScans: UINT;              {the total number of scan lines}
Bits: Pointer;               {a pointer to the DIB bitmap bit values}
var BitsInfo: TBitmapInfo;   {a pointer to the DIB bitmap information structure}
Usage: UINT;                 {color type flags}
): Integer;                  {returns the number of scan lines copied}
```

Description

This function creates a device-independent bitmap from the image stored in a device-dependent bitmap by retrieving the bit values from the specified device-dependent bitmap and storing them in a buffer in the format defined by the TBitmapInfo structure pointed to by the BitsInfo parameter. The Bitmap parameter can also specify the handle to a device-independent bitmap, in which case this function can be used to create a copy of the DIB in the desired format specified by the TBitmapInfo structure. If the color format of the requested DIB does not match the color format of the specified bitmap, a color palette will be generated for the DIB using default colors for the requested color format. If the BitsInfo parameter indicates a 16 bits per pixel or higher color format for the DIB, no color table is generated.

5

Chapter

Parameters

DC: A handle to a device context. The device-dependent bitmap specified by the Bitmap parameter uses the currently realized palette of this device context for its color information.

Bitmap: A handle to the device-dependent bitmap from which the bit values are copied.

StartScan: Specifies the starting scan line to retrieve from the device-dependent bitmap.

NumScans: Specifies the total number of scan lines to retrieve from the device-dependent bitmap.

Bits: A pointer to a buffer that receives the bitmap bit values. The application is responsible for allocating enough memory for this pointer to store the bitmap image, and for freeing this memory when it is no longer needed. The first six members of the TBitmapInfoHeader structure contained in the TBitmapInfo structure pointed to by the BitsInfo parameter must be initialized to indicate the dimensions and color format of the requested DIB bit values. If this parameter is NIL, the function fills the TBitmapInfo structure pointed to by the BitsInfo parameter with the dimensions and color format of the device-dependent bitmap specified by the Bitmap parameter. In this case, the biSize member of the TBitmapInfoHeader structure must be set to SizeOf(TBitmapInfoHeader) or the function will fail. In addition, if the biBitCount member is set to zero, the TBitmapInfo structure is filled in without the bitmap's color table. This is useful for querying bitmap attributes.

BitsInfo: A pointer to a TBitmapInfo data structure describing desired format for the DIB, including information about its dimensions and color table. The TBitmapInfo data structure is defined as:

TBitmapInfo = packed record
    bmiHeader: TBitmapInfoHeader;   {bitmap header information}
    bmiColors: array[0..0] of TRGBQuad;   {the color table used by the bitmap}
end;

The TBitmapInfoHeader data structure is defined as:

TBitmapInfoHeader = packed record
    biSize: DWORD;   {the size of the structure in bytes}
    biWidth: Longint;   {the width of the bitmap in pixels}
    biHeight: Longint;   {the height of the bitmap in pixels}
    biPlanes: Word;   {the number of color planes}
    biBitCount: Word;   {the bits per pixel required to describe a color}
    biCompression: DWORD;   {compression flags}
    biSizeImage: DWORD;   {the size of the image in bytes}
    biXPelsPerMeter: Longint;   {horizontal pixels per meter of the target device}
    biYPelsPerMeter: Longint;   {vertical pixels per meter of the target device}

```
        biClrUsed: DWORD;          {the number of color indices used}
        biClrImportant: DWORD;     {the number of important color indices}
    end;
```

The TRGBQuad data structure is defined as:

```
TRGBQuad = packed record
        rgbBlue: Byte;             {blue color intensity}
        rgbGreen: Byte;            {green color intensity}
        rgbRed: Byte;              {red color intensity}
        rgbReserved: Byte;         {reserved value}
    end;
```

For an explanation of these data structures, see the CreateDIBSection function.

Usage: A flag indicating the type of color information stored in the bmiColors member of the TBitmapInfo structure pointed to by the BitsInfo parameter. This parameter can be one value from Table 5-9.

Return Value

If the function succeeds and the Bits parameter is not NIL, it returns the number of scan lines copied from the device-dependent bitmap. If the function succeeds and the Bits parameter is NIL, the TBitmapInfo structure pointed to by the BitsInfo parameter is initialized with the dimensions and format of the device-dependent bitmap, and the function returns the total number of scan lines in the device-dependent bitmap. If the function fails, it returns zero.

See Also

CreateDIBitmap, CreateDIBSection, GetBitmapBits, SetDIBits

Example

Listing 5-13: Creating a DIB from a Device-dependent Bitmap

```
procedure TForm1.Button1Click(Sender: TObject);
var
  TheBitmap: HBITMAP;                    // a handle to a regular bitmap
  RegularBitmapInfo: Windows.TBitmap;    // a Windows bitmap information structure

  BitmapInfo: PBitmapInfo;               // a pointer to a DIB info structure
  BitmapBits: Pointer;                   // a pointer to DIB bit values
begin
  {get a handle to a system bitmap}
  TheBitmap:=LoadBitmap(0, MakeIntResource(OBM_CHECKBOXES));

  {fill in a Windows TBITMAP information structure}
  GetObject(TheBitmap, SizeOf(Windows.TBitmap), @RegularBitmapInfo);

  {get the memory for the DIB bitmap header}
  GetMem(BitmapInfo, SizeOf(TBitmapInfo)+256*SizeOf(TRGBQuad));
```

5

Chapter

```
{initialize the bitmap information}
BitmapInfo^.bmiHeader.biWidth          := RegularBitmapInfo.bmWidth;
BitmapInfo^.bmiHeader.biHeight         := RegularBitmapInfo.bmHeight;
BitmapInfo^.bmiHeader.biPlanes         := 1;
BitmapInfo^.bmiHeader.biBitCount       := 8;        // 256 colors
BitmapInfo^.bmiHeader.biCompression    := BI_RGB; // no compression
BitmapInfo^.bmiHeader.biSizeImage      := 0;        // let Windows determine size
BitmapInfo^.bmiHeader.biXPelsPerMeter  := 0;
BitmapInfo^.bmiHeader.biYPelsPerMeter  := 0;
BitmapInfo^.bmiHeader.biClrUsed        := 0;
BitmapInfo^.bmiHeader.biClrImportant   := 0;
BitmapInfo^.bmiHeader.biSize           := SizeOf(TBitmapInfoHeader);

{allocate enough memory to hold the bitmap bit values}
GetMem(BitmapBits,RegularBitmapInfo.bmWidth*RegularBitmapInfo.bmHeight);

{retrieve the bit values from the regular bitmap in a DIB format}
GetDIBits(Form1.Canvas.Handle, TheBitmap, 0, RegularBitmapInfo.bmHeight,
          BitmapBits, BitmapInfo^, 0);

{display this new DIB bitmap}
SetDIBitsToDevice(Form1.Canvas.Handle, (Form1.Width div 2)-
                  (BitmapInfo^.bmiHeader.biWidth div 2), 25,
                  BitmapInfo^.bmiHeader.biWidth,
                  BitmapInfo^.bmiHeader.biHeight, 0, 0, 0,
                  BitmapInfo^.bmiHeader.biHeight, BitmapBits, BitmapInfo^,
                  DIB_RGB_COLORS);

{delete the regular bitmap}
DeleteObject(TheBitmap);

{clean up allocated memory}
FreeMem(BitmapInfo, SizeOf(TBitmapInfo)+256*SizeOf(TRGBQuad));
FreeMem(BitmapBits,RegularBitmapInfo.bmWidth*RegularBitmapInfo.bmHeight);
end;
```

*Figure 5-14:
The DIB image
created from a
device-
dependent
bitmap*

Table 5-9: GetDIBits Usage Values

Value	Description
DIB_PAL_COLORS	The bmiColors member of the TBitmapInfo structure is an array of 16-bit indices into the currently realized logical palette of the specified device context. This value should not be used if the bitmap will be saved to disk.
DIB_RGB_COLORS	The bmiColors member of the TBitmapInfo structure is an array of literal RGB color values.

GetEnhMetaFile *Windows.Pas*

Syntax

```
GetEnhMetaFile(
p1: PChar                {an enhanced metafile filename}
): HENHMETAFILE;         {returns a handle to an enhanced metafile}
```

Description

This function creates an enhanced metafile and returns its handle, based on the enhanced metafile information stored in the specified file. When the application no longer needs the enhanced metafile, it should be deleted by using the DeleteObject function. This function will only open metafiles in the enhanced format.

Parameters

p1: A null-terminated string containing the filename of the enhanced metafile to open.

Return Value

If the function succeeds, it returns a handle to an enhanced metafile; otherwise it returns zero.

See Also

CreateEnhMetaFile, DeleteEnhMetaFile, GetEnhMetaFileHeader, GetEnhMetaFileDescription

Example

Listing 5-14: Opening Enhanced Metafiles

```
procedure TForm1.FileListBox1DblClick(Sender: TObject);
var
  TheMetafile: HENHMETAFILE;      // a handle to the original metafile
  CopyMetafile: HENHMETAFILE;     // a handle to the copied metafile
  MetafileInfo: TEnhMetaHeader;   // the metafile header structure
  MetafileDescription: PChar;     // holds the metafile description
  DescriptionSize: UINT;          // holds the size of the description
  CorrectedRect: TRect;           // an aspect ratio corrected rectangle
```

5

Chapter

```
          ScaleVert,                            // these are used to compute the
          ScaleHorz,                            // corrected aspect ratio
          ScaleLeast: Real;
      begin
          {open and retrieve a handle to the selected metafile}
          TheMetafile:=GetEnhMetaFile(PChar(FileListBox1.FileName));

          {retrieve the size of the description string}
          DescriptionSize:=GetEnhMetaFileDescription(TheMetaFile, 0, nil);

          {dynamically allocate a buffer large enough to hold the description}
          MetafileDescription:=StrAlloc(DescriptionSize+1);

          {retrieve the metafile description string, if one exists}
          GetEnhMetaFileDescription(TheMetaFile, DescriptionSize, MetafileDescription);

          {retrieve the metafile header info}
          GetEnhMetaFileHeader(TheMetafile, SizeOf(MetafileInfo), @MetafileInfo);

          {find the smallest ratio between the size of the metafile bounding rectangle
           and the TImage rectangle}
          ScaleVert:=Image1.Height / (MetafileInfo.rclBounds.Bottom-
                                      MetafileInfo.rclBounds.Top);
          ScaleHorz:=Image1.Width  / (MetafileInfo.rclBounds.Right-
                                      MetafileInfo.rclBounds.Left);

          {find the smallest ratio}
          if ScaleVert<ScaleHorz then
             ScaleLeast:=ScaleVert
          else
             ScaleLeast:=ScaleHorz;

          {determine the new bounding rectangle using this scaling factor}
          CorrectedRect.Left   :=Trunc(MetafileInfo.rclBounds.Left*ScaleLeast);
          CorrectedRect.Top    :=Trunc(MetafileInfo.rclBounds.Top*ScaleLeast);
          CorrectedRect.Right  :=Trunc(MetafileInfo.rclBounds.Right*ScaleLeast);
          CorrectedRect.Bottom :=Trunc(MetafileInfo.rclBounds.Bottom*ScaleLeast);

          {adjust the new bounding rectangle so it starts in the
           upper left-hand corner}
          CorrectedRect.Left:=0;
          CorrectedRect.Top:=0;
          CorrectedRect.Right:=CorrectedRect.Right-CorrectedRect.Left;
          CorrectedRect.Bottom:=CorrectedRect.Bottom-CorrectedRect.Top;

          {start displaying the metafile information}
          with ListBox1.Items do
          begin
             Clear;
             Add('Description -');
             if DescriptionSize>0 then
             begin
                {the description is a string in the form of the program name used
                 to create the metafile followed by a null terminator, followed
                 by the name of the metafile, followed by two null terminators. this
```

```
            line will display the first part of the description (the name of the
            program used to create the metafile)}
            Add(string(MetafileDescription));

            {by advancing the address of the string one past the first null
             terminator, we gain access to the second half containing the
             name of the metafile}
            Add(string(PChar(MetafileDescription+StrLen(MetafileDescription)+1)));
        end
        else
            Add('No description found.');
        Add('Type: '+IntToStr(MetafileInfo.iType));
        Add('Size: '+IntToStr(MetafileInfo.nSize));
        Add('Bounding Rectangle -');
        Add('        Left: '+IntToStr(MetafileInfo.rclBounds.Left));
        Add('         Top: '+IntToStr(MetafileInfo.rclBounds.Top));
        Add('       Right: '+IntToStr(MetafileInfo.rclBounds.Right));
        Add('      Bottom: '+IntToStr(MetafileInfo.rclBounds.Bottom));
        Add('Frame Rectangle - (1 = .01 millimeters)');
        Add('        Left: '+IntToStr(MetafileInfo.rclFrame.Left));
        Add('         Top: '+IntToStr(MetafileInfo.rclFrame.Top));
        Add('       Right: '+IntToStr(MetafileInfo.rclFrame.Right));
        Add('      Bottom: '+IntToStr(MetafileInfo.rclFrame.Bottom));
        Add('Signature: '+IntToStr(MetafileInfo.dSignature));
        Add('Version: '+IntToStr(MetafileInfo.nVersion));
        Add('Bytes: '+IntToStr(MetafileInfo.nBytes));
        Add('Records: '+IntToStr(MetafileInfo.nRecords));
        Add('Handles: '+IntToStr(MetafileInfo.nHandles));
        Add('Reserved: '+IntToStr(MetafileInfo.sReserved));
        Add('Description Size: '+IntToStr(MetafileInfo.nDescription));
        Add('Description Offset: '+IntToStr(MetafileInfo.offDescription));
        Add('Palette Entries: '+IntToStr(MetafileInfo.nPalEntries));
        Add('Reference Resolution, Pixels - ');
        Add('          Horizontal: '+IntToStr(MetafileInfo.szlDevice.cx));
        Add('            Vertical: '+IntToStr(MetafileInfo.szlDevice.cy));
end;

{erase any previous images}
Image1.Canvas.Fillrect(Image1.Canvas.Cliprect);
Image2.Canvas.Fillrect(Image2.Canvas.Cliprect);

{display the metafile as it originally appears}
PlayEnhMetaFile(Image1.Canvas.Handle, TheMetafile, CorrectedRect);

{make a copy of the original metafile in memory}
CopyMetafile:=CopyEnhMetaFile(TheMetafile, nil);

{display this copied metafile}
PlayEnhMetaFile(Image2.Canvas.Handle, CopyMetafile, Image1.Canvas.Cliprect);

{delete the handles to both metafiles, as they are no longer needed}
DeleteEnhMetaFile(TheMetafile);
DeleteEnhMetaFile(CopyMetafile);

{return the memory allocated for the description string}
```

5

Chapter

```
        StrDispose(MetafileDescription);
end;
```

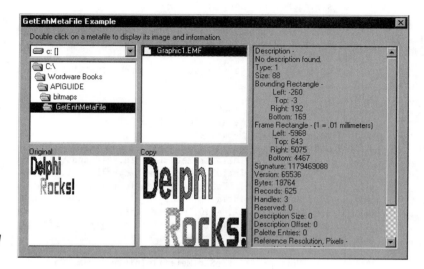

*Figure 5-15:
An enhanced
metafile*

GetEnhMetaFileDescription   Windows.Pas

Syntax

```
GetEnhMetaFileDescription(
p1: HENHMETAFILE;      {a handle to a metafile}
p2: UINT;              {the size of the buffer pointed to by the p3 parameter}
p3: PChar              {a pointer to a buffer}
): UINT;               {returns the length of the description}
```

Description

This function extracts a description string from an enhanced metafile, copying it to the specified buffer. This description is optional, so some enhanced metafiles may not contain one. The description string contains two individual strings, separated by a null character and terminated by two null characters (i.e., "CreateEnhMetaFile Example Program"+Chr(0)+"Example Metafile"+Chr(0)+Chr(0)). Typically, the first string contains the name of the graphics package that created the enhanced metafile, and the second string contains the title of the enhanced metafile picture. See the CreateEnhMetaFile function for information on including a description in an enhanced metafile. Under Windows 95, the maximum length for the description string is 16,384 bytes.

Parameters

p1: A handle to the metafile whose description string is to be retrieved.

p2: Specifies the size of the text buffer pointed to by the p3 parameter, in characters. If the description string is longer than this value, it will be truncated.

p3: A pointer to a text buffer that receives the description string. This parameter can be NIL.

Return Value

If the function succeeds, it returns the number of characters copied into the buffer. If the function succeeds and the p3 parameter contains a value of NIL, it returns the length of the description string in characters. If the description string does not exist, it returns zero. If the function fails, it returns GDI_ERROR.

See Also

CreateEnhMetaFile

Example

Please see Listing 5-14 under GetEnhMetaFile.

GetEnhMetaFileHeader   Windows.Pas

Syntax

```
GetEnhMetaFileHeader(
p1: HENHMETAFILE;        {a handle to an enhanced metafile}
p2: UINT;                {the size of the buffer pointed to by the p3 parameter}
p3: PEnhMetaHeader       {a pointer to a TEnhMetaHeader record}
): UINT;                 {returns the number of bytes copied}
```

Description

This function retrieves the record containing header information for the specified enhanced metafile. The header information completely describes the enhanced metafile, including such things as its color palette, its dimensions, and its size.

Parameters

p1: A handle to the enhanced metafile whose header information is to be retrieved.

p2: Specifies the size of the buffer pointed to by the p3 parameter, in bytes. This should be set to SizeOf(TEnhMetaHeader).

p3: A pointer to a TEnhMetaHeader structure that receives the information about the specified enhanced metafile. This parameter can be NIL. The TEnhMetaHeader structure is defined as:

```
TEnhMetaHeader = packed record
    iType: DWORD;            {the record type identifier}
    nSize: DWORD;            {the enhanced metafile record size, in bytes}
    rclBounds: TRect;        {the bounding rectangle dimensions}
    rclFrame: TRect;         {the rectangular picture dimensions}
    dSignature: DWORD;       {the enhanced metafile signature}
    nVersion: DWORD;         {the enhanced metafile version}
```

5

Chapter

```
        nBytes: DWORD;              {the size of the enhanced metafile in bytes}
        nRecords: DWORD;           {the number of records in the enhanced metafile}
        nHandles: Word;            {the number of handles in the handle table}
        sReserved: Word;           {a reserved value}
        nDescription: DWORD;       {the number of characters in the description string}
        offDescription: DWORD;     {the offset to the description string}
        nPalEntries: DWORD;        {the number of entries in the color palette}
        szlDevice: TSize;          {the reference device resolution in pixels}
        szlMillimeters: TSize;     { the reference device resolution in millimeters}
end;
```

iType: This is set to the enhanced metafile record identifier EMR_HEADER.

nSize: Specifies the size of the TEnhMetaHeader record structure in bytes.

rclBounds: A TRect structure containing the coordinates, in device units, of the smallest rectangle that completely contains the picture stored in the enhanced metafile. These dimensions are provided by the GDI.

rclFrame: A TRect structure containing the coordinates, in .01 millimeter units, of the rectangle surrounding the picture stored in the enhanced metafile. These coordinates are provided by the function that originally created the enhanced metafile.

dSignature: This is set to the metafile signature constant ENHMETA_SIGNATURE.

nVersion: The metafile version. The most current version at the time of this writing is $10000.

nBytes: The size of the enhanced metafile in bytes.

nRecords: The number of records stored in the metafile.

nHandles: The number of handles stored in the enhanced metafile handle table. Note: Index 0 of this table is reserved.

sReserved: This member is reserved and is set to zero.

nDescription: The number of characters in the optional enhanced metafile description string. If the enhanced metafile does not contain a description string, this member is set to zero.

offDescription: The offset from the beginning of the TEnhMetaHeader record to the array containing the characters of the optional enhanced metafile description string. If the enhanced metafile does not contain a description string, this member is set to zero.

nPalEntries: The number of entries in the enhanced metafile's color palette. If the enhanced metafile does not contain a color palette, this member is set to zero.

szlDevice: A TSize structure containing the horizontal and vertical resolution of the reference device for the enhanced metafile, in pixels.

szlMillimeters: A TSize structure containing the horizontal and vertical resolution of the reference device for the enhanced metafile, in millimeters.

Return Value

If the function succeeds, it returns the number of bytes that were copied to the TEnhMetaHeader record structure pointed to by the p3 parameter. If the function succeeds and the p3 parameter is set to NIL, it returns the size of the buffer needed to hold the header information. If the function fails, it returns zero.

See Also

CreateEnhMetaFile, GetEnhMetaFile, GetEnhMetaFileDescription, PlayEnhMetaFile

Example

Please see Listing 5-14 under GetEnhMetaFile.

GetStretchBltMode   Windows.Pas

Syntax

```
GetStretchBltMode(
DC: HDC                        {a handle to a device context}
): Integer;                    {returns the bitmap stretch mode}
```

Description

This function retrieves the current bitmap stretch mode. This mode defines how rows and columns of a bitmap are added or removed when the StretchBlt function is called.

Parameters

DC: A handle to the device context whose stretch mode is to be retrieved.

Return Value

If the function succeeds, it returns the current bitmap stretch mode. This can be one value from Table 5-10. If the function fails, it returns zero.

See Also

SetStretchBltMode, StretchBlt

Example

Please see Listing 5-15 under LoadBitmap.

Table 5-10: GetStretchBltMode Return Values

Value	Description
BLACKONWHITE	Performs a Boolean AND operation using the color values for eliminated and existing pixels. If the bitmap is a monochrome bitmap, this mode preserves black pixels at the expense of white pixels.
COLORONCOLOR	Deletes pixels without making any attempt to preserve pixel information.

Value	Description
HALFTONE	Maps pixels from the source bitmap into blocks of pixels on the destination bitmap. The destination pixel color is the average of the colors from the source pixels. This mode requires more processing time than the other flags, but produces higher quality images. If this flag is used, the application must call the SetBrushOrgEx function to reset the brush origin or brush misalignment will occur.
STRETCH_ANDSCANS	The same as BLACKONWHITE.
STRETCH_DELETESCANS	The same as COLORONCOLOR.
STRETCH_HALFTONE	The same as HALFTONE.
STRETCH_ORSCANS	The same as WHITEONBLACK.
WHITEONBLACK	Performs a Boolean OR operation using the color values for eliminated and existing pixels. If the bitmap is a monochrome bitmap, this mode preserves white pixels at the expense of black pixels.

LoadBitmap   Windows.Pas

Syntax

```
LoadBitmap(
hInstance: HINST;          {an instance handle}
lpBitmapName: PAnsiChar    {a bitmap resource name}
): HBITMAP;                {returns a handle to a bitmap}
```

Description

This function loads a bitmap from the executable file's resources, returning its handle. When the application is finished with the bitmap, it should be deleted by calling the DeleteObject function. This function assumes the bitmap will contain only 16 colors. Use the LoadResource function to load bitmaps with a higher color resolution.

Parameters

hInstance: A handle to a module instance whose executable file contains the bitmap resource to load.

lpBitmapName: A pointer to a null-terminated string containing the resource name of the bitmap to load. The MakeIntResource function can be used with a resource identifier to provide a value for this parameter. To load one of the predefined bitmap resources used by the Win32 API, set the hInstance parameter to zero and use the MakeIntResource function with one of the values from Table 5-11 for this parameter.

Return Value

If the function succeeds, it returns a handle to the bitmap loaded from the executable file's resources; otherwise it returns zero.

See Also

BitBlt, CreateBitmap, CreateBitmapIndirect, CreateCompatibleBitmap, CreateDIBitmap, CreateDIBSection, DeleteObject, LoadResource, StretchBlt

Example

Listing 5-15: Loading a Predefined Bitmap

```
procedure TForm1.ComboBox1Change(Sender: TObject);
var
   TheBitmap: HBITMAP;              // holds the bitmap
   BitmapInfo: Windows.TBitmap;    // holds the bitmap information
   OffscreenDC: HDC;               // a handle to an offscreen device context

{this defines all of the system bitmaps available in Windows}
type
   TBitmapTypes = array[0..25] of Integer;
const
   BitmapTypes: TBitmapTypes = (OBM_CLOSE,OBM_UPARROW,OBM_DNARROW,OBM_RGARROW,
                                OBM_LFARROW,OBM_REDUCE,OBM_ZOOM,OBM_RESTORE,
                                OBM_REDUCED,OBM_ZOOMD,OBM_RESTORED,OBM_UPARROWD,
                                OBM_DNARROWD,OBM_RGARROWD,OBM_LFARROWD,
                                OBM_MNARROW,OBM_COMBO,OBM_UPARROWI,OBM_DNARROWI,
                                OBM_RGARROWI,OBM_LFARROWI,OBM_BTSIZE,
                                OBM_CHECK,OBM_CHECKBOXES,OBM_BTNCORNERS,
                                OBM_SIZE);
begin
   {erase the last images}
   Image1.Canvas.Brush.Color:=clBtnFace;
   Image2.Canvas.Brush.Color:=clBtnFace;
   Image1.Canvas.Fillrect(Image1.Canvas.Cliprect);
   Image2.Canvas.Fillrect(Image2.Canvas.Cliprect);

   {load the selected bitmap}
   TheBitmap:=LoadBitmap(0, MakeIntResource(BitmapTypes[ComboBox1.ItemIndex]));

   {create an offscreen device context and select the bitmap into it}
   OffscreenDC:=CreateCompatibleDC(0);
   SelectObject(OffscreenDC, TheBitmap);

   {fill in a BITMAP information structure}
   GetObject(TheBitmap, SizeOf(Windows.TBitmap), @BitmapInfo);

   {draw the bitmap into Image1}
   BitBlt(Image1.Canvas.Handle, 45,45,Image1.Width, Image1.Height,OffscreenDC,
          0,0,SRCCOPY);

   {verify the stretch mode in Image2 is what we want}
   if GetStretchBltMode(Image2.Canvas.Handle)<>COLORONCOLOR then
      SetStretchBltMode(Image2.Canvas.Handle, COLORONCOLOR);

   {draw the bitmap into Image2, stretching it to fill the image}
   StretchBlt(Image2.Canvas.Handle, 0, 0, Image2.Width, Image2.Height,
              OffscreenDC, 0, 0, BitmapInfo.bmWidth, BitmapInfo.bmHeight,
```

5

Chapter

```
        SRCCOPY);

    {delete the bitmap}
    DeleteObject(TheBitmap);

    {delete the offscreen device context}
    DeleteDC(OffscreenDC);
  end;
```

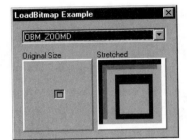

Figure 5-16:
A predefined
bitmap
resource

Table 5-II: LoadBitmap lpBitmapName Values

Value	Description
OBM_BTNCORNERS	Loads the bitmap resource for the system corner marker.
OBM_BTSIZE	Loads the bitmap resource for the sizing button.
OBM_CHECK	Loads the bitmap resource for the default check mark.
OBM_CHECKBOXES	Loads the collection of system check box symbols.
OBM_CLOSE	Loads the default system menu icon resource.
OBM_COMBO	Loads the bitmap resource for the combo box drop-down arrow.
OBM_DNARROW	Loads the bitmap resource for a scroll bar down arrow in an up state.
OBM_DNARROWD	Loads the bitmap resource for a scroll bar down arrow in a down state.
OBM_DNARROWI	Loads the bitmap resource for a scroll bar down arrow in a disabled state.
OBM_LFARROW	Loads the bitmap resource for a scroll bar left arrow in an up state.
OBM_LFARROWD	Loads the bitmap resource for a scroll bar left arrow in a down state.
OBM_LFARROWI	Loads the bitmap resource for a scroll bar left arrow in a disabled state.
OBM_MNARROW	Loads the bitmap resource used to indicate a menu item that contains a submenu.
OBM_REDUCE	Loads the bitmap resource for a minimize button in an up state.

Value	Description
OBM_REDUCED	Loads the bitmap resource for a minimize button in a down state.
OBM_RESTORE	Loads the bitmap resource for a restore button in an up state.
OBM_RESTORED	Loads the bitmap resource for a restore button in a down state.
OBM_RGARROW	Loads the bitmap resource for a scroll bar right arrow in an up state.
OBM_RGARROWD	Loads the bitmap resource for a scroll bar right arrow in a down state.
OBM_RGARROWI	Loads the bitmap resource for a scroll bar right arrow in a disabled state.
OBM_SIZE	Loads the bitmap resource for the sizing corner.
OBM_UPARROW	Loads the bitmap resource for a scroll bar up arrow in an up state.
OBM_UPARROWD	Loads the bitmap resource for a scroll bar up arrow in a down state.
OBM_UPARROWI	Loads the bitmap resource for a scroll bar up arrow in a disabled state.
OBM_ZOOM	Loads the bitmap resource for a maximize button in an up state.
OBM_ZOOMD	Loads the bitmap resource for a maximize button in a down state.

LoadImage　　　Windows.Pas

Syntax

```
LoadImage(
hInst: HINST;              {a handle of the instance containing the image}
ImageName: PChar;          {the image name}
ImageType: UINT;           {the image type flag}
X: Integer;                {width of new image}
Y: Integer;                {height of new image}
Flags: UINT                {the load operation flags}
): THandle;                {returns a handle to the loaded image}
```

Description

This function loads an icon, cursor, enhanced metafile, or bitmap from either a file or from the executable resources. The image can be sized as desired, and numerous options affect the final loaded image.

5

Chapter

Parameters

hInst: A handle to the module instance containing the image to be loaded.

ImageName: A pointer to a null-terminated string containing the name of the image resource to be loaded. If the Flags parameter contains the LR_LOADFROMFILE flag, this parameter contains a pointer to a null-terminated string specifying the filename of the image to load.

ImageType: A flag indicating the type of image to be loaded. This parameter can be one value from Table 5-12.

X: Indicates the desired width of the image in pixels. If this parameter is set to zero and the Flags parameter does not contain the LR_DEFAULTSIZE flag, the loaded image width is set to the width of the original resource. If this parameter is set to zero and the Flags parameter contains the LR_DEFAULTSIZE flag, the width is set to the value returned from GetSystemMetrics(SM_CXICON) or GetSystemMetrics(SM_CXCURSOR) if the loaded image is an icon or cursor.

Y: Indicates the desired height of the image in pixels. If this parameter is set to zero and the Flags parameter does not contain the LR_DEFAULTSIZE flag, the loaded image height is set to the height of the original resource. If this parameter is zero and the Flags parameter contains the LR_DEFAULTSIZE flag, the height is set to the value returned from GetSystemMetrics(SM_CYICON) or GetSystemMetrics(SM_CYCURSOR) if the loaded image is an icon or cursor.

Flags: A value indicating additional actions performed when the image is loaded. This parameter can be one or more values from Table 5-13.

Return Value

If the function succeeds, it returns a handle to the loaded image; otherwise it returns zero.

See Also

CopyImage, GetSystemMetrics, LoadBitmap, LoadCursor, LoadIcon

Example

Listing 5-16: Loading Bitmap Images from Files

```
procedure TForm1.FileListBox1Click(Sender: TObject);
var
  TheBitmap: THandle;          // holds a newly loaded bitmap image
  BitmapInfo: Windows.TBitmap; // holds the bitmap information
  TheOffscreenDC: HDC;         // holds a handle to a memory device context
begin
  {create a memory device context}
  TheOffscreenDC := CreateCompatibleDC(0);

  {load the specified bitmap file}
  TheBitmap := LoadImage(0,PChar(FileListBox1.FileName),IMAGE_BITMAP,0,0,
```

```
                LR_LOADFROMFILE);

  {retrieve information about the bitmap (width and height will be used)}
  GetObject(TheBitmap, SizeOf(Windows.TBitmap), @BitmapInfo);

  {select the bitmap into the memory device context}
  SelectObject(TheOffscreenDC, TheBitmap);

  {copy the image to Image1 at its original size}
  BitBlt(Image1.Canvas.Handle,0,0,Image1.Width,Image1.Height,TheOffscreenDC,
       0,0,SRCCOPY);

  {copy the image to Image2, and compress it to fit}
  StretchBlt(Image2.Canvas.Handle,0,0,Image2.Width,Image2.Height,TheOffscreenDC,
          0,0,BitmapInfo.bmWidth,BitmapInfo.bmHeight,SRCCOPY);

  {update the images on screen}
  Image1.Refresh;
  Image2.Refresh;

  {delete the loaded image and the offscreen device context}
  DeleteDC(TheOffscreenDC);
  DeleteObject(TheBitmap);
end;
```

Figure 5-17:
The loaded
bitmap image

Table 5-12: LoadImage ImageType Values

Value	Description
IMAGE_BITMAP	The image is a bitmap.
IMAGE_CURSOR	The image is a cursor.
IMAGE_ENHMETAFILE	The image is an enhanced metafile.
IMAGE_ICON	The image is an icon.

Table 5-13: LoadImage Flags Values

Value	Description
LR_CREATEDIBSECTION	If the ImageType parameter contains the value IMAGE_BITMAP, this function returns a handle to a DIB section bitmap.
LR_DEFAULTCOLOR	Loads the image in its defined color format. This is the default flag.
LR_DEFAULTSIZE	For icon or cursor images only, this flag causes the function to load the image using the default width and height as reported by the GetSystemMetrics function.
LR_LOADFROMFILE	Indicates that the null-terminated string pointed to by the ImageName parameter contains a filename, and the image is loaded from disk.
LR_LOADMAP3DCOLORS	Searches the pixels of the loaded image, and replaces dark gray pixels (RGB(128,128,128)) with the COLOR_3DSHADOW system color, replaces gray pixels (RGB(192,192,192)) with the COLOR_3DFACE system color, and replaces light gray pixels (RGB(223,223,223)) with the COLOR_3DLIGHT system color.
LR_LOADTRANSPARENT	Retrieves the color value of the first pixel in the image, replacing all pixels in the image of the same color with the COLOR_WINDOW system color. This has the same effect as blitting the image to the canvas using the BrushCopy function. If the LR_LOADMAP3DCOLORS flag is included, LR_LOADTRANSPARENT takes precedence, but replaces the indicated pixel color with the COLOR_3DFACE system color.
LR_MONOCHROME	Creates a black and white version of the original image.
LR_SHARED	For resources, this flag causes the function to return the same handle for identical resources loaded multiple times. Without this flag, LoadImage returns a different handle when the same resource is loaded. Do not specify this flag for images loaded from files or for images that will change after loading.

PatBlt   *Windows.Pas*

Syntax

```
PatBlt(
DC: HDC;              {a handle to a device context}
X: Integer;           {the horizontal start coordinate of rectangle to be filled}
Y: Integer;           {the vertical start coordinate of rectangle to be filled}
```

Width: Integer;	{the width of the rectangle to be filled}
Height: Integer;	{the height of the rectangle to be filled}
Rop: DWORD	{the raster operation flag}
): BOOL;	{returns TRUE or FALSE}

Description

This function fills a rectangle using the brush currently selected into the specified device context, combining the colors of the brush and the destination using the specified raster operation. Some devices may not support the PatBlt function; use the GetDeviceCaps function to determine if the target device supports bit block transfers.

Parameters

DC: A handle to the device context upon which the filled rectangle is drawn.

X: The horizontal coordinate of the upper left-hand corner of the rectangle to be filled, in logical units.

Y: The vertical coordinate of the upper left-hand corner of the rectangle to be filled, in logical units.

Width: The width of the rectangle to be filled, in logical units.

Height: The height of the rectangle to be filled, in logical units.

Rop: A raster operation code. This determines how the pixels of the brush used to paint the rectangle are combined with the pixels on the device context, and can be one value from Table 5-14.

Return Value

If the function succeeds, it returns TRUE; otherwise it returns FALSE. To get extended error information, call the GetLastError function.

See Also

GetDeviceCaps, CreateBrush, CreatePatternBrush

Example

Listing 5-17: Filling a Background

```
procedure TForm1.Button1Click(Sender: TObject);
var
  BitmapPattern: HBITMAP;    // holds the bitmap brush pattern
  PatternBrush: HBRUSH;      // holds the handle to the patterned brush
  OldBrush: HBRUSH;          // tracks the original brush
begin
  {load a bitmap from the resource file}
  BitmapPattern := LoadBitmap(hInstance, 'BRUSHPATTERN');

  {use it to create a patterned brush}
  PatternBrush := CreatePatternBrush(BitmapPattern);
```

5

Chapter

```
{select this new brush into the main form's device context}
OldBrush := SelectObject(Canvas.Handle, PatternBrush);

{paint a pattern filled rectangle}
PatBlt(Canvas.Handle, 0, 0, Width, Height, PATINVERT);

{replace the original brush handle}
SelectObject(Canvas.Handle, OldBrush);

{we no longer need the patterned brush or the bitmap, so delete them}
DeleteObject(PatternBrush);
DeleteObject(BitmapPattern);
end;
```

Figure 5-18: The pattern brush result

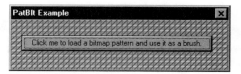

Table 5-14: PatBlt Rop Values

Value	Description
BLACKNESS	Fills the pixels in the specified rectangle in the destination with the color in index 0 of the physical palette. By default, this color is black.
DSTINVERT	Inverts the colors of the pixels in the specified rectangle in the destination.
PATCOPY	Copies the pattern contained in the brush selected into the destination device context directly into the destination.
PATINVERT	Combines the pixel colors of the pattern contained in the brush selected into the destination device context with the colors of the pixels in the destination using the Boolean XOR operator.
WHITENESS	Fills the pixels in the specified rectangle in the destination with the color in index 255 of the physical palette. By default, this color is white.

PlayEnhMetaFile   Windows.Pas

Syntax

```
PlayEnhMetaFile(
DC: HDC;                    {a handle to a device context}
p2: HENHMETAFILE;          {a handle to an enhanced metafile}
const p3: TRect            {a pointer to a rectangle structure}
): BOOL;                   {returns TRUE or FALSE}
```

Description

This function displays the enhanced metafile identified by the p2 parameter on the specified device context. The metafile can be clipped by defining a clipping region in the device context before playing the metafile. If the enhanced metafile contains a color palette, the application can maintain color consistency by creating and realizing a color palette into the device context before playing the metafile. Use the GetEnhMetaFilePaletteEntries to retrieve the color palette of the enhanced metafile. An enhanced metafile can be embedded into a newly created enhanced metafile by using this function to play the metafile into the device context for the new metafile. The state of the specified device context is preserved by this function. If an object was created but not deleted when the original metafile was created, this function deletes the errant object after the metafile is played.

Parameters

DC: A handle to the device context upon which the enhanced metafile will be drawn.

p2: A handle to the enhanced metafile to draw.

p3: A pointer to a TRect structure. The enhanced metafile will be drawn within the coordinates specified by this structure. These coordinates are specified in logical units. The rclFrame member of the enhanced metafile header is used to map the metafile into the specified rectangular coordinates.

Return Value

If the function succeeds, it returns TRUE; otherwise it returns FALSE. To get extended error information, call the GetLastError function.

See Also

CreateEnhMetaFile, GetEnhMetaFile, GetEnhMetaFileHeader, GetEnhMetaFilePalette-Entries, PlayEnhMetaFileRecord

Example

Please see Listing 5-10 under CreateEnhMetaFile.

PlayEnhMetaFileRecord   Windows.Pas

Syntax

```
PlayEnhMetaFileRecord(
DC: HDC;                      {a handle to a device context}
var p2: THandleTable;         {a pointer to a metafile handle table}
const p3: TEnhMetaRecord;     {a pointer to a metafile record}
p4: UINT                      {the number of handles in the metafile handle table}
): BOOL;                      {returns TRUE or FALSE}
```

5

Chapter

Description

This function executes the GDI functions identified by the enhanced metafile record. PlayEnhMetaFileRecord is intended to be used with the EnumEnhMetaFile function to process and play an enhanced metafile one record at a time. The DC, p2, and p3 parameters must exactly match the device context, handle table, and handle table count passed to the callback function used by the EnumEnhMetaFile function. If the record passed in the p3 parameter is not recognized, it is ignored and the function returns a value of TRUE.

Parameters

DC: A handle to the device context upon which the enhanced metafile is being played.

p2: A pointer to a table of GDI object handles. These objects define the enhanced metafile picture.

p3: A pointer to the TEnhMetaRecord structure defining the enhanced metafile record to be played. The TEnhMetaRecord is defined as:

```
TEnhMetaRecord = packed record
    iType: DWORD;                    {the enhanced metafile record identifier}
    nSize: DWORD;                    {the size of the record in bytes}
    dParm: array[0..0] of DWORD;     {an array of parameters}
end;
```

See the EnumEnhMetaFile callback function for an explanation of this structure.

p4: A count of the number of handles stored in the enhanced metafile handle table.

Return Value

If the function succeeds, it returns TRUE; otherwise it returns FALSE.

See Also

EnumEnhMetaFile, PlayEnhMetaFile

Example

Please see Listing 5-11 under EnumEnhMetaFile.

SetBitmapBits   *Windows.Pas*

Syntax

```
SetBitmapBits(
    p1: HBITMAP;        {a handle to a bitmap}
    p2: DWORD;          {the number of bytes in the bits array}
    bits: Pointer       {a pointer to an array of bytes}
): Longint;             {returns the number of bytes used to set the bitmap}
```

Description

This function sets the image for the specified bitmap from the values stored in the bits array. The SetBitmapBits function is included for compatibility purposes. Win32-based applications should use the SetDIBits function.

Parameters

p1: A handle to the bitmap whose image will be set from the values in the array pointed to by the bits parameter.

p2: Specifies the number of bytes pointed to by the bits parameter.

bits: A pointer to an array of bytes containing the image data for the bitmap.

Return Value

If the function succeeds, it returns the number of bytes used to set the bitmap bits; otherwise it returns zero.

See Also

CreateBitmap, DestroyBitmap, GetBitmapBits, SetDIBits

Example

Listing 5-18: Setting the Bitmap Bits

```
{This example will run properly only with a 256-color video driver.}
procedure TForm1.Button1Click(Sender: TObject);
var
   BitmapBits: array[0..9999] of byte;   // holds the new bitmap bit information
   BitmapImage: TBitmap;                  // the bitmap image
   Loop: Integer;                         // a general loop counter
const
   Started: Boolean = FALSE;              // controls the overall loop
begin
   {toggle the loop control variable}
   Started:=not Started;

   {change the button caption to reflect the new state}
   if Started then
     Button1.Caption := 'Stop'
   else
     Button1.Caption := 'Start';

   {create a 100X100 pixel bitmap}
   BitmapImage := TBitmap.Create;
   BitmapImage.Height := 100;
   BitmapImage.Width := 100;

   {force this to be a device-dependent bitmap}
   BitmapImage.HandleType := bmDDB;

   {this loop continues until the button is pressed again}
```

5

Chapter

```
while Started do
begin
  {fill the bitmap bit information with white}
  FillChar(BitmapBits, SizeOf(BitmapBits), 255);

  {set 10000 random pixels to black}
  for Loop := 0 to 1000 do
  begin
    BitmapBits[Random(100)*100+Random(100)]:=0;
    BitmapBits[Random(100)*100+Random(100)]:=0;
    BitmapBits[Random(100)*100+Random(100)]:=0;
    BitmapBits[Random(100)*100+Random(100)]:=0;
    BitmapBits[Random(100)*100+Random(100)]:=0;
    BitmapBits[Random(100)*100+Random(100)]:=0;
    BitmapBits[Random(100)*100+Random(100)]:=0;
    BitmapBits[Random(100)*100+Random(100)]:=0;
    BitmapBits[Random(100)*100+Random(100)]:=0;
    BitmapBits[Random(100)*100+Random(100)]:=0;
  end;

  {blast the new bits into the bitmap}
  SetBitmapBits(BitmapImage.Handle, 10000, @BitmapBits);

  {copy the bitmap to the canvas of the form}
  BitBlt(Form1.Canvas.Handle, 84, 8, 100, 100, BitmapImage.Canvas.Handle, 0,
         0, SRCCOPY);

  {this is required for proper Windows operation}
  Application.ProcessMessages;
end;

{free our bitmap}
BitmapImage.Free
end;
```

Figure 5-19:
Using
SetBitmapBits
to produce a
TV snow effect

SetBitmapDimensionEx   Windows.Pas

Syntax

```
SetBitmapDimensionEx(
hBitmap: HBITMAP;          {a handle to a bitmap}
Width: Integer;            {the preferred width of the bitmap}
```

Height: Integer;	{the preferred height of the bitmap}
Size: PSize	{a pointer to a TSize structure}
): BOOL;	{returns TRUE or FALSE}

Description

This function sets the preferred width and height of the specified bitmap, in terms of 0.1 millimeter units. These dimensions are for application specific use, do not affect the appearance of the bitmap image, and are not used by Windows. Once set, these dimensions can be retrieved using the GetBitmapDimensionEx function.

Parameters

hBitmap: A handle to a bitmap whose preferred dimensions are to be set. This cannot be a handle to a bitmap returned by the CreateDIBSection function.

Width: An integer specifying the bitmap's preferred width in terms of 0.1 millimeter units.

Height: An integer specifying the bitmap's preferred height in terms of 0.1 millimeter units.

Size: A pointer to a TSize structure that will receive the previously set dimensions. This parameter can be NIL.

Return Value

If the function succeeds, it returns TRUE; otherwise it returns FALSE. To get extended error information, call the GetLastError function.

See Also

GetBitmapDimensionEx

Example

Please see Listing 5-5 under CreateBitmap.

SetDIBits   *Windows.Pas*

Syntax

SetDIBits(	
DC: HDC;	{a handle to a device context}
Bitmap: HBITMAP;	{a handle to a regular bitmap}
StartScan: UINT;	{the starting scan line}
NumScans: UINT;	{the total number of scan lines}
Bits: Pointer;	{a pointer to the DIB bitmap bit values}
var BitsInfo: TBitmapInfo;	{a pointer to the DIB bitmap information structure}
Usage: UINT;	{color type flags}
): Integer;	{returns the number of scan lines copied}

5

Chapter

Description

This function copies the bit values from the specified area in the DIB bit values pointed to by the Bits parameter directly into the device-dependent bitmap indicated by the Bitmap parameter. Note that optimal bitmap copy speed is obtained when the DIB bitmap bits specify indices into the system palette.

Parameters

DC: A handle to a device context. If the DIB_PAL_COLORS flag is specified in the Usage parameter, the bit values copied from the DIB use the colors in the currently realized palette of this device context. If the DIB_PAL_COLORS flag is not specified, this parameter is ignored.

Bitmap: A handle to the bitmap whose bit values are being set.

StartScan: Specifies the scan line to start the copy operation from in the DIB image pointed to by the Bits parameter.

NumScans: Specifies the number of scan lines to copy to the device-dependent bitmap from the image pointed to by the Bits parameter.

Bits: A pointer to the image representing the DIB, in the form of an array of bytes.

BitsInfo: A pointer to a TBitmapInfo data structure describing the DIB, including information about its dimensions and color table. The TBitmapInfo data structure is defined as:

```
TBitmapInfo = packed record
        bmiHeader: TBitmapInfoHeader;        {bitmap header information}
        bmiColors: array[0..0] of TRGBQuad;  {the color table used by the bitmap}
end;
```

The TBitmapInfoHeader data structure is defined as:

```
TBitmapInfoHeader = packed record
        biSize: DWORD;                {the size of the structure in bytes}
        biWidth: Longint;             {the width of the bitmap in pixels}
        biHeight: Longint;            {the height of the bitmap in pixels}
        biPlanes: Word;               {the number of color planes}
        biBitCount: Word;             {the bits per pixel required to describe a
                                       color}
        biCompression: DWORD;         {compression flags}
        biSizeImage: DWORD;           {the size of the image in bytes}
        biXPelsPerMeter: Longint;     {horizontal pixels per meter of the target
                                       device}
        biYPelsPerMeter: Longint;     {vertical pixels per meter of the target device}
        biClrUsed: DWORD;             {the number of color indices used}
        biClrImportant: DWORD;        {the number of important color indices}
end;
```

The TRGBQuad data structure is defined as:

```
TRGBQuad = packed record
    rgbBlue: Byte;        {blue color intensity}
    rgbGreen: Byte;       {green color intensity}
    rgbRed: Byte;         {red color intensity}
    rgbReserved: Byte;    {reserved value}
end;
```

For an explanation of these data structures, see the CreateDIBSection function.

Usage: A flag indicating the type of color information stored in the bmiColors member of the TBitmapInfo structure pointed to by the BitsInfo parameter. This parameter can be one value from Table 5-15.

Return Value

If the function succeeds, it returns the number of scan lines that were copied to the device-dependent bitmap; otherwise it returns zero. To get extended error information, call the GetLastError function.

See Also

BitBlt, CreateBitmap, GetDIBits, SetBitmapBits

Example

Listing 5-19: Setting the Image of a DDB from a DIB

```
{This example will run properly only with a 256-color video driver.}
procedure TForm1.Button1Click(Sender: TObject);
var
  TheBitmap: HBitmap;        // a handle for a regular bitmap
  OffScreen: HDC;            // an offscreen device context
  Dib: HBITMAP;              // holds a handle to the device-independent bitmap
  DibInfo: PBitmapInfo;      // a pointer to the bitmap information data structure
  BitsPtr: PByte;            // holds a pointer to the bitmap bits
  ReferenceDC: HDC;          // a handle to the reference device context
  Loop: Integer;             // a general loop counter

  SystemPalette: array[0..255] of TPaletteEntry; // required for converting the
                                                 // system palette into a DIB
                                                 // compatible palette
const
  Started: Boolean = FALSE;  // controls the overall loop
begin
  {toggle the loop control variable}
  Started := not Started;

  {change the button caption to reflect the new state}
  if Started then
    Button1.Caption := 'Stop'
  else
```

```
  Button1.Caption := 'Start';

{create a 128 X 128 pixel bitmap}
TheBitmap := CreateBitmap(128, 128, 1, 8, nil);

{create an offscreen device context that is
 compatible with the screen}
OffScreen := CreateCompatibleDC(0);

{select the new bitmap into the offscreen device context}
SelectObject(OffScreen, TheBitmap);

{get the memory needed for the bitmap information data structure}
GetMem(DibInfo, SizeOf(TBitmapInfo)+256*SizeOf(TRGBQuad));

{initialize the bitmap information}
DibInfo^.bmiHeader.biWidth         := 128;   // create a 128 X 128 pixel
DibInfo^.bmiHeader.biHeight        := -128;  // oriented top-down
DibInfo^.bmiHeader.biPlanes        := 1;
DibInfo^.bmiHeader.biBitCount      := 8;     // 256 colors
DibInfo^.bmiHeader.biCompression   := BI_RGB; // no compression
DibInfo^.bmiHeader.biSizeImage     := 0;        // let Windows determine size
DibInfo^.bmiHeader.biXPelsPerMeter := 0;
DibInfo^.bmiHeader.biYPelsPerMeter := 0;
DibInfo^.bmiHeader.biClrUsed       := 0;
DibInfo^.bmiHeader.biClrImportant  := 0;
DibInfo^.bmiHeader.biSize          := SizeOf(TBitmapInfoHeader);

{retrieve the current system palette}
GetSystemPaletteEntries(Form1.Canvas.Handle, 0, 256, SystemPalette);

{the system palette is returned as an array of TPaletteEntry structures,
 which store the palette colors in the form of Red, Green, and Blue. however,
 the TBitmapInfo structure's bmiColors member takes an array of TRGBQuad
 structures, which store the palette colors in the form of Blue, Green, and
 Red.  therefore, we must translate the TPaletteEntry structures into the
 appropriate TRGBQuad structures to get the correct color entries.}
for Loop := 0 to 255 do
begin
  DibInfo^.bmiColors[Loop].rgbBlue     := SystemPalette[Loop].peBlue;
  DibInfo^.bmiColors[Loop].rgbRed      := SystemPalette[Loop].peRed;
  DibInfo^.bmiColors[Loop].rgbGreen    := SystemPalette[Loop].peGreen;
  DibInfo^.bmiColors[Loop].rgbReserved := 0;
end;

{create a memory-based device context}
ReferenceDC := CreateCompatibleDC(0);

{create the DIB based on the memory device context and the
 initialized bitmap information}
Dib := CreateDIBSection(ReferenceDC, DibInfo^, DIB_RGB_COLORS,
                        Pointer(BitsPtr), 0, 0);
```

```
    {delete the reference device context}
    DeleteDC(ReferenceDC);

    {this loop continues until the button is pressed again}
    while Started do
    begin
      {fill the bitmap bit information with white}
      FillMemory(BitsPtr, 128*128, $FF);

      {set 10000 random pixels to black. this loop has been 'unrolled' somewhat
       for optimization}
      for Loop := 0 to 1000 do
      begin
        PByte(Longint(BitsPtr)+Random(128)*128+Random(128))^ := 0;
        PByte(Longint(BitsPtr)+Random(128)*128+Random(128))^ := 0;
        PByte(Longint(BitsPtr)+Random(128)*128+Random(128))^ := 0;
        PByte(Longint(BitsPtr)+Random(128)*128+Random(128))^ := 0;
        PByte(Longint(BitsPtr)+Random(128)*128+Random(128))^ := 0;
        PByte(Longint(BitsPtr)+Random(128)*128+Random(128))^ := 0;
        PByte(Longint(BitsPtr)+Random(128)*128+Random(128))^ := 0;
        PByte(Longint(BitsPtr)+Random(128)*128+Random(128))^ := 0;
        PByte(Longint(BitsPtr)+Random(128)*128+Random(128))^ := 0;
        PByte(Longint(BitsPtr)+Random(128)*128+Random(128))^ := 0;
        PByte(Longint(BitsPtr)+Random(128)*128+Random(128))^ := 0;
        PByte(Longint(BitsPtr)+Random(128)*128+Random(128))^ := 0;
      end;

      {copy the bit values from the DIB directly into the DDB bitmap}
      SetDIBits(Form1.Canvas.Handle, TheBitmap, 0, 128, BitsPtr, DibInfo^,
                DIB_RGB_COLORS);

      {copy the bitmap to the canvas of the form}
      BitBlt(Form1.Canvas.Handle, (Form1.Width div 2)-64, 8, 128, 128,
             Offscreen, 0, 0, SRCCOPY);

      {this is required for proper Windows operation}
      Application.ProcessMessages;
    end;

    {destroy the offscreen device context}
    DeleteDC(Offscreen);

    {free our bitmaps}
    DeleteObject(TheBitmap);
    DeleteObject(Dib);
    FreeMem(DibInfo, SizeOf(TBitmapInfo)+256*SizeOf(TRGBQuad));
  end;
```

5

Chapter

Figure 5-20: The DDB image was set from bits stored in a DIB.

Table 5-15: SetDIBits Usage Values

Value	Description
DIB_PAL_COLORS	The bmiColors member of the TBitmapInfo structure is an array of 16-bit indices into the currently realized logical palette of the specified device context. This value should not be used if the bitmap will be saved to disk.
DIB_RGB_COLORS	The bmiColors member of the TBitmapInfo structure is an array of literal RGB color values.

SetDIBitsToDevice   **Windows.Pas**

Syntax

```
SetDIBitsToDevice(
DC: HDC;                    {a handle to a device context}
DestX: Integer;            {the horizontal coordinate of the destination rectangle}
DestY: Integer;            {the vertical coordinate of the destination rectangle}
Width: DWORD;              {the width of the DIB}
Height: DWORD;             {the height of the DIB}
SrcX: Integer;             {the horizontal coordinate of the source rectangle}
SrcY: Integer;             {the vertical coordinate of the source rectangle}
nStartScan: UINT;          {the starting scan line}
NumScans: UINT;            {the total number of scan lines}
Bits: Pointer;             {a pointer to the bitmap bit values}
var BitsInfo: TBitmapInfo; {a pointer to the DIB bitmap information data structure}
Usage: UINT               {color type flags}
): Integer;                {returns the number of scan lines copied}
```

Description

This function copies pixels from the specified section of the DIB image onto the destination device context. This copy operation can be banded for large device-independent bitmaps by repeatedly calling SetDIBitsToDevice, passing a different portion of the DIB in the nStartScan and NumScans parameters. Note that optimal bitmap copy speed is obtained when the DIB bitmap bits specify indices into the system palette. This function will fail when called by a process running in the background while an MS-DOS process runs full screen in the foreground.

Parameters

DC: The device context upon which the DIB image is copied and displayed.

DestX: The horizontal coordinate of the upper left corner of the destination rectangle in the destination device context, measured in logical units.

DestY: The vertical coordinate of the upper left corner of the destination rectangle in the destination device context, measured in logical units.

Width: The width of the DIB image, measured in logical units.

Height: The height of the DIB image, measured in logical units.

SrcX: The horizontal coordinate of the lower left corner of the DIB, measured in logical units.

SrcY: The vertical coordinate of the lower left corner of the DIB, measured in logical units.

nStartScan: Specifies the scan line to start the copy operation from in the DIB image pointed to by the Bits parameter

NumScans: Specifies the number of scan lines to copy to the destination from the image pointed to by the Bits parameter.

Bits: A pointer to the image representing the DIB, in the form of an array of bytes.

BitsInfo: A pointer to a TBitmapInfo data structure describing the DIB, including information about its dimensions and color table. The TBitmapInfo data structure is defined as:

```
TBitmapInfo = packed record
      bmiHeader: TBitmapInfoHeader;        {bitmap header information}
      bmiColors: array[0..0] of TRGBQuad;  {the color table used by the bitmap}
end;
```

The TBitmapInfoHeader data structure is defined as:

```
TBitmapInfoHeader = packed record
        biSize: DWORD;           {the size of the structure in bytes}
        biWidth: Longint;        {the width of the bitmap in pixels}
        biHeight: Longint;       {the height of the bitmap in pixels}
        biPlanes: Word;          {the number of color planes}
        biBitCount: Word;        {the bits per pixel required to describe a
                                  color}
        biCompression: DWORD;    {compression flags}
        biSizeImage: DWORD;      {the size of the image in bytes}
        biXPelsPerMeter: Longint; {horizontal pixels per meter of the target
                                  device}
```

Chapter 5

```
        biYPelsPerMeter: Longint;     {vertical pixels per meter of the target device}
        biClrUsed: DWORD;             {the number of color indices used}
        biClrImportant: DWORD;        {the number of important color indices}
    end;
```

The TRGBQuad data structure is defined as:

```
    TRGBQuad = packed record
        rgbBlue: Byte;                {blue color intensity}
        rgbGreen: Byte;               {green color intensity}
        rgbRed: Byte;                 {red color intensity}
        rgbReserved: Byte;            {reserved value}
    end;
```

For an explanation of these data structures, see the CreateDIBSection function.

Usage: A flag indicating the type of color information stored in the bmiColors member of the TBitmapInfo structure pointed to by the BitsInfo parameter. This parameter can be one value from Table 5-16.

Return Value

If the function succeeds, it returns the number of scan lines that were copied to the destination device context; otherwise it returns zero. To get extended error information, call the GetLastError function.

See Also

SetDIBits, StretchDIBits

Example

Please see Listing 5-9 under CreateDIBSection.

Table 5-16: SetDIBitsToDevice Usage Values

Value	Description
DIB_PAL_COLORS	The bmiColors member of the TBitmapInfo structure is an array of 16-bit indices into the currently realized logical palette of the specified device context. This value should not be used if the bitmap will be saved to disk.
DIB_RGB_COLORS	The bmiColors member of the TBitmapInfo structure is an array of literal RGB color values.

SetStretchBltMode   Windows.Pas

Syntax

```
    SetStretchBltMode(
        DC: HDC;                      {a handle to a device context}
```

p2: Integer   {the bitmap stretch mode flag}
): Integer;   {returns the previous stretch mode}

Description

This function sets the bitmap stretching mode on the specified device context. This mode defines how rows and columns of a bitmap are added or removed when the StretchBlt function is called.

Parameters

DC: A handle to the device context whose bitmap stretch mode is to be modified.

p2: The bitmap stretch mode identifier. This parameter can be one value from Table 5-17. The display device driver may support additional stretching modes.

Return Value

If the function succeeds, it returns the previous stretch mode flag; otherwise it returns zero.

See Also

GetStretchBltMode, SetBrushOrgEx, StretchBlt

Example

Please see Listing 5-15 under LoadBitmap.

Table 5-17: SetStretchBltMode p2 Values

Value	Description
BLACKONWHITE	Performs a Boolean AND operation using the color values for eliminated and existing pixels. If the bitmap is a monochrome bitmap, this mode preserves black pixels at the expense of white pixels.
COLORONCOLOR	Deletes pixels without making any attempt to preserve pixel information.
HALFTONE	Maps pixels from the source bitmap into blocks of pixels on the destination bitmap. The destination pixel color is the average of the colors from the source pixels. This mode requires more processing time than the other flags, but produces higher quality images. If this flag is used, the application must call the SetBrushOrgEx function to reset the brush origin or brush misalignment will occur.
STRETCH_ANDSCANS	The same as BLACKONWHITE.
STRETCH_DELETESCANS	The same as COLORONCOLOR.
STRETCH_HALFTONE	The same as HALFTONE.
STRETCH_ORSCANS	The same as WHITEONBLACK.

5

Chapter

Value	Description
WHITEONBLACK	Performs a Boolean OR operation using the color values for eliminated and existing pixels. If the bitmap is a monochrome bitmap, this mode preserves white pixels at the expense of black pixels.

StretchBlt   Windows.Pas

Syntax

```
StretchBlt(
DestDC: HDC;          {a handle to the destination device context}
X: Integer;           {the horizontal coordinate of the destination rectangle}
Y: Integer;           {the vertical coordinate of the destination rectangle}
Width: Integer;       {the width of the destination rectangle}
Height: Integer;      {the height of the destination rectangle}
SrcDC: HDC;           {a handle to the source device context}
XSrc: Integer;        {the horizontal coordinate of the source rectangle}
YSrc: Integer;        {the vertical coordinate of the source rectangle}
SrcWidth: Integer;    {the width of the source rectangle}
SrcHeight: Integer;   {the height of the source rectangle}
Rop: DWORD            {the raster operation code}
): BOOL;              {returns TRUE or FALSE}
```

Description

This function copies a rectangle of pixels from the bitmap in the specified source device context into the bitmap in the specified destination device context. The copied bitmap area can be stretched or compressed as desired. The stretch mode set by the Set-StretchBltMode function determines how the bitmap is stretched or compressed. If the color formats of the source and destination device contexts differ, this function converts the color format of the source into the color format of the destination. If the specified raster operation indicates that colors from the source and destination are merged, the merge takes place after the source bitmap is stretched or compressed. Note that if the sign of the source and destination width and height differ, StretchBlt creates a mirror image of the copied bitmap area.

Parameters

DestDC: A handle to the device context to which the pixels are copied.

X: The horizontal coordinate of the upper left corner of the destination rectangle in the destination device context, measured in logical units.

Y: The vertical coordinate of the upper left corner of the destination rectangle in the destination device context, measured in logical units.

Width: The width of the destination rectangle, measured in logical units.

Height: The height of the destination rectangle, measured in logical units.

SrcDC: A handle to the device context from which the pixels are copied. This cannot be the handle to a metafile device context.

XSrc: The horizontal coordinate of the upper left corner of the source rectangle in the source device context, measured in logical units.

YSrc: The vertical coordinate of the upper left corner of the source rectangle in the source device context, measured in logical units.

SrcWidth: The width of the source rectangle, measured in logical units.

SrcHeight: The height of the source rectangle, measured in logical units.

Rop: A raster operation code that determines how the colors of the pixels in the source are combined with the colors of the pixels in the destination. This parameter can be one value from Table 5-18.

Return Value

If the function succeeds, it returns TRUE; otherwise it returns FALSE. To get extended error information, call the GetLastError function.

See Also

BitBlt, GetDC, CreateCompatibleDC, CreateBitmap, LoadBitmap, SetStretchBltMode

Example

Please see Listing 5-16 under LoadImage, and other examples throughout this chapter.

Table 5-18: StretchBlt Rop Values

Value	Description
BLACKNESS	Fills the pixels in the specified rectangle in the destination with the color in index 0 of the physical palette. By default, this color is black.
DSTINVERT	Inverts the colors of the pixels in the specified rectangle in the destination.
MERGECOPY	Combines the pixel colors of the source rectangle with the pixel colors of the pattern contained in the brush selected into the destination device context using the Boolean AND operator.
MERGEPAINT	Inverts the pixel colors of the source rectangle and combines them with the pixel colors of the destination rectangle using the Boolean OR operator.
NOTSRCCOPY	Inverts the pixel colors of the source rectangle and copies them into the destination rectangle.
NOTSRCERASE	Combines the pixel colors of the source and destination rectangles using the Boolean OR operator, then inverts the resulting color.

5

Chapter

Value	Description
PATCOPY	Copies the pattern contained in the brush selected into the destination device context directly into the destination.
PATINVERT	Combines the pixel colors of the pattern contained in the brush selected into the destination device context with the colors of the pixels in the destination using the Boolean XOR operator.
PATPAINT	Combines the colors of the pattern contained in the brush selected into the destination device context with the inverted pixel colors of the source rectangle using the Boolean OR operator, then combines the result with the pixel colors of the destination rectangle using the Boolean OR operator.
SRCAND	Combines the pixel colors of the source and destination rectangles using the Boolean AND operator.
SRCCOPY	Copies the pixel colors of the source rectangle directly into the destination rectangle.
SRCERASE	Combines the pixel colors of the source rectangle with the inverted colors of the destination rectangle using the Boolean AND operator.
SRCINVERT	Combines the pixel colors of the source and destination rectangles using the Boolean XOR operator.
SRCPAINT	Combines the pixel colors of the source and destination rectangles using the Boolean OR operator.
WHITENESS	Fills the pixels in the specified rectangle in the destination with the color in index 255 of the physical palette. By default, this color is white.

StretchDIBits   Windows.Pas

Syntax

```
StretchDIBits(
  DC: HDC;                        {a handle to a device context}
  DestX: Integer;                 {the horizontal coordinate of the destination rectangle}
  DestY: Integer;                 {the vertical coordinate of the destination rectangle}
  DestWidth: Integer;             {the width of the destination rectangle}
  DestHeight: Integer;            {the height of the destination rectangle}
  SrcX: Integer;                  {the horizontal coordinate of the source rectangle}
  SrcY: Integer;                  {the vertical coordinate of the source rectangle}
  SrcWidth: Integer;              {the width of the source rectangle}
  SrcHeight: Integer;             {the height of the source rectangle}
  Bits: Pointer;                  {a pointer to the bitmap bit values}
  var BitsInfo: TBitmapInfo;      {a pointer to the DIB bitmap information data structure}
  Usage: UINT                     {color type flag}
  Rop: DWORD                      {the raster operation code}
): Integer;                       {returns the number of scan lines copied}
```

Description

This function copies pixels from the specified rectangular area of the DIB image into the specified rectangular area of the destination device context. The copied bitmap area can be stretched or compressed as desired. The stretch mode set by the Set-StretchBltMode function determines how the bitmap is stretched or compressed. Optimal bitmap copy speed is obtained when the DIB bitmap bits specify indices into the system palette. Note that if the signs of the source and destination width and height differ, StretchDIBits creates a mirror image of the copied bitmap area. This function will reliably copy a bitmap image onto a printer device context.

Parameters

DC: The device context upon which the DIB image is copied and displayed.

DestX: The horizontal coordinate of the upper left corner of the destination rectangle in the destination device context, measured in logical units.

DestY: The vertical coordinate of the upper left corner of the destination rectangle in the destination device context, measured in logical units.

DestWidth: The width of the destination rectangle, measured in logical units.

DestHeight: The height of the destination rectangle, measured in logical units.

SrcX: The horizontal coordinate of the upper left corner of the source rectangle in the source device context, measured in logical units.

SrcY: The vertical coordinate of the upper left corner of the source rectangle in the source device context, measured in logical units.

SrcWidth: The width of the source rectangle, measured in logical units.

SrcHeight: The height of the source rectangle, measured in logical units.

Bits: A pointer to the image representing the DIB, in the form of an array of bytes.

BitsInfo: A pointer to a TBitmapInfo data structure describing the DIB, including information about its dimensions and color table. The TBitmapInfo data structure is defined as:

TBitmapInfo = packed record
    bmiHeader: TBitmapInfoHeader;   {bitmap header information}
    bmiColors: array[0..0] of TRGBQuad;   {the color table used by the bitmap}
end;

The TBitmapInfoHeader data structure is defined as:

TBitmapInfoHeader = packed record
    biSize: DWORD;   {the size of the structure in bytes}
    biWidth: Longint;   {the width of the bitmap in pixels}
    biHeight: Longint;   {the height of the bitmap in pixels}
    biPlanes: Word;   {the number of color planes}

5

Chapter

biBitCount: Word;	{the bits per pixel required to describe a color}
biCompression: DWORD;	{compression flags}
biSizeImage: DWORD;	{the size of the image in bytes}
biXPelsPerMeter: Longint;	{horizontal pixels per meter of the target device}
biYPelsPerMeter: Longint;	{vertical pixels per meter of the target device}
biClrUsed: DWORD;	{the number of color indices used}
biClrImportant: DWORD;	{the number of important color indices}

    end;

The TRGBQuad data structure is defined as:

    TRGBQuad = packed record

rgbBlue: Byte;	{blue color intensity}
rgbGreen: Byte;	{green color intensity}
rgbRed: Byte;	{red color intensity}
rgbReserved: Byte;	{reserved value}

    end;

For an explanation of these data structures, see the CreateDIBSection function.

Usage: A flag indicating the type of color information stored in the bmiColors member of the TBitmapInfo structure pointed to by the BitsInfo parameter. This parameter can be one value from Table 5-19.

Rop: A raster operation code that determines how the colors of the pixels in the source are combined with the colors of the pixels in the destination. This parameter can be one value from Table 5-20.

Return Value

If the function succeeds, it returns the number of scan lines that were copied to the destination device context; otherwise it returns GDI_ERROR. To get extended error information, call the GetLastError function.

See Also

SetDIBits, SetDIBitsToDevice, SetStretchBltMode

Example

Please see Listing 5-9 under CreateDIBSection.

Table 5-19: StretchDIBits Usage Values

Value	Description
DIB_PAL_COLORS	The bmiColors member of the TBitmapInfo structure is an array of 16-bit indices into the currently realized logical palette of the specified device context. This value should not be used if the bitmap will be saved to disk.
DIB_RGB_COLORS	The bmiColors member of the TBitmapInfo structure is an array of literal RGB color values.

Table 5-20: StretchDIBits Rop Values

Value	Description
BLACKNESS	Fills the pixels in the specified rectangle in the destination with the color in index 0 of the physical palette. By default, this color is black.
DSTINVERT	Inverts the colors of the pixels in the specified rectangle in the destination.
MERGECOPY	Combines the pixel colors of the source rectangle with the pixel colors of the pattern contained in the brush selected into the destination device context using the Boolean AND operator.
MERGEPAINT	Inverts the pixel colors of the source rectangle and combines them with the pixel colors of the destination rectangle using the Boolean OR operator.
NOTSRCCOPY	Inverts the pixel colors of the source rectangle and copies them into the destination rectangle.
NOTSRCERASE	Combines the pixel colors of the source and destination rectangles using the Boolean OR operator, then inverts the resulting color.
PATCOPY	Copies the pattern contained in the brush selected into the destination device context directly into the destination.
PATINVERT	Combines the pixel colors of the pattern contained in the brush selected into the destination device context with the colors of the pixels in the destination using the Boolean XOR operator.
PATPAINT	Combines the colors of the pattern contained in the brush selected into the destination device context with the inverted pixel colors of the source rectangle using the Boolean OR operator, then combines the result with the pixel colors of the destination rectangle using the Boolean OR operator.
SRCAND	Combines the pixel colors of the source and destination rectangles using the Boolean AND operator.
SRCCOPY	Copies the pixel colors of the source rectangle directly into the destination rectangle.

5

Chapter

Value	Description
SRCERASE	Combines the pixel colors of the source rectangle with the inverted colors of the destination rectangle using the Boolean AND operator.
SRCINVERT	Combines the pixel colors of the source and destination rectangles using the Boolean XOR operator.
SRCPAINT	Combines the pixel colors of the source and destination rectangles using the Boolean OR operator.
WHITENESS	Fills the pixels in the specified rectangle in the destination with the color in index 255 of the physical palette. By default, this color is white.

Chapter 6

Icon, Cursor, and Caret Functions

Windows, being the graphical environment that it is, displays information in a variety of ways, most obviously by means of simple graphics. Various images are used to portray the type of file being viewed in the Explorer, or what type of action is available to the user depending on the current position of the mouse cursor. The Windows functions concerned with the creating and manipulation of icon, cursor, and caret images give the developer a variety of means by which to communicate specific information or available actions.

Carets

The caret is a small, flashing image used to indicate which window currently has the keyboard focus and can accept text input. Since only one window at a time can have the keyboard focus, there is only one caret in the system. In Delphi, the default caret used by components that accept text is a thin, vertical line, and Delphi encapsulates the caret functions so completely that the developer will likely never have to be concerned with them. However, if a new caret shape is desired, the Windows caret functions allow the developer to specify a caret shape in terms of a desired width and height, or based on a bitmap. See the CreateCaret function for an example of creating a new caret shape based on a bitmap. The following example demonstrates how to create a solid black box caret.

Listing 6-I: Creating a Solid Black Box Caret

```
procedure TForm1.Button1Click(Sender: TObject);
begin
   {we must set focus to the window we want to type in. when
    this window receives focus manually (i.e., by using the Tab
    key), Delphi automatically reassigns the appropriate caret}
   Memo1.SetFocus;

   {hide the current caret}
   HideCaret(0);
```

```
{destroy the current caret}
DestroyCaret;

{create the new caret shape (a solid black box)}
CreateCaret(Memo1.Handle, 0, 10, 12);

{display the new caret image}
ShowCaret(0);
end;
```

Figure 6-1:
The black box
caret shape

Icon and Cursor Masks

Windows does not have a native API function that copies a bitmap to a destination while interpreting some of the pixels as "transparent." However, icons and cursors have irregular shapes that, when drawn to the screen, allow the background to show through. This is accomplished by means of Boolean raster operations and masks.

Each icon and cursor is composed of two bitmap images known as masks: an AND mask and an OR mask. These images are combined using Boolean raster operations with the background image of the destination in two steps to create a final image, exhibiting "transparent" pixels.

Figure 6-2:
The icon and
cursor image
is a
composite of
an AND
mask and an
OR mask.

First, the AND mask is combined with the background image on the destination device context using the Boolean AND operator. The white pixels of the AND mask will preserve those pixels in the destination, while the black pixels of the AND mask will change the pixels in the destination to black, thereby carving out a space for the final image, like so:

*Figure 6-3:
First step -
Combine the
AND mask
with the
destination
(Boolean
AND)*

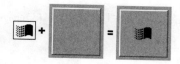

Once the AND mask is combined with the destination, the OR mask is combined with the background image on the destination device context using the Boolean OR operator. The black pixels of the OR mask will preserve those pixels in the destination, while the colored pixels, which should fall within the black pixels created by the first step, should show up as they appear in the OR mask, thereby creating the final image with the illusion of transparent pixels, like so:

*Figure 6-4:
Last step -
Combine the
OR mask
with the
destination
(Boolean OR)*

It is this method of bitmap merging that allows icons and cursors to have irregular shapes with the background showing through the "transparent" areas. The same technique can be used to display bitmaps transparently by using a combination of masks with the BitBlt function and the SRCAND and SRCPAINT raster operation codes. The GetIconInfo function can be used to retrieve the AND and OR masks for both icons and cursors.

Icon to Bitmap Conversion

The complementary nature of the Windows bitmap, cursor, and icon functions provides the developer a means by which a bitmap can be converted into an icon or cursor, or vice versa. With a few simple API calls, combined with Delphi's power and ease of use, the developer can create applications that could potentially use bitmaps, cursors, and icons interchangeably. The following example demonstrates a method by which any bitmap can be converted into an icon, or any icon converted into a bitmap.

Listing 6-2: Converting Icons to Bitmaps and Back

```
var
  Form1: TForm1;
  CurIcon: TIcon;        // holds an icon
  CurBitmap: TBitmap;    // holds a bitmap

implementation

{$R *.DFM}

procedure TForm1.FileListBox1DblClick(Sender: TObject);
begin
  {open the selected file as an icon (automatically converts bitmaps
```

```
     to icons)}
   CurIcon.Handle := ExtractIcon(hInstance, PChar(FileListBox1.FileName), 0);

   {enable the save image button}
   Button1.Enabled := TRUE;

   {erase the paintbox}
   PaintBox1.Canvas.Brush.Color := clBtnFace;
   PaintBox1.Canvas.FillRect(PaintBox1.ClientRect);

   {if the user wants to convert icons to bitmaps...}
   if RadioButton1.Checked then
   begin
     {erase the current bitmap image}
     CurBitmap.Canvas.Brush.Color := clBtnFace;
     CurBitmap.Canvas.FillRect(PaintBox1.ClientRect);

     {draw the icon onto the bitmap}
     DrawIcon(CurBitmap.Canvas.Handle, 0, 0, CurIcon.Handle);

     {display the bitmap image}
     PaintBox1.Canvas.Draw((PaintBox1.Width div 2)-16,
                       (PaintBox1.Height div 2)-16, CurBitmap);
   end
   else
     {display the icon}
     DrawIcon(PaintBox1.Canvas.Handle, (PaintBox1.Width div 2)-16,
           (PaintBox1.Height div 2)-16, CurIcon.Handle);
   end;

procedure TForm1.RadioButton1Click(Sender: TObject);
begin
   {if the user wants to convert icons to bitmaps...}
   if Sender=RadioButton1 then
   begin
     {filter files by icons only}
     FileListBox1.Mask := '*.ico';

     {initialize the save picture dialog accordingly}
     SavePictureDialog1.Filter := 'Bitmaps (*.bmp)|*.bmp';
     SavePictureDialog1.DefaultExt := '*.bmp';
   end
   else
   begin
     {otherwise, filter files by bitmaps only}
     FileListBox1.Mask := '*.bmp';

     {initialize the save picture dialog accordingly}
     SavePictureDialog1.Filter := 'Icons (*.ico)|*.ico';
     SavePictureDialog1.DefaultExt := '*.ico';
   end;

   {erase the current paintbox image}
   PaintBox1.Canvas.Brush.Color := clBtnFace;
```

```
      PaintBox1.Canvas.FillRect(PaintBox1.ClientRect);

      {disable the save image button until the user selects a file to convert}
      Button1.Enabled := FALSE;
    end;

procedure TForm1.FormCreate(Sender: TObject);
begin
  {create the icon to hold converted bitmaps}
  CurIcon := TIcon.Create;

  {create and initialize the bitmap to hold converted icons}
  CurBitmap := TBitmap.Create;
  CurBitmap.Width := GetSystemMetrics(SM_CXICON);
  CurBitmap.Height := GetSystemMetrics(SM_CYICON);

  {initialize the save picture dialog for saving bitmaps}
  SavePictureDialog1.Filter := 'Bitmaps (*.bmp)|*.bmp';
  SavePictureDialog1.DefaultExt := '*.bmp';
end;

procedure TForm1.Button1Click(Sender: TObject);
begin
  {delete the last specified filename}
  SavePictureDialog1.FileName := '';

  {show the dialog box}
  if SavePictureDialog1.Execute then
    if RadioButton1.Checked then
      {as indicated, save the file as a bitmap...}
      CurBitmap.SaveToFile(SavePictureDialog1.FileName)
    else
      {...or icon}
      CurIcon.SaveToFile(SavePictureDialog1.FileName);
end;

procedure TForm1.FormDestroy(Sender: TObject);
begin
  {free the resources}
  CurIcon.Free;
  CurBitmap.Free;
end;
```

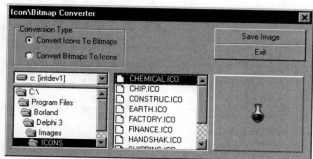

Figure 6-5:
Converting an
icon

Icon, Cursor, and Caret Functions

The following icon, cursor, and caret functions are covered in this chapter:

Table 6-1: Icon, Cursor, and Caret Functions

Function	Description
CopyIcon	Creates a copy of an existing icon.
CreateCaret	Creates a new caret.
CreateCursor	Creates a new cursor.
CreateIcon	Creates a new icon.
CreateIconFromResource	Creates a new icon or cursor from resource information.
CreateIconFromResourceEx	Creates a new icon or cursor from resource information with a specified width and height.
CreateIconIndirect	Creates an icon or cursor from a data structure.
DestroyCaret	Destroys a caret.
DestroyCursor	Destroys a cursor.
DestroyIcon	Destroys an icon.
DrawIcon	Draws an icon at a specified location.
DrawIconEx	Draws an icon or cursor at a specified location.
ExtractAssociatedIcon	Retrieves a handle to an icon for the executable file associated with a specified file.
ExtractIcon	Retrieves a handle to an icon from a specified file.
ExtractIconEx	Retrieves a handle to the large and small icons from a specified file.
GetCursor	Retrieves a handle to the current cursor.
GetIconInfo	Retrieves information about an icon or cursor.
HideCaret	Hides the caret.
LoadCursor	Loads a cursor from the executable's resources.
LoadCursorFromFile	Loads a cursor from a file.
LoadIcon	Loads an icon from the executable's resources.
LookupIconIdFromDirectory	Searches through resource data for a compatible icon or cursor.
LookupIconIdFromDirectoryEx	Searches through resource data for a compatible icon or cursor with the specified width and height.
SetCursor	Sets the cursor to the specified cursor.
SetSystemCursor	Sets a system cursor to the specified cursor.
ShowCaret	Displays the caret if it was hidden.
ShowCursor	Displays or hides the cursor.

CopyIcon   *Windows.Pas*

Syntax

```
CopyIcon(
hIcon: HICON                    {a handle to the icon to copy}
): HICON;                       {returns a handle to an icon}
```

Description

This function makes an exact duplicate of the specified icon, returning its handle. This can be used to copy icons belonging to other modules.

Parameters

hIcon: A handle to the icon being copied.

Return Value

If the function succeeds, it returns a handle to an exact copy of the specified icon; otherwise it returns zero. To get extended error information, call the GetLastError function.

See Also

DrawIcon, DrawIconEx

Example

Listing 6-3: Copying the Application Icon

```
procedure TForm1.Button1Click(Sender: TObject);
var
  IconCopy: HICON;          // holds a handle to the duplicated icon
begin
  {make a copy of the application icon...}
  IconCopy := CopyIcon(Application.Icon.Handle);

  {...and display it}
  DrawIcon(PaintBox1.Canvas.Handle, (PaintBox1.Width div 2)-16,
           (PaintBox1.Height div 2)-16, IconCopy);
end;
```

Figure 6-6:
The duplicated application icon

6

Chapter

CreateCaret   Windows.Pas

Syntax

```
CreateCaret(
hWnd: HWND;            {a handle to the owner windows}
hBitmap: HBITMAP;      {a handle to a bitmap}
nWidth: Integer;       {the width of the caret}
nHeight: Integer       {the height of the caret}
): BOOL;               {returns TRUE or FALSE}
```

Description

This function creates a new shape for the caret. The caret is assigned to a window, and can be either a line, a block, or a bitmap. If a bitmap is specified, the bitmap determines the width and height of the caret shape. Otherwise, the width and height are in terms of logical units, and the exact dimensions are dependent upon the current mapping mode. The developer can retrieve the default width and height values used for a caret by calling the GetSystemMetrics function using the SM_CXBORDER and SM_CYBORDER flags. The CreateCaret function automatically destroys the previous caret shape, and the caret will not be visible until the ShowCaret function is called.

Parameters

hWnd: A handle to the window that will own the caret.

hBitmap: A handle to the bitmap used as the caret shape. If this parameter is zero, the caret will be a solid rectangle. If this parameter is set to (hBitmap) 1, the caret will be gray.

nWidth: The width of the caret, in logical units. If this parameter is set to zero, the system-defined window border width is used as the default width of the cursor. If the hBitmap parameter is set to the handle of a bitmap, the bitmap determines the width and this parameter is ignored.

nHeight: The height of the caret, in logical units. If this parameter is set to zero, the system-defined window border height is used as the default height of the cursor. If the hBitmap parameter is set to the handle of a bitmap, the bitmap determines the height and this parameter is ignored.

Return Value

If the function succeeds, it returns TRUE; otherwise it returns FALSE. To get extended error information, call the GetLastError function.

See Also

CreateBitmap, CreateDIBitmap, DestroyCaret, GetSystemMetrics, HideCaret, LoadBitmap, LoadImage, ShowCaret

Example

Listing 6-4: Creating a New Caret Shape

```
procedure TForm1.Button1Click(Sender: TObject);
var
    TheCaretBitmap: HBitmap;       // a handle to the new caret bitmap
begin
    {load the caret bitmap from an external file}
    TheCaretBitmap := LoadImage(0,'NewCaret.bmp',IMAGE_BITMAP,0,0,
                          LR_DEFAULTSIZE OR LR_LOADFROMFILE);

    {we must set focus to the window we want to type in. when
     this window receives focus manually (i.e., by using the Tab
     key), Delphi automatically reassigns the appropriate caret}
    Memo1.SetFocus;

    {hide the current caret}
    HideCaret(0);

    {destroy the current caret}
    DestroyCaret;

    {create the new caret shape from the loaded bitmap}
    CreateCaret(Memo1.Handle,TheCaretBitmap,0,0);

    {display the new caret image}
    ShowCaret(0);
end;
```

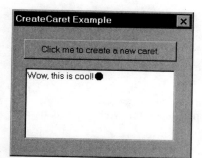

Figure 6-7:
The new caret

CreateCursor   *Windows.Pas*

Syntax

```
CreateCursor(
hInst: HINST;              {a handle to the current application instance}
xHotSpot: Integer;         {the horizontal position of the cursor hot spot}
yHotSpot: Integer;         {the vertical position of the cursor hot spot}
nWidth: Integer;           {the width of the cursor in pixels}
nHeight: Integer;          {the height of the cursor in pixels}
```

6

Chapter

pvANDPlane: Pointer;	{a pointer to the AND image data}
pvXORPlane: Pointer	{a pointer to the XOR image data}
): HCURSOR;	{returns a handle to the cursor}

Description

This function creates a new cursor with the specified dimensions, image, and hot spot. This cursor can be added to Delphi's screen cursors array to make it persistent.

Parameters

hInst: A handle to the current application instance.

xHotSpot: The horizontal coordinate of the cursor's hot spot.

yHotSpot: The vertical coordinate of the cursor's hot spot.

nWidth: The width of the cursor in pixels. Use GetSystemMetrics(SM_CXCURSOR) to determine the display driver supported cursor width.

nHeight: The height of the cursor in pixels. Use GetSystemMetrics(SM_CYCURSOR) to determine the display driver supported cursor height.

pvANDPlane: A pointer to an array of bytes containing the bit values for the AND mask of the cursor. This array contains information in the format of a device-dependent monochrome bitmap.

pvXORPlane: A pointer to an array of bytes containing the bit values for the XOR mask of the cursor. This array contains information in the format of a device-dependent monochrome bitmap.

Return Value

If the function succeeds, it returns a handle to the new cursor; otherwise it returns zero. To get extended error information, call the GetLastError function.

See Also

CreateIcon, DestroyCursor, GetCursor, GetSystemMetrics, SetCursor

Example

Listing 6-5: Creating a New Cursor

```
var
  Form1: TForm1;
  OldCursor: HCURSOR;    // preserves the old cursor
  NewCursor: HCURSOR;    // a handle to the new cursor

implementation

procedure TForm1.Button1Click(Sender: TObject);
var
  MaskSize: Integer;    // holds the computed size of the cursor
  AndMask,              // cursor bit arrays
```

```
   XorMask: ^Byte;
   AndImage,                    // intermediate bitmaps used to define the cursor shape
   XorImage: TBitmap;
begin
  {compute the size of the cursor bit arrays}
  MaskSize := (GetSystemMetrics(SM_CXICON) div 8)*GetSystemMetrics(SM_CYICON);

  {create the bitmap used to define the AND mask shape}
  AndImage := TBitmap.Create;
  with AndImage do
  begin
    {we are creating a black and white cursor}
    Monochrome := TRUE;

    {set the dimensions to those reported by the system}
    Width := GetSystemMetrics(SM_CXICON);
    Height := GetSystemMetrics(SM_CYICON);

    {create the shape of an X}
    Canvas.Brush.Color := clWhite;
    Canvas.Pen.Color := clBlack;
    Canvas.FillRect(Canvas.ClipRect);
    Canvas.MoveTo(0,0);
    Canvas.LineTo(Width,Height);
    Canvas.MoveTo(Width,0);
    Canvas.LineTo(0,Height);
  end;

  {create the bitmap used to define the XOR mask shape}
  XorImage := TBitmap.Create;
  with XorImage do
  begin
    {we are creating a black and white cursor}
    Monochrome := TRUE;

    {set the dimensions to those reported by the system}
    Width := GetSystemMetrics(SM_CXICON);
    Height := GetSystemMetrics(SM_CYICON);

    {fill the bitmap with black}
    Canvas.Brush.Color := clBlack;
    Canvas.Pen.Color := clBlack;
    Canvas.FillRect(Canvas.ClipRect);
  end;

  {allocate the memory for the bit arrays}
  GetMem(AndMask,MaskSize);
  GetMem(XorMask,MaskSize);

  {transfer the images in the bitmaps to the bit arrays}
  GetBitmapBits(AndImage.Handle, MaskSize, AndMask);
  GetBitmapBits(XorImage.Handle, MaskSize, XorMask);

  {create a new cursor based on the images transferred into
   the bit arrays}
```

6

Chapter

```
NewCursor := CreateCursor(hInstance, 0, 0, GetSystemMetrics(SM_CXICON),
                    GetSystemMetrics(SM_CYICON), AndMask, XorMask);

  {if the cursor for the window class is not set to zero, SetCursor will
   succeed but the cursor will be reset to the class cursor as soon as
   the mouse is moved.  therefore, we must set the class cursor for the
   button and the form to zero}
  SetClassLong(Form1.Handle, GCL_HCURSOR, 0);
  SetClassLong(Button1.Handle, GCL_HCURSOR, 0);

  {now that the class cursor has been deleted, set the new cursor shape}
  SetCursor(NewCursor);

  {the temporary bitmaps are no longer needed, so dispose of them}
  AndImage.Free;
  XorImage.Free;
end;

procedure TForm1.FormCreate(Sender: TObject);
begin
  {retrieve and save a handle to the original cursor}
  OldCursor := GetCursor;
end;

procedure TForm1.FormDestroy(Sender: TObject);
begin
  {set the cursor back to the original cursor shape}
  SetCursor(OldCursor);

  {delete the new cursor}
  DestroyCursor(NewCursor);
end;
```

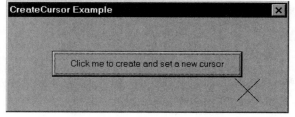

*Figure 6-8:
The new
cursor*

CreateIcon   Windows.Pas

Syntax

```
CreateIcon(
hInstance: HINST;          {a handle to the application instance}
nWidth: Integer;           {the width of the icon}
nHeight: Integer;          {the height of the icon}
cPlanes: Byte;             {the number of color planes}
cBitsPixel: Byte;          {the number of bits describing an XOR mask pixel}
```

lpbANDbits: Pointer;	{a pointer to the AND mask data}
lpbXORbits: Pointer	{a pointer to the XOR mask data}
): HICON;	{returns a handle to an icon}

Description

This function dynamically creates a new icon with the specified dimensions and image.

Parameters

hInstance: A handle to the instance of the application creating the icon.

nWidth: The width of the icon in pixels. This parameter must be set to the value returned by GetSystemMetrics(SM_CXICON).

nHeight: The height of the icon in pixels. This parameter must be set to the value returned by GetSystemMetrics(SM_CYICON).

cPlanes: The number of color planes used in the XOR icon mask.

cBitsPixel: The number of bits required to describe the color of one pixel (i.e., 8 bits for 256-color images, 24 bits for 16.7 million-color images, etc.).

lpbANDbits: A pointer to an array of bytes containing the image for the AND mask of the icon. The image information contained in this array must describe a monochrome bitmap.

lpbXORbits: A pointer to an array of bytes containing the image for the XOR mask of the icon. This image information can describe either a monochrome bitmap or a device-dependent color bitmap.

Return Value

If the function succeeds, it returns the handle to a new icon; otherwise it returns zero. To get extended error information, call the GetLastError function.

See Also

CreateIconFromResource, CreateIconFromResourceEx, CreateIconIndirect, DrawIcon, DrawIconEx, GetSystemMetrics, LoadIcon

Example

Listing 6-6: Creating an Icon at Runtime

```
procedure TForm1.Button1Click(Sender: TObject);
var
  AndMaskSize,          // holds the computed size of the icon
  XorMaskSize: Integer;

  AndMask,              // icon bit arrays
  XorMask: ^Byte;

  AndImage,             // intermediate bitmaps used to define the icon shape
  XorImage: TBitmap;
```

6

Chapter

```
begin
  {compute the size of the Icon bit arrays}
  XorMaskSize := GetSystemMetrics(SM_CXICON)*GetSystemMetrics(SM_CYICON);
  {the AND mask is a monochrome bitmap. thus, each bit represents a
   pixel, so divide the width by 8 to get the correct number of bytes}
  AndMaskSize :=(GetSystemMetrics(SM_CXICON) div 8)*GetSystemMetrics(SM_CYICON);

  {create the bitmap used to define the XOR mask shape}
  XorImage := TBitmap.Create;
  with XorImage do
  begin
    {set the dimensions to those reported by the system}
    Width := GetSystemMetrics(SM_CXICON);
    Height := GetSystemMetrics(SM_CYICON);

    {fill the background with black}
    Canvas.Brush.Color := clBlack;
    Canvas.FillRect(Canvas.ClipRect);

    {draw a red box}
    Canvas.Brush.Color := clRed;
    Canvas.Pen.Color := clBlack;
    Canvas.FillRect(Rect(5,5,GetSystemMetrics(SM_CXICON)-5,
                         GetSystemMetrics(SM_CYICON)-5));
  end;

  {create the bitmap used to define the AND mask shape}
  AndImage := TBitmap.Create;
  with AndImage do
  begin
    {the AND mask is always black and white}
    Monochrome := TRUE;

    {set the dimensions to those reported by the system}
    Width := GetSystemMetrics(SM_CXICON);
    Height := GetSystemMetrics(SM_CYICON);

    {fill the background with white}
    Canvas.Brush.Color := clWhite;
    Canvas.FillRect(Canvas.ClipRect);

    {draw a black box the same size as the red box
     in the XOR bitmask}
    Canvas.Brush.Color := clBlack;
    Canvas.Pen.Color := clBlack;
    Canvas.FillRect(Rect(5,5,GetSystemMetrics(SM_CXICON)-5,
                         GetSystemMetrics(SM_CYICON)-5));
  end;

  {allocate the memory for the bit arrays}
  GetMem(AndMask,AndMaskSize);
  GetMem(XorMask,XorMaskSize);

  {transfer the images in the bitmaps to the bit arrays}
  GetBitmapBits(AndImage.Handle, AndMaskSize, AndMask);
```

```
GetBitmapBits(XorImage.Handle, XorMaskSize, XorMask);

{create a new icon based on the images transferred into
 the bit arrays}
NewIcon := CreateIcon(hInstance, GetSystemMetrics(SM_CXICON),
                      GetSystemMetrics(SM_CYICON), 1, 8, AndMask, XorMask);

{point the application's icon to this new icon}
Application.Icon.Handle := NewIcon;

{display the icon on the form}
DrawIcon(PaintBox1.Canvas.Handle,
         PaintBox1.Width div 2-(GetSystemMetrics(SM_CXICON) div 2),
         PaintBox1.Height div 2-(GetSystemMetrics(SM_CYICON) div 2), NewIcon);

{the temporary bitmaps are no longer needed, so dispose of them}
AndImage.Free;
XorImage.Free;
end;
```

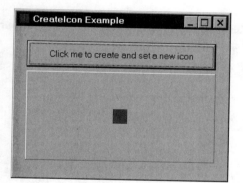

Figure 6-9:
The new icon

CreateIconFromResource   *Windows.Pas*

Syntax

```
CreateIconFromResource(
presbits: PByte;          {a pointer to icon or cursor bits}
dwResSize: DWORD;         {the number of bytes pointed to by presbits}
fIcon: BOOL;              {indicates an icon or cursor}
dwVer: DWORD              {the format version number}
): HICON;                 {returns a handle to an icon or cursor}
```

Description

This function creates a new icon or cursor from the specified resource bits defining the icon or cursor image.

6

Chapter

Parameters

presbits: A pointer to a buffer containing the icon or cursor resource bits. The return value from the LoadResource or LookupIconIdFromDirectory functions can be used as the input for this parameter.

dwResSize: The size of the buffer pointed to by the presbits parameter, in bytes.

fIcon: A flag indicating whether an icon or cursor is created. A value of TRUE causes the function to create an icon; FALSE creates a cursor.

dwVer: Specifies the icon and cursor format version number. Win32 applications should set this value to $30000.

Return Value

If the function succeeds, it returns a handle to an icon or cursor; otherwise it returns zero. To get extended error information, call the GetLastError function.

See Also

CreateIcon, CreateIconFromResourceEx, CreateIconIndirect, LoadResource, LookupIconIdFromDirectory, LookupIconIdFromDirectoryEx

Example

Listing 6-7: Creating an Icon from Resource Information

```
procedure TForm1.Button1Click(Sender: TObject);
var
  IconBits: HGLOBAL;        // a handle to the icon image
  IconBitsPtr: Pointer;     // a pointer to the icon image
  ResHandle: HRSRC;         // a handle to the icon resource information
  ResId: Integer;           // holds the resource id for the icon
  TheIcon: HICON;           // a handle to the created icon
begin
  {retrieve a handle to the icon resource}
  ResHandle := FindResource(0, 'TARGET', RT_GROUP_ICON);

  {retrieve a handle to the icon resource image}
  IconBits := LoadResource(0, ResHandle);

  {retrieve a pointer to the icon image}
  IconBitsPtr := LockResource(IconBits);

  {find the icon that fits the current display device}
  ResId := LookupIconIdFromDirectory(IconBitsPtr, TRUE);

  {retrieve a handle to this icon}
  ResHandle := FindResource(0, MakeIntResource(ResId), RT_ICON);

  {load the icon resource image}
  IconBits := LoadResource(0, ResHandle);

  {retrieve a pointer to the icon image}
```

```
    IconBitsPtr := LockResource(IconBits);

    {create a new icon from the correct icon resource information}
    TheIcon := CreateIconFromResource(IconBitsPtr, SizeOfResource(0, ResHandle),
                                TRUE, $30000);

    {display the icon}
    DrawIcon(PaintBox1.Canvas.Handle,
            PaintBox1.Width div 2-(GetSystemMetrics(SM_CXICON) div 2),
            PaintBox1.Height div 2-(GetSystemMetrics(SM_CYICON) div 2), TheIcon);
  end;
```

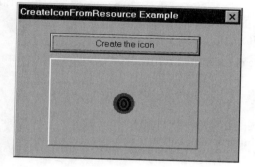

Figure 6-10:
The new icon

CreateIconFromResourceEx   Windows.Pas

Syntax

```
CreateIconFromResourceEx(
presbits: PByte;                {a pointer to icon or cursor bits}
dwResSize: DWORD;               {the number of bytes pointed to by presbits}
fIcon: BOOL;                    {indicates an icon or cursor}
dwVer: DWORD;                   {the format version number}
cxDesired: Integer;             {the preferred width of the icon or cursor}
cyDesired: Integer;             {the preferred height of the icon or cursor}
Flags: UINT                     {color flags}
): HICON;                       {returns a handle to an icon or cursor}
```

Description

This function creates a new icon or cursor from the specified resource bits defining the icon or cursor image. Unlike the CreateIconFromResource function, this function allows the developer to determine the dimensions and color format of the icon or cursor.

Parameters

presbits: A pointer to a buffer containing the icon or cursor resource bits. The return value from the LoadResource or LookupIconIdFromDirectory functions can be used as the input for this parameter.

6

Chapter

dwResSize: The size of the buffer pointed to by the presbits parameter, in bytes.

fIcon: A flag indicating whether an icon or cursor is created. A value of TRUE causes the function to create an icon; FALSE creates a cursor.

dwVer: Specifies the icon and cursor format version number. Win32 applications should set this value to $30000.

cxDesired: Specifies the preferred width of the icon or cursor in pixels. If this parameter is zero, the function uses the value returned from GetSystemMetrics(SM_CXICON).

cyDesired: Specifies the preferred height of the icon or cursor in pixels. If this parameter is zero, the function uses the value returned from GetSystemMetrics(SM_CYICON).

Flags: A value indicating the color format for the icon or cursor. This parameter can be one value from Table 6-2.

Return Value

If the function succeeds, it returns a handle to an icon or cursor; otherwise it returns zero. To get extended error information, call the GetLastError function.

See Also

CreateIcon, CreateIconFromResource, CreateIconIndirect, LoadResource, LookupIconId-FromDirectory, LookupIconIdFromDirectoryEx

Example

Listing 6-8: More Options for Creating an Icon from Resource Information

```
procedure TForm1.Button1Click(Sender: TObject);
var
  IconBits: HGLOBAL;      // a handle to the icon image
  IconBitsPtr: Pointer;   // a pointer to the icon image
  ResHandle: HRSRC;       // a handle to the icon resource information
  ResId: Integer;         // holds the resource id for the icon
  TheIcon: HICON;         // a handle to the created icon
begin
  {retrieve a handle to the icon resource}
  ResHandle := FindResource(0, 'TARGET', RT_GROUP_ICON);

  {retrieve a handle to the icon resource image}
  IconBits := LoadResource(0, ResHandle);

  {retrieve a pointer to the icon image}
  IconBitsPtr := LockResource(IconBits);

  {find the icon that fits the current display device}
  ResId := LookupIconIdFromDirectoryEx(IconBitsPtr, TRUE,
                              0, 0, LR_DEFAULTCOLOR);

  {retrieve a handle to this icon}
```

```
ResHandle := FindResource(0, MakeIntResource(ResId), RT_ICON);

{load the icon resource image}
IconBits := LoadResource(0, ResHandle);

{retrieve a pointer to the icon image}
IconBitsPtr := LockResource(IconBits);

{create a new icon from the correct icon resource information}
TheIcon := CreateIconFromResourceEx(IconBitsPtr, SizeOfResource(0, ResHandle),
                           TRUE, $30000, 0, 0, LR_DEFAULTCOLOR);
{display the icon}
DrawIcon(PaintBox1.Canvas.Handle,
         PaintBox1.Width div 2-(GetSystemMetrics(SM_CXICON) div 2),
         PaintBox1.Height div 2-(GetSystemMetrics(SM_CYICON) div 2), TheIcon);
end;
```

Table 6-2: CreateIconFromResourceEx Flags Values

Value	Description
LR_DEFAULTCOLOR	Create a color cursor or icon using the default system colors.
LR_MONOCHROME	Create a monochrome cursor or icon.

CreateIconIndirect   Windows.Pas

Syntax

```
CreateIconIndirect(
var piconinfo: TIconInfo        {a pointer to an icon information data structure}
): HICON;                       {returns a handle to an icon}
```

Description

This function dynamically creates a new icon from the dimensions and images defined in the piconinfo variable. After the icon is created, the application must manage the bitmaps used in the icon definition and delete them when they are no longer used. Icons created with this function must be destroyed by using the DestroyIcon function.

Parameters

piconinfo: A pointer to a TIconInfo data structure that describes the icon image. The TIconInfo structure is defined as:

```
TIconInfo = packed record
     fIcon: BOOL;              {indicates icon or cursor information}
     xHotspot: DWORD;          {the hot spot horizontal coordinate}
     yHotspot: DWORD;          {the hot spot vertical coordinate}
     hbmMask: HBITMAP;         {a bitmap handle}
     hbmColor: HBITMAP;        {a bitmap handle}
end;
```

6

Chapter

See GetIconInfo for a description of the data structure members.

Return Value

If the function succeeds, it returns a handle to the new icon; otherwise it returns zero. To get extended error information, call the GetLastError function.

See Also

CreateIcon, CreateIconFromResource, CreateIconFromResourceEx, DrawIcon, DrawIconEx, DestroyIcon, LoadIcon

Example

Listing 6-9: Creating an Icon Indirectly

```
var
  Form1: TForm1;
  NewIcon: HICON;  // holds the new icon

implementation

procedure TForm1.Button1Click(Sender: TObject);
var
  AndImage,                 // bitmaps used to define the icon shape
  XorImage: TBitmap;
  IconInfo: TIconInfo;  // the icon information data structure
begin
  {create the bitmap used to define the XOR mask shape}
  XorImage := TBitmap.Create;
  with XorImage do
  begin
    {set the dimensions to those reported by the system}
    Width := GetSystemMetrics(SM_CXICON);
    Height := GetSystemMetrics(SM_CYICON);

    {fill the background with black}
    Canvas.Brush.Color := clBlack;
    Canvas.FillRect(Canvas.ClipRect);

    {draw a red box}
    Canvas.Brush.Color := clRed;
    Canvas.Pen.Color := clBlack;
    Canvas.FillRect(Rect(5,5,GetSystemMetrics(SM_CXICON)-5,
                         GetSystemMetrics(SM_CYICON)-5));
  end;

  {create the bitmap used to define the AND mask shape}
  AndImage := TBitmap.Create;
  with AndImage do
  begin
    {the AND mask is always black and white}
    Monochrome := TRUE;

    {set the dimensions to those reported by the system}
```

```
        Width := GetSystemMetrics(SM_CXICON);
        Height := GetSystemMetrics(SM_CYICON);

        {fill the background with white}
        Canvas.Brush.Color := clWhite;
        Canvas.FillRect(Canvas.ClipRect);

        {draw a black box the same size as the red box
         in the XOR bitmask}
        Canvas.Brush.Color := clBlack;
        Canvas.Pen.Color := clBlack;
        Canvas.FillRect(Rect(5,5,GetSystemMetrics(SM_CXICON)-5,
                             GetSystemMetrics(SM_CYICON)-5));
      end;

      {initialize the icon information structure to define the new icon}
      IconInfo.fIcon := TRUE;
      IconInfo.xHotspot := 0;
      IconInfo.yHotspot := 0;
      IconInfo.hbmMask:=AndImage.Handle;
      IconInfo.hbmColor:=XorImage.Handle;

      {create a new icon based on the icon information data structure}
      NewIcon := CreateIconIndirect(IconInfo);

      {point the application's icon to this new icon}
      Application.Icon.Handle := NewIcon;

      {display the icon on the form}
      DrawIcon(PaintBox1.Canvas.Handle,
              PaintBox1.Width div 2-(GetSystemMetrics(SM_CXICON) div 2),
              PaintBox1.Height div 2-(GetSystemMetrics(SM_CYICON) div 2), NewIcon);

      {the temporary bitmaps are no longer needed, so dispose of them}
      AndImage.Free;
      XorImage.Free;
    end;

procedure TForm1.FormDestroy(Sender: TObject);
begin
  {delete the new icon}
  DestroyIcon(NewIcon);
end;
```

DestroyCaret   *Windows.Pas*

Syntax

DestroyCaret: BOOL;   {returns a TRUE or FALSE}

Description

This function deletes the caret's current shape, frees it from the window, and removes it from the screen. If a bitmap was used to define the caret's shape, the bitmap is not freed. DestroyCaret fails if the window that owns the caret is not in the current task.

Return Value

If the function succeeds, it returns TRUE; otherwise it returns FALSE. To get extended error information, call the GetLastError function.

See Also

CreateCaret, HideCaret, ShowCaret

Example

Please see Listing 6-4 under CreateCaret.

DestroyCursor   *Windows.Pas*

Syntax

```
DestroyCursor(
hCursor: HICON        {a handle to the cursor being destroyed}
): BOOL;              {returns TRUE or FALSE}
```

Description

This function destroys the cursor identified by the given cursor handle and frees its memory. This function should only be used to destroy cursors created with the Create-Cursor function.

Parameters

hCursor: A handle to the cursor to be destroyed. This cursor handle must not be in use at the time this function is called.

Return Value

If the function succeeds, it returns TRUE; otherwise it returns FALSE. To get extended error information, call the GetLastError function.

See Also

CreateCursor

Example

Please see Listing 6-5 under CreateCursor.

DestroyIcon   *Windows.Pas*

Syntax

```
DestroyIcon(
hIcon: HICON          {a handle to the icon being destroyed}
): BOOL;              {returns TRUE or FALSE}
```

Description

This function destroys the icon identified by the given icon handle and frees its memory. This function should only be used to destroy icons created with the CreateIconIndirect function.

Parameters

hIcon: A handle to the icon to be destroyed. This icon handle must not be in use at the time this function is called.

Return Value

If the function succeeds, it returns TRUE; otherwise it returns FALSE. To get extended error information, call the GetLastError function.

See Also

CreateIconIndirect

Example

Please see Listing 6-9 under CreateIconIndirect.

DrawIcon	**Windows.Pas**

Syntax

```
DrawIcon(
hDC: HDC;          {a handle to a device context}
X: Integer;        {the horizontal coordinate of the icon or cursor}
Y: Integer;        {the vertical coordinate of the icon or cursor}
hIcon: HICON       {a handle to the icon or cursor to draw}
): BOOL;           {returns TRUE or FALSE}
```

Description

This function draws an icon or cursor, including animated cursors, onto the specified device context.

Parameters

hDC: A handle to the device context upon which the icon or cursor will be drawn.

X: Indicates the horizontal position of the upper left corner of the icon or cursor within the specified device context, subject to the current mapping mode.

Y: Indicates the vertical position of the upper left corner of the icon or cursor within the specified device context, subject to the current mapping mode.

hIcon: A handle to the icon or cursor to be drawn.

Return Value

If the function succeeds, it returns TRUE; otherwise it returns FALSE. To get extended error information, call the GetLastError function.

See Also

DrawIconEx, LoadCursor, LoadIcon, LoadImage

Example

Please see Listing 6-6 under CreateIcon.

DrawIconEx   *Windows.Pas*

Syntax

```
DrawIconEx(
hdc: HDC;                        {a handle to a device context}
xLeft: Integer;                  {the horizontal coordinate for displaying the icon}
yTop: Integer;                   {the vertical coordinate for displaying the icon}
hIcon: HICON;                    {a handle to the icon to display}
cxWidth: Integer;                {the width of the icon}
cyWidth: Integer;                {the height of the icon}
istepIfAniCur: UINT;             {the frame index of an animated cursor}
hbrFlickerFreeDraw: HBRUSH;      {a handle to a brush}
diFlags: UINT                    {icon display flags}
): BOOL;                         {returns TRUE or FALSE}
```

Description

This function draws an icon or cursor, including animated cursors, onto the specified device context. The icon or cursor can be stretched or compressed as desired.

Parameters

hdc: A handle to the device context upon which the icon or cursor will be drawn.

xLeft: Indicates the horizontal position of the upper left corner of the icon or cursor within the specified device context, subject to the current mapping mode.

yTop: Indicates the vertical position of the upper left corner of the icon or cursor within the specified device context, subject to the current mapping mode.

hIcon: A handle to the icon or cursor to be drawn.

cxWidth: Specifies how wide to draw the icon or cursor, in logical units. If this parameter is zero and the diFlags parameter is set to DI_DEFAULTSIZE, the function uses the SM_CXICON or SM_CXCURSOR system metric values for the width. If this parameter is zero and the diFlags parameter is not set to DI_DEFAULTSIZE, the function uses the actual width of the icon or cursor resource.

cyWidth: Specifies how tall to draw the icon or cursor, in logical units. If this parameter is zero and the diFlags parameter is set to DI_DEFAULTSIZE, the function uses the SM_CYICON or SM_CYCURSOR system metric values for the height. If this parameter is zero and the diFlags parameter is not set to DI_DEFAULTSIZE, the function uses the actual height of the icon or cursor resource.

istepIfAniCur: Specifies which frame of an animated cursor to draw. If the hIcon parameter does not specify a handle to an animated icon, this parameter is ignored.

hbrFlickerFreeDraw: A handle to a brush. If the brush handle is valid, the function creates an offscreen bitmap using the brush for the background color, draws the icon or cursor into this offscreen bitmap, then copies it onto the device context specified by the hdc parameter. This eliminates any flicker when displaying the icon or cursor. If this parameter is zero, the icon or cursor is drawn directly into the specified device context.

diFlags: A flag controlling drawing behavior. This parameter can be one or more values from Table 6-3.

Return Value

If the function succeeds, it returns TRUE; otherwise it returns FALSE. To get extended error information, call the GetLastError function.

See Also

DrawIcon, LoadCursor, LoadIcon, LoadImage

Example

Please see Listing 6-14 under LoadCursorFromFile.

Table 6-3: DrawIconEx diFlags Values

Value	Description
DI_COMPAT	Draws the default cursor image for the specified standard cursor, even if the cursor has been replaced by a call to the SetSystemCursor function.
DI_DEFAULTSIZE	Draws the icon or cursor with the system metric defined width and height for icons and cursors.
DI_IMAGE	Draws only the OR mask of the icon or cursor.
DI_MASK	Draws only the AND mask of the icon or cursor.
DI_NORMAL	Combines the DI_IMAGE and DI_MASK values to draw the cursor or icon as it is normally displayed.

ExtractAssociatedIcon   *ShellAPI.Pas*

Syntax

```
ExtractAssociatedIcon(
hInst: HINST;                    {a handle to the application instance}
```

6

Chapter

lpIconPath: PChar;	{a pointer to a filename string}
var lpiIcon: Word	{the icon index}
): HICON;	{returns a handle to an icon}

Description

This function returns the handle to an icon extracted from the file referenced by the lpIconPath parameter. If this parameter does not point to an executable file, the icon is extracted from the executable file associated with the specified file. If this file does not have an associated executable file, this function returns the handle to a default icon assigned by Windows. In addition, if the filename specifies a bitmap or cursor file, this function will create an icon from the image and return its handle.

Parameters

hInst: A handle to the application instance.

lpIconPath: A pointer to a null-terminated string containing the filename from which to extract the icon.

lpiIcon: A pointer to a variable containing the index of the icon to extract. The index is zero based, so a value of 0 will retrieve the first icon in the file.

Return Value

If the function succeeds, it returns the handle to an icon; otherwise it returns zero.

See Also

DrawIcon, DrawIconEx, ExtractIcon, LoadIcon

Example

Listing 6-10: Extracting Icons Associated with a File

```
procedure TForm1.FileListBox1Click(Sender: TObject);
var
   IconIndex: Word;
   TheIcon: TIcon;
begin
   {extract the first icon found}
   IconIndex:=0;

   {create the temporary icon object}
   TheIcon:=TIcon.Create;

   {extract a handle to the icon of the executable
    associated with the selected file}
   TheIcon.Handle:=ExtractAssociatedIcon(hInstance,PChar(FileListBox1.FileName),
                                     IconIndex);

   {copy the icon into the image object}
   Image1.Picture.Assign(TheIcon);
```

```
    {free the temporary icon object}
    TheIcon.Free;
end;
```

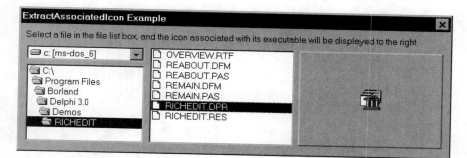

*Figure 6-11:
An icon
associated
with a file*

ExtractIcon   ShellAPI.Pas

Syntax

```
ExtractIcon(
hInst: HINST;                   {a handle to the application instance}
lpszExeFileName: PChar;         {a pointer to a filename string}
nIconIndex: UINT                {the icon index}
): HICON;                       {returns a handle to an icon}
```

Description

This function returns a handle to an icon extracted from an executable file, DLL, or icon file. In addition, if the filename specifies a bitmap or cursor file, this function will create an icon from the image and return its handle. This function can be used to convert bitmaps or cursors into icons.

Parameters

hInst: A handle to the application instance.

lpszExeFileName: A pointer to a null-terminated string containing the filename from which to extract the icon.

nIconIndex: The index of the icon to retrieve. The index is zero based, so a value of 0 will retrieve the first icon in the file, if any exist. If this value is -1, the return value will be the total number of icons stored in the specified file.

Return Value

If the function succeeds, it returns a handle to an icon. If the function fails or there are no icons stored in the specified file, it returns zero.

See Also

DrawIcon, DrawIconEx, ExtractAssociatedIcon, LoadIcon

6

Chapter

Example

Listing 6-11: Extracting the Icon from a File

```
procedure TForm1.FileListBox1DblClick(Sender: TObject);
var
   TheIcon: TIcon;        // this will hold the returned icon
   NumIcons: Integer;     // holds the icon count
begin
   {determine the number of icons stored in this file}
   NumIcons:=ExtractIcon(hInstance,PChar(FileListBox1.FileName), -1);

   {display this number}
   Label2.Caption:=IntToStr(NumIcons)+' icon(s) in this file';

   {create an icon object}
   TheIcon:=TIcon.Create;

   {find the icon in the selected application, if one exists}
   TheIcon.Handle:=ExtractIcon(hInstance, PChar(FileListBox1.FileName), 0);

   {display the icon. if no icon exists, the currently
    displayed icon will be cleared}
   Image1.Picture.Assign(TheIcon);

   {free our icon object}
   TheIcon.Free;
end;
```

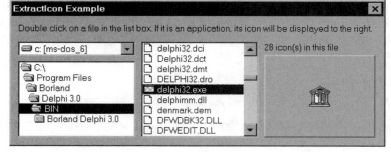

Figure 6-12:
The extracted
icon

ExtractIconEx   ShellAPI.Pas

Syntax

```
ExtractIconEx(
lpszFile: PChar;                    {a pointer to a filename string}
nIconIndex: Integer;                {the icon index}
var phiconLarge: HICON;             {a pointer to a large icon handle}
var phiconSmall: HICON;             {a pointer to a small icon handle}
nIcons: UINT                        {the number of icons to retrieve}
): UINT;                            {returns the number of icons stored in the file}
```

Description

This function returns the handle to both a large and small icon stored in an executable file, DLL, or icon file.

Parameters

lpszFile: A pointer to a null-terminated string containing the filename of an executable file, DLL, or icon file from which to extract the icons.

nIconIndex: The index of the icon to retrieve. The index is zero based, so a value of 0 will retrieve the first large and small icon in the file, if any exist. If this value is -1, the return value will be the total number of icons stored in the specified file.

phiconLarge: A pointer to an icon handle. If the function succeeds, this value will point to the handle of a large icon extracted from the given file.

phiconSmall: A pointer to an icon handle. If the function succeeds, this value will point to the handle of a small icon extracted from the given file.

nIcons: A value indicating the number of icons to extract.

Return Value

If the function succeeds and the value of nIconIndex is -1, it returns the total number of icons stored in the file. This function counts a large icon and its associated small icon as one icon (i.e., if there are 3 large icons and 3 small icons in a file, this function would return a 3). If the function extracts icons, it returns the total number of large and small icons extracted (i.e., if it extracted 1 small and 1 large icon, it returns 2). If the function fails or there are no icons stored in the indicated file, it returns zero.

See Also

DrawIcon, DrawIconEx, ExtractIcon, LoadIcon

Example

Listing 6-12: Extracting Large and Small Icons

```
var
  Form1: TForm1;
  LargeIconsBitmap: TBitmap;   // this holds the icon images
  SmallIconsBitmap: TBitmap;

implementation

{$R *.DFM}

procedure TForm1.FileListBox1DblClick(Sender: TObject);
var
  NumIcons: Integer;        // holds the icon count
  LIcon: HICON;             // holds the handles to extracted icons
  SIcon: HICON;
  LoopCount: Integer;       // a general loop counter
```

6

Chapter

```
begin
   {determine the number of icons stored in this file}
   NumIcons:=ExtractIconEx(PChar(FileListBox1.FileName), -1, LIcon, SIcon, 0);

   {display this number}
   Label4.Caption:='Total Number of Icons: '+IntToStr(NumIcons);

   {resize the images and clear the canvases of the offscreen bitmaps.
    we add a 1 to the width in case there are no icons. this prevents
    the height of these objects from being reset to 1.}
   Image1.Width:=NumIcons*40+1;
   Image2.Width:=NumIcons*40+1;
   LargeIconsBitmap.Width:=NumIcons*40+1;
   LargeIconsBitmap.Canvas.FillRect(LargeIconsBitmap.Canvas.ClipRect);
   SmallIconsBitmap.Width:=NumIcons*40+1;
   SmallIconsBitmap.Canvas.FillRect(SmallIconsBitmap.Canvas.ClipRect);

   {extract each large and small icon from the file}
   for LoopCount:=0 to NumIcons-1 do
   begin
      {find the icon in the selected application, if one exists}
      ExtractIconEx(PChar(FileListBox1.FileName), LoopCount, LIcon, SIcon, 1);

      {display the large icon}
      DrawIcon(LargeIconsBitmap.Canvas.Handle, (LoopCount*40)+4, 2, LIcon);

      {draw the small icon to the correct dimensions}
      DrawIconEx(SmallIconsBitmap.Canvas.Handle, (LoopCount*40)+4, 2, SIcon,
               GetSystemMetrics(SM_CXSMICON), GetSystemMetrics(SM_CYSMICON),
               0, 0, DI_NORMAL);
   end;

   {assign the offscreen bitmaps to the images for display}
   Image1.Picture.Bitmap.Assign(LargeIconsBitmap);
   Image2.Picture.Bitmap.Assign(SmallIconsBitmap);
end;

procedure TForm1.FormCreate(Sender: TObject);
begin
   {create the offscreen bitmaps to hold the images of the icons.}
   LargeIconsBitmap:=TBitmap.Create;
   LargeIconsBitmap.Height:=53;
   LargeIconsBitmap.Width:=40;

   SmallIconsBitmap:=TBitmap.Create;
   SmallIconsBitmap.Height:=53;
   SmallIconsBitmap.Width:=40;
end;

procedure TForm1.FormDestroy(Sender: TObject);
begin
   {free the offscreen bitmaps}
   LargeIconsBitmap.Free;
   SmallIconsBitmap.Free;
end;
```

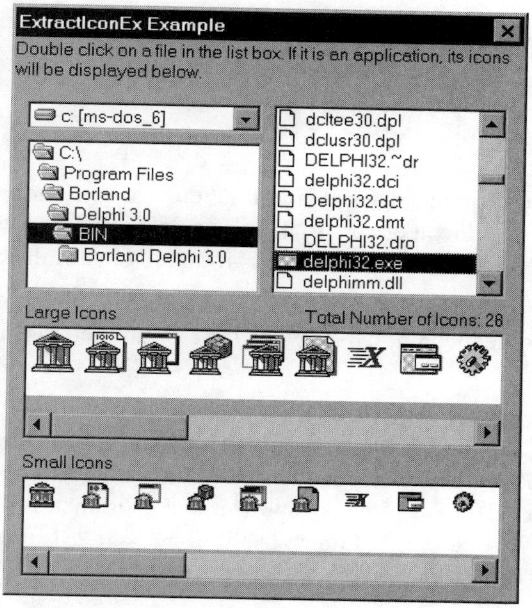

Figure 6-13:
The large and small icons extracted from a file

GetCursor   *Windows.Pas*

Syntax

GetCursor: HCURSOR;   {returns a handle to a cursor}

Description

This function retrieves a handle to the current cursor.

Return Value

If the function succeeds, it returns a handle to the current cursor; otherwise it returns zero.

See Also

CreateCursor, SetCursor

Example

Please see Listing 6-5 under CreateCursor.

GetIconInfo   *Windows.Pas*

Syntax

```
GetIconInfo(
hIcon: HICON;                    {a handle to an icon or cursor}
var piconinfo: TIconInfo         {a pointer to an icon information structure}
): BOOL;                         {returns TRUE or FALSE}
```

Description

This function retrieves information about an icon or cursor, including hot spots and mask images.

Parameters

hIcon: A handle to an icon or cursor whose information is to be retrieved. To retrieve information about a standard icon or cursor, this parameter may be set to one value from Table 6-4. See the LoadCursor function for an explanation of the cursor values.

piconinfo: A pointer to a TIconInfo structure. This structure is filled with the requested information on the specified icon or cursor when the function returns. The TIconInfo structure is defined as:

```
TIconInfo = packed record
    fIcon: BOOL;                {indicates icon or cursor information}
    xHotspot: DWORD;            {the hot spot horizontal coordinate}
    yHotspot: DWORD;            {the hot spot vertical coordinate}
    hbmMask: HBITMAP;           {a bitmap handle}
    hbmColor: HBITMAP;          {a bitmap handle}
end;
```

fIcon: A flag indicating if the structure contains information on an icon or a cursor. If this member contains TRUE, the structure contains information on an icon; otherwise it contains information on a cursor.

xHotspot: Specifies the horizontal coordinate of the cursor's hot spot. If the structure contains information on an icon, the hot spot is always in the center of the icon and this member is ignored.

yHotspot: Specifies the vertical coordinate of the cursor's hot spot. If the structure contains information on an icon, the hot spot is always in the center of the icon and this member is ignored.

hbmMask: A handle to the AND mask bitmap of the icon or cursor. If the structure contains information on a black and white icon or cursor, the AND mask is formatted so that the upper half contains the AND mask and the lower half contains the OR mask. In this case, the hbmColor member may contain a zero. The application must delete this bitmap when it is no longer needed.

hbmColor: A handle to the OR mask bitmap of the icon or cursor. For animated cursors, this will be the first frame of the cursor's color images. The application must delete this bitmap when it is no longer needed.

Return Value

If the function succeeds, it returns TRUE; otherwise it returns FALSE. To get extended error information, call the GetLastError function.

See Also

CreateIcon, CreateIconFromResource, CreateIconIndirect, DestroyIcon, DrawIcon, DrawIconEx, LoadIcon

Example

Listing 6-13: Retrieving Information on System Cursors and Icons

```
procedure TForm1.ComboBox1Change(Sender: TObject);
var
   TheIcon: HICON;              // holds an icon
   TheCursor: HCURSOR;          // holds a cursor

   TheIconInfo: TIconInfo;      // holds the cursor or icon information

{this specifies the system icons and cursors}
type
   TIconTypes = array[0..8] of PAnsiChar;
   TCursorTypes = array[0..12] of PAnsiChar;
const
   IconTypes: TIconTypes = (IDI_APPLICATION,IDI_ASTERISK,IDI_ERROR,
                            IDI_EXCLAMATION,IDI_HAND,IDI_INFORMATION,
                            IDI_QUESTION,IDI_WARNING,IDI_WINLOGO);
   CursorTypes: TCursorTypes = (IDC_ARROW,IDC_IBEAM,IDC_WAIT,IDC_CROSS,
                                IDC_UPARROW,IDC_SIZENWSE,IDC_SIZENESW,
                                IDC_SIZEWE,IDC_SIZENS,IDC_SIZEALL,
                                IDC_NO,IDC_APPSTARTING,IDC_HELP);
begin
   {erase the last image}
   Image1.Canvas.Brush.Color:=clBtnFace;
   Image1.Canvas.Fillrect(Image1.Canvas.Cliprect);
   if TheIconInfo.hbmMask<>0 then DeleteObject(TheIconInfo.hbmMask);
   if TheIconInfo.hbmColor<>0 then DeleteObject(TheIconInfo.hbmColor);

   {if we have selected icons, get an icon...}
   if RadioButton1.Checked then
   begin
      {load the selected system icon}
      TheIcon:=LoadIcon(0, IconTypes[ComboBox1.ItemIndex]);

      {fill the information structure for this icon}
      GetIconInfo(TheIcon, TheIconInfo);

      {now draw the icon on the TImage canvas}
      DrawIconEx(Image1.Canvas.Handle,25,25,TheIcon,0,0,0,
                 Image1.Canvas.Brush.Handle,DI_DEFAULTSIZE OR DI_NORMAL);
   end
   else
   {...otherwise, get a cursor}
   begin
      {load the selected system cursor}
      TheCursor:=LoadCursor(0, CursorTypes[ComboBox2.ItemIndex]);

      {fill the information structure for this cursor}
```

```
          GetIconInfo(TheCursor, TheIconInfo);

          {now draw the cursor on the TImage canvas}
          DrawIconEx(Image1.Canvas.Handle,25,25,TheCursor,0,0,0,
                     Image1.Canvas.Brush.Handle,DI_DEFAULTSIZE OR DI_NORMAL);
     end;

     {clear the listbox}
     ListBox1.Items.Clear;

     {fill the listbox with the icon or cursor information}
     if TheIconInfo.fIcon then
        ListBox1.Items.Add('This is an icon')
     else
        ListBox1.Items.Add('This is a cursor');

     {specify hotspots}
     ListBox1.Items.Add('X Hotspot: '+IntToStr(TheIconInfo.xHotspot));
     ListBox1.Items.Add('Y Hotspot: '+IntToStr(TheIconInfo.yHotspot));

     {display the AND and OR masks for this cursor or icon}
     Image2.Picture.Bitmap.Handle:=TheIconInfo.hbmMask;
     Image3.Picture.Bitmap.Handle:=TheIconInfo.hbmColor;
end;
```

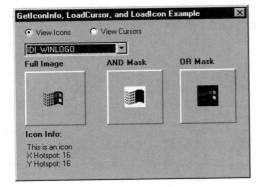

Figure 6-14: The icon and cursor information

Table 6-4: GetIconInfo hIcon Values

Value	Description
IDI_APPLICATION	The default application icon.
IDI_ASTERISK	The information system icon.
IDI_ERROR	The stop system icon.
IDI_EXCLAMATION	The exclamation point system icon.
IDI_HAND	Same as the IDI_ERROR value.
IDI_INFORMATION	Same as the IDI_ASTERISK value.
IDI_QUESTION	The system question mark icon.
IDI_WARNING	Same as the IDI_EXCLAMATION value.

Value	Description
IDI_WINLOGO	The Windows logo icon.
IDC_ARROW	The cursor file identified by the Arrow key.
IDC_IBEAM	The cursor file identified by the IBeam key.
IDC_WAIT	The cursor file identified by the Wait key.
IDC_CROSS	The cursor file identified by the Crosshair key.
IDC_UPARROW	The cursor file identified by the UpArrow key.
IDC_SIZENWSE	The cursor file identified by the SizeNWSE key.
IDC_SIZENESW	The cursor file identified by the SizeNESW key.
IDC_SIZEWE	The cursor file identified by the SizeWE key.
IDC_SIZENS	The cursor file identified by the SizeNS key.
IDC_SIZEALL	The cursor file identified by the SizeAll key.
IDC_NO	The cursor file identified by the No key.
IDC_APPSTARTING	The cursor file identified by the AppStarting key.
IDC_HELP	The cursor file identified by the Help key.

HideCaret   Windows.Pas

Syntax

```
HideCaret(
hWnd: HWND          {a handle to the window that owns the caret}
): BOOL;            {returns TRUE or FALSE}
```

Description

This function hides the caret from the screen but does not destroy it or lose the insertion point. Hiding is cumulative. For each time the HideCaret function is called, a subsequent ShowCaret function must be called to display the caret.

Parameters

hWnd: A handle to the window that owns the caret. If this parameter is set to FALSE, the function searches all windows in the current task. If no window in the current task owns the caret, the HideCaret function fails.

Return Value

If the function succeeds, it returns TRUE; otherwise it returns FALSE. To get extended error information, call the GetLastError function.

See Also

CreateCaret, DestroyCaret, ShowCaret

Example

Please see Listing 6-4 under CreateCaret.

LoadCursor   Windows.Pas

Syntax

```
LoadCursor(
hInstance: HINST;              {an instance handle}
lpCursorName: PAnsiChar        {the cursor resource name or identifier}
): HCURSOR;                    {returns a handle to a cursor}
```

Description

This function retrieves a handle to a cursor from cursor resources stored in the executable file associated with the given instance handle. If the cursor is not currently loaded, it will load the specified cursor resource and return its handle; otherwise it returns a handle to the existing cursor.

Parameters

hInstance: A handle to the module instance whose executable file contains the cursor resource to be loaded.

lpCursorName: A pointer to a null-terminated string containing the name of the cursor resource to load. The MakeIntResource function can be used with a resource identifier to provide a value for this parameter. To load one of the user-defined cursors, set the hInstance parameter to zero and set this parameter to one of the values from Table 6-5. The user-defined cursors are set from the Mouse applet under the Control Panel and are stored in the registry under the key HKEY_CURRENT_USER\Control Panel\Cursors.

Return Value

If the function succeeds, it returns a handle to a cursor loaded from the executable file resources; otherwise it returns zero. To get extended error information, call the GetLastError function.

See Also

GetCursor, GetIconInfo, LoadImage, SetCursor, ShowCursor

Example

Please see Listing 6-13 under GetIconInfo.

Table 6-5: LoadCursor lpCursorName Values

Value	Description
IDC_APPSTARTING	The cursor file identified by the AppStarting key.
IDC_ARROW	The cursor file identified by the Arrow key.
IDC_CROSS	The cursor file identified by the Crosshair key.
IDC_HELP	The cursor file identified by the Help key.
IDC_IBEAM	The cursor file identified by the IBeam key.

Value	Description
IDC_NO	The cursor file identified by the No key.
IDC_SIZEALL	The cursor file identified by the SizeAll key.
IDC_SIZENESW	The cursor file identified by the SizeNESW key.
IDC_SIZENS	The cursor file identified by the SizeNS key.
IDC_SIZENWSE	The cursor file identified by the SizeNWSE key.
IDC_SIZEWE	The cursor file identified by the SizeWE key.
IDC_UPARROW	The cursor file identified by the UpArrow key.
IDC_WAIT	The cursor file identified by the Wait key.

LoadCursorFromFile   Windows.Pas

Syntax

```
LoadCursorFromFile(
lpFileName: PAnsiChar          {a cursor filename}
): HCURSOR;                    {returns a handle to a cursor}
```

Description

This function creates a cursor based on the cursor data stored in the specified file, returning a handle to the new cursor. The cursor file can be a normal cursor file (*.cur), or it can contain animated cursor data (*.ani).

Parameters

lpFileName: A null-terminated string identifying the cursor file used to create the cursor.

Return Value

If the function succeeds, it returns a handle to the new cursor; otherwise it returns zero. To get extended error information, call the GetLastError function.

See Also

LoadCursor, SetCursor, SetSystemCursor

Example

Listing 6-14: Loading a Cursor from a File

```
procedure TForm1.FileListBox1Click(Sender: TObject);
var
   TheCursor: HCURSOR;    // a handle to a cursor loaded from a file
begin
   {erase the last image}
   Image1.Canvas.Brush.Color:=clBtnFace;
   Image1.Canvas.Fillrect(Image1.Canvas.Cliprect);
```

6

Chapter

```
{load the cursor from the selected file}
TheCursor:=LoadCursorFromFile(PChar(FileListBox1.FileName));

{now draw the cursor on the TImage canvas}
DrawIconEx(Image1.Canvas.Handle,35,35,TheCursor,0,0,0,0,DI_DEFAULTSIZE OR
           DI_NORMAL);

{we no longer need the cursor, so delete it}
DeleteObject(TheCursor);
end;
```

Figure 6-15:
The loaded
cursor

LoadIcon   Windows.Pas

Syntax

```
LoadIcon(
hInstance: HINST;                {an instance handle}
lpIconName: PChar                {an icon resource name}
): HICON;                        {returns a handle to an icon}
```

Description

This function retrieves a handle to an icon from icon resources stored in the executable file associated with the given instance handle. If the icon is not currently loaded, it will load the specified icon resource and return its handle; otherwise it returns a handle to the existing icon. The icon must have the same dimensions as those reported by the SM_CXICON and SM_CYICON system metric values. Use the LoadImage function to load icons of other sizes.

Parameters

hInstance: A handle to the module instance whose executable file contains the icon resource to be loaded.

lpIconName: A pointer to a null-terminated string containing the name of the icon resource to load. The MakeIntResource function can be used with a resource identifier to provide a value for this parameter. To load one of the predefined icons used by the Win32 API, set the hInstance parameter to zero and set this parameter to one of the values from Table 6-6.

Return Value

If the function succeeds, it returns a handle to an icon loaded from the executable file resources; otherwise it returns zero. To get extended error information, call the GetLastError function.

See Also

CreateIcon, LoadImage

Example

Please see Listing 6-13 under GetIconInfo.

Table 6-6: LoadIcon lpIconName Values

Value	Description
IDI_APPLICATION	The default application icon.
IDI_ASTERISK	The information system icon.
IDI_ERROR	The stop system icon.
IDI_EXCLAMATION	The exclamation point system icon.
IDI_HAND	Same as the IDI_ERROR value.
IDI_INFORMATION	Same as the IDI_ASTERISK value.
IDI_QUESTION	The system question mark icon.
IDI_WARNING	Same as the IDI_EXCLAMATION value.
IDI_WINLOGO	The Windows logo icon.

LookupIconIdFromDirectory   Windows.Pas

Syntax

```
LookupIconIdFromDirectory(
presbits: PByte;          {a pointer to icon or cursor resource bits}
fIcon: BOOL               {indicates an icon or cursor}
): Integer;               {returns an integer resource identifier}
```

Description

This function searches through icon or cursor resource information to find the icon or cursor that is the most appropriate for the current display device. It is intended for use with resource files containing icon and cursor images in several device-dependent and device-independent formats. The return value from this function can be used with the MakeIntResource and FindResource functions to locate the cursor or icon in the module's resources.

Parameters

presbits: A pointer to icon or cursor resource bits. Use the return value from the Lock-Resource function for this parameter.

fIcon: A flag indicating whether an icon or cursor is desired. A value of TRUE indicates an icon should be found; FALSE indicates a cursor.

Return Value

If the function succeeds, it returns an integer resource identifier for the most appropriate icon or cursor for the current display device; otherwise it returns zero.

See Also

CreateIconFromResource, FindResource, FindResourceEx, LoadCursor, LookupIconIdFromDirectoryEx

Example

Please see Listing 6-7 under CreateIconFromResource.

LookupIconIdFromDirectoryEx   Windows.Pas

Syntax

```
LookupIconIdFromDirectoryEx(
presbits: PByte;          {a pointer to icon or cursor resource bits}
fIcon: BOOL               {indicates an icon or cursor}
cxDesired: Integer;       {the preferred width of the icon or cursor}
cyDesired: Integer;       {the preferred height of the icon or cursor}
Flags: UINT               {color flags}
): Integer;               {returns an integer resource identifier}
```

Description

This function searches through icon or cursor resource information to find the icon or cursor that is the most appropriate for the current display device. It is intended for use with resource files containing icon and cursor images in several device-dependent and device-independent formats. The return value from this function can be used with the MakeIntResource and FindResource functions to locate the cursor or icon in the module's resources. Unlike the LookupIconIdFromDirectory function, this function allows the developer to specify the dimensions and color format of the icon or cursor.

Parameters

presbits: A pointer to icon or cursor resource bits. Use the return value from the Lock-Resource function for this parameter.

fIcon: A flag indicating whether an icon or cursor is desired. A value of TRUE indicates an icon should be found; FALSE indicates a cursor.

cxDesired: Specifies the preferred width of the icon or cursor in pixels. If this parameter is zero, the function uses the value returned from GetSystemMetrics(SM_CXICON).

cyDesired: Specifies the preferred height of the icon or cursor in pixels. If this parameter is zero, the function uses the value returned from GetSystemMetrics(SM_CYICON).

Flags: A value indicating the color format for the icon or cursor. This parameter can be one value from Table 6-7.

Return Value

If the function succeeds, it returns an integer resource identifier for the most appropriate icon or cursor for the current display device; otherwise it returns zero.

See Also

CreateIconFromResourceEx, FindResource, FindResourceEx, LoadCursor, LookupIconIdFromDirectory

Example

Please see Listing 6-8 under CreateIconFromResourceEx.

Table 6-7: LookupIconIdFromDirectoryEx Flags Values

Value	Description
LR_DEFAULTCOLOR	Create a color cursor or icon using the default system colors.
LR_MONOCHROME	Create a monochrome cursor or icon.

SetCursor   Windows.Pas

Syntax

```
SetCursor(
hCursor: HICON          {a handle to a cursor}
): HCURSOR;             {returns a handle to the previous cursor}
```

Description

This function sets the shape of the mouse cursor to the cursor associated with the specified cursor handle. A new cursor is set only if the new cursor is different than the current cursor. When using the SetCursor function to change the cursor, the class cursor for the application's window (and child windows) must be set to zero. If the class cursor of a window is not set to zero, Windows restores the class cursor shape every time the mouse is moved over that particular window. Use the ShowCursor function to increase the internal display count to display the new cursor.

Parameters

hCursor: A handle to the cursor replacing the current mouse cursor shape. This cursor handle must be retrieved from the CreateCursor, LoadCursor, or LoadImage functions. In addition, the width and height of the cursor must match those returned by the GetSystemMetrics function, and the color depth must be equal or less than the color depth of the current display.

Return Value

If the function succeeds, it returns a handle to the previous cursor if one existed; otherwise it returns zero.

See Also

CreateCursor, GetCursor, ShowCursor

Example

Please see Listing 6-5 under CreateCursor.

SetSystemCursor   Windows.Pas

Syntax

```
SetSystemCursor(
hcur: HICON;              {a handle to the new cursor}
id: DWORD                 {a system cursor identifier}
): BOOL;                  {returns TRUE or FALSE}
```

Description

This function replaces the image of the specified system cursor with the image of the cursor identified by the hcur parameter. The Windows registry is not updated with this new cursor selection, and the original system cursor is reset when Windows is rebooted.

Parameters

hcur: A handle to the cursor replacing the specified system cursor.

id: A system cursor identifier. This system cursor image is replaced by the cursor indicated by the hcur parameter. This parameter can be one value from Table 6-8.

Return Value

If the function succeeds, it returns TRUE; otherwise it returns FALSE. To get extended error information, call the GetLastError function.

See Also

CreateCursor, GetCursor, LoadCursor, LoadCursorFromFile, SetCursor

Example

Listing 6-15: Setting a New System Cursor

```
var
  Form1: TForm1;
  CurSysCursor: HCURSOR;    // holds the current system cursor

procedure TForm1.Button1Click(Sender: TObject);
begin
  {save a handle to the current system cursor}
  CurSysCursor := GetCursor;

  {set a new system cursor}
  SetSystemCursor(Screen.Cursors[crHandPoint],OCR_NORMAL);
end;

procedure TForm1.FormDestroy(Sender: TObject);
begin
  {restore the previous system cursor}
  SetSystemCursor(CurSysCursor, OCR_NORMAL);
end;
```

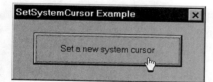

Figure 6-16:
The new
system cursor

Table 6-8: SetSystemCursor id Values

Value	Description
OCR_APPSTARTING	The small hourglass with arrow cursor.
OCR_CROSS	The crosshair cursor.
OCR_IBEAM	The text insert cursor.
OCR_NO	The international no symbol cursor.
OCR_NORMAL	The normal arrow cursor.
OCR_SIZEALL	The all directions sizing arrow cursor.
OCR_SIZENESW	The northeast to southwest sizing arrow cursor.
OCR_SIZENS	The vertical sizing arrow cursor.
OCR_SIZENWSE	The northwest to southeast sizing arrow cursor.
OCR_SIZEWE	The horizontal sizing arrow cursor.
OCR_UP	The up arrow cursor.
OCR_WAIT	The hourglass cursor.

6

Chapter

ShowCaret   *Windows.Pas*

Syntax

```
ShowCaret(
hWnd: HWND              {a handle to a window}
): BOOL;                {returns TRUE or FALSE}
```

Description

Displays the caret on the screen at the current insertion point. The caret appears only if the specified window owns it, it has a shape, and HideCaret has not been called two or more times sequentially. Hiding is cumulative. For each time the HideCaret function is called, a subsequent ShowCaret function must be called to display the caret.

Parameters

hWnd: A handle to the window that owns the caret. If this parameter is set to FALSE, the function searches all windows in the current task. If no window in the current task owns the caret, the ShowCaret function fails.

Return Value

If the function succeeds, it returns TRUE; otherwise it returns FALSE. To get extended error information, call the GetLastError function.

See Also

CreateCaret, DestroyCaret, HideCaret

Example

Please see Listing 6-4 under CreateCaret.

ShowCursor   *Windows.Pas*

Syntax

```
ShowCursor(
bShow: BOOL             {the cursor visibility flag}
): Integer;             {returns the cursor display counter}
```

Description

This function displays or hides the cursor by incrementing or decrementing an internal display counter. When the internal display counter goes below 0, the mouse cursor is hidden. If a mouse is installed, the initial display counter is set to 0; otherwise it is set to -1.

Parameters

bShow: A Boolean value indicating if the internal cursor display counter should be incremented or decremented. A value of TRUE increments the display counter; FALSE decrements it.

Return Value

If the function succeeds, it returns the new internal display counter. If the function fails, it returns zero. A return value of zero does not necessarily mean the function failed; a comparison with previous return values should be made to determine failure in this case.

See Also

GetCursor, GetCursorPos, SetCursor, SetCursorPos

Example

Listing 6-16: Hiding and Displaying the Cursor

```
procedure TForm1.Button1Click(Sender: TObject);
const
    RefCount: Integer = 0;    // holds the count of successive show/hides
begin
  {if the Show button was pressed...}
  if TButton(Sender).Caption='Show' then
  begin
    {...show the cursor and increase the reference count}
    ShowCursor(TRUE);
    Inc(RefCount);
  end
  else
  {if the Hide button was pressed...}
  begin
    {...hide the cursor and decrease the reference count}
    ShowCursor(FALSE);
    Inc(RefCount,-1);
  end;

  {display the current reference count}
  Edit1.Text := IntToStr(RefCount);
end;
```

Figure 6-17:
The cursor
reference
count

Chapter 7

Palette Functions

Color is an important part of the user interface. It can communicate data in very intuitive and effective ways, and adds to the overall aesthetic appeal of the application. Current computer systems ship with video hardware that can support color depths in the millions. Although it is common for users to have video drivers set to display more than 256 colors, it is good practice to develop an application for 256-color displays as this is the most commonly supported color depth across computer systems. Additionally, most games are developed for 256-color display drivers for speed and special color animation effects. As a result, most functions in this chapter will be useless when the color depth of the video driver is set to more than 256 colors.

The functions in this chapter demonstrate working with colors and color palettes in a 256-color video mode. Most examples in this chapter will not work unless the video driver has been set to display 256 colors.

The Windows Palette Manager

Windows maintains one systemwide palette that contains all of the colors that can be displayed. The first ten and last ten palette entries are reserved for the system, and contain the twenty static colors that are used for specific elements of a window, such as the title bar, the borders, or the bevels of 3-D user interface elements. The remaining 236 colors can be set by the application, although it cannot modify the colors in the system palette directly.

To modify the colors in the system palette, an application must create a logical palette by using the CreatePalette function. Once the palette is created, it must be selected into a specific device context by using the SelectPalette function. It is merged with the system palette by calling the RealizePalette function. When the RealizePalette function is called, the Windows palette manager looks at each palette entry in the logical palette and maps it to an existing entry in the system palette. If no matching entry is found, the color in the logical palette is placed into the first unused entry in the system palette. If an existing entry is not found and there are no more unused palette slots, the Windows palette manager maps the color to the closest matching entry in the system palette. This continues until all colors in the logical palette have been merged with the colors in the system palette. If the specified device context identifies an active window, the logical palette is treated as a foreground palette and the Windows palette manager will mark all nonstatic entries in the system palette as unused when the RealizePalette function is called. This allows the logical palette to potentially replace all nonstatic colors of the system palette. Otherwise, the logical palette is treated as a background palette, and can set unused palette slots only if any remain after the foreground palette has been realized.

Identity Palettes

Many applications, such as games or image manipulation utilities, must have explicit control over where their palette entries are mapped into the system palette. In this instance, the application can create what is known as an identity palette. To create an identity palette, start by preparing a 256-entry logical palette. Use the GetSystem-PaletteEntries function to retrieve the first and last ten entries from the system palette, and place these into the first and last ten entries of the logical palette. Once this is done, set the remaining 236 colors of the logical palette to the desired colors, using the PC_NOCOLLAPSE flag in the peFlags member of the TPaletteEntry structure for each palette entry. When this palette is realized, the first and last ten colors should map directly into the static system colors, and the remaining 236 will be forced into unused slots without being remapped to existing colors.

Color Specifiers

Colors within a palette are identified by color specifiers. A color specifier is a 32-bit value that can indicate the relative intensities of the red, green, and blue components of the color in the lower 3 bytes, or can indicate a specific palette index in the lowest byte. The high-order byte indicates how the other three bytes are to be interpreted, as illustrated in Table 7-1. A color specifier can be used in any palette function where a value of type COLORREF, TColor, or a DWORD is required.

Table 7-1: Color Specifier High-order Byte Values

Value	Description
$00	Indicates that the lowest 3 bytes contain relative intensity values for the blue, green, and red components of the color. The color specifier will be in the form of:
	$00bbggrr
	This color specifier will result in a color generated by dithering the twenty static colors to create the closest approximation to the requested color.

Value	Description
$01	Indicates that the lowest byte specifies an index into the currently realized logical palette. The color specifier will be in the form of: $010000nn This color specifier will result in the color stored at the indicated index into the currently realized logical palette.
$02	Indicates that the lowest 3 bytes contain relative intensity values for the blue, green, and red components of the color. The color specifier will be in the form of: $02bbggrr This color specifier will result in a color selected from the currently realized logical palette that most closely matches the requested color.

The following example demonstrates the use of the three types of color specifiers to indicate various colors.

Listing 7-I: Using Color Specifiers

```
{Whoops! Delphi incorrectly imports the GetSystemPaletteEntries function.
Here's the correct declaration that gives all of the functionality available
with this API function}
function GetSystemPaletteEntries(DC: HDC; StartIndex, NumEntries: UINT;
                                PaletteEntries: Pointer): UINT; stdcall;

var
  Form1: TForm1;
  FormPalette: HPALETTE;              // a handle to a logical palette

implementation

{$R *.DFM}

{link in the GetSystemPaletteEntries function}
function GetSystemPaletteEntries; external gdi32 name 'GetSystemPaletteEntries';

procedure TForm1.FormCreate(Sender: TObject);
var
  ThePalette: PLogPalette;  // a logical palette definition structure
  iLoop: Integer;           // general loop counter
begin
  {get enough memory to hold the colors in the first 10 system
   palette slots, plus 236 of our own. this memory is temporary,
   and is no longer needed once the palette is created.}
  GetMem(ThePalette, SizeOf(TLogPalette)+246*SizeOf(TPaletteEntry));

  {initialize the palette version number}
  ThePalette^.palVersion := $300;

  {we will have a total of 246 entries in our palette}
  ThePalette^.palNumEntries := 246;
```

```
{get the first 10 system palette entries}
GetSystemPaletteEntries(Form1.Canvas.Handle, 0, 10, @(ThePalette^.palPalEntry));

{we only want 236 new palette entries, and we want them to start
 immediately after the first 10 system palette entries. by
 retrieving the first 10 system palette entries, when we realize
 our new palette, the first 10 logical palette entries will be
 mapped to the first 10 system palette entries, and our
 palette entries will follow}
for iLoop := 0 to 235 do
begin
  {create a gradient red palette}
  ThePalette^.palPalEntry[iLoop+10].peRed    := Trunc(255-((255 / 235)*iLoop));
  ThePalette^.palPalEntry[iLoop+10].peGreen := 0;
  ThePalette^.palPalEntry[iLoop+10].peBlue   := 0;
  {do not match this palette entry to any other palette entry}
  ThePalette^.palPalEntry[iLoop+10].peFlags := PC_NOCOLLAPSE;
end;

{create the palette}
FormPalette := CreatePalette(ThePalette^);

{free the temporary memory}
FreeMem(ThePalette, SizeOf(TLogPalette)+246*SizeOf(TPaletteEntry));
end;

function TForm1.GetPalette: HPALETTE;
begin
  {when something requests the palette of the form,
   pass it back the new logical palette}
  Result := FormPalette;
end;

procedure TForm1.ScrollBar1Change(Sender: TObject);
begin
  {select our new logical palette into the device context}
  SelectPalette(Canvas.Handle, FormPalette, FALSE);

  {map our logical palette into the system palette}
  RealizePalette(Canvas.Handle);

  {display the requested color settings}
  Label1.Caption := 'Red: '+IntToStr(ScrollBar1.Position);

  {display the dithered color}
  Canvas.Brush.Color := RGB(ScrollBar1.Position, 0, 0);
  Canvas.Rectangle(24, 80, 113, 145);
  Label5.Caption := IntToHex(Canvas.Brush.Color, 8);

  {display the color at the specific index}
  Canvas.Brush.Color := $01000000 or RGB(ScrollBar1.Position, 0, 0);
  Canvas.Rectangle(120, 80, 209, 145);
  Label6.Caption := IntToHex(Canvas.Brush.Color, 8);

  {display the closest matching color}
```

```
Canvas.Brush.Color := $02000000 or RGB(ScrollBar1.Position, 0, 0);
Canvas.Rectangle(216, 80, 305, 145);
Label7.Caption := IntToHex(Canvas.Brush.Color, 8);
end;

procedure TForm1.FormDestroy(Sender: TObject);
begin
  {we no longer need the logical palette, so delete it}
  DeleteObject(FormPalette);
end;
```

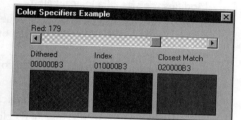

Figure 7-1:
The various
color specifier
results

Palette Functions

The following palette functions are covered in this chapter:

Table 7-2: Palette Functions

Function	Description
AnimatePalette	Replaces entries in a logical palette.
CreateHalftonePalette	Creates a halftone palette.
CreatePalette	Creates a logical palette.
GetBValue	Retrieves the blue intensity of a color specifier.
GetDIBColorTable	Retrieves the color palette from a device-independent bitmap.
GetEnhMetaFilePaletteEntries	Retrieves the color palette from an enhanced metafile.
GetGValue	Retrieves the green intensity of a color specifier.
GetNearestColor	Retrieves a color specifier from the system palette that most closely matches the requested color.
GetNearestPaletteIndex	Retrieves the index from the currently realized logical palette that most closely matches the requested color.
GetPaletteEntries	Retrieves a range of palette entries from a logical palette.
GetRValue	Retrieves the red intensity of a color specifier.
GetSysColor	Retrieves the color specifier for the indicated system color.
GetSystemPaletteEntries	Retrieves a range of palette entries from the system palette.

Function	Description
GetSystemPaletteUse	Indicates if the system palette contains static colors.
PaletteIndex	Retrieves a color specifier from the currently realized logical palette at the indicated index.
PaletteRGB	Retrieves a color specifier from the currently realized logical palette that most closely matches the requested color.
RealizePalette	Realizes a logical palette into the system palette.
ResizePalette	Modifies the size of a logical palette.
RGB	Retrieves a color specifier for the requested color that will be generated by dithering the twenty static colors.
SelectPalette	Selects a logical palette into a device context.
SetDIBColorTable	Sets the color palette of a device-independent bitmap.
SetPaletteEntries	Sets a range of palette entries in a logical palette.
SetSysColor	Sets a system color to the specified color specifier.
SetSystemPaletteUse	Toggles the number of static colors used by the system palette.

AnimatePalette   *Windows.Pas*

Syntax

```
AnimatePalette(
p1: HPALETTE;          {a handle to a logical color palette}
p2: UINT;              {the first entry to be replaced}
p3: UINT;              {the number of entries to be replaced}
p4: PPaletteEntry      {a pointer to an array of palette entries}
): BOOL;               {returns TRUE or FALSE}
```

Description

This function replaces color entries in the specified logical palette with the new entries pointed to by the p4 parameter. Only the corresponding entries in the specified logical palette with the peFlags member set to PC_RESERVED are replaced.

Parameters

p1: A handle to the logical palette whose entries are to be replaced.

p2: Specifies the index into the logical palette where palette entry replacement will start.

p3: Specifies the number of palette entries to replace.

p4: A pointer to an array of TPaletteEntry structures that will replace the specified entries in the logical palette. The TPaletteEntry structure is defined as:

TPaletteEntry = packed record
      peRed: Byte;   {the red color intensity}
      peGreen: Byte;   {the green color intensity}
      peBlue: Byte;   {the blue color intensity}
      peFlags: Byte;   {palette entry usage flags}
end;

Please see the CreatePalette function for a description of this data structure.

Return Value

If the function succeeds, it returns TRUE; otherwise it returns FALSE. To get extended error information, call the GetLastError function.

See Also

CreatePalette, SelectPalette

Example

Listing 7-2: Color Gradient Animation

```
{Whoops! Delphi incorrectly imports the GetSystemPaletteEntries function.
 Here's the correct declaration that gives all of the functionality available
 with this API function}
function GetSystemPaletteEntries(DC: HDC; StartIndex, NumEntries: UINT;
                                 PaletteEntries: Pointer): UINT; stdcall;

var
  Form1: TForm1;
  FormPalette: HPALETTE;                          // holds our new logical palette
  AnimPalette: array[0..31] of TPaletteEntry;  // tracks moving palette entries

implementation

{link in the GetSystemPaletteEntries function}
function GetSystemPaletteEntries; external gdi32 name 'GetSystemPaletteEntries';

function TForm1.GetPalette: HPALETTE;
begin
  {any time the form is queried for its palette,
   return the new logical palette}
  Result := FormPalette;
end;

procedure TForm1.CreateThePalette;
var
  ThePalette: PLogPalette;      // holds a logical palette data structure
  iLoop: Integer;               // general loop counter
begin
  {get enough memory to hold the colors in the first 10 system
   palette slots, plus 32 of our own}
  GetMem(ThePalette, SizeOf(TLogPalette)+42*SizeOf(TPaletteEntry));
```

```
{get the first 10 system palette entries}
GetSystemPaletteEntries(Form1.Canvas.Handle, 0, 10,
                        @(ThePalette^.palPalEntry));

{initialize palette information}
ThePalette^.palVersion := $300;
ThePalette^.palNumEntries := 42;

{create a red gradient palette}
for iLoop := 0 to 31 do
begin
  ThePalette^.palPalEntry[iLoop+10].peRed   := 255-((255 div 32)*iLoop);
  ThePalette^.palPalEntry[iLoop+10].peGreen := 0;
  ThePalette^.palPalEntry[iLoop+10].peBlue  := 0;
  ThePalette^.palPalEntry[iLoop+10].peFlags := PC_RESERVED;

  {this will track the moving palette entries, so set it
   to match the logical palette}
  AnimPalette[iLoop] := ThePalette^.palPalEntry[iLoop+10];
end;

{create the new logical palette}
FormPalette := CreatePalette(ThePalette^);

{the palette data structure is no longer needed so return the memory}
FreeMem(ThePalette, SizeOf(TLogPalette)+42*SizeOf(TPaletteEntry));
end;

procedure TForm1.FormCreate(Sender: TObject);
begin
  {create the new logical palette}
  CreateThePalette;
end;

procedure TForm1.Button1Click(Sender: TObject);
begin
  {begin the palette animation}
  Timer1.Enabled := TRUE;
end;

procedure TForm1.FormPaint(Sender: TObject);
var
  iLoop: Integer;  // general loop counter
begin
  {select and realize the new red gradient palette}
  SelectPalette(Canvas.Handle, FormPalette, FALSE);
  RealizePalette(Canvas.Handle);

  {draw a series of rectangles that display the red gradient}
  for iLoop := 0 to 31 do
  begin
    Canvas.Brush.Color := PaletteIndex(iLoop+10);
    Canvas.FillRect(Rect(30, iLoop*10+56, 290, (iLoop*10)+76));
```

7

```
        end;
end;

procedure TForm1.Timer1Timer(Sender: TObject);
var
  PaletteEntry: TPALETTEENTRY;        // temporary palette entry storage
  iLoop: Integer;                     // general loop counter
begin
  {the AnimPalette array begins as an exact duplicate of the logical
   palette. we rotate the palette entries from the beginning of the
   array to the end by saving off the first entry in the array...}
  PaletteEntry := AnimPalette[0];

  {...moving all of the other entries down one...}
  for iLoop := 0 to 30 do
    AnimPalette[iLoop] := AnimPalette[iLoop+1];

  {...and then placing the first entry into the last entry of the array}
  AnimPalette[31] := PaletteEntry;

  {we then set this new array of palette entries into the exact area
   of the logical palette where we first set up the red gradient. the
   visual result looks very cool.}
  AnimatePalette(FormPalette, 10, 42, @AnimPalette);
end;

procedure TForm1.FormDestroy(Sender: TObject);
begin
  {we no longer need the logical palette, so delete it}
  DeleteObject(FormPalette);
end;
```

Figure 7-2:
A moving color
gradient

CreateHalftonePalette   *Windows.Pas*

Syntax

```
CreateHalftonePalette(
DC: HDC                    {a handle to a device context}
): HPALETTE;               {returns the handle to a logical palette}
```

Description

This function creates a logical palette based on the specified device context. A halftone palette should be created when an application uses the SetStretchBltMode function with the HALFTONE stretching mode flag. This palette should be selected and realized into the device context before the StretchBlt or StretchDIBits functions are called. When the palette is no longer needed, it should be destroyed using the DeleteObject function.

Parameters

DC: A handle to a device context used as a reference for the colors of the halftone palette.

Return Value

If the function succeeds, it returns the handle to a new logical palette; otherwise it returns zero. To get extended error information, call the GetLastError function.

See Also

CreatePalette, DeleteObject, RealizePalette, SelectPalette, SetStretchBltMode, Stretch-DIBits, StretchBlt

Example

Listing 7-3: Creating a Halftone Palette

```
{Whoops! Delphi incorrectly imports the GetPaletteEntries function. Here's
 the correct declaration that gives all of the functionality available
 with this API function}
function GetPaletteEntries(Palette: HPALETTE; StartIndex, NumEntries: UINT;
        PaletteEntries: Pointer): UINT; stdcall;

var
  Form1: TForm1;
  SysPalette: array[0..255] of TPaletteEntry;  // holds palette entry info
  FormPalette: HPALETTE;                        // a handle to a logical palette

implementation

{$R *.DFM}

{link in the GetPaletteEntries function}
function GetPaletteEntries; external gdi32 name 'GetPaletteEntries';
```

7

```
function TForm1.GetPalette: HPALETTE;
begin
  {when the form is asked to return its palette, it returns
   the application created logical palette}
  Result := FormPalette;
end;

procedure TForm1.SetThePalette;
begin
  {create a halftone color palette}
  FormPalette := CreateHalftonePalette(Form1.Canvas.Handle);
end;

procedure TForm1.FormCreate(Sender: TObject);
var
  iLoop: Integer;    // general loop control variable
begin
  {create the halftone palette}
  SetThePalette;

  {select and realize the halftone palette into the form's device context}
  SelectPalette(Canvas.Handle, FormPalette, FALSE);
  RealizePalette(Canvas.Handle);

  {retrieve the color values of the halftone palette}
  GetPaletteEntries(FormPalette, 0, 256, @SysPalette);

  {display the halftone palette color values}
  for iLoop := 0 to 255 do
  begin
    ListBox1.Items.Add('Palette slot: '+IntToStr(iLoop));
    ListBox1.Items.Add('     Red: '+IntToStr(SysPalette[iLoop].peRed));
    ListBox1.Items.Add('   Green: '+IntToStr(SysPalette[iLoop].peGreen));
    ListBox1.Items.Add('    Blue: '+IntToStr(SysPalette[iLoop].peBlue));

    case SysPalette[iLoop].peFlags of
      PC_EXPLICIT:   ListBox1.Items.Add('   Flags: PC_EXPLICIT');
      PC_NOCOLLAPSE: ListBox1.Items.Add('   Flags: PC_NOCOLLAPSE');
      PC_RESERVED:   ListBox1.Items.Add('   Flags: PC_RESERVED');
      else ListBox1.Items.Add('   Flags: NULL');
    end;
  end;
end;

procedure TForm1.FormPaint(Sender: TObject);
var
  iOutLoop, iInLoop: Integer;   // loop control variables
begin
  {select and realize the halftone palette into the form's device context}
  SelectPalette(Canvas.Handle, FormPalette, FALSE);
  RealizePalette(Canvas.Handle);

  {draw a series of rectangles to display the halftone palette}
  for iOutLoop := 0 to 15 do
    for iInLoop := 0 to 15 do
```

```
  begin
    Canvas.Brush.Color := PaletteIndex((iOutLoop*16)+iInLoop);
    Canvas.Rectangle((iInLoop*20)+15, (iOutLoop*20)+32, (iInLoop*20)+35,
                       (iOutLoop*20)+52);
  end;
end;

procedure TForm1.FormDestroy(Sender: TObject);
begin
  {we no longer need the halftone palette, so delete it}
  DeleteObject(FormPalette);
end;
```

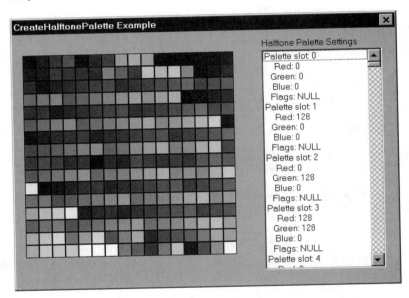

Figure 7-3:
The halftone
palette

CreatePalette   Windows.Pas

Syntax

```
CreatePalette(
const LogPalette: TLogPalette     {a pointer to a TLogPalette data structure}
): HPalette;                      {returns a handle to a logical palette}
```

Description

This function creates a logical palette from the color palette description contained in the TLogPalette structure pointed to by the LogPalette parameter. This new palette can be used by calling the SelectPalette and RealizePalette functions. When the palette is no longer needed, it should be deleted by using the DeleteObject function.

7

Parameters

LogPalette: A pointer to a TLogPalette data structure. This structure contains information about the format and colors of the desired palette. The TLogPalette data structure is defined as:

TLogPalette = packed record
      palVersion: Word;   {the palette version number}
      palNumEntries: Word;   {the number of palette entries}
      palPalEntry: array[0..0] of TPaletteEntry;   {an array of TPaletteEntry
                                      structures}
end;

palVersion: Specifies the Windows palette version number. As of this writing, this member should always be set to $300.

palNumEntries: Specifies the desired number of palette entries in the logical palette.

palPalEntry: An array of TPaletteEntry structures. These structures define the red, green, and blue color intensities and palette entry usage for each entry in the logical color palette. The colors in this array should be arranged in the order of importance, as the foremost entries are most likely to be placed in the system palette. The TPaletteEntry structure is defined as:

TPaletteEntry = packed record
      peRed: Byte;   {the red color intensity}
      peGreen: Byte;   {the green color intensity}
      peBlue: Byte;   {the blue color intensity}
      peFlags: Byte;   {palette entry usage flags}
end;

peRed: Specifies the intensity of the red component.

peGreen: Specifies the intensity of the green component.

peBlue: Specifies the intensity of the blue component.

peFlags: A flag indicating how this palette entry is to be used. This member can be one value from Table 7-3.

Return Value

If the function succeeds, it returns a handle to the new logical palette; otherwise it returns zero. To get extended error information, call the GetLastError function.

See Also

DeleteObject, RealizePalette, SelectPalette

Example

Listing 7-4: Creating a New Palette

```
{Whoops! Delphi incorrectly imports the GetPaletteEntries function. Here's
 the correct declaration that gives all of the functionality available
 with this API function}
function GetPaletteEntries(Palette: HPALETTE; StartIndex, NumEntries: UINT;
        PaletteEntries: Pointer): UINT; stdcall;

{Whoops! Delphi incorrectly imports the GetSystemPaletteEntries function.
 Here's the correct declaration that gives all of the functionality available
 with this API function}
function GetSystemPaletteEntries(DC: HDC; StartIndex, NumEntries: UINT;
                                PaletteEntries: Pointer): UINT; stdcall;


var
  Form1: TForm1;
  FormPalette: HPALETTE;              // a handle to a logical palette

implementation

{$R *.DFM}

{link in the GetPaletteEntries function}
function GetPaletteEntries; external gdi32 name 'GetPaletteEntries';

{link in the GetSystemPaletteEntries function}
function GetSystemPaletteEntries; external gdi32 name 'GetSystemPaletteEntries';

procedure TForm1.FormCreate(Sender: TObject);
begin
  {create the new palette}
  CreateThePalette;

  {display information on the new palette entries}
  DisplayPaletteEntries;
end;

function TForm1.GetPalette: HPALETTE;
begin
  {when something requests the palette of the form
   pass it back the new logical palette}
  Result := FormPalette;
end;

procedure TForm1.CreateThePalette;
var
  ThePalette: PLogPalette;   // a logical palette definition structure
  iLoop: Integer;            // general loop counter
begin
  {get enough memory to hold the colors in the first 10 system
   palette slots, plus 32 of our own. this memory is temporary,
   and is no longer needed once the palette is created.}
```

```
GetMem(ThePalette, SizeOf(TLogPalette)+42*SizeOf(TPaletteEntry));

{initialize the palette version number}
ThePalette^.palVersion := $300;

{we will have a total of 42 entries in our palette}
ThePalette^.palNumEntries := 42;

{get the first 10 system palette entries}
GetSystemPaletteEntries(Form1.Canvas.Handle, 0, 10,
                        @(ThePalette^.palPalEntry));

{we only want 32 new palette entries, and we want them to start
 immediately after the first 10 system palette entries. by
 retrieving the first 10 system palette entries, when we realize
 our new palette, the first 10 logical palette entries will be
 mapped to the first 10 system palette entries, and our
 palette entries will follow}
for iLoop := 0 to 31 do
begin
  {create a gradient red palette}
  ThePalette^.palPalEntry[iLoop+10].peRed   := 255-((255 div 32)*iLoop);
  ThePalette^.palPalEntry[iLoop+10].peGreen := 0;
  ThePalette^.palPalEntry[iLoop+10].peBlue  := 0;
  {do not match this palette entry to any other palette entry}
  ThePalette^.palPalEntry[iLoop+10].peFlags := PC_NOCOLLAPSE;
end;

{create the palette}
FormPalette := CreatePalette(ThePalette^);

{free the temporary memory}
FreeMem(ThePalette, SizeOf(TLogPalette)+42*SizeOf(TPaletteEntry));
end;

procedure TForm1.DisplayPaletteEntries;
var
  PaletteEntries: array[0..31] of TPaletteEntry;  // holds palette entries
  iLoop: Integer;
begin
  {get our 32 palette entries from the logical palette}
  GetPaletteEntries(FormPalette, 10, 32, @PaletteEntries);

  {display the palette entry information}
  ListBox1.Items.Clear;
  for iLoop := 0 to 31 do
  begin
    ListBox1.Items.Add('Palette slot: '+IntToStr(iLoop+10));
    ListBox1.Items.Add('     Red: '+IntToStr(PaletteEntries[iLoop].peRed));
    ListBox1.Items.Add('   Green: '+IntToStr(PaletteEntries[iLoop].peGreen));
    ListBox1.Items.Add('    Blue: '+IntToStr(PaletteEntries[iLoop].peBlue));

    case PaletteEntries[iLoop].peFlags of
      PC_EXPLICIT:   ListBox1.Items.Add('   Flags: PC_EXPLICIT');
      PC_NOCOLLAPSE: ListBox1.Items.Add('   Flags: PC_NOCOLLAPSE');
```

```
            PC_RESERVED:   ListBox1.Items.Add('   Flags: PC_RESERVED');
            else ListBox1.Items.Add('   Flags: NULL');
        end;
    end;
end;

procedure TForm1.FormPaint(Sender: TObject);
var
    OldPalette: HPALETTE;          // a handle to the previous palette
    iLoop: Integer;               // general loop control variable
begin
    {select our new logical palette into the device context}
    OldPalette := SelectPalette(Canvas.Handle, FormPalette, FALSE);

    {map our logical palette into the system palette}
    RealizePalette(Canvas.Handle);

    {display a red gradient}
    for iLoop := 0 to 31 do
    begin
        Canvas.Brush.Color := $01000000 or iLoop+10;
        Canvas.FillRect(Rect(10, iLoop*10+16, 260, (iLoop*10)+36));
    end;

    {select the previous palette back into the device context}
    SelectPalette(Canvas.Handle, OldPalette, FALSE);
end;

procedure TForm1.Button1Click(Sender: TObject);
var
    PaletteEntries: array[0..31] of TPaletteEntry;  // holds palette entries
    iLoop: Integer;
begin
    {set up a green gradient}
    for iLoop := 0 to 31 do
    begin
        PaletteEntries[iLoop].peRed   := 0;
        PaletteEntries[iLoop].peGreen := 255-((255 div 32)*iLoop);
        PaletteEntries[iLoop].peBlue  := 0;
        PaletteEntries[iLoop].peFlags := PC_NOCOLLAPSE;
    end;

    {reset the logical palette to this green gradient}
    SetPaletteEntries(FormPalette, 10, 32, PaletteEntries);

    {display the new palette entries}
    DisplayPaletteEntries;

    {redraw the form}
    Invalidate;
end;
```

```
procedure TForm1.FormDestroy(Sender: TObject);
begin
  {we no longer need the logical palette, so delete it}
  DeleteObject(FormPalette);
end;
```

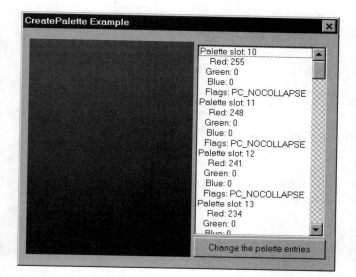

Figure 7-4: The gradient palette

Table 7-3: CreatePalette LogPalette.palPalEntry.peFlags Values

Value	Description
PC_EXPLICIT	Indicates that the low-order byte of the logical palette entry designates a system palette index.
PC_NOCOLLAPSE	Indicates that this color entry is placed in an unused system palette entry. It will not be mapped into another color entry if a duplicate color entry already exists in the logical palette. If there are no unused system palette entries left, the color is mapped normally as if no peFlags value was specified. Other colors can be mapped to this color entry normally.
PC_RESERVED	Indicates that this color entry is used for palette animation. It is placed into an unused system palette entry, and will not be mapped into another color entry if a duplicate color entry already exists in the logical palette. Other colors are prevented from mapping to this color entry if they are identical. If there are no unused system palette entries left, this color entry will not be placed into the system palette and will therefore be unavailable.

GetBValue   Windows.Pas

Syntax

```
GetBValue(
rgb: DWORD          {a 32-bit color specifier}
): Byte;            {returns the blue intensity}
```

Description

This function retrieves the blue color intensity value from the given 32-bit color specifier.

Parameters

rgb: The 32-bit color specifier from which the blue color intensity is retrieved.

Return Value

If this function succeeds, it returns the blue color intensity of the 32-bit color specifier. This value is in the range 0 through 255. If the function fails, it returns zero.

See Also

GetGValue, GetRValue, PaletteIndex, PaletteRGB, RGB

Example

Listing 7-5: Displaying Red, Green, and Blue Color Intensities

```
procedure TForm1.ColorGrid1Change(Sender: TObject);
begin
  {display the red, green, and blue intensities of the selected color}
  Label4.Caption := IntToStr(GetRValue(ColorGrid1.ForegroundColor));
  Label5.Caption := IntToStr(GetGValue(ColorGrid1.ForegroundColor));
  Label6.Caption := IntToStr(GetBValue(ColorGrid1.ForegroundColor));
end;
```

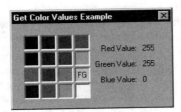

Figure 7-5: The color component intensity values

GetDIBColorTable   Windows.Pas

Syntax

```
GetDIBColorTable(
DC: HDC;            {a handle to a device context with a selected DIB}
p2: UINT;           {the color palette index of the first entry to retrieve}
```

p3: UINT;	{the number of palette entries to retrieve}
var RGBQuadStructs	{a pointer to a buffer receiving an array of TRGBQuad}
): UINT;	{returns the number of color palette entries retrieved}

Description

This function retrieves the specified range of color palette entries from the device-independent bitmap currently selected into the device context identified by the DC parameter. These entries are in the form of an array of TRGBQuad data structures, stored in a buffer pointed to by the RGBQuadStructs parameter. This function is useful only for DIBs that have a color format of 1, 4, or 8 bits per pixel, as DIBs with color formats greater than 8 bits per pixel do not contain a color palette.

Parameters

DC: A handle to a device context. The DIB from which the color palette entries are to be retrieved must be selected into this device context.

p2: Specifies the zero-based index of the first entry in the palette to retrieve.

p3: Specifies the number of palette entries to retrieve.

RGBQuadStructs: A pointer to a buffer that receives an array of TRGBQuad structures describing the color values of the specified DIB's palette entries. This buffer must be large enough to hold the number of TRGBQuad structures indicated by the p3 parameter. The TRGBQuad structure is defined as:

```
TRGBQuad = packed record
     rgbBlue: Byte;           {blue color intensity}
     rgbGreen: Byte;          {green color intensity}
     rgbRed: Byte;            {red color intensity}
     rgbReserved: Byte;       {reserved value}
end;
```

Please see the CreateDIBSection function for a description of this data structure.

Return Value

If the function succeeds, the RGBQuadStructs buffer is filled with an array of TRGBQuad structures, and the function returns the number of palette entries retrieved. If the function fails, the RGBQuadStructs buffer will be empty and the function returns zero. To get extended error information, call the GetLastError function.

See Also

CreatePalette, CreateDIBSection, SelectObject, SetDIBColorTable, SetPaletteEntries

Example

Listing 7-6: Retrieving a Device-Independent Bitmap's Color Palette

```
var
  Form1: TForm1;
```

```
      FormPalette: HPALETTE;      // holds our generic logical palette

implementation

function TForm1.GetPalette: HPALETTE;
begin
  {when the form is queried about a color palette, return
    the application created palette}
  Result := FormPalette;
end;

procedure TForm1.FormCreate(Sender: TObject);
var
  ThePalette: PLogPalette;      // a logical palette data structure
begin
  {allocate enough memory to create a 256-color logical palette}
  GetMem(ThePalette, SizeOf(TLogPalette)+256*SizeOf(TPaletteEntry));

  {initialize the appropriate members}
  ThePalette^.palVersion := $300;
  ThePalette^.palNumEntries := 256;

  {this palette is used to transfer the colors of the DIB into
    the form's device context.  therefore, since the colors of
    the palette will be based on the color palette stored in the
    selected DIB, we do not need to initialize this new color palette}
  FormPalette := CreatePalette(ThePalette^);

  {we have the logical color palette, so delete the
    unneeded memory}
  FreeMem(ThePalette, SizeOf(TLogPalette)+256*SizeOf(TPaletteEntry));
end;

procedure TForm1.FormDestroy(Sender: TObject);
begin
  {delete our generic logical palette}
  DeleteObject(FormPalette);
end;

procedure TForm1.FileListBox1Click(Sender: TObject);
var
  InLoop, OutLoop: Integer;                        // loop control variables
  NumColors: Integer;                              // the number of colors in the
                                                   // DIB color table
  PalEntries: array[0..255] of TPaletteEntry;      // holds color information in a
                                                   // logical palette format
  Colors: array[0..255] of TRGBQuad;               // holds the retrieved DIB
                                                   // palette entries
  TheDC: hdc;                                       // a handle to a device context
  OldBrush, NewBrush: HBRUSH;                       // brush handles used to display
                                                   // the DIB palette
begin
  {Delphi 3's TBitmap now encapsulates a DIB.  therefore, load
    a DIB into the Image1 object}
```

```
Image1.Picture.Bitmap.LoadFromFile(FileListBox1.FileName);

{the loaded DIB is automatically selected into Image1's device
 context, so retrieve the DIB color palette values}
NumColors := GetDIBColorTable(Image1.Canvas.Handle, 0, 256, Colors);

{the members of a TRGBQuad structure are in the opposite order of
 the members of a TPaletteEntry structure. we need to create an
 array of TPaletteEntry structures so the form's palette can be
 set to that of the DIB.  therefore, we must translate the
 TRGBQuad structures into the appropriate TPaletteEntry format.}
for InLoop := 0 to NumColors-1 do
begin
  PalEntries[InLoop].peRed   := Colors[InLoop].rgbRed;
  PalEntries[InLoop].peGreen := Colors[InLoop].rgbGreen;
  PalEntries[InLoop].peBlue  := Colors[InLoop].rgbBlue;
  PalEntries[InLoop].peFlags := PC_NOCOLLAPSE;
end;

{set the form's palette to match that of the selected DIB}
SetPaletteEntries(FormPalette, 10, NumColors, PalEntries);

{select and realize this new palette}
TheDC := GetDC(Form1.Handle);
SelectPalette(TheDC, FormPalette, FALSE);
RealizePalette(TheDC);

{clear the list box and prepare to display the color palette information}
ListBox1.Items.Clear;
ListBox1.Items.Add('Number of colors: '+IntToStr(NumColors));

{draw a grid of colored squares representing the
 palette of the selected DIB. since only 236 colors
 can be set in the system palette, this code will not
 display the first or last 10 colors of the logical
 palette}
for OutLoop := 0 to 15 do
  for InLoop := 0 to 15 do
  begin
    if ((OutLoop*16)+InLoop>NumColors-1) or ((OutLoop*16)+InLoop>245) then
      {if there are fewer than 236 colors, or we are displaying
       the last 10 system colors, display a solid black square}
      NewBrush := CreateSolidBrush(clBlack)
    else
    begin
      {display the color values for this palette index}
      ListBox1.Items.Add('Index: '+IntToStr((OutLoop*16)+InLoop));
      ListBox1.Items.Add('   Red: '+IntToStr(Colors[
                                   (OutLoop*16)+InLoop].rgbRed));
      ListBox1.Items.Add('  Green: '+IntToStr(Colors[
                                   (OutLoop*16)+InLoop].rgbGreen));
      ListBox1.Items.Add('   Blue: '+IntToStr(Colors[
                                   (OutLoop*16)+InLoop].rgbBlue));

      {create a colored brush for this specific palette index,
```

```
          skipping the first 10 system colors}
       NewBrush := CreateSolidBrush($01000000 or (OutLoop*16)+InLoop+10);
     end;

     {Select the new brush into the device context}
     OldBrush := SelectObject(TheDC, NewBrush);

     {draw a rectangle using the specific palette index color}
     Rectangle(TheDC, (InLoop*15)+15, (OutLoop*15)+256,
                      (InLoop*15)+30, (OutLoop*15)+271);

     {delete the colored brush}
     SelectObject(TheDC, OldBrush);
     DeleteObject(NewBrush);
   end;

  {release the device context}
  ReleaseDC(Form1.Handle, TheDC);
end;
```

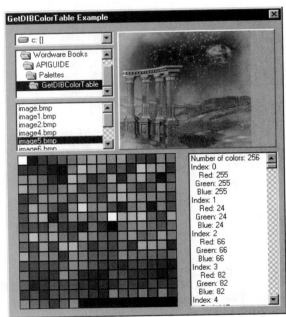

Figure 7-6:
Displaying a
DIB color
palette

GetEnhMetaFilePaletteEntries   Windows.Pas

Syntax

GetEnhMetaFilePaletteEntries(
p1: HENHMETAFILE;   {a handle to an enhanced metafile}
p2: UINT;   {the number of palette entries to retrieve}
p3: Pointer   {a pointer to a buffer receiving palette entry info}

): UINT;   {returns the number of entries copied}

Description

This function retrieves the specified number of palette entries from the enhanced metafile indicated by the p1 parameter, if it contains a palette. The retrieved entries always start at index 0 of the enhanced metafile's palette entry table. Once the palette entries are retrieved, the developer can use the CreatePalette, SelectPalette, and RealizePalette functions before calling the PlayEnhMetaFile function to display the enhanced metafile in its original colors.

Parameters

p1: A handle to the enhanced metafile whose color palette entries are to be retrieved.

p2: Specifies the number of palette entries to retrieve.

p3: A pointer to a buffer that receives an array of TPaletteEntry structures describing the color values of the metafile's palette entries. This buffer must be large enough to hold the number of TPaletteEntry structures indicated by the p2 parameter. If this parameter is set to NIL and the specified enhanced metafile contains a color palette, the function returns the number of entries in the metafile's palette. The TPaletteEntry structure is defined as:

```
TPaletteEntry = packed record
     peRed: Byte;          {the red color intensity}
     peGreen: Byte;        {the green color intensity}
     peBlue: Byte;         {the blue color intensity}
     peFlags: Byte;        {palette entry usage flags}
end;
```

Please see the CreatePalette function for a description of this data structure.

Return Value

If the function succeeds and the specified enhanced metafile contains a palette, the buffer pointed to by the p3 parameter is filled with an array of TPaletteEntry structures, and the function returns the number of palette entries retrieved. If the function succeeds and the metafile does not contain a palette, it returns zero. If the function fails, it returns GDI_ERROR.

See Also

CreatePalette, GetEnhMetaFile, PlayEnhMetaFile, RealizePalette, SelectPalette

Example

Listing 7-7: Retrieving an Enhanced Metafile Color Palette

```
procedure TForm1.FileListBox1Click(Sender: TObject);
var
  TheMetafile: HENHMETAFILE;        // a handle to an enhanced metafile
  MetafilePalette: PLogPalette;     // a logical palette description structure
```

```
    MetafilePaletteHandle: HPALETTE;      // a handle to a palette
    NumPaletteEntries: Integer;           // the number of entries in the palette
    iLoop: Integer;                       // general loop control variable
begin
  {erase the last image in the paintbox}
  PaintBox1.Canvas.FillRect(PaintBox1.Canvas.ClipRect);

  {open the selected metafile}
  TheMetafile := GetEnhMetaFile(PChar(FileListBox1.FileName));

  {retrieve the number of entries in this metafile's palette}
  NumPaletteEntries := GetEnhMetaFilePaletteEntries(TheMetafile, 0, nil);

  {allocate enough memory to create a logical palette
   large enough for all of the metafile palette entries}
  GetMem(MetafilePalette, SizeOf(TLogPalette)+
         NumPaletteEntries*SizeOf(TPaletteEntry));

  {if there are any entries in the metafile, retrieve them}
  if NumPaletteEntries>0 then
    GetEnhMetaFilePaletteEntries(TheMetafile, NumPaletteEntries,
                          @(MetafilePalette^.palPalEntry));

  {initialize the appropriate logical palette information}
  MetafilePalette^.palVersion := $300;
  MetafilePalette^.palNumEntries := NumPaletteEntries;

  {create a logical palette based on the palette
   stored in the enhanced metafile}
  MetafilePaletteHandle := CreatePalette(MetafilePalette^);

  {select and realize this palette into the form's canvas}
  SelectPalette(Form1.Canvas.Handle, MetafilePaletteHandle, FALSE);
  RealizePalette(Form1.Canvas.Handle);

  {now, display the enhanced metafile.  this metafile
   will play back using its original colors}
  PlayEnhMetaFile(PaintBox1.Canvas.Handle, TheMetafile, PaintBox1.BoundsRect);

  {initialize the list box to display the enhanced
   metafile's palette entry information}
  ListBox1.Items.Clear;
  ListBox1.Items.Add('Palette Entries: '+IntToStr(NumPaletteEntries));

  {display the enhanced metafile's palette entries}
  for iLoop := 0 to NumPaletteEntries-1 do
  begin
    ListBox1.Items.Add('Palette slot: '+IntToStr(iLoop));
    ListBox1.Items.Add('     Red: '+IntToStr(
                    MetafilePalette^.palPalEntry[iLoop].peRed));
    ListBox1.Items.Add('   Green: '+IntToStr(
                    MetafilePalette^.palPalEntry[iLoop].peGreen));
    ListBox1.Items.Add('    Blue: '+IntToStr(
                    MetafilePalette^.palPalEntry[iLoop].peBlue));
```

```
case MetafilePalette^.palPalEntry[iLoop].peFlags of
  PC_EXPLICIT:   ListBox1.Items.Add('   Flags: PC_EXPLICIT');
  PC_NOCOLLAPSE: ListBox1.Items.Add('   Flags: PC_NOCOLLAPSE');
  PC_RESERVED:   ListBox1.Items.Add('   Flags: PC_RESERVED');
  else ListBox1.Items.Add('   Flags: NULL');
  end;
end;

{the logical palette description data structure is no
 longer needed, so free its memory}
FreeMem(MetafilePalette, SizeOf(TLogPalette)+
        NumPaletteEntries*SizeOf(TPaletteEntry));

{enhanced metafile is no longer needed, so delete it}
DeleteEnhMetaFile(TheMetafile);
DeleteObject(MetafilePaletteHandle);

{delete the logical palette}
DeleteObject(MetafilePaletteHandle);
end;
```

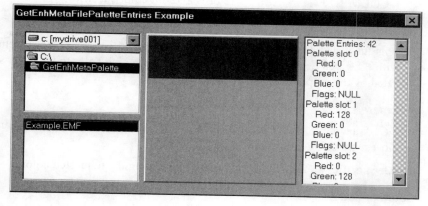

*Figure 7-7:
Displaying an
enhanced
metafile in its
original colors*

GetGValue   *Windows.Pas*

Syntax

GetGValue(
rgb: DWORD   {a 32-bit color specifier}
): Byte;   {returns the green intensity}

Description

This function retrieves the green color intensity value from the given 32-bit color specifier.

Parameters

rgb: The 32-bit color specifier from which the green color intensity is retrieved.

Return Value

If this function succeeds, it returns the green color intensity of the 32-bit color specifier. This value is in the range 0 through 255. If the function fails, it returns zero.

See Also

GetBValue, GetRValue, PaletteIndex, PaletteRGB, RGB

Example

Please see Listing 7-5 under GetBValue.

GetNearestColor   **Windows.Pas**

Syntax

```
GetNearestColor(
DC: HDC;                    {a handle to a device context}
p2: COLORREF               {a 32-bit color specifier}
): COLORREF;               {returns a 32-bit color specifier}
```

Description

This function returns a 32-bit color specifier from the system color palette associated with the given device context for the closest matching color to the color specifier indicated by the p2 parameter.

Parameters

DC: A handle to a device context whose associated system palette is searched for the closest matching color to the requested color.

p2: Specifies a 32-bit color specifier representing the requested color.

Return Value

If the function succeeds, it returns the closest matching 32-bit color specifier from the system color palette for the requested color; otherwise it returns CLR_INVALID. To get extended error information, call the GetLastError function.

See Also

GetNearestPaletteIndex, RGB

Example

Listing 7-8: Finding the Closest Matching Color

```
procedure TForm1.ScrollBar1Change(Sender: TObject);
begin
  {display the requested color settings}
  Label1.Caption := 'Red: '+IntToStr(ScrollBar1.Position);
  Label2.Caption := 'Green: '+IntToStr(ScrollBar2.Position);
```

```
Label3.Caption := 'Blue: '+IntToStr(ScrollBar3.Position);

{color the first shape with the requested color}
Shape1.Brush.Color := RGB(ScrollBar1.Position,
                          ScrollBar2.Position,
                          ScrollBar3.Position);

{find the closest matching pure color for the requested
 color in the system palette}
Shape2.Brush.Color := GetNearestColor(Canvas.Handle, Shape1.Brush.Color);
end;
```

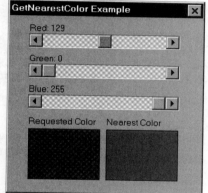

Figure 7-8:
Displaying the
closest
matching color

GetNearestPaletteIndex   Windows.Pas

Syntax

GetNearestPaletteIndex(
p1: HPALETTE;   {a handle to a logical palette}
p2: COLORREF   {a 32-bit explicit RGB color value}
): UINT;   {returns a zero-based index into the logical palette}

Description

This function returns the index into the logical palette identified by the p1 parameter of the closest matching color entry for the requested color specified by the p2 parameter. Note that if the logical palette contains palette entries with the peFlags member set to PC_EXPLICIT, the return value is undefined.

Parameters

p1: A handle to the logical palette that is searched for a color closely matching the requested color.

p2: A 32-bit explicit RGB color value representing the requested color.

Return Value

If the function succeeds, it returns the zero-based index into the logical palette of the closest matching color for the requested color. If the function fails, it returns CLR_INVALID. To get extended error information, call the GetLastError function.

See Also

GetNearestColor, GetPaletteEntries, GetSystemPaletteEntries, PaletteRGB, RGB

Example

Listing 7-9: Finding the Color Palette Index for the Requested Color

```
{Whoops! Delphi incorrectly imports the GetSystemPaletteEntries function.
 Here's the correct declaration that gives all of the functionality available
 with this API function}
function GetSystemPaletteEntries(DC: HDC; StartIndex, NumEntries: UINT;
                                PaletteEntries: Pointer): UINT; stdcall;

var
  Form1: TForm1;
  SysPalette: array[0..255] of TPaletteEntry;  // holds a copy of the
                                               // system palette entries

  FormPalette: HPALETTE;                        // a handle to a logical palette

implementation

{link in the GetSystemPaletteEntries function}
function GetSystemPaletteEntries; external gdi32 name 'GetSystemPaletteEntries';

function TForm1.GetPalette: HPalette;
begin
  {when the form is queried about its palette,
   return the application created palette}
  Result := FormPalette;
end;

procedure TForm1.SetThePalette;
var
  ThePalette: PLogPalette;  // a logical palette description structure
begin
  {allocate enough memory for a 256 entry color palette}
  GetMem(ThePalette, SizeOf(TLogPalette)+256*SizeOf(TPaletteEntry));

  {retrieve the palette entries of the system palette}
  GetSystemPaletteEntries(Form1.Canvas.Handle, 0, 256,
                          @(ThePalette^.palPalEntry));

  {initialize the appropriate logical palette information}
  ThePalette^.palVersion := $300;
  ThePalette^.palNumEntries := 256;
```

```
  {create an exact duplicate of the current system palette}
  FormPalette := CreatePalette(ThePalette^);

  {we no longer need the logical palette description
   structure memory, so delete it}
  FreeMem(ThePalette, SizeOf(TLogPalette)+256*SizeOf(TPaletteEntry));
end;

procedure TForm1.FormCreate(Sender: TObject);
var
  iLoop: Integer;    // general loop counter
begin
  {create an exact duplicate of the current system palette}
  SetThePalette;

  {retrieve the system palette color entries}
  GetSystemPaletteEntries(Form1.Canvas.Handle, 0, 256, @SysPalette);

  {display the color palette entry information}
  for iLoop := 0 to 255 do
  begin
    ListBox1.Items.Add('Palette slot: '+IntToStr(iLoop));
    ListBox1.Items.Add('      Red: '+IntToStr(SysPalette[iLoop].peRed));
    ListBox1.Items.Add('    Green: '+IntToStr(SysPalette[iLoop].peGreen));
    ListBox1.Items.Add('     Blue: '+IntToStr(SysPalette[iLoop].peBlue));

    case SysPalette[iLoop].peFlags of
      PC_EXPLICIT:   ListBox1.Items.Add('    Flags: PC_EXPLICIT');
      PC_NOCOLLAPSE: ListBox1.Items.Add('    Flags: PC_NOCOLLAPSE');
      PC_RESERVED:   ListBox1.Items.Add('    Flags: PC_RESERVED');
      else ListBox1.Items.Add('    Flags: NULL');
    end;
  end;
end;

procedure TForm1.FormPaint(Sender: TObject);
var
  iOutLoop, iInLoop: Integer;
begin
  {select and realize the duplicate of the system
   palette into the form's device context}
  SelectPalette(Canvas.Handle, FormPalette, FALSE);
  RealizePalette(Canvas.Handle);

  {draw a grid of rectangles to display the color palette}
  for iOutLoop := 0 to 15 do
    for iInLoop := 0 to 15 do
    begin
      Canvas.Brush.Color := PaletteIndex((iOutLoop*16)+iInLoop);
      Canvas.Rectangle((iInLoop*20)+15, (iOutLoop*20)+144,
                       (iInLoop*20)+35, (iOutLoop*20)+164);
    end;
end;
```

```
procedure TForm1.FormDestroy(Sender: TObject);
begin
  {we no longer need the created logical palette, so delete it}
  DeleteObject(FormPalette);
end;

procedure TForm1.ScrollBar1Change(Sender: TObject);
begin
  {display the requested color settings}
  Label1.Caption := 'Red: '+IntToStr(ScrollBar1.Position);
  Label2.Caption := 'Green: '+IntToStr(ScrollBar2.Position);
  Label3.Caption := 'Blue: '+IntToStr(ScrollBar3.Position);

  {find the index of the nearest matching color}
  Label8.Caption := IntToStr(GetNearestPaletteIndex(FormPalette, RGB(
                                          ScrollBar1.Position,
                                          ScrollBar2.Position,
                                          ScrollBar3.Position)));

  {display the matching color entry}
  ListBox1.TopIndex := ListBox1.Items.IndexOf('Palette slot: '+Label8.Caption);
end;
```

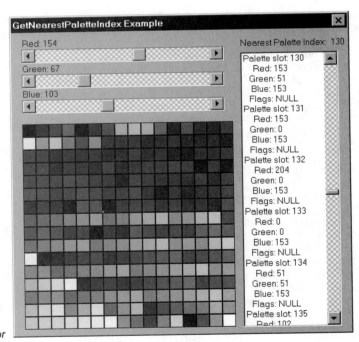

*Figure 7-9:
The palette
index for the
closest
matching color*

GetPaletteEntries   *Windows.Pas*

Syntax

```
GetPaletteEntries(
Palette: HPALETTE;              {a handle to a logical palette}
StartIndex: UINT;              {the starting palette index}
NumEntries: UINT;              {the number of palette entries to retrieve}
PaletteEntries: Pointer        {a pointer to an array of TPaletteEntry structures}
): UINT;                       {returns the number of palette entries retrieved}
```

Description

This function retrieves a range of color palette entries from the specified logical palette. These palette entries are returned in the form of an array of TPaletteEntry structures stored in the buffer pointed to by the PaletteEntries parameter.

Parameters

Palette: A handle to the logical palette from which palette entries are retrieved.

StartIndex: The zero-based index of the first entry to retrieve from the logical palette.

NumEntries: Specifies the number of entries to retrieve. If the logical color palette contains fewer entries than this parameter indicates, the remaining entries in the buffer pointed to by the PaletteEntries parameter are not altered.

PaletteEntries: A pointer to a buffer that receives an array of TPaletteEntry structures describing the color values retrieved from the specified logical palette's entries. This buffer must be large enough to hold the number of TPaletteEntry structures indicated by the NumEntries parameter. If this parameter is set to NIL, the function returns the number of palette entries in the specified logical palette. The TPaletteEntry structure is defined as:

```
TPaletteEntry = packed record
     peRed: Byte;         {the red color intensity}
     peGreen: Byte;       {the green color intensity}
     peBlue: Byte;        {the blue color intensity}
     peFlags: Byte;       {palette entry usage flags}
end;
```

Please see the CreatePalette function for a description of this data structure.

Return Value

If the function succeeds, the buffer pointed to by the PaletteEntries parameter is filled with an array of TPaletteEntry structures, and the function returns the number of palette entries retrieved from the logical palette. If the function succeeds and the PaletteEntries parameter is set to NIL, the function returns the number of entries the specified logical palette contains. If the function fails, it returns zero. To get extended error information, call the GetLastError function.

See Also

CreatePalette, GetSystemPaletteEntries, RealizePalette, SelectPalette, SetPaletteEntries

Example

Please see Listing 7-4 under CreatePalette or Listing 7-3 under CreateHalftonePalette.

GetRValue   Windows.Pas

Syntax

```
GetRValue(
rgb: DWORD          {a 32-bit color specifier}
): Byte;            {returns the red intensity}
```

Description

This function retrieves the red color intensity value from the given 32-bit color specifier.

Parameters

rgb: The 32-bit color specifier from which the red color intensity is retrieved.

Return Value

If this function succeeds, it returns the red color intensity of the 32-bit color specifier. This value is in the range 0 through 255. If the function fails, it returns zero.

See Also

GetBValue, GetGValue, PaletteIndex, PaletteRGB, RGB

Example

Please see Listing 7-5 under GetBValue.

GetSysColor   Windows.Pas

Syntax

```
GetSysColor(
nIndex: Integer       {display element flag}
): DWORD;             {returns an RGB color value}
```

Description

This function retrieves the RGB color value for the specified display element. The display element flags identify various parts of a window, and its color is associated with one of the twenty static system-defined colors.

7

Parameters

nIndex: Specifies a display element whose RGB color value is to be retrieved. This parameter can be one value from Table 7-4.

Return Value

If the function succeeds, it returns a 32-bit explicit RGB value for the specified display element. This color will correspond to one of the twenty static system colors. If the function fails, it returns zero.

See Also

GetBValue, GetGValue, GetRValue, GetSystemPaletteEntries, PaletteRGB, RGB, SetSysColors

Example

Listing 7-10: Retrieving and Setting Display Element System Colors

```
{define a constant array of all available display element flags}
const
   DisplayElements: array[0..24] of integer = (COLOR_3DDKSHADOW,COLOR_3DLIGHT,
                                    COLOR_ACTIVEBORDER,COLOR_ACTIVECAPTION,
                                    COLOR_APPWORKSPACE,COLOR_BACKGROUND,
                                    COLOR_BTNFACE,COLOR_BTNHIGHLIGHT,
                                    COLOR_BTNSHADOW,COLOR_BTNTEXT,
                                    COLOR_CAPTIONTEXT,COLOR_GRAYTEXT,
                                    COLOR_HIGHLIGHT,COLOR_HIGHLIGHTTEXT,
                                    COLOR_INACTIVEBORDER,COLOR_INACTIVECAPTION,
                                    COLOR_INACTIVECAPTIONTEXT,COLOR_INFOBK,
                                    COLOR_INFOTEXT,COLOR_MENU,COLOR_MENUTEXT,
                                    COLOR_SCROLLBAR,COLOR_WINDOW,
                                    COLOR_WINDOWFRAME,COLOR_WINDOWTEXT);

implementation

procedure TForm1.ComboBox1Change(Sender: TObject);
var
   DisplayColor: TColor;    // holds the display element system color
begin
   {retrieve the color of the selected display element}
   DisplayColor := GetSysColor(DisplayElements[ComboBox1.ItemIndex]);

   {adjust the scroll bar positions accordingly}
   ScrollBar1.Position := GetRValue(DisplayColor);
   ScrollBar2.Position := GetGValue(DisplayColor);
   ScrollBar3.Position := GetBValue(DisplayColor);
end;

procedure TForm1.ScrollBar1Change(Sender: TObject);
begin
   {display the selected color in the shape}
   Shape1.Brush.Color := RGB(ScrollBar1.Position,
                             ScrollBar2.Position,
```

```
                                 ScrollBar3.Position);

      {display the colors' component values}
      Label1.Caption := 'Red: '+IntToStr(ScrollBar1.Position);
      Label2.Caption := 'Green: '+IntToStr(ScrollBar2.Position);
      Label3.Caption := 'Blue: '+IntToStr(ScrollBar3.Position);
end;

procedure TForm1.Button1Click(Sender: TObject);
var
   Elements: array[0..0] of Integer;   // holds the display element to change
   NewColor: array[0..0] of TColor;    // holds the new color for the element
begin
   {identify the display element to change}
   Elements[0] := DisplayElements[ComboBox1.ItemIndex];

   {identify the new color for the selected element}
   NewColor[0] := RGB(ScrollBar1.Position, ScrollBar2.Position,
                      ScrollBar3.Position);

   {change the display element's color. the screen will repaint
    to display the new color}
   SetSysColors(1, Elements, NewColor);
end;
```

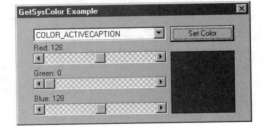

Figure 7-10:
The new
system color

Table 7-4: GetSysColor nIndex Values

Value	Description
COLOR_3DDKSHADOW	The dark shadow color for three-dimensional display elements.
COLOR_3DLIGHT	The lighted edge color for three-dimensional display elements.
COLOR_ACTIVEBORDER	The active window border color.
COLOR_ACTIVECAPTION	The active window caption color.
COLOR_APPWORKSPACE	The background color used in multiple document interface applications.
COLOR_BACKGROUND	The desktop color.
COLOR_BTNFACE	The color of pushbutton faces.
COLOR_BTNHIGHLIGHT	The color of a highlighted pushbutton.

Value	Description
COLOR_BTNSHADOW	The shaded edge color on pushbuttons.
COLOR_BTNTEXT	The text color on pushbuttons.
COLOR_CAPTIONTEXT	The text color used in caption, size box, and scroll bar arrow box controls.
COLOR_GRAYTEXT	The color of disabled text. This will be set to zero if the display driver cannot support solid gray.
COLOR_HIGHLIGHT	The color used for selected items in a control.
COLOR_HIGHLIGHTTEXT	The color used for the text of selected items in a control.
COLOR_INACTIVEBORDER	The inactive window border color.
COLOR_INACTIVECAPTION	The inactive window caption color.
COLOR_INACTIVECAPTIONTEXT	The text color in an inactive caption bar.
COLOR_INFOBK	The background color for tooltip controls.
COLOR_INFOTEXT	The text color for tooltip controls.
COLOR_MENU	The menu background color.
COLOR_MENUTEXT	The text color used in menus.
COLOR_SCROLLBAR	The scroll bar "gray" area color.
COLOR_WINDOW	The window background color.
COLOR_WINDOWFRAME	The window frame color.
COLOR_WINDOWTEXT	The color of text used in a window.

GetSystemPaletteEntries Windows.Pas

Syntax

```
GetSystemPaletteEntries(
DC: HDC;                        {a handle to a device context}
StartIndex: UINT;               {the starting palette index}
NumEntries: UINT;               {the number of palette entries to retrieve}
PaletteEntries: Pointer         {a pointer to an array of TPaletteEntry structures}
): UINT;                        {returns the number of palette entries retrieved}
```

Description

This function retrieves the specified range of palette entries from the system palette associated with the device context identified by the DC parameter.

Parameters

DC: A handle to a device context. The color palette entries are retrieved from the system palette associated with this device context.

StartIndex: The zero-based index of the first entry to retrieve from the system palette.

NumEntries: Specifies the number of entries to retrieve.

PaletteEntries: A pointer to a buffer that receives an array of TPaletteEntry structures describing the color values retrieved from the system palette's entries. This buffer must be large enough to hold the number of TPaletteEntry structures indicated by the NumEntries parameter. If this parameter is set to NIL, the function returns the number of palette entries in the system palette. The TPaletteEntry structure is defined as:

```
TPaletteEntry = packed record
    peRed: Byte;          {the red color intensity}
    peGreen: Byte;        {the green color intensity}
    peBlue: Byte;         {the blue color intensity}
    peFlags: Byte;        {palette entry usage flags}
end;
```

Please see the CreatePalette function for a description of this data structure.

Return Value

If the function succeeds, the buffer pointed to by the PaletteEntries parameter is filled with an array of TPaletteEntry structures, and the function returns the number of palette entries retrieved from the system palette. If the function fails, it returns zero. To get extended error information, call the GetLastError function.

See Also

GetPaletteEntries, GetSystemPaletteUse, RealizePalette, SelectPalette, SetSystemPaletteUse

Example

Listing 7-II: Retrieving System Palette Entries

```
{Whoops! Delphi incorrectly imports the GetSystemPaletteEntries function.
 Here's the correct declaration that gives all of the functionality available
 with this API function}
function GetSystemPaletteEntries(DC: HDC; StartIndex, NumEntries: UINT;
                                 PaletteEntries: Pointer): UINT; stdcall;

var
   Form1: TForm1;
   SysPalette: array[0..255] of TPaletteEntry; // holds retrieved system palette
   FormPalette: HPALETTE;                       // handle to a logical palette

implementation

{link in the GetSystemPaletteEntries function}
function GetSystemPaletteEntries; external gdi32 name 'GetSystemPaletteEntries';

function TForm1.GetPalette: HPALETTE;
begin
   {when the form is queried about its palette, return
    the application created logical palette}
```

```
    Result := FormPalette;
end;

procedure TForm1.SetThePalette;
var
  ThePalette: PLogPalette;  // a logical palette description data structure
  iLoop: Integer;            // general loop counter
begin
  {allocate enough memory for a 256-color palette}
  GetMem(ThePalette, SizeOf(TLogPalette)+256*SizeOf(TPaletteEntry));

  {retrieve all of the system palette entries}
  GetSystemPaletteEntries(Form1.Canvas.Handle, 0, 256,
                      @(ThePalette^.palPalEntry));

  {initialize the logical palette information}
  ThePalette^.palVersion := $300;
  ThePalette^.palNumEntries := 256;

  {create a logical palette that is the exact duplicate
   of the current system palette}
  FormPalette := CreatePalette(ThePalette^);

  {we no longer need the logical palette description
   memory, so delete it}
  FreeMem(ThePalette, SizeOf(TLogPalette)+256*SizeOf(TPaletteEntry));
end;

procedure TForm1.FormCreate(Sender: TObject);
var
  iLoop: Integer;         // general loop counter
begin
  {create the logical palette}
  SetThePalette;

  {retrieve the current system palette use...}
  GetSystemPaletteUse(Form1.Canvas.Handle);

  {...and display it}
  ListBox1.Items.Add('System Palette State:');
  case GetSystemPaletteUse(Form1.Canvas.Handle) of
    SYSPAL_NOSTATIC: ListBox1.Items.Add('   No static colors');
    SYSPAL_STATIC:   ListBox1.Items.Add('   Static colors');
    SYSPAL_ERROR:    ListBox1.Items.Add('   No color palette');
  end;

  {retrieve the current system palette entries}
  GetSystemPaletteEntries(Form1.Canvas.Handle, 0, 256, @SysPalette);

  {display the color settings for all 256 entries
   in the system palette}
  for iLoop := 0 to 255 do
  begin
    ListBox1.Items.Add('Palette slot: '+IntToStr(iLoop));
    ListBox1.Items.Add('     Red: '+IntToStr(SysPalette[iLoop].peRed));
```

```
       ListBox1.Items.Add('   Green: '+IntToStr(SysPalette[iLoop].peGreen));
       ListBox1.Items.Add('    Blue: '+IntToStr(SysPalette[iLoop].peBlue));

     case SysPalette[iLoop].peFlags of
       PC_EXPLICIT:   ListBox1.Items.Add('   Flags: PC_EXPLICIT');
       PC_NOCOLLAPSE: ListBox1.Items.Add('   Flags: PC_NOCOLLAPSE');
       PC_RESERVED:   ListBox1.Items.Add('   Flags: PC_RESERVED');
       else ListBox1.Items.Add('   Flags: NULL');
     end;
   end;
 end;

procedure TForm1.FormPaint(Sender: TObject);
var
   iOutLoop, iInLoop: Integer;   // loop control variables
begin
   {select and realize the logical palette into Form1's device context}
   SelectPalette(Canvas.Handle, FormPalette, FALSE);
   RealizePalette(Canvas.Handle);

   {draw a series of rectangles to display the system palette}
   for iOutLoop := 0 to 15 do
     for iInLoop := 0 to 15 do
     begin
       Canvas.Brush.Color := PaletteIndex((iOutLoop*16)+iInLoop);
       Canvas.Rectangle((iInLoop*20)+15, (iOutLoop*20)+32,
                        (iInLoop*20)+35, (iOutLoop*20)+52);

     end;
 end;
```

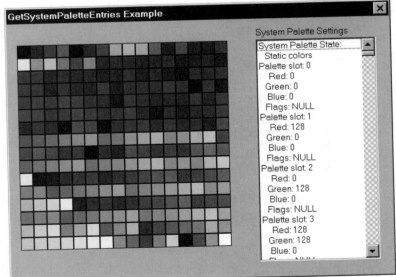

*Figure 7-11:
The currently
realized
system palette*

GetSystemPaletteUse   *Windows.Pas*

Syntax

```
GetSystemPaletteUse(
DC: HDC                   {a handle to a device context}
): UINT;                  {returns a flag indicating the system palette state}
```

Description

This function retrieves a value indicating the current static color usage state of the system palette associated with the specified device context.

Parameters

DC: A handle to a device context whose associated system palette state is to be retrieved. This must identify a device context that supports color palettes.

Return Value

If the function succeeds, it returns the current state of the system palette associated with the specified device context, and can be one value from Table 7-5. If the function fails, it returns zero. To get extended error information, call the GetLastError function.

See Also

GetSystemPaletteEntries, RealizePalette, SelectPalette, SetSystemPaletteUse

Example

Please see Listing 7-11 under GetSystemPaletteEntries.

Table 7-5: GetSystemPaletteUse Return Values

Value	Description
SYSPAL_NOSTATIC	The system palette contains only two static colors: black and white.
SYSPAL_STATIC	The system palette contains the default static colors. These colors will not change when a palette is realized. This is the default system palette state.
SYSPAL_ERROR	The specified device context is invalid or does not support color palettes.

PaletteIndex   *Windows.Pas*

Syntax

```
PaletteIndex(
i: Word                   {an index to a logical palette entry}
): COLORREF;              {returns a 32-bit color specifier}
```

Description

This function converts an explicit palette entry index into a 32-bit color specifier. This value can be used in functions expecting a color specifier to instruct the function to use the color found at the requested logical palette index. This function is equivalent to using the Boolean OR operator with an explicit palette index and the value $01000000 to specify a logical palette index.

Parameters

i: The index of the desired logical palette entry.

Return Value

If the function succeeds, it returns a 32-bit color specifier indicating an index into the currently realized logical palette; otherwise it returns zero.

See Also

CreatePalette, PaletteRGB, RGB

Example

Please see Listing 7-11 under GetSystemPaletteEntries.

PaletteRGB   *Windows.Pas*

Syntax

```
PaletteRGB(
  r: Byte;          {red color intensity}
  g: Byte;          {green color intensity}
  b: Byte           {blue color intensity}
): COLORREF;        {returns a 32-bit color specifier}
```

Description

This function returns a 32-bit color specifier containing the closest matching color for the requested color from the currently realized logical palette. This number contains a $02 in the high-order byte, and the red, green, and blue values in the three low-order bytes from the closest matching logical palette color entry. This function is equivalent to the GetNearestColor function.

Parameters

r: Specifies the red color intensity. This must be a value between 0 and 255.

g: Specifies the green color intensity. This must be a value between 0 and 255.

b: Specifies the blue color intensity. This must be a value between 0 and 255.

Return Value

If the function succeeds, it returns a 32-bit color specifier for the closest matching color from the currently realized logical palette; otherwise it returns zero.

See Also

CreatePalette, PaletteIndex, RGB

Example

Listing 7-12: Finding the Closest Matching Color

```
procedure TForm1.ScrollBar1Change(Sender: TObject);
begin
  {color the shape with the specified color, dithered}
  Shape1.Brush.Color := RGB(ScrollBar1.Position, ScrollBar2.Position,
                            ScrollBar3.Position);

  {color the shape with the color in the current palette that is the
   closest match to the requested color}
  Shape2.Brush.Color := PaletteRGB(ScrollBar1.Position, ScrollBar2.Position,
                                   ScrollBar3.Position);
end;
```

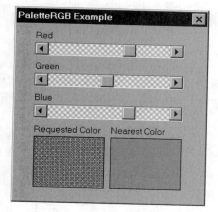

*Figure 7-12:
Found a color
match*

RealizePalette   *Windows.Pas*

Syntax

```
RealizePalette(
DC: HDC                    {a handle to a device context}
): UINT;                   {returns the number of palette entries realized}
```

Description

This function maps the palette entries from the logical palette associated with the specified device context into the system palette of the device associated with the device context. If the DC parameter identifies a memory device context, the logical palette is mapped into the color palette of the bitmap selected into the device context. If the DC parameter identifies a display device context, the logical palette is mapped into the physical palette of the device. A logical palette must be associated with the specified device context by using the SelectPalette function before calling RealizePalette.

The color matching process that takes place when RealizePalette is called depends on whether the device context's palette is a foreground or background palette. The palette state is determined when the SelectPalette function is called. If the palette is a background palette, the logical palette's entries are mapped to the closest matching entries already in the system palette, and no system palette entries are replaced. This is the default for applications running in the background. If the palette is a foreground palette, the logical palette's entries are still mapped to the closest matching entries already in the system palette. If an exact match is found, that logical palette entry is mapped to the matching system palette entry. However, if an exact match is not found, the first unused entry in the system palette is set to the color values of the specific logical palette entry. This can be affected by the peFlags value of the palette entry. See the CreatePalette function for more details.

Parameters

DC: A handle to a device context whose associated logical palette is mapped to the system palette of the device that the device context represents.

Return Value

If the function succeeds, it returns the number of logical palette entries that were mapped to the system palette of the specified device context. If the function fails, it returns GDI_ERROR. To get extended error information, call the GetLastError function.

See Also

CreatePalette, SelectPalette

Example

Please see Listing 7-4 under CreatePalette, and many other examples throughout this chapter.

ResizePalette   *Windows.Pas*

Syntax

```
ResizePalette(
p1: HPALETTE;              {a handle to the logical palette to be resized}
p2: UINT                   {the new number of logical palette entries}
): BOOL;                   {returns TRUE or FALSE}
```

Description

This function increases or decreases the number of palette entries in the specified logical palette. If a logical palette is increased in size, the new palette entries are initialized to black and their peFlags member is set to zero.

Parameters

p1: A handle to the logical palette whose palette entry count is being modified.

p2: The new number of palette entries the logical palette will contain.

Return Value

If the function succeeds, it returns TRUE; otherwise it returns FALSE. To get extended error information, call the GetLastError function.

See Also

CreatePalette, RealizePalette, SelectPalette

Example

Listing 7-13: Resizing a Palette

```
{Whoops! Delphi incorrectly imports the GetSystemPaletteEntries function.
 Here's the correct declaration that gives all of the functionality available
 with this API function}
function GetSystemPaletteEntries(DC: HDC; StartIndex, NumEntries: UINT;
                                PaletteEntries: Pointer): UINT; stdcall;

var
  Form1: TForm1;
  FormPalette: HPALETTE;            // a handle to a logical palette

implementation

{link in the GetSystemPaletteEntries function}
function GetSystemPaletteEntries; external gdi32 name 'GetSystemPaletteEntries';

function TForm1.GetPalette: HPALETTE;
begin
  {when something requests the palette of the form,
   pass it back the new logical palette}
  Result := FormPalette;
end;

procedure TForm1.FormCreate(Sender: TObject);
var
  ThePalette: PLogPalette;    // a logical palette definition structure
  iLoop: Integer;             // general loop counter
begin
  {get enough memory to hold the colors in the first 10 system
   palette slots, plus 22 of our own. this memory is temporary,
   and is no longer needed once the palette is created.}
```

```
    GetMem(ThePalette, SizeOf(TLogPalette)+32*SizeOf(TPaletteEntry));

    {initialize the palette version number}
    ThePalette^.palVersion := $300;

    {we will have a total of 32 entries in our palette}
    ThePalette^.palNumEntries := 32;

    {get the first 10 system palette entries}
    GetSystemPaletteEntries(Form1.Canvas.Handle, 0, 10,
                            @(ThePalette^.palPalEntry));

    {we only want 22 new palette entries, and we want them to start
     immediately after the first 10 system palette entries. by
     retrieving the first 10 system palette entries, when we realize
     our new palette, the first 10 logical palette entries will be
     mapped to the first 10 system palette entries, and our
     palette entries will follow}
    for iLoop := 0 to 21 do
    begin
      {create a gradient red palette}
      ThePalette^.palPalEntry[iLoop+10].peRed   := 255-((255 div 32)*iLoop);
      ThePalette^.palPalEntry[iLoop+10].peGreen := 0;
      ThePalette^.palPalEntry[iLoop+10].peBlue  := 0;
      {do not match this palette entry to any other palette entry}
      ThePalette^.palPalEntry[iLoop+10].peFlags := PC_NOCOLLAPSE;
    end;

    {create the palette}
    FormPalette := CreatePalette(ThePalette^);

    {free the temporary memory}
    FreeMem(ThePalette, SizeOf(TLogPalette)+42*SizeOf(TPaletteEntry));
end;

procedure TForm1.FormPaint(Sender: TObject);
var
  OldPalette: HPALETTE;      // a handle to the previous palette
  iLoop: Integer;            // general loop control variable
begin
  {select our new logical palette into the device context}
  OldPalette := SelectPalette(Canvas.Handle, FormPalette, FALSE);

  {map our logical palette into the system palette}
  RealizePalette(Canvas.Handle);

  {display a red gradient}
  for iLoop := 0 to 31 do
  begin
    Canvas.Brush.Color := $01000000 or iLoop+10;
    Canvas.FillRect(Rect(10, iLoop*10+16, 260, (iLoop*10)+36));
  end;

  {select the previous palette back into the device context}
  SelectPalette(Canvas.Handle, OldPalette, FALSE);
```

```
end;

procedure TForm1.Button1Click(Sender: TObject);
var
  PaletteEntries: array[0..9] of TPaletteEntry;   // holds palette entries
  iLoop: Integer;
begin
  ResizePalette(FormPalette, 42);

  {set up a green gradient}
  for iLoop := 0 to 9 do
  begin
    PaletteEntries[iLoop].peRed   := 0;
    PaletteEntries[iLoop].peGreen := 255-((255 div 32)*iLoop);
    PaletteEntries[iLoop].peBlue  := 0;
    PaletteEntries[iLoop].peFlags := PC_NOCOLLAPSE;
  end;

  {reset the logical palette to this green gradient}
  SetPaletteEntries(FormPalette, 32, 10, PaletteEntries);

  {redraw the form}
  Invalidate;
end;

procedure TForm1.FormDestroy(Sender: TObject);
begin
  {we no longer need the logical palette, so delete it}
  DeleteObject(FormPalette);
end;
```

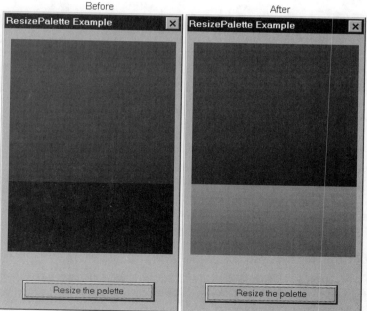

*Figure 7-13:
The resized
palette*

RGB   *Windows.Pas*

Syntax

```
RGB(
  r: Byte;                {red color intensity}
  g: Byte;                {green color intensity}
  b: Byte                 {blue color intensity}
  ): COLORREF;            {returns a 32-bit color specifier}
```

Description

This function returns a 32-bit color specifier containing a $00 in the high-order byte and the specified red, green, and blue values in the three low-order bytes. Windows displays this color by dithering the 20 system colors to achieve the closest possible match to the requested color.

Parameters

r: Specifies the red color intensity. This must be a value between 0 and 255.

g: Specifies the green color intensity. This must be a value between 0 and 255.

b: Specifies the blue color intensity. This must be a value between 0 and 255.

Return Value

If the function succeeds, it returns a 32-bit color specifier indicating the color should be displayed by dithering the 20 system colors to obtain a close match. If the function fails, it returns zero.

See Also

CreatePalette, PaletteIndex, PaletteRGB

Example

Please see Listing 7-8 under GetNearestColor and Listing 7-12 under PaletteRGB.

SelectPalette   *Windows.Pas*

Syntax

```
SelectPalette(
  DC: HDC;                        {a handle to a device context}
  Palette: HPALETTE;              {a handle to a logical color palette}
  ForceBackground: Bool           {palette mode flag}
  ): HPALETTE;                    {returns a handle to the previously selected palette}
```

Description

This function associates a logical palette with the specified device context. A logical palette can be associated with multiple device contexts, but a change to the logical palette affects all device contexts associated with it.

Parameters

DC: A handle to a device context which is to be associated with the specified logical palette.

Palette: A handle to a logical palette.

ForceBackground: Specifies whether the logical palette is a foreground or background palette. A value of TRUE indicates that the palette is a background palette. When the RealizePalette function is called, the logical palette's entries are mapped to the closest matching entries already in the system palette, and no system palette entries are replaced. This is the default for applications running in the background. A value of FALSE indicates that the palette is a foreground palette. When the RealizePalette function is called, the logical palette's entries are still mapped to the closest matching entries already in the system palette. If an exact match is found, that logical palette entry is mapped to the matching system palette entry. However, if an exact match is not found, the first unused entry in the system palette is set to the color values of the specific logical palette entry. This can be affected by the peFlags value of the palette entry. See the CreatePalette function for more details.

Return Value

If the function succeeds, it returns a handle to the device context's previously selected logical palette; otherwise it returns zero. To get extended error information, call the GetLastError function.

See Also

CreatePalette, RealizePalette

Example

Please see Listing 7-4 under CreatePalette, and many other examples throughout this chapter.

SetDIBColorTable	**Windows.Pas**

Syntax

```
SetDIBColorTable(
DC: HDC;                {a handle to a device context}
p2: UINT;               {the color palette index of the first entry to modify}
p3: UINT;               {the number of palette entries to modify}
var RGBQuadStructs      {a pointer to an array of TRGBQuad data structures}
): UINT;                {returns the number of color palette entries modified}
```

Description

This function replaces the specified range of color palette entries in the device-independent bitmap currently selected into the device context identified by the DC parameter with the palette entries pointed to by the RGBQuadStructs parameter. This function is useful only for DIBs that have a color format of 1, 4, or 8 bits per pixel, as DIBs with color formats greater than 8 bits per pixel do not contain a color palette.

Parameters

DC: A handle to a device context. The DIB whose color palette entries are to be modified must be selected into this device context.

p2: Specifies the zero-based index of the first entry in the DIB's color palette to be modified.

p3: Specifies the number of palette entries in the DIB to modify.

RGBQuadStructs: A pointer to an array of TRGBQuad structures describing the color values replacing the specified DIB's palette entries. This array must hold at least the number of TRGBQuad structures as the p3 parameter indicates. The TRGBQuad structure is defined as:

```
TRGBQuad = packed record
     rgbBlue: Byte;          {blue color intensity}
     rgbGreen: Byte;         {green color intensity}
     rgbRed: Byte;           {red color intensity}
     rgbReserved: Byte;      {reserved value}
end;
```

Please see the CreateDIBSection function for a description of this data structure.

Return Value

If the function succeeds, it returns the number of color palette entries replaced in the device-independent bitmap; otherwise it returns zero. To get extended error information, call the GetLastError function.

See Also

CreateDIBSection, CreatePalette, GetDIBColorTable

Example

Listing 7-14: Modifying a Device-Independent Bitmap's Color Table

```
procedure TForm1.Button1Click(Sender: TObject);
var
  Dib: TBitmap;                              // holds the device-independent bitmap
  NewColors: array[0..63] of TRGBQuad;       // holds the new color table for the DIB
  OffscreenDC: HDC;                          // a handle to an offscreen DC
  OldBitmap: HBITMAP;                        // a handle to the previous DC bitmap
  iLoop: Integer;                            // a general loop counter
begin
  {Delphi 3's TBitmap object now encapsulates a DIB, so create
   a bitmap and load in a test bitmap image}
  Dib := TBitmap.Create;
  Dib.LoadFromFile('Gradient.bmp');
```

```
{create a green gradient in the NewColors array}
for iLoop := 0 to 63 do
begin
  NewColors[iLoop].rgbBlue := 0;
  NewColors[iLoop].rgbGreen := (256 div 64)*iLoop;
  NewColors[iLoop].rgbRed := 0;
  NewColors[iLoop].rgbReserved := 0;
end;

{create an offscreen device context compatible with the display}
OffscreenDC := CreateCompatibleDC(0);

{select the DIB into this device context}
OldBitmap := SelectObject(OffscreenDC, Dib.Handle);

{replace its color table with the new green gradient colors}
SetDIBColorTable(OffscreenDC, 0, 64, NewColors);

{select the previous bitmap back into the offscreen DC}
SelectObject(OffscreenDC, OldBitmap);

{the offscreen DC is no longer needed, so delete it}
DeleteDC(OffscreenDC);

{the DIB's color table has now been modified, so save it to disk}
Dib.SaveToFile('NewGrad.bmp');
Dib.Free;

{load and display the DIB with its new color table}
Image1.Picture.Bitmap.LoadFromFile('NewGrad.bmp');
Label1.Caption := 'After';
end;
```

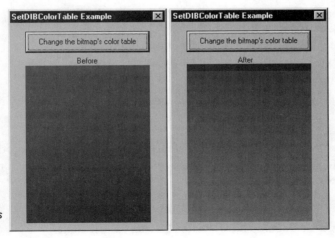

Figure 7-14:
This DIB's
color table has
been modified

SetPaletteEntries Windows.Pas

Syntax

```
SetPaletteEntries(
Palette: HPALETTE;          {a handle to a logical palette}
StartIndex: UINT;           {the starting palette index}
NumEntries: UINT;           {the number of palette entries to replace}
var PaletteEntries          {a pointer to an array of TPaletteEntry structures}
): UINT;                    {returns the number of palette entries replaced}
```

Description

This function replaces a range of color palette entries in the specified logical palette with the values in the TPaletteEntry array pointed to by the PaletteEntries parameter. Once the palette entries have been replaced, the RealizePalette function must be called for the changes to take effect.

Parameters

Palette: A handle to the logical palette whose palette entries are to be replaced.

StartIndex: The zero-based index of the first entry to replace in the logical palette.

NumEntries: Specifies the number of entries to replace.

PaletteEntries: A pointer to an array of TPaletteEntry structures describing the color values replacing the specified logical palette's entries. This array must hold at least the number of TPaletteEntry structures as the NumEntries parameter indicates. The TPaletteEntry structure is defined as:

```
TPaletteEntry = packed record
      peRed: Byte;            {the red color intensity}
      peGreen: Byte;          {the green color intensity}
      peBlue: Byte;           {the blue color intensity}
      peFlags: Byte;          {palette entry usage flags}
end;
```

Please see the CreatePalette function for a description of this data structure.

Return Value

If the function succeeds, it returns the number of palette entries replaced in the specified logical palette; otherwise it returns zero. To get extended error information, call the GetLastError function.

See Also

CreatePalette, GetPaletteEntries, RealizePalette, SelectPalette

Example

Please see Listing 7-4 under CreatePalette.

7

Chapter

SetSysColors   *Windows.Pas*

Syntax

SetSysColors(
cElements: Integer;   {the number of display elements to change}
const lpaElements;   {a pointer to an array of display element values}
const lpaRgbValues   {a pointer to an array of RGB values}
): BOOL;   {returns TRUE or FALSE}

Description

This function replaces the RGB color value of the display elements in the array pointed to by the lpaElements parameter with the 32-bit explicit RGB color values in the array pointed to by the lpaRgbValues parameter. A display element identifies various parts of a window, and its color is associated with one of the twenty static system-defined colors. When the color of a display element is changed, its associated static system color is also changed. The arrays pointed to by the lpaElements and lpaRgbValues parameters should contain the same number of entries. This function causes a WM_SYSCOLORCHANGE message to be sent to all windows informing them of the change, and Windows repaints the affected portions of the windows appropriately. These new system colors are in effect for the current Windows session only, and will be restored to their previous settings when Windows is rebooted.

Parameters

cElements: Specifies the number of display elements in the array pointed to by the lpaElements parameter.

lpaElements: A pointer to an array of integers. Each element in the array identifies a display element whose color is to be changed, and contains one of the display element flags from Table 7-6.

lpaRgbValues: A pointer to an array of long integers. Each element in this array corresponds to an element in the lpaElements array at the same index, and contains the new 32-bit explicit RGB color value for this corresponding display element.

Return Value

If the function succeeds, it returns TRUE; otherwise it returns FALSE. To get extended error information, call the GetLastError function.

See Also

GetBValue, GetGValue, GetRValue, GetSysColor, GetSystemPaletteEntries, PaletteRGB, RGB

Example

Please see Listing 7-10 under GetSysColor.

Table 7-6: SetSysColors lpaElements Values

Value	Description
COLOR_3DDKSHADOW	The dark shadow color for three-dimensional display elements.
COLOR_3DLIGHT	The lighted edge color for three-dimensional display elements.
COLOR_ACTIVEBORDER	The active window border color.
COLOR_ACTIVECAPTION	The active window caption color.
COLOR_APPWORKSPACE	The background color used in multiple document interface applications.
COLOR_BACKGROUND	The desktop color.
COLOR_BTNFACE	The color of pushbutton faces.
COLOR_BTNHIGHLIGHT	The color of a highlighted pushbutton.
COLOR_BTNSHADOW	The shaded edge color on pushbuttons.
COLOR_BTNTEXT	The text color on pushbuttons.
COLOR_CAPTIONTEXT	The text color used in caption, size box, and scroll bar arrow box controls.
COLOR_GRAYTEXT	The color of disabled text. This will be set to zero if the display driver cannot support solid gray.
COLOR_HIGHLIGHT	The color used for selected items in a control.
COLOR_HIGHLIGHTTEXT	The color used for the text of selected items in a control.
COLOR_INACTIVEBORDER	The inactive window border color.
COLOR_INACTIVECAPTION	The inactive window caption color.
COLOR_INACTIVECAPTIONTEXT	The text color in an inactive caption bar.
COLOR_INFOBK	The background color for tooltip controls.
COLOR_INFOTEXT	The text color for tooltip controls.
COLOR_MENU	The menu background color.
COLOR_MENUTEXT	The text color used in menus.
COLOR_SCROLLBAR	The scroll bar "gray" area color.
COLOR_WINDOW	The window background color.
COLOR_WINDOWFRAME	The window frame color.
COLOR_WINDOWTEXT	The color of text used in a window.

SetSystemPaletteUse   Windows.Pas

Syntax

```
SetSystemPaletteUse(
DC: HDC                {a handle to a device context}
p2: UINT               {a system palette usage flag}
```

): UINT;   {returns the previous system palette usage flag}

Description

This function sets the static color usage state of the system palette associated with the specified device context. By default, the system contains twenty static colors that will not change when a logical palette is realized.

Parameters

DC: A handle to a device context whose associated system palette state is to be modified. This must identify a device context that supports color palettes.

p2: A flag specifying the new static color state for the system palette. This parameter can be one value from Table 7-7.

Return Value

If the function succeeds, it returns the previous system palette usage flag, and will be one value from Table 7-7. If the function fails, it returns SYSPAL_ERROR, indicating that the specified device context was invalid or does not support a color palette. To get extended error information, call the GetLastError function.

See Also

GetSysColor, GetSystemPaletteUse, RealizePalette, SelectPalette, SetPaletteEntries, SetSysColors

Example

Listing 7-15: Using 254 Colors in the System Palette

```
{Whoops! Delphi incorrectly imports the GetSystemPaletteEntries function.
 Here's the correct declaration that gives all of the functionality available
 with this API function}
function GetSystemPaletteEntries(DC: HDC; StartIndex, NumEntries: UINT;
                                PaletteEntries: Pointer): UINT; stdcall;

var
  Form1: TForm1;
  SysPalette: array[0..255] of TPaletteEntry;  // holds a copy of the palette
  FormPalette: HPALETTE;                        // a handle to the new palette

implementation

{link in the GetSystemPaletteEntries function}
function GetSystemPaletteEntries; external gdi32 name 'GetSystemPaletteEntries';

procedure TForm1.SetThePalette;
var
  ThePalette: PLogPalette;  // a pointer to a logical palette description
  iLoop: Integer;           // general loop counter
  TheDC: HDC;               // a handle to a device context
begin
```

```
  {get enough memory to define a 256-color logical palette}
  GetMem(ThePalette, SizeOf(TLogPalette)+256*SizeOf(TPaletteEntry));

  {retrieve a handle to the form's device context}
  TheDC := GetDC(Form1.Handle);

  {retrieve the current system palette entries}
  GetSystemPaletteEntries(TheDC, 0, 256, @(ThePalette^.palPalEntry));

  {set the system palette to only use 2 static colors}
  SetSystemPaletteUse(TheDC, SYSPAL_NOSTATIC);

  {initialize the appropriate logical palette information}
  ThePalette^.palVersion := $300;
  ThePalette^.palNumEntries := 256;

  {create a 254-color red gradient palette}
  for iLoop := 0 to 253 do
  begin
    ThePalette^.palPalEntry[iLoop+1].peRed   := 255-iLoop;
    ThePalette^.palPalEntry[iLoop+1].peGreen := 0;
    ThePalette^.palPalEntry[iLoop+1].peBlue  := 0;
    ThePalette^.palPalEntry[iLoop+1].peFlags := 0;
  end;

  {create the red gradient palette}
  FormPalette := CreatePalette(ThePalette^);

  {select and realize the palette.  all but the first and last
   system colors will be replaced with the colors in the new
   logical palette.}
  SelectPalette(TheDC, FormPalette, FALSE);
  RealizePalette(TheDC);

  {free the logical palette description structure and the device context}
  FreeMem(ThePalette, SizeOf(TLogPalette)+256*SizeOf(TPaletteEntry));
  ReleaseDC(Form1.Handle, TheDC);
end;

procedure TForm1.FormCreate(Sender: TObject);
var
  iLoop: Integer;    // general loop counter
  TheDC: HDC;        // a handle to a device context
begin
  {create and realize the new palette}
  SetThePalette;

  {get a handle to the form's device context}
  TheDC := GetDC(Form1.Handle);

  {display the current static color usage state of the system palette}
  ListBox1.Items.Add('System Palette State:');
  case GetSystemPaletteUse(TheDC) of
     SYSPAL_NOSTATIC: ListBox1.Items.Add('   No static colors');
     SYSPAL_STATIC:   ListBox1.Items.Add('   Static colors');
```

```
          SYSPAL_ERROR:     ListBox1.Items.Add('   No color palette');
     end;

   {retrieve the system palette entries}
   GetSystemPaletteEntries(TheDC, 0, 256, @SysPalette);

   {display the color values of the system palette}
   for iLoop := 0 to 255 do
   begin
     ListBox1.Items.Add('Palette slot: '+IntToStr(iLoop));
     ListBox1.Items.Add('      Red: '+IntToStr(SysPalette[iLoop].peRed));
     ListBox1.Items.Add('    Green: '+IntToStr(SysPalette[iLoop].peGreen));
     ListBox1.Items.Add('     Blue: '+IntToStr(SysPalette[iLoop].peBlue));

     case SysPalette[iLoop].peFlags of
       PC_EXPLICIT:    ListBox1.Items.Add('   Flags: PC_EXPLICIT');
       PC_NOCOLLAPSE:  ListBox1.Items.Add('   Flags: PC_NOCOLLAPSE');
       PC_RESERVED:    ListBox1.Items.Add('   Flags: PC_RESERVED');
       else ListBox1.Items.Add('   Flags: NULL');
     end;
   end;

   {delete the device context handle}
   ReleaseDC(Form1.Handle, TheDC);
end;

procedure TForm1.FormPaint(Sender: TObject);
var
   iOutLoop, iInLoop: Integer;    // general loop counters
   TheDC: HDC;                    // a handle to a device context
   OldBrush, NewBrush: HBRUSH;    // handles to brushes
begin
   {get a handle to the form's device context}
   TheDC := GetDC(Form1.Handle);

   {select and realize the new logical palette}
   SelectPalette(TheDC, FormPalette, FALSE);
   RealizePalette(TheDC);

   {draw a grid of rectangles displaying the current logical palette,
    which is an exact duplicate of the system palette}
   for iOutLoop := 0 to 15 do
     for iInLoop := 0 to 15 do
     begin
       {use explicit palette indices}
       NewBrush := CreateSolidBrush($01000000 or (iOutLoop*16)+iInLoop);
       OldBrush := SelectObject(TheDC, NewBrush);
       Rectangle(TheDC, (iInLoop*20)+15, (iOutLoop*20)+32,
                 (iInLoop*20)+35, (iOutLoop*20)+52);
       SelectObject(TheDC, OldBrush);
       DeleteObject(NewBrush);
     end;

   {delete the device context handle}
   ReleaseDC(Form1.Handle, TheDC);
```

```
end;

procedure TForm1.FormDestroy(Sender: TObject);
var
  TheDC: HDC;     // a handle to a device context
begin
  {reset the static color usage state to the default of 20 static colors}
  TheDC := GetDC(Form1.Handle);
  SetSystemPaletteUse(TheDC, SYSPAL_STATIC);
  ReleaseDC(Form1.Handle, TheDC);

  {delete the logical palette}
  DeleteObject(FormPalette);
end;
```

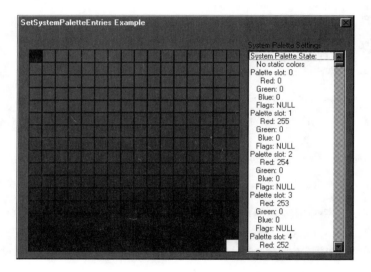

Figure 7-15:
An all-red
palette

Table 7-7: SetSystemPaletteUse p2 Values

Value	Description
SYSPAL_NOSTATIC	The system palette contains only two static colors: black and white.
SYSPAL_STATIC	The system palette contains the default static colors. These colors will not change when a palette is realized. This is the default system palette state.

Chapter 8

Text Output Functions

Drawing text to the screen is the most common graphical function performed by Windows in almost any application. As such, the API functions for manipulating and displaying text are very numerous and robust. Although Delphi encapsulates some of the text output API functions, the Delphi developer can dramatically extend the textual drawing capabilities of an application by utilizing the functions described in this chapter.

Fonts

Currently, Windows supports three types of fonts: raster, vector, and True Type. The differences between font types lie in the method by which the font's glyphs define the shape of a character. A glyph for a raster font is a bitmap of a specific size containing an image for each individual character. Vector fonts store their glyphs as a series of endpoints used to create line segments defining the outline of the character. True Type font glyphs are stored as a series of lines, curves, and hints that are used to draw the character outline. Due to the fact that raster fonts store their glyphs as bitmaps, raster fonts generally lose a lot of resolution when scaled. Vector fonts can generally be scaled up or down, but will start losing resolution when scaled to a certain degree past their original size, and are slow to draw. However, True Type fonts can be drawn relatively fast because the GDI subsystem is optimized for drawing them. In addition, the hints stored in True Type font glyph definitions provide scaling correction for the curves and lines of the character outline, allowing True Type fonts to be scaled to any size with no loss of resolution.

Font Families

Windows categorizes all fonts into five families. A font family is a collection of fonts sharing similar stroke widths and serif attributes. When considering a choice of font, font families allow the developer to indicate the general style desired, leaving the actual font selection to Windows. For example, using the appropriate functions and specifying only a font family, the developer can enumerate all symbol fonts installed on the system. Font families also allow the developer to create a logical font based on only specific characteristics, allowing Windows to select the most appropriate font from the specified font family based on those characteristics.

The five font family categories defined by Windows are:

Table 8-1: Font Families

Family Name	Constant	Description
Decorative	FF_DECORATIVE	Indicates a novelty or decorative font, such as Old English.
Modern	FF_MODERN	Indicates a monospaced font with consistent stroke widths, with or without serifs, such as Courier New.
Roman	FF_ROMAN	Indicates a proportional font with variable stroke widths, containing serifs, such as Times New Roman.
Script	FF_SCRIPT	Indicates a font resembling handwriting, such as Brush Script.
Swiss	FF_SWISS	Indicates a proportional font with variable stroke widths, without serifs, such as Arial.

Character Sets

By definition, a font defines the image for each individual character within a collection of characters. This collection of characters is called a character set. Each character set contains the symbols, numbers, punctuation marks, letters, and other printable or displayable images of a written language, with each character identified by a number.

There are five major character sets: Windows, Unicode, OEM, Symbol, and vendor specific. The Windows character set is equivalent to the ANSI character set. The Unicode character set is used for Eastern languages that contain thousands of symbols in their alphabet, and currently is the only character set that uses two bytes to identify a single character. The OEM character set is generally equivalent to the Windows character set except that it usually contains characters at the upper and lower ranges of the available character space that can only be displayed in a full-screen DOS session. The Symbol character set contains characters useful in representing mathematical or scientific equations, or graphical characters used for illustration. Vendor-specific character sets usually provide characters that are not available under the other character sets, and are most likely to be implemented at the printer or output device level.

In many cases, a font will define a default character. When a string contains a character that is not defined in the character set of a device context's selected font, the default character is substituted for the offending character when the text is displayed. Most True Type fonts define the default character as an unfilled rectangle (" □ ").

For purposes of line breaks and justification, most fonts define a break character. The break character identifies the character that is most commonly used to separate words in a line of text. Most fonts using the Windows character set define the break character as the space (" ") character.

Character Dimensions

Font sizes are typically measured in units called points. One point equals .013837 of an inch, commonly approximated to 1/72 of an inch. Note that a logical inch in Windows is approximately 30 to 40 percent larger than a physical inch in order to facilitate more legible fonts on the screen.

A character glyph image is defined by specific dimensions as illustrated by Figure 8-1. The baseline of a glyph is an imaginary line that defines the "base" upon which a character stands. The descent is the space below the baseline containing the descenders of certain characters such as "g" and "y." Internal leading defines space above the character where accent and diacritical marks reside. External leading actually lies outside of the glyph image; it will never contain glyph image data and is used solely for extra vertical spacing between lines. The ascent is defined as the distance from the baseline to the top of the internal leading space. The height is the sum of the ascent and the descent, and defines the total vertical space that can be occupied by glyph image data. These character dimensions can be retrieved by calling the GetOutlineTextMetrics or GetTextMetrics functions. The measurements retrieved by these functions will be in logical units, so their actual value is dependent upon the current mapping mode of the device context specified in the called function.

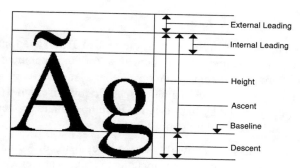

Figure 8-1:
The
dimensions of
a glyph

The Windows Font Table

Windows stores a reference to all nondevice fonts in an internal array known as the font table. Any font in this internal table is available for use by any Windows application. An application can programmatically add a font resource to this internal table by calling the AddFontResource function. Once this function has completed successfully, the application installing the font should inform all other applications of the change to the font table by sending the WM_FONTCHANGE message with the SendMessage function, specifying HWND_BROADCAST as the value of the hWnd parameter. When the application has terminated, or the font is no longer needed, it should be removed by a call to the RemoveFontResource function. Note that the font will not actually be removed from the internal font tables until all device contexts have unselected the font, if the font had been selected into the device context prior to the call to RemoveFontResource.

The AddFontResource function only installs the font to the internal font table for the duration of the installing application, or until the font is completely released as described above. In previous versions of Windows, permanently installing a font required an application to modify the Fonts section of the Win.ini file. Under Windows 95 and NT 4.0, an application can permanently install a font by simply copying the font file into the Fonts directory under the Windows directory.

When an application calls the CreateFont or CreateFontIndirect functions, a new font is not actually created. These functions return a handle to a logical font definition which is used by the Windows font mapper to select an appropriate physical font from the Windows font table. The Windows font mapper takes the desired font characteristics defined by the logical font and uses an internal algorithm to compare them with the characteristics of physical fonts currently installed on the system. This font mapping algorithm takes place when the logical font is selected into a device context by a call to the SelectObject function, and results in a selection of the font that most closely matches the desired characteristics. Subsequently, the selected font returned by the font mapper may not exactly match the requested font.

Font Embedding

Most advanced word processors offer the ability to embed True Type fonts into a document. Embedding a True Type font into a document allows the document to be viewed or edited by the word processing application on another system in its original appearance if the destination system does not have the specific font installed. However, as fonts are owned and copyrighted by their original developer, there are certain caveats that must be followed when embedding a font.

The developer of the font may not allow the font to be embedded. A font may allow embedding, but in a read-only context. If a document contains any embedded read-only fonts, the document may be viewed or printed, but the document itself must be read-only and may not be modified, nor can the font be unembedded and installed permanently into the system. Some fonts may be licensed as read-write, indicating that the font can be embedded into a document and permanently installed on the destination system. An application can determine the embedding status of a font by using the GetOutlineTextMetrics function. In any event, unless specific permission is granted from the font developer, fonts can only be embedded in a document and may not be embedded within an application, nor can an application be distributed with documents containing embedded fonts.

To embed a font within a document, the application must retrieve the data for the entire font file by calling the GetFontData function, setting the p2 and p3 parameters to zero. The font data is then written to the output file along with the text of the document in the file format determined by the application. Typically, applications use a file format that contains the name of each font embedded within the document and an indication of read-only or read-write licensing. Note that if a read-only font is embedded in a document, it must be encrypted, although the encryption algorithm does not need to be very complex.

When the application opens a document that contains an embedded font, it must first determine if the font allows read-only embedding or read-write embedding. The font data is then extracted from the document file and written to disk using file manipulation functions such as CreateFile and WriteFile. If the font is a read-write font, it can be directly written out to a file with a TTF extension in the Fonts subdirectory under the Windows directory to permanently install the font to the system. If the font is read-only, it must be unencrypted and written out to a hidden file. This hidden file should not have a TTF extension. Once the read-only font is extracted and written to disk, it can be installed to the internal Windows font table using the CreateScalableFontResource and AddFontResource functions, specifying a value of one for the p1 parameter of the CreateScalableFontResource function to indicate a read-only font. Note that read-only fonts will not be identified by the EnumFontFamilies or EnumFontFamiliesEx functions. When the document containing the read-only embedded font is closed, the FOT file created by the CreateScalableFontResource function and the file created when extracting the read-only font must be deleted, and the font must be removed from the Windows font table by calling the RemoveFontResource function.

The following example demonstrates embedding a True Type font into a text document. The document is written to disk in a proprietary format. Note that checks for read-only licensing have been omitted for the sake of code clarity.

Listing 8-1: Embedding True Type Fonts into a Document

```
{==============================================================================
    The Ventilate font used in this example was generously donated by and is
    copyright © 1997 by Brian J. Bonislawsky - Astigmatic One Eye.  Used with
    permission.

    Astigmatic One Eye is a great source for shareware and freeware fonts of
    all types.  Check them out at http://www.comptechdev.com/cavop/aoe/

    Note that this example makes use of a document that already contains an
    embedded True Type font.
    ============================================================================}

procedure TForm1.Button1Click(Sender: TObject);
var
  SavedFile: THandle;      // holds a handle to the open file
  TextSize: LongInt;       // holds the size of the text in the memo
  TheText: PChar;          // holds the text in the memo
```

```
    BytesWritten: DWORD;      // holds the number of bytes written to the file
    FontData: Pointer;        // points to retrieved font data
    FontDataSize: Integer;    // holds the size of the font data
    MemoDC: HDC;              // a handle to a common device context
    OldFont: THandle;         // holds the previously selected font in the DC
begin
  {create the file that will contain the saved document and embedded font}
  SavedFile := CreateFile('ProprietaryFileFormat.PFF', GENERIC_WRITE, 0, NIL,
                          CREATE_ALWAYS, FILE_ATTRIBUTE_NORMAL or
                          FILE_FLAG_SEQUENTIAL_SCAN, 0);

  {retrieve the size of the text in the memo, adding one
   for the null terminator}
  TextSize := Length(Memo1.Text)+1;

  {retrieve enough memory to hold all of the text}
  GetMem(TheText, TextSize);

  {copy the text to a null-terminated text buffer}
  StrPCopy(TheText, Memo1.Text);

  {explicitly set the end of the text}
  TheText[TextSize] := #0;

  {our proprietary file format is such that the first four bytes of the file
   contain the number of bytes following that contain the text of the
   document.  After these 'text' bytes, the next four bytes indicate how many
   bytes following contain the embedded True Type font information.  therefore,
   we write out the first four bytes of the document as an integer containing
   the size of the document's text, and then write out that many indicated bytes
   containing the text of the document}
  WriteFile(SavedFile, TextSize, SizeOf(TextSize), BytesWritten, NIL);
  WriteFile(SavedFile, TheText^, TextSize, BytesWritten, NIL);

  {in order to get the font file data for embedding, the font must be selected
   into a device context.  we retrieve a device context for the memo, but since
   this returns a common DC with default settings, we must select the memo's
   font into the retrieved device context.}
  MemoDC := GetDC(Memo1.Handle);
  OldFont := SelectObject(MemoDC, Memo1.Font.Handle);

  {at this point, the selected font should be checked to see if it allows
   embedding.  if the font does not allow embedding, the document should
   simply be saved and the following code should be skipped.  if the font
   allows embedding in a read-only format, once the font data is retrieved,
   it should be encrypted before being written out to the document file}

  {retrieve the size of buffer required to hold the entire font file data}
  FontDataSize := GetFontData(MemoDC, 0, 0, NIL, 0);

  {allocate the required memory}
  GetMem(FontData, FontDataSize);
```

```
{retrieve the entire font file data}
GetFontData(MemoDC, 0, 0, FontData, FontDataSize);

{now, write out an integer indicating how many bytes following contain the
  font data, and then write out that many bytes containing the actual font
  data}
WriteFile(SavedFile, FontDataSize, SizeOf(FontDataSize), BytesWritten, NIL);
WriteFile(SavedFile, FontData^, FontDataSize, BytesWritten, NIL);

{select the original font back into the device context, and delete the DC}
SelectObject(MemoDC, OldFont);
ReleaseDC(Memo1.Handle, MemoDC);

{flush the file buffers to force the file to be written to disk}
FlushFileBuffers(SavedFile);

{close the file handle}
CloseHandle(SavedFile);

{the file has been saved, so free all allocated memory that
  is no longer needed}
FreeMem(TheText, TextSize);
FreeMem(FontData, FontDataSize);
end;

procedure TForm1.Button2Click(Sender: TObject);
var
  SavedFile: THandle;                  // holds a handle to the open file
  TextSize: LongInt;                   // holds the size of the text in the memo
  TheText: PChar;                      // holds the text in the memo
  BytesRead: DWORD;                    // the number of bytes read from the file
  BytesWritten: DWORD;                 // the number of bytes written to the file
  FontData: Pointer;                   // points to retrieved font data
  FontDataSize: Integer;               // holds the size of the font data
  NewFontFile: THandle;                // holds the font file handle
  CurDir: array[0..MAX_PATH] of char;  // holds the current directory path
begin
  {open the document containing the embedded font}
  SavedFile := CreateFile('ProprietaryFileFormat.PFF', GENERIC_READ, 0, NIL,
                    OPEN_EXISTING, FILE_ATTRIBUTE_NORMAL or
                    FILE_FLAG_SEQUENTIAL_SCAN, 0);

  {read in the number of bytes occupied by the text of the document}
  ReadFile(SavedFile, TextSize, SizeOf(TextSize), BytesRead, NIL);

  {allocate the required buffer size to hold the text of the document}
  GetMem(TheText, TextSize);

  {initialize the buffer to null characters}
  FillMemory(TheText, TextSize, 0);
```

8

Chapter

```
{explicitly set the file pointer to point past the first four bytes, so that
 reading begins at the start of the document text}
SetFilePointer(SavedFile, SizeOf(TextSize), nil, FILE_BEGIN);

{read in the indicated number of 'document text' bytes from the file}
ReadFile(SavedFile, TheText^, TextSize, BytesRead, NIL);

{explicitly set the file pointer past the document text. it should now be
 pointing to the integer indicating the size of the embedded font data}
SetFilePointer(SavedFile, SizeOf(TextSize)+TextSize, nil, FILE_BEGIN);

{read in the embedded font data size}
ReadFile(SavedFile, FontDataSize, SizeOf(FontData), BytesRead, NIL);

{retrieve enough memory to hold the font data}
GetMem(FontData, FontDataSize);

{explicitly set the file pointer to point past the four bytes containing the
 size of the font data. it should now be pointing to the start of the font
 data}
SetFilePointer(SavedFile, SizeOf(TextSize)+TextSize+SizeOf(FontData),
               nil, FILE_BEGIN);

{read the font data into the font data buffer}
ReadFile(SavedFile, FontData^, FontDataSize, BytesRead, NIL);

{we are done with the document file, so close it}
CloseHandle(SavedFile);

{at this point, the application should determine, based on the information
 stored in the document file, if the font is read-only or read-write. if it
 is read-write, it can be written directly to the Fonts directory under the
 Windows directory. if it is read-only, it should be written to a hidden
 file. in this example, we will write the font out as a regular TTF file
 in the application's directory.}

{create the file that will contain the font information}
NewFontFile := CreateFile('TempFont.TTF', GENERIC_WRITE, 0, NIL,
                          CREATE_ALWAYS, FILE_ATTRIBUTE_NORMAL or
                          FILE_FLAG_SEQUENTIAL_SCAN, 0);

{write the font data into the font file}
WriteFile(NewFontFile, FontData^, FontDataSize, BytesWritten, NIL);

{flush the file buffers to ensure that the file is written to disk}
FlushFileBuffers(NewFontFile);

{close the font file}
CloseHandle(NewFontFile);

{retrieve the current directory}
GetCurrentDirectory(MAX_PATH, @CurDir[0]);
```

```
    {since the font was written out as a regular TTF file, create font resource
     file, indicating that it is a read-write file}
    CreateScalableFontResource(0, PChar(CurDir+'\TempFont.fot'),
                               PChar(CurDir+'\TempFont.ttf'),
                               nil);

    {add the font to the internal font table}
    AddFontResource(PChar(CurDir+'\TempFont.fot'));

    {inform other applications that the font table has changed}
    SendMessage(HWND_BROADCAST, WM_FONTCHANGE, 0, 0);

    {assign the retrieved document text to the memo}
    Memo1.Text := Copy(string(TheText), 0, StrLen(TheText));

    {free the allocated text buffer}
    FreeMem(TheText, TextSize);

    {the installed font was the Ventilate font, so set the memo's
     font accordingly}
    Memo1.Font.Name := 'Ventilate';
    Memo1.Font.Size := 16;

    {free the buffer allocated to hold the font data}
    FreeMem(FontData, FontDataSize);

    {now that the font has been installed, enable the document save button}
    Button1.Enabled := TRUE;
  end;

procedure TForm1.FormDestroy(Sender: TObject);
var
  CurDir: array[0..MAX_PATH] of char; // holds the current directory
begin
  {retrieve the current directory}
  GetCurrentDirectory(MAX_PATH, @CurDir[0]);

  {remove the font from the internal font table}
  RemoveFontResource(PChar(CurDir+'\TempFont.fot'));

  {inform all applications of the change to the font table}
  SendMessage(HWND_BROADCAST, WM_FONTCHANGE, 0, 0);

  {the application (and the document) are being closed, so delete the font
   resource file and the font file from the hard disk as if this were a
   read-only font}
  DeleteFile(CurDir+'\TempFont.fot');
  DeleteFile(CurDir+'\TempFont.ttf');
end;
```

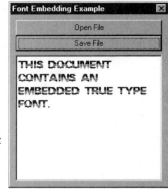

Figure 8-2:
This document
uses an
embedded
true type font.

Text Output Functions

The following text output functions are covered in this chapter:

Table 8-2: Text Output Functions

Function	Description
AddFontResource	Adds the font resource contained in the specified file to the internal Windows font table.
CreateFont	Creates a logical font.
CreateFontIndirect	Creates a logical font based on information specified in a data structure.
CreateScalableFontResource	Creates a font resource file from a True Type font file.
DrawText	Draws formatted text onto a device context within a specified rectangle.
DrawTextEx	Draws formatted text onto a device context within a specified rectangle according to specified margin widths.
EnumFontFamilies	Enumerates installed fonts.
EnumFontFamiliesEx	Enumerates installed fonts matching specified font characteristics.
GetCharABCWidths	Retrieves character widths and spacing for True Type fonts.
GetCharWidth	Retrieves character widths.
GetFontData	Retrieves True Type font file information.
GetGlyphOutline	Retrieves a bitmap or outline of a True Type character.
GetKerningPairs	Retrieves character kerning pairs.
GetOutlineTextMetrics	Retrieves text metrics for True Type fonts.
GetRasterizerCaps	Retrieves information concerning True Type font availability.

Function	Description
GetTabbedTextExtent	Retrieves the width and height of a character string containing tabs.
GetTextAlign	Retrieves text alignment.
GetTextCharacterExtra	Retrieves intercharacter spacing.
GetTextColor	Retrieves the color used when drawing text.
GetTextExtentExPoint	Retrieves the number of characters in a specified string that will fit within a specified space.
GetTextExtentPoint32	Retrieves the width and height of a specified string.
GetTextFace	Retrieves the name of a font selected into a device context.
GetTextMetrics	Retrieves text metrics for a font.
RemoveFontResource	Deletes a font resource from the internal Windows font table.
SetTextAlign	Sets text alignment.
SetTextCharacterExtra	Sets intercharacter spacing.
SetTextColor	Sets the color used when drawing text.
SetTextJustification	Sets text justification.
TabbedTextOut	Draws a string onto a device context, expanding tab characters.
TextOut	Draws text onto a device context.

8

Chapter

AddFontResource   Windows.Pas

Syntax

AddFontResource(
p1: PChar   {the font resource filename}
): Integer;   {returns the number of fonts added}

Description

This function adds the font resource contained in the specified font resource file to the internal system font tables, making the font available to all applications. If the font is successfully added to the internal tables, the application that added the font should inform all other applications of the change. This is accomplished by sending the WM_FONTCHANGE message with the SendMessage function, specifying HWND_BROADCAST as the value of the hWnd parameter. When the font is no longer needed, it must be removed from the internal system font tables by a call to the RemoveFontResource function.

Parameters

p1: A pointer to a null-terminated string containing the name of the font resource to add. The specified file can contain font resources (*.FON), a raw bitmapped font

(*.FNT), raw True Type font information (*.TTF), or a True Type font resource (*.FOT).

Return Value

If the function succeeds, it returns the number of fonts that were added to the internal system font tables; otherwise it returns zero. To get extended error information, call the GetLastError function.

See Also

CreateScalableFontResource, GetFontData, RemoveFontResource

Example

Please see Listing 8-4 under CreateScalableFontResource.

CreateFont   *Windows.Pas*

Syntax

```
CreateFont(
nHeight: Integer;              {the font height in logical units}
nWidth: Integer;              {the average character width in logical units}
nEscapement: Integer;              {the escapement vector angle}
nOrientation: Integer;              {the character baseline angle}
fnWeight: Integer;              {the bolding weight}
fdwItalic: DWORD;              {the italics flag}
fdwUnderline: DWORD;              {the underline flag}
fdwStrikeOut: DWORD;              {the strikeout flag}
fdwCharSet: DWORD;              {the character set}
fdwOutputPrecision: DWORD;              {the output precision flag}
fdwClipPrecision: DWORD;              {the clipping precision flags}
fdwQuality: DWORD;              {the output quality flag}
fdwPitchAndFamily: DWORD;              {the pitch and font family flags}
lpszFace: PChar              {the font typeface name}
): HFONT;              {returns a handle to the new font}
```

Description

This function creates a logical font matching the specified font attributes. This font can be selected into any device context that supports text output functions. When the font is no longer needed, it should be deleted by using the DeleteObject function.

Parameters

nHeight: Specifies the height of the character or character cells within the font. Character height is a measurement of the character cell height value minus the internal leading value. This value is expressed in logical units, and will be dependent on the current mapping mode. The Windows font mapper interprets the value of the nHeight parameter as described in Table 8-3, and will retrieve the largest font available up to the specified size. For the MM_TEXT mapping mode, use the following formula to express a font height for any specific point size:

```
nHeight := -MulDiv(PointSize, GetDeviceCaps(hDeviceContext, LOGPIXELSY), 72);
```

nWidth: Specifies the average width of characters within the font. This value is expressed in logical units, and will be dependent on the current mapping mode. If this parameter is set to zero, the Windows font mapper will choose an appropriate font based on the absolute values of the difference between the current device's aspect ratio and the digitized aspect ratio of all appropriate fonts.

nEscapement: Specifies the angle between the baseline of a line of text and the X axis, in tenths of a degree. Under Windows NT, if the graphics mode is set to GM_ADVANCED, the angle of a line of text and the angle of each character within that line of text can be set independently. If the graphics mode is set to GM_COMPATIBLE, the nEscapement parameter specifies the angle for both the line of text and the characters within that line of text, and the nEscapement and nOrientation parameters should be set to the same value. Under Windows 95, the nEscapement parameter always specifies the angle for both the line of text and the characters within that line of text, and the nEscapement and nOrientation parameters should be set to the same value.

nOrientation: Specifies the angle between the baseline of each individual character and the X axis, in tenths of a degree. Under Windows 95, the nEscapement parameter always specifies the angle for both the line of text and the characters within that line of text, and the nEscapement and nOrientation parameters should be set to the same value.

fnWeight: Specifies the boldness of the font. The value of this parameter can be in the range of 0 to 1000, or can be set to one value from Table 8-4. A weight of zero indicates the default boldness value for the specified font.

fdwItalic: Specifies the italics attribute for the font. If this parameter is set to TRUE, the font will be italicized.

fdwUnderline: Specifies the underlining attribute for the font. If this parameter is set to TRUE, the font will be underlined.

fdwStrikeOut: Specifies the strikeout attribute for the font. If this parameter is set to TRUE, the font will be struck out.

fdwCharSet: Specifies the character set which the Windows font mapper uses to choose an appropriate font, and can be set to one value from Table 8-5. The font typeface name specified in the lpszFace parameter must be a font that defines characters for the specified character set. If this parameter is set to DEFAULT_CHARSET, the font size and typeface name will be used to find an appropriate font. However, if the specified typeface name is not found, any font from any character set matching the specified values can be used, and can lead to unexpected results.

fdwOutputPrecision: Specifies how closely the resulting font must match the given height, width, character orientation, escapement, pitch, and font type values. This parameter can be set to one value from Table 8-6. Note that the OUT_DEVICE_PRECIS, OUT_RASTER_PRECIS, and OUT_TT_PRECIS flags control the Windows font mapper behavior when more then one font exists with the name specified by the lpszFace parameter.

fdwClipPrecision: Specifies how characters partially outside of the clipping region are drawn. This parameter can be set to one or more values from Table 8-7.

fdwQuality: Specifies how closely the Windows font mapper matches the specified font attributes with an actual font. This parameter can be set to one value from Table 8-8.

fdwPitchAndFamily: The font pitch and font family flags. This parameter can contain a combination of one value from the pitch flags table (Table 8-9) and one value from the font family flags table (Table 8-10). The values from these tables are combined by using the Boolean OR operator. The pitch describes how the width of individual character glyphs vary, and the family describes the general look and feel of the font. If the specified typeface name is unavailable, the function returns the most closest matching font from the specified font family.

lpszFace: A pointer to a null-terminated string containing the typeface name of the font. The font typeface name cannot exceed 32 characters in length, including the null terminator. Use the EnumFontFamilies function to retrieve a list of all installed font typeface names. If this parameter is NIL, the Windows font mapper will choose the first font from the specified font family matching the specified attributes.

Return Value

If the function succeeds, it returns a handle to the newly created logical font; otherwise it returns zero. To get extended error information, call the GetLastError function.

See Also

CreateFontIndirect, DeleteObject, SelectObject, EnumFontFamilies, EnumFontFamiliesEx

Example

Listing 8-2: Creating Various Fonts

```
procedure TForm1.FormPaint(Sender: TObject);
var
  NewFont, OldFont: HFont;     // holds the old and new fonts
begin
  {set the background mode for transparency}
  SetBkMode(Form1.Canvas.Handle, TRANSPARENT);

  {create a bold font}
  NewFont := CreateFont(-MulDiv(16, GetDeviceCaps(Form1.Canvas.Handle,
                        LOGPIXELSY), 72), 0, 0, 0, FW_BOLD, 0, 0, 0,
                        DEFAULT_CHARSET, OUT_TT_ONLY_PRECIS,
```

```
                              CLIP_DEFAULT_PRECIS, DEFAULT_QUALITY, DEFAULT_PITCH or
                              FF_DONTCARE, 'Arial');

{select the font into the form's device context}
OldFont := SelectObject(Form1.Canvas.Handle, NewFont);

{output a line of text}
TextOut(Form1.Canvas.Handle, 8, Label1.Top+Label1.Height, 'Delphi Rocks!',
        Length('Delphi Rocks!'));

{select the old font back into the device context and delete the new font}
SelectObject(Form1.Canvas.Handle, OldFont);
DeleteObject(NewFont);

{create a strikeout font}
NewFont := CreateFont(-MulDiv(16, GetDeviceCaps(Form1.Canvas.Handle,
                      LOGPIXELSY), 72), 0, 0, 0, FW_DONTCARE, 0, 0, 1,
                      DEFAULT_CHARSET, OUT_TT_ONLY_PRECIS,
                      CLIP_DEFAULT_PRECIS, DEFAULT_QUALITY, DEFAULT_PITCH or
                      FF_ROMAN, '');

{select the font into the form's device context}
OldFont := SelectObject(Form1.Canvas.Handle, NewFont);

{output a line of text}
TextOut(Form1.Canvas.Handle, 8, Label2.Top+Label2.Height, 'Delphi Rocks!',
        Length('Delphi Rocks!'));

{select the old font back into the device context and delete the new font}
SelectObject(Form1.Canvas.Handle, OldFont);
DeleteObject(NewFont);

{create an underlined font}
NewFont := CreateFont(-MulDiv(16, GetDeviceCaps(Form1.Canvas.Handle,
                      LOGPIXELSY), 72), 0, 0, 0, FW_DONTCARE, 0, 1, 0,
                      DEFAULT_CHARSET, OUT_TT_ONLY_PRECIS,
                      CLIP_DEFAULT_PRECIS, DEFAULT_QUALITY, DEFAULT_PITCH or
                      FF_DECORATIVE, '');

{select the font into the form's device context}
OldFont := SelectObject(Form1.Canvas.Handle, NewFont);

{output a line of text}
TextOut(Form1.Canvas.Handle, 8, Label3.Top+Label3.Height, 'Delphi Rocks!',
        Length('Delphi Rocks!'));

{select the old font back into the device context and delete the new font}
SelectObject(Form1.Canvas.Handle, OldFont);
DeleteObject(NewFont);

{create an italicized font}
NewFont := CreateFont(-MulDiv(16, GetDeviceCaps(Form1.Canvas.Handle,
                      LOGPIXELSY), 72), 0, 0, 0, FW_DONTCARE, 1, 0, 0,
                      DEFAULT_CHARSET, OUT_TT_ONLY_PRECIS,
                      CLIP_DEFAULT_PRECIS, DEFAULT_QUALITY, DEFAULT_PITCH or
```

8

Chapter

```
                            FF_SCRIPT, '');

  {select the font into the form's device context}
  OldFont := SelectObject(Form1.Canvas.Handle, NewFont);

  {output a line of text}
  TextOut(Form1.Canvas.Handle, 8, Label4.Top+Label4.Height, 'Delphi Rocks!',
          Length('Delphi Rocks!'));

  {select the old font back into the device context and delete the new font}
  SelectObject(Form1.Canvas.Handle, OldFont);
  DeleteObject(NewFont);
end;
```

*Figure 8-3:
Various fonts
created with
the
CreateFont
function*

Table 8-3: CreateFont nHeight Font Mapper Interpretation Values

Value	Description
nHeight>0	The font mapper converts the value of nHeight into device units, matching the result against the cell height of available fonts.
nHeight=0	The font mapper uses a default font height when searching for a matching font.
nHeight<0	The font mapper converts the value of nHeight into device units, matching the absolute value of the result against the character height of available fonts.

Table 8-4: CreateFont fnWeight Values

Value	Description
FW_DONTCARE	Uses the default bolding value (0).
FW_THIN	Extra thin font weight (100).
FW_EXTRALIGHT	Thin font weight (200).
FW_LIGHT	Below average bolding (300).
FW_NORMAL	Normal bolding (400).

Value	Description
FW_MEDIUM	Above average bolding (500).
FW_SEMIBOLD	Light bolding (600).
FW_BOLD	Bolded font (700).
FW_EXTRABOLD	Extra bolding (800).
FW_HEAVY	Very heavy bolding (900).

Table 8-5: CreateFont fdwCharSet Values

Value	Description
ANSI_CHARSET	The ANSI character set.
DEFAULT_CHARSET	The default character set.
SYMBOL_CHARSET	The symbol character set.
SHIFTJIS_CHARSET	The shiftjis character set.
GB2312_CHARSET	The GB2312 character set.
HANGEUL_CHARSET	The Korean character set.
CHINESEBIG5_CHARSET	The Chinese character set.
OEM_CHARSET	The original equipment manufacturer character set.
JOHAB_CHARSET	Windows 95 only: The Johab character set.
HEBREW_CHARSET	Windows 95 only: The Hebrew character set.
ARABIC_CHARSET	Windows 95 only: The Arabic character set.
GREEK_CHARSET	Windows 95 only: The Grecian character set.
TURKISH_CHARSET	Windows 95 only: The Turkish character set.
VIETNAMESE_CHARSET	Windows 95 only: The Vietnamese character set.
THAI_CHARSET	Windows 95 only: The Thai character set.
EASTEUROPE_CHARSET	Windows 95 only: The eastern Europe character set.
RUSSIAN_CHARSET	Windows 95 only: The Russian character set.
MAC_CHARSET	Windows 95 only: The Macintosh character set.
BALTIC_CHARSET	Windows 95 only: The Baltic character set.

Table 8-6: CreateFont fdwOutputPrecision Values

Value	Description
OUT_DEFAULT_PRECIS	The default font mapper behavior.
OUT_DEVICE_PRECIS	Chooses a device font when more than one font of the specified name exists.
OUT_OUTLINE_PRECIS	Windows NT only: Chooses a font from True Type and other vector-based fonts.
OUT_RASTER_PRECIS	Chooses a raster font when more than one font of the specified name exists.

8

Chapter

Value	Description
OUT_STROKE_PRECIS	Windows NT only: Not used by the font mapper. However, this flag is returned when True Type and other vector fonts are enumerated.
	Windows 95 only: Chooses a font from vector-based fonts.
OUT_TT_ONLY_PRECIS	Chooses a font only from True Type fonts. If no True Type fonts exist, the font mapper reverts to default behavior.
OUT_TT_PRECIS	Chooses a True Type font when more than one font of the specified name exists.

Table 8-7: CreateFont fdwClipPrecision Values

Value	Description
CLIP_DEFAULT_PRECIS	The default clipping behavior.
CLIP_STROKE_PRECIS	This flag is used only when enumerating fonts.
CLIP_EMBEDDED	This flag must be included when using a read-only embedded font.
CLIP_LH_ANGLES	Specifies that font rotation is dependent upon the coordinate system. If this flag is not specified, device fonts always rotate counterclockwise.

Table 8-8: CreateFont fdwQuality Values

Value	Description
DEFAULT_QUALITY	Uses the default font quality.
DRAFT_QUALITY	Raster font scaling is enabled, and bold, italic, underline, and strikeout fonts are fabricated as needed. Exact attribute matching is a higher priority than font quality.
PROOF_QUALITY	Raster font scaling is disabled, and the physical font closest to the specified size is chosen. Bold, italic, underline, and strikeout fonts are fabricated as needed. Font quality is a higher priority than exact attribute matching.

Table 8-9: CreateFont fdwPitchAndFamily Pitch Flags Values

Value	Description
DEFAULT_PITCH	The default font pitch is used.
FIXED_PITCH	The width of all character glyphs are equal.
VARIABLE_PITCH	The width of all character glyphs is dependent upon the individual glyph image.

Table 8-10: CreateFont fdwPitchAndFamily Font Family Flags Values

Value	Description
FF_DECORATIVE	Indicates a novelty or decorative font, such as Old English.
FF_DONTCARE	The general font style is unknown or unimportant.
FF_MODERN	Indicates a monospaced font with consistent stroke widths, with or without serifs, such as Courier New.
FF_ROMAN	Indicates a proportional font with variable stroke widths, containing serifs, such as Times New Roman.
FF_SCRIPT	Indicates a font resembling handwriting, such as Brush Script.
FF_SWISS	Indicates a proportional font with variable stroke widths, without serifs, such as Arial.

CreateFontIndirect   Windows.Pas

Syntax

```
CreateFontIndirect(
const p1: TLogFont          {a pointer to a logical font structure}
): HFONT;                   {returns a handle to the new font}
```

Description

This function creates a logical font matching the font attributes specified by the TLog-Font structure pointed to by the p1 parameter. This font can be selected into any device context that supports text output functions. When the font is no longer needed, it should be deleted by using the DeleteObject function.

Parameters

p1: A pointer to a TLogFont data structure describing the attributes of the desired font. The TLogFont structure is defined as:

```
TLogFont = packed record
    lfHeight: Longint;          {font height in logical units}
    lfWidth: Longint;           {the average character width}
    lfEscapement: Longint;      {the escapement vector angle}
    lfOrientation: Longint;     {the character baseline angle}
    lfWeight: Longint;          {the bolding weight}
    lfItalic: Byte;             {the italics flag}
    lfUnderline: Byte;          {the underline flag}
    lfStrikeOut: Byte;          {the strikeout flag}
    lfCharSet: Byte;            {the character set}
    lfOutPrecision: Byte;       {the output precision flag}
    lfClipPrecision: Byte;      {the clipping precision flags}
```

8

Chapter

```
lfQuality: Byte;                          {the output quality flag}
lfPitchAndFamily: Byte;                   {the pitch and family flags}
lfFaceName: array[0..LF_FACESIZE - 1]
of AnsiChar;                              {the font typeface name}
end;
```

lfHeight: Specifies the height of the character or character cells within the font. Character height is a measurement of the character cell height value minus the internal leading value. This value is expressed in logical units, and will be dependent on the current mapping mode. The Windows font mapper interprets the value of the lfHeight member as described in Table 8-11, and will retrieve the largest font available up to the specified size. For the MM_TEXT mapping mode, use the following formula to express a font height for any specific point size:

```
lfHeight := -MulDiv(PointSize, GetDeviceCaps(hDeviceContext, LOGPIXELSY), 72);
```

lfWidth: Specifies the average width of characters within the font. This value is expressed in logical units, and will be dependent on the current mapping mode. If this member is set to zero, the Windows font mapper will choose an appropriate font based on the absolute values of the difference between the current device's aspect ratio and the digitized aspect ratio of all appropriate fonts.

lfEscapement: Specifies the angle between the baseline of a line of text and the X axis, in tenths of a degree. Under Windows NT, if the graphics mode is set to GM_ADVANCED, the angle of a line of text and the angle of each character within that line of text can be set independently. If the graphics mode is set to GM_COMPATIBLE, the lfEscapement member specifies the angle for both the line of text and the characters within that line of text, and the lfEscapement and lfOrientation members should be set to the same value. Under Windows 95, the lfEscapement member always specifies the angle for both the line of text and the characters within that line of text, and the lfEscapement and lfOrientation members should be set to the same value.

lfOrientation: Specifies the angle between the baseline of each individual character and the X axis, in tenths of a degree. Under Windows 95, the lfEscapement member always specifies the angle for both the line of text and the characters within that line of text, and the lfEscapement and lfOrientation members should be set to the same value.

lfWeight: Specifies the boldness of the font. The value of this member can be in the range of 0 to 1000, or can be set to one value from Table 8-12. A weight of zero indicates the default boldness value for the specified font.

lfItalic: Specifies the italics attribute for the font. If this member is set to TRUE, the font will be italicized.

lfUnderline: Specifies the underlining attribute for the font. If this member is set to TRUE, the font will be underlined.

lfStrikeOut: Specifies the strikeout attribute for the font. If this member is set to TRUE, the font will be struck out.

lfCharSet: Specifies the character set which the Windows font mapper uses to choose an appropriate font, and can be set to one value from Table 8-13. The font typeface name specified in the lfFaceName member must be a font that defines characters for the specified character set. If this member is set to DEFAULT_CHARSET, the font size and typeface name will be used to find an appropriate font. However, if the specified typeface name is not found, any font from any character set matching the specified values can be used, and can lead to unexpected results.

lfOutPrecision: Specifies how closely the resulting font must match the given height, width, character orientation, escapement, pitch, and font type values. This member can be set to one value from Table 8-14. Note that the OUT_DEVICE_PRECIS, OUT_RASTER_PRECIS, and OUT_TT_PRECIS flags control the Windows font mapper behavior when more then one font exists with the name specified by the lfFaceName member.

lfClipPrecision: Specifies how characters partially outside of the clipping region are drawn. This member can be set to one or more values from Table 8-15.

lfQuality: Specifies how closely the Windows font mapper matches the specified font attributes with an actual font. This member can be set to one value from Table 8-16.

lfPitchAndFamily: The font pitch and font family flags. This member can contain a combination of one value from the pitch flags table (Table 8-17) and one value from the font family flags table (Table 8-18). The values from these tables are combined by using the Boolean OR operator. The pitch describes how the width of individual character glyphs vary, and the family describes the general look and feel of the font. If the specified typeface name is unavailable, the function returns the most closest matching font from the specified font family.

lfFaceName: A pointer to a null-terminated string containing the typeface name of the font. The font typeface name cannot exceed 32 characters in length, including the null terminator. Use the EnumFontFamilies function to retrieve a list of all installed font typeface names. If this member is NIL, the Windows font mapper will choose the first font from the specified font family matching the specified attributes.

Return Value

If the function succeeds, it returns a handle to the newly created logical font; otherwise it returns zero.

See Also

CreateFont, DeleteObject, EnumFontFamilies, EnumFontFamiliesEx, SelectObject

Example

Listing 8-3: Creating a Font Indirectly

```
procedure TForm1.FormPaint(Sender: TObject);
var
```

8

Chapter

```
  FontInfo: TLogFont;        // the logical font information
  NewFont, OldFont: HFont;   // holds the old and new fonts
begin
  {set the background mode for transparency}
  SetBkMode(Form1.Canvas.Handle, TRANSPARENT);

  {initialize the logical font information, setting the weight and escapement
   values to those specified by the trackbars.}
  with FontInfo do
  begin
    lfHeight := 24;
    lfWidth := 0;
    lfEscapement := TrackBar1.Position*10;
    lfOrientation := TrackBar1.Position*10;
    lfWeight := TrackBar2.Position;
    lfItalic := 0;
    lfUnderline := 0;
    lfStrikeOut := 0;
    lfFaceName := 'Arial';
  end;

  {create the new font}
  NewFont := CreateFontIndirect(FontInfo);

  {select the new font into the form's device context}
  OldFont := SelectObject(Form1.Canvas.Handle, NewFont);

  {output a string of rotated text}
  TextOut(Form1.Canvas.Handle, Form1.Width div 2, 140, 'Delphi Rocks!',
  Length('Delphi Rocks!'));

  {select the original font back into the device context,
   and delete the new one}
  SelectObject(Form1.Canvas.Handle, OldFont);
  DeleteObject(NewFont);
end;
```

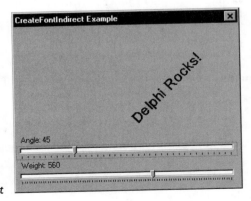

Figure 8-4:
A rotated font

Table 8-11: CreateFontIndirect pl.lfHeight Font Mapper Interpretation Values

Value	Description
lfHeight>0	The font mapper converts the value of nHeight into device units, matching the result against the cell height of available fonts.
lfHeight=0	The font mapper uses a default font height when searching for a matching font.
lfHeight<0	The font mapper converts the value of nHeight into device units, matching the absolute value of the result against the character height of available fonts.

Table 8-12: CreateFontIndirect pl.lfWeight Values

Value	Description
FW_DONTCARE	Uses the default bolding value (0).
FW_THIN	Extra thin font weight (100).
FW_EXTRALIGHT	Thin font weight (200).
FW_LIGHT	Below average bolding (300).
FW_NORMAL	Normal bolding (400).
FW_MEDIUM	Above average bolding (500).
FW_SEMIBOLD	Light bolding (600).
FW_BOLD	Bolded font (700).
FW_EXTRABOLD	Extra bolding (800).
FW_HEAVY	Very heavy bolding (900).

Table 8-13: CreateFontIndirect pl.lfCharSet Values

Value	Description
ANSI_CHARSET	The ANSI character set.
DEFAULT_CHARSET	The default character set.
SYMBOL_CHARSET	The symbol character set.
SHIFTJIS_CHARSET	The shiftjis character set.
GB2312_CHARSET	The GB2312 character set.
HANGEUL_CHARSET	The Korean character set.
CHINESEBIG5_CHARSET	The Chinese character set.
OEM_CHARSET	The original equipment manufacturer character set.
JOHAB_CHARSET	Windows 95 only: The Johab character set.
HEBREW_CHARSET	Windows 95 only: The Hebrew character set.
ARABIC_CHARSET	Windows 95 only: The Arabic character set.
GREEK_CHARSET	Windows 95 only: The Grecian character set.

8

Chapter

Value	Description
TURKISH_CHARSET	Windows 95 only: The Turkish character set.
VIETNAMESE_CHARSET	Windows 95 only: The Vietnamese character set.
THAI_CHARSET	Windows 95 only: The Thai character set.
EASTEUROPE_CHARSET	Windows 95 only: The eastern Europe character set.
RUSSIAN_CHARSET	Windows 95 only: The Russian character set.
MAC_CHARSET	Windows 95 only: The Macintosh character set.
BALTIC_CHARSET	Windows 95 only: The Baltic character set.

Table 8-14: CreateFontIndirect pl.lfOutputPrecision Values

Value	Description
OUT_DEFAULT_PRECIS	The default font mapper behavior.
OUT_DEVICE_PRECIS	Chooses a device font when more than one font of the specified name exists.
OUT_OUTLINE_PRECIS	Windows NT only: Chooses a font from True Type and other vector-based fonts.
OUT_RASTER_PRECIS	Chooses a raster font when more than one font of the specified name exists.
OUT_STROKE_PRECIS	Windows NT only: Not used by the font mapper. However, this flag is returned when True Type and other vector fonts are enumerated. Windows 95 only: Chooses a font from vector-based fonts.
OUT_TT_ONLY_PRECIS	Chooses a font only from True Type fonts. If no True Type fonts exist, the font mapper reverts to default behavior.
OUT_TT_PRECIS	Chooses a True Type font when more than one font of the specified name exists.

Table 8-15: CreateFontIndirect pl.lfClipPrecision Values

Value	Description
CLIP_DEFAULT_PRECIS	The default clipping behavior.
CLIP_STROKE_PRECIS	This flag is used only when enumerating fonts.
CLIP_EMBEDDED	This flag must be included when using a read-only embedded font.
CLIP_LH_ANGLES	Specifies that font rotation is dependent upon the coordinate system. If this flag is not specified, device fonts always rotate counterclockwise.

Table 8-16: CreateFontIndirect pl.lfQuality Values

Value	Description
DEFAULT_QUALITY	Uses the default font quality.
DRAFT_QUALITY	Raster font scaling is enabled, and bold, italic, underline, and strikeout fonts are fabricated as needed. Exact attribute matching is a higher priority than font quality.
PROOF_QUALITY	Raster font scaling is disabled, and the physical font closest to the specified size is chosen. Bold, italic, underline, and strikeout fonts are fabricated as needed. Font quality is a higher priority than exact attribute matching.

Table 8-17: CreateFontIndirect pl.lfPitchAndFamily Pitch Flags Values

Value	Description
DEFAULT_PITCH	The default font pitch is used.
FIXED_PITCH	The width of all character glyphs are equal.
VARIABLE_PITCH	The width of all character glyphs is dependent upon the individual glyph image.

Table 8-18: CreateFontIndirect pl.lfPitchAndFamily Font Family Flags Values

Value	Description
FF_DECORATIVE	Indicates a novelty or decorative font, such as Old English.
FF_DONTCARE	The general font style is unknown or unimportant.
FF_MODERN	Indicates a monospaced font with consistent stroke widths, with or without serifs, such as Courier New.
FF_ROMAN	Indicates a proportional font with variable stroke widths, containing serifs, such as Times New Roman.
FF_SCRIPT	Indicates a font resembling handwriting, such as Brush Script.
FF_SWISS	Indicates a proportional font with variable stroke widths, without serifs, such as Arial.

CreateScalableFontResource *Windows.Pas*

Syntax

```
CreateScalableFontResource(
p1: DWORD;              {read-only flag}
p2: PChar;              {the font resource filename}
```

p3: PChar;   {the scalable font filename}
p4: PChar   {the scalable font file path}
): BOOL;   {returns TRUE or FALSE}

Description

This function is used to create a font resource file that is subsequently used by the Add-FontResource function to add a True Type font to the internal Windows font tables. This makes the True Type font available to all applications. When an application is finished using the True Type font, it should remove it from the system by calling the RemoveFontResource function.

Parameters

p1: Indicates if the font is a read-only embedded font. If this parameter is set to zero, the font has read and write permission. A value of one indicates that this is a read-only font, and the font will be hidden from other applications and will not appear when the EnumFontFamilies or EnumFontFamiliesEx functions are called.

p2: A pointer to a null-terminated string containing the filename and extension (usually .FOT) of the font resource file that will be created by this function.

p3: A pointer to a null-terminated string containing the name of the True Type font file used to create the scalable font resource file. If this string contains only a True Type font filename and extension, the p4 parameter must point to a string containing the path to the specified file.

p4: A pointer to a null-terminated string containing the path to the scaleable font file. If the p3 parameter contains a full path and filename to the True Type font, this parameter must be set to NIL.

Return Value

If the function succeeds, it returns TRUE; otherwise it returns FALSE. To get extended error information, call the GetLastError function.

See Also

AddFontResource, EnumFontFamilies, EnumFontFamiliesEx, RemoveFontResource

Example

Listing 8-4: Installing a New True Type Font

```
{=============================================================================
    The Ventilate font used in this example was generously donated by and is
    copyright © 1997 by Brian J. Bonislawsky - Astigmatic One Eye.  Used with
    permission.

    Astigmatic One Eye is a great source for shareware and freeware fonts of
    all types.  Check them out at http://www.comptechdev.com/cavop/aoe/
==============================================================================}
```

```
procedure TForm1.FormCreate(Sender: TObject);
var
  CurDir: array[0..MAX_PATH] of char;     // holds the current directory
begin
  {retrieve the current directory}
  GetCurrentDirectory(MAX_PATH, @CurDir[0]);

  {create a font resource file}
  CreateScalableFontResource(0, PChar(CurDir+'\Ventilat.fot'),
                             PChar(CurDir+'\Ventilat.ttf'),
                             nil);

  {add the font to the internal Windows font tables, making it available
   to any application}
  AddFontResource(PChar(CurDir+'\ventilat.fot'));

  {inform all applications of the change to the font tables}
  SendMessage(HWND_BROADCAST, WM_FONTCHANGE, 0, 0);
end;

procedure TForm1.FormDestroy(Sender: TObject);
var
  CurDir: array[0..MAX_PATH] of char;     // holds the current directory
begin
  {retrieve the current directory}
  GetCurrentDirectory(MAX_PATH, @CurDir[0]);

  {remove the font resource from the internal Windows font tables}
  RemoveFontResource(PChar(CurDir+'\ventilat.fot'));

  {inform all applications of the change to the font tables}
  SendMessage(HWND_BROADCAST, WM_FONTCHANGE, 0, 0);
end;

procedure TForm1.FormPaint(Sender: TObject);
var
  NewFont, OldFont: HFont;       // holds the old and new fonts
begin
  {set the background mode for transparency}
  SetBkMode(Form1.Canvas.Handle, TRANSPARENT);

  {create a font from the newly installed font resource}
  NewFont := CreateFont(-MulDiv(48, GetDeviceCaps(Form1.Canvas.Handle,
                        LOGPIXELSY), 72), 0, 0, 0, FW_DONTCARE, 0, 0, 0,
                        DEFAULT_CHARSET, OUT_TT_ONLY_PRECIS,
                        CLIP_DEFAULT_PRECIS, DEFAULT_QUALITY, DEFAULT_PITCH or
                        FF_DONTCARE, 'Ventilate');

  {select the font into the form's device context}
  OldFont := SelectObject(Form1.Canvas.Handle, NewFont);

  {output a line of text}
  TextOut(Form1.Canvas.Handle, 8, 8, 'Delphi Rocks!', Length('Delphi Rocks!'));

  {select the old font back into the device context and delete the new font}
```

```
    SelectObject(Form1.Canvas.Handle, OldFont);
    DeleteObject(NewFont);
  end;
```

*Figure 8-5:
Using the new
font*

DrawText   Windows.Pas

Syntax

```
DrawText(
  hDC: HDC;              {a handle to a device context}
  lpString: PChar;       {the output string}
  nCount: Integer;       {the length of the output string}
  var lpRect: TRect;     {the formatting rectangle}
  uFormat: UINT          {the text formatting flags}
  ): Integer;            {returns the height of the output text}
```

Description

This function draws the specified string of text onto the device context specified by the hDC parameter. The text is drawn within the specified rectangle, and is formatted according to the formatting flags identified by the uFormat parameter. The device context's selected font, text color, background color, and background mode are used when drawing the text. Unless otherwise specified by a specific formatting flag, the text is assumed to have multiple lines, and will be clipped by the boundaries of the specified rectangle.

Note that strings containing the mnemonic prefix character (&) will underline the character that follows it, and two mnemonic prefix characters will be interpreted as a literal & character.

Parameters

hDC: A handle to the device context upon which the text is to be drawn.

lpString: A pointer to a null-terminated string containing the text to be drawn.

nCount: Specifies the length of the string pointed to by the lpString parameter, in characters. If this parameter is set to -1, the string pointed to by the lpString parameter is assumed to be a null-terminated string, and the function will automatically calculate the string length.

lpRect: Specifies the rectangular coordinates, in logical units, within which the text will be drawn and formatted.

uFormat: A series of flags specifying how the text will be output and formatted within the specified rectangle. This parameter can contain one or more values from Table 8-19.

Return Value

If the function succeeds, it returns the height of the text in logical units; otherwise it returns zero.

See Also

DrawTextEx, GrayString, TabbedTextOut, TextOut

Example

Listing 8-5: Drawing Formatted Text

```
procedure TForm1.FormPaint(Sender: TObject);
var
  BoundingRect: TRect;                         // the text formatting rectangle
  CurDirectory: array[0..MAX_PATH] of char;   // the directory string
begin
  {create the text formatting bounding rectangle}
  BoundingRect := Rect(Label1.Left, Label1.Top+Label1.Height+3,
                  Form1.Width-(Label1.Left*2), Label1.Top+Label1.Height+83);

  {draw this rectangle visually on the form}
  Form1.Canvas.Rectangle(BoundingRect.Left, BoundingRect.Top,
                  BoundingRect.Right, BoundingRect.Bottom);

  {set the form's background mode for transparency}
  SetBkMode(Form1.Canvas.Handle, TRANSPARENT);

  {draw text at the bottom left of the rectangle}
  DrawText(Form1.Canvas.Handle, 'Delphi Rocks!', -1, BoundingRect,
        DT_BOTTOM or DT_SINGLELINE);

  {draw text in the very center of the rectangle}
  DrawText(Form1.Canvas.Handle, 'Delphi Rocks!', -1, BoundingRect,
        DT_CENTER or DT_VCENTER or DT_SINGLELINE);

  {draw text at the top right of the rectangle}
  DrawText(Form1.Canvas.Handle, 'Delphi Rocks!', -1, BoundingRect,
        DT_TOP or DT_RIGHT);

  {create a new text formatting bounding rectangle}
  BoundingRect := Rect(Label2.Left, Label2.Top+Label2.Height+3,
                  Label2.Width+Label2.Left, Label2.Top+Label2.Height+73);

  {draw the rectangle visually}
  Form1.Canvas.Rectangle(BoundingRect.Left, BoundingRect.Top,
                  BoundingRect.Right, BoundingRect.Bottom);

  {draw word wrapped text within the rectangle}
  DrawText(Form1.Canvas.Handle, 'Delphi is the most awesome Windows '+
        'development environment on the market.', -1, BoundingRect,
```

8

Chapter

```
                    DT_WORDBREAK);

       {create a new text formatting bounding rectangle}
       BoundingRect := Rect(Label3.Left, Label3.Top+Label3.Height+3,
                          Label3.Width+Label3.Left, Label3.Top+Label3.Height+25);

       {retrieve the current directory}
       GetCurrentDirectory(MAX_PATH, CurDirectory);

       {draw the directory string within the rectangle, reducing it as necessary}
       DrawText(Form1.Canvas.Handle, CurDirectory, -1, BoundingRect,
              DT_PATH_ELLIPSIS);
     end;
```

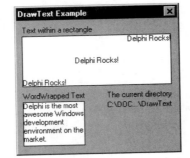

Figure 8-6:
Formatted
text output

Table 8-19: DrawText uFormat Values

Value	Description
DT_BOTTOM	The output text is justified to the bottom of the rectangle. This flag must be combined with the DT_SINGLELINE flag.
DT_CALCRECT	Automatically determines the width and height of the rectangle. For multiline text, the bottom of the rectangle is extended to include the last line of text. For single-line text, the right side of the rectangle is extended to include the last character. The function returns the height of the text, but the text is not drawn.
DT_CENTER	Centers the text horizontally within the rectangle.
DT_EDITCONTROL	Duplicates the text display behavior of an edit control. Specifically, the function will not draw the last line of text if it is only partially visible.
DT_END_ELLIPSIS	If the string is too large to fit within the specified rectangle, this flag causes the function to replace characters at the end of the string with ellipses (...) such that the resulting string will fit within the rectangle.
DT_EXPANDTABS	Tab characters are expanded when the text is drawn. By default, a tab character expands to eight characters.

Value	Description
DT_EXTERNALLEADING	The returned font height will include the external leading value for the selected font.
DT_LEFT	The output text is justified to the left of the rectangle.
DT_MODIFYSTRING	Modifies the specified string to match the displayed text. This flag is only useful when combined with the DT_END_ELLIPSES or DT_PATH_ELLIPSIS flags.
DT_NOCLIP	Causes the text to be drawn without clipping it to the boundaries of the specified rectangle. This has a side effect of increased performance.
DT_NOPREFIX	Turns off mnemonic prefix character processing. Specifically, any mnemonic prefix characters in the string will be interpreted as a literal & character, and will not cause the following character to be underlined.
DT_PATH_ELLIPSIS	If the string is too large to fit within the specified rectangle, this flag causes the function to replace characters in the middle of the string with ellipses (...) such that the resulting string will fit within the rectangle. If the string contains backslashes (\), as in the case of a path, the function will attempt to preserve as much text as possible following the last backslash in the string.
DT_RIGHT	The output text is justified to the right of the rectangle.
DT_RTLREADING	Draws the text in a right-to-left reading order. This flag can only be used when the font selected into the specified device context is a Hebrew or Arabic font; otherwise it is ignored.
DT_SINGLELINE	The specified text is interpreted as a single line, and carriage returns and line feed characters are ignored.
DT_TABSTOP	Specifies the number of characters that result from expanding a tab. The high-order byte of the low-order word of the uFormat parameter (bits 8-15) should be set to the number of characters to which tabs are expanded.
DT_TOP	The output text is justified to the top of the rectangle. This flag must be combined with the DT_SINGLELINE flag.
DT_VCENTER	Centers the text vertically within the window.
DT_WORDBREAK	Implements a word wrapping algorithm such that any word that would extend past the edge of the rectangle causes a line break to be inserted, with the breaking word drawn on the following line.

Chapter **8**

DrawTextEx   **Windows.Pas**

Syntax

```
DrawTextEx(
DC: HDC;                        {a handle to a device context}
lpchText: PChar;               {the output string}
cchText: Integer;              {the length of the output string}
var p4: TRect;                 {the formatting rectangle}
dwDTFormat: UINT;              {the text formatting flags}
DTParams: PDrawTextParams      {additional formatting options}
): Integer;                    {returns the height of the output text}
```

Description

This function draws the specified string of text onto the device context specified by the DC parameter. The text is drawn within the specified rectangle, and is formatted according to the formatting flags identified by the dwDTFormat parameter and the additional formatting options identified by the DTParams parameter. The device context's selected font, text color, background color, and background mode are used when drawing the text. Unless otherwise specified by a specific formatting flag, the text is assumed to have multiple lines, and will be clipped by the boundaries of the specified rectangle.

Note that strings containing the mnemonic prefix character (&) will underline the character that follows it, and two mnemonic prefix characters will be interpreted as a literal & character.

Parameters

DC: A handle to the device context upon which the text is to be drawn.

lpchText: A pointer to a null-terminated string containing the text to be drawn.

cchText: Specifies the length of the string pointed to by the lpchText parameter, in characters. If this parameter is set to -1, the string pointed to by the lpchText parameter is assumed to be a null-terminated string, and the function will automatically calculate the string length.

p4: Specifies the rectangular coordinates, in logical units, within which the text will be drawn and formatted.

dwDTFormat: A series of flags specifying how the text will be output and formatted within the specified rectangle. This parameter can contain one or more values from Table 8-20.

DTParams: A pointer to a TDrawTextParams structure that contains additional text formatting options. If this parameter is set to NIL, DrawTextEx behaves exactly like the DrawText function. The TDrawTextParams structure is defined as:

```
TDrawTextParams = packed record
    cbSize: UINT;              {the size of the TDrawTextParams structure}
    iTabLength: Integer;       {the tab stop size}
    iLeftMargin: Integer;      {the left margin}
    iRightMargin: Integer;     {the right margin}
    uiLengthDrawn: UINT;       {receives the number of characters drawn}
end;
```

cbSize: Specifies the size of the TDrawTextParams structure. This member should be set to SizeOf(TDrawTextParams).

iTabLength: Specifies the width of each tab stop, in units equal to the average character width.

iLeftMargin: Specifies the left margin within the formatting rectangle, in logical units.

iRightMargin: Specifies the right margin within the formatting rectangle, in logical units.

uiLengthDrawn: Receives the number of characters drawn by the DrawTextEx function, including white space.

Return Value

If the function succeeds, it returns the height of the text in logical units; otherwise it returns zero.

See Also

DrawText, GrayString, TabbedTextOut, TextOut

Example

Listing 8-6: Drawing Text with Margins

```
{the large string to be drawn}
const
  TheString = 'The companion CD-ROM that accompanies this book is a multimedia'+
    ' experience containing all of the source code from the book, a complete '+
    'Delphi Syntax compliant help file, shareware, freeware, and an assortment '+
    'of third party development and evaluation tools. Using the CD-Browser you '+
    'can navigate through the CD and choose which applications and chapter code'+
    ' to install with a single mouse click. Using the CD browser is simple; on '+
    'a Windows 95 or Windows NT system, simply insert the CD and the browser '+
    'will begin automatically.';

var
  Form1: TForm1;
  ResizingMargins: Boolean;      // indicates if margins are being resized

implementation

{$R *.DFM}
```

```
procedure TForm1.PaintBox1Paint(Sender: TObject);
var
  BoundingRect: TRect;              // the text formatting bounding rectangle
  DrawingParams: TDrawTextParams;  // additional text formatting options
begin
  with PaintBox1.Canvas do
  begin
    {erase the last image}
    Brush.Color := clWhite;
    FillRect(ClipRect);

    {the text formatting rectangle is the size of the paintbox}
    BoundingRect := ClipRect;

    with DrawingParams do
    begin
      {set the size of the optional formatting parameters structure}
      cbSize := SizeOf(TDrawTextParams);

      {initialize the tab length and margins to those specified
       by the panels}
      iTabLength := 0;
      iLeftMargin := (Panel1.Left-PaintBox1.Left);
      iRightMargin := 200-Panel2.Width;
    end;

    {draw the text, with margins}
    DrawTextEx(PaintBox1.Canvas.Handle, TheString, Length(TheString),
             BoundingRect, DT_WORDBREAK, @DrawingParams);
  end;
end;

procedure TForm1.FormCreate(Sender: TObject);
begin
  {we are not initially resizing margins}
  ResizingMargins := FALSE;
end;

procedure TForm1.Panel1MouseDown(Sender: TObject; Button: TMouseButton;
  Shift: TShiftState; X, Y: Integer);
begin
  {the user is dragging a panel and resizing margins}
  ResizingMargins := TRUE;
end;

procedure TForm1.Panel1MouseUp(Sender: TObject; Button: TMouseButton;
  Shift: TShiftState; X, Y: Integer);
begin
  {margins have been resized, so update the screen}
  ResizingMargins := FALSE;
  PaintBox1.Refresh;
end;

procedure TForm1.Panel1MouseMove(Sender: TObject; Shift: TShiftState; X,
  Y: Integer);
```

```
begin
  {resize the panel if the user has started to resize margins}
  if ResizingMargins then
  begin
    Panel1.Left  := Panel1.Left+X;
    Panel1.Width := Panel2.Left - Panel1.Left;
  end;

  {confine the panel to a maximum size}
  if Panel1.Left<PaintBox1.Left then
  begin
    Panel1.Left  := PaintBox1.Left;
    Panel1.Width := 200;
  end;
end;

procedure TForm1.Panel2MouseMove(Sender: TObject; Shift: TShiftState; X,
  Y: Integer);
begin
  {resize the panel if the user has started to resize margins}
  if ResizingMargins then
    Panel2.Width := X;

  {confine the panel to a maximum size}
  if Panel2.Width>200 then
    Panel2.Width := 200;
end;
```

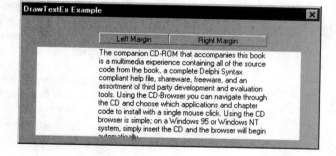

*Figure 8-7:
Formatted
text with
margins*

Table 8-20: DrawTextEx dwDTFormat Values

Value	Description
DT_BOTTOM	The output text is justified to the bottom of the rectangle. This flag must be combined with the DT_SINGLELINE flag.
DT_CALCRECT	Automatically determines the width and height of the rectangle. For multiline text, the bottom of the rectangle is extended to include the last line of text. For single-line text, the right side of the rectangle is extended to include the last character. The function returns the height of the text, but the text is not drawn.

Value	Description
DT_CENTER	Centers the text horizontally within the rectangle.
DT_EDITCONTROL	Duplicates the text display behavior of an edit control. Specifically, the function will not draw the last line of text if it is only partially visible.
DT_END_ELLIPSIS	If the string is too large to fit within the specified rectangle, this flag causes the function to replace characters at the end of the string with ellipses (...) such that the resulting string will fit within the rectangle.
DT_EXPANDTABS	Tab characters are expanded when the text is drawn. By default, a tab character expands to eight characters.
DT_EXTERNALLEADING	The returned font height will including the external leading value for the selected font.
DT_LEFT	The output text is justified to the left of the rectangle.
DT_MODIFYSTRING	Modifies the specified string to match the displayed text. This flag is only useful when combined with the DT_END_ELLIPSES or DT_PATH_ELLIPSIS flags.
DT_NOCLIP	Causes the text to be drawn without clipping it to the boundaries of the specified rectangle. This has a side effect of increased performance.
DT_NOPREFIX	Turns off mnemonic prefix character processing. Specifically, any mnemonic prefix characters in the string will be interpreted as a literal & character, and will not cause the following character to be underlined.
DT_PATH_ELLIPSIS	If the string is too large to fit within the specified rectangle, this flag causes the function to replace characters in the middle of the string with ellipses (...) such that the resulting string will fit within the rectangle. If the string contains backslashes (\), as in the case of a path, the function will attempt to preserve as much text as possible following the last backslash in the string.
DT_RIGHT	The output text is justified to the right of the rectangle.
DT_RTLREADING	Draws the text in a right-to-left reading order. This flag can only be used when the font selected into the specified device context is a Hebrew or Arabic font; otherwise it is ignored.
DT_SINGLELINE	The specified text is interpreted as a single line, and carriage returns and line feed characters are ignored.
DT_TABSTOP	Specifies the number of characters that result from expanding a tab. The high-order byte of the low-order word of the dwDTFormat parameter (bits 8-15) should be set to the number of characters to which tabs are expanded.
DT_TOP	The output text is justified to the top of the rectangle. This flag must be combined with the DT_SINGLELINE flag.

Value	Description
DT_VCENTER	Centers the text vertically within the window.
DT_WORDBREAK	Implements a word wrapping algorithm such that any word that would extend past the edge of the rectangle causes a line break to be inserted, with the breaking word drawn on the following line.

EnumFontFamilies   *Windows.Pas*

Syntax

```
EnumFontFamilies(
DC: HDC;                    {a handle to a device context}
p2: PChar;                  {the font typeface name}
p3: TFNFontEnumProc;        {a pointer to the callback function}
p4: LPARAM                  {32-bit application-defined data}
): BOOL;                    {returns TRUE or FALSE}
```

Description

This function passes font information for every font available in the specified device context with the specified typeface to an application-defined callback function. This includes True Type, raster, and vector fonts, but excludes any read-only True Type fonts. The enumeration will continue until all fonts have been enumerated or the callback function returns zero.

Parameters

DC: A handle to the device context whose fonts are to be enumerated. The function enumerates all fonts available on the specified device context.

p2: A pointer to a null-terminated string containing the typeface name whose associated fonts are to be enumerated. If this parameter is set to NIL, the function enumerates one randomly selected font from each typeface.

p3: The address of the application-defined callback function.

p4: Contains a 32-bit application-defined value that is passed to the enumeration function.

Return Value

If the last value returned by the callback function is a nonzero value, the function returns TRUE. If the last value returned by the callback function is zero, the function returns FALSE. This function does not indicate an error upon failure.

Callback Syntax

```
EnumFontFamProc(
LogFont: PEnumLogFont;      {a pointer to logical font attributes}
TextMetrics: PNewTextMetric;   {a pointer to physical font attributes}
```

FontType: Integer;	{the font type flags}
lParam: LPARAM	{the 32-bit application-defined data}
): Integer;	{returns a nonzero value to continue enumeration}

Description

This function receives a pointer to a TEnumLogFont structure and a TNewTextMetric structure for each font enumerated, and may perform any desired task.

Parameters

LogFont: A pointer to a TEnumLogFont structure containing logical font attributes for the currently enumerated font. The TEnumLogFont structure is defined as:

TEnumLogFont = packed record	
elfLogFont: TLogFont;	{the logical font info}
elfFullName: array[0..LF_FULLFACESIZE - 1]	
of AnsiChar;	{the full font name}
elfStyle: array[0..LF_FACESIZE - 1] of AnsiChar;	{the font style}
end;	

elfLogFont: Specifies a TLogFont structure describing the logical attributes of the font. The TLogFont structure is defined as:

TLogFont = packed record	
lfHeight: Longint;	{the font height}
lfWidth: Longint;	{character width}
lfEscapement: Longint;	{escapement angle}
lfOrientation: Longint;	{baseline angle}
lfWeight: Longint;	{the bolding weight}
lfItalic: Byte;	{the italics flag}
lfUnderline: Byte;	{the underline flag}
lfStrikeOut: Byte;	{the strikeout flag}
lfCharSet: Byte;	{the character set}
lfOutPrecision: Byte;	{output precision flag}
lfClipPrecision: Byte;	{clipping precision}
lfQuality: Byte;	{output quality flag}
lfPitchAndFamily: Byte;	{pitch and family flags}
lfFaceName: array[0..LF_FACESIZE - 1]	
of AnsiChar;	{font typeface name}
end;	

Please see the CreateFontIndirect function for a description of this data structure.

elfFullName: A null-terminated string containing the full, unique name for the enumerated font.

elfStyle: A null-terminated string containing the style of the font.

TextMetrics: A pointer to a TNewTextMetric structure containing physical font attributes for the currently enumerated font. Note that if the currently enumerated font is not a True Type font, this parameter will point to a TTextMetric structure. All measurements returned by this structure are in logical units and depend on the current mapping mode of the specified device context. The TNewTextMetric structure is defined as:

```
TNewTextMetric = record
    tmHeight: Longint;              {the height of a character}
    tmAscent: Longint;             {the ascent of a character}
    tmDescent: Longint;            {the descent of a character}
    tmInternalLeading: Longint;    {the internal leading}
    tmExternalLeading: Longint;    {the external leading}
    tmAveCharWidth: Longint;       {the average character width}
    tmMaxCharWidth: Longint;       {the maximum character width}
    tmWeight: Longint;             {the boldness value}
    tmOverhang: Longint;           {the overhang width}
    tmDigitizedAspectX: Longint;   {the horizontal aspect}
    tmDigitizedAspectY: Longint;   {the vertical aspect}
    tmFirstChar: AnsiChar;         {the first character}
    tmLastChar: AnsiChar;          {the last character}
    tmDefaultChar: AnsiChar;       {the default character}
    tmBreakChar: AnsiChar;         {the word break character}
    tmItalic: Byte;                {the italics flag}
    tmUnderlined: Byte;            {the underlined flag}
    tmStruckOut: Byte;             {the strikeout flag}
    tmPitchAndFamily: Byte;        {the pitch and family flags}
    tmCharSet: Byte;               {the character set}
    ntmFlags: DWORD;               {attribute bitmask}
    ntmSizeEM: UINT;               {the em square size, in notional units}
    ntmCellHeight: UINT;           {the cell height, in notional units}
    ntmAvgWidth: UINT;             {the average character width, in notional
                                    units}
end;
```

Except for the last four members, this data structure is identical to the TTextMetric data structure. Please see the GetTextMetrics function for a description of the TTextMetric structure containing the other members.

ntmFlags: A bitmask specifying various attributes of the font. Each bit in the mask identifies a different font attribute as described in Table 8-21. If a specific bit is set, that attribute is present in the currently enumerated font.

ntmSizeEM: Specifies the size of the em square for the font, in notional units. A notional unit is the unit for which the font was originally designed.

ntmCellHeight: Specifies the height of a character cell for the font, in notional units.

ntmAvgWidth: Specifies the average character width for the font, in notional units.

FontType: Specifies a series of flags indicating the type of font being enumerated. This parameter may contain one or more values from Table 8-22. Note that if neither the RASTER_FONTTYPE nor the TRUETYPE_FONTTYPE flag is present, the enumerated font is a vector font.

lParam: Specifies the 32-bit application-defined value passed to the EnumFontFamilies function in the p4 parameter.

Return Value

The callback function should return a nonzero value to continue enumeration, or a zero to terminate enumeration.

See Also

CreateFontIndirect, EnumFontFamiliesEx, GetTextMetrics

Example

Listing 8-7: Enumerating Available Fonts

```
{the callback function prototype}
function FontEnumProc(LogFont: PEnumLogFont; TextMetrics: PNewTextMetric;
                      FontType: Integer; lParam: LPARAM): Integer; stdcall;

var
  Form1: TForm1;

implementation

{$R *.DFM}

procedure TForm1.FormActivate(Sender: TObject);
var
  RasterStatus: TRasterizerStatus;    // holds raster capabilities
begin
  {set the size of the raster status structure}
  RasterStatus.nSize := SizeOf(TRasterizerStatus);

  {retrieve the rasterizer status}
  GetRasterizerCaps(RasterStatus, SizeOf(TRasterizerStatus));

  {indicate if True Type fonts are enabled and available}
  if (RasterStatus.wFlags and TT_ENABLED) = TT_ENABLED then
    CheckBox1.Checked := TRUE;
  if (RasterStatus.wFlags and TT_AVAILABLE) = TT_AVAILABLE then
    CheckBox2.Checked := TRUE;

  {enumerate all installed fonts}
  EnumFontFamilies(Form1.Canvas.Handle, NIL, @FontEnumProc, 0);
end;

function FontEnumProc(LogFont: PEnumLogFont; TextMetrics: PNewTextMetric;
                      FontType: Integer; lParam: LPARAM): Integer; stdcall;
begin
```

```
  {add the font name and its font type to the list box}
  Form1.ListBox1.Items.AddObject(TEnumLogFont(LogFont^).elfLogFont.lfFaceName,
                                 TObject(FontType));

  {continue enumeration}
  Result := 1;
end;

procedure TForm1.ListBox1DrawItem(Control: TWinControl; Index: Integer;
  Rect: TRect; State: TOwnerDrawState);
begin
  {indicate if the font is a True Type or other type of font}
  if Integer(ListBox1.Items.Objects[Index]) = TRUETYPE_FONTTYPE then
    ListBox1.Canvas.Draw(Rect.Left, Rect.Top, Image2.Picture.Bitmap)
  else
    ListBox1.Canvas.Draw(Rect.Left, Rect.Top, Image1.Picture.Bitmap);

  {draw the font name}
  Rect.Left := Rect.Left + 18;
  Rect.Top  := Rect.Top + 2;
  TextOut(ListBox1.Canvas.Handle, Rect.Left, Rect.Top,
          PChar(ListBox1.Items[Index]), Length(ListBox1.Items[Index]));
end;
```

*Figure 8-8:
The available
font names*

Table 8-21: EnumFontFamilies EnumFontFamProc TextMetrics.ntmFlags Bit Values

Bit Position	Description
0	Indicates an italic font.
1	Indicates an underscored font.
2	Indicates a negative image font.
3	Indicates an outline font.
4	Indicates a struckout font.
5	Indicates a bold font.

Table 8-22: EnumFontFamilies EnumFontFamProc FontType Values

Value	Description
DEVICE_FONTTYPE	Indicates a device resident font, or that the specified device supports download True Type fonts.
RASTER_FONTTYPE	Indicates a raster, or bitmap, font.
TRUETYPE_FONTTYPE	Indicates a True Type font.

EnumFontFamiliesEx   *Windows.Pas*

Syntax

```
EnumFontFamiliesEx(
DC: HDC;                  {a handle to a device context}
var p2: TLogFont;         {a TLogFont structure}
p3: TFNFontEnumProc;      {a pointer to the callback function}
p4: LPARAM;               {32-bit application-defined data}
p5: DWORD                 {this parameter is reserved}
): BOOL;                  {returns TRUE or FALSE}
```

Description

This function passes font information for every font available in the specified device context that matches the attributes defined by the TLogFont structure to an application-defined callback function. This includes True Type, raster, and vector fonts, but excludes any read-only True Type fonts. The enumeration will continue until all fonts have been enumerated or the callback function returns zero.

Parameters

DC: A handle to the device context whose fonts are to be enumerated. The function enumerates all fonts available on the specified device context.

p2: A pointer to a TLogFont structure containing information that determines which fonts to enumerate. The TLogFont structure is defined as:

```
TLogFont = packed record
    lfHeight: Longint;                {the font height in logical units}
    lfWidth: Longint;                 {the average character width}
    lfEscapement: Longint;            {the escapement vector angle}
    lfOrientation: Longint;           {the character baseline angle}
    lfWeight: Longint;                {the bolding weight}
    lfItalic: Byte;                   {the italics flag}
    lfUnderline: Byte;                {the underline flag}
    lfStrikeOut: Byte;                {the strikeout flag}
    lfCharSet: Byte;                  {the character set}
    lfOutPrecision: Byte;             {the output precision flag}
    lfClipPrecision: Byte;            {the clipping precision flags}
```

```
        lfQuality: Byte;                           {the output quality flag}
        lfPitchAndFamily: Byte;                    {the pitch and family flags}
        lfFaceName: array[0..LF_FACESIZE - 1]
          of AnsiChar;                             {the font typeface name}
    end;
```

Please see the CreateFontIndirect function for a description of this data structure. Only the lfCharSet, lfFaceName, and lfPitchAndFamily members determine the behavior of the EnumFontFamiliesEx function.

lfCharSet: If this member is set to DEFAULT_CHARSET, the function enumerates every font in every character set. If this member is set to a specific character set, only fonts that define characters for the indicated character set will be enumerated.

lfFaceName: If this member is set to an empty string, one randomly selected font from each typeface is enumerated. If this member is set to a valid typeface name, only fonts with the specified typeface name will be enumerated.

lfPitchAndFamily: This member is only used with Hebrew or Arabic fonts, and must be set to zero for any other font type. For Hebrew and Arabic fonts, this member can be set to MONO_FONT to enumerate only fonts containing all code page characters.

p3: The address of the application-defined callback function.

p4: Contains a 32-bit application-defined value that is passed to the enumeration function.

p5: This parameter is reserved for future use, and must be set to zero.

Return Value

If the last value returned by the callback function is a nonzero value, the function returns TRUE. If the last value returned by the callback function is zero, the function returns FALSE. This function does not indicate an error upon failure.

Callback Syntax

```
EnumFontFamExProc(
    LogFont: PEnumLogFontEx;        {a pointer to logical font attributes}
    TextMetrics: PNewTextMetric;   {a pointer to physical font attributes}
    FontType: Integer;             {the font type flags}
    lParam: LPARAM                 {the 32-bit application-defined data}
): Integer;                        {returns a nonzero value to continue enumeration}
```

Description

This function receives a pointer to a TEnumLogFontEx structure and a TNewTextMetricEx structure for each font enumerated, and may perform any desired task.

Parameters

LogFont: A pointer to a TEnumLogFontEx structure containing logical font attributes for the currently enumerated font. The TEnumLogFontEx structure is defined as:

```
TEnumLogFontEx = packed record
      elfLogFont: TLogFont;                              {the logical font info}
      elfFullName: array[0..LF_FULLFACESIZE - 1] of Char;   {the full font name}
      elfStyle: array[0..LF_FACESIZE - 1] of Char;          {the font style}
      elfScript: array[0..LF_FACESIZE - 1] of Char;         {the font script}
end;
```

elfLogFont: Specifies a TLogFont structure describing the logical attributes of the font. Please see the CreateFontIndirect function for a description of this data structure.

elfFullName: A null-terminated string containing the full, unique name for the enumerated font.

elfStyle: A null-terminated string containing the style of the font.

elfScript: A null-terminated string containing the script of the font.

TextMetrics: A pointer to a TNewTextMetricEx structure containing physical font attributes for the currently enumerated font. Note that if the currently enumerated font is not a True Type font, this parameter will point to a TTextMetric structure. Also note that under Windows 95, the TNewTextMetricEx structure is not implemented, and this parameter will instead point to a TNewTextMetric structure. The TNewTextMetricEx structure is defined as:

```
TNewTextMetricEx = packed record
      ntmTm: TNewTextMetric;              {a TNewTextMetric structure}
      ntmFontSig: TFontSignature;         {a TFontSignature structure}
end;
```

ntmTm: A TNewTextMetric structure containing physical font attributes for the currently enumerated font. The TNewTextMetric structure is defined as:

```
TNewTextMetric = record
      tmHeight: Longint;                  {the height of a character}
      tmAscent: Longint;                  {the ascent of a character}
      tmDescent: Longint;                 {the descent of a character}
      tmInternalLeading: Longint;         {the internal leading}
      tmExternalLeading: Longint;         {the external leading}
      tmAveCharWidth: Longint;            {the average character width}
      tmMaxCharWidth: Longint;            {the maximum character width}
      tmWeight: Longint;                  {the boldness value}
      tmOverhang: Longint;                {the overhang width}
      tmDigitizedAspectX: Longint;        {the horizontal aspect}
      tmDigitizedAspectY: Longint;        {the vertical aspect}
      tmFirstChar: AnsiChar;              {the first character}
```

```
      tmLastChar: AnsiChar;           {the last character}
      tmDefaultChar: AnsiChar;        {the default character}
      tmBreakChar: AnsiChar;          {the word break character}
      tmItalic: Byte;                 {the italics flag}
      tmUnderlined: Byte;             {the underlined flag}
      tmStruckOut: Byte;              {the strikeout flag}
      tmPitchAndFamily: Byte;         {the pitch and family flags}
      tmCharSet: Byte;                {the character set}
      ntmFlags: DWORD;                {attribute bitmask}
      ntmSizeEM: UINT;                {the em square size, in notional units}
      ntmCellHeight: UINT;            {the cell height, in notional units}
      ntmAvgWidth: UINT;              {the average character width}
end;
```

Please see the EnumFontFamilies function for a description of this data structure.

ntmFontSig: A TFontSignature structure identifying the code pages and Unicode subranges for which the currently enumerated font provides glyph images. The TFontSignature structure is defined as:

```
TFontSignature = packed record
      fsUsb: array[0..3] of DWORD;    {the Unicode subset bitmask}
      fsCsb: array[0..1] of DWORD;    {the code page bitmask}
end;
```

fsUsb: A 128-bit Unicode subset bitmask that identifies 126 Unicode subranges, where each bit except the two most significant bits identifies a single subrange. The most significant bit is always set, and the second most significant bit is currently reserved and will not be set.

fsCsb: A 64-bit code page bitmask identifying a specific character set or code page, where each bit identifies a single code page. The low-order double word specifies Windows code pages, and the high-order double word specifies non-Windows code pages. The code page for each individual bit is listed in Table 8-23.

FontType: Specifies a series of flags indicating the type of font being enumerated. This parameter may contain one or more values from Table 8-24. Note that if neither the RASTER_FONTTYPE nor the TRUETYPE_FONTTYPE flag is present, the enumerated font is a vector font.

lParam: Specifies the 32-bit application-defined value passed to the EnumFontFamilies-Ex function in the p4 parameter.

Return Value

The callback function should return a nonzero value to continue enumeration or a zero to terminate enumeration.

See Also

CreateFontIndirect, EnumFontFamilies, GetTextMetrics

Example

Listing 8-8: Enumerating Only Symbol Fonts

```
{the callback function prototype}
function FontEnumExProc(LogFont: PEnumLogFontEx; TextMetrics: PNewTextMetric;
                       FontType: Integer; lParam: LPARAM): Integer; stdcall;

var
  Form1: TForm1;

implementation

{$R *.DFM}

procedure TForm1.FormActivate(Sender: TObject);
var
  FontInfo: TLogFont;    // holds the font enumeration information
begin
  {initialize the font information to enumerate all fonts belonging
   to the symbol character set}
  FontInfo.lfCharSet        := SYMBOL_CHARSET;
  FontInfo.lfFaceName       := '';
  FontInfo.lfPitchAndFamily := 0;

  {enumerate the fonts}
  EnumFontFamiliesEx(Form1.Canvas.Handle, FontInfo, @FontEnumExProc, 0, 0);
end;

function FontEnumExProc(LogFont: PEnumLogFontEx; TextMetrics: PNewTextMetric;
                       FontType: Integer; lParam: LPARAM): Integer; stdcall;
begin
  {add the font typeface name and its type to the list box}
  Form1.ListBox1.Items.AddObject(TEnumLogFontEx(LogFont^).elfLogFont.lfFaceName,
                                 TObject(FontType));

  {continue enumeration}
  Result := 1;
end;

procedure TForm1.ListBox1DrawItem(Control: TWinControl; Index: Integer;
  Rect: TRect; State: TOwnerDrawState);
begin
  {indicate if the font is a True Type or other type of font}
  if Integer(ListBox1.Items.Objects[Index]) = TRUETYPE_FONTTYPE then
    ListBox1.Canvas.Draw(Rect.Left, Rect.Top, Image2.Picture.Bitmap)
  else
    ListBox1.Canvas.Draw(Rect.Left, Rect.Top, Image1.Picture.Bitmap);

  {draw the font name}
  Rect.Left := Rect.Left + 18;
```

```
Rect.Top  := Rect.Top + 2;
TextOut(ListBox1.Canvas.Handle, Rect.Left, Rect.Top,
        PChar(ListBox1.Items[Index]), Length(ListBox1.Items[Index]));
end;
```

Figure 8-9:
All available
symbol fonts

8

Chapter

Table 8-23: EnumFontFamiliesEx EnumFontFamExProc TextMetrics.ntmFontSig.fsCsb Values

Bit	Code Page	Description
0	1252	Latin 1.
1	1250	Latin 2 (Eastern Europe).
2	1251	Cyrillic.
3	1253	Greek.
4	1254	Turkish.
5	1255	Hebrew.
6	1256	Arabic.
7	1257	Baltic.
8-16		Reserved for ANSI.
17	874	Thai.
18	932	JIS/Japan.
19	936	Chinese simplified characters.
20	949	Korean Unified Hangeul Code.
21	950	Chinese traditional characters.
22-29		Reserved for alternate ANSI and OEM use.
30-21		Reserved by the system.
32-47		Reserved for OEM use.
48	869	IBM Greek.
49	866	MS-DOS Russian.
50	865	MS-DOS Nordic.
51	864	Arabic.
52	863	MS-DOS Canadian French.
53	862	Hebrew.
54	861	MS-DOS Icelandic.
55	860	MS-DOS Portuguese.
56	857	IBM Turkish.

Bit	Code Page	Description
57	855	IBM Cyrillic.
58	852	Latin 2.
59	776	Baltic.
60	737	Greek.
61	708	Arabic (ASMO 708).
62	850	WE/Latin 1.
63	437	United States.

Table 8-24: EnumFontFamiliesEx EnumFontFamExProc FontType Values

Value	Description
DEVICE_FONTTYPE	Indicates a device resident font, or that the specified device supports download True Type fonts.
RASTER_FONTTYPE	Indicates a raster, or bitmap, font.
TRUETYPE_FONTTYPE	Indicates a True Type font.

GetCharABCWidths   Windows.Pas

Syntax

```
GetCharABCWidths(
DC: HDC;                {a handle to a device context}
p2: UINT;               {the first character in the range}
p3: UINT;               {the last character in the range}
const ABCStructs        {points to an array of TABC structures}
): BOOL;                {returns TRUE or FALSE}
```

Description

This function retrieves various spacing width values for the currently selected True Type font in the device context identified by the DC parameter. These values are retrieved from a range of consecutive characters within the font. For each character in the range, a matching TABC structure in the array of TABC structures pointed to by the ABCStructs parameter receives three width values. The "A" spacing value is the distance added to the current position before placing the next character glyph when outputting a line of text. The "B" spacing value is the actual width of the character glyph. The "C" spacing value is the distance added to the right of the glyph to provide white space for separating characters. A negative value for the "A" or "C" spacing values indicates a font with an underhang or overhang. Note that this function succeeds only for True Type fonts. To retrieve the width for non-True Type font characters, use the GetCharWidth function.

Parameters

DC: A handle to the device context whose character widths for the currently selected font are to be retrieved.

p2: Specifies the value of the first character in the range of characters.

p3: Specifies the value of the last character in the range of characters.

ABCStructs: A pointer to an array of TABC structures that receive the ABC spacing widths of each character in the defined range. There must be at least as many TABC structures in the array as there are characters in the range defined by the p2 and p3 parameters. The TABC structure is defined as:

```
TABC = packed record
      abcA: Integer;        {the next character offset}
      abcB: UINT;           {the width of the glyph}
      abcC: Integer;        {the white space}
end;
```

abcA: Specifies the distance added to the current position before placing the next character glyph when outputting a line of text, in logical units.

abcB: Specifies the actual width of the character glyph, in logical units.

abcC: Specifies the distance added to the right of the glyph to provide white space for separating characters, in logical units.

Return Value

If the function succeeds, it returns TRUE; otherwise it returns FALSE. To get extended error information, call the GetLastError function.

See Also

GetCharWidth, GetOutlineTextMetrics, GetTextMetrics

Example

Listing 8-9: Retrieving ABC Widths for All Uppercase Letters

```
procedure TForm1.FormActivate(Sender: TObject);
var
  CharWidths: array[0..25]of TABC;    // holds character ABC widths
  Count: Integer;                      // general loop control variable
begin
  {initialize the string grid}
  StringGrid1.Cells[0,0] := 'Character';
  StringGrid1.Cells[1,0] := '''A'' Width';
  StringGrid1.Cells[2,0] := '''B'' Width';
  StringGrid1.Cells[3,0] := '''C'' Width';

  {retrieve ABC widths for all uppercase letters}
  GetCharABCWidths(Form1.Canvas.Handle, Ord('A'), Ord('Z'), CharWidths);

  {display the ABC widths for all uppercase letters}
```

8

Chapter

```
for Count := 0 to 26 do
begin
  StringGrid1.Cells[0, Count+1] := Char(Ord('A')+Count);
  StringGrid1.Cells[1, Count+1] := IntToStr(CharWidths[Count].abcA);
  StringGrid1.Cells[2, Count+1] := IntToStr(CharWidths[Count].abcB);
  StringGrid1.Cells[3, Count+1] := IntToStr(CharWidths[Count].abcC);
end;
end;
```

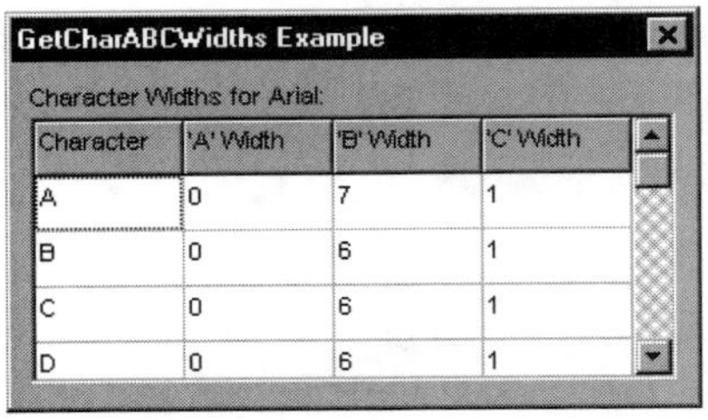

*Figure 8-10:
The uppercase
letter ABC
widths*

Character	'A' Width	'B' Width	'C' Width
A	0	7	1
B	0	6	1
C	0	6	1
D	0	6	1

Character Widths for Arial:

GetCharABCWidths Example

GetCharWidth   Windows.Pas

Syntax

```
GetCharWidth(
DC: HDC;                {a handle to a device context}
p2: UINT;               {the first character in the range}
p3: UINT;               {the last character in the range}
const Widths            {a pointer to an array of integers}
): BOOL;                {returns TRUE or FALSE}
```

Description

This function retrieves the width of each character in a range of characters for the currently selected font in the device context identified by the DC parameter. For each character in the range, a matching integer in the array of integers pointed to by the Widths parameter receives the character width. This function is useful for both True Type and non-True Type fonts. However, True Type fonts should use the GetCharABCWidths function to retrieve more accurate values.

Parameters

DC: A handle to the device context whose character widths for the currently selected font are to be retrieved.

p2: Specifies the value of the first character in the range of characters.

p3: Specifies the value of the last character in the range of characters.

Widths: A pointer to an array of integers that receive the character widths of each character in the defined range. There must be at least as many integers in the array as there are characters in the range defined by the p2 and p3 parameters.

Return Value

If this function succeeds, it returns TRUE; otherwise it returns FALSE. To get extended error information, call the GetLastError function.

See Also

GetCharABCWidths, GetTextExtentExPoint, GetTextExtentPoint32

Example

Listing 8-10: Retrieving Character Widths for All Uppercase Letters

```
procedure TForm1.FormActivate(Sender: TObject);
var
  CharWidths: array[0..25] of Integer;    // holds the character widths
  Count: Integer;                         // general loop control variable
begin
  {initialize the string grid}
  StringGrid1.Cells[0,0] := 'Character';
  StringGrid1.Cells[1,0] := 'Width';

  {retrieve the widths of all uppercase letters}
  GetCharWidth(Form1.Canvas.Handle, Ord('A'), Ord('Z'), CharWidths);

  {display the character widths}
  for Count := 0 to 26 do
  begin
    StringGrid1.Cells[0, Count+1] := Char(Ord('A')+Count);
    StringGrid1.Cells[1, Count+1] := IntToStr(CharWidths[Count]);
  end;
end;
```

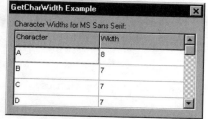

Figure 8-11:
The uppercase letter character widths

GetFontData   *Windows.Pas*

Syntax

```
GetFontData(
DC: HDC;                {a handle to a device context}
p2: DWORD;              {the font metric table}
p3: DWORD;              {the offset into the font metric table}
p4: Pointer;            {a pointer to a buffer receiving the information}
```

p5: DWORD	{the amount of data to retrieve}
): DWORD;	{returns the number of bytes retrieved}

Description

This function retrieves information from the font metric table specified by the p2 parameter for the True Type font currently selected into the device context identified by the DC parameter. GetFontData can be used to retrieve an entire True Type font file for purposes of embedding a font into a document.

Parameters

DC: Specifies a handle to the device context whose currently selected font's information is to be retrieved.

p2: Specifies the font metric table from which data is to be retrieved. The True Type font metric tables are described in the True Type font file specification published by Microsoft. If this parameter is set to zero, the function retrieves information starting at the beginning of the font file.

p3: Specifies the offset from the beginning of the specified metric table where the function begins retrieving information. If this parameter is set to zero, the function retrieves information starting at the beginning of the specified metric table.

p4: A pointer to a buffer that receives the retrieved information. If this parameter is set to NIL, the function returns the size of buffer required to hold the requested information.

p5: Specifies the amount of information to retrieve, in bytes. If this parameter is set to zero, the function returns the size of the metric table specified by the p2 parameter.

Return Value

If the function succeeds, it returns the number of bytes of font data retrieved; otherwise it returns GDI_ERROR.

See Also

AddFontResource, CreateScalableFontResource, GetTextMetrics, RemoveFontResource

Example

Please see Listing 8-1 demonstrating font embedding in the introduction.

GetGlyphOutline   Windows.Pas

Syntax

GetGlyphOutline(	
DC: HDC;	{a handle to a device context}
p2: UINT;	{the character}
p3: UINT;	{data format flags}

const p4: TGlyphMetrics;	{a pointer to a TGlyphMetrics structure}
p5: DWORD;	{the size of the data buffer}
p6: Pointer;	{a pointer to the data buffer}
const p7: TMat2	{the rotation matrix}
): DWORD;	{returns an error code}

Description

This function retrieves outline information for the specified character in the True Type (only) font currently selected into the device context identified by the DC parameter. The outline information retrieved is in the form of either a monochrome bitmap or a series of lines and curves describing the glyph shape in its native format. This information is stored in the buffer pointed to by the p6 parameter.

Parameters

DC: A handle to the device context whose currently selected True Type font is used when retrieving the outline information.

p2: Identifies the code of the character whose outline is to be retrieved.

p3: Specifies the format of the retrieved outline information. This parameter can contain one value from Table 8-25.

p4: A pointer to a TGlyphMetrics structure which receives information concerning the physical attributes of the character glyph. The TGlyphMetrics structure is defined as:

```
TGlyphMetrics = packed record
      gmBlackBoxX: UINT;        {the smallest rectangle width}
      gmBlackBoxY: UINT;        {the smallest rectangle height}
      gmptGlyphOrigin: TPoint;  {the smallest rectangle origin}
      gmCellIncX: SHORT;        {the next character cell horizontal offset}
      gmCellIncY: SHORT;        {the next character cell vertical offset}
end;
```

gmBlackBoxX: Indicates the width of the smallest rectangle that the glyph image would completely fit inside, in device units.

gmBlackBoxY: Indicates the height of the smallest rectangle that the glyph image would completely fit inside, in device units.

gmptGlyphOrigin: Indicates the horizontal and vertical coordinates within the character cell of the origin of the smallest rectangle that the glyph image would completely fit inside, in device units.

gmCellIncX: Indicates the horizontal offset from the beginning of the current character cell to the beginning of the next character cell, in device units.

gmCellIncY: Indicates the vertical offset from the beginning of the current character cell to the beginning of the next character cell, in device units.

p5: Specifies the size of the data buffer pointed to by the p6 parameter. If this parameter is set to zero, the function returns the required size of the buffer.

p6: A pointer to a buffer that receives the glyph outline information. If this parameter is set to NIL, the function returns the required size of the buffer.

p7: A pointer to a TMat2 structure defining a 3X3 transformation matrix, used to rotate the font to any angle. The TMat2 structure is defined as:

```
TMat2 = packed record
      eM11: TFixed;          {a fixed point angle}
      eM12: TFixed;          {a fixed point angle}
      eM21: TFixed;          {a fixed point angle}
      eM22: TFixed;          {a fixed point angle}
end;
```

eM11: Identifies the angle of font rotation, in the form of a TFixed structure, for the M11 value of a 3X3 transformation matrix.

eM12: Identifies the angle of font rotation, in the form of a TFixed structure, for the M12 value of a 3X3 transformation matrix.

eM21: Identifies the angle of font rotation, in the form of a TFixed structure, for the M21 value of a 3X3 transformation matrix.

eM22: Identifies the angle of font rotation, in the form of a TFixed structure, for the M22 value of a 3X3 transformation matrix.

The TFixed structure defines a real number in a fixed point format. The TFixed structure is defined as:

```
TFixed = packed record
      fract: Word;           {the fractional portion}
      value: SHORT;          {the integer portion}
end;
```

fract: Identifies the fractional portion of the real number.

value: Identifies the integer portion of the real number.

Return Value

If the function succeeds, it returns a nonzero value, and the buffer pointed to by the p6 parameter will contain the glyph outline information. If the function fails, it returns GDI_ERROR.

See Also

GetOutlineTextMetrics

Example

Listing 8-11: Retrieving Glyph Bitmaps

```
var
  Form1: TForm1;
  SelectedChar: Byte;   // holds the selected character
```

```
    Angle: Integer;        // holds the rotation angle

implementation

{$R *.DFM}

function MakeFixed(Value: Double): TFixed;
var
  TheValue: longint;  // intermediate storage variable
begin
  {convert the indicated number into a TFixed record}
  TheValue := Trunc(Value*65536);
  Result := TFixed(Longint(TheValue));
end;

procedure DrawGlyph;
var
  BitmapSize: Longint;              // holds the required size of the bitmap
  BitmapBits: Pointer;              // a pointer to the bitmap
  BitmapInfo: Windows.TBitmap;      // Windows bitmap information
  GlyphBitmap: HBITMAP;             // a handle to the final bitmap
  GlyphMetrics: TGlyphMetrics;      // holds glyph metric information
  Matrix: TMat2;                    // holds the rotation matrix
begin
  {initialize the rotation matrix. note that all angle values
   must be converted to radians}
  Matrix.eM11 := MakeFixed(Cos(Angle*(PI/180)));
  Matrix.eM12 := MakeFixed(Sin(Angle*(PI/180)));
  Matrix.eM21 := MakeFixed(-Sin(Angle*(PI/180)));
  Matrix.eM22 := MakeFixed(Cos(Angle*(PI/180)));

  {retrieve the required size of the bitmap}
  BitmapSize := GetGlyphOutline(Form1.Canvas.Handle, SelectedChar, GGO_BITMAP,
                                GlyphMetrics, 0, NIL, Matrix);

  {allocate enough memory to hold the bitmap}
  GetMem(BitmapBits, BitmapSize);

  {retrieve the glyph bitmap}
  GetGlyphOutline(Form1.Canvas.Handle, SelectedChar, GGO_BITMAP, GlyphMetrics,
                  BitmapSize, BitmapBits, Matrix);

  {initialize the bitmap information structure to create
   an actual Windows bitmap}
  with BitmapInfo do
  begin
    bmType := 0;
    bmWidth := (GlyphMetrics.gmBlackBoxX+31) and not 31;
    bmHeight := GlyphMetrics.gmBlackBoxY;
    bmWidthBytes := bmWidth shr 3;
    bmPlanes := 1;
    bmBitsPixel := 1;
    bmBits := BitmapBits;
  end;
```

8

Chapter

```
      {create the Windows bitmap}
      GlyphBitmap := CreateBitmapIndirect(BitmapInfo);

      {assign the final bitmap to the image for display}
      Form1.Image1.Picture.Bitmap.Handle := GlyphBitmap;
      Form1.Image1.Picture.Bitmap.Width := GlyphMetrics.gmBlackBoxX;

      {free the allocated bitmap memory}
      FreeMem(BitmapBits, BitmapSize);
   end;

procedure TForm1.FormCreate(Sender: TObject);
begin
   {create the image's bitmap and initialize variables}
   Image1.Picture.Bitmap := TBitmap.Create;
   SelectedChar := Ord('A');
   Angle := 0;
end;

procedure TForm1.FormActivate(Sender: TObject);
begin
   {draw the bitmap upon activation}
   DrawGlyph;
end;

procedure TForm1.SpeedButton1Click(Sender: TObject);
begin
   {select the indicated character and draw its bitmap}
   SelectedChar := Ord(PChar(TSpeedButton(Sender).Caption)[0]);
   DrawGlyph;
end;

procedure TForm1.ScrollBar1Change(Sender: TObject);
begin
   {change the rotation angle and update the screen}
   Angle := ScrollBar1.Position;
   Label2.Caption := IntToStr(Angle);
   DrawGlyph;
end;
```

*Figure 8-12:
The rotated
glyph*

Table 8-25: GetGlyphOutline p3 Values

Value	Description
GGO_BITMAP	Retrieves the glyph outline in the form of a double word aligned, row oriented monochrome bitmap.
GGO_NATIVE	Retrieves the glyph outline in its native format (a series of lines and curves), measured in the font's design units. The p7 parameter is ignored.
GGO_METRICS	Retrieves only the TGlyphMetrics information for the p4 parameter.

GetKerningPairs   Windows.Pas

Syntax

```
GetKerningPairs(
DC: HDC;              {a handle to a device context}
Count: DWORD;         {the number of TKerningPair structures in the array}
var KerningPairs      {a pointer to an array of TKerningPair structures}
): DWORD;             {returns the number of kerning pairs retrieved}
```

Description

This function retrieves the character kerning pairs for the currently selected font in the device context identified by the DC parameter.

Parameters

DC: A handle to the device context whose currently selected font's kerning pairs are to be retrieved.

Count: Specifies the number of TKerningPair structures in the array pointed to by the KerningPairs parameter. If the selected font contains more kerning pairs than this parameter indicates, the function fails.

KerningPairs: A pointer to an array of TKerningPair structures that receives the character kerning pairs of the currently selected font. This array must contain at least as many TKerningPair structures as indicated by the Count parameter. If this parameter is set to NIL, the function returns the total number of kerning pairs in the font. The TKerningPair structure is defined as:

```
TKerningPair = packed record
    wFirst: Word;              {the first kerning pair character}
    wSecond: Word;             {the second kerning pair character}
    iKernAmount: Integer;      {the kerning amount}
end;
```

wFirst: Specifies the value of the first character in the kerning pair.

wSecond: Specifies the value of the second character in the kerning pair.

iKernAmount: Specifies the intercharacter space adjustment, in logical units, if the two characters appear side by side in the same typeface and size. Typically, this value is negative, causing the characters to be spaced closer together.

Return Value

If the function succeeds, it returns the number of kerning pairs retrieved; otherwise it returns zero.

See Also

GetTextCharacterExtra, SetTextCharacterExtra

Example

Listing 8-12: Retrieving Kerning Pairs for the Currently Selected Font

```
{Whoops!  Delphi incorrectly imports this function, so we must reimport it
 manually to obtain the full functionality of this function}
function GetKerningPairs(DC: HDC; Count: DWORD;
                         KerningPairs: Pointer): DWORD; stdcall;

var
  Form1: TForm1;

implementation

{$R *.DFM}

{reimport the function}
function GetKerningPairs; external gdi32 name 'GetKerningPairs';

procedure TForm1.FormActivate(Sender: TObject);
type
  TKerningPairs = array[0..0] of TKerningPair;  // holds the kerning pairs
var
  FaceName: array[0..255] of char;   // holds the selected font typeface name
  KerningPairs: ^TKerningPairs;      // a pointer to the kerning pair array
  NumPairs: DWORD;                   // holds the number of pairs
  Count: Integer;                    // general loop control variable
begin
  {retrieve the name of the currently selected font and display it}
  GetTextFace(Form1.Canvas.Handle, 255, @FaceName[0]);
  Label2.Caption := FaceName;

  {retrieve the total number of kerning pairs in the selected font}
  NumPairs := GetKerningPairs(Form1.Canvas.Handle, 0, nil);

  {allocate enough memory to hold all of the kerning pairs}
  GetMem(KerningPairs, SizeOf(TKerningPair)*NumPairs);

  {retrieve the kerning pairs for the font}
```

```
GetKerningPairs(Form1.Canvas.Handle, NumPairs, KerningPairs);

{display every kerning pair and its kerning amount}
Memo1.Lines.Clear;
Memo1.Lines.Add('Pair'+#9+'Kern Amount');
for Count := 0 to NumPairs-1 do
  Memo1.Lines.Add(Char(KerningPairs^[Count].wFirst)+
                  Char(KerningPairs^[Count].wSecond)+#9+
                  IntToStr(KerningPairs^[Count].iKernAmount));

{free the kerning pairs array memory}
  FreeMem(KerningPairs,SizeOf(TKerningPair)*NumPairs);
end;
```

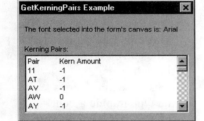

Figure 8-13:
The kerning
pairs

GetOutlineTextMetrics   *Windows.Pas*

Syntax

```
GetOutlineTextMetrics(
DC: HDC;                        {a handle to a device context}
p2: UINT;                       {the size of the TOutlineTextMetric buffer}
OTMetricStructs: Pointer        {a pointer to the TOutlineTextMetric buffer}
): UINT;                        {returns an error code}
```

Description

This function retrieves metric information, such as height, ascent, descent, and other physical measurements, for the currently selected True Type (only) font in the device context identified by the DC parameter. This function provides True Type specific information in addition to the information retrieved by the GetTextMetrics function.

Parameters

DC: A handle to the device context whose currently selected True Type font's text metrics are retrieved.

p2: Specifies the size of the buffer pointed to by the OTMetricStructs parameter, in bytes.

OTMetricStructs: A pointer to a buffer that receives a TOutlineTextMetric structure describing the text metrics of the True Type font. If this parameter is set to NIL, the function returns the required size for the TOutlineTextMetric buffer. Due to the strings located at the end of this structure, the structure can vary in size. The developer should first query the function for the appropriate size, then dynamically allocate the buffer. Note that the sizes returned by the members of this structure are in logical units and depend on the mapping mode of the specified device context. The TOutlineTextMetric structure is defined as:

```
TOutlineTextMetric = record
      otmSize: UINT;                          {the size of the structure}
      otmTextMetrics: TTextMetric;            {contains additional font information}
      otmFiller: Byte;                        {a byte aligning value}
      otmPanoseNumber: TPanose;               {specifies PANOSE information}
      otmfsSelection: UINT;                   {inherent font attributes}
      otmfsType: UINT;                        {licensing and embedding flags}
      otmsCharSlopeRise: Integer;             {italic cursor slope enumerator}
      otmsCharSlopeRun: Integer;              {italic cursor slope denominator}
      otmItalicAngle: Integer;                {the italics angle}
      otmEMSquare: UINT;                      {em square dimensions}
      otmAscent: Integer;                     {the typographic ascent}
      otmDescent: Integer;                    {the typographic descent}
      otmLineGap: UINT;                       {the typographic line spacing}
      otmsCapEmHeight: UINT;                  {unused}
      otmsXHeight: UINT;                      {unused}
      otmrcFontBox: TRect;                    {the bounding box}
      otmMacAscent: Integer;                  {the Macintosh ascent}
      otmMacDescent: Integer;                 {the Macintosh descent}
      otmMacLineGap: UINT;                    {the Macintosh line spacing}
      otmusMinimumPPEM: UINT;                 {the smallest recommended size}
      otmptSubscriptSize: TPoint;             {the recommended subscript size}
      otmptSubscriptOffset: TPoint;           {the recommended subscript offset}
      otmptSuperscriptSize: TPoint;           {the recommended superscript size}
      otmptSuperscriptOffset: TPoint;         {the recommended superscript offset}
      otmsStrikeoutSize: UINT;                {the strikeout line width}
      otmsStrikeoutPosition: Integer;         {the strikeout offset}
      otmsUnderscoreSize: Integer;            {the underscore line width}
      otmsUnderscorePosition: Integer;        {the underscore position}
      otmpFamilyName: PAnsiChar;              {the font family name offset}
      otmpFaceName: PAnsiChar;                {the font face name offset}
      otmpStyleName: PAnsiChar;               {the font style name offset}
      otmpFullName: PAnsiChar;                {the full font name offset}
end;
```

otmSize: Specifies the size of the allocated TOutlineTextMetric structure, in bytes.

otmTextMetrics: Specifies a TTextMetric structure containing additional physical information for the font. The TTextMetric structure is defined as:

```
TTextMetric = record
    tmHeight: Longint;                  {the height of a character}
    tmAscent: Longint;                  {the ascent of a character}
    tmDescent: Longint;                 {the descent of a character}
    tmInternalLeading: Longint;         {the internal leading}
    tmExternalLeading: Longint;         {the external leading}
    tmAveCharWidth: Longint;            {the average character width}
    tmMaxCharWidth: Longint;            {the maximum character width}
    tmWeight: Longint;                  {the boldness value}
    tmOverhang: Longint;                {the overhang width}
    tmDigitizedAspectX: Longint;        {the horizontal aspect}
    tmDigitizedAspectY: Longint;        {the vertical aspect}
    tmFirstChar: AnsiChar;              {the first character}
    tmLastChar: AnsiChar;               {the last character}
    tmDefaultChar: AnsiChar;            {the default character}
    tmBreakChar: AnsiChar;              {the word break character}
    tmItalic: Byte;                     {the italics flag}
    tmUnderlined: Byte;                 {the underlined flag}
    tmStruckOut: Byte;                  {the strikeout flag}
    tmPitchAndFamily: Byte;             {the pitch and family flags}
    tmCharSet: Byte;                    {the character set}
end;
```

Please see the GetTextMetrics function for a description of this data structure.

otmFiller: Specifies a value used solely for byte aligning the structure.

otmPanoseNumber: A TPanose structure containing the PANOSE font classification information for the True Type font. This is used to associate the font with other fonts having a similar appearance but varying names. The TPanose structure is defined as:

```
TPanose = packed record
    bFamilyType: Byte;                  {the family type}
    bSerifStyle: Byte;                  {the serif style}
    bWeight: Byte;                      {the boldness}
    bProportion: Byte;                  {the proportionality}
    bContrast: Byte;                    {the contrast}
    bStrokeVariation: Byte;             {the stroke variation}
    bArmStyle: Byte;                    {the arm style}
    bLetterform: Byte;                  {the letter form}
    bMidline: Byte;                     {the midline position}
    bXHeight: Byte;                     {the xheight}
end;
```

bFamilyType: Specifies the family type, and can contain one value from Table 8-26.

bSerifStyle: Specifies the serif style, and can contain one value from Table 8-27.

bWeight: Specifies the font weight (boldness), and can contain one value from Table 8-28.

bProportion: Specifies the font proportionality, and can contain one value from Table 8-29.

bContrast: Specifies font contrast, and can contain one value from Table 8-30.

bStrokeVariation: Specifies the stroke variation within the font, and can contain one value from Table 8-31.

bArmStyle: Specifies glyph arm style, and can contain one value from Table 8-32.

bLetterform: Specifies the glyph letter form, and can contain one value from Table 8-33.

bMidline: Specifies the midline, and can contain one value from Table 8-34.

bXHeight: Specifies the xheight, and can contain one value from Table 8-35.

otmfsSelection: Specifies a bitmask indicating certain attributes inherently built into the font pattern, such as bold or italics. The bits of this member indicate the various attributes, as shown in Table 8-36.

otmfsType: Specifies a bitmask indicating the licensing attributes of the font. If bit 1 is set, the font may not be embedded in a document; if it is not set, embedding is allowed. If bit 2 is set, the font may be embedded only as a read-only font.

otmsCharSlopeRise: Used with the otmsCharSlopeRun member, this value specifies the numerator of the ratio used to create an italics cursor that has the same slope as the italicized font, as indicated by the otmItalicAngle member.

otmsCharSlopeRun: Used with the otmsCharSlopeRise member, this value specifies the denominator of the ratio used to create an italics cursor that has the same slope as the italicized font, as indicated by the otmItalicAngle member.

otmItalicAngle: Specifies the italics angle for the font, in tenths of a degree rotating counterclockwise from vertical. Most fonts have a negative value, indicating a font leaning to the right. This member will be set to zero for nonitalicized fonts.

otmEMSquare: Specifies the horizontal and vertical dimensions, in logical units, of the font's em square.

otmAscent: The typographic value that specifies the maximum extent to which characters in this font rise above the baseline.

otmDescent: The typographic value that specifies the maximum extent to which characters in this font descend below the baseline.

otmLineGap: Specifies the typographic line spacing.

otmsCapEmHeight: This member is no longer used.

otmsXHeight: This member is no longer used.

otmrcFontBox: Specifies the font's bounding box.

otmMacAscent: The maximum extent to which characters in this font rise above the baseline on the Macintosh computer.

otmMacDescent: The maximum extent to which characters in this font descend below the baseline on the Macintosh computer.

otmMacLineGap: The line spacing used by this font on the Macintosh computer.

otmusMinimumPPEM: Specifies the smallest recommended font size in pixels per em square.

otmptSubscriptSize: A TPoint structure that specifies the recommended subscript width and height.

otmptSubscriptOffset: A TPoint structure that specifies the recommended horizontal and vertical subscript offset from the origin of the character to the origin of the subscript.

otmptSuperscriptSize: A TPoint structure that specifies the recommended superscript width and height.

otmptSuperscriptOffset: A TPoint structure that specifies the recommended horizontal and vertical superscript offset from the baseline of the character to the baseline of the superscript.

otmsStrikeoutSize: Specifies the width of the strikeout line.

otmsStrikeoutPosition: Specifies the offset of the strikeout line from the baseline.

otmsUnderscoreSize: Specifies the width of the underscore line.

otmsUnderscorePosition: Specifies the offset of the underscore line from the baseline.

otmpFamilyName: Specifies the offset from the beginning of the TOutlineText-Metric structure to the beginning of the string containing the font family name.

otmpFaceName: Specifies the offset from the beginning of the TOutlineText-Metric structure to the beginning of the string containing the font face name.

otmpStyleName: Specifies the offset from the beginning of the TOutlineText-Metric structure to the beginning of the string containing the font style name.

otmpFullName: Specifies the offset from the beginning of the TOutlineText-Metric structure to the beginning of the string containing the full, unique font name.

Return Value

If the function succeeds, it returns a nonzero value; otherwise it returns zero. To get extended error information, call the GetLastError function.

See Also

GetGlyphOutline, GetTextMetrics

Example

Listing 8-13: Retrieving True Type Font Text Metrics

{note: the form must have a True Type font set as its selected font before
this example will work properly}

```
procedure TForm1.FormActivate(Sender: TObject);
var
  FontInfo: POutlineTextMetric;        // a pointer to the text metric info
  FaceName: array[0..255] of char;     // holds the font face name
  TheSize: LongInt;                    // holds the required buffer size
begin
  {retrieve and display the selected font's face name}
  GetTextFace(Form1.Canvas.Handle, 256, FaceName);
  Label2.Caption := FaceName;

  {retrieve the required buffer size}
  TheSize := GetOutlineTextMetrics(Form1.Canvas.Handle, 0, nil);

  {allocate the buffer}
  GetMem(FontInfo, TheSize);

  {set the size member}
  FontInfo^.otmSize := TheSize;

  {retrieve the True Type font attributes}
  GetOutlineTextMetrics(Form1.Canvas.Handle, TheSize,
                        FontInfo);

  {clear the list box and begin displaying the physical font attributes}
  ListBox1.Items.Clear;
  with FontInfo^.otmTextMetrics, ListBox1.Items do
  begin
    {display the various font measurements}
    Label15.Caption := IntToStr(tmHeight);
    Label14.Caption := IntToStr(tmAscent);
    Label13.Caption := IntToStr(tmDescent);
    Label12.Caption := IntToStr(tmInternalLeading);
    Label11.Caption := IntToStr(tmExternalLeading);

    {display the average and maximum character width}
    Add('Average Char Width: '+IntToStr(tmAveCharWidth));
    Add('Max Char Width: '+IntToStr(tmMaxCharWidth));

    {display the boldness setting}
    case tmWeight of
      FW_DONTCARE:    Add('Weight: Don't care');
      FW_THIN:        Add('Weight: Thin');
      FW_EXTRALIGHT:  Add('Weight: Extra light');
      FW_LIGHT:       Add('Weight: Light');
      FW_NORMAL:      Add('Weight: Normal');
      FW_MEDIUM:      Add('Weight: Medium');
      FW_SEMIBOLD:    Add('Weight: Semibold');
      FW_BOLD:        Add('Weight: Bold');
```

```
    FW_EXTRABOLD:  Add('Weight: Extra bold');
    FW_HEAVY:      Add('Weight: Heavy');
  end;

  {display the overhang measurement}
  Add('Overhang: '+IntToStr(tmOverhang));

  {display the horizontal and vertical aspect}
  Add('Digitized Aspect X: '+IntToStr(tmDigitizedAspectX));
  Add('Digitized Aspect Y: '+IntToStr(tmDigitizedAspectY));

  {display the important font characters}
  Add('First Character: '+Char(tmFirstChar));
  Add('Last Char: '+Char(tmLastChar));
  Add('Default Char: '+Char(tmDefaultChar));
  Add('Break Char: '+Char(tmBreakChar));

  {indicate italic, underlined, or strikeout attributes}
  CheckBox1.Checked := (tmItalic>0);
  CheckBox2.Checked := (tmUnderlined>0);
  CheckBox3.Checked := (tmStruckOut>0);

  {display the font pitch}
  Add('Pitch: ');
  if ((tmPitchAndFamily and $0F) and TMPF_FIXED_PITCH)= TMPF_FIXED_PITCH then
    Add('      Fixed pitch');
  if ((tmPitchAndFamily and $0F) and TMPF_VECTOR) = TMPF_VECTOR then
    Add('      Vector');
  if ((tmPitchAndFamily and $0F) and TMPF_TRUETYPE) = TMPF_TRUETYPE then
    Add('      True Type');
  if ((tmPitchAndFamily and $0F) and TMPF_DEVICE) = TMPF_DEVICE then
    Add('      Device');
  if (tmPitchAndFamily and $0F) = 0 then
    Add('      Monospaced bitmap font');

  {display the font family}
  case (tmPitchAndFamily and $F0) of
    FF_DECORATIVE: Add('Family: Decorative');
    FF_DONTCARE:   Add('Family: Don''t care');
    FF_MODERN:     Add('Family: Modern');
    FF_ROMAN:      Add('Family: Roman');
    FF_SCRIPT:     Add('Family: Script');
    FF_SWISS:      Add('Family: Swiss');
  end;

  {display the character set}
  case tmCharSet of
    ANSI_CHARSET:          Add('Character set: ANSI');
    DEFAULT_CHARSET:       Add('Character set: Default');
    SYMBOL_CHARSET:        Add('Character set: Symbol');
    SHIFTJIS_CHARSET:      Add('Character set: ShiftJis');
    GB2312_CHARSET:        Add('Character set: GB2312');
    HANGEUL_CHARSET:       Add('Character set: Hangeul');
    CHINESEBIG5_CHARSET:   Add('Character set: Chinese Big5');
    OEM_CHARSET:           Add('Character set: OEM');
```

```
      else
        Add('Windows 95 only character set');
      end;
end;

{display True Type specific information}
with FontInfo^, ListBox1.Items do
begin
  Add('');
  Add('');
  Add('True Type specific information');
  Add('-------------------------------');
  Add('');
  Add('Panose Information: ');

  {display the Panose family type}
  case otmPanoseNumber.bFamilyType of
    PAN_ANY:                 Add('      Family Type: Any');
    PAN_NO_FIT:              Add('      Family Type: No fit');
    PAN_FAMILY_TEXT_DISPLAY: Add('      Family Type: Text and display');
    PAN_FAMILY_SCRIPT:       Add('      Family Type: Script');
    PAN_FAMILY_DECORATIVE:   Add('      Family Type: Decorative');
    PAN_FAMILY_PICTORIAL:    Add('      Family Type: Pictorial');
  end;

  {display the Panose serif style}
  case otmPanoseNumber.bSerifStyle of
    PAN_ANY:                     Add('      Serif Style: Any');
    PAN_NO_FIT:                  Add('      Serif Style: No fit');
    PAN_SERIF_COVE:              Add('      Serif Style: Cove');
    PAN_SERIF_OBTUSE_COVE:       Add('      Serif Style: Obtuse cove');
    PAN_SERIF_SQUARE_COVE:       Add('      Serif Style: Square cove');
    PAN_SERIF_OBTUSE_SQUARE_COVE: Add('      Serif Style: Obtuse square cove');
    PAN_SERIF_SQUARE:            Add('      Serif Style: Square');
    PAN_SERIF_THIN:              Add('      Serif Style: Thin');
    PAN_SERIF_BONE:              Add('      Serif Style: Bone');
    PAN_SERIF_EXAGGERATED:       Add('      Serif Style: Exaggerated');
    PAN_SERIF_TRIANGLE:          Add('      Serif Style: Triangle');
    PAN_SERIF_NORMAL_SANS:       Add('      Serif Style: Normal sans serif');
    PAN_SERIF_OBTUSE_SANS:       Add('      Serif Style: Obtuse sans serif');
    PAN_SERIF_PERP_SANS:         Add('      Serif Style: Perp sans serif');
    PAN_SERIF_FLARED:            Add('      Serif Style: Flared');
    PAN_SERIF_ROUNDED:           Add('      Serif Style: Rounded');
  end;

  {display the Panose weight}
  case otmPanoseNumber.bWeight of
    PAN_ANY:                 Add('      Weight: Any');
    PAN_NO_FIT:              Add('      Weight: No fit');
    PAN_WEIGHT_VERY_LIGHT:   Add('      Weight: Very light');
    PAN_WEIGHT_LIGHT:        Add('      Weight: Light');
    PAN_WEIGHT_THIN:         Add('      Weight: Thin');
    PAN_WEIGHT_BOOK:         Add('      Weight: Book');
    PAN_WEIGHT_MEDIUM:       Add('      Weight: Medium');
    PAN_WEIGHT_DEMI:         Add('      Weight: Demi');
```

```
      PAN_WEIGHT_BOLD:         Add('     Weight: Bold');
      PAN_WEIGHT_HEAVY:        Add('     Weight: Heavy');
      PAN_WEIGHT_BLACK:        Add('     Weight: Black');
      PAN_WEIGHT_NORD:         Add('     Weight: Nord');
    end;

    {display the Panose proportion}
    case otmPanoseNumber.bProportion of
      PAN_ANY:                     Add('     Proportion: Any');
      PAN_NO_FIT:                  Add('     Proportion: No fit');
      PAN_PROP_OLD_STYLE:          Add('     Proportion: Old style');
      PAN_PROP_MODERN:             Add('     Proportion: Modern');
      PAN_PROP_EVEN_WIDTH:         Add('     Proportion: Even width');
      PAN_PROP_EXPANDED:           Add('     Proportion: Expanded');
      PAN_PROP_CONDENSED:          Add('     Proportion: Condensed');
      PAN_PROP_VERY_EXPANDED:      Add('     Proportion: Very expanded');
      PAN_PROP_VERY_CONDENSED:     Add('     Proportion: Very condensed');
      PAN_PROP_MONOSPACED:         Add('     Proportion: Monospaced');
    end;

    {display the Panose contrast}
    case otmPanoseNumber.bContrast of
      PAN_ANY:                     Add('     Contrast: Any');
      PAN_NO_FIT:                  Add('     Contrast: No fit');
      PAN_CONTRAST_NONE:           Add('     Contrast: None');
      PAN_CONTRAST_VERY_LOW:       Add('     Contrast: Very low');
      PAN_CONTRAST_LOW:            Add('     Contrast: Low');
      PAN_CONTRAST_MEDIUM_LOW:     Add('     Contrast: Medium low');
      PAN_CONTRAST_MEDIUM:         Add('     Contrast: Medium');
      PAN_CONTRAST_MEDIUM_HIGH:    Add('     Contrast: Medium high');
      PAN_CONTRAST_HIGH:           Add('     Contrast: High');
      PAN_CONTRAST_VERY_HIGH:      Add('     Contrast: Very high');
    end;

    {display the Panose stroke variation}
    case otmPanoseNumber.bStrokeVariation of
      PAN_ANY:                  Add('     Stroke variation: Any');
      PAN_NO_FIT:               Add('     Stroke variation: No fit');
      PAN_STROKE_GRADUAL_DIAG:  Add('     Stroke variation: Gradual diagonal');
      PAN_STROKE_GRADUAL_TRAN:  Add('     Stroke variation: Gradual transition');
      PAN_STROKE_GRADUAL_VERT:  Add('     Stroke variation: Gradual vertical');
      PAN_STROKE_GRADUAL_HORZ:  Add('     Stroke variation: Gradual horizontal');
      PAN_STROKE_RAPID_VERT:    Add('     Stroke variation: Rapid vertical');
      PAN_STROKE_RAPID_HORZ:    Add('     Stroke variation: Rapid horizontal');
      PAN_STROKE_INSTANT_VERT:  Add('     Stroke variation: Instant vertical');
    end;

    {display the Panose arm style}
    case otmPanoseNumber.bArmStyle of
      PAN_ANY:                       Add('     Arm style: Any');
      PAN_NO_FIT:                    Add('     Arm style: No fit');
      PAN_STRAIGHT_ARMS_HORZ:        Add('     Arm style: Straight '+
                                         'horizontal');
      PAN_STRAIGHT_ARMS_WEDGE:       Add('     Arm style: Straight wedge');
      PAN_STRAIGHT_ARMS_VERT:        Add('     Arm style: Straight vertical');
```

8

Chapter

```
    PAN_STRAIGHT_ARMS_SINGLE_SERIF: Add('       Arm style: Straight '+
                                         'single_serif');
    PAN_STRAIGHT_ARMS_DOUBLE_SERIF: Add('       Arm style: Straight '+
                                         'double-serif');
    PAN_BENT_ARMS_HORZ:             Add('       Arm style: Nonstraight '+
                                         'horizontal');
    PAN_BENT_ARMS_WEDGE:            Add('       Arm style: Nonstraight wedge');
    PAN_BENT_ARMS_VERT:             Add('       Arm style: Nonstraight '+
                                         'vertical');
    PAN_BENT_ARMS_SINGLE_SERIF:     Add('       Arm style: Nonstraight '+
                                         'single-serif');
    PAN_BENT_ARMS_DOUBLE_SERIF:     Add('       Arm style: Nonstraight '+
                                         'double-serif');
  end;

  {display the Panose letter form}
  case otmPanoseNumber.bLetterform of
    PAN_ANY:                      Add('       Letter form: Any');
    PAN_NO_FIT:                   Add('       Letter form: No fit');
    PAN_LETT_NORMAL_CONTACT:      Add('       Letter form: Normal contact');
    PAN_LETT_NORMAL_WEIGHTED:     Add('       Letter form: Normal weighted');
    PAN_LETT_NORMAL_BOXED:        Add('       Letter form: Normal boxed');
    PAN_LETT_NORMAL_FLATTENED:    Add('       Letter form: Normal flattened');
    PAN_LETT_NORMAL_ROUNDED:      Add('       Letter form: Normal rounded');
    PAN_LETT_NORMAL_OFF_CENTER:   Add('       Letter form: Normal off center');
    PAN_LETT_NORMAL_SQUARE:       Add('       Letter form: Normal square');
    PAN_LETT_OBLIQUE_CONTACT:     Add('       Letter form: Oblique contact');
    PAN_LETT_OBLIQUE_WEIGHTED:    Add('       Letter form: Oblique weighted');
    PAN_LETT_OBLIQUE_BOXED:       Add('       Letter form: Oblique boxed');
    PAN_LETT_OBLIQUE_FLATTENED:   Add('       Letter form: Oblique flattened');
    PAN_LETT_OBLIQUE_ROUNDED:     Add('       Letter form: Oblique rounded');
    PAN_LETT_OBLIQUE_OFF_CENTER:  Add('       Letter form: Oblique off center');
    PAN_LETT_OBLIQUE_SQUARE:      Add('       Letter form: Oblique square');
  end;

  {display the Panose midline}
  case otmPanoseNumber.bMidline of
    PAN_ANY:                        Add('   Midline: Any');
    PAN_NO_FIT:                     Add('   Midline: No fit');
    PAN_MIDLINE_STANDARD_TRIMMED:   Add('   Midline: Standard trimmed');
    PAN_MIDLINE_STANDARD_POINTED:   Add('   Midline: Standard pointed');
    PAN_MIDLINE_STANDARD_SERIFED:   Add('   Midline: Standard serifed');
    PAN_MIDLINE_HIGH_TRIMMED:       Add('   Midline: High trimmed');
    PAN_MIDLINE_HIGH_POINTED:       Add('   Midline: High pointed');
    PAN_MIDLINE_HIGH_SERIFED:       Add('   Midline: High serifed');
    PAN_MIDLINE_CONSTANT_TRIMMED:   Add('   Midline: Constant trimmed');
    PAN_MIDLINE_CONSTANT_POINTED:   Add('   Midline: Constant pointed');
    PAN_MIDLINE_CONSTANT_SERIFED:   Add('   Midline: Constant serifed');
    PAN_MIDLINE_LOW_TRIMMED:        Add('   Midline: Low trimmed');
    PAN_MIDLINE_LOW_POINTED:        Add('   Midline: Low pointed');
    PAN_MIDLINE_LOW_SERIFED:        Add('   Midline: Low serifed');
  end;

  {display the Panose xheight}
  case otmPanoseNumber.bXHeight of
```

```
PAN_ANY:                         Add('    XHeight: Any');
PAN_NO_FIT:                      Add('    XHeight: No fit');
PAN_XHEIGHT_CONSTANT_SMALL: Add('    XHeight: Constant small');
PAN_XHEIGHT_CONSTANT_STD:   Add('    XHeight: Constant standard');
PAN_XHEIGHT_CONSTANT_LARGE: Add('    XHeight: Constant large');
PAN_XHEIGHT_DUCKING_SMALL:  Add('    XHeight: Ducking small');
PAN_XHEIGHT_DUCKING_STD:    Add('    XHeight: Ducking standard');
PAN_XHEIGHT_DUCKING_LARGE:  Add('    XHeight: Ducking large');
end;

{display the inherent font attributes}
Add('Selection: ');
if (otmfsSelection and $01)>0 then
  Add('     Italic');
if (otmfsSelection and $02)>0 then
  Add('     Underscore');
if (otmfsSelection and $04)>0 then
  Add('     Negative');
if (otmfsSelection and $08)>0 then
  Add('     Outline');
if (otmfsSelection and $10)>0 then
  Add('     Strikeout');
if (otmfsSelection and $20)>0 then
  Add('     Bold');

{display font embedding information}
Add('Type:');
if (otmfsType and $02)>0 then
  Add('     Embedding Forbidden');
if (otmfsType and $02)<1 then
  Add('     Embedding Allowed');
if (otmfsType and $04)>0 then
  Add('     Embedding Read-Only');

{display italics attributes}
Add('Slope Rise: '+IntToStr(otmsCharSlopeRise));
Add('Slope Run: '+IntToStr(otmsCharSlopeRun));
Add('Italic Angle: '+IntToStr(otmItalicAngle));

{display important physical attributes}
Add('EM Square: '+IntToStr(otmEMSquare));
Add('Typographic Ascent: '+IntToStr(otmAscent));
Add('Typographic Descent: '+IntToStr(otmDescent));
Add('Typographic Line Gap: '+IntToStr(otmLineGap));

{display the bounding box coordinates}
Add('Font Bounding Box: ');
Add('     Left: '+IntToStr(otmrcFontBox.Left));
Add('     Top: '+IntToStr(otmrcFontBox.Top));
Add('     Right: '+IntToStr(otmrcFontBox.Right));
Add('     Bottom: '+IntToStr(otmrcFontBox.Bottom));

{display the Macintosh attributes}
Add('Mac Ascent: '+IntToStr(otmMacAscent));
Add('MacDescent: '+IntToStr(otmMacDescent));
```

```
        Add('Mac Line Gap: '+IntToStr(otmMacLineGap));

        {display the minimum size}
        Add('Minimum Size: '+IntToStr(otmusMinimumPPEM));

        {display subscript suggestions}
        Add('Subscript Size: ');
        Add('      Horizontal: '+IntToStr(otmptSubscriptSize.X));
        Add('      Vertical: '+IntToStr(otmptSubscriptSize.Y));
        Add('Subscript Offset: ');
        Add('      Horizontal: '+IntToStr(otmptSubscriptOffset.X));
        Add('      Vertical: '+IntToStr(otmptSubscriptOffset.Y));

        {display superscript suggestions}
        Add('Superscript Size: ');
        Add('      Horizontal: '+IntToStr(otmptSuperscriptSize.X));
        Add('      Vertical: '+IntToStr(otmptSuperscriptSize.Y));
        Add('Superscript Offset: ');
        Add('      Horizontal: '+IntToStr(otmptSuperscriptOffset.X));
        Add('      Vertical: '+IntToStr(otmptSuperscriptOffset.Y));

        {display line sizes and positions}
        Add('Strikeout Size: '+IntToStr(otmsStrikeoutSize));
        Add('Strikeout Position: '+IntToStr(otmsStrikeoutPosition));
        Add('Underscore Size: '+IntToStr(otmsUnderscoreSize));
        Add('Underscore Position: '+IntToStr(otmsUnderscorePosition));

        {display font family, face, and name strings}
        Add('Family Name: '+PChar(Longint(FontInfo)+FontInfo^.otmpFamilyName));
        Add('Face Name: '+PChar(Longint(FontInfo)+FontInfo^.otmpFaceName));
        Add('Style Name: '+PChar(Longint(FontInfo)+FontInfo^.otmpStyleName));
      end;

      {display the full font name}
      Label17.Caption := PChar(Longint(FontInfo)+FontInfo^.otmpFullName);

      {free the allocated text metric buffer}
      FreeMem(FontInfo, TheSize);
    end;
```

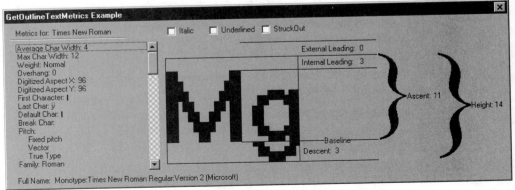

Figure 8-14: The True Type font information

Table 8-26: GetOutlineTextMetrics OTMetricStructs.otmPanoseNumber.bFamilyType Values

Value	Description
PAN_ANY	Any family.
PAN_NO_FIT	No fit.
PAN_FAMILY_TEXT_DISPLAY	Text and display family.
PAN_FAMILY_SCRIPT	Script family.
PAN_FAMILY_DECORATIVE	Decorative family.
PAN_FAMILY_PICTORIAL	Pictorial family.

Table 8-27: GetOutlineTextMetrics OTMetricStructs.otmPanoseNumber.bSerifStyle Values

Value	Description
PAN_ANY	Any serif style.
PAN_NO_FIT	No fit.
PAN_SERIF_COVE	Cove serifs.
PAN_SERIF_OBTUSE_COVE	Obtuse cove serifs.
PAN_SERIF_SQUARE_COVE	Square cove serifs.
PAN_SERIF_OBTUSE_SQUARE_COVE	Obtuse square cove serifs.
PAN_SERIF_SQUARE	Square serifs.
PAN_SERIF_THIN	Thin serifs.
PAN_SERIF_BONE	Bone serifs.
PAN_SERIF_EXAGGERATED	Exaggerated serifs.
PAN_SERIF_TRIANGLE	Triangle serifs.
PAN_SERIF_NORMAL_SANS	Normal sans serif.
PAN_SERIF_OBTUSE_SANS	Obtuse sans serif.
PAN_SERIF_PERP_SANS	Perp sans serif.
PAN_SERIF_FLARED	Flared serifs.
PAN_SERIF_ROUNDED	Rounded serifs.

Table 8-28: GetOutlineTextMetrics OTMetricStructs.otmPanoseNumber.bWeight Values

Value	Description
PAN_ANY	Any boldness.
PAN_NO_FIT	No fit.
PAN_WEIGHT_VERY_LIGHT	Very light boldness.
PAN_WEIGHT_LIGHT	Light boldness.
PAN_WEIGHT_THIN	Thin boldness.
PAN_WEIGHT_BOOK	Book boldness.
PAN_WEIGHT_MEDIUM	Medium boldness.
PAN_WEIGHT_DEMI	Demibold.
PAN_WEIGHT_BOLD	Bold.

8

Chapter

Value	Description
PAN_WEIGHT_HEAVY	Heavy boldness.
PAN_WEIGHT_BLACK	Black boldness.
PAN_WEIGHT_NORD	Nord boldness.

Table 8-29: GetOutlineTextMetrics OTMetricStructs.otmPanoseNumber.bProportion Values

Value	Description
PAN_ANY	Any proportion.
PAN_NO_FIT	No fit.
PAN_PROP_OLD_STYLE	Old style proportion.
PAN_PROP_MODERN	Modern proportion.
PAN_PROP_EVEN_WIDTH	Even width proportion.
PAN_PROP_EXPANDED	Expanded proportion.
PAN_PROP_CONDENSED	Condensed proportion.
PAN_PROP_VERY_EXPANDED	Very expanded proportion.
PAN_PROP_VERY_CONDENSED	Very condensed proportion.
PAN_PROP_MONOSPACED	Monospaced proportion.

Table 8-30: GetOutlineTextMetrics OTMetricStructs.otmPanoseNumber.bContrast Values

Value	Description
PAN_ANY	Any contrast.
PAN_NO_FIT	No fit.
PAN_CONTRAST_NONE	No contrast.
PAN_CONTRAST_VERY_LOW	Very low contrast.
PAN_CONTRAST_LOW	Low contrast.
PAN_CONTRAST_MEDIUM_LOW	Medium low contrast.
PAN_CONTRAST_MEDIUM	Medium contrast.
PAN_CONTRAST_MEDIUM_HIGH	Medium high contrast.
PAN_CONTRAST_HIGH	High contrast.
PAN_CONTRAST_VERY_HIGH	Very high contrast.

Table 8-31: GetOutlineTextMetrics OTMetricStructs.otmPanoseNumber.bStrokeVariation Values

Value	Description
PAN_ANY	Any stroke variation.
PAN_NO_FIT	No fit.
PAN_STROKE_GRADUAL_DIAG	Gradual, diagonal stroke variation.
PAN_STROKE_GRADUAL_TRAN	Gradual, transitional stroke variation.
PAN_STROKE_GRADUAL_VERT	Gradual, vertical stroke variation.

Value	Description
PAN_STROKE_GRADUAL_HORZ	Gradual, horizontal stroke variation.
PAN_STROKE_RAPID_VERT	Rapid, vertical stroke variation.
PAN_STROKE_RAPID_HORZ	Rapid, horizontal stroke variation.
PAN_STROKE_INSTANT_VERT	Instant, vertical stroke variation.

Table 8-32: GetOutlineTextMetrics OTMetricStructs.otmPanoseNumber.bArmStyle Values

Value	Description
PAN_ANY	Any arm style.
PAN_NO_FIT	No fit.
PAN_STRAIGHT_ARMS_HORZ	Straight arms, horizontal arm style.
PAN_STRAIGHT_ARMS_WEDGE	Straight arms, wedge arm style.
PAN_STRAIGHT_ARMS_VERT	Straight arms, vertical arm style.
PAN_STRAIGHT_ARMS_SINGLE_SERIF	Straight arms, single serif arm style.
PAN_STRAIGHT_ARMS_DOUBLE_SERIF	Straight arms, double serif arm style.
PAN_BENT_ARMS_HORZ	Bent arms, horizontal arm style.
PAN_BENT_ARMS_WEDGE	Bent arms, wedge arm style.
PAN_BENT_ARMS_VERT	Bent arms, vertical arm style.
PAN_BENT_ARMS_SINGLE_SERIF	Bent arms, single serif arm style.
PAN_BENT_ARMS_DOUBLE_SERIF	Bent arms, double serif arm style.

Table 8-33: GetOutlineTextMetrics OTMetricStructs.otmPanoseNumber.bLetterform Values

Value	Description
PAN_ANY	Any letter form.
PAN_NO_FIT	No fit.
PAN_LETT_NORMAL_CONTACT	Normal, contact letter form.
PAN_LETT_NORMAL_WEIGHTED	Normal, weighted letter form.
PAN_LETT_NORMAL_BOXED	Normal, boxed letter form.
PAN_LETT_NORMAL_FLATTENED	Normal, flattened letter form.
PAN_LETT_NORMAL_ROUNDED	Normal, rounded letter form.
PAN_LETT_NORMAL_OFF_CENTER	Normal, off center letter form.
PAN_LETT_NORMAL_SQUARE	Normal, square letter form.
PAN_LETT_OBLIQUE_CONTACT	Oblique, contact letter form.
PAN_LETT_OBLIQUE_WEIGHTED	Oblique, weighted letter form.
PAN_LETT_OBLIQUE_BOXED	Oblique, boxed letter form.
PAN_LETT_OBLIQUE_FLATTENED	Oblique, flattened letter form.
PAN_LETT_OBLIQUE_ROUNDED	Oblique, rounded letter form.
PAN_LETT_OBLIQUE_OFF_CENTER	Oblique, off center letter form.
PAN_LETT_OBLIQUE_SQUARE	Oblique, square letter form.

8

Chapter

Table 8-34: GetOutlineTextMetrics OTMetricStructs.otmPanoseNumber.bMidline Values

Value	Description
PAN_ANY	Any midline.
PAN_NO_FIT	No fit.
PAN_MIDLINE_STANDARD_TRIMMED	Standard, trimmed midline.
PAN_MIDLINE_STANDARD_POINTED	Standard, pointed midline.
PAN_MIDLINE_STANDARD_SERIFED	Standard, serifed midline.
PAN_MIDLINE_HIGH_TRIMMED	High, trimmed midline.
PAN_MIDLINE_HIGH_POINTED	High, pointed midline.
PAN_MIDLINE_HIGH_SERIFED	High, serifed midline.
PAN_MIDLINE_CONSTANT_TRIMMED	Constant, trimmed midline.
PAN_MIDLINE_CONSTANT_POINTED	Constant, pointed midline.
PAN_MIDLINE_CONSTANT_SERIFED	Constant, serifed midline.
PAN_MIDLINE_LOW_TRIMMED	Low, trimmed midline.
PAN_MIDLINE_LOW_POINTED	Low, pointed midline.
PAN_MIDLINE_LOW_SERIFED	Low, serifed midline.

Table 8-35: GetOutlineTextMetrics OTMetricStructs.otmPanoseNumber.bXHeight Values

Value	Description
PAN_ANY	Any xheight.
PAN_NO_FIT	No fit.
PAN_XHEIGHT_CONSTANT_SMALL	Constant, small xheight.
PAN_XHEIGHT_CONSTANT_STD	Constant, standard xheight.
PAN_XHEIGHT_CONSTANT_LARGE	Constant, large xheight.
PAN_XHEIGHT_DUCKING_SMALL	Ducking, small xheight.
PAN_XHEIGHT_DUCKING_STD	Ducking, standard xheight.
PAN_XHEIGHT_DUCKING_LARGE	Ducking, large xheight.

Table 8-36: GetOutlineTextMetrics OTMetricStructs.otmfsSelection Values

Bit	Description
0	Indicates an italic font.
1	Indicates an underscored font.
2	Indicates a negative font.
3	Indicates an outline font.
4	Indicates a struckout font.
5	Indicates a bold font.

GetRasterizerCaps   *Windows.Pas*

Syntax

GetRasterizerCaps(
var p1: TRasterizerStatus;   {a pointer to a TRasterizerStatus structure}
p2: UINT   {the size of the TRasterizerStatus structure}
): BOOL;   {returns TRUE or FALSE}

Description

This function returns information in the TRasterizerStatus structure pointed to by the p1 parameter that indicates if True Type fonts are installed or enabled on the system.

Parameters

p1: A pointer to a TRasterizerStatus structure that receives information concerning availability of True Type fonts on the system. The TRasterizerStatus structure is defined as:

TRasterizerStatus = packed record
    nSize: SHORT;   {the size of the TRasterizerStatus structure}
    wFlags: SHORT;   {True Type availability flags}
    nLanguageID: SHORT;   {the language identifier}
end;

nSize: Specifies the size of the TRasterizerStatus structure, in bytes. This member should be set to SizeOf(TRasterizerStatus).

wFlags: A series of flags specifying True Type font availability. This member can contain one or more values from Table 8-37.

nLanguageID: Specifies the language identifier, as indicated by the system's Setup.inf file.

p2: Specifies the number of bytes to copy into the TRasterizerStatus structure. The actual number of bytes copied is the value of this parameter or the size of the TRasterizerStatus structure, whichever is less.

Return Value

If the function succeeds, it returns TRUE; otherwise it returns FALSE. To get extended error information, call the GetLastError function.

See Also

GetOutlineTextMetrics, GetTextMetrics

Example

Please see Listing 8-7 under EnumFontFamilies.

8

Chapter

Table 8-37: GetRasterizerCaps pl.wFlags Values

Value	Description
TT_AVAILABLE	At least one True Type font is installed and available on the system.
TT_ENABLED	True Type fonts are supported by the system.

GetTabbedTextExtent   Windows.Pas

Syntax

```
GetTabbedTextExtent(
hDC: HDC;                        {a handle to a device context}
lpString: PChar;                 {the string whose dimensions are to be determined}
nCount: Integer;                 {the number of characters in the string}
nTabPositions: Integer;          {the number of tab stops}
lpnTabStopPositions: Pointer     {a pointer to an array of tab stop positions}
): DWORD;                        {returns the width and height of the string}
```

Description

This function returns the width and height of a string containing tab characters. The font currently selected into the specified device context is used as the basis for the string dimensions, and any tab characters in the string are expanded to the tab stop positions as indicated by the array pointed to by the lpnTabStopPositions parameter. The current clipping region of the specified device context does not affect the computed dimensions. In instances where a string containing kerning pairs is output to a device supporting character kerning, the dimensions returned by this function may not match the sum of the individual character dimensions in the string.

Parameters

hDC: A handle to a device context whose currently selected font is used to determine the length of the string.

lpString: A pointer to a null-terminated string containing the text with tab characters

nCount: Specifies the length of the string pointed to by the lpString parameter, in characters.

nTabPositions: Specifies the number of entries in the array of tab stops pointed to by the lpnTabStopPositions parameter.

lpnTabStopPositions: A pointer to an array of integers. Each integer entry in the array indicates a tab stop position, in device units. The tab stops must be arranged in an increasing order, with the smallest tab stop position as the first entry in the array and each tab stop position increasing thereafter. If this parameter is set to NIL and the nTabPositions parameter is set to zero, tab characters are expanded to eight times the average character width of the selected font.

Return Value

If the function succeeds, it returns the width and height of the string, where the height is in the high-order word of the return value and the width is in the low-order word. If the function fails, it returns zero.

See Also

GetTextExtentPoint32, TabbedTextOut

Example

Please see Listing 8-17 under TabbedTextOut.

GetTextAlign   Windows.Pas

Syntax

```
GetTextAlign(
DC: HDC                    {a handle to a device context}
): UINT;                   {returns the text alignment flags}
```

Description

This function retrieves a set of flags indicating the current text alignment defined for the specified device context. The alignment is based on a bounding rectangle surrounding all characters within the string. The string's bounding rectangle dimensions can be retrieved by calling the GetTextExtentPoint32 function. Text alignment is based on the starting point of the string, as defined by text output functions such as TextOut.

Parameters

DC: A handle to the device context whose text alignment is to be retrieved.

Return Value

If the function succeeds, it returns one or more text alignment flags from Table 8-38; otherwise it returns GDI_ERROR. To get extended error information, call the GetLastError function. Unlike most functions, the returned flags do not represent individual bits, and cannot simply be combined with the return value to determine if a particular flag is present. Instead, the flags must be inspected in the following groups of related flags:

TA_LEFT, TA_RIGHT, and TA_CENTER
TA_BOTTOM, TA_TOP, and TA_BASELINE
TA_NOUPDATECP and TA_UPDATECP

For vertical baseline fonts, the related flags are:

TA_LEFT, TA_RIGHT, and VTA_BASELINE
TA_BOTTOM, TA_TOP, and VTA_CENTER
TA_NOUPDATECP and TA_UPDATECP

To determine if any particular flag is present in the return value, the related group of flags must be combined using the OR Boolean operator, and the result combined with the return value using the Boolean AND operator. For example, to determine if the text is right aligned, assume that TextAlignment contains the return value from a call to the GetTextAlign function and use the formula:

```
if (TextAlignment and (TA_LEFT or TA_CENTER or TA_RIGHT)) = TA_RIGHT then
    Label2.Caption := 'Right';
```

See Also

DrawText, DrawTextEx, GetTextExtentPoint32, SetTextAlign, TextOut

Example

Please see Listing 8-16 under SetTextAlign.

Table 8-38: GetTextAlign Return Values

Value	Description
TA_BASELINE	The starting point is on the text baseline.
TA_BOTTOM	The starting point is on the bottom of the bounding rectangle for the text.
TA_TOP	The starting point is on the top of the bounding rectangle for the text.
TA_CENTER	The starting point is the horizontal center of the bounding rectangle for the text.
TA_LEFT	The starting point is on the left of the bounding rectangle for the text.
TA_RIGHT	The starting point is on the right of the bounding rectangle for the text.
TA_RTLREADING	Windows 95 only: Indicates that the text is in a right to left reading order. This value is meaningful only when the selected font is either Hebrew or Arabic.
TA_NOUPDATECP	Does not update the current position after drawing text.
TA_UPDATECP	Updates the current position after drawing text.
VTA_BASELINE	Vertical baseline fonts only: The starting point is on the text baseline.
VTA_CENTER	Vertical baseline fonts only: The starting point is the vertical center of the bounding rectangle for the text.

GetTextCharacterExtra   Windows.Pas

Syntax

```
GetTextCharacterExtra(
DC: HDC                      {a handle to a device context}
): Integer;                  {returns the intercharacter spacing amount}
```

Description

This function retrieves the amount of extra space, in logical units, added between characters when drawing a line of text on the specified device context.

Parameters

DC: A handle to the device context whose extra character spacing value is to be retrieved.

Return Value

If the function succeeds, it returns the amount of extra space added between characters; otherwise, it returns $80000000.

See Also

DrawText, DrawTextEx, SetTextCharacterExtra, TextOut

Example

Please see Listing 8-16 under SetTextAlign.

GetTextColor   *Windows.Pas*

Syntax

```
GetTextColor(
DC: HDC                {a handle to a device context}
): COLORREF;           {returns a 32-bit color specifier}
```

Description

This function retrieves the current color used when drawing text on the device context identified by the DC parameter.

Parameters

DC: A handle to the device context whose text color is to be retrieved.

Return Value

If the function succeeds, it returns the 32-bit color specifier identifying the color used when drawing text. If the function fails, it returns CLR_INVALID.

See Also

SetTextColor, TextOut

Example

Please see Listing 8-16 under SetTextAlign.

GetTextExtentExPoint   *Windows.Pas*

Syntax

```
GetTextExtentExPoint(
DC: HDC;                {a handle to a device context}
p2: PChar;              {the string from which to retrieve character extents}
p3: Integer;            {the number of characters in the string}
p4: Integer;            {the maximum string width}
p5: PInteger;           {an integer receiving the maximum character count}
p6: Pointer;            {points to an array of integers receiving the extents}
var p7: TSize           {a TSize structure receiving the string dimensions}
): BOOL;                {returns TRUE or FALSE}
```

Description

This function retrieves the maximum number of characters from the string pointed to by the p2 parameter that will fit within the maximum allowed width specified by the p4 parameter. In addition, it fills an array of integers corresponding to each character in the string with the offset from the beginning of the string to the beginning of the character when it is drawn on the specified device context. The font currently selected into the specified device context is used to determine the maximum allowable characters and the offsets.

Parameters

DC: A handle to a device context whose currently selected font's attributes are used in determining the text extents.

p2: A pointer to a null-terminated string whose text extents are to be retrieved.

p3: Specifies the size of the string pointed to by the p2 parameter, in bytes.

p4: Specifies the maximum allowable width of the output string on the device context, in logical units.

p5: A pointer to an integer that will receive the maximum number of characters that will fit in the logical space on the specified device context as defined by the p4 parameter. If this parameter is set to NIL, the p4 parameter is ignored.

p6: A pointer to an array of integers that receive the individual character extents for each character in the string pointed to by the p2 parameter. Each entry in the array is associated with the character in the identical position in the string, and contains the offset from the beginning of the string to the origin of the character when it is drawn to the screen. This offset will always fall within the maximum width as specified by the p4 parameter. Although there should be as many array entries as there are characters in the p2 string, the function only fills array entries for the number of characters as received by the p5 parameter. This parameter can be set to NIL if individual character extents are not needed.

p7: A pointer to a TSize structure that receives the width and height of the specified string, in logical units.

Return Value

If the function succeeds, it returns TRUE; otherwise it returns FALSE. To get extended error information, call the GetLastError function.

See Also

GetTextExtentPoint32

Example

Listing 8-14: Programmatically Justifying Text

```
{Whoops!  Delphi incorrectly imports this function, so we must reimport it
manually to obtain the full functionality of this function}
function GetTextExtentExPoint(DC: HDC; p2: PChar;
  p3, p4: Integer; p5: PInteger; p6: Pointer; var p7: TSize): BOOL; stdcall;

var
  Form1: TForm1;

implementation

{$R *.DFM}

{reimport the function}
function GetTextExtentExPoint; external gdi32 name 'GetTextExtentExPointA';

procedure TForm1.PaintBox1Paint(Sender: TObject);
var
  TheString: PChar;        // holds the output string
  StrPointer: PChar;       // a pointer within the output string
  DisplayString: PChar;    // holds the actual displayed string
  MaxChars: Integer;       // receives the maximum displayable characters
  StringSize: TSize;       // receives the string dimensions
  LineNum: Integer;        // a line number counter
  ExtraSpace: Integer;     // holds the extra space to add
  NumBreaks: Integer;      // holds the number of spaces in a string
  Count: Integer;          // a general loop control variable
begin
  {erase the image on the paintbox canvas}
  with PaintBox1.Canvas do
  begin
    Brush.Color := clWhite;
    FillRect(ClipRect);
  end;

  {initialize the original string}
  TheString:='Delphi is the most awesome Windows development environment ever!';

  {initialize the line number and the string pointer}
  LineNum := 0;
```

```
StrPointer := TheString;

{retrieve enough memory for the displayed string}
GetMem(DisplayString, Length(TheString));

{loop through the string until the entire string is displayed}
while Length(StrPointer)>0 do
begin
  {retrieve the maximum number of characters that can fit on
   one line within the small paintbox}
  GetTextExtentExPoint(PaintBox1.Canvas.Handle, TheString,
                       Length(TheString), PaintBox1.Width, @MaxChars,
                       nil, StringSize);

  {if the remaining string is longer than what can be displayed on one line,
   and the last character to be displayed is not a space, continue
   decreasing the maximum displayable characters until we hit a space}
  while (Length(StrPointer)>MaxChars) and (StrPointer[MaxChars]<>' ') do
    Inc(MaxChars, -1);

  {copy only the computed amount of characters into the displayable string.
   this new string should fit within the paintbox without breaking any words}
  StrLCopy(DisplayString, StrPointer, MaxChars);

  {if the remaining string is longer that what can be displayed, move
   the string pointer beyond the end of the displayed string; otherwise,
   point the string pointer to an empty string}
  if Length(StrPointer)>MaxChars then
    StrPointer := @StrPointer[MaxChars+1]
  else
    StrPointer := #0;

  {retrieve the width and height of the string}
  GetTextExtentPoint32(PaintBox1.Canvas.Handle, DisplayString,
                       Length(DisplayString), StringSize);

  {to justify the text so that it fills the entire line, compute the amount
   of space left between the size of the string and the width of the
   paintbox}
  ExtraSpace := PaintBox1.Width - StringSize.cx;

  {count the number of break characters in the displayed string. note that
   this assumes that the break character is a space (' ')}
  NumBreaks := 0;
  for Count := 0 to Length(DisplayString)-1 do
    if DisplayString[Count] = ' ' then
      Inc(NumBreaks);

  {if there is at least one space, set the text justification. this will add
   the computed amount of extra space evenly among all of the spaces in the
   line, thus performing a full justification when the string is drawn to
   the device context}
  if NumBreaks>0 then
    SetTextJustification(PaintBox1.Canvas.Handle, ExtraSpace, NumBreaks);
```

```
  {draw the fully justified string to the paint box device context}
  TextOut(PaintBox1.Canvas.Handle, 0, LineNum*Stringsize.cy, DisplayString,
          Length(DisplayString));

  {reset the text justification to its original value for the next pass}
  SetTextJustification(PaintBox1.Canvas.Handle, 0, 0);

  {track the current text line number}
  Inc(LineNum);
end;

  {free the display string memory}
  FreeMem(DisplayString, Length(TheString));
end;
```

Figure 8-15:
The justified
text

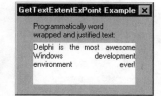

GetTextExtentPoint32   Windows.Pas

Syntax

```
GetTextExtentPoint32(
DC: HDC;                   {a handle to a device context}
Str: PChar;                {a pointer to a string}
Count: Integer;            {the number of characters in the string}
var Size: TSize            {points to a TSize structure receiving the dimensions}
): BOOL;                   {returns TRUE or FALSE}
```

Description

This function retrieves the width and height of the string pointed to by the Str parameter, in logical units. The width and height are based on the attributes of the string currently selected into the device context identified by the DC parameter. The clipping region of the specified device context does not affect the computed dimensions. In instances where a string containing kerning pairs is output to a device supporting character kerning, the dimensions returned by this function may not match the sum of the individual character dimensions in the string.

Parameters

DC: A handle to the device context whose currently selected font is used to determine the string's width and height.

Str: A pointer to a string whose width and height are to be retrieved. This does not have to be a null-terminated string, as the Count parameter specifies the string length.

Count: Specifies the number of characters in the string pointed to by the Str parameter.

Size: A pointer to a TSize structure that receives the width and height of the specified string based on the attributes of the font selected into the specified device context.

Return Value

If the function succeeds, it returns TRUE; otherwise it returns FALSE. To get extended error information, call the GetLastError function.

See Also

GetTabbedTextExtent, GetTextExtentExPoint, SetTextCharacterExtra

Example

Please see Listing 8-14 under GetTextExtentExPoint.

GetTextFace   *Windows.Pas*

Syntax

```
GetTextFace(
DC: HDC;                    {a handle to a device context}
Count: Integer;            {the buffer length}
Buffer: PChar              {a buffer receiving the typeface name}
): Integer;                {returns the number of characters copied}
```

Description

This function retrieves the typeface name of the font currently selected into the device context identified by the DC parameter.

Parameters

DC: A handle to the device context whose currently selected font's typeface name is to be retrieved.

Count: Specifies the size of the buffer pointed to by the Buffer parameter, in characters. If the retrieved typeface name string is longer than the value specified by this parameter, the string is truncated.

Buffer: A pointer to a null-terminated string buffer that receives the typeface name of the currently selected font. If this parameter is set to NIL, the function returns the size of the required buffer in characters, including the null terminator.

Return Value

If the function succeeds, it returns the number of characters copied to the buffer pointed to by the Buffer parameter. If the function fails, it returns zero. To get extended error information, call the GetLastError function.

See Also

EnumFontFamilies, EnumFontFamiliesEx, GetTextAlign, GetTextColor, GetTextMetrics

Example

Please see Listing 8-15 under GetTextMetrics.

GetTextMetrics　*Windows.Pas*

Syntax

```
GetTextMetrics(
DC: HDC;                    {a handle to a device context}
var TM: TTextMetric        {a pointer to a TTextMetric structure}
): BOOL;                    {returns TRUE or FALSE}
```

Description

This function retrieves metric information, such as height, ascent, descent, and other physical measurements, for the currently selected font in the device context identified by the DC parameter.

Parameters

DC: A handle to the device context whose currently selected font's metric information is to be retrieved.

TM: A pointer to a TTextMetric data structure that receives the physical measurements and other attributes for the currently selected font of the specified device context. Note that all measurements are in logical units and are dependent on the mapping mode of the specified device context. The TTextMetric structure is defined as:

```
TTextMetric = record
      tmHeight: Longint;              {the height of a character}
      tmAscent: Longint;             {the ascent of a character}
      tmDescent: Longint;            {the descent of a character}
      tmInternalLeading: Longint;    {the internal leading}
      tmExternalLeading: Longint;    {the external leading}
      tmAveCharWidth: Longint;       {the average character width}
      tmMaxCharWidth: Longint;       {the maximum character width}
      tmWeight: Longint;             {the boldness value}
      tmOverhang: Longint;           {the overhang width}
      tmDigitizedAspectX: Longint;   {the horizontal aspect}
      tmDigitizedAspectY: Longint;   {the vertical aspect}
      tmFirstChar: AnsiChar;         {the first character}
      tmLastChar: AnsiChar;          {the last character}
      tmDefaultChar: AnsiChar;       {the default character}
      tmBreakChar: AnsiChar;         {the word break character}
```

```
        tmItalic: Byte;              {the italics flag}
        tmUnderlined: Byte;          {the underlined flag}
        tmStruckOut: Byte;           {the strikeout flag}
        tmPitchAndFamily: Byte;      {the pitch and family flags}
        tmCharSet: Byte;             {the character set}
end;
```

tmHeight: Specifies the height of characters within the font. The character height is measured as tmAscent+tmDescent.

tmAscent: Specifies the ascent of the characters within the font. The ascent is measured from the baseline to the top of the character, including the internal leading.

tmDescent: Specifies the descent of the characters within the font. The descent is measured from the baseline to the bottom of the character, and includes descenders for characters such as "g" or "y."

tmInternalLeading: Specifies the amount of space inside of the ascent for such things as accent and diacritical marks. The font designer may set this value to zero.

tmExternalLeading: Specifies the amount of extra space above the top of the font. This space is intended for added extra room between rows of text, and does not contain any marks. The font designer may set this value to zero.

tmAveCharWidth: Specifies the average width of characters within the font, excluding any overhang required for italic or bold characters.

tmMaxCharWidth: Specifies the width of the widest character within the font.

tmWeight: Specifies the boldness of the font. The value of this member can be in the range of 0-1000, or can be set to one value from Table 8-39.

tmOverhang: Specifies the extra width per string that is added when synthesizing bold or italic fonts. For bold fonts, this value indicates the overstrike offset. For italic fonts, this value indicates the shearing distance. Use the value returned by a call to the GetTextExtentPoint32 function on a single character minus the value of this member to determine the actual character width.

tmDigitizedAspectX: Specifies the horizontal aspect of the device for which the font was originally designed.

tmDigitizedAspectY: Specifies the vertical aspect of the device for which the font was originally designed.

tmFirstChar: Specifies the value of the first defined character.

tmLastChar: Specifies the value of the last defined character.

tmDefaultChar: Specifies the value of the default character. This character is used when text output with this font contains a character not defined within the font.

tmBreakChar: Specifies the value of the character used for word breaks and text justification.

tmItalic: Specifies the italics attribute for the font. If this member is set to TRUE, the font is italicized.

tmUnderlined: Specifies the underlining attribute for the font. If this member is set to TRUE, the font is underlined.

tmStruckOut: Specifies the strikeout attribute for the font. If this member is set to TRUE, the font is struck out.

tmPitchAndFamily: Specifies the font pitch and font family. The low-order 4 bits specify the pitch of the font, and can contain one or more values from Table 8-40. The high-order 4 bits indicate the font family. Combining this member with a value of $F0 using the Boolean AND operator will retrieve a value matching one flag from Table 8-41.

tmCharSet: Specifies the character set of the font. This member may contain one value from Table 8-42.

Return Value

If the function succeeds, it returns TRUE; otherwise it returns FALSE. To get extended error information, call the GetLastError function.

See Also

EnumFontFamilies, EnumFontFamiliesEx, GetTextAlign, GetTextExtentExPoint, Get-TextExtentPoint32, GetTextFace, SetTextJustification

Example

Listing 8-15: Retrieving Font Metric Information

```
procedure TForm1.FormActivate(Sender: TObject);
var
  FontInfo: TTextMetric;            // holds the font metric information
  FaceName: array[0..255] of char;  // holds the font name
begin
  {retrieve the name of the currently selected font and display it}
  GetTextFace(Form1.Canvas.Handle, 256, FaceName);
  Label2.Caption := FaceName;

  {retrieve the physical attributes for the selected font}
  GetTextMetrics(Form1.Canvas.Handle, FontInfo);

  {clear the list box and begin displaying the physical font attributes}
  ListBox1.Items.Clear;
  with FontInfo, ListBox1.Items do
  begin
    {display the various font measurements}
    Label15.Caption := IntToStr(tmHeight);
    Label14.Caption := IntToStr(tmAscent);
    Label13.Caption := IntToStr(tmDescent);
    Label12.Caption := IntToStr(tmInternalLeading);
    Label11.Caption := IntToStr(tmExternalLeading);
```

```
{display the average and maximum character width}
Add('Average Char Width: '+IntToStr(tmAveCharWidth));
Add('Max Char Width: '+IntToStr(tmMaxCharWidth));

{display the boldness setting}
case tmWeight of
  FW_DONTCARE:    Add('Weight: Don't care');
  FW_THIN:        Add('Weight: Thin');
  FW_EXTRALIGHT:  Add('Weight: Extra light');
  FW_LIGHT:       Add('Weight: Light');
  FW_NORMAL:      Add('Weight: Normal');
  FW_MEDIUM:      Add('Weight: Medium');
  FW_SEMIBOLD:    Add('Weight: Semibold');
  FW_BOLD:        Add('Weight: Bold');
  FW_EXTRABOLD:   Add('Weight: Extra bold');
  FW_HEAVY:       Add('Weight: Heavy');
end;

{display the overhang measurement}
Add('Overhang: '+IntToStr(tmOverhang));

{display the horizontal and vertical aspect.
 note: there is a bug in the GetTextMetrics function that causes these
 two values to be swapped. the AspectX value is returned in the AspectY
 member, and vice versa}
Add('Digitized Aspect X: '+IntToStr(tmDigitizedAspectY));
Add('Digitized Aspect Y: '+IntToStr(tmDigitizedAspectX));

{display the important font characters}
Add('First Character: '+Char(tmFirstChar));
Add('Last Char: '+Char(tmLastChar));
Add('Default Char: '+Char(tmDefaultChar));
Add('Break Char: '+Char(tmBreakChar));

{indicate italic, underlined, or strikeout attributes}
CheckBox1.Checked := (tmItalic>0);
CheckBox2.Checked := (tmUnderlined>0);
CheckBox3.Checked := (tmStruckOut>0);

{display the font pitch}
Add('Pitch: ');
if ((tmPitchAndFamily and $0F) and TMPF_FIXED_PITCH)= TMPF_FIXED_PITCH then
  Add('      Fixed pitch');
if ((tmPitchAndFamily and $0F) and TMPF_VECTOR) = TMPF_VECTOR then
  Add('      Vector');
if ((tmPitchAndFamily and $0F) and TMPF_TRUETYPE) = TMPF_TRUETYPE then
  Add('      True Type');
if ((tmPitchAndFamily and $0F) and TMPF_DEVICE) = TMPF_DEVICE then
  Add('      Device');
if (tmPitchAndFamily and $0F) = 0 then
  Add('      Monospaced bitmap font');

{display the font family}
case (tmPitchAndFamily and $F0) of
  FF_DECORATIVE: Add('Family: Decorative');
```

```
    FF_DONTCARE:    Add('Family: Don't care');
    FF_MODERN:      Add('Family: Modern');
    FF_ROMAN:       Add('Family: Roman');
    FF_SCRIPT:      Add('Family: Script');
    FF_SWISS:       Add('Family: Swiss');
  end;

  {display the character set}
  case tmCharSet of
    ANSI_CHARSET:          Add('Character set: ANSI');
    DEFAULT_CHARSET:       Add('Character set: Default');
    SYMBOL_CHARSET:        Add('Character set: Symbol');
    SHIFTJIS_CHARSET:      Add('Character set: ShiftJis');
    GB2312_CHARSET:        Add('Character set: GB2312');
    HANGEUL_CHARSET:       Add('Character set: Hangeul');
    CHINESEBIG5_CHARSET: Add('Character set: Chinese Big5');
    OEM_CHARSET:           Add('Character set: OEM');
  else
    Add('Windows 95 only character set');
  end;
 end;
end;
```

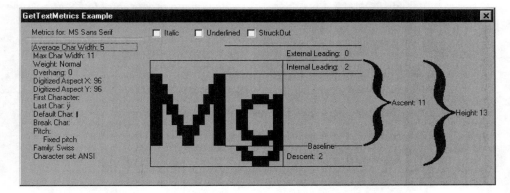

Figure 8-16:
The current
font metric
information

Table 8-39: GetTextMetrics TM.tmWeight Values

Value	Description
FW_THIN	Extra thin font weight (100).
FW_EXTRALIGHT	Thin font weight (200).
FW_LIGHT	Below average bolding (300).
FW_NORMAL	Normal bolding (400).
FW_MEDIUM	Above average bolding (500).
FW_SEMIBOLD	Light bolding (600).
FW_BOLD	Bolded font (700).
FW_EXTRABOLD	Extra bolding (800).
FW_HEAVY	Very heavy bolding (900).

Table 8-40: GetTextMetrics TM.tmPitchAndFamily Font Pitch Values

Value	Description
TMPF_FIXED_PITCH	If this flag is present, the font is a variable pitch font. If this flag is not present, this font is a fixed pitch, or monospaced, font.
TMPF_VECTOR	Indicates a vector font.
TMPF_TRUETYPE	Indicates a True Type font.
TMPF_DEVICE	Indicates a device font.

Table 8-41: GetTextMetrics TM.tmPitchAndFamily Font Family Values

Value	Description
FF_DECORATIVE	Indicates a novelty or decorative font, such as Old English.
FF_DONTCARE	The general font style is unknown or unimportant.
FF_MODERN	Indicates a monospaced font with consistent stroke widths, with or without serifs, such as Courier New.
FF_ROMAN	Indicates a proportional font with variable stroke widths, containing serifs, such as Times New Roman.
FF_SCRIPT	Indicates a font resembling handwriting, such as Brush Script.
FF_SWISS	Indicates a proportional font with variable stroke widths, without serifs, such as Arial.

Table 8-42: GetTextMetrics TM.tmCharSet Values

Value	Description
ANSI_CHARSET	The ANSI character set.
DEFAULT_CHARSET	The default character set.
SYMBOL_CHARSET	The symbol character set.
SHIFTJIS_CHARSET	The shiftjis character set.
GB2312_CHARSET	The GB2312 character set.
HANGEUL_CHARSET	The Korean character set.
CHINESEBIG5_CHARSET	The Chinese character set.
OEM_CHARSET	The original equipment manufacturer character set.
JOHAB_CHARSET	Windows 95 only: The Johab character set.
HEBREW_CHARSET	Windows 95 only: The Hebrew character set.
ARABIC_CHARSET	Windows 95 only: The Arabic character set.
GREEK_CHARSET	Windows 95 only: The Grecian character set.
TURKISH_CHARSET	Windows 95 only: The Turkish character set.
VIETNAMESE_CHARSET	Windows 95 only: The Vietnamese character set.
THAI_CHARSET	Windows 95 only: The Thai character set.

Value	Description
EASTEUROPE_CHARSET	Windows 95 only: The eastern Europe character set.
RUSSIAN_CHARSET	Windows 95 only: The Russian character set.
MAC_CHARSET	Windows 95 only: The Macintosh character set.
BALTIC_CHARSET	Windows 95 only: The Baltic character set.

RemoveFontResource   Windows.Pas

Syntax

```
RemoveFontResource(
p1: PChar                {the font resource filename}
): BOOL;                 {returns TRUE or FALSE}
```

Description

This function removes the font resource contained in the specified font resource file from the internal system font tables. If the font is successfully removed, the application that removed the font should inform all other applications of the change. This is accomplished by sending the WM_FONTCHANGE message with the SendMessage function, specifying HWND_BROADCAST as the value of the hWnd parameter. The font resource will not actually be removed until it is no longer selected into any device context.

Parameters

p1: A pointer to a null-terminated string containing the name of the font resource file whose font resource is to be removed from the internal system font tables.

Return Value

If the function succeeds, it returns TRUE; otherwise it returns FALSE. To get extended error information, call the GetLastError function.

See Also

AddFontResource, CreateScalableFontResource, GetFontData, WM_FONTCHANGE

Example

Please see Listing 8-4 under CreateScalableFontResource.

SetTextAlign   Windows.Pas

Syntax

```
SetTextAlign(
DC: HDC;                 {a handle to a device context}
Flags: UINT              {the text alignment flags}
): UINT;                 {returns the previous alignment flags}
```

Description

This function sets the alignment used when drawing text on the specified device context. The alignment is based on a bounding rectangle surrounding all characters within the string. The string's bounding rectangle dimensions can be retrieved by calling the GetTextExtentPoint32 function. Text alignment is based on the starting point of the string, as defined by text output functions such as TextOut.

Parameters

DC: A handle to the device context whose text alignment is to be set.

Flags: A series of flags indicating the new text alignment for the specified device context. This parameter can be set to one or more values from Table 8-43 by combining them with the Boolean OR operator. However, only one flag each from those that modify horizontal or vertical alignment can be chosen, and only one flag from those that modify the current position can be chosen.

Return Value

If this function succeeds, it returns the previous text alignment flags; otherwise it returns GDI_ERROR. To get extended error information, call the GetLastError function.

See Also

DrawText, DrawTextEx, GetTextAlign, TabbedTextOut, TextOut

Example

Listing 8-16: Manipulating Text

```
var
  Form1: TForm1;
  HorzAlignmentValue: UINT;          // holds the horizontal alignment
  VertAlignmentValue: UINT;          // holds the vertical alignment
  IntercharacterSpacing: Integer;    // holds the intercharacter spacing

implementation

{$R *.DFM}

procedure TForm1.PaintBox1Paint(Sender: TObject);
var
  TextAlignment: UINT;    // holds the text alignment
begin
  {set the text alignment}
  SetTextAlign(PaintBox1.Canvas.Handle,
               HorzAlignmentValue or VertAlignmentValue);

  {set the intercharacter spacing}
  SetTextCharacterExtra(PaintBox1.Canvas.Handle, SpinEdit1.Value);

  {retrieve and display the current intercharacter spacing}
```

```
Label7.Caption := IntToStr(GetTextCharacterExtra(PaintBox1.Canvas.Handle));

{set the text color}
SetTextColor(PaintBox1.Canvas.Handle, ColorGrid1.ForegroundColor);

{retrieve and display the current text color}
Label9.Caption := IntToHex(GetTextColor(PaintBox1.Canvas.Handle), 8);

{draw some text (affected by alignment, spacing, and color) to
 the device context}
TextOut(PaintBox1.Canvas.Handle, PaintBox1.Width div 2,
        PaintBox1.Height div 2, 'ABCabc', Length('ABCabc'));

{retrieve the current text alignment}
TextAlignment := GetTextAlign(PaintBox1.Canvas.Handle);

{display the horizontal alignment}
if (TextAlignment and (TA_LEFT or TA_CENTER or TA_RIGHT)) = TA_LEFT then
  Label2.Caption := 'Left';
if (TextAlignment and (TA_LEFT or TA_CENTER or TA_RIGHT)) = TA_CENTER then
  Label2.Caption := 'Center';
if (TextAlignment and (TA_LEFT or TA_CENTER or TA_RIGHT)) = TA_RIGHT then
  Label2.Caption := 'Right';

{display the vertical alignment}
if (TextAlignment and (TA_TOP or TA_BASELINE or TA_BOTTOM)) = TA_TOP then
  Label4.Caption := 'Top';
if (TextAlignment and (TA_TOP or TA_BASELINE or TA_BOTTOM)) = TA_BASELINE then
  Label4.Caption := 'Baseline';
if (TextAlignment and (TA_TOP or TA_BASELINE or TA_BOTTOM)) = TA_BOTTOM then
  Label4.Caption := 'Bottom';
end;

procedure TForm1.RadioButton1Click(Sender: TObject);
begin
  {indicate the selected horizontal alignment}
  HorzAlignmentValue := 0;
  case TRadioButton(Sender).Tag of
    1: HorzAlignmentValue := TA_LEFT;
    2: HorzAlignmentValue := TA_CENTER;
    3: HorzAlignmentValue := TA_RIGHT;
  end;

  {refresh the screen}
  PaintBox1.Refresh;
end;

procedure TForm1.RadioButton4Click(Sender: TObject);
begin
  {indicate the selected vertical alignment}
  VertAlignmentValue := 0;
  case TRadioButton(Sender).Tag of
    1: VertAlignmentValue := TA_TOP;
    2: VertAlignmentValue := TA_BASELINE;
    3: VertAlignmentValue := TA_BOTTOM;
```

8

Chapter

```
  end;

  {refresh the screen}
  PaintBox1.Refresh;
end;
```

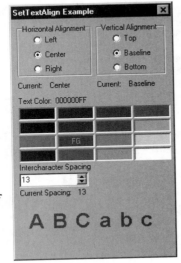

Figure 8-17:
The effects of
text
alignment,
color, and
spacing

Table 8-43: SetTextAlign Flags Values

Value	Description
TA_BASELINE	The starting point is on the text baseline.
TA_BOTTOM	The starting point is on the bottom of the bounding rectangle for the text.
TA_TOP	The starting point is on the top of the bounding rectangle for the text.
TA_CENTER	The starting point is the horizontal center of the bounding rectangle for the text.
TA_LEFT	The starting point is on the left of the bounding rectangle for the text.
TA_RIGHT	The starting point is on the right of the bounding rectangle for the text.
TA_RTLREADING	Windows 95 only: Indicates that the text is in a right to left reading order. This value is meaningful only when the selected font is either Hebrew or Arabic.
TA_NOUPDATECP	Does not update the current position after drawing text.
TA_UPDATECP	Updates the current position after drawing text.
VTA_BASELINE	Vertical baseline fonts only: The starting point is on the text baseline.

Value	Description
VTA_CENTER	Vertical baseline fonts only: The starting point is the vertical center of the bounding rectangle for the text.

SetTextCharacterExtra   Windows.Pas

Syntax

```
SetTextCharacterExtra(
DC: HDC;                    {a handle to a device context}
CharExtra: Integer         {the extra character spacing amount}
): Integer;                {returns the previous intercharacter spacing amount}
```

Description

This function sets the amount of extra space, in logical units, added between characters when drawing a line of text on the specified device context.

Parameters

DC: A handle to the device context whose extra character spacing value is to be set.

CharExtra: Specifies the amount of space to add between characters, in logical units. If the specified device context's current mapping mode is not set to MM_TEXT, this value will be translated for the current mapping mode and rounded to the nearest pixel.

Return Value

If the function succeeds, it returns the previous extra space; otherwise it returns $80000000.

See Also

DrawText, DrawTextEx, GetTextCharacterExtra, TextOut

Example

Please see Listing 8-16 under SetTextAlign.

SetTextColor   Windows.Pas

Syntax

```
SetTextColor(
DC: HDC;                    {a handle to a device context}
Color: COLORREF            {the new 32-bit text color specifier}
): COLORREF;               {returns the previous text color specifier}
```

Description

This function sets the current color used when drawing text on the device context identified by the DC parameter.

Parameters

DC: A handle to the device context whose text color is to be set.

Color: Specifies a 32-bit color specifier defining the new color in which to draw text. The actual color used is the closest matching color for the specified color in the currently realized palette of the specified device context.

Return Value

If the function succeeds, it returns the previous text color specifier; otherwise it returns CLR_INVALID. To get extended error information, call the GetLastError function.

See Also

DrawText, DrawTextEx, GetTextColor, RealizePalette, RGB, SetBkColor, SetBkMode, TabbedTextOut, TextOut

Example

Please see Listing 8-16 under SetTextAlign.

SetTextJustification   *Windows.Pas*

Syntax

```
SetTextJustification(
DC: HDC;                      {a handle to a device context}
BreakExtra: Integer;         {the total extra space}
BreakCount: Integer          {the number of break characters}
): Integer;                   {returns a zero or nonzero value}
```

Description

This function specifies the amount of extra space, in logical units, that should be added to each break character in a string of text when drawing the string on the specified device context. Most fonts define the break character as the space (" "), but some non-Latin fonts may define a different character. Use the GetTextMetrics function to retrieve any specific font's defined break character. The GetTextExtentPoint32 function can be used to retrieve the width of the output text so that the appropriate extra space can be determined. The TextOut function distributes the specified extra character space evenly among all break characters in an output line of text.

Parameters

DC: A handle to the device context whose extra space for justification is to be set.

BreakExtra: Specifies the total extra space that will be added to the output line of text, in logical units. If the specified device context's current mapping mode is not set to MM_TEXT, this value will be translated for the current mapping mode and rounding to the nearest pixel.

BreakCount: Specifies the total number of break characters in the string to be justified.

Return Value

If the function succeeds, it returns a nonzero value; otherwise it returns zero. To get extended error information, call the GetLastError function.

See Also

DrawText, DrawTextEx, GetTextExtentExPoint, GetTextExtentPoint32, GetText-Metrics, TextOut

Example

Please see Listing 8-14 under GetTextExtentExPoint.

TabbedTextOut   Windows.Pas

Syntax

```
TabbedTextOut(
hDC: HDC;                          {a handle to a device context}
X: Integer;                        {the horizontal text origin}
Y: Integer;                        {the vertical text origin}
lpString: PChar;                   {the string to be drawn onto the device context}
nCount: Integer;                   {the number of characters in the string}
nTabPositions: Integer;            {the number of entries in the tab stops array}
lpnTabStopPositions: Pointer       {a pointer to an array of tab stop positions}
nTabOrigin: Integer                {the horizontal tab stop origin}
): Longint;                        {returns the string dimensions}
```

Description

This function outputs the specified string of text onto the device context identified by the hDC parameter, expanding any tab characters in the string to the tab stop positions indicated by the array of integers pointed to by the lpnTabStopPositions parameter. The tabs are expanded to the values in this array as they are encountered, with the first tab character in the string expanding to the position indicated by the first entry in the array, the second tab character expanding to the position indicated by the second entry in the array, and so on. The currently selected font in the specified device context is used when drawing the text. The function will not update the current position unless the Set-TextAlign function has been called with the TA_UPDATECP flag specified.

Parameters

hDC: A handle to the device context upon which the text is drawn.

8

Chapter

X: The horizontal coordinate of the output line of text, in logical units. If the current position is set to be updated, this parameter is ignored on subsequent calls.

Y: The vertical coordinate of the output line of text, in logical units. If the current position is set to be updated, this parameter is ignored on subsequent calls.

lpString: A pointer to the string containing tab characters that is to be drawn onto the specified device context. This does not have to be a null-terminated string, as the nCount parameter specifies the string length.

nCount: Specifies the number of characters in the string pointed to by the lpString parameter.

nTabPositions: Specifies the number of entries in the array of tab stops pointed to by the lpnTabStopPositions parameter.

lpnTabStopPositions: A pointer to an array of integers. Each integer entry in the array indicates a tab stop position, in device units. The tab stops must be arranged in an increasing order, with the smallest tab stop position as the first entry in the array and each tab stop position increasing thereafter. If this parameter is set to NIL and the nTabPositions parameter is set to zero, tab characters are expanded to eight times the average character width of the selected font. Under Windows 95, a negative tab stop position indicates a right aligned tab stop.

nTabOrigin: Specifies the horizontal coordinate from which to start expanding tabs, in logical units.

Return Value

If the function succeeds, it returns the dimensions of the output string in logical units, with the height of the string in the high-order word of the return value and the width in the low-order word. If the function fails, it returns zero.

See Also

DrawText, DrawTextEx, GetTabbedTextExtent, GrayString, SetTextAlign, TextOut

Example

Listing 8-17: Outputting Text Like a Table

```
{Whoops! Delphi incorrectly imports this function, so we must reimport it
 manually to obtain the full functionality of this function}
function TabbedTextOut(hDC: HDC; X, Y: Integer; lpString: PChar; nCount,
nTabPositions: Integer;
  lpnTabStopPositions: Pointer; nTabOrigin: Integer): Longint; stdcall;

{Whoops! Delphi incorrectly imports this function, so we must reimport it
 manually to obtain the full functionality of this function}
function GetTabbedTextExtent(hDC: HDC; lpString: PChar;
  nCount, nTabPositions: Integer; lpnTabStopPositions: Pointer): DWORD; stdcall;
```

```
var
  Form1: TForm1;

implementation

{$R *.DFM}

{reimport the function}
function GetTabbedTextExtent; external user32 name 'GetTabbedTextExtentA';

{reimport the function}
function TabbedTextOut; external user32 name 'TabbedTextOutA';

procedure TForm1.PaintBox1Paint(Sender: TObject);
const
  {define some static arrays of strings}
  NameCol:  array[0..8] of string = ('Name', 'John', 'David', 'Larry', 'Phil',
                                     'Kenneth', 'Rod', 'Ovais', 'Mike');
  IDCol:    array[0..8] of string = ('ID Number', '100', '101', '102', '103',
                                     '104', '105', '106', '107');
  ScoreCol: array[0..8] of string = ('Score', '9,000,000', '8,345,678',
                                     '7,325,876', '8,324,689', '5,234,761',
                                     '5,243,864', '8,358,534', '6,538,324');
var
  TabStops: array[0..2] of Integer;  // holds the tab stops
  FontSize: TSize;                   // holds the font size
  Count: Integer;                    // a general loop control variable
begin
  {define our tab stops}
  TabStops[0] := 10;
  TabStops[1] := PaintBox1.Width div 2;
  TabStops[2] := -PaintBox1.Width;          // a right aligned tab stop

  {retrieve the height of a string}
  GetTextExtentPoint32(PaintBox1.Canvas.Handle, 'ABC', Length('ABC'), FontSize);

  with PaintBox1.Canvas do
  begin
    {erase the last image}
    Brush.Color := clWhite;
    FillRect(ClipRect);

    {output the above string arrays, using tab stops to format the
     strings like a table}
    for Count := 0 to 8 do
      TabbedTextOut(Handle, 0, FontSize.cy*Count,
                    PChar(NameCol[Count]+#9+IDCol[Count]+#9+ScoreCol[Count]),
                    Length(NameCol[Count]+#9+IDCol[Count]+#9+ScoreCol[Count]),
                    3, @TabStops, 0);
  end;

  {retrieve the length of a string containing tabs, in pixels.  this value
   should equal the width of the paintbox.}
```

```
Label3.Caption := IntToStr(LoWord(GetTabbedTextExtent(PaintBox1.Canvas.Handle,
                              PChar(NameCol[0]+#9+IDCol[0]+#9+ScoreCol[0]),
                              Length(NameCol[0]+#9+IDCol[0]+#9+ScoreCol[0]),
                              3, @TabStops))));
end;
```

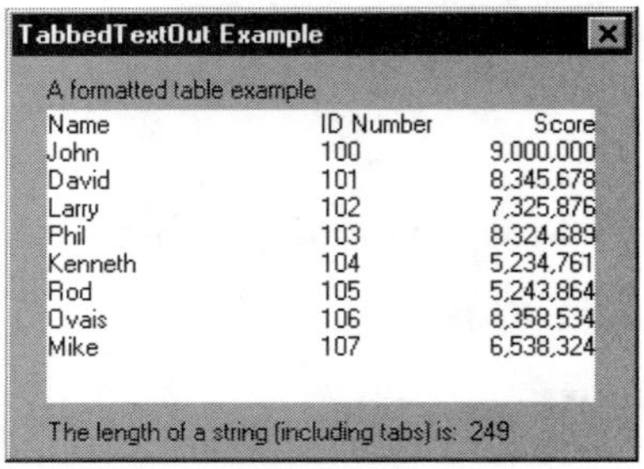

Figure 8-18:
Text output
with tab stops

TextOut   Windows.Pas

Syntax

```
TextOut(
DC: HDC;                    {a handle to a device context}
X: Integer;                 {the horizontal text origin}
Y: Integer;                 {the vertical text origin}
Str: PChar;                 {the string to be drawn onto the device context}
Count: Integer              {the number of characters in the string}
): BOOL;                    {returns TRUE or FALSE}
```

Description

This function outputs the specified string of text onto the device context identified by the DC parameter. The currently selected font in the specified device context is used when drawing the text. The function will not update the current position unless the SetTextAlign function has been called with the TA_UPDATECP flag specified.

Parameters

DC: A handle to the device context upon which the text is drawn.

X: The horizontal coordinate of the output line of text, in logical units. If the current position is set to be updated, this parameter is ignored on subsequent calls.

Y: The vertical coordinate of the output line of text, in logical units. If the current position is set to be updated, this parameter is ignored on subsequent calls.

Str: A pointer to the string to be drawn onto the specified device context. This does not have to be a null-terminated string, as the Count parameter specifies the string length.

Count: Specifies the number of characters in the string pointed to by the Str parameter.

Return Value

If the function succeeds, it returns TRUE; otherwise it returns FALSE. To get extended error information, call the GetLastError function.

See Also

DrawText, DrawTextEx, GetTextAlign, SetTextAlign, TabbedTextOut

Example

Please see Listing 8-2 under CreateFont, and other examples throughout this chapter.

Chapter 9

Resource Functions

Resources provide a mechanism by which the developer can bind extra data needed by the application into the application itself. This eliminates many external files that would otherwise be required, providing a smaller footprint for product distribution while protecting elements such as graphics from being tampered with by the user. Delphi's encapsulation of certain aspects of Windows programming makes the use of some resource types obsolete. For example, a developer no longer has to create menu resources or dialog box resources as this functionality has been greatly simplified by Delphi. However, Delphi developers can still take advantage of certain resource types to reap the benefits of using resources as listed above. This chapter covers the resource API functions that are most commonly used in Delphi applications.

Note that some examples in this chapter will have an extra listing for the resource script file.

Creating Resources

To use resources, the developer must first create a resource script file. This is little more than a text file with the extension .RC. A resource script file can be created manually using Notepad. However, Borland sells a product known as Resource Workshop that can greatly simplify the creation of resource files. This product has editors for every standard resource type, such as bitmaps, and can create compiled resource files for both 16-bit and 32-bit applications. Coverage of the resource scripting commands is beyond the scope of this book.

Once the resource script file has been created, it must be compiled into a binary format that is used by Delphi's linker to bind the resources into the executable. Resource Workshop can compile resources from within its IDE. For those without this product, Delphi ships with a DOS command line resource compiler called BRCC32.Exe, located in the BIN directory. To compile the resource script file, pass the name of the script file to BRCC32 on the command line (i.e., "BRCC32 <resource script file>.RC"). This will create a file with the same name as the script file but with an extension of .RES. This is the compiled binary resource data that will be linked into the application.

Note: It is very important that the name of the compiled binary file be different from the name of the project to which the resource will be bound. Delphi automatically creates a resource file for the project with the name <project name>.RES. This file is maintained by Delphi and is recreated when anything is added to or removed from the project, such as visual controls. For this reason, no resources should be added to the Delphi maintained resource file. Modifying this file in any way can have drastic side effects, such as duplicate resource error messages when the project is compiled, or worse.

Resource Names and Types

When defining a resource name or type in a resource script file, it is common practice to use a text string that describes the resource in some logical manner (i.e., Splash BITMAP "Splash.bmp"). Alternatively, the resource name (or type, in the case of user-defined resources) can be expressed as an integer identifier. This has the advantage of providing a small performance boost when searching for and loading resources. When using any resource function that requires a resource name or type, the developer can specify the resource's integer identifier for these parameters by converting it into a suitable value using the MakeIntResource function. The resource integer identifier can also be specified as a literal string, with the first character as the number symbol ("#") followed by the resource type integer identifier (i.e., "#256").

Binding Resources

Once the resource file has been compiled, it is linked into the Delphi application by specifying the $R compiler directive somewhere in the source code. The location of this compiler directive is irrelevant, and it can be located anywhere in the project. The syntax of this directive is "{$R <compiled resource filename>.RES}". When the project is built, the compiled resources are linked in and bound to the resulting executable.

Resources do not have to be bound only to executable files. Resources can also be bound to DLLs. This is a very common practice and is especially useful when localizing applications for international markets. In fact, the MoreIcons.DLL file shipped with Windows contains only resources, no executable code. Using resources in this manner allows an application to be updated by simply compiling a new resource DLL, which has a smaller footprint than an executable and would thus be easier to distribute.

Using Resources

To use a resource, an application must first retrieve a handle to the resource by using the FindResource or FindResourceEx functions. The resource is loaded into memory by passing this resource handle to the LoadResource function, which returns a handle to the global memory block containing the resource data. The application retrieves a pointer to the resource data by passing the global memory block handle to the LockResource function. Note that under the Win32 API it is no longer necessary to unlock a locked resource or to free a resource loaded with the LoadResource function.

The FindResource, LoadResource, and LockResource method of obtaining a resource is only necessary if the application needs direct access to the binary resource data. All standard resource types have functions that can load a resource and return a handle to the resource object in its native format. The following table lists the most commonly used functions for loading standard resource types.

Table 9-1: Standard Resource Loading Functions

Function	Description
LoadBitmap	Loads a bitmap resource, returning a handle to the bitmap.
LoadCursor	Loads a cursor resource, returning a handle to the cursor.
LoadIcon	Loads an icon resource, returning a handle to the icon.
LoadImage	Loads an icon, cursor, or bitmap resource, returning a handle to the icon, cursor, or bitmap.
LoadString	Loads a string resource from a string table, storing it in a null-terminated string buffer.

User-Defined Resources

In addition to the standard resource types, developers can create user-defined resource types. The simplest method of utilizing user-defined resource types is with single-line resource statements. This format is similar to other single-line resource types, consisting of the name of the resource, followed by the resource type, followed by the filename of the external file containing the resource data to be compiled. The resource compiler creates a resource file as if the data were a standard resource type. However, user-defined resources can only be accessed by using the FindResource, LoadResource, and LockResource functions. For example, to include digitized audio files (WAV files) in a resource, the resource script file could contain the line DRocks WAV "Delphi.wav," where DRocks is the resource name, WAV is our user-defined resource type, and "Delphi.wav" is the external audio file. When loading the resource, simply use DRocks as the resource name and WAV as the resource type in the calls to the FindResource, LoadResource, and LockResource functions. The following example demonstrates this technique.

Listing 9-1: User-defined Resources Script File

```
DRocks WAV "Delphi.wav"
```

Listing 9-2: Loading a User-defined Resource

```
implementation
```

```
uses MMSystem;

{$R *.DFM}
{$R WAVES.RES}

procedure TForm1.Button1Click(Sender: TObject);
var
  TheResource: HRSRC;      // a handle to the resource
  TheWave: Pointer;        // a pointer to the resource data
begin
  {find and load the user-defined resource (a digitized audio file)}
  TheResource := LoadResource(hInstance, FindResource(hInstance,
                                              'DRocks', 'WAV'));

  {retrieve a pointer to the wave file data}
  TheWave := LockResource(TheResource);

  {play the wave file}
  sndPlaySound(TheWave, SND_MEMORY or SND_SYNC);
end;
```

Multiline user-defined resources are just as easy to create and utilize. In this case, the RCDATA standard resource type is used. RCDATA defines a multiline user resource, and the values between the BEGIN and END block of this resource definition can contain any desired data. Again, there is no standard means of loading this type of resource other than the FindResource, LoadResource, and LockResource sequence. Like single-line user-defined resource types, the application must have intimate knowledge of the format of the resource data. The following example demonstrates how to use multiline user-defined resources

Listing 9-3: Multiline User-defined Resources Script File

```
CustomInfo RCDATA
BEGIN
  0x0000001B,
  "John Ayres\0",
  "Lead Author\0",
END
```

Listing 9-4: Using Multiline User-defined Resources

```
implementation

{$R *.DFM}
{$R CustomInfo.RES}

procedure TForm1.Button1Click(Sender: TObject);
var
  TheResource: HRSRC;      // a handle to the resource
  TheInfo: Pointer;        // a pointer to the resource data
begin
  {find and load the resource.  this will be a multiline, user-defined
   resource}
  TheResource := LoadResource(hInstance, FindResource(hInstance, 'CustomInfo',
```

```
                                                RT_RCDATA));

{retrieve a pointer to the resource}
TheInfo := LockResource(TheResource);

{extract the first element of the user-defined resource (an age value)}
Label1.Caption := IntToStr(LongInt(TheInfo^));

{extract the second element of the user-defined resource (a name in the form
 of a null-terminated string)}
TheInfo := Pointer(LongInt(TheInfo)+SizeOf(LongInt));
Label2.Caption := PChar(TheInfo);

{extract the third element of the user-defined resource (a title in the form
 of a null-terminated string). note that we add one to the length of the
 previous string to position the pointer past the null terminating character
 of the first string.}
TheInfo := Pointer(LongInt(TheInfo)+StrLen(TheInfo)+1);
Label3.Caption := PChar(TheInfo);
end;
```

Figure 9-1:
The multiline
user-defined
resource data

Resource Functions

The following resource functions are covered in this chapter:

Table 9-2: Resource Functions

Function	Description
EnumResourceLanguages	Finds all languages in which a specific resource is available.
EnumResourceNames	Finds all resources available for a specific resource type.
EnumResourceTypes	Finds all resource types available in a specific module.
FindResource	Finds a specific resource.
FindResourceEx	Finds a specific resource according to a specific language.
LoadResource	Loads a resource.
LoadString	Loads a string from a string table.
LockResource	Obtains a pointer to resource data.
MakeIntResource	Converts an integer identifier into a value suitable for use in resource functions.
SizeofResource	Retrieves the size of a resource.

EnumResourceLanguages   Windows.Pas

Syntax

```
EnumResourceLanguages(
hModule: HMODULE;              {the instance handle of the module}
lpType: PChar;                 {the resource type}
lpName: PChar;                 {the resource name}
lpEnumFunc: ENUMRESLANGPROC;   {a pointer to the callback function}
lParam: LongInt               {an application-defined value}
): BOOL;                       {returns TRUE or FALSE}
```

Description

This function enumerates all resources matching the specified type and name for every language in which the resource is available, passing the language for each resource found to the callback function pointed to by the lpEnumFunc parameter. Resources will continue to be enumerated until the callback function returns a value of FALSE or all resources have been enumerated.

 Note: As of this writing, there is a small problem in Delphi when linking an application with a resource file that has multiple resources in the same name but different languages. Delphi will return a Duplicate Resource error when linking in the RES file if the resource names have an even number of characters. An odd number of characters in the resource name will work as expected. Borland has been made aware of this problem.

Parameters

hModule: Specifies the instance handle of the module containing the resources to be enumerated. If this parameter is set to zero, the function enumerates the resources associated with the calling process.

lpType: A pointer to a null-terminated string containing the type of resource to enumerate. This parameter can point to a string containing a custom resource type, or it can be set to one value from Table 9-3. To specify a resource type integer identifier, the high-order word of this pointer must be zero, and the low-order word must contain the resource type integer identifier. This can be accomplished by using the MakeIntResource function. Alternatively, an integer identifier can be expressed as a string with the first character as the number symbol ("#") followed by the resource type integer identifier (i.e., "#256").

lpName: A pointer to a null-terminated string containing the name of the resource to enumerate. To specify a resource name integer identifier, the high-order word of this pointer must be zero, and the low-order word must contain the resource name integer identifier. This can be accomplished by using the MakeIntResource function.

Alternatively, an integer identifier can be expressed as a string with the first character as the number symbol ("#") followed by the resource type integer identifier (i.e., "#256").

lpEnumFunc: A pointer to the callback function. This function is called once for each resource found matching the specified name and type.

lParam: A 32-bit application-defined value that is passed to the callback function.

Return Value

If the function succeeds, it returns TRUE; otherwise it returns FALSE. To retrieve extended error information, call the GetLastError function.

Callback Syntax

```
EnumResLangProc(
hModule: HMODULE;        {the instance handle of the module}
lpszType: PChar;         {the resource type}
lpszName: PChar;         {the resource name}
wIDLanguage: LANGID;     {the language identifier of the resource}
lParam: LongInt          {an application-defined value}
):BOOL;                  {returns TRUE or FALSE}
```

Description

This callback function receives a language identifier for each language in which a specific resource name and type is available. This callback function may perform any desired task.

Parameters

hModule: Specifies the instance handle of the module containing the resources to be enumerated, as passed to the hModule parameter of the EnumResourceLanguages function.

lpszType: A pointer to a null-terminated string containing the type of resource to enumerate, as passed to the lpType parameter of the EnumResourceLanguages function. If the resource type was specified as an integer identifier, the high-order word of this pointer will be zero, and the low-order word will contain the resource type integer identifier.

lpszName: A pointer to a null-terminated string containing the name of the resource to enumerate, as passed to the lpName parameter of the EnumResourceLanguages function. If the resource name is an integer identifier, the high-order word of this pointer will be zero, and the low-order word will contain the resource name integer identifier.

wIDLanguage: Specifies a language identifier for a language in which the indicated resource is available.

9

Chapter

lParam: Specifies the 32-bit application-defined value as passed to the lParam parameter of the EnumResourceLanguages function. This value is intended for application specific use inside the callback function.

Return Value

If the callback function should continue enumeration, it should return TRUE; otherwise it should return FALSE.

See Also

EnumResourceNames, EnumResourceTypes

Example

Listing 9-5: The Multilingual Resource File

```
LANGUAGE LANG_ENGLISH,SUBLANG_ENGLISH_US
Hello BITMAP "hienglsh.bmp"

LANGUAGE LANG_SPANISH, SUBLANG_SPANISH_MEXICAN
Hello BITMAP "hispansh.bmp"
```

Listing 9-6: Enumerating All Languages in Which a Specific Resource is Available

```
var
  Form1: TForm1;
  NumResources: Integer;     // holds a count of the resources enumerated

{the enumeration callback function prototype}
function ResLangCallBack(hModule: HMODULE; lpszType: PChar; lpszName: PChar;
                      wIDLanguage: LANGID; lParam: Integer): BOOL; stdcall;

implementation

{$R *.DFM}
{$R reslangs.res}

function ResLangCallBack(hModule: HMODULE; lpszType: PChar; lpszName: PChar;
                      wIDLanguage: LANGID; lParam: Integer): BOOL;

var
  LanName: array[0..255] of Char;   // holds a language name
  ResHandle: THandle;               // holds a resource handle
  TheBitmap: TBitmap;               // a bitmap object
  ResPtr: Pointer;                  // a pointer to the resource data
  WinBitmap: HBitmap;               // a handle to a Windows bitmap
begin
  {retrieve the name of the language in which the enumerated resource
   is available}
  VerLanguageName(wIDLanguage, LanName, 255);
```

```
   {retrieve a handle to the resource data}
   ResHandle := LoadResource(hInstance, FindResourceEx(hInstance, lpszType,
                            lpszName, wIDLanguage));

   {retrieve a pointer to the resource data}
   ResPtr := LockResource(ResHandle);

   {if a resource was located...}
   if ResHandle <> 0 then
   begin
     {we know specifically that these are 256-color images, so create a DIB
      from the bitmap resource information}
     WinBitmap := CreateDIBitmap(Form1.Canvas.Handle, Windows.TBitmapInfo(
                            ResPtr^).bmiHeader, CBM_INIT, Pointer(Integer(
                            ResPtr)+SizeOf(Windows.TBitmapInfo)+(SizeOf(
                            tRGBQuad)*255)), Windows.TBitmapInfo(ResPtr^),
                            DIB_RGB_COLORS);

     {create a Delphi bitmap object}
     TheBitmap := TBitmap.Create;

     {assign the DIB to the Delphi bitmap object}
     TheBitmap.Handle := WinBitmap;

     {display the language in which the resource is available and the
      bitmap resource itself}
     SetBkMode(Form1.Canvas.Handle, TRANSPARENT);
     Form1.Canvas.TextOut(16, 128+(64*NumResources)+(3*NumResources), LanName);
     Form1.Canvas.Draw(168, 128+(64*NumResources)+(3*NumResources), TheBitmap);

     {free the bitmap as it is no longer needed}
     TheBitmap.Free;

     {increment the number of resources loaded}
     Inc(NumResources);
   end;

   {indicate that enumeration should continue}
   ResLangCallBack := TRUE;
end ;

procedure TForm1.Button1Click(Sender: TObject);
begin
   {initialize the count of loaded resources}
   NumResources := 0;

   {enumerate all languages in which the bitmap resource named 'Hello'
    is available}
   EnumResourceLanguages(hInstance, RT_BITMAP, 'Hello', @ResLangCallBack, 0);
end;
```

9

Chapter

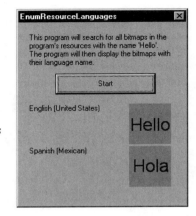

*Figure 9-2:
All languages
in which a
specific
bitmap
resource is
available*

Table 9-3: EnumResourceLanguages lpType and EnumResLangProc lpszType Values

Value	Description
RT_ACCELERATOR	An accelerator table resource.
RT_ANICURSOR	An animated cursor resource.
RT_ANIICON	An animated icon resource.
RT_BITMAP	A bitmap resource.
RT_CURSOR	A hardware-dependent cursor resource.
RT_DIALOG	A dialog box resource.
RT_FONT	A font resource.
RT_FONTDIR	A font directory resource.
RT_GROUP_CURSOR	A hardware-independent cursor resource.
RT_GROUP_ICON	A hardware-independent icon resource.
RT_ICON	A hardware-dependent icon resource.
RT_MENU	A menu resource.
RT_MESSAGETABLE	A message table entry resource.
RT_RCDATA	An application-defined resource.
RT_STRING	A string table entry resource.
RT_VERSION	A version resource.

EnumResourceNames   Windows.Pas

Syntax

```
EnumResourceNames(
hModule: HMODULE;                  {the instance handle of the module}
lpType: PChar;                     {the resource type}
lpEnumFunc: ENUMRESNAMEPROC; {a pointer to the callback function}
```

lParam: Longint   {an application-defined value}
): BOOL;   {returns TRUE or FALSE}

Description

This function enumerates all resources of the type specified by the lpType parameter, passing the name of each resource found to the callback function pointed to by the lpEnumFunc parameter. Resources will continue to be enumerated until the callback function returns a value of FALSE or all resources have been enumerated.

Parameters

hModule: Specifies the instance handle of the module containing the resources to be enumerated. If this parameter is set to zero, the function enumerates the resources associated with the calling process.

lpType: A pointer to a null-terminated string containing the type of resource to enumerate. This parameter can point to a string containing a custom resource type, or it can be set to one value from Table 9-4. To specify a resource type integer identifier, the high-order word of this pointer must be zero, and the low-order word must contain the resource type integer identifier. This can be accomplished by using the MakeIntResource function. Alternatively, an integer identifier can be expressed as a string with the first character as the number symbol ("#") followed by the resource type integer identifier (i.e., "#256").

lpEnumFunc: A pointer to the callback function. This function is called once for each resource found matching the specified type.

lParam: A 32-bit application-defined value that is passed to the callback function.

Return Value

If the function succeeds, it returns TRUE; otherwise it returns FALSE. To retrieve extended error information, call the GetLastError function.

Callback Syntax

EnumResNameProc(
hModule: HMODULE;   {the instance handle of the module}
lpszType: PChar;   {the resource type}
lpszName:PChar;   {the resource name}
lParam: LongInt   {an application-defined value}
):BOOL;   {returns TRUE or FALSE}

Description

This function receives the name of each resource of the type specified by the lpszType parameter that is found in the module identified by the hModule parameter. This callback function may perform any desired task.

9

Chapter

Parameters

hModule: Specifies the instance handle of the module containing the resources to be enumerated, as passed to the hModule parameter of the EnumResourceNames function.

lpszType: A pointer to a null-terminated string containing the type of resource to enumerate, as passed to the lpType parameter of the EnumResourceNames function. If the resource type was specified as an integer identifier, the high-order word of this pointer will be zero, and the low-order word will contain the resource type integer identifier.

lpszName: A pointer to a null-terminated string containing the name of the enumerated resource of the type specified by the lpszType parameter. If the resource name is an integer identifier, the high-order word of this pointer will be zero, and the low-order word will contain the resource name integer identifier.

lParam: Specifies the 32-bit application-defined value as passed to the lParam parameter of the EnumResourceNames function. This value is intended for application specific use inside the callback function.

Return Value

If the callback function should continue enumeration, it should return TRUE; otherwise it should return FALSE.

See Also

EnumResourceLanguages, EnumResourceTypes

Example

Please see Listing 9-7 under EnumResourceTypes.

Table 9-4: EnumResourceNames lpType and EnumResNameProc lpszType Values

Value	Description
RT_ACCELERATOR	An accelerator table resource.
RT_ANICURSOR	An animated cursor resource.
RT_ANIICON	An animated icon resource.
RT_BITMAP	A bitmap resource.
RT_CURSOR	A hardware-dependent cursor resource.
RT_DIALOG	A dialog box resource.
RT_FONT	A font resource.
RT_FONTDIR	A font directory resource.
RT_GROUP_CURSOR	A hardware-independent cursor resource.
RT_GROUP_ICON	A hardware-independent icon resource.
RT_ICON	A hardware-dependent icon resource.
RT_MENU	A menu resource.

Value	Description
RT_MESSAGETABLE	A message table entry resource.
RT_RCDATA	An application-defined resource.
RT_STRING	A string table entry resource.
RT_VERSION	A version resource.

EnumResourceTypes   *Windows.Pas*

Syntax

```
EnumResourceTypes(
hModule: HMODULE;                    {the instance handle of the module}
lpEnumFunc: ENUMRESTYPEPROC;         {a pointer to the callback function}
lParam: Longint                      {an application-defined value}
): BOOL;                             {returns TRUE or FALSE}
```

Description

This function enumerates all resources in the module identified by the hModule parameter. For each unique resource type found in the module, it passes a string containing the resource type to the callback function pointed to by the lpEnumFunc parameter. Resources will continue to be enumerated until the callback function returns a value of FALSE or all resources have been enumerated.

Parameters

hModule: Specifies the instance handle of the module containing the resources to be enumerated. If this parameter is set to zero, the function enumerates the resources associated with the calling process.

lpEnumFunc: A pointer to the callback function. This function is called once for each unique resource type found.

lParam: A 32-bit application-defined value that is passed to the callback function.

Return Value

If the function succeeds, it returns TRUE; otherwise it returns FALSE. To retrieve extended error information, call the GetLastError function.

Callback Syntax

```
EnumResTypeProc(
hModule: HMODULE;          {the instance handle of the module}
lpszType: PChar;           {the resource type}
lParam: LongInt            {an application-defined value}
):BOOL;                    {returns TRUE or FALSE}
```

9

Chapter

Description

This function receives a string containing a type of resource for each unique resource type found in the module identified by the hModule parameter. This callback function may perform any desired task.

Elements

hModule: Specifies the instance handle of the module containing the resources to be enumerated, as passed to the hModule parameter of the EnumResourceTypes function.

lpszType: A pointer to a null-terminated string containing a type of resource found in the specified module. This string can contain a custom resource type, or it can contain one value from Table 9-5. If the resource type is specified as an integer identifier, the high-order word of this pointer will be zero, and the low-order word will contain the resource type integer identifier.

lParam: Specifies the 32-bit application-defined value as passed to the lParam parameter of the EnumResourceTypes function. This value is intended for application specific use inside the callback function.

Return Value

If the callback function should continue enumeration, it should return TRUE; otherwise it should return FALSE.

See Also

EnumResourceLanguages, EnumResourceNames

Example

Listing 9-7: Enumerating the Types and Names of All Included Resources

```
{the EnumResourceTypes callback function prototype}
function EnumResTypeProc(hModule: HMODULE; lpszType: PChar;
                        lParam: LongInt): BOOL; stdcall;

{the EnumResourceNames callback function prototype}
function EnumResNameProc(hModule: HMODULE; lpszType: PChar; lpszName: PChar;
                        lParam: LongInt): BOOL; stdcall;

implementation

{$R *.DFM}

function EnumResTypeProc(hModule: HMODULE; lpszType: PChar;
                        lParam: LongInt): BOOL;
var
  TypeName: string;        // holds a type description
  ParentNode: TTreeNode;   // holds a tree node
begin
  {indicate that we want enumeration to continue}
```

```
  Result := TRUE;

  {if the resource type is one of the standard resource types, the pointer will
   contain a resource identifier matching one of the standard resource types.
   we must typecast this as a LongInt so that the case statement will
   function correctly.  however, for any resource types that are not standard
   (such as user-defined resource types), we assume that the lpszType parameter
   is actually pointing to a string}
  case LongInt(lpszType) of
    LongInt(RT_CURSOR)       : Typename := 'Cursor';
    LongInt(RT_BITMAP)       : Typename := 'Bitmap';
    LongInt(RT_ICON)         : Typename := 'Icon';
    LongInt(RT_MENU)         : Typename := 'Menu';
    LongInt(RT_DIALOG)       : Typename := 'Dialog';
    LongInt(RT_STRING)       : Typename := 'String';
    LongInt(RT_FONTDIR)      : Typename := 'Font Directory';
    LongInt(RT_FONT)         : Typename := 'Font';
    LongInt(RT_ACCELERATOR)  : Typename := 'Accelerator';
    LongInt(RT_RCDATA)       : Typename := 'RC Data';
    LongInt(RT_MESSAGETABLE) : Typename := 'Message Table';
    LongInt(RT_GROUP_CURSOR) : Typename := 'Cursor Group';
    LongInt(RT_GROUP_ICON)   : Typename := 'Icon Group';
    LongInt(RT_VERSION)      : Typename := 'Version Table';
    LongInt(RT_DLGINCLUDE)   : Typename := 'Dialog Include';
    LongInt(RT_PLUGPLAY)     : Typename := 'Plug and Play';
    LongInt(RT_VXD)          : Typename := 'VXD';
    LongInt(RT_ANICURSOR)    : Typename := 'Animated Cursor';
    LongInt(RT_ANIICON)      : Typename := 'Animated Icon';
  else
    TypeName := lpszType;
  end;

  {add a node to the treeview, specifying its text as the enumerated
   resource type}
  ParentNode := Form1.TreeView1.Items.Add(nil, TypeName);

  {now, enumerate the names of every resource of this type contained
   in the executable}
  EnumResourceNames(hInstance, lpszType, @EnumResNameProc, LongInt(ParentNode));
end;

function EnumResNameProc(hModule: HMODULE; lpszType: PChar; lpszName: PChar;
                         lParam: LongInt): BOOL;
begin
  {if the high-order word of the pointer to the resource name is zero, the
   pointer actually contains a resource identifier. therefore, add the
   resource identifier number to the treeview}
  if Hi(LongInt(lpszName)) = 0 then
    TTreeNode(lParam).Owner.AddChild(TTreeNode(lParam), IntToStr(
                                  LongInt(lpszName)))
  else
    {otherwise, the pointer contains an actual resource name, so add it to
     the treeview}
    TTreeNode(lParam).Owner.AddChild(TTreeNode(lParam), lpszName);
```

9

Chapter

```
   {indicate that we wish to continue enumeration}
   Result := TRUE;
end;

procedure TForm1.Button1Click(Sender: TObject);
begin
   {enumerate all resource types found in the executable}
   EnumResourceTypes(hInstance, @EnumResTypeProc, 0);
end;
```

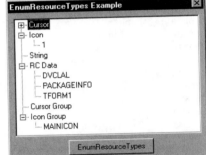

Figure 9-3:
Standard
resources
included in a
regular Delphi
project

Table 9-5: EnumResTypeProc lpszType Values

Value	Description
RT_ACCELERATOR	An accelerator table resource.
RT_ANICURSOR	An animated cursor resource.
RT_ANIICON	An animated icon resource.
RT_BITMAP	A bitmap resource.
RT_CURSOR	A hardware-dependent cursor resource.
RT_DIALOG	A dialog box resource.
RT_FONT	A font resource.
RT_FONTDIR	A font directory resource.
RT_GROUP_CURSOR	A hardware-independent cursor resource.
RT_GROUP_ICON	A hardware-independent icon resource.
RT_ICON	A hardware-dependent icon resource.
RT_MENU	A menu resource.
RT_MESSAGETABLE	A message table entry resource.
RT_RCDATA	An application-defined resource.
RT_STRING	A string table entry resource.
RT_VERSION	A version resource.

FindResource   Windows.Pas

Syntax

```
FindResource(
hModule: HMODULE;        {the instance handle of the module}
lpName: PChar;           {the name of the resource}
lpType: PChar            {the resource type}
): HRSRC;                {returns a handle to the resource information block}
```

Description

This function locates the resource with the indicated type and name in the module specified by the hModule parameter. The handle returned from this function is used with the LoadResource function.

Parameters

hModule: Specifies the instance handle of the module containing the resource to be found. If this parameter is set to zero, the function searches the resources associated with the calling process.

lpName: A pointer to a null-terminated string containing the name of the resource to find. To specify a resource name integer identifier, the high-order word of this pointer must be zero, and the low-order word must contain the resource name integer identifier. This can be accomplished by using the MakeIntResource function. Alternatively, an integer identifier can be expressed as a string with the first character as the number symbol ("#") followed by the resource type integer identifier (i.e., "#256").

lpType: A pointer to a null-terminated string containing the type of resource to find. This parameter can point to a string containing a custom resource type, or it can be set to one value from Table 9-6. To specify a resource type integer identifier, the high-order word of this pointer must be zero, and the low-order word must contain the resource type integer identifier. This can be accomplished by using the MakeIntResource function. Alternatively, an integer identifier can be expressed as a string with the first character as the number symbol ("#") followed by the resource type integer identifier (i.e., "#256").

Return Value

If the function succeeds, it returns a handle to an information block for the located resource. This handle is passed to the LoadResource function to actually load the resource into memory. If the function fails, it returns zero. To retrieve extended error information, call the GetLastError function.

See Also

FindResourceEx, FormatMessage, LoadBitmap, LoadCursor, LoadIcon, LoadResource, LoadString, LockResource, SizeofResource

9

Chapter

Example

Please see Listing 9-2 and Listing 9-4 under the user-defined resource examples in the chapter introduction.

Table 9-6: FindResource lpType Values

Value	Description
RT_ACCELERATOR	An accelerator table resource.
RT_ANICURSOR	An animated cursor resource.
RT_ANIICON	An animated icon resource.
RT_BITMAP	A bitmap resource.
RT_CURSOR	A hardware-dependent cursor resource.
RT_DIALOG	A dialog box resource.
RT_FONT	A font resource.
RT_FONTDIR	A font directory resource.
RT_GROUP_CURSOR	A hardware-independent cursor resource.
RT_GROUP_ICON	A hardware-independent icon resource.
RT_ICON	A hardware-dependent icon resource.
RT_MENU	A menu resource.
RT_MESSAGETABLE	A message table entry resource.
RT_RCDATA	An application-defined resource.
RT_STRING	A string table entry resource.
RT_VERSION	A version resource.

FindResourceEx   Windows.Pas

Syntax

```
FindResourceEx(
hModule: HMODULE;          {the instance handle of the module}
lpType: PChar;             {the resource type}
lpName: PChar;             {the name of the resource}
wLanguage: Word            {the language of the resource}
): HRSRC;                  {returns a handle to the resource information block}
```

Description

This function locates the resource with the indicated type, name, and language in the module specified by the hModule parameter. The handle returned from this function is used with the LoadResource function.

Parameters

hModule: Specifies the instance handle of the module containing the resource to be found. If this parameter is set to zero, the function searches the resources associated with the calling process.

lpType: A pointer to a null-terminated string containing the type of resource to find. This parameter can point to a string containing a custom resource type, or it can be set to one value from Table 9-7. To specify a resource type integer identifier, the high-order word of this pointer must be zero, and the low-order word must contain the resource type integer identifier. This can be accomplished by using the MakeIntResource function. Alternatively, an integer identifier can be expressed as a string with the first character as the number symbol ("#") followed by the resource type integer identifier (i.e., "#256").

lpName: A pointer to a null-terminated string containing the name of the resource to find. To specify a resource name integer identifier, the high-order word of this pointer must be zero, and the low-order word must contain the resource name integer identifier. This can be accomplished by using the MakeIntResource function. Alternatively, an integer identifier can be expressed as a string with the first character as the number symbol ("#") followed by the resource type integer identifier (i.e., "#256").

wLanguage: Specifies the language identifier of the resource to find. If this parameter is set to MakeLangId(LANG_NEUTRAL, SUBLANG_NEUTRAL), the function uses the current language of the calling thread.

Return Value

If the function succeeds, it returns a handle to an information block for the located resource. This handle is passed to the LoadResource function to actually load the resource into memory. If the function fails, it returns zero. To retrieve extended error information, call the GetLastError function.

See Also

FindResource, FormatMessage, LoadBitmap, LoadCursor, LoadIcon, LoadResource, LoadString, LockResource, SizeofResource

Example

Please see Listing 9-6 under EnumResourceLanguages.

Table 9-7: FindResourceEx lpType Values

Value	Description
RT_ACCELERATOR	An accelerator table resource.
RT_ANICURSOR	An animated cursor resource.
RT_ANIICON	An animated icon resource.

Value	Description
RT_BITMAP	A bitmap resource.
RT_CURSOR	A hardware-dependent cursor resource.
RT_DIALOG	A dialog box resource.
RT_FONT	A font resource.
RT_FONTDIR	A font directory resource.
RT_GROUP_CURSOR	A hardware-independent cursor resource.
RT_GROUP_ICON	A hardware-independent icon resource.
RT_ICON	A hardware-dependent icon resource.
RT_MENU	A menu resource.
RT_MESSAGETABLE	A message table entry resource.
RT_RCDATA	An application-defined resource.
RT_STRING	A string table entry resource.
RT_VERSION	A version resource.

LoadResource   *Windows.Pas*

Syntax

```
LoadResource(
hModule: HINST;          {the instance handle of the module}
hResInfo: HRSRC          {the resource handle}
): HGLOBAL;              {returns a global memory block handle}
```

Description

This function loads the resource identified by the hResInfo parameter into memory. A pointer to the resource data can be retrieved by passing the return value of this function to the LockResource function. Under Windows 95 and Windows NT, any resource loaded with the LoadResource function will automatically be freed by the system.

Parameters

hModule: Specifies the instance handle of the module containing the resource to be loaded. If this parameter is set to zero, the function loads the resource from the calling process.

hResInfo: Specifies a handle to a resource information block. This handle is retrieved from the FindResource and FindResourceEx functions.

Return Value

If the function succeeds, it returns a global memory block handle identifying the resource data. This handle can be used in a subsequent call to the LockResource function to retrieve a pointer to the resource data. If the function fails, it returns zero. To retrieve extended error information, call the GetLastError function.

See Also

FindResource, FindResourceEx, LoadLibrary, LockResource, SizeofResource

Example

Please see Listing 9-11 under MakeIntResource.

LoadString   Windows.Pas

Syntax

```
LoadString(
hInstance: HINST;          {the instance handle of the module}
uID: UINT;                 {the integer identifier of the string to load}
lpBuffer: PChar;           {a pointer to a buffer receiving the string}
nBufferMax: Integer        {the size of the buffer in characters}
): Integer;                {returns the number of characters copied to the buffer}
```

Description

This function retrieves the string associated with the specified integer identifier from the resources in the module identified by the hInstance parameter. The function appends a null terminator to the string once it is copied into the buffer.

Parameters

hInstance: Specifies the instance handle of the module containing the string to be loaded. If this parameter is set to zero, the function loads the resource from the calling process.

uID: Specifies the integer identifier of the string resource to load.

lpBuffer: A pointer to a null-terminated string buffer, allocated by the application, that receives the string resource.

nBufferMax: Specifies the size of the buffer pointed to by the lpBuffer parameter, in characters. If the string resource is longer than this value, it is truncated.

Return Value

If the function succeeds, it returns the number of characters copied to the buffer, not including the null terminator. If the function fails, it returns zero. To retrieve extended error information, call the GetLastError function.

See Also

FindResource, FindResourceEx, LoadBitmap, LoadCursor, LoadIcon, LoadResource, LockResource

Example

Listing 9-8: The String Table Resource File

```
STRINGTABLE
{
 1, "An error has occurred."
 2, "A really, really bad error has occurred."
 3, "A massive, critical failure has occurred."
}
```

Listing 9-9: Using Strings in a String Table for Error Messages

```
implementation

{$R *.DFM}
{$R Strings.RES}

procedure TForm1.Button1Click(Sender: TObject);
var
  Buffer: array[0..255] of char;  // holds a string from a string table
begin
  {simulate an error condition.  we have 3 strings in the string table,
   numbered 1-3. our error code will match the string number}
  SetLastError(Random(3)+1);

  {initialize the buffer to hold the string}
  FillMemory(@Buffer, 256, 0);

  {retrieve the last error code set (from above). this will correspond to
   a string resource integer identifier from the string table, so load
   that string}
  LoadString(hInstance, GetLastError, Buffer, 255);

  {display the string (a simulated error message)}
  Panel1.Caption := Buffer
end;
```

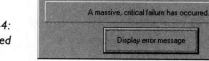

Figure 9-4:
The loaded
string

LockResource   *Windows.Pas*

Syntax

```
LockResource(
hResData: HGLOBAL          {the handle of the resource to lock}
): Pointer;                {returns a pointer to the resource data}
```

Description

This function locks a resource, returning a pointer to the first byte of the resource data. This function is used with the return value from the LoadResource function. It is not necessary to unlock resources locked by this function.

Parameters

hResData: Specifies a handle to a global memory block containing resource data. This handle is returned by the LoadResource function.

Return Value

If the function succeeds, it returns a pointer to the first byte of the resource data. If the function fails, it returns NIL. To retrieve extended error information, call the GetLastError function.

See Also

FindResource, FindResourceEx, LoadResource

Example

Please see Listing 9-11 under MakeIntResource.

MakeIntResource Windows.Pas

Syntax

```
MakeIntResource(
wInteger: Integer          {the resource integer identifier}
):PChar;                   {returns the resource identifier}
```

Description

This function converts a resource integer identifier into a value usable in the resource name and type parameters of resource API functions.

Parameters

wInteger: Specifies the integer identifier of the desired resource.

Return Value

This function returns a pointer value that specifies a resource integer identifier. The high-order word of the pointer is zero, and the low-order word will contain the resource integer identifier. This value can be used in place of a resource name or type in any resource API function. This function does not indicate an error condition.

See Also

EnumResourceLanguages, EnumResourceNames, FindResource, FindResourceEx

Example

Listing 9-10: The MakeIntResource Example Resource File

```
#define CoolPic 256

CoolPic BITMAP "image6.bmp"
```

Listing 9-11: Loading a 256-Color Bitmap from a Resource

```
implementation

{$R *.DFM}
{$R intresource.RES}

{this function loads a 256-color bitmap resource while retaining its original
 palette. this functionality is now present in the TBitmap methods
 LoadFromResourceID and LoadFromResourceName. note that this example should be
 run under a 256-color video driver to see the full effect}
procedure TForm1.Button1Click(Sender: TObject);
var
  ResHandle: HGLOBAL;             // a handle to the loaded resource
  ResPointer: Pointer;            // a pointer to the resource data
  FileHeader: TBitmapFileHeader;  // holds bitmap file header information
  ResSize: LongInt;               // holds the size of the resource
  InfoStream: TMemoryStream;      // used to load the resource into a bitmap
begin
  {initialize the file header type to the characters 'BM'. this is the only
   member of the bitmap header required to be initialized}
  FileHeader.bfType := $4D42;

  {find and load the bitmap resource, specifying the name as a string
   identifying the resource's integer identifier}
  ResHandle := LoadResource(hInstance, FindResource(hInstance, '#256',
                                                      RT_BITMAP));

  {retrieve the size of the resource. this time, find the resource by
   specifying the name as an integer identifier using MakeIntResource. either
   method is perfectly legal}
  ResSize := SizeofResource(hInstance, FindResource(hInstance,
                                MakeIntResource(256), RT_BITMAP));

  {retrieve a pointer to the resource data}
  ResPointer := LockResource(ResHandle);

  {create a memory stream and initialize its size to hold the entire resource
   and the bitmap file header information}
  InfoStream := TMemoryStream.Create;
  InfoStream.SetSize(ResSize+SizeOf(TBitmapFileHeader));

  {write the bitmap file header to the stream}
  InfoStream.Write(FileHeader, SizeOf(TBitmapFileHeader));
```

```
{write the resource data to the stream}
InfoStream.Write(ResPointer^, ResSize);

{reposition the stream pointer to the beginning}
InfoStream.Seek(0, 0);

{create the image's bitmap}
Image1.Picture.Bitmap := TBitmap.Create;

{load the resource information into the new bitmap, thereby displaying it}
Image1.Picture.Bitmap.LoadFromStream(InfoStream);

{we no longer need the stream, so free it}
InfoStream.Free;
end;
```

*Figure 9-5:
The loaded
bitmap
resource*

SizeofResource   Windows.Pas

Syntax

```
SizeofResource(
hModule: HINST;          {the instance handle of the module}
hResInfo: HRSRC          {the resource handle}
): DWORD;                {returns the size of the resource}
```

Description

This function retrieves the size of the resource specified by the hResInfo parameter, in bytes. This function is used with the return value from the FindResource or FindResourceEx functions. The value returned may be larger than the actual size of the resource due to memory alignment.

Parameters

hModule: Specifies the instance handle of the module containing the resource. If this parameter is set to zero, the function uses the resources in the calling process.

hResInfo: Specifies the handle of the resource for which the size is retrieved. This handle is returned by the FindResource and FindResourceEx functions.

Return Value

If the function succeeds, it returns the size of the resource, in bytes. If the function fails, it returns zero. To retrieve extended error information, call the GetLastError function.

See Also

FindResource, FindResourceEx, LoadResource, LockResource

Example

Please see Listing 9-11 under MakeIntResource.

Chapter 10

Window Movement Functions

The Win32 API includes a group of functions that allow a developer to programmatically control the size and positioning of windows. While a window can be moved or resized easily using its Left, Top, Width, or Height properties, these functions give the developer extended control above and beyond what Delphi encapsulates.

Z-order

Many of the window movement functions are concerned with modifying the Z-order of a window. The Z-order of a window refers to the order in which the windows overlap each other. It is based on the Z axis, which can be thought of as an imaginary line running into the screen at a 90 degree angle. The windows are stacked according to their position on this Z axis. Those windows that are said to be closer to the top of the Z-order overlap and appear on top of other windows, while those that are overlapped are said to be closer to the bottom of the Z-order. Figure 10-1 illustrates this concept.

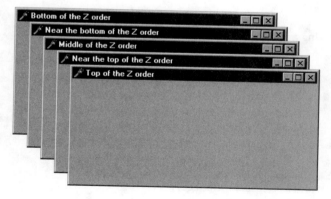

Figure 10-1: The window Z-order

Windows maintains the Z-order of all windows in a single list. A window's Z-order is determined by the order in which it appeared on the screen in relation to the other windows. When a window is created, it is placed above the previously created windows in the Z-order, so the first window created is at the bottom of the Z-order and the last window created is at the top. However, the window's position in the Z-order list is dependent upon its type. All windows can be classified as follows:

Topmost windows: A topmost window overlaps all other non-topmost windows. This is true even if it is not the active or foreground window. This type of window contains the WS_EX_TOPMOST extended style, and appears in the Z-order before all non-topmost windows.

Top-level windows: A top-level window is any normal window that is not a child window. This type of window does not contain the WS_EX_TOPMOST extended style, and is always overlapped by and appears below any topmost window in the Z-order.

Child windows: A child window contains the WS_CHILD style. Child windows have a Z-order amongst themselves within a parent window, but otherwise reflect the same Z-order position as their parent.

When a window is activated, it is brought to the top of the Z-order of all windows of the same type, bringing any child windows with it. If a window owns any other windows, those windows are positioned above the activated window in the Z-order so they are always displayed above their owners.

Special Effects

Imaginative utilization of the window movement functions can give an application that professional touch. For example, if an application occupies a relatively small amount of screen space, but has floating toolbars or other pop-up windows that are constantly open, a developer can use the window movement functions to cause the toolbar windows to move with the main window when the user drags it to a new location. This is a nice effect at the cost of only a few lines of code. The following example demonstrates this technique.

Listing 10-1: Moving a Toolbar with Its Owner Window

```
unit WinMoveU;

interface

uses
  Windows, Messages, SysUtils, Classes, Graphics, Controls, Forms, Dialogs,
  Unit2;

type
  TForm1 = class(TForm)
    procedure FormShow(Sender: TObject);
  private
    { Private declarations }
    {we must override the WM_MOVE message}
    procedure WMMove(var Msg: TWMMove); message WM_MOVE;
  public
    { Public declarations }
  end;
```

```
var
  Form1: TForm1;

implementation

{$R *.DFM}

procedure TForm1.FormShow(Sender: TObject);
begin
  {show the toolbar window}
  Form2.Show;
end;

{this is fired every time the main window is moved}
procedure TForm1.WMMove(var Msg: TWMMove);
begin
  {if the toolbar window exists...}
  if Form2<>NIL then
    {...move the toolbar window alongside the main window.}
    MoveWindow(Form2.Handle, Form1.Left+Form1.Width+5, Form1.Top, Form2.Width,
               Form2.Height, TRUE);
end;

end.
```

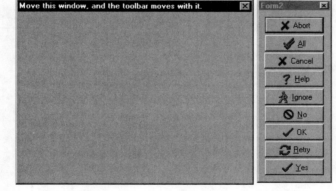

Figure 10-2: The main window and its toolbar

10

Chapter

Window Movement Functions

The following window movement functions are covered in this chapter:

Table 10-1: Window Movement Functions

Function	Description
AdjustWindowRect	Calculates the size of a window based on the desired client area size.
AdjustWindowRectEx	Calculates the size of a window with an extended style based on the desired client area size.

Function	Description
BeginDeferWindowPos	Begins a process of moving multiple windows simultaneously.
BringWindowToTop	Brings the specified window to the top of the Z-order.
CascadeWindows	Arranges the specified windows in a cascading format.
CloseWindow	Minimizes the specified window.
DeferWindowPos	Defines a new size and position for the specified window.
EndDeferWindowPos	Ends the process of moving multiple windows simultaneously.
GetWindowPlacement	Retrieves the show state and positioning of the specified window.
MoveWindow	Moves a window.
OpenIcon	Restores a window from a minimized state.
SetWindowPlacement	Sets the show state and positioning of the specified window.
SetWindowPos	Changes the size, position, and Z-order of the specified window.
ShowOwnedPopups	Toggles the visibility of all pop-ups owned by the specified window.
ShowWindow	Displays a window.
ShowWindowAsync	Displays a window and immediately returns to the calling function.
TileWindows	Arranges the specified windows in a cascading format.

AdjustWindowRect   *Windows.Pas*

Syntax

```
AdjustWindowRect(
var lpRect: TRect;          {a pointer to the client rectangle structure}
dwStyle: DWORD;            {window style flags}
bMenu: BOOL                {menu flag}
): BOOL;                   {returns TRUE or FALSE}
```

Description

This calculates a window rectangle size based on the specified client rectangle size in lpRect. The window rectangle will include the size of the border, caption bar, and menu bar. This rectangle can be used with the CreateWindow or CreateWindowEx functions to create a window with the exact desired client area size. The returned coordinates are in terms of top left and bottom right screen coordinates, but the CreateWindow function needs these parameters in terms of a top and left coordinate and a window width and height. Therefore, the developer must subtract the left coordinate from the right to get the appropriate width, and subtract the top coordinate from the bottom to get the appropriate height.

Parameters

lpRect: The address of a TRect structure that contains the top left and bottom right coordinates of the desired client area, relative to the screen. If this function succeeds, this information will be modified to contain the top left and bottom right coordinates of a window rectangle containing the specified client area, also relative to the screen.

dwStyle: A 32-bit number representing the window styles used by the specified window.

bMenu: If this window has a menu, this parameter should be TRUE; otherwise it should be FALSE.

Return Value

If this function succeeds, it returns TRUE; otherwise it returns FALSE. To get extended error information, call the GetLastError function.

See Also

AdjustWindowRectEx, CreateWindow, CreateWindowEx

Example

Listing 10-2: Creating a Window with a Client Area 300 x 300 Pixels

```
procedure TForm1.CreateParams(var Params: TCreateParams);
var
    TheRect: TRect; // stores our rectangle coordinates
begin
    {fill in the standard parameters}
    inherited CreateParams(Params);

    {our window will start at coordinates 100,100 and our client
     rectangle will be 300 pixels high and 300 pixels wide}
    TheRect.Left:=100;
    TheRect.Top:=100;
    TheRect.Right:=400;
    TheRect.Bottom:=400;

    {adjust our rectangular coordinates to get a window with a
     300 by 300 pixel client area}
    AdjustWindowRect(TheRect, Params.Style, FALSE);

    {the results from AdjustWindowRect are in terms of exact coordinates,
     but the CreateWindowEx function needs this in terms of a top and left
     coordinate and a width and height measurement}
    Params.X:=TheRect.Left;
    Params.Y:=TheRect.Top;
    Params.Width:=TheRect.Right-TheRect.Left;      // determine window width
    Params.Height:=TheRect.Bottom-TheRect.Top;     // determine window height

end;
```

10

Chapter

Figure 10-3:
The result of
the
AdjustWindow-
Rect function
on the window

AdjustWindowRectEx   Windows.Pas

Syntax

```
AdjustWindowRectEx(
var lpRect: TRect;              {a pointer to the client rectangle structure}
dwStyle: DWORD;                {window style flags}
bMenu: BOOL                    {menu flag}
dwExStyle: DWORD               {extended style flags}
): BOOL;                       {returns TRUE or FALSE}
```

Description

This calculates a window rectangle size based on the specified client rectangle size in lpRect. The window rectangle will include the size of the border, caption bar, and menu bar. This rectangle can be used with the CreateWindow or CreateWindowEx functions to create a window with the exact desired client area size. The returned coordinates are in terms of top left and bottom right screen coordinates, but the CreateWindow function needs these parameters in terms of a top and left coordinate and a window width and height. Therefore, the developer must subtract the left coordinate from the right to get the appropriate width, and subtract the top coordinate from the bottom to get the appropriate height. This is functionally equivalent to AdjustWindowRect.

Parameters

lpRect: The address of a TRect structure that contains the top left and bottom right coordinates of the desired client area, relative to the screen. If this function succeeds, this information will be modified to contain the top left and bottom right coordinates of a window rectangle containing the specified client area, also relative to the screen.

dwStyle: A 32-bit number representing the window styles used by the specified window.

bMenu: If this window will have a menu, this parameter should be TRUE; otherwise it should be FALSE.

dwExStyle: A 32-bit number representing the extended window styles used by the specified window.

Return Value

If this function succeeds, it returns TRUE; otherwise it returns FALSE. To get extended error information, call the GetLastError function.

See Also

AdjustWindowRect, CreateWindow, CreateWindowEx

Example

Listing l0-3: Giving an Extended Window Style Window a Client Area of 300 x 300 Pixels

```
procedure TForm1.CreateParams(var Params: TCreateParams);
var
   TheRect: TRect; // stores our rectangle coordinates
begin
   {fill in the standard parameters}
   inherited CreateParams(Params);

   {our window will start at coordinates 100,100 and our client
    rectangle will be 300 pixels high and 300 pixels wide}
   TheRect.Left:=100;
   TheRect.Top:=100;
   TheRect.Right:=400;
   TheRect.Bottom:=400;

   {adjust our rectangular coordinates to get a window with a
    300 by 300 pixel client area}
   AdjustWindowRectEx(TheRect, Params.Style, FALSE, Params.ExStyle);

   {the results from AdjustWindowRectEx are in terms of exact coordinates,
    but the CreateWindowEx function needs this in terms of a top and left
    coordinate and a width and height measurement}
   Params.X:=TheRect.Left;
   Params.Y:=TheRect.Top;
   Params.Width:=TheRect.Right-TheRect.Left;     // determine window width
   Params.Height:=TheRect.Bottom-TheRect.Top;    // determine window height
end;
```

BeginDeferWindowPos   Windows.Pas

Syntax

```
BeginDeferWindowPos(
nNumWindows: Integer     {the number of windows to be moved}
): HDWP;                 {returns a handle to a position structure}
```

Description

This is the first function in a series of functions used to reposition and resize multiple windows simultaneously with a minimum of screen refresh. It allocates memory to an internal structure that tracks the target position and size for the windows to be modified. The DeferWindowPos function fills this structure with information on the new size and position for each window. The EndDeferWindowPos function then uses the information to move and resize the windows simultaneously. The screen is not updated until the EndDeferWindowPos function is called.

Parameters

nNumWindows: Specifies the number of windows that will have position information stored in the multiple window position structure. The DeferWindowPos function can increase the size of this structure if necessary, but if there is not enough memory to increase the size, the entire sequence fails.

Return Value

If this function succeeds, it returns a handle to the multiple window position structure; otherwise it returns zero.

See Also

DeferWindowPos, EndDeferWindowPos, GetWindowPlacement, MoveWindow, SetWindowPlacement, SetWindowPos, ShowWindow, WM_MOVE, WM_SIZE, WM_WINDOWPOSCHANGED, WM_WINDOWPOSCHANGING

Example

Listing 10-4: Repositioning Multiple Windows

```
procedure TForm1.FormShow(Sender: TObject);
begin
   {display the other two forms}
   Form2.Show;
   Form3.Show;
end;

procedure TForm1.Button1Click(Sender: TObject);
var
   WindowPosInfo: HDWP;  // holds the internal window position structure
begin
   {allocate memory for moving three windows}
   WindowPosInfo:=BeginDeferWindowPos(3);

   {set up the first window}
   WindowPosInfo:=DeferWindowPos(WindowPosInfo, Form1.Handle, HWND_NOTOPMOST,
                         50,50,400,100,SWP_SHOWWINDOW);
```

```
{set up the second window}
WindowPosInfo:=DeferWindowPos(WindowPosInfo, Form2.Handle, HWND_NOTOPMOST,
                        50,150,400,100,SWP_SHOWWINDOW);

{set up the third window}
WindowPosInfo:=DeferWindowPos(WindowPosInfo, Form3.Handle, HWND_NOTOPMOST,
                        50,250,400,100,SWP_SHOWWINDOW);

{complete the sequence and reposition the windows}
EndDeferWindowPos(WindowPosInfo);
end;
```

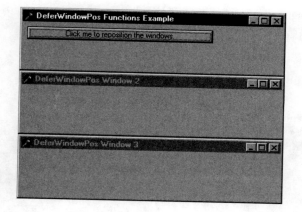

Figure 10-4:
The
repositioned
windows

BringWindowToTop   *Windows.Pas*

Syntax

```
BringWindowToTop(
hWnd: HWND          {a handle to a window}
): BOOL;            {returns TRUE or FALSE}
```

Description

This function will bring the specified window to the top of its relative Z-order, bringing it in front of other windows in the same Z-order (i.e., a child window is in front of other child windows, a top-level window is in front of other top-level windows, and a topmost window is in front of other topmost windows). If the window is a top-level or topmost window, it will be activated, but it will not be restored from a minimized state. This function cannot be used to make a window a topmost window. An application should call SetForegroundWindow to make itself the foreground application.

Parameters

hWnd: The handle of the window to bring to the top of the Z-order.

Return Value

If this function succeeds, it returns TRUE; otherwise it returns FALSE. To get extended error information, call the GetLastError function.

See Also

EnableWindow, IsWindowVisible, SetActiveWindow, SetFocus, SetForegroundWindow, SetWindowPos, WM_ENABLE, WM_SETFOCUS

Example

Listing 10-5: Rearranging the Z-order of Child Windows

```
procedure TForm1.Button1Click(Sender: TObject);
begin
    {bring Panel1 to the top of the child window Z-order}
    BringWindowToTop(Panel1.Handle);
end;
```

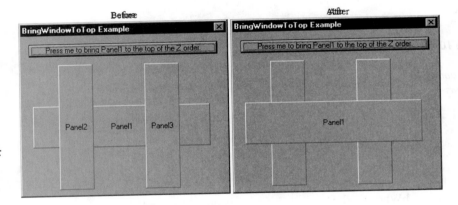

Figure 10-5: The rearranged Z-order

CascadeWindows   Windows.Pas

Syntax

CascadeWindows(
hwndParent: HWND;   {a handle to the parent window}
wHow: UINT;   {control flags}
lpRect: PRect;   {rectangular area to arrange windows in}
cKids: UINT;   {the number of windows to arrange}
lpKids: Pointer   {the address of an array of window handles}
): WORD;   {returns the number of windows arranged}

Description

This function arranges the windows associated by the handles in the lpKids array or the child windows of the specified window by cascading them.

Parameters

hwndParent: A handle to the parent window. If this parameter is zero, the desktop window is used as the parent window. If this is being used to cascade MDI child windows, this parameter should be set to the ClientHandle property of the particular form.

wHow: This can be set to MDITILE_SKIPDISABLED to bypass cascading any disabled child windows. If this parameter is set to zero, all child windows are cascaded.

lpRect: A pointer to a TRect structure describing a rectangular area in screen coordinates in which the windows are arranged. If this parameter is NIL, the client area of the parent window is used.

cKids: Specifies the number of elements in the lpKids array. If the lpKids parameter is NIL, this parameter is ignored.

lpKids: A pointer to an array of window handles identifying the windows to be arranged. Specifying NIL for this parameter will arrange all of the child windows of the parent window.

Return Value

If the function succeeds, it returns the number of windows that were arranged; otherwise it returns zero.

See Also

BeginDeferWindowPos, DeferWindowPos, EndDeferWindowPos, MoveWindow, SetWindowPlacement, TileWindows, WM_MDICASCADE, WM_MDITILE

Example

Listing 10-6: Cascading MDI Child Windows

```
procedure TForm1.Cascade1Click(Sender: TObject);
begin
   {this will tile all of the MDI child windows except the one that
    is disabled}
   CascadeWindows(Form1.ClientHandle,MDITILE_SKIPDISABLED,nil,0,nil);
end;
```

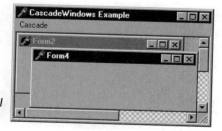

Figure 10-6:
Cascaded MDI
child windows

CloseWindow   Windows.Pas

Syntax

```
CloseWindow(
hWnd: HWND          {a handle to a window}
): BOOL;            {returns TRUE or FALSE}
```

Description

CloseWindow minimizes the specified window, but does not destroy it.

Parameters

hWnd: The handle of the window to be minimized.

Return Value

If this function succeeds, it returns TRUE; otherwise it returns FALSE. To get extended error information, call the GetLastError function.

See Also

ArrangeIconicWindows, DestroyWindow, IsIconic, IsWindowVisible, IsZoomed, OpenIcon, ShowWindow, WM_SIZE

Example

Listing 10-7: CloseWindow Example Using OpenIcon and IsIconic

```
{this continually minimizes and restores the form}
procedure TForm1.Timer1Timer(Sender: TObject);
begin
  {if our form is minimized...}
  if IsIconic(Form1.Handle) then
      {...restore it...}
      OpenIcon(Form1.Handle)
  else
      {...otherwise minimize it}
      CloseWindow(Form1.Handle);
end;
```

DeferWindowPos   Windows.Pas

Syntax

```
DeferWindowPos(
hWinPosInfo: HDWP;        {the handle to a position structure}
hWnd: HWND;              {the handle of a window to position}
hWndInsertAfter: HWND;   {the handle of the preceding window}
X: Integer;             {the horizontal coordinate}
Y: Integer;             {the vertical coordinate}
CX: Integer;            {the width, in pixels}
CY: Integer;            {the height, in pixels}
```

uFlags: UINT	{size and position flags}
): HDWP;	{returns a handle to a position structure}

Description

This function updates the specified multiple window position structure for the new size and position of the indicated window. Use the BeginDeferWindowPos function to allocate memory for this structure. The DeferWindowPos function can increase the size of this structure if necessary, but if there is not enough memory for the increased size, the entire sequence fails. When the EndDeferWindowPos function is called, it uses this structure to move and resize multiple windows simultaneously. The screen is not refreshed until after the EndDeferWindowPos function is completed.

Note that owned windows of a topmost window are also made topmost so that they are displayed above their owner, but owner windows of the specified window are not changed. Thus, a non-topmost window can own a topmost window, but a topmost window cannot own a non-topmost window. If a topmost window is repositioned to a non-topmost window, its owned windows are also changed to non-topmost.

Parameters

hWinPosInfo: The handle to the multiple window position structure that was returned by BeginDeferWindowPos or the last call to DeferWindowPos.

hWnd: The handle of the window to be moved or resized.

hWndInsertAfter: Identifies the window that will precede the repositioned window in the Z-order. This is either a window handle or one value from Table 10-2. This parameter is ignored if the SWP_NOZORDER flag is set in the Flags parameter. If this parameter is set to zero, the window will be placed at the top of the Z-order. If a window's Z-order position is placed above all other topmost windows, that window becomes a topmost window. This has the same effect as specifying the HWND_TOPMOST flag for this parameter.

X: The horizontal coordinate of the window's upper left corner. If this is a child window, the coordinates are relative to the parent window's client area.

Y: The vertical coordinate of the window's upper left corner. If this is a child window, the coordinates are relative to the parent window's client area.

CX: The window's new width, in pixels.

CY: The window's new height, in pixels.

uFlags: Specifies a combination of values from Table 10-3 that will affect the size and position of the window. Two or more values can be specified by using the Boolean OR operator.

Return Value

If this function succeeds, it returns a handle to the updated multiple window position structure. This structure could be different from the one passed to the function, and

10

Chapter

should be used in subsequent calls to DeferWindowPos and EndDeferWindowPos. Otherwise, this function returns zero. If the function fails, the application should abandon the window positioning operation and should not call EndDeferWindowPos.

See Also

BeginDeferWindowPos, EndDeferWindowPos, GetWindowPlacement, MoveWindow, SetWindowPlacement, SetWindowPos, ShowWindow, WM_MOVE, WM_SIZE, WM_WINDOWPOSCHANGED, WM_WINDOWPOSCHANGING,

Example

Please see Listing 10-4 under BeginDeferWindowPos

Table 10-2: DeferWindowPos hWndInsertAfter Values

Value	Description
HWND_BOTTOM	Places the window at the bottom of the Z-order. If this window was a topmost window, it loses its topmost status and is placed below all other windows.
HWND_NOTOPMOST	Places the window above all non-topmost windows, but behind all topmost windows. If the window is already a non-topmost window, this flag has no effect.
HWND_TOP	Places the window at the top of the Z-order.
HWND_TOPMOST	Places the window above all non-topmost windows; it will retain its topmost position even when deactivated.

Table 10-3: DeferWindowPos uFlags Values

Value	Description
SWP_DRAWFRAME	Draws the frame defined in the window's class description around the window.
SWP_FRAMECHANGED	Causes a WM_NCCALCSIZE message to be sent to the window, even if the window size is not changing.
SWP_HIDEWINDOW	Hides the window.
SWP_NOACTIVATE	Does not activate the window. If this flag is not set, the window is activated and moved to the top of the topmost or non-topmost group depending on the hWndInsertAfter parameter.
SWP_NOCOPYBITS	Discards the entire client area. If this flag is not set, the valid area of the client area is saved and copied back into the client area after all movement and positioning is completed.
SWP_NOMOVE	Retains the current position, ignoring the X and Y parameters.
SWP_NOOWNERZORDER	Does not change the owner window's position in the Z-order.

Value	Description
SWP_NOREDRAW	When this flag is set, no repainting occurs, and the application must explicitly invalidate or redraw any parts of the window that need to be redrawn, including the nonclient area and scroll bars.
SWP_NOREPOSITION	The same as the SWP_NOOWNERZORDER flag.
SWP_NOSENDCHANGING	The window will not receive WM_WINDOWPOSCHANGING messages.
SWP_NOSIZE	Retains the current size, ignoring the CX and CY parameters.
SWP_NOZORDER	Retains the current Z-order, effectively causing the WndInsertAfter parameter to be ignored.
SWP_SHOWWINDOW	Displays the window.

EndDeferWindowPos   Windows.Pas

Syntax

EndDeferWindowPos(
hWinPosInfo: HDWP   {the handle of a position structure}
): BOOL;   {returns TRUE or FALSE}

Description

This is the last function called in a series of functions used to simultaneously move and resize multiple windows with a minimum of screen refresh. The BeginDeferWindow-Pos function is called first, which allocates memory for a multiple window position internal structure that tracks the new position and size of each window to be moved. The DeferWindowPos function is then called for each window to be modified. The EndDeferWindowPos function is called last. This function sends the WM_WINDOWPOSCHANGING and WM_WINDOWPOSCHANGED messages to each window and updates the screen only when all windows have been modified.

Parameters

hWinPosInfo: A handle to the multiple window position internal structure. This handle is returned from the BeginDeferWindowPos and DeferWindowPos functions.

Return Value

If this function succeeds, it returns TRUE; otherwise it returns FALSE. To get extended error information, call the GetLastError function.

See Also

BeginDeferWindowPos, DeferWindowPos, GetWindowPlacement, MoveWindow, SetWindowPlacement, SetWindowPos, ShowWindow, WM_MOVE, WM_SIZE, WM_WINDOWPOSCHANGED, WM_WINDOWPOSCHANGING,

10

Chapter

Example

Please see Listing 10-4 under BeginDeferWindowPos.

GetWindowPlacement   Windows.Pas

Syntax

```
GetWindowPlacement(
hWnd: HWND;                                      {a handle of a window}
WindowPlacement: PWindowPlacement  {a pointer to a position data structure}
): BOOL;                                              {returns TRUE or FALSE}
```

Description

This function retrieves the show state and the normal, minimized, and maximized positions of the specified window.

Parameters

hWnd: A handle to the window whose placement information is to be retrieved.

WindowPlacement: A pointer to a TWindowPlacement data structure that will receive the show state and window placement information. This structure is defined as:

```
TWindowPlacement = packed record
      length: UINT;               {the size of the structure in bytes}
      flags: UINT;                {positioning flags}
      showCmd: UINT;              {show state flags}
      ptMinPosition: TPoint;      {minimized coordinates}
      ptMaxPosition: TPoint;      {maximized coordinates}
      rcNormalPosition: TRect;    {restored position coordinates}
end;
```

Before calling this function, the Length member must be set to SizeOf(TWindowPlacement). The members of this structure are filled with the placement information after this function is called. Please refer to the SetWindowPlacement function for a description of this data structure.

Return Value

If this function succeeds, it returns TRUE; otherwise it returns FALSE. To get extended error information, call the GetLastError function.

See Also

SetWindowPlacement, SetWindowPos, ShowWindow

Example

Please see Listing 10-9 under SetWindowPlacement.

MoveWindow   Windows.Pas

Syntax

```
MoveWindow(
hWnd: HWND;        {a handle to a window to be moved}
X: Integer;        {the new horizontal coordinate}
Y: Integer;        {the new vertical coordinate}
nWidth: Integer;   {the new window width}
nHeight: Integer;  {the new window height}
bRepaint: BOOL     {the repaint flag}
): BOOL;           {returns TRUE or FALSE}
```

Description

This function changes the position and dimensions of the specified window. If the specified window is a top-level window, the coordinates are relative to the screen. If the specified window is a child window, coordinates are relative to the parent window's client area.

This function sends the following messages to the specified window: WM_WINDOWPOSCHANGING, WM_WINDOWPOSCHANGED, WM_MOVE, WM_SIZE, and WM_NCCALCSIZE.

Parameters

hWnd: A handle to the window to be modified.

X: The new horizontal coordinate for the left side of the window.

Y: The new vertical coordinate for the top side of the window.

nWidth: Specifies the new width of the window.

nHeight: Specifies the new height of the window.

bRepaint: Determines how this window will be repainted. If this parameter is TRUE, the MoveWindow function calls the UpdateWindow function. This sends a WM_PAINT message to the window, causing it to be repainted immediately after the window is moved. If this parameter is FALSE, no repainting will occur, including the entire nonclient area and any part of the parent window uncovered by a child window. The application must explicitly invalidate or redraw any areas that need to be updated as a result of the MoveWindow function. A WM_PAINT message is placed in the message queue of the specified window, but its message loop will only dispatch the WM_PAINT message after all other messages have been dispatched.

Return Value

If this function succeeds, it returns TRUE; otherwise it returns FALSE.

10

Chapter

See Also

BeginDeferWindowPos, DeferWindowPos, EndDeferWindowPos, SetWindowPlacement, SetWindowPos

Example

Listing 10-8: Moving a Window

```
procedure TForm1.Timer1Timer(Sender: TObject);
const
   XPos: Integer = 5;  // our initial horizontal position
begin
   {increment the horizontal position}
   Inc(XPos);

   {move the edit box to the right}
   MoveWindow(Edit1.Handle, XPos, Edit1.Top, Edit1.Width, Edit1.Height, TRUE);
end;
```

OpenIcon   Windows.Pas

Syntax

```
OpenIcon(
hWnd: HWND                {a handle to a minimized window}
): BOOL;                  {returns TRUE or FALSE}
```

Description

This function restores and activates the specified minimized window. A WM_QUERYOPEN message is sent to the window when this function is called.

Parameters

hWnd: A handle to the window to be restored and activated.

Return Value

If this function succeeds, it returns TRUE; otherwise it returns FALSE. To get extended error information, call the GetLastError function.

See Also

ArrangeIconicWindows, CloseWindow, DestroyWindow, IsIconic, IsWindowVisible, IsZoomed, ShowWindow, WM_SIZE, WM_QUERYOPEN

Example

Please see Listing 10-7 under CloseWindow.

SetWindowPlacement   Windows.Pas

Syntax

```
SetWindowPlacement(
hWnd: HWND;                                    {a handle to a window}
WindowPlacement: PWindowPlacement  {a pointer to a window placement structure}
): BOOL;                                        {returns TRUE or FALSE}
```

Description

This function sets the show state and the normal, minimized, and maximized coordinates of the specified window.

Parameters

hWnd: A handle to the window whose placement information is to be set.

WindowPlacement: A pointer to a TWindowPlacement data structure that contains the show state and window placement information. This structure is defined as:

```
TWindowPlacement = packed record
        length· UINT;                {the size of the structure in bytes}
        flags: UINT;                 {positioning flags}
        showCmd: UINT;               {show state flags}
        ptMinPosition: TPoint;       {minimized coordinates}
        ptMaxPosition: TPoint;       {maximized coordinates}
        rcNormalPosition: TRect;     {restored position coordinates}
end;
```

length: The size of the structure, in bytes. Before calling this function, this member must be set to SizeOf(TWindowPlacement).

flags: Specifies flags that control the position of a minimized window and the method by which the window is restored. This member can be either or both of the flags in Table 10-4.

showCmd: Specifies the current show state of the window, and can be one of the values in Table 10-5.

ptMinPosition: The coordinates of the top left corner of the window when it is minimized, stored in the members of a TPoint structure.

ptMaxPosition: The coordinates of the top left corner of the window when it is maximized, stored in the members of a TPoint structure.

rcNormalPosition: The coordinates of the window in a normal, restored position, stored in the members of a TRect structure.

Return Value

If this function succeeds, it returns TRUE; otherwise it returns FALSE. To get extended error information, call the GetLastError function.

10

Chapter

See Also

GetWindowPlacement, SetWindowPos, ShowWindow

Example

Listing 10-9: Window Placement Information

```
{get the window placement}
procedure TForm1.Button1Click(Sender: TObject);
var
    PlacementInfo: TWindowPlacement;
begin
    {we must set the length to the size of the data structure first}
    PlacementInfo.Length:=SizeOf(TWindowPlacement);

    {get the window placement information}
    GetWindowPlacement(Form1.Handle, @PlacementInfo);

    {empty the list box}
    ListBox1.Items.Clear;

    {display all of the information in the window placement structure}
    ListBox1.Items.Add('Length: '+IntToStr(PlacementInfo.length));
    ListBox1.Items.Add('Flags: '+IntToStr(PlacementInfo.Flags));
    ListBox1.Items.Add('Show Command: '+IntToStr(PlacementInfo.showCmd));
    ListBox1.Items.Add('Min: '+IntToStr(PlacementInfo.ptMinPosition.X)+','+
                        IntToStr(PlacementInfo.ptMinPosition.Y));
    ListBox1.Items.Add('Max: '+IntToStr(PlacementInfo.ptMaxPosition.X)+','+
                        IntToStr(PlacementInfo.ptMaxPosition.Y));
    ListBox1.Items.Add('Normal position: '+
                    IntToStr(PlacementInfo.rcNormalPosition.Left)+','+
                    IntToStr(PlacementInfo.rcNormalPosition.Top)+','+
                    IntToStr(PlacementInfo.rcNormalPosition.Right)+','+
                    IntToStr(PlacementInfo.rcNormalPosition.Bottom));

end;

{set the window placement}
procedure TForm1.Button2Click(Sender: TObject);
var
    PlacementInfo: TWindowPlacement;
begin
    {we must set the length to the size of the data structure first}
    PlacementInfo.Length:=SizeOf(TWindowPlacement);

    {fill in the rest of the window structure members}
    PlacementInfo.flags:=WPF_SETMINPOSITION;
    PlacementInfo.showCmd:=SW_SHOW;
    PlacementInfo.ptMinPosition.X:=100;
    PlacementInfo.ptMinPosition.Y:=100;
    PlacementInfo.ptMaxPosition.X:=50;
    PlacementInfo.ptMaxPosition.Y:=50;
```

```
PlacementInfo.rcNormalPosition.Left:=100;
PlacementInfo.rcNormalPosition.Top:=100;
PlacementInfo.rcNormalPosition.Right:=250;
PlacementInfo.rcNormalPosition.Bottom:=250;

{set the window placement information}
SetWindowPlacement(Form1.Handle, @PlacementInfo);
end;
```

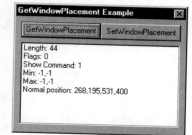

Figure 10-7: Getting the window placement information

Table 10-4: SetWindowPlacement WindowPlacement.flags Values

Value	Description
WPF_RESTORETOMAXIMIZED	The window will be maximized the next time it is restored, regardless of whether or not it was maximized before being minimized. This is valid only the next time that the window is restored, and when the SW_SHOWMINIMIZED flag is set for the ShowCmd member. This does not change the default restoration behavior.
WPF_SETMINPOSITION	The coordinates of the minimized window may be specified. This flag must be included if coordinates are set in the ptMinPosition member.

Table 10-5: SetWindowPlacement WindowPlacement.showCmd Values

Value	Description
SW_HIDE	The window is hidden and another window is activated.
SW_MINIMIZE	The window is minimized and the next top-level window in the system window list is activated.
SW_RESTORE	The window is activated and displayed in its original size and position.
SW_SHOW	The window is activated and displayed in its current size and position.

10

Chapter

Value	Description
SW_SHOWDEFAULT	The window is shown based on the wShowWindow member of the TStartupInfo structure passed to the CreateProcess function by the program that started the application. This is used to set the initial show state of an application's main window. This flag should be used when showing the window for the first time if the application could be run from a shortcut. This flag will cause the window to be shown using the Run settings under the shortcut properties.
SW_SHOWMAXIMIZED	The window is activated and displayed in a maximized state.
SW_SHOWMINIMIZED	The window is activated and displayed as an icon.
SW_SHOWMINNOACTIVE	The window is displayed as an icon. The active window remains active.
SW_SHOWNA	The window is displayed in its current state. The active window remains active.
SW_SHOWNOACTIVE	The window is displayed in its most recent state. The active window remains active.
SW_SHOWNORMAL	This is the same as SW_RESTORE.

SetWindowPos   Windows.Pas

Syntax

```
SetWindowPos(
hWnd: HWND;                        {a handle to a window}
hWndInsertAfter: HWND;             {a window handle or positioning flag}
X: Integer;                        {the horizontal position}
Y: Integer;                        {the vertical position}
CX: Integer;                       {the width of the window}
CY: Integer;                       {the height of the window}
uFlags: UINT                       {size and positioning flags}
): BOOL;                           {returns TRUE or FALSE}
```

Description

This function changes the size, position, and Z-order of the specified window. The Z-order of child, pop-up, and top-level windows is determined by the order in which these windows appeared on the screen. The topmost window is the first window in the Z-order.

Note that owned windows of a topmost window are also made topmost so that they are displayed above their owner, but owner windows of the specified window are not changed. Thus, a non-topmost window can own a topmost window, but a topmost window cannot own a non-topmost window. If a topmost window is repositioned to a non-topmost window, its owned windows are also changed to non-topmost.

Parameters

hWnd: The handle of the window to be moved or resized.

hWndInsertAfter: Identifies the window that will precede the repositioned window in the Z-order. This is either a window handle or one value from Table 10-6. This parameter is ignored if the SWP_NOZORDER flag is set in the Flags parameter. If this parameter is set to zero, the window will be placed at the top of the Z-order. If a window's Z-order position is placed above all other topmost windows, that window becomes a topmost window. This has the same effect as specifying the HWND_TOPMOST flag for this parameter.

X: The horizontal coordinate of the window's upper left corner. If this is a child window, the coordinates are relative to the parent window's client area.

Y: The vertical coordinate of the window's upper left corner. If this is a child window, the coordinates are relative to the parent window's client area.

CX: The window's new width, in pixels.

CY: The window's new height, in pixels.

uFlags: Specifies a combination of values from Table 10-7 that will affect the size and position of the window. Two or more values can be specified by using the Boolean OR operator.

Return Value

If the function succeeds, it returns TRUE; otherwise it returns FALSE. To get extended error information, call the GetLastError function.

See Also

BeginDeferWindowPos, DeferWindowPos, EndDeferWindowPos, MoveWindow, SetActiveWindow, SetForegroundWindow, SetWindowPlacement, ShowWindow, WM_MOVE, WM_SIZE

Example

Listing 10-10: Setting the Window Position

```
procedure TForm1.Button1Click(Sender: TObject);
begin
   {resize the memo so that it takes up the entire client area below the button}
   SetWindowPos(Memo1.Handle,0,0,Button1.Top+Button1.Height+5,Form1.ClientWidth,
            Form1.ClientHeight-(Button1.Top+Button1.Height+5),
            SWP_SHOWWINDOW);
end;
```

10

Chapter

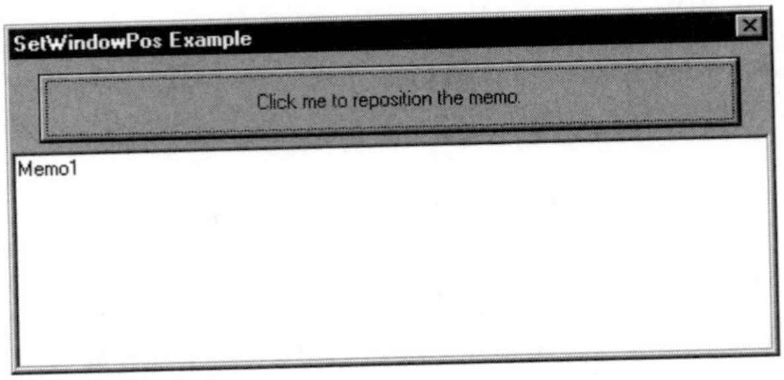

Figure 10-8:
The
repositioned
memo

Table 10-6: SetWindowPos hWndInsertAfter Values

Value	Description
HWND_BOTTOM	Places the window at the bottom of the Z-order. If this window was a topmost window, it loses its topmost status and is placed below all other windows.
HWND_NOTOPMOST	Places the window above all non-topmost windows, but behind all topmost windows. If the window is already a non-topmost window, this flag has no effect.
HWND_TOP	Places the window at the top of the Z-order.
HWND_TOPMOST	Places the window above all non-topmost windows; it will retain its topmost position even when deactivated.

Table 10-7: SetWindowPos uFlags Values

Value	Description
SWP_DRAWFRAME	Draws the frame defined in the window's class description around the window.
SWP_FRAMECHANGED	Causes a WM_NCCALCSIZE message to be sent to the window, even if the window size is not changing.
SWP_HIDEWINDOW	Hides the window.
SWP_NOACTIVATE	Does not activate the window. If this flag is not set, the window is activated and moved to the top of the topmost or non-topmost group depending on the hWndInsertAfter parameter.
SWP_NOCOPYBITS	Discards the entire client area. If this flag is not set, the valid area of the client area is saved and copied back into the client area after all movement and positioning is completed.
SWP_NOMOVE	Retains the current position, ignoring the X and Y parameters.
SWP_NOOWNERZORDER	Does not change the owner window's position in the Z-order.

Value	Description
SWP_NOREDRAW	When this flag is set, no repainting occurs, and the application must explicitly invalidate or redraw any parts of the window that need to be redrawn, including the nonclient area and scroll bars.
SWP_NOREPOSITION	The same as the SWP_NOOWNERZORDER flag.
SWP_NOSENDCHANGING	The window will not receive WM_WINDOWPOSCHANGING messages.
SWP_NOSIZE	Retains the current size, ignoring the CX and CY parameters.
SWP_NOZORDER	Retains the current Z-order, effectively causing the WndInsertAfter parameter to be ignored.
SWP_SHOWWINDOW	Displays the window.

ShowOwnedPopups   Windows.Pas

Syntax

```
ShowOwnedPopups(
hWnd: HWND;          {a handle to a window}
fShow: BOOL          {the window visibility flag}
): BOOL;             {returns TRUE or FALSE}
```

Description

This function will show or hide all pop-up windows owned by the specified window. Pop-up windows will only be shown if hidden by a previous call to ShowOwnedPopups (a window hidden with the ShowWindow function will not be displayed when ShowOwnedPopups is called).

Parameters

hWnd: A handle to the window owning the pop-ups to be shown.

fShow: Determines if pop-up windows are shown or hidden. A value of TRUE displays all hidden pop-up windows owned by the specified window. A value of FALSE will hide all visible pop-up windows.

Return Value

If this function succeeds, it returns TRUE; otherwise it returns FALSE. To get extended error information, call the GetLastError function.

See Also

IsWindowVisible, SetWindowPos, ShowWindow

10

Chapter

Example

Listing 10-11: Toggling the Show State of Owned Pop-up Windows

This code belongs in the unit for the main form:

```
var
  Form1: TForm1;
  ShowIt: Boolean;    // our toggle variable

implementation

uses Unit2;

{$R *.DFM}

procedure TForm1.Button1Click(Sender: TObject);
begin
   {toggle our show state variable}
   ShowIt:=not ShowIt;

   {show or hide all pop-ups owned by the main form}
   ShowOwnedPop-ups(Form1.Handle, ShowIt);
end;

procedure TForm1.FormShow(Sender: TObject);
begin
   {show the second form when the program starts}
   Form2.Show;
end;

initialization
   {initialize our toggle variable}
   ShowIt:=TRUE;
```

This code goes in the unit for Form2:

```
uses Unit2;

{we must override CreateParams to set this window's owner}
procedure TForm2.CreateParams(var Params: TCreateParams);
begin
   {fill in the default creation parameters}
   inherited CreateParams(Params);

   {set this form's owner to the main form}
   Params.WndParent:=Form1.Handle;
end;
```

ShowWindow   Windows.Pas

Syntax

```
ShowWindow(
hWnd: HWND;            {a handle to a window}
nCmdShow: Integer      {the show state of the window}
): BOOL;               {returns TRUE or FALSE}
```

Description

This function sets the specified window's display state. When displaying an application's main window, the developer should specify the SW_SHOWDEFAULT flag. This will display the window as instructed by application startup information. For example, if a Windows 95 shortcut has its properties set to run the application minimized, the SW_SHOWDEFAULT flag will show the window minimized. Without this flag, these shortcut properties are ignored.

Parameters

hWnd: A handle to the window to be shown.

nCmdShow: Specifies how the window will be shown. This can be one of the values from Table 10-8.

Return Value

If the function succeeded and the window was previously visible, it returns TRUE. If the function fails or the window was previously hidden, it returns FALSE.

See Also

CreateProcess, CreateWindow, SetWindowPlacement, SetWindowPos, ShowOwnedPopups, ShowWindowAsync, WM_SHOWWINDOW

Example

Listing 10-12: Showing a Window Based on Shortcut Properties

```
procedure TForm1.FormCreate(Sender: TObject);
begin
   {this example is run from a shortcut, and this line will
    show the window based on the shortcut properties}
   ShowWindow(Form1.Handle, SW_SHOWDEFAULT);
end;
```

10

Chapter

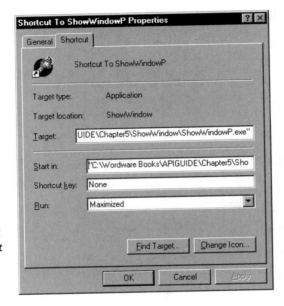

Figure 10-9: The shortcut settings start this application maximized.

Table 10-8: ShowWindow nCmdShow Values

Value	Description
SW_HIDE	The window is hidden and another window is activated.
SW_MINIMIZE	The window is minimized and the next top-level window in the system window list is activated.
SW_RESTORE	The window is activated and displayed in its original size and position.
SW_SHOW	The window is activated and displayed in its current size and position.
SW_SHOWDEFAULT	The window is shown based on the wShowWindow member of the TStartupInfo structure passed to the CreateProcess function by the program that started the application. This is used to set the initial show state of an application's main window. This flag should be used when showing the window for the first time if the application could be run from a shortcut. This flag will cause the window to be shown using the Run settings under the shortcut properties.
SW_SHOWMAXIMIZED	The window is activated and displayed in a maximized state.
SW_SHOWMINIMIZED	The window is activated and displayed as an icon.
SW_SHOWMINNOACTIVE	The window is displayed as an icon. The active window remains active.
SW_SHOWNA	The window is displayed in its current state. The active window remains active.

Value	Description
SW_SHOWNOACTIVE	The window is displayed in its most recent state. The active window remains active.
SW_SHOWNORMAL	This is the same as SW_RESTORE.

ShowWindowAsync — Windows.Pas

Syntax

```
ShowWindowAsync(
hWnd: HWND;              {a handle to a window}
nCmdShow: Integer        {the show state of the window}
): BOOL;                 {returns TRUE or FALSE}
```

Description

This function is similar to ShowWindow. Its purpose is to set the display state of a window created by a different thread. This function posts a WM_SHOWWINDOW message to the message queue of the specified window. This allows the calling application to continue execution if the application associated with the specified window is hung.

Parameters

hWnd: A handle to the window to be shown.

nCmdShow: Specifies how the window will be shown. This can be one of the values from Table 10-9.

Return Value

If the function succeeded and the window was previously visible, it returns TRUE. If the function fails or the window was previously hidden, it returns FALSE.

See Also

CreateProcess, CreateWindow, SetWindowPlacement, SetWindowPos, ShowOwnedPopups, ShowWindow, WM_SHOWWINDOW

Example

Listing 10-13: Showing a Window Asynchronously

```
procedure TForm1.Button1Click(Sender: TObject);
var
   TheWindow: HWND;
begin
   {find a handle to the Windows Explorer window. Windows Explorer must be
    running}
   TheWindow:=FindWindow('ExploreWClass',nil);
```

10

Chapter

```
   {show it}
   ShowWindowAsync(TheWindow, SW_MAXIMIZE);
end;
```

Table 10-9: ShowWindowAsync nCmdShow Values

Value	Description
SW_HIDE	The window is hidden and another window is activated.
SW_MINIMIZE	The window is minimized and the next top-level window in the system window list is activated.
SW_RESTORE	The window is activated and displayed in its original size and position.
SW_SHOW	The window is activated and displayed in its current size and position.
SW_SHOWDEFAULT	The window is shown based on the wShowWindow member of the TStartupInfo structure passed to the CreateProcess function by the program that started the application. This is used to set the initial show state of an application's main window. This flag should be used when showing the window for the first time if the application could be run from a shortcut. This flag will cause the window to be shown using the Run settings under the shortcut properties.
SW_SHOWMAXIMIZED	The window is activated and displayed in a maximized state.
SW_SHOWMINIMIZED	The window is activated and displayed as an icon.
SW_SHOWMINNOACTIVE	The window is displayed as an icon. The active window remains active.
SW_SHOWNA	The window is displayed in its current state. The active window remains active.
SW_SHOWNOACTIVE	The window is displayed in its most recent state. The active window remains active.
SW_SHOWNORMAL	This is the same as SW_RESTORE.

TileWindows   Windows.Pas

Syntax

```
TileWindows(
hwndParent: HWND;        {a handle to a parent window}
wHow: UINT;              {tiling flags}
lpRect: PRect;           {the area to arrange the windows in}
cKids: UINT;             {the number of windows to tile}
lpKids: Pointer          {the address to an array of window handles}
): WORD;                 {returns the number of windows arranged}
```

Description

This function arranges the windows associated by the handles in the lpKids array or the child windows of the specified window by tiling them. The windows can be tiled in a horizontal or vertical fashion, and can be restricted to a rectangular area within the specified parent window.

Parameters

hwndParent: A handle to the parent window. If this parameter is zero, the desktop window is assumed to be the parent window.

wHow: Specifies how the windows are tiled. MDITILE_HORIZONTAL tiles windows horizontally, and MDITILE_VERTICAL tiles windows vertically. The MDITILE_SKIPDISABLED flag can be combined with either of the previous flags to exclude any windows that are disabled from the tiling process. See Table 10-10.

lpRect: A pointer to a TRect structure containing the coordinates of the area in which the windows are arranged. If this parameter is NIL, the entire client area of the parent window is used.

cKids: Specifies the number of elements in the array pointed to by the lpKids parameter. If the lpKids parameter is NIL, this parameter is ignored.

lpKids: A pointer to an array of window handles identifying the windows to be tiled. If this parameter is NIL, all of the child windows of the specified parent window are tiled.

Return Value

If the function succeeds, it returns the number of windows tiled; otherwise it returns zero.

See Also

BeginDeferWindowPos, CascadeWindows, DeferWindowPos, EndDeferWindowPos, MoveWindow, SetWindowPlacement, WM_MDICASCADE, WM_MDITILE

Example

Listing 10-14: Vertically Tiling MDI Child Windows

```
procedure TForm1.TileWindows1Click(Sender: TObject);
begin
   {this will tile all of the MDI child windows vertically}
   TileWindows(Form1.ClientHandle,MDITILE_VERTICAL,nil,0,nil);
end;
```

10

Chapter

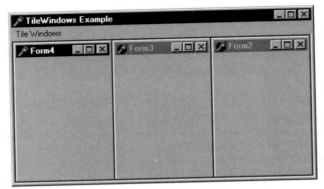

Figure 10-10:
Tiled windows

Table 10-10: TileWindow wHow Values

Value	Description
MDITILE_HORIZONTAL	The windows are tiled horizontally.
MDITILE_SKIPDISABLED	Any disabled windows are not tiled.
MDITILE_VERTICAL	The windows are tiled vertically.

Chapter 11

Shell Functions

The Windows shell provides the developer with a suite of functions concerned with file management and manipulation. These functions allow a developer to interrogate a file for information such as its type, its icon, or its associated executable file. Functions to move, copy, rename, delete, or launch a file give applications functionality similar to that provided by the Windows Explorer. File drag and drop functions enable a user to drag files from the Windows Explorer onto an application for opening, printing, or any other desired action. These functions are at the heart of application launch bars and other file management and manipulation utilities. The new Windows 95 and NT 4.0 shells also provide the developer with new user interface elements for a more specialized look and feel.

File-based Applications

The Shell drag and drop functions and file manipulation functions can greatly enhance the functionality of file-based applications. The ability to drag a file onto an application to open it is essential for a well behaved, robust file-based application. The DragAcceptFiles, DragQueryFile, and DragFinish functions are all a developer needs to implement a very user friendly and intuitive method for users to open files.

The following launch bar example demonstrates the use of a variety of the Shell functions. When files are dragged from the Explorer and dropped on the launch bar window, the application looks at each file dropped and creates a speed button for each executable file. An icon is extracted from the executable file and used as the glyph on the speed button. Then, the ShellExecute function is used in the OnClick event of the button to launch the executable file.

Listing 11-1: An Application Launch Bar with File Drag and Drop Functionality

```
unit LaunchU;

interface
```

```
uses
  Windows, Messages, SysUtils, Classes, Graphics,
  Controls, Forms, Dialogs, Buttons, ShellAPI, ExtCtrls;

type
  TForm1 = class(TForm)
    procedure FormCreate(Sender: TObject);
    procedure SpeedButtonClick(Sender: TObject);
  private
    { Private declarations }
    {the message handler required to process dropped files}
    procedure WMDropFiles(var Msg: TWMDropFiles); message WM_DROPFILES;
  public
    { Public declarations }
  end;

var
  Form1: TForm1;

implementation

{$R *.DFM}

procedure TForm1.FormCreate(Sender: TObject);
begin
  {register the form as a file drop target}
  DragAcceptFiles(Form1.Handle, TRUE);
end;

procedure TForm1.WMDropFiles(var Msg: TWMDropFiles);
var
  NumDroppedFiles: UINT;     // holds the number of files dropped
  TextBuffer: PChar;         // holds the filename
  BufferSize: UINT;          // the buffer size required to hold the filename
  Count: Integer;            // a general loop control variable
  LargeIcon, SmallIcon: HICON;  // holds handles to the icons for the file
begin
  {retrieve the number of files dropped on the form}
  NumDroppedFiles := DragQueryFile(Msg.Drop,$FFFFFFFF,nil,0);

  {for every file dropped on the form...}
  for Count := 0 to NumDroppedFiles-1 do
  begin
    {get the size of the filename and allocate a string large
     enough to hold it (add one to the text buffer size for
     the null terminator)}
    BufferSize := DragQueryFile(Msg.Drop,Count,nil,0);
    TextBuffer := StrAlloc(BufferSize+1);

    {the filename}
    DragQueryFile(Msg.Drop, Count, TextBuffer, BufferSize+1);

    {if the file is an executable...}
    if (ExtractFileExt(UpperCase(string(TextBuffer)))='.EXE') then
      {...create a speed button for it and initialize properties}
```

```
      with TSpeedButton.Create(Form1) do
      begin
        Parent := Form1;

        {the hint is used to store the path and filename of the
         executable dropped on the form. the shorthint part holds
         only the filename (this is what is displayed when the mouse
         cursor is moved over the button), and the longhint part
         holds the full path and filename. this part is used to
         launch the executable.}
        Hint := ExtractFileName(string(TextBuffer))+'|'+TextBuffer;
        ShowHint := TRUE;

        {set the left side of the button. if it is the first one
         on the form, its left side is set to 4.}
        if Form1.ComponentCount=1 then
          Left := 4
        else
          Left := TSpeedButton(Form1.Components[Form1.ComponentCount-2]).Left+
                  TSpeedButton(Form1.Components[Form1.ComponentCount-2]).Width+4;

        Top := 4;

        {set the OnClick method so the button does something}
        OnClick := SpeedButtonClick;

        {this extracts the small icon from the executable
         and displays it in the glyph for the speedbutton}
        with Glyph do
        begin
          ExtractIconEx(TextBuffer,0,LargeIcon,SmallIcon, 1);

          {we must set the width and height of the glyph
           so it is large enough to display the small icon}
          Width  := GetSystemMetrics(SM_CXSMICON);
          Height := GetSystemMetrics(SM_CYSMICON);
          DrawIconEx(Glyph.Canvas.Handle, 0, 0, SmallIcon,
                     GetSystemMetrics(SM_CXSMICON),
                     GetSystemMetrics(SM_CYSMICON),0,0,DI_NORMAL);

          DeleteObject(SmallIcon);
        end;
      end;

    {delete our filename text buffer}
    StrDispose(TextBuffer);
  end;

  {dispose of the memory allocated for the dropfile structure}
  DragFinish(Msg.Drop);
end;

procedure TForm1.SpeedButtonClick(Sender: TObject);
begin
  {when the button is pressed, the longhint portion of the hint
```

11

Chapter

```
    contains the full path and filename of the executable. extract
    this path and filename and launch the file.}
    ShellExecute(Form1.Handle, 'open', PChar(GetLongHint(TControl(Sender).Hint)),
              nil,nil,SW_SHOWNORMAL);

end;

end.
```

Figure II-I:
Files dropped
on the launch
bar

A file-based application may want to give the user the ability to go directly to a Windows Explorer window centered on the application's directory. With one line of code, the developer can do just this using the ShellExecute command. When the ShellExecute "explores" a folder, it opens a new Windows Explorer window with the specified directory selected. The following example demonstrates this technique.

Note: If Delphi 3 is not installed in its default directory, this example will need to be modified.

Listing II-2: Exploring a Folder

```
procedure TForm1.Button1Click(Sender: TObject);
begin
  {open a new explorer window with the Delphi 3 folder selected}
  ShellExecute(Form1.Handle, 'explore', 'C:\Program Files\Borland\Delphi 3',
              nil, nil, SW_SHOWNORMAL);
end;
```

Applications that produce temporary files should provide the functionality to delete these files without user intervention. A file-based application may also need to provide a mechanism allowing the user to copy, move, rename, or delete files within a controlled environment. The SHFileOperation function provides the ability to accomplish any file manipulation requirements. The following example demonstrates deleting a file to the recycle bin.

Listing 11-3: Deleting a File to the Recycle Bin

```
procedure TForm1.FileListBox1DblClick(Sender: TObject);
var
  FileOperation: TSHFileOpStruct;   // holds information on the file to delete
begin
  {initialize the TSHFileOpStruct with the necessary information.
   the FOF_ALLOWUNDO flag indicates the deleted file will go to
   the recycle bin}
  FileOperation.fFlags          := FOF_ALLOWUNDO or FOF_SIMPLEPROGRESS;
  FileOperation.Wnd             := Form1.Handle;
  FileOperation.wFunc           := FO_DELETE;
  FileOperation.pFrom           := PChar(FileListBox1.FileName+#0#0);
  FileOperation.pTo             := nil;
  FileOperation.hNameMappings   := nil;
  FileOperation.lpszProgressTitle := 'Deleting Files';

  {delete the specified file}
  SHFileOperation(FileOperation);

  {update the file list box information}
  FileListBox1.Update;
end;
```

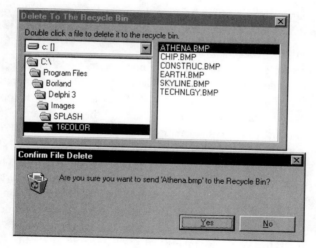

Figure 11-2:
File delete
confirmation

Item Identifier Lists

Each object in a shell's name space (such as files, folders, servers, workgroups, printers, etc.) is uniquely identified by an object called an *item identifier*. An item identifier is a variable length binary data structure whose content and format are known only to the creator of the item identifier. Item identifiers can be retrieved from a number of the file management functions.

The organization of the shell's name space is analogous to the organization of files in a directory structure. The root of the shell's name space is the Desktop, and every object

11

Chapter

under it can potentially contain other objects. An object's item identifier is unique and meaningful only within the context of its parent. Since container objects have an item identifier that uniquely identifies it within its parent container, any object can be uniquely identified by a list of item identifiers. Therefore, an Item Identifier List uniquely identifies an object within the shell's name space by tracing a path from it to the desktop. Many of the file management and manipulation functions use item identifier lists to specify files or folders.

Item identifier lists are commonly used with the shell Component Object Model (COM) objects. These objects provide a more advanced and complex interface to the Windows shell than the functions listed in this chapter. Entire books have been written concerning the Component Object Model and how to interface with such objects. Therefore, an explanation of COM is beyond the scope of this chapter.

The Application Bar

The Windows 95 and NT shells introduce a new user interface item known as an application bar. An appbar is a window that is associated with a particular edge of the screen. The space occupied by the appbar is reserved for its own use, and the system prevents other windows from using this area. There are several popular applications that ship with appbars, most of which provide the user with an alternative form of file management than that offered by the Start menu. The Windows taskbar is a special type of appbar.

The SHAppBarMessage function provides the interface to the Windows shell for registering an appbar and controlling its position. The application communicates with the shell through this function by sending it application bar messages. An appbar is registered by using the SHAppBarMessage function to send the system an ABM_NEW message. When an application creates an appbar, it should use the ABM_QUERYPOS message to retrieve an approved area for the appbar to reside. The ABM_SETPOS message is then used to inform the system that the appbar is occupying the specified rectangular area of the screen. The MoveWindow function is used to physically move the appbar window into the approved area. Once the appbar is in position, it receives appbar notification messages through the application-defined message identifier to inform it of events that might affect its appearance. These events include such things as a change in the state of the Windows taskbar or the launching or shutdown of a full screen application.

The appbar gives the Delphi developer an alternative to using a top-level window as the primary user interface. The following example demonstrates how Delphi can create a Windows application bar.

Listing 11-4: Creating an Appbar Using Delphi

```
unit AppBarMessageU;

interface
```

```
uses
  Windows, Messages, SysUtils, Classes, Graphics, Controls, Forms, Dialogs,
  StdCtrls, ShellAPI;

const
  {the application-defined appbar message identifier}
  WM_DELAPPBAR = WM_USER+1;

type
  TForm1 = class(TForm)
    Button1: TButton;
    Button2: TButton;
    procedure FormActivate(Sender: TObject);
    procedure FormDestroy(Sender: TObject);
    procedure FormCreate(Sender: TObject);
    procedure FormPaint(Sender: TObject);
  private
    { Private declarations }
    procedure CreateParams(var Params: TCreateParams); override;
  public
    { Public declarations }
    {the appbar message handler}
    procedure WMDelAppBar(var Msg: TMessage); message WM_DELAPPBAR;
  end;

var
  Form1: TForm1;
  {the TAppBarData structure must be global to the unit}
  AppBarInfo: TAppBarData;

implementation

{$R *.DFM}

{we must override the CreateParams method to ensure the
 appropriate styles are used}
procedure TForm1.CreateParams(var Params: TCreateParams);
begin
  inherited CreateParams(Params);
  {the appbar must be a pop-up tool window
   to function properly}
  Params.ExStyle := WS_EX_TOOLWINDOW;
  Params.Style := WS_POPUP or WS_CLIPCHILDREN;
end;

procedure TForm1.FormCreate(Sender: TObject);
begin
  {provide the TAppBarData structure with the
   handle to the appbar window}
  AppBarInfo.hWnd := Form1.Handle;

  {register the new appbar}
  SHAppBarMessage(ABM_NEW, AppBarInfo);

  {ask the system for an approved position}
```

```
      SHAppBarMessage(ABM_QUERYPOS, AppBarInfo);

      {adjust the new position to account for
       the appbar window height}
      AppBarInfo.rc.Bottom := AppBarInfo.rc.Top+50;

      {inform the system of the new appbar position}
      SHAppBarMessage(ABM_SETPOS, AppBarInfo);

      {physically move the appbar window into position}
      MoveWindow(AppBarInfo.hWnd, AppBarInfo.rc.Left, AppBarInfo.rc.Top,
                 AppBarInfo.rc.Right-AppBarInfo.rc.Left,
                 AppBarInfo.rc.Bottom-AppBarInfo.rc.Top, TRUE);
    end;

procedure TForm1.FormDestroy(Sender: TObject);
begin
  {provide the TAppBarData structure with
   the required information}
  AppBarInfo.cbSize := SizeOf(TAppBarData);
  AppBarInfo.hWnd := Form1.Handle;
  AppBarInfo.lParam := 0;

  {unregister the appbar}
  SHAppBarMessage(ABM_REMOVE, AppBarInfo);
end;

procedure TForm1.FormActivate(Sender: TObject);
begin
  {activate the appbar}
  SHAppBarMessage(ABM_ACTIVATE, AppBarInfo);
end;

procedure TForm1.FormPaint(Sender: TObject);
var
  Loop: Integer;
begin
  {this will fill the appbar with a gradient from yellow to red}
  for Loop := 0 to (Width div 20) do
  begin
    Canvas.Brush.Color := RGB(255,255-((255 div 20)*Loop),0);
    Canvas.Brush.Style := bsSolid;
    Canvas.FillRect(Rect((Width div 20)*Loop,0,((Width div 20)*Loop)+
                    (Width div 20),Height));
  end;

  {paint a caption on the appbar}
  Canvas.Font.Name    := 'Arial';
  Canvas.Font.Size    := 20;
  Canvas.Font.Color   := clBlue;
  Canvas.Font.Style   := [fsBold];
  Canvas.Brush.Style := bsClear;
  Canvas.TextOut(10,10,'Delphi App Bar');
end;
```

```
{this message handler is called whenever an event has
  occurred that could affect the appbar}
procedure TForm1.WMDelAppBar(var Msg: TMessage);
begin
  {the wParam parameter of the message contains the
   appbar notification message identifier}
  case Msg.wParam of
    ABN_FULLSCREENAPP: ShowMessage('FullScreenApp notification message
                                    received.');
    ABN_POSCHANGED:    ShowMessage('PosChanged notification message received.');
    ABN_STATECHANGE:   ShowMessage('StateChange notification message
                                    received.');
    ABN_WINDOWARRANGE: ShowMessage('WindowArrange notification message
                                    received.');
  end;
end;

initialization
  {initialize the TAppBarData structure with the required information}
  AppBarInfo.uEdge := ABE_TOP;
  AppBarInfo.rc := Rect(0,0,GetSystemMetrics(SM_CXSCREEN),50);
  AppBarInfo.cbSize := SizeOf(TAppBarData);
  AppBarInfo.uCallbackMessage := WM_DELAPPBAR;

end.
```

*Figure 11-3:
The Delphi
Appbar in
action*

Shell Functions

The following Shell functions are covered in this chapter:

Table 11-1: Shell Functions

Function	Description
DragAcceptFiles	Registers a window as a drop target for dragged files.
DragFinish	Completes the file drag and drop process.
DragQueryFile	Retrieves information about a dropped file.
DragQueryPoint	Retrieves the mouse coordinates at the time of a file drop.
FindExecutable	Retrieves the name of the executable file associated with a specified file.
SHAddToRecentDocs	Adds or clears a registered document type to the Documents menu item under the Start button.

Function	Description
SHAppBarMessage	Registers and controls an application bar.
SHBrowseForFolder	Creates a dialog box allowing the user to choose a shell folder.
ShellAbout	Displays the shell About dialog box.
ShellExecute	Launches an executable file.
ShellExecuteEx	Launches an executable file. This function provides more options than ShellExecute.
Shell_NotifyIcon	Registers a tray notification icon.
SHFileOperation	Copies, moves, renames, or deletes a file.
SHFreeNameMappings	Frees a name mapping object.
SHGetFileInfo	Retrieves information about the specified file.
SHGetPathFromIDList	Retrieves a path name from an item identifier list.
SHGetSpecialFolderLocation	Retrieves the location of unique folders.

DragAcceptFiles   ShellAPI.Pas

Syntax

```
DragAcceptFiles(
Wnd: HWND;              {a handle to a window}
Accept: BOOL            {the acceptance flag}
);                      {this procedure does not return a value}
```

Description

This procedure registers a window to accept or decline dropped files. If an application registers a window to accept dropped files, it receives a WM_DROPFILES message when files are dragged and dropped onto the window.

Parameters

Wnd: A handle to the window that will accept or decline dropped files.

Accept: A Boolean value that determines if the window will accept or decline dropped files. A value of TRUE registers the window as accepting dropped files; a value of FALSE will decline dropped files.

See Also

DragFinish, DragQueryFile, DragQueryPoint, WM_DROPFILES

Example

Listing 11-5: Retrieving Information on Dropped Files

Note that this example requires this line to be added to the public section of the form's class definition:

```
procedure WMDropFiles(var DropFileMsg: TWMDropFiles); message WM_DROPFILES;
```

When a file is dropped onto the form, Windows sends the form a WM_DROPFILES message. This line declares a procedure that will handle this message.

```
procedure TForm1.FormCreate(Sender: TObject);
begin
   {this registers the window to accept files}
   DragAcceptFiles(Handle,TRUE);
end;

procedure TForm1.WMDropFiles(var DropFileMsg: TWMDropFiles);
var
   FileCount: Integer;                    // holds the number of files dropped
   TheFileName: array[0..500] of char;    // holds a filename
   DropPoint: TPoint;                     // holds drop point coordinates
   LoopCount: Integer;                    // a general loop count variable
begin
   {clear our list box that displays file information}
   ListBox1.Items.Clear;

   {get the number of files that were dropped and display it}
   FileCount:=DragQueryFile(DropFileMsg.Drop,$FFFFFFFF,nil,0);
   ListBox1.Items.Add('Number of files dropped: '+IntToStr(FileCount));
   ListBox1.Items.Add('');

   {get the coordinates relative to the window where the files were dropped}
   DragQueryPoint(DropFileMsg.Drop, DropPoint);
   ListBox1.Items.Add('Mouse Drop Point: '+IntToStr(DropPoint.X)+', '+
                      IntToStr(DropPoint.Y));
   ListBox1.Items.Add('');
   ListBox1.Items.Add('----------------------------------------');
   ListBox1.Items.Add('');

   {retrieve the full path and filename of each file that was dropped}
   for LoopCount:=0 to FileCount-1 do
   begin
      DragQueryFile(DropFileMsg.Drop, LoopCount, TheFileName, 500);
      ListBox1.Items.Add('File '+IntToStr(LoopCount)+': '+string(TheFileName));
   end;

   {release the memory that was allocated
    for the file drop information structure}
   DragFinish(DropFileMsg.Drop);
end;
```

11

Chapter

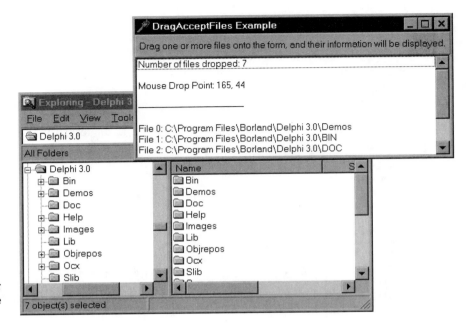

Figure 11-4:
Dropped file
information

DragFinish   ShellAPI.Pas

Syntax

```
DragFinish(
Drop: HDROP          {a handle to a file drop information structure}
);                   {this procedure does not return a value}
```

Description

This procedure frees memory that Windows allocated for the data structure holding dropped file information.

Parameters

Drop: A handle to the dropped file information data structure. This handle is passed in the wParam member of the WM_DROPFILES message. This is also accessible from Delphi as the Drop member of the TWMDropFiles message structure passed to the WM_DROPFILES message handling routine.

See Also

DragAcceptFiles, WM_DROPFILES

Example

Please see Listing 11-5 under DragAcceptFiles.

DragQueryFile   ShellAPI.Pas

Syntax

```
DragQueryFile(
Drop: HDROP;          {a handle to a file drop information structure}
FileIndex: UINT;      {the index to a filename}
FileName: PChar;      {a pointer to a buffer to hold a filename}
cb: UINT              {the size of the filename buffer}
): UINT;              {returns an unsigned integer based on the parameters}
```

Description

This function retrieves the filename of a dropped file. The FileIndex parameter indicates the position of the dropped file in the list of dropped files identified by the Drop parameter for which to retrieve the filename. The full path and filename of the dropped file is stored in the buffer pointed to by the FileName parameter.

Parameters

Drop: A handle to the dropped file information data structure. This handle is passed in the wParam member of the WM_DROPFILES message. This is also accessible from Delphi as the Drop member of the TWMDropFiles message structure passed to the WM_DROPFILES message handling routine.

FileIndex: This identifies the index of the dropped file. If this parameter is $FFFFFFFF, this function returns the total number of files dropped. The array of files is zero-based, and a value between zero and the total number of files dropped will cause the full path and filename of the corresponding file to be copied into the buffer pointed to by the FileName parameter.

FileName: This points to a buffer that receives the filename of a dropped file. If this parameter is NIL, this function returns the required size of the buffer, in characters.

cb: Specifies the size of the buffer pointed to by the FileName parameter, in characters.

Return Value

If this function succeeds, the return value is dependent on the values passed in the parameters. If the value of the FileIndex parameter is $FFFFFFFF, this function returns the total number of files dropped. If the FileIndex parameter is between zero and the total number of files dropped, and the value of the FileName parameter is NIL, this function returns the size of the buffer required to hold the full path and filename of the corresponding file, in characters. This does not include the null-terminating character. If this function copies a filename to the buffer pointed to by the FileName parameter, it returns the total number of characters copied, excluding the null-terminating character. If the function fails, it returns zero.

See Also

DragAcceptFiles, DragQueryPoint, WM_DROPFILES

11

Chapter

Example

Please see Listing 11-5 under DragAcceptFiles.

DragQueryPoint   ShellAPI.Pas

Syntax

```
DragQueryPoint(
Drop: HDROP;              {a handle to a file drop information structure}
var Point: TPoint         {a pointer to a structure for coordinate information}
): BOOL;                  {returns TRUE or FALSE}
```

Description

This function fills a TPoint structure with the coordinates of the mouse cursor at the time files were dropped onto the window.

Parameters

Drop: A handle to the dropped file information data structure. This handle is passed in the wParam member of the WM_DROPFILES message. This is also accessible from Delphi as the Drop member of the TWMDropFiles message structure passed to the WM_DROPFILES message handling routine.

Point: A pointer to a TPoint structure that will be filled with the X and Y coordinates of the mouse cursor at the time the files were dropped. These coordinates are relative to the window in which the drop occurred.

Return Value

If this function succeeds and the drop point was within the client area of the window, it returns TRUE. If the function fails, or the drop point was not within the client area, it returns FALSE.

See Also

DragAcceptFiles, DragQueryFile, WM_DROPFILES

Example

Please see Listing 11-5 under DragAcceptFiles.

FindExecutable   ShellAPI.Pas

Syntax

```
FindExecutable(
FileName: PChar;          {a pointer to a filename string}
Directory: PChar;         {a pointer to a default directory string}
Result: PChar             {a pointer to a buffer that receives a filename}
): HINST;                 {returns an integer value}
```

Description

This function retrieves the name and path of the executable file associated with the filename passed in the FileName parameter.

Parameters

FileName: A pointer to a null-terminated string that contains a filename. This parameter can specify either a document or an executable file. If this parameter contains the name of an executable file, the Result parameter will contain an exact copy of this parameter when the function returns.

Directory: A pointer to a null-terminated string specifying a path to use as the default directory.

Result: A pointer to a buffer that receives a null-terminated string identifying the executable file associated with the file or document indicated by the FileName parameter. This executable file is launched when an "open" action is performed on the file specified by the FileName parameter, either by right-clicking on the file and selecting Open in the Windows Explorer or using the ShellExecute function. The registry records which executable file is associated with specific file types. When the FindExecutable function is called, it first looks in the registry under the key HKEY_LOCAL_MACHINE\SOFTWARE\Classes\<file type>. The value at this location is the name of another key. FindExecutable then takes this value and looks under the key HKEY_LOCAL_MACHINE\SOFTWARE\Classes\<key name>\Shell\Open\Command. The value at this location contains the full path and filename of the associated executable. For example, if the FileName parameter specified a file with the extension .PAS, FindExecutable would first look under HKEY_LOCAL_MACHINE\SOFTWARE\Classes\.pas. The value at this location is "DelphiUnit". FindExecutable takes this value and looks under the key HKEY_LOCAL_MACHINE\SOFTWARE\Classes\DelphiUnit\Shell\Open\Command. If Delphi 3 has been installed into the default location, the value found at this location will be "C:\Program Files\Borland\Delphi 3\Bin\Delphi32.EXE" "%1." Note that if the path and filename of the executable file stored in this registry key contains spaces, as in this example, and it is not surrounded by double quotes, the FindExecutable function replaces any spaces in the value with a null character.

Return Value

If the function succeeds, it returns a value greater than 32. If the function fails, it returns a value from Table 11-2.

See Also

ShellExecute, ShellExecuteEx

11

Chapter

Example

Listing 11-6: Finding an Executable File and Opening Documents

```
procedure TForm1.Edit1KeyPress(Sender: TObject; var Key: Char);
begin
   {set a new edit mask based on the contents of Edit1}
   if ((Key=Chr(13)) AND (Edit1.Text<>'')) then
   begin
      FileListBox1.Mask := '*.'+Edit1.Text;
      {this prevents the speaker from beeping}
      Key := #0;
   end;
end;

procedure TForm1.Button1Click(Sender: TObject);
begin
   {launch the executable file found by FindExecutable}
   if Label1.Caption<>'' then
      ShellExecute(Form1.Handle, 'open', PChar(Label1.Caption),
                   nil, nil, SW_SHOWNORMAL);
end;

procedure TForm1.Button2Click(Sender: TObject);
begin
   {open the selected file by starting its associated application}
   ShellExecute(Form1.Handle, 'open', PChar(FileListBox1.Filename),
                nil, nil, SW_SHOWNORMAL);
end;

procedure TForm1.FileListBox1Click(Sender: TObject);
var
   Buffer: array[0..500] of char;    // a buffer for a path and filename
begin
   {find the executable associated with the selected file}
   FindExecutable(PChar(FileListBox1.FileName),nil,@Buffer);

   {if an executable was not found...}
   if StrLen(Buffer)<1 then
   begin
      {...display a message and disable the launch buttons...}
      Label1.Caption:='No Associated executable';
      Button1.Enabled:=FALSE;
      Button2.Enabled:=FALSE;
   end
   else
   begin
      {...otherwise display the executable path and filename}
      Label1.Caption:=string(Buffer);
      Button1.Enabled:=TRUE;
      Button2.Enabled:=TRUE;
   end;
end;
```

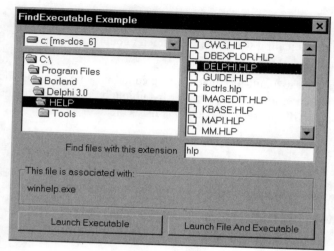

Figure 11-5:
Found an
executable file

Table 11-2: FindExecutable Return Value Error Codes

Value	Description
0	Not enough memory or resources.
ERROR_GEN_FAILURE	The specified file does not have an associated executable file.
ERROR_FILE_NOT_FOUND	The file specified by the FileName parameter could not be found.
ERROR_PATH_NOT_FOUND	The default directory path specified by the Directory parameter could not be found.
ERROR_BAD_FORMAT	The associated executable file is invalid or corrupt.

SHAddToRecentDocs   *ShlObj.Pas*

Syntax

SHAddToRecentDocs(
uFlags: UINT;   {a value indicating the contents of the pv parameter}
pv: Pointer   {a pointer to a buffer or an item id list}
);   {this procedure does not return a value}

Description

This function adds or removes files to the recent documents list. This list is accessed through the Start button in the Documents menu item. Only registered documents (those that have an associated executable file) can be added to this list.

11

Chapter

Parameters

uFlags: A value indicating what the pv parameter contains. This parameter can contain one value from Table 11-3.

pv: Either a pointer to a null-terminated string containing the path and filename of a document or a pointer to an item identifier list uniquely identifying the document. If this parameter is NIL, the recent documents list is cleared.

See Also

SHGetFileInfo

Example

Listing II-7: Adding a Document to the Recent Documents List

```
procedure TForm1.Button1Click(Sender: TObject);
begin
  {clear all documents from the recent docs list}
  SHAddToRecentDocs(SHARD_PATH,nil);
end;

procedure TForm1.FileListBox1DblClick(Sender: TObject);
var
  TheFileName: string;
begin
  {retrieve the filename of the selected document}
  TheFileName := FileListBox1.FileName;

  {add it to the recent docs list. note that the file
   must be registered (must have an associated executable)
   before it is added to the list}
  SHAddToRecentDocs(SHARD_PATH, pchar(TheFileName));
end;
```

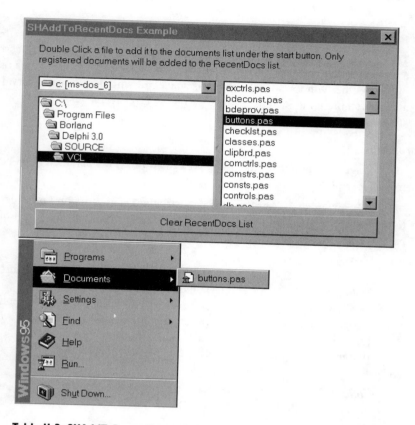

Figure 11-6:
A document
was added to
the list.

Table II-3: SHAddToRecentDocs uFlags Values

Value	Description
SHARD_PATH	The pv parameter contains the address of a null-terminated string containing the path and filename of a document.
SHARD_PIDL	The pv parameter contains the address of an item identifier list uniquely identifying the document.

SHAppBarMessage   *ShellAPI.Pas*

Syntax

```
SHAppBarMessage(
dwMessage: DWORD;              {the appbar message}
var pData: TAppBarData         {a pointer to a TAppBarData data structure}
): UINT;                       {returns a message-dependent value}
```

Chapter

11

Description

This function creates an application bar. An appbar is a window that is associated with a particular edge of the screen and reserves that screen space for its own use. Windows prevents other windows from using this space, moving them if necessary. Note that the application bar window must use the WS_EX_TOOLWINDOW and WS_POPUP styles to work properly.

Parameters

dwMessage: The application bar message identifier. This parameter can be one value from Table 11-4.

pData: A pointer to a TAppBarData data structure. This structure provides information to the SHAppBarMessage function, and receives information as a result of the function call. The TAppBarData structure is defined as:

```
TAppBarData = record
        cbSize: DWORD;              {the size of the TAppBarData structure}
        hWnd: HWND;                 {a handle to a window}
        uCallbackMessage: UINT;     {an application-defined message identifier}
        uEdge: UINT;                {a screen edge flag}
        rc: TRect;                  {a rectangle in screen coordinates}
        lParam: LPARAM;             {a message-dependent value}
end;
```

cbSize: The size of the TAppBarData data structure, in bytes. This member should be set to SizeOf(TAppBarData).

hWnd: A handle to the appbar window.

uCallbackMessage: An application-defined message identifier. This message is sent to the window identified by the hWnd parameter to notify it of events. The wParam parameter of this message will contain one of the notification messages from Table 11-5.

uEdge: A flag indicating which edge of the screen is associated with the appbar. This member can be one value from Table 11-6.

rc: A TRect structure that holds the coordinates of the appbar window. These coordinates are in terms of the screen.

lParam: A message-dependent value. See Table 11-5 for an explanation of when this member is used.

Return Value

If the function succeeds, it returns a message specific value; otherwise it returns zero. See Table 11-5 for a description of possible return values.

See Also

CreateWindow, CreateWindowEx, MoveWindow

Example

Listing II-8: Retrieving the Windows Taskbar Coordinates

```
procedure TForm1.Button1Click(Sender: TObject);
var
  AppBarInfo: TAppBarData;    // holds the appbar information
begin
  {initialize the appbar data structure with the information needed}
  AppBarInfo.cbSize := SizeOf(TAppBarData);
  AppBarInfo.hWnd    := Form1.Handle;

  {retrieve the coordinates of the Windows taskbar...}
  SHAppBarMessage(ABM_GETTASKBARPOS, AppBarInfo);

  {...and display them}
  Button1.Caption := 'Left: '+IntToStr(AppBarInfo.rc.Left)+
                     ' Top: '+IntToStr(AppBarInfo.rc.Top)+
                     ' Right: '+IntToStr(AppBarInfo.rc.Right)+
                     ' Bottom: '+IntToStr(AppBarInfo.rc.Bottom);
end;
```

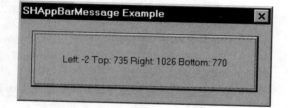

Figure 11-7: The taskbar coordinates

Table II-4: SHAppBarMessage dwMessage Values

Value	Description
ABM_ACTIVATE	Notifies Windows that an appbar has been activated. The appbar should call this message when it receives a WM_ACTIVATE message. The cbSize and hWnd members of the TAppBarData structure must be initialized. All other members are ignored. This message is ignored if the hWnd parameter identifies an autohide appbar, as the system automatically sets their Z-order. The function will always return a value greater than zero when using this message.

11

Chapter

Value	*Description*
ABM_GETAUTOHIDEBAR	Retrieves the window handle of the autohide appbar associated with the specified screen edge. The cbSize, hWnd, and uEdge members of the TAppBarData structure must be initialized. All other members are ignored. If the function succeeds, it returns a handle to the appbar window associated with the specified screen edge. If the function fails or there is no appbar associated with the specified screen edge, the function returns zero.
ABM_GETSTATE	Retrieves the autohide and always-on-top states of the Windows taskbar. The cbSize and hWnd members of the TAppBarData structure must be initialized. All other members are ignored. If the function succeeds, it returns either ABS_ALWAYSONTOP, a constant indicating the taskbar is in the always-on-top state, or ABS_AUTOHIDE, a constant indicating the taskbar is in the autohide state. The function can return both values if necessary. If the function fails or the Windows taskbar is in neither state, it returns zero.
ABM_GETTASKBARPOS	Retrieves the bounding rectangular coordinates of the Windows taskbar. The cbSize and hWnd members of the TAppBarData structure must be initialized. All other members are ignored. If the function succeeds, it returns a value greater than zero, and the rc member will contain the bounding rectangle, in screen coordinates, of the Windows taskbar. If the function fails, it returns zero.
ABM_NEW	Registers a new appbar with the system. The function specifies the application-defined message identifier that is used to send the appbar notification messages. This message should be called before any other appbar messages. To register an autohide appbar, use the ABM_SETAUTOHIDEBAR message. The cbSize, hWnd, and uCallbackMessage members of the TAppBarData structure must be initialized. All other members are ignored. If the function succeeds, it returns a nonzero value. If the function fails or the specified appbar is already registered, it returns zero.

Value	Description
ABM_QUERYPOS	Requests a bounding rectangle and screen edge position for the appbar. The system adjusts the specified rectangle so the appbar will not interfere with the Windows taskbar or any other appbar. The appbar should send this message before sending the ABM_SETPOS message. The cbSize, hWnd, uEdge, and rc members of the TAppBarData structure must be initialized. All other members are ignored. When the function returns, the rc member contains the adjusted coordinates for the new appbar position. This message causes the function to always return a nonzero value.
ABM_REMOVE	Unregisters an appbar from the system. The cbSize and hWnd members of the TAppBarData structure must be initialized. All other members are ignored. The function will always return a nonzero value when using this message. The ABN_POSCHANGED notification message is sent to all other appbars after this message is processed.
ABM_SETAUTOHIDEBAR	Registers or unregisters an autohide appbar. The system only allows one autohide appbar per screen edge. The lParam member of the TAppBarData structure is set to a nonzero value to register an autohide appbar or to zero to unregister the appbar. The cbSize, hWnd, uEdge, and lParam members of the TAppBarData structure must be initialized. All other members are ignored. If the function succeeds, it returns a nonzero value. If the function fails or an appbar is already registered for the specified edge, the function returns zero.
ABM_SETPOS	Sets a bounding rectangle and screen edge position for the appbar. The system adjusts the specified rectangle so the appbar will not interfere with the Windows taskbar or any other appbar. The cbSize, hWnd, uEdge, and rc members of the TAppBarData structure must be initialized. All other members are ignored. When the function returns, the rc member contains the adjusted coordinates for the new appbar position. This message causes the function to always return a nonzero value. The system sends all appbars the ABN_POSCHANGED notification message after this message is processed.

11

Chapter

Value	Description
ABM_WINDOWPOSCHANGED	Notifies the system that the appbar's position has changed. The appbar should call this message when responding to the WM_WINDOWPOSCHANGED message. The cbSize and hWnd members of the TAppBarData structure must be initialized. All other members are ignored. This message causes the function to always return a nonzero value. This message is ignored if the hWnd member identifies an autohide appbar.

Table 11-5: SHAppBarMessage pData.uCallbackMessage wParam Notification Messages

Value	Description
ABN_FULLSCREENAPP	Notifies an appbar when a full screen application is opening or closing. When a full screen application starts, the appbar must go to the bottom of the Z-order. When the full screen application shuts down, the appbar can restore its original position in the Z-order. If the lParam parameter is a nonzero value, it indicates that the full screen app is opening. If the lParam parameter is zero, the full screen app is shutting down.
ABN_POSCHANGED	Notifies the appbar of an event that may affect its size and position, such as adding, removing, or resizing another appbar, or changing the Windows taskbar position or state. Upon receiving this message, the appbar should send the ABM_QUERYPOS message followed by the ABM_SETPOS message to determine if its position has changed. The MoveWindow function is then called to physically move the appbar window into its new position.
ABN_STATECHANGE	Notifies the appbar that taskbar's autohide or always-on-top state has changed.
ABN_WINDOWARRANGE	Notifies the appbar that the user has selected the Cascade, Tile Horizontally, or Tile Vertically command from the Windows taskbar context menu. If the lParam parameter is a nonzero value, it indicates that the arrangement command has started, and no windows have been moved. A value of zero indicates that the arrangement command has finished and all windows are in their final positions. The appbar receives this message twice, once before the operation starts and again after the operation has finished.

Table II-6: SHAppBarMessage pData.uEdge Values

Value	Description
ABE_BOTTOM	The bottom edge of the screen.
ABE_LEFT	The left edge of the screen.
ABE_RIGHT	The right edge of the screen.
ABE_TOP	The top edge of the screen.

SHBrowseForFolder   **ShlObj.Pas**

Syntax

SHBrowseForFolder(
var lpbi: TBrowseInfo   {a pointer to a TBrowseInfo data structure}
): PItemIDList;   {returns a pointer to an item identifier list}

Description

This function displays a dialog box allowing the user to choose a shell folder.

Parameters

lpbi: A pointer to a TBrowseInfo structure. This structure holds information used to display the dialog box, and receives information from the dialog box indicating the user's choice. This structure is defined as:

TBrowseInfo = packed record
    hwndOwner: HWND;   {a handle to a window}
    pidlRoot: PItemIDList;   {a pointer to an item identifier list}
    pszDisplayName: PAnsiChar;   {a pointer to a string}
    lpszTitle: PAnsiChar;   {a pointer to a string}
    ulFlags: UINT;   {control flags}
    lpfn: TFNBFFCallBack;   {the address to a callback function}
    lParam: LPARAM;   {an application-defined value}
    iImage: Integer;   {a system image list image index}
end;

hwndOwner: A handle to the window that owns the dialog box.

pidlRoot: A pointer to an item identifier list specifying the root folder from which the user starts the browse. If this member is NIL, the root of the name space is used as the starting point.

pszDisplayName: A pointer to a buffer that receives a null-terminated string containing the display name of the selected folder. The size of this buffer is assumed to be MAX_PATH bytes.

lpszTitle: A pointer to a null-terminated string containing the text displayed in the caption of the dialog box.

11

Chapter

ulFlags: An array of flags specifying the types of folders listed and other options. This member can be one or more of the values from Table 11-7.

lpfn: A pointer to a callback function. This function is called whenever a user action generates an event in the dialog box, such as selecting a folder. This member can be set to NIL. The callback function syntax is described below.

lParam: An application-defined value that is passed to the callback function if one is defined.

iImage: Receives an index into the system image list of the image that represents the selected folder.

Return Value

If the function succeeds, it returns a pointer to an item identifier list specifying the chosen folder. The location of the folder is relative to the root of the name space. If the function fails or the user chooses the Cancel button, the function returns NIL.

Callback Syntax

```
BrowseCallbackProc(
hWnd: HWND;              {a handle to the dialog box window}
uMsg: UINT;              {a dialog box event message}
lParam: LPARAM;          {a message specific value}
lpData: LPARAM           {an application-defined value}
): Integer;              {returns an integer value}
```

Description

The callback function is run whenever the user causes an event to take place in the Browse for Folder dialog box. This callback function can perform any desired task.

Parameters

hWnd: A handle to the dialog box window. The callback function can use this parameter to send a special message to the dialog box window. The available messages are listed in Table 11-8.

uMsg: A value indicating the type of event that has occurred. This parameter can be one value from Table 11-9.

lParam: A message specific value. This value is dependent on the uMsg parameter.

lpData: The application-defined value that was passed in the lParam member of the TBrowseInfo structure.

Return Value

The callback function should always return a zero.

See Also

FindExecutable, ShellExecute, ShellExecuteEx, SHFileOperation

Example

Listing II-9: Browsing for a Folder

```
{the callback function used by the browse for folder dialog
  box. notice the export directive.}
function BrowseCallback(hWnd: HWND; uMsg: UINT; lParam: LPARAM;
                        lpData: LPARAM): Integer; stdcall; export;

var
  Form1: TForm1;

implementation

{$R *.DFM}

procedure TForm1.Button1Click(Sender: TObject);
var
  IDList: PItemIDList;                         // an item identifier list
  BrowseInfo: TBrowseInfo;                     // the browse info structure
  PathName: array[0..MAX_PATH] of char;        // the path name
  DisplayName: array[0..MAX_PATH] of char;     // the file display name
begin
  {initialize the browse information structure}
  BrowseInfo.hwndOwner      := Form1.Handle;
  BrowseInfo.pidlRoot       := nil;
  BrowseInfo.pszDisplayName := DisplayName;
  BrowseInfo.lpszTitle      := 'Choose a file or folder';
  BrowseInfo.ulFlags        := BIF_STATUSTEXT;          // display a status line
  BrowseInfo.lpfn           := @BrowseCallback;
  BrowseInfo.lParam         := 0;

  {show the Browse for Folder dialog box}
  IDList := SHBrowseForFolder(BrowseInfo);

  {retrieve the path from the item identifier list
   that was returned}
  SHGetPathFromIDList(IDList, @PathName);

  {display the path name and display name of
   the selected folder}
  Label2.Caption := PathName;
  Label4.Caption := BrowseInfo.pszDisplayName;
end;

{this callback function is called whenever an action takes
 place inside the Browse for Folder dialog box}
function BrowseCallback(hWnd: HWND; uMsg: UINT; lParam: LPARAM;
                        lpData: LPARAM): Integer;
var
  PathName: array[0..MAX_PATH] of Char;   // holds the path name
begin
  {if the selection in the browse for folder
   dialog box has changed...}
  if uMsg=BFFM_SELCHANGED then
```

```
begin
  {...retrieve the path name from the item identifier list}
  SHGetPathFromIDList(PItemIDList(lParam), @PathName);

  {display this path name in the status line of the dialog box}
  SendMessage(hWnd, BFFM_SETSTATUSTEXT, 0, Longint(PChar(@PathName)));

  Result := 0;
  end;
end;
```

Figure 11-8:
The Browse
for Folder
dialog box

Table 11-7: SHBrowseForFolder lpbi.ulFlags Values

Value	Description
BIF_BROWSEFORCOMPUTER	Allows the user to select only computers.
BIF_BROWSEFORPRINTER	Allows the user to select only printers.
BIF_DONTGOBELOWDOMAIN	The dialog box will not contain network folders below the domain level.
BIF_RETURNFSANCESTORS	Allows the user to select only file system ancestors.
BIF_RETURNONLYFSDIRS	Allows the user to select only file system directories.
BIF_STATUSTEXT	Includes a status line in the dialog box. The callback function can send a message to the dialog box specifying what to display on this line.

Table 11-8: BrowseCallbackProc Browse For Folder Dialog Box Messages

Value	Description
BFFM_ENABLEOK	Enables the OK button if the wParam parameter of the message contains a nonzero value. If the wParam parameter contains a zero, the OK button is disabled.
BFFM_SETSELECTION	Selects a specific folder. If the wParam parameter of the message contains TRUE, the lParam parameter must contain a pointer to a string describing the path of the folder. If the wParam parameter is FALSE, the lParam parameter must contain a pointer to an item identifier list specifying the selected folder.
BFFM_SETSTATUSTEXT	Sets the text of the status line in the dialog box. The lParam parameter of the message must contain a pointer to a null-terminated string for the status line. This message is only valid if the BIF_STATUSTEXT flag was specified in the ulFlags member of the TbrowseInfo structure.

Table 11-9: BrowseCallbackProc uMsg Values

Value	Description
BFFM_INITIALIZED	The Browse for Folder dialog box has finished initializing. The lParam parameter contains zero.
BFFM_SELCHANGED	The user has selected a folder. The lParam parameter contains a pointer to an item identifier list specifying the chosen folder.

ShellAbout   ShellAPI.Pas

Syntax

```
ShellAbout(
Wnd: HWND;              {a handle to a parent window}
szApp: PChar;           {a pointer to the title bar text}
szOtherStuff: PChar;    {a pointer to descriptive text}
Icon: HICON             {a handle to an icon}
): Integer;             {returns an integer value}
```

11

Chapter

Description

This function displays the shell About dialog box. This is the About box that is displayed when About Windows 95 is selected in the Windows Explorer. This dialog box displays an icon and text that is specific to Windows or Windows NT.

Parameters

Wnd: A handle to a parent window. If this parameter is zero, the About box acts like a modeless dialog box. If a handle is specified, the About box will be modal.

szApp: A pointer to text that is displayed in the title bar and on the first line of the About box.

szOtherStuff: A pointer to text that is displayed after the copyright information.

Icon: A handle to an icon that is displayed in the dialog box. If this parameter is zero, the dialog box will display the Windows or Windows NT icon.

Return Value

If the function succeeds, it returns a nonzero value; otherwise it returns zero.

See Also

GetSystemInfo

Example

Listing 11-10: Displaying the ShellAbout Dialog Box

```
procedure TForm1.Button1Click(Sender: TObject);
begin
  {call the Microsoft shell about box}
  ShellAbout(Form1.Handle, 'ShellAbout Example',
    'This is a simple example of how to use the ShellAbout API function.',0);
end;
```

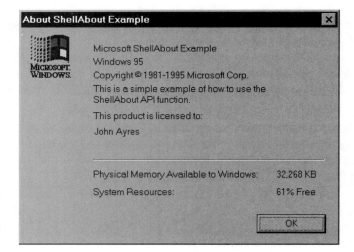

Figure 11-9: The shell About dialog box

ShellExecute   ShellAPI.Pas

Syntax

ShellExecute(
hWnd: HWND;   {a handle to a parent window}
Operation: PChar;   {a pointer to a string describing the action}
FileName: PChar;   {a pointer to a filename or folder name}
Parameters: PChar;   {a pointer to executable file parameters}
Directory: PChar;   {a pointer to the default directory name}
ShowCmd: Integer   {file display flags}
): HINST;   {returns an instance handle}

Description

This function performs the specified action on the specified file, and can be used to print a document, launch an executable file, or open a directory folder.

Parameters

hWnd: A handle to a parent window that receives message boxes if an error occurs.

Operation: A pointer to a null-terminated string specifying the action to perform on the file or folder indicated by the FileName parameter. Table 11-10 lists the standard actions that can be performed on a file or folder. However, these actions are not limited to those listed in the table. This parameter is dependent on the actions registered for the document or application in the registry, and new actions can be created through the Options menu in the Windows Explorer. If this parameter is NIL, the "open" operation is used by default.

FileName: A pointer to a null-terminated string containing the name of a document, executable file, or folder.

Parameters: If the FileName parameter indicates an executable file, this parameter contains a pointer to a null-terminated string specifying the command line parameters to pass to the executable file. The parameters must be separated by spaces. If the FileName parameter specifies a document or folder, this parameter should be NIL.

Directory: A pointer to a null-terminated string containing the path to the default directory. If this parameter is NIL, the current directory is used as the working directory.

ShowCmd: A flag that determines how the executable file indicated by the FileName parameter is to be displayed when it is launched. This parameter can be one value from Table 11-11.

Return Value

If the function succeeds, it returns the instance handle of the application that was launched or the handle to a dynamic data exchange server application. If the function fails, it returns a value from Table 11-12. This value will be less than 32.

11

Chapter

See Also

FindExecutable, ShellExecuteEx

Example

Listing 11-11: Viewing Text Files

```
procedure TForm1.FileListBox1DblClick(Sender: TObject);
begin
  {this will open the file that was double-clicked in the file list box. if
   this file is too big for Notepad, Windows will ask if you want to launch
   Wordpad}
  ShellExecute(Form1.Handle, 'open', PChar(FileListBox1.FileName), nil, nil,
               SW_SHOWNORMAL);
end;
```

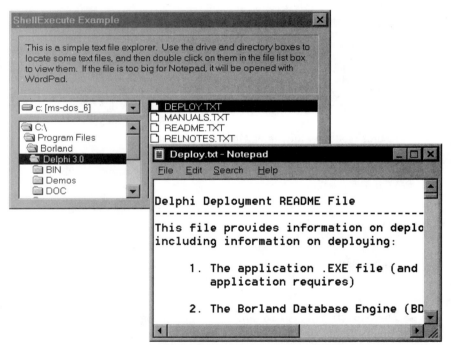

Figure 11-10: Viewing a text file in Notepad

Table 11-10: ShellExecute Operation Values

Value	Description
"open"	Opens the file or folder or launches the executable file identified by the FileName parameter.
"print"	Prints the document identified by the FileName parameter. If the FileName parameter identifies an executable file, it is launched as if a value of "open" had been specified.

Value	Description
"explore"	Opens a Windows Explorer window onto the folder identified by the FileName parameter.

Table 11-11: ShellExecute ShowCmd Values

Value	Description
SW_HIDE	The window is hidden and another window is activated.
SW_MINIMIZE	The window is minimized and the next top-level window in the relative Z-order is activated.
SW_RESTORE	The window is activated and displayed in its original size and position.
SW_SHOW	The window is activated and displayed in its current size and position.
SW_SHOWDEFAULT	The window is shown based on the wShowWindow member of the TStartupInfo structure passed to the CreateProcess function by the program that started the application. This is used to set the initial show state of an application's main window. This flag should be used when showing the window for the first time if the application could be run from a shortcut. This flag will cause the window to be shown using the Run settings under the shortcut properties.
SW_SHOWMAXIMIZED	The window is activated and displayed in a maximized state.
SW_SHOWMINIMIZED	The window is activated and displayed as an icon.
SW_SHOWMINNOACTIVE	The window is displayed as an icon. The active window remains active.
SW_SHOWNA	The window is displayed in its current state. The active window remains active.
SW_SHOWNOACTIVE	The window is displayed in its most recent state. The active window remains active.
SW_SHOWNORMAL	This is the same as SW_RESTORE.

Table 11-12: ShellExecute Return Value Error Codes

Value	Description
0	Not enough memory or resources.
ERROR_FILE_NOT_FOUND	The file specified by the FileName parameter could not be found.
ERROR_PATH_NOT_FOUND	The directory specified by the Directory parameter could not be found.
ERROR_BAD_FORMAT	The executable file is invalid or corrupt.
SE_ERR_ACCESSDENIED	Access to the specified file was denied.

11

Chapter

Value	Description
SE_ERR_ASSOCINCOMPLETE	There is an incomplete or invalid executable file association for the specified file.
SE_ERR_DDEBUSY	The requested DDE transaction could not be completed due to other DDE transactions in progress.
SE_ERR_DDEFAIL	The requested DDE transaction failed.
SE_ERR_DDETIMEOUT	The requested DDE transaction failed because the DDE request timed out.
SE_ERR_DLLNOTFOUND	A required dynamic link library could not be found.
SE_ERR_FNF	The file specified by the FileName parameter could not be found.
SE_ERR_NOASSOC	There is no executable file associated with the given filename extension.
SE_ERR_OOM	The operation could not be completed due to insufficient memory.
SE_ERR_PNF	The directory specified by the Directory parameter could not be found.
SE_ERR_SHARE	A sharing violation has occurred.

ShellExecuteEx   *ShellAPI.Pas*

Syntax

```
ShellExecuteEx(
lpExecInfo: PShellExecuteInfo      {a pointer to a file execution information structure}
):BOOL;                            {returns TRUE or FALSE}
```

Description

Similar to ShellExecute, this function performs an action on a file, and can be used to print a document, launch an executable file, or open a directory folder.

Parameters

lpExecInfo: A pointer to a TShellExecuteInfo structure. This structure contains information about the action to perform on a particular file, and will receive information once the action is completed. The TShellExecuteInfo structure is defined as:

```
TShellExecuteInfo = record
      cbSize: DWORD;               {size of the structure in bytes}
      fMask: ULONG;                {flags indicating how to use other members}
      Wnd: HWND;                   {a handle to a parent window}
      lpVerb: PAnsiChar;           {a pointer to a string describing the action}
      lpFile: PAnsiChar;           {a pointer to a filename or folder name}
      lpParameters: PAnsiChar;     {a pointer to executable file parameters}
      lpDirectory: PAnsiChar;      {a pointer to the default directory name}
```

```
nShow: Integer;          {file display flags}
hInstApp: HINST;         {a handle to an application instance}
{the following fields are optional}
lpIDList: Pointer;       {a pointer to an item identifier list}
lpClass: PAnsiChar;      {a pointer to the name of a file class or GUID}
hkeyClass: HKEY;         {a handle to the file class registry key}
dwHotKey: DWORD;         {the hot key associated with the application}
hIcon: THandle;          {a handle to an icon for the file class}
hProcess: THandle;       {a process handle for the newly launched
                          application}
end;
```

cbSize: The size of the TShellExecuteInfo structure, in bytes. This member should be set to SizeOf(TShellExecuteInfo).

fMask: A series of flags that indicate if the optional members of the structure should be used. This member can be one or more values from Table 11-13. Two or more values can be specified by using the Boolean OR operator (i.e., SEE_MASK_CLASSKEY OR SEE_MASK_CLASSNAME).

Wnd: A handle to a parent window that receives message boxes if an error occurs.

lpVerb: A pointer to a null-terminated string specifying the action to perform on the file or folder indicated by the lpFile member. Table 11-14 lists the standard actions that can be performed on a file or folder. However, these actions are not limited to those listed in the table. This member is dependent on the actions registered for the document or application in the registry, and new actions can be created through the Options menu in the Windows Explorer. If this member is NIL, the "open" operation is used by default.

lpFile: A pointer to a null-terminated string containing the name of a document, executable file, or folder.

lpParameters: If the lpFile member indicates an executable file, this member contains a pointer to a null-terminated string specifying the command line parameters to pass to the executable file. The parameters must be separated by spaces. If the lpFile member specifies a document or folder, this parameter should be NIL.

lpDirectory: A pointer to a null-terminated string containing the path to the default directory. If this parameter is NIL, the current directory is used as the working directory.

nShow: A flag that determines how the executable file indicated by the lpFile member is to be displayed when it is launched. This parameter can be one value from Table 11-15.

hInstApp: If the function succeeds, upon return this member contains either the handle to the executable file that was launched or the handle to a DDE server application. If the function fails, this member will contain one of the values from Table 11-16.

11

Chapter

The following fields are optional. These members do not have to be set in order for the ShellExecuteEx function to work properly.

lpIDList: A pointer to an item identifier list that uniquely identifies the executable file to launch. This member is ignored if the fMask member does not contain SEE_MASK_IDLIST.

lpClass: A pointer to a null-terminated string containing the name of a file class or globally unique identifier (GUID). This member is ignored if the fMask member does not contain SEE_MASK_CLASSNAME.

hkeyClass: A handle to the registry key for the file class. This member is ignored if the fMask member does not contain SEE_MASK_CLASSKEY.

dwHotKey: The hot key to associate with the launched executable file. The low-order word contains the virtual key code, and the high-order word contains a modifier flag. The modifier flag can be one or more values from Table 11-17. Two or more values can be specified by using the Boolean OR operator (i.e., HOTKEYF_ALT OR HOTKEYF_SHIFT). This member is ignored if the fMask member does not contain SEE_MASK_HOTKEY.

hIcon: A handle to an icon to use for the file class. This member is ignored if the fMask member does not contain SEE_MASK_ICON.

hProcess: If the function succeeds, upon return this member contains a process handle of the application that was started. This member is set to zero if the fMask member does not contain SEE_MASK_NOCLOSEPROCESS.

Return Value

If the function succeeds, it returns TRUE, and the hInstApp member of the TShellExecuteInfo structure contains an instance handle to the application that was started. If the function fails, it returns FALSE, and the hInstApp member will be set to one of the values from Table 11-16. To get extended error information, call the GetLastError function.

See Also

ShellExecute

Example

Listing 11-12: Another Way to View Text Files

```
procedure TForm1.FileListBox1DblClick(Sender: TObject);
var
   ExecInfo: TShellExecuteInfo;
begin
   {this will open the file that was double clicked in the file list box. if
    this file is too big for Notepad, Windows will ask if you want to launch
    Wordpad}

   {fill in the TShellExecuteInfo structure information}
   ExecInfo.cbSize      := SizeOf(TShellExecuteInfo);
   ExecInfo.fMask       := SEE_MASK_NOCLOSEPROCESS;
```

```
ExecInfo.Wnd          := Form1.Handle;
ExecInfo.lpVerb       := 'Open';
ExecInfo.lpFile       := PChar(FileListBox1.FileName);
ExecInfo.lpParameters := '';
ExecInfo.lpDirectory  := '';
ExecInfo.nShow        := SW_SHOWNORMAL;

{open the specified file}
ShellExecuteEx(@ExecInfo);
end;
```

Table 11-13: ShellExecuteEx lpExecInfo.fMask Values

Value	Description
SEE_MASK_CLASSKEY	Use the class key specified by the hkeyClass member.
SEE_MASK_CLASSNAME	Use the class name specified by the lpClass member.
SEE_MASK_CONNECTNETDRV	The lpFile member specifies a Universal Naming Convention path.
SEE_MASK_DOENVSUBST	Expand any environment variables included in the lpFile or lpDirectory members.
SEE_MASK_FLAG_DDEWAIT	If a DDE conversation is started, wait for it to end before returning.
SEE_MASK_FLAG_NO_UI	Do not display error message boxes if errors occur.
SEE_MASK_HOTKEY	Use the hot key specified by the dwHotKey member.
SEE_MASK_ICON	Use the icon specified by the hIcon member.
SEE_MASK_IDLIST	Use the item identifier list specified by the lpIDList member.
SEE_MASK_INVOKEIDLIST	Use the item identifier list specified by the lpIDList member. If the lpIDList member is NIL, the function creates an item identifier list and launches the application. This flag overrides the SEE_MASK_IDLIST flag.
SEE_MASK_NOCLOSEPROCESS	Causes the hProcess member to receive a handle to the process started. The process continues to run after the ShellExecuteEx function ends.

Table 11-14: ShellExecuteEx lpExecInfo.lpVerb Values

Value	Description
"open"	Opens the file or folder or launches the executable identified by the FileName parameter.
"print"	Prints the document identified by the FileName parameter. If the FileName parameter identifies an executable file, it is launched as if a value of "open" had been specified.

Value	Description
"explore"	Opens a Windows Explorer window onto the folder identified by the FileName parameter.

Table II-15: ShellExecuteEx lpExecInfo.nShow Values

Value	Description
SW_HIDE	The window is hidden and another window is activated.
SW_MINIMIZE	The window is minimized and the next top-level window in the relative Z-order is activated.
SW_RESTORE	The window is activated and displayed in its original size and position.
SW_SHOW	The window is activated and displayed in its current size and position.
SW_SHOWDEFAULT	The window is shown based on the wShowWindow member of the TStartupInfo structure passed to the CreateProcess function by the program that started the application. This is used to set the initial show state of an application's main window. This flag should be used when showing the window for the first time if the application could be run from a shortcut. This flag will cause the window to be shown using the Run settings under the shortcut properties.
SW_SHOWMAXIMIZED	The window is activated and displayed in a maximized state.
SW_SHOWMINIMIZED	The window is activated and displayed as an icon.
SW_SHOWMINNOACTIVE	The window is displayed as an icon. The active window remains active.
SW_SHOWNA	The window is displayed in its current state. The active window remains active.
SW_SHOWNOACTIVE	The window is displayed in its most recent state. The active window remains active.
SW_SHOWNORMAL	This is the same as SW_RESTORE.

Table II-16: ShellExecuteEx lpExecInfo.hInstApp Error Codes

Value	Description
SE_ERR_ACCESSDENIED	Access to the specified file was denied.
SE_ERR_ASSOCINCOMPLETE	There is an incomplete or invalid executable file association for the specified file.
SE_ERR_DDEBUSY	The requested DDE transaction could not be completed due to other DDE transactions in progress.

Value	Description
SE_ERR_DDEFAIL	The requested DDE transaction failed.
SE_ERR_DDETIMEOUT	The requested DDE transaction failed because the DDE request timed out.
SE_ERR_DLLNOTFOUND	A required dynamic link library could not be found.
SE_ERR_FNF	The file specified by the FileName parameter could not be found.
SE_ERR_NOASSOC	There is no executable file associated with the given filename extension.
SE_ERR_OOM	The operation could not be completed due to insufficient memory.
SE_ERR_PNF	The directory specified by the Directory parameter could not be found.
SE_ERR_SHARE	A sharing violation has occurred.

Table 11-17: ShellExecuteEx lpExecInfo.dwHotKey Modifier Flag Values

Value	Description
HOTKEYF_ALT	The Alt key must be held down.
HOTKEYF_CONTROL	The Ctrl key must be held down.
HOTKEYF_SHIFT	The Shift key must be held down.

Shell_NotifyIcon   ShellAPI.Pas

Syntax

```
Shell_NotifyIcon(
dwMessage: DWORD;            {a notify icon message}
lpData: PNotifyIconData      {a pointer to a notify icon data structure}
): BOOL;                     {returns TRUE or FALSE}
```

Description

This function adds, modifies, or removes a notification icon from the taskbar system tray.

Parameters

dwMessage: A notification icon message identifier. This can be one value from Table 11-18.

lpData: A pointer to a TNotifyIconData data structure. This structure is defined as:

```
TNotifyIconData = record
    cbSize: DWORD;          {the size of the TNotifyIconData structure}
    Wnd: HWND;              {a handle to a window}
```

```
        uID: UINT;                              {an application-defined identifier}
        uFlags: UINT;                           {modification flags}
        uCallbackMessage: UINT;                 {an application-defined message identifier}
        hIcon: HICON;                           {a handle to an icon}
        szTip: array [0..63] of AnsiChar;       {a tooltip string}
end;
```

cbSize: The size of the TNotifyIconData structure, in bytes. This member should be set to SizeOf(TNotifyIconData).

Wnd: A handle to the window that receives notification messages when an event happens to the icon in the system tray.

uID: An application-defined identifier for the notification icon.

uFlags: An array of flags that indicate which other members of the TNotifyIcon-Data structure are valid and should be used. This member can be any combination of the values in Table 11-19.

uCallbackMessage: An application-defined message. This message is sent to the window associated with the window handle set in the Wnd member whenever a mouse event happens in the icon in the system tray.

hIcon: A handle to an icon to display in the system tray.

szTip: A pointer to a null-terminated string used as the tooltip text for the notification icon.

Return Value

If the function succeeds, it returns TRUE; otherwise it returns FALSE.

See Also

SHAppBarMessage

Example

Listing 11-13: Adding an Icon to the System Tray

```
const
 {the application-defined notification message}
  WM_TRAYICONCLICKED = WM_USER+1;

type
  TForm1 = class(TForm)
    ListBox1: TListBox;
    Label1: TLabel;
    procedure FormCreate(Sender: TObject);
    procedure FormDestroy(Sender: TObject);
  private
    { Private declarations }
    {the message handler for the tray icon notification message}
    procedure WMTrayIconClicked(var Msg: TMessage); message WM_TRAYICONCLICKED;
```

```
    public
      { Public declarations }
    end;

var
  Form1: TForm1;
  IconData: TNotifyIconData;  // the tray notification icon data structure

const
  DELTRAYICON = 1;                // the tray icon id

implementation

{$R *.DFM}

procedure TForm1.FormCreate(Sender: TObject);
begin
  {initialize the tray notification icon structure}
  with IconData do
  begin
    cbSize            := SizeOf(TNotifyIconData);
    Wnd               := Form1.Handle;
    uID               := DELTRAYICON;
    uFlags            := NIF_ICON or NIF_MESSAGE or NIF_TIP;
    uCallbackMessage  := WM_TRAYICONCLICKED;
    hIcon             := Application.Icon.Handle;
    szTip             := 'Delphi TrayIcon';
  end;

  {notify the system that we are adding a tray notification icon}
  Shell_NotifyIcon(NIM_ADD, @IconData);
end;

procedure TForm1.WMTrayIconClicked(var Msg: TMessage);
begin
  {the tray icon has received a message, so display it}
  case Msg.lParam of
    WM_LBUTTONDBLCLK: listbox1.Items.add('double click');
    WM_LBUTTONDOWN:   listbox1.Items.add('mouse down');
    WM_LBUTTONUP:     listbox1.Items.add('mouse up');
  end;
End;

procedure TForm1.FormDestroy(Sender: TObject);
begin
  {remove the icon from the system}
  Shell_NotifyIcon(NIM_DELETE, @IconData);
end;
```

11

Chapter

Figure 11-11:
The new
notification
icon

Table II-18: Shell_NotifyIcon dwMessage Values

Value	Description
NIM_ADD	Add a notification icon to the taskbar system tray.
NIM_DELETE	Delete a notification icon from the taskbar system tray.
NIM_MODIFY	Modify a notification icon in the taskbar system tray.

Table II-19: Shell_NotifyIcon lpData.uFlags Values

Value	Description
NIF_ICON	The icon handle in the hIcon member is valid.
NIF_MESSAGE	The message identifier in the uCallbackMessage member is valid.
NIF_TIP	The tooltip string pointed to by the szTip member is valid.

SHFileOperation   ShellAPI.Pas

Syntax

SHFileOperation(
const lpFileOp: TSHFileOpStruct   {a pointer to a file operation data structure}
): Integer;   {returns an integer value}

Description

This function copies, deletes, moves, or renames files or folders.

Parameters

lpFileOp: A TSHFileOpStruct that contains information about the files and the action to perform. This structure is defined as:

TSHFileOpStruct = record
    Wnd: HWND;   {a handle to a window}
    wFunc: UINT;   {a flag indicating the operation}

```
        pFrom: PAnsiChar;            {a pointer to the source filenames}
        pTo: PAnsiChar;             {a pointer to the destination names}
        fFlags: FILEOP_FLAGS;        {operation control flags}
        fAnyOperationsAborted: BOOL;  {aborted operation flag}
        hNameMappings: Pointer;      {a handle to a filename mapping object}
        lpszProgressTitle: PAnsiChar; {the progress dialog box title}
    end;
```

Wnd: The handle of the window used as the parent of the dialog box displaying the progress of the file operation.

wFunc: A flag indicating the operation to perform. This member can be one value from Table 11-20.

pFrom: A pointer to a buffer containing the filenames upon which to perform the indicated operation. If multiple filenames are specified, each must be separated with a null-terminating character, and the entire buffer must end with two null-terminating characters. If the filenames do not contain a path, the source directory is assumed to be the directory as reported by the GetCurrentDirectory function.

pTo: A pointer to a buffer containing the name of the destination file or directory. If the fFlags member contains FOF_MULTIDESTFILES, this buffer can contain multiple destination filenames, one for each source file. Each destination filename must be separated with a null-terminating character, and the entire buffer must end with two null-terminating characters. If the filenames do not contain a path, the destination directory is assumed to be the directory as reported by the GetCurrentDirectory function.

fFlags: An array of flags indicating the type of operation to perform on the specified files. This member can contain one or more values from Table 11-21.

fAnyOperationsAborted: This member receives a value of TRUE if any file operations were aborted by the user before completion. Otherwise, it receives a value of FALSE.

hNameMappings: If the fFlags member contains the FOF_WANTMAPPINGHANDLE flag, this member receives a pointer to a filename mapping object containing an array of TSHNameMapping structures. These structures contain the old and new path and filename for each file that was moved, copied, or renamed. The filename mapping object must be deleted using the SHFreeNameMappings function.

The TSHNameMapping structures are defined as:

```
TSHNameMapping = record
        pszOldPath: PAnsiChar;       {a pointer to a string}
        pszNewPath: PAnsiChar;       {a pointer to a string}
        cchOldPath: Integer;         {a string size value}
        cchNewPath: Integer;         {a string size value}
    end;
```

11

Chapter

pszOldPath: A null-terminated string specifying the original path and filename.

pszNewPath: A null-terminated string specifying the new path and filename.

cchOldPath: The number of characters in the pszOldPath member.

cchNewPath: The number of characters in the pszNewPath member.

lpszProgressTitle: A null-terminated string used as the title for the progress dialog box. This member is used only if the fFlags member contains the FOF_SIMPLEPROGRESS flag.

Return Value

If the function succeeds, it returns a number greater than zero; otherwise it returns zero.

See Also

GetCurrentDirectory, SetCurrentDirectory, ShellExecute, SHFreeNameMappings

Example

Listing 11-14: Copying a File

```
procedure TForm1.Button1Click(Sender: TObject);
var
  FileOpInfo: TSHFileOpStruct;  // holds information about the file
begin
  with FileOpInfo do
  begin
    Wnd    := Form1.Handle;
    wFunc  := FO_COPY;                               // perform a copy
    pFrom  := PChar(FileListBox1.FileName+#0+#0);    // the source
    pTo    := PChar(DirectoryListBox2.Directory);    // the destination directory
    fFlags := FOF_WANTMAPPINGHANDLE;
  end;

  {perform the file operation}
  SHFileOperation(FileOpInfo);

  {the fFlags member contains FOF_WANTMAPPINGHANDLE, indicating
   that a handle to an array of TSHNameMapping structures was
   returned in the FileOpInfo.hNameMappings member. this must
   be freed using the SHFreeNameMappings function.}
  SHFreeNameMappings(GlobalHandle(FileOpInfo.hNameMappings));
end;
```

*Figure 11-12:
Copying a
bitmap file*

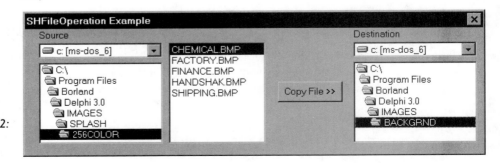

Table II-20: SHFileOperation lpFileOp.wFunc Values

Value	Description
FO_COPY	Copy the files specified by the pFrom member to the location specified by the pTo member.
FO_DELETE	Delete the files specified by the pFrom member. The pTo member is ignored.
FO_MOVE	Move the files specified by the pFrom member to the location specified by the pTo member.
FO_RENAME	Rename the files specified by the pFrom member. The pTo member is ignored.

Table II-2I: SHFileOperation lpFileOp.fFlags Values

Value	Description
FOF_ALLOWUNDO	The specified file is deleted to the recycle bin.
FOF_FILESONLY	The operation is performed only on files if a wild card filename is specified (i.e., *.pas).
FOF_MULTIDESTFILES	The pTo member contains one destination file for each source file instead of one directory to which all source files are deposited.
FOF_NOCONFIRMATION	The user is never asked for confirmation, and the operation continues as if a response of Yes to All was indicated.
FOF_NOCONFIRMMKDIR	Automatically creates a new directory if one is needed.
FOF_NOERRORUI	There is not visual indication if an error occurs.
FOF_RENAMEONCOLLISION	The source file is automatically given a new name, such as "Copy #I of..", in a move, copy, or rename operation if a file in the target directory already has the same name.
FOF_SILENT	Does not display a progress dialog box.
FOF_SIMPLEPROGRESS	Displays a progress dialog box, but does not show filenames.
FOF_WANTMAPPINGHANDLE	The hNameMappings member receives a handle to a filename mapping object.

SHFreeNameMappings   ShellAPI.Pas

Syntax

```
SHFreeNameMappings(
hNameMappings: THandle          {a handle to a filename mapping object}
);                               {this procedure does not return a value}
```

Description

This function frees the filename mapping object as returned by the SHFileOperation function.

Parameters

hNameMappings: A handle to the filename mapping object to free.

See Also

SHFileOperation

Example

Please see Listing 11-14 under SHFileOperation.

SHGetFileInfo   ShellAPI.Pas

Syntax

SHGetFileInfo(	
pszPath: PAnsiChar;	{a pointer to a filename string}
dwFileAttributes: DWORD;	{file attribute flags}
var psfi: TSHFileInfo;	{a pointer to a TSHFileInfo structure}
cbFileInfo: UINT;	{the size of the TSHFileInfo structure}
uFlags: UINT	{information retrieval flags}
): DWORD;	{returns a double word value}

Description

This function retrieves information about a file, folder, directory, or drive root.

Parameters

pszPath: A pointer to a null-terminated string containing the path and filename of the file whose information is to be retrieved. This can be either a long filename or in the DOS 8.3 filename format. If the uFlags parameter contains the SHGFI_PIDL flag, this parameter can point to an item identifier list for the file.

dwFileAttributes: An array of flags indicating the file attribute flags. This parameter may contain one or more of the values from Table 11-22. If the uFlags parameter does not contain the SHGFI_USEFILEATTRIBUTES flag, this parameter is ignored.

psfi: A pointer to a TSHFileInfo data structure. This structure contains the requested information about the specified file. The TSHFileInfo structure is defined as:

TSHFileInfo = record	
hIcon: HICON;	{an icon handle}
iIcon: Integer;	{an icon index}
dwAttributes: DWORD;	{attribute flags}
szDisplayName: array [0..MAX_PATH-1]	
of AnsiChar;	{display name string}

```
        szTypeName: array [0..79] of AnsiChar;        {file type string}
end;
```

hIcon: A handle to the icon that represents the specified file.

iIcon: The index of the file's icon within the system image list.

dwAttributes: An array of flags that indicates the file's attributes. This member can be one or more of the values from the dwFileAttributes table (Table 11-22).

szDisplayName: A null-terminated string indicating the display name of the specified file as it appears in the shell.

szTypeName: A null-terminated string describing the type of the specified file.

cbFileInfo: The size, in bytes, of the TSHFileInfo structure pointed to by the psfi parameter. This parameter should be set to SizeOf(TSHFileInfo).

uFlags: An array of flags indicating the type of information to retrieve. This parameter can be one or more of the values from Table 11-23.

Return Value

If the function succeeds, it returns a value greater than zero. Otherwise, it returns zero. See the uFlags values table (Table 11-23) for descriptions of the return value.

See Also

ExtractAssociatedIcon, ExtractIcon, FindExecutable

Example

Listing II-I5: Retrieving Information about a File

```pascal
procedure TForm1.FileListBox1DblClick(Sender: TObject);
var
  FileInfo: TSHFileInfo;         // holds information about a file
  TempIcon: TIcon;               // a temporary icon object
begin
  {retrieve information about the selected file}
  SHGetFileInfo(PChar(FileListBox1.Filename),0,FileInfo,SizeOf(TSHFileInfo),
    SHGFI_DISPLAYNAME or SHGFI_ICON or SHGFI_TYPENAME);

  {display the information about the selected file}
  with ListBox1.Items do
  begin
    Clear;
    Add('Display Name: '+FileInfo.szDisplayName);
    Add('Type Name: '+FileInfo.szTypeName);
    Add('Icon index: '+IntToStr(FileInfo.iIcon));
  end;

  {create a temporary icon object so we can
   display the file icon in the image object}
  TempIcon := TIcon.Create;
  TempIcon.Handle := FileInfo.hIcon;
  Image1.Picture.Assign(TempIcon);
```

```
  TempIcon.Free;
end;
```

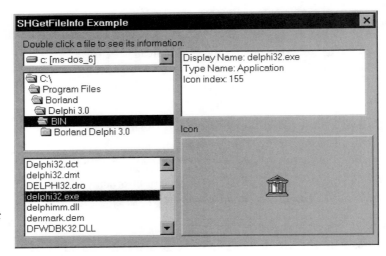

Figure 11-13:
The file
information

Table 11-22: SHGetFileInfo dwFileAttributes Values

Value	Description
FILE_ATTRIBUTE_READONLY	The file is read only.
FILE_ATTRIBUTE_HIDDEN	The file is hidden.
FILE_ATTRIBUTE_SYSTEM	The file is a system file.
FILE_ATTRIBUTE_DIRECTORY	The file is a directory folder.
FILE_ATTRIBUTE_ARCHIVE	The file is an archive file.
FILE_ATTRIBUTE_NORMAL	The file does not have any attributes.
FILE_ATTRIBUTE_TEMPORARY	The file is a temporary file.
FILE_ATTRIBUTE_COMPRESSED	The file is compressed.

Table 11-23: SHGetFileInfo uFlags Values

Value	Description
SHGFI_ATTRIBUTES	Retrieves the attributes of the specified file. These values are copied to the dwAttributes member of the TSHFileInfo structure pointed to by the psfi parameter.
SHGFI_DISPLAYNAME	Retrieves the display name of the specified file. This string is copied to the szDisplayName member of the TSHFileInfo structure pointed to by the psfi parameter.

Value	*Description*
SHGFI_ICON	Retrieves a handle to the icon that represents the specified file. The icon handle is copied to the hIcon member of the TSHFileInfo structure pointed to by the psfi parameter. The index of the icon in the system image list is copied to the iIcon member of the TSHFileInfo structure pointed to by the psfi parameter. The function returns the handle to the system image list.
SHGFI_ICONLOCATION	Retrieves the name of the file containing the icon that represents the specified file. This filename is copied to the szDisplayName member of the TSHFileInfo structure pointed to by the psfi parameter.
SHGFI_LARGEICON	Retrieves the specified file's large icon. This flag must be used in conjunction with the SHGFI_ICON flag.
SHGFI_LINKOVERLAY	Adds the link overlay graphic to the specified file's icon. This flag must be used in conjunction with the SHGFI_ICON flag.
SHGFI_OPENICON	Retrieves the specified file's open icon. This flag must be used in conjunction with the SHGFI_ICON flag.
SHGFI_PIDL	Indicates that the pszPath parameter points to an item identifier list instead of a path name.
SHGFI_SELECTED	The file's icon is combined with the system's highlight color. This flag must be used in conjunction with the SHGFI_ICON flag.
SHGFI_SHELLICONSIZE	Retrieves the specified file's icon modified to the size displayed by the shell. This flag must be used in conjunction with the SHGFI_ICON flag.
SHGFI_SMALLICON	Retrieves the specified file's small icon. This flag must be used in conjunction with the SHGFI_ICON flag.
SHGFI_SYSICONINDEX	Retrieves the index of the specified file's icon within the system image list. The icon index is copied to the iIcon member of the TSHFileInfo structure pointed to by the psfi parameter. The function returns the handle to the system image list.
SHGFI_TYPENAME	Retrieves a string describing the specified file's type. This string is copied to the szTypeName of the TSHFileInfo structure pointed to by the psfi parameter.
SHGFI_USEFILEATTRIBUTES	Indicates the function should retrieve information only on files that have the attributes specified by the dwFileAttributes parameter.

11

Chapter

SHGetPathFromIDList

ShlObj.Pas

Syntax

SHGetPathFromIDList(
pidl: PItemIDList;   {a pointer to an item identifier list}
pszPath: PChar   {a pointer to a buffer}
): BOOL;   {returns TRUE or FALSE}

Description

This function retrieves a string containing the path name of the file or folder identified by the item identifier list.

Parameters

pidl: A pointer to an item identifier list that specifies a file or directory in the file system. This function will fail if the item identifier list specifies a folder that is not in the file system, such as the Printers or Control Panel folders.

pszPath: A pointer to a buffer that receives the name of the path. The size of the buffer is assumed to be MAX_PATH bytes.

Return Value

If the function succeeds, it returns TRUE; otherwise it returns FALSE.

See Also

SHBrowseForFolder, SHGetFileInfo

Example

Please see Listing 11-9 under SHBrowseForFolder.

SHGetSpecialFolderLocation

ShlObj.Pas

Syntax

SHGetSpecialFolderLocation(
hwndOwner: HWND;   {a handle to a window}
nFolder: Integer;   {a folder location flag}
var ppidl: PItemIDList   {a pointer to an item identifier list}
): HResult;   {returns an OLE result}

Description

This function retrieves an item identifier list specifying the location of the special folder. Note that only those folders that are registered under the key HKEY_CURRENT_USER\Software\Microsoft\Windows\CurrentVersion\Explorer\Shell Folders will return an item identifier list specifying a file system folder that SHGetPathFromIDList can use to retrieve a physical path name.

Parameters

hwndOwner: A handle to the owning window for dialog or message boxes.

nFolder: A flag indicating the folder for which to retrieve the location. This parameter can be one value from Table 11-24.

ppidl: A pointer to an item identifier list that specifies the indicated folder's location relative to the root of the name space.

Return Value

If the function succeeds, it returns NOERROR; otherwise it returns an OLE-defined error result.

See Also

SHBrowseForFolder, SHGetFileInfo, SHGetPathFromIDList

Example

Listing 11-16: Retrieving the Location of the Windows Desktop Directory

```
procedure TForm1.Button1Click(Sender: TObject);
var
  IDList: PItemIDList;                       // the item identifier list
  PathName: array[0..MAX_PATH] of char; // the path name of the specified folder
begin
  {retrieve the item identifier list specifying the
   location of the Windows desktop directory}
  SHGetSpecialFolderLocation(Form1.Handle, CSIDL_DESKTOPDIRECTORY, IDList);

  {retrieve the path name}
  SHGetPathFromIDList(IDList, @PathName);

  {display the path name}
  Label1.Caption := PathName;
end;
```

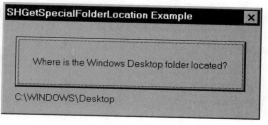

Figure 11-14: Retrieving the location of the Windows Desktop directory

11

Chapter

Table 11-24: SHGetSpecialFolderLocation nFolder Values

Value	Description
CSIDL_BITBUCKET	Retrieves the location of the recycle bin. This directory is not in the registry, and has the hidden and system attributes to prevent the user from moving or deleting it.
CSIDL_CONTROLS	Retrieves the virtual folder containing the icons for control panel applets.
CSIDL_DESKTOP	Retrieves the virtual folder for the root of the name space, the Windows desktop.
CSIDL_DESKTOPDIRECTORY	Retrieves the file system directory where desktop items are physically stored.
CSIDL_DRIVES	Retrieves the My Computer virtual folder, which contains storage devices, printers, and the control panel, and may contain mapped network drives.
CSIDL_FONTS	Retrieves the virtual folder containing fonts.
CSIDL_NETHOOD	Retrieves the file system directory containing network neighborhood objects.
CSIDL_NETWORK	Retrieves the network neighborhood virtual folder representing the top level of the network hierarchy.
CSIDL_PERSONAL	Retrieves the file system directory that serves as a common repository for documents, most commonly the C:\My Documents directory.
CSIDL_PRINTERS	Retrieves the virtual folder containing installed printers.
CSIDL_PROGRAMS	Retrieves the file system directory containing the program groups.
CSIDL_RECENT	Retrieves the file system directory where the links for the most recent documents are physically stored.
CSIDL_SENDTO	Retrieves the file system directory containing the Send To context menu options.
CSIDL_STARTMENU	Retrieves the file system directory containing links and executable files that appear on the Start menu.
CSIDL_STARTUP	Retrieves the file system directory containing links and executable files that are launched during Windows startup
CSIDL_TEMPLATES	Retrieves the file system directory that serves as a common repository for document templates.

Chapter 12

Menu Functions

Every complex Windows application uses a menu as part of its user interface navigational tools. Delphi does a wonderful job in encapsulating the menu architecture,
eliminating the need for a developer to define a menu structure in a resource file and
programmatically importing it into the application. However, the low-level Windows
API functions for manipulating menus give the developer some added functionality that
is not natively included in Delphi.

General Menu Information

All menu items have a unique identifier that the application uses to determine which
menu item was selected. This menu item identifier is automatically assigned by Delphi
when a TMenu object is used to create the application's menu structure. However,
when programmatically adding menu items using the Windows API, the developer
must explicitly set the menu item's identifier. If this identifier matches any other menu
identifier in the application, the application can become confused, causing it to behave
in unexpected ways when menu items are selected. Use the GetMenuItemID function
to retrieve the menu item identifiers of all Delphi-created menu items to ensure that the
new menu item identifier will not cause an identifier naming collision.

Whenever a user selects a menu item, the menu item sends a WM_COMMAND message to its owning window. The wID parameter of this message will contain the menu
item identifier of the selected menu. When a menu item is added using the Windows
API, the application must provide a message override function for the
WM_COMMAND message. This allows the application to respond to the messages
sent from both Windows API added menu items as well as Delphi's own TMenuItem
objects.

The System Menu

The most common use for the Windows API menu functions in Delphi is to add items
to a window's system menu. The system menu is the drop-down menu displayed when
the icon in the upper left-hand corner of a window is clicked.

12

Chapter

To add a menu item to the system menu, an application must first use the GetSystemMenu function to retrieve a handle to the system menu. Once this is done, the other menu functions can be used with this handle as if it were a normal menu. Menu items added to the system menu will send a WM_SYSCOMMAND message to the window instead of a WM_COMMAND message. Additionally, Windows assigns menu item identifiers to the default system menu items that are greater than $F000. Thus, any menu items added to the system menu by the application must have menu item identifiers that are less than $F000. When the handler for the WM_SYSCOMMAND message determines if the message was sent by a menu item added by the application, it must combine the value of the message's wParam parameter with the value $FFF0 by using the Boolean AND operator. This is necessary as Windows uses the last four bits of the wParam parameter internally, and they must be masked out of the value in order to test their equality to an application-defined menu item identifier.

Note that if the application adds items to the system menu and then changes any property of the form that causes the form to be recreated, such as changing the border style, the system menu reverts to its default configuration and all changes are lost. See the CreatePopupMenu function for an example of adding items to the system menu.

Pop-up Menus

There are two forms that a menu can take: the form of a menu bar and the form of a pop-up menu. A menu bar is a menu that has been assigned to a window, and its menu items are displayed in a horizontal row right under the window's caption bar. A pop-up menu is any menu that is dynamically displayed, such as when a menu item in the menu bar is selected or when the user right-clicks on the form to display a pop-up menu. All drop-down menus, pop-up menus, or submenus fall into this category. Any drop-down menu or submenu can be displayed as a pop-up menu by retrieving its handle using the GetSubMenu function and then displaying it using the TrackPopupMenu function. See the CreatePopupMenu function for an example of this technique.

Menu items in a pop-up menu send the WM_COMMAND message when selected. However, Delphi defines a private object known as a PopupList when using the TPopupMenu object. All WM_COMMAND messages sent from a TPopupMenu are handled by this PopupList object. Therefore, the form never receives these messages. When using the TrackPopupMenu or TrackPopupMenuEx functions with a Delphi TPopupMenu object, these messages are sent directly to the indicated window, bypassing Delphi's native functionality. This requires the developer to handle menu item selection as if the menu items had been programmatically added using Windows API functions. If the developer sends these messages back to the pop-up menu by using the TPopupMenu's DispatchCommand method, a developer can assign OnClick events to menu items in a TPopupMenu as normal.

Owner-drawn Menus

Owner-drawn menus allow the developer to perform some very interesting special effects with menus. The developer has complete control of the menu item's appearance, drawing the menu item in any manner desired. The AppendMenu, InsertMenu, Insert-MenuItem, ModifyMenu, and SetMenuItemInfo functions can define a menu as owner drawn. When owner-drawn menus are used, the owning window receives a WM_MEASUREITEM message for each menu item the first time that the menu is displayed. When the menu is actually drawn to the screen, the owning window receives a WM_DRAWITEM message for each owner-drawn menu item. Both messages contain pointers to data structures that contain information about which menu item is being measured or drawn. The following example demonstrates how to use owner-drawn menu items to display a bitmap in the background of a menu.

Listing 12-1: Displaying a Bitmap in the Background of a Menu

```
procedure TForm1.FormCreate(Sender: TObject);
var
  iCount: Integer;           // a general loop control variable
  MenuInfo: TMenuItemInfo;   // holds menu item information
  ABitmap: TBitmap;          // holds a bitmap
begin
  {for each menu item in the drop-down menu...}
  for iCount := 0 to GetMenuItemCount(MainMenu2.Handle)-1 do
  begin
    {create a bitmap. this will contain the image displayed when this
     menu item is drawn}
    ABitmap := TBitmap.Create;

    {set the bitmap to be 18 pixels high and as wide as the original image}
    ABitmap.Width  := Image1.Width;
    ABitmap.Height := 18;

    {copy a slice of the original image into the bitmap}
    ABitmap.Canvas.CopyRect(Rect(0, 0, ABitmap.Width, ABitmap.Height),
                      Image1.Canvas, Rect(0, ABitmap.Height*iCount,
                      ABitmap.Width, (ABitmap.Height*iCount)+
                      ABitmap.Height));

    {transparently draw the caption of the menu item on the bitmap slice}
    SetBkMode(ABitmap.Canvas.Handle, TRANSPARENT);
    ABitmap.Canvas.Font.Color := clRed;
    ABitmap.Canvas.TextOut(5, 2, MainMenu2.Items[iCount].Caption);

    {initialize the menu item information structure to indicate that we are
     defining an owner-drawn menu. place a pointer to the bitmap slice for
     this menu item in the menu item's dwItemData member. this pointer will
     be retrieved and used when processing the WM_DRAWITEM message}
    MenuInfo.cbSize := SizeOf(TMenuItemInfo);
    MenuInfo.fMask := MIIM_DATA or MIIM_TYPE;
```

```
      MenuInfo.fType := MFT_OWNERDRAW;
      MenuInfo.dwItemData := Longint(Pointer(ABitmap));

      {modify the existing menu item, turning it into an owner-drawn menu item}
      SetMenuItemInfo(MainMenu2.Handle, iCount, TRUE, MenuInfo);
    end;
end;

{the overridden WM_MEASUREITEM message}
procedure TForm1.WMMeasureItem(var Msg: TWMMeasureItem);
begin
  {call the inherited method}
  inherited;

  {indicate that the new menu item is 18 pixels high, and as wide as the
   original bitmap}
  Msg.MeasureItemStruct^.itemWidth  := Image1.Width;
  Msg.MeasureItemStruct^.itemHeight := 18;

  {indicate that the message has been handled}
  Msg.Result := 1;
end;

{the overridden WM_DRAWITEM message}
procedure TForm1.WMDrawItem(var Msg: TWMDrawItem);
begin
  {call the inherited method}
  inherited;

  {set the handle of the canvas to the device context handle provided by
   the message}
  Canvas.Handle := Msg.DrawItemStruct^.hDC;

  {if the item is selected or the mouse cursor is over the item...}
  if (Msg.DrawItemStruct^.itemAction and ODA_SELECT<>0) and
     (Msg.DrawItemStruct^.itemState and ODS_SELECTED<>0) then
    {...indicate that the bitmap will be drawn inverted...}
    Canvas.CopyMode := cmNotSrcCopy
  else
    {...or that it will be drawn normally}
    Canvas.CopyMode := cmSrcCopy;

  {draw the slice of the bitmap (obtained from the ItemData member of the
   message)}
  Canvas.Draw(Msg.DrawItemStruct^.rcItem.Left, Msg.DrawItemStruct^.rcItem.Top,
            TBitmap(Pointer(Msg.DrawItemStruct^.ItemData)));

  {reset the canvas handle. a new canvas handle will be automatically
   created when it is needed}
  Canvas.Handle := 0;
end;

procedure TForm1.FormDestroy(Sender: TObject);
var
  iCount: Integer;              // a general loop control variable
```

```
MenuInfo: TMenuItemInfo;  // holds menu item information
begin
  {initialize the menu item information structure, indicating that we
   only wish to retrieve a pointer to the menu item's associated bitmap}
  MenuInfo.cbSize := SizeOf(TMenuItemInfo);
  MenuInfo.fMask := MIIM_DATA;

  {for each item in the menu...}
  for iCount := 0 to 6 do
  begin
    {retrieve the menu item information, specifically retrieving the
     associated pointer to the bitmap}
    GetMenuItemInfo(MainMenu2.Handle, iCount, TRUE, MenuInfo);

    {free the bitmap}
    TBitmap(MenuInfo.dwItemData).Free;
  end;
end;

procedure TForm1.Item11Click(Sender: TObject);
begin
  {indicate which menu item was selected}
  Label2.Caption := TMenuItem(Sender).Caption;
end;
```

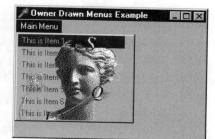

*Figure 12-1:
The
owner-drawn
menu items*

Menu Functions

The following menu functions are covered in this chapter:

Table 12-1: Menu Functions

Value	Description
AppendMenu	Appends a menu item to a menu.
CheckMenuItem	Checks or unchecks a menu item.
CheckMenuRadioItem	Checks a menu item in a group of menu items, and unchecks all others. The check mark is displayed as a bullet.
CreateMenu	Creates a new, empty menu.
CreatePopupMenu	Creates a new, empty pop-up menu.
DeleteMenu	Deletes a menu item and its associated submenu.

12

Chapter

Value	Description
DestroyMenu	Destroys a menu.
EnableMenuItem	Enables or disables a menu item.
GetMenu	Retrieves a handle to a window's assigned menu.
GetMenuDefaultItem	Retrieves a menu's default item.
GetMenuItemCount	Retrieves the number of menu items in a menu.
GetMenuItemID	Retrieves a menu item's identifier.
GetMenuItemInfo	Retrieves information about a menu item.
GetMenuItemRect	Retrieves a menu item's screen coordinates.
GetMenuState	Retrieves the state of a menu item.
GetMenuString	Retrieves a menu item's text.
GetSubMenu	Retrieves a handle to the submenu activated by a menu item.
GetSystemMenu	Retrieves a handle to the system menu.
HiliteMenuItem	Highlights or unhighlights a menu item in a menu bar.
InsertMenu	Inserts a menu item.
InsertMenuItem	Inserts a menu item. This function has more options than InsertMenu.
IsMenu	Indicates if a specified handle is a handle to a menu.
ModifyMenu	Modifies an existing menu item.
RemoveMenu	Removes a menu item from a menu.
SetMenu	Assigns a menu to a window.
SetMenuDefaultItem	Sets a menu's default item.
SetMenuItemBitmaps	Sets a menu item's checked and unchecked bitmaps.
SetMenuItemInfo	Sets a menu item's information.
TrackPopupMenu	Displays a pop-up menu.
TrackPopupMenuEx	Displays a pop-up menu without obscuring a specified rectangular area.

AppendMenu   Windows.Pas

Syntax

```
AppendMenu(
hMenu: HMenu,              {a handle to the menu being appended}
uFlags: Integer,           {menu item flags}
uIDNewItem: Integer,       {menu item identifier or submenu handle}
lpNewItem: PChar           {menu item data}
): BOOL;                   {returns TRUE or FALSE}
```

Description

This function appends a new menu item to the end of a menu, drop-down menu, pop-up menu, or submenu, setting specific attributes of the menu as desired.

Parameters

hMenu: A handle to the menu to which the new menu item will be appended.

uFlags: A combination of flags indicating certain attributes of the new menu item. This parameter may be set to one or more values from Table 12-2.

uIDNewItem: Specifies the identifier of the new menu item. If the uFlags parameter contains the MF_POPUP flag, this parameter is set to the handle of the drop-down menu or submenu.

lpNewItem: A pointer to extra data associated with the new menu item. The contents of this parameter are dependent upon the flags specified in the uFlags parameter. If the uFlags parameter contains the MF_BITMAP flag, this parameter contains a handle to a bitmap. If the uFlags parameter contains the MF_STRING flag, this parameter points to a null-terminated string. If the uFlags parameter contains the MF_OWNERDRAW flag, this parameter contains an application-defined 32-bit value. This value will be contained in the itemData member of the data structures pointed to by the WM_MEASUREITEM and WM_DRAWITEM messages that the window receives when the menu is created or drawn.

Return Value

If the function succeeds, it returns TRUE; otherwise it returns FALSE. To get extended error information, call the GetLastError function.

See Also

CreateMenu, CreatePopupMenu, DeleteMenu, DestroyMenu, InsertMenu, InsertMenuItem, ModifyMenu, RemoveMenu

Example

Listing 12-2: Appending an About Box Menu Item to the System Menu

```
const
  MNUID_ABOUT = $1000;    // the identifier of the new menu item

var
  Form1: TForm1;

implementation

uses AboutBoxU;

{$R *.DFM}

procedure TForm1.FormCreate(Sender: TObject);
begin
  {add an About menu to the end of the system menu}
  AppendMenu(GetSystemMenu(Form1.Handle, FALSE), MF_STRING, MNUID_ABOUT,
          'About...');
```

```
{do the same for the application so it will show up when the icon is right-
 clicked on the task bar}
AppendMenu(GetSystemMenu(Application.Handle, FALSE), MF_STRING, MNUID_ABOUT,
           'About...');

{since these are menu items added from API functions, we must manually
 intercept their messages and proceed appropriately}
Application.OnMessage := ApplicationMessage;
end;

procedure TForm1.ApplicationMessage(var Msg: TMsg; var Handled: Boolean);
begin
  {if the message came from a system menu item, and it specifically came
   from our new menu item, display the About box}
  if (Msg.Message=WM_SYSCOMMAND) and (Msg.wParam and $FFF0=MNUID_ABOUT) then
    AboutBox.ShowModal;
end;
```

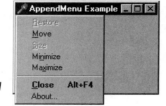

Figure 12-2:
The appended
menu item

Table 12-2: AppendMenu uFlags Values

Value	Description
MF_BITMAP	Indicates that a bitmap is used to represent the menu item. The handle to the bitmap is specified in the lpNewItem parameter. This flag cannot be combined with the MF_STRING or MF_OWNERDRAW flags.
MF_CHECKED	Places the menu's check mark bitmap next to the menu item. By default, this is an image of a check mark. This flag cannot be combined with the MF_UNCHECKED flag.
MF_DISABLED	Disables the menu item so it cannot be selected, but does not gray it. This flag cannot be combined with the MF_ENABLED or MF_GRAYED flags.
MF_ENABLED	Enables the menu item so it can be selected, and restores it if it was grayed. This flag cannot be combined with the MF_DISABLED or MF_GRAYED flags.
MF_GRAYED	Disables the menu item so it cannot be selected, and draws the menu item in gray. This flag cannot be combined with the MF_ENABLED or MF_DISABLED flags.

Value	Description
MF_MENUBARBREAK	Places the menu item on a new line for menu bars. For submenus and drop-down menus, the menu item is placed in a new column, and the columns are separated by a vertical line. This flag cannot be combined with the MF_MENUBREAK flag.
MF_MENUBREAK	Places the menu item on a new line for menu bars. For submenus and drop-down menus, the menu item is placed in a new column. There is no visual indication of column separation. This flag cannot be combined with the MF_MENUBARBREAK flag.
MF_OWNERDRAW	Indicates an owner-drawn menu item. When the menu item is displayed for the first time, the owning window receives a WM_MEASUREITEM message, allowing the application to specify the menu item's width and height. The owning window receives a WM_DRAWITEM message when the menu item is to be drawn, allowing the application to draw the menu item in any appearance desired. This flag cannot be combined with the MF_BITMAP or MF_STRING flags.
MF_POPUP	Indicates that the menu item opens a drop-down menu or submenu. The handle to the drop-down menu or submenu is specified in the uIDNewItem parameter.
MF_SEPARATOR	Indicates a menu separator. This menu item is drawn as a horizontal line, and is valid only when used with drop-down menus, pop-up menus, or submenus. This menu item cannot be highlighted, grayed, or disabled, and the uIDNewItem and lpNewItem parameters are ignored.
MF_STRING	Indicates that a string is used to represent the menu item. A pointer to the null-terminated string displayed in the menu item is specified in the lpNewItem parameter. This flag cannot be combined with the MF_BITMAP or MF_OWNERDRAW flags.
MF_UNCHECKED	Places the menu's unchecked check mark bitmap next to the menu item. By default, this is a blank image. This flag cannot be combined with the MF_CHECKED flag.

CheckMenuItem   *Windows.Pas*

Syntax

```
CheckMenuItem(
hMenu: HMENU;            {a handle to a menu}
uIDCheckItem: UINT;      {the identifier or position of the menu item to check}
uCheck: UINT             {menu item flags}
): DWORD;                {returns the previous checked state}
```

12

Chapter

Description

This function sets the checked state of the specified menu item. The menu item cannot be in a menu bar; it must be in a submenu, drop-down menu, or pop-up menu. If the specified menu item opens a submenu, the uIDCheckItem parameter must contain the menu item identifier.

Parameters

hMenu: A handle to the menu containing the item to be checked or unchecked.

uIDCheckItem: Specifies the menu item whose checked attributed is to be changed. This parameter contains either a menu item identifier or a zero-based position, as determined by the contents of the uCheck parameter.

uCheck: A combination of flags that determine how the uIDCheckItem parameter is interpreted and if the menu item is checked or unchecked. This parameter can contain either the MF_BYCOMMAND or the MF_BYPOSITION flags combined with either the MF_CHECKED or the MF_UNCHECKED flags, as described in Table 12-3.

Return Value

If the function succeeds, it returns either the MF_CHECKED or MF_UNCHECKED flag that indicates the previous menu item checked state; otherwise it returns $FFFFFFFF.

See Also

CheckMenuRadioItem, GetMenuItemID, GetMenuItemInfo, GetMenuState, GetSystemMetrics, SetMenuItemBitmaps, SetMenuItemInfo

Example

Please see Listing 12-3 under CreateMenu.

Table 12-3: CheckMenuItem uCheck Values

Value	Description
MF_BYCOMMAND	Indicates that the uIDCheckItem parameter contains a menu item identifier. This flag is used by default if none are specified, and cannot be combined with the MF_BYPOSITION flag.
MF_BYPOSITION	Indicates that the uIDCheckItem parameter contains a zero-based position. This flag cannot be combined with the MF_BYCOMMAND flag.
MF_CHECKED	Places the menu's check mark bitmap next to the menu item. By default, this is an image of a check mark. This flag cannot be combined with the MF_UNCHECKED flag.
MF_UNCHECKED	Places the menu's unchecked check mark bitmap next to the menu item. By default, this is a blank image. This flag cannot be combined with the MF_CHECKED flag.

CheckMenuRadioItem   Windows.Pas

Syntax

```
CheckMenuRadioItem(
hMenu: HMENU;          {a handle to a menu}
First: UINT;           {the first menu item identifier or position in the group}
Last: UINT;            {the last menu item identifier or position in the group}
Check: UINT;           {the identifier or position of the menu item to check}
Flags: UINT            {menu item flags}
): BOOL;               {returns TRUE or FALSE}
```

Description

This function sets the checked attribute of the menu item identified by the Check parameter, while clearing the checked attribute from all other menu items in the group of menu items identified by the First and Last parameters. Specifically, the MFT_RADIOCHECK and MFS_CHECKED flags are set for the menu item identified by the Check parameter, and cleared from the others. Please see the GetMenuItemInfo for an explanation of these flags. By default, the checked menu item will display a small round circle (a bullet) instead of a check mark.

Parameters

hMenu: A handle to the menu containing the group of menu items to be modified.

First: Specifies the first menu item in the group. This parameter contains either a menu item identifier or a zero-based position, as determined by the contents of the Flags parameter.

Last: Specifies the last menu item in the group. This parameter contains either a menu item identifier or a zero-based position, as determined by the contents of the Flags parameter.

Check: Specifies the menu item to be checked. This parameter contains either a menu item identifier or a zero-based position, as determined by the contents of the Flags parameter.

Flags: A flag indicating how the First, Last, and Check parameters are to be interpreted. If this parameter contains the MF_BYCOMMAND flag, the First, Last, and Check parameters contain menu item identifiers. If this parameter contains the MF_BYPOSITION flag, these parameters contain a zero-based position.

Return Value

If the function succeeds, it returns TRUE; otherwise it returns FALSE. To get extended error information, call the GetLastError function.

See Also

CheckMenuItem, GetMenuItemInfo, GetMenuState, SetMenuItemBitmaps, SetMenuItemInfo

12

Chapter

Example

Please see Listing 12-4 under CreatePopupMenu.

CreateMenu   *Windows.Pas*

Syntax

CreateMenu: HMENU;   {returns a handle to a newly created menu}

Description

This function creates an empty menu and returns its handle. Menu items and submenus can be added to the menu by using the AppendMenu, InsertMenu, and InsertMenuItem functions. When the application is finished with the menu, it should be deleted by using the DestroyMenu function. However, if the menu is assigned to a window by using the SetMenu function, Windows will automatically free the menu resources when the application terminates.

 Note: Windows 95 can handle a maximum of 16,364 menu handles.

Return Value

If the function succeeds, it returns a handle to the newly created menu; otherwise it returns zero.

See Also

AppendMenu, CreatePopupMenu, DestroyMenu, InsertMenu, InsertMenuItem, IsMenu, SetMenu

Example

Listing 12-3: Creating a Menu the Old-fashioned Way

```
const
  {these are the menu item identifiers}
  MNUID_MAINMENU = 1;
  MNUID_ITEM1    = 2;
  MNUID_ITEM2    = 3;
  MNUID_ITEM3    = 4;
  MNUID_ITEM4    = 5;

var
  Form1: TForm1;
  MainMenu, SubMenu1: HMENU;   // holds a handle to the main and drop-down menus

implementation

{$R *.DFM}
```

```
procedure TForm1.FormCreate(Sender: TObject);
var
  MenuInfo: TMenuItemInfo;   // holds menu item information
begin
  {start by creating the main menu and a drop-down menu}
  MainMenu := CreateMenu;
  SubMenu1 := CreatePopupMenu;

  {initialize the menu item information structure to indicate that the
   menu item identifier is valid and that the menu will contain a string}
  MenuInfo.cbSize := SizeOf(TMenuItemInfo);
  MenuInfo.fMask := MIIM_TYPE or MIIM_ID;
  MenuInfo.fType := MFT_STRING;

  {insert the first menu item into the drop-down menu}
  MenuInfo.wID := MNUID_ITEM1;
  MenuInfo.dwTypeData := 'Item 1';
  InsertMenuItem(SubMenu1, 0, TRUE, MenuInfo);

  {insert the second menu item at the end of the drop-down menu}
  MenuInfo.wID := MNUID_ITEM2;
  MenuInfo.dwTypeData := 'Item 2';
  InsertMenuItem(SubMenu1, $FFFF, TRUE, MenuInfo);

  {insert the third menu item at the end of the drop-down menu}
  MenuInfo.wID := MNUID_ITEM3;
  MenuInfo.dwTypeData := 'Item 3';
  InsertMenuItem(SubMenu1, $FFFF, TRUE, MenuInfo);

  {insert the fourth menu item at the end of the drop-down menu}
  MenuInfo.wID := MNUID_ITEM4;
  MenuInfo.dwTypeData := 'Item 4';
  InsertMenuItem(SubMenu1, $FFFF, TRUE, MenuInfo);

  {reset the menu item info structure to indicate that we are inserting
   a menu item that will activate a drop-down menu}
  MenuInfo.wID := MNUID_MAINMENU;
  MenuInfo.fMask := MIIM_TYPE or MIIM_ID or MIIM_SUBMENU;
  MenuInfo.dwTypeData := 'Main Menu';
  MenuInfo.hSubMenu := SubMenu1;

  {insert the menu item into the main menu}
  InsertMenuItem(MainMenu, 0, TRUE, MenuInfo);

  {set the window menu to the main menu that was created.  this causes the
   application to draw the menu bar containing the main menu item}
  SetMenu(Form1.Handle, MainMenu);
end;

{the overridden WM_COMMAND message handler}
procedure TForm1.WMCommand(var Msg: TWMCommand);
begin
  {if this message was sent from a menu item (zero indicates a menu)...}
  if Msg.NotifyCode=0 then
  begin
```

```
                        {...retrieve the state of the menu and check it accordingly}
                        if (GetMenuState(MainMenu, Msg.ItemID, MF_BYCOMMAND)
                            and MF_CHECKED)=MF_CHECKED then
                          CheckMenuItem(MainMenu, Msg.ItemID, MF_BYCOMMAND or MF_UNCHECKED)
                        else
                          CheckMenuItem(MainMenu, Msg.ItemID, MF_BYCOMMAND or MF_CHECKED);

                        {indicate that the message was handled}
                        Msg.Result:=0;
                      end
                      else
                        {otherwise, it was not one of our new menu items that generated the
                        message, so let Windows handle it}
                        inherited;
                    end;

                    procedure TForm1.Timer1Timer(Sender: TObject);
                    begin
                      {to draw attention to the menu, we can toggle its highlighted state on or
                      off.  therefore, check its state and highlight it accordingly}
                      if (GetMenuState(MainMenu, 0, MF_BYPOSITION) and MF_HILITE)=MF_HILITE then
                        HiliteMenuItem(Form1.Handle, MainMenu, 0, MF_BYPOSITION or MF_UNHILITE)
                      else
                        HiliteMenuItem(Form1.Handle, MainMenu, 0, MF_BYPOSITION or MF_HILITE);
                    end;

                    procedure TForm1.FormDestroy(Sender: TObject);
                    begin
                      {we are done with the menus, so remove and destroy both the drop-down menu
                      and the main menu}
                      DeleteMenu(MainMenu, 0, MF_BYPOSITION);

                      {note that since the menu was assigned to a window by using the SetMenu
                      function, the menu resources are removed automatically, and the following
                      line of code is unnecessary}
                      DestroyMenu(MainMenu);
                    end;
```

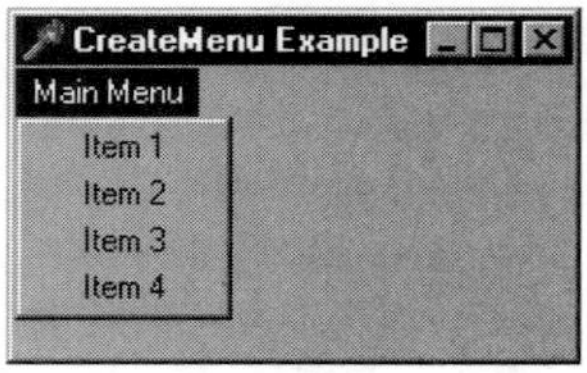

Figure 12-3:
The menu
structure

CreatePopupMenu   Windows.Pas

Syntax

CreatePopupMenu: HMENU;   {returns a handle to the newly created pop-up
                                  menu}

Description

This function creates an empty pop-up menu and returns its handle. The resulting menu can be used as a pop-up menu, submenu, or drop-down menu. Menu items and submenus can be added by using the AppendMenu, InsertMenu, and InsertMenuItem functions. If the menu is to be used as a pop-up menu, it can be displayed by using the TrackPopupMenu or TrackPopupMenuEx functions. When the application is finished with the menu, it should be deleted by using the DestroyMenu function.

 Note: Windows 95 can handle a maximum of 16,364 menu handles.

Return Value

If the function succeeds, it returns a handle to the newly created menu; otherwise it returns zero.

See Also

AppendMenu, CreateMenu, DestroyMenu, InsertMenu, InsertMenuItem, IsMenu, TrackPopupMenu, TrackPopupMenuEx

Example

Listing 12-4: Creating a Pop-up Menu and Using it in the System Menu

```
const
  {the menu item identifiers. since these menu items will be placed in the
   system menu, and the WM_SYSCOMMAND message uses the last 4 bits of the
   wParam parameter internally, the menu item identifiers must be greater
   than 15}
  MNUID_BLACK  = $1000;
  MNUID_NORMAL = $2000;

var
  Form1: TForm1;
  SysPopup: HMENU;     // holds a handle to our pop-up menu

implementation

{$R *.DFM}

procedure TForm1.FormCreate(Sender: TObject);
begin
  {create the pop-up menu. this will be used as a drop-down menu in
   the system menu}
  SysPopup := CreatePopupMenu;

  {append the two menu items to it}
  AppendMenu(SysPopup, MF_STRING, MNUID_BLACK, 'Black');
```

12

Chapter

```
        AppendMenu(SysPopup, MF_STRING, MNUID_NORMAL, 'Normal');

        {insert a separator first}
        InsertMenu(GetSystemMenu(Form1.Handle, FALSE), 0,
                MF_BYPOSITION or MF_SEPARATOR, 0, NIL);

        {insert a menu item at the beginning of the system menu that will display
         the created drop-down menu}
        InsertMenu(GetSystemMenu(Form1.Handle, FALSE), 0,
                MF_BYPOSITION or MF_POPUP OR MF_STRING, SysPopup, 'Color');

        {exclusively check the 'normal' menu item}
        CheckMenuRadioItem(SysPopup, 0, 1, 1, MF_BYPOSITION);

        {set up a message handler to receive messages from the pop-up menu items}
        Application.OnMessage := ApplicationMessage;
    end;

procedure TForm1.ApplicationMessage(var Msg: TMsg; var Handled: Boolean);
begin
    {if this is a message from a menu, and it is the 'black' menu item...}
    if ((Msg.Message=WM_SYSCOMMAND) or (Msg.Message=WM_COMMAND)) and
        (Msg.wParam and $FFF0=MNUID_BLACK) then
    begin
        {exclusively check the 'black' menu item and change
         the form color accordingly}
        CheckMenuRadioItem(SysPopup, 0, 1, 0, MF_BYPOSITION);
        Form1.Color := clBlack;
    end;

    {if this is a message from a menu, and it is the 'normal' menu item...}
    if ((Msg.Message=WM_SYSCOMMAND) or (Msg.Message=WM_COMMAND)) and
        (Msg.wParam and $FFF0=MNUID_NORMAL) then
    begin
        {exclusively check the 'normal' menu item and change
         the form color accordingly}
        CheckMenuRadioItem(SysPopup, 0, 1, 1, MF_BYPOSITION);
        Form1.Color := clBtnFace;
    end;
end;

procedure TForm1.FormMouseDown(Sender: TObject; Button: TMouseButton;
    Shift: TShiftState; X, Y: Integer);
var
    MenuPoint: TPoint;  // used to translate mouse coordinates
begin
    {if the right mouse button was pressed...}
    if Button = mbRight then
    begin
        {...translate the mouse coordinates to screen coordinates}
        MenuPoint.X := X;
        MenuPoint.Y := Y;
        MenuPoint := ClientToScreen(MenuPoint);
```

```
    {retrieve the drop-down menu from the system menu, and
      display the drop-down menu as a pop-up menu}
    TrackPopupMenu(GetSubMenu(GetSystemMenu(Form1.Handle, FALSE), 0),
                   TPM_CENTERALIGN or TPM_LEFTBUTTON, MenuPoint.X, MenuPoint.Y,
                   0, Form1.Handle, NIL);
  end;
end;

procedure TForm1.FormDestroy(Sender: TObject);
begin
  {we no longer need the pop-up menu, so delete it}
  DeleteMenu(GetSystemMenu(Form1.Handle, FALSE), 0, MF_BYPOSITION);
end;
```

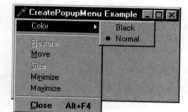

Figure 12-4:
The submenu
in the system
menu

DeleteMenu   Windows.Pas

Syntax

```
DeleteMenu(
hMenu: HMENU;          {a handle to a menu}
uPosition: UINT;       {the identifier or position of the menu item to delete}
uFlags: UINT           {menu item flags}
): BOOL;               {returns TRUE or FALSE}
```

Description

This function deletes the specified menu item from the specified menu. If the menu item opens a drop-down menu or submenu, this function deletes the drop-down menu or submenu handle, freeing its associated resources.

Parameters

hMenu: A handle to the menu containing the menu item to be deleted.

uPosition: Specifies the menu item to be deleted. This parameter contains either a menu item identifier or a zero-based position, as determined by the contents of the uFlags parameter.

uFlags: A flag indicating how the uPosition parameter is interpreted. If this parameter contains the MF_BYCOMMAND flag, the uPosition parameter contains a menu item identifier. If this parameter contains the MF_BYPOSITION flag, the uFlags parameter contains a zero-based position.

12

Chapter

Return Value

If this function succeeds, it returns TRUE; otherwise it returns FALSE. To get extended error information, call the GetLastError function.

See Also

AppendMenu, CreatePopupMenu, DestroyMenu, InsertMenu, InsertMenuItem, RemoveMenu

Example

Please see Listing 12-4 under CreatePopupMenu.

DestroyMenu   *Windows.Pas*

Syntax

```
DestroyMenu(
hMenu: HMENU              {a handle to the menu to be destroyed}
): BOOL;                  {returns TRUE or FALSE}
```

Description

This function destroys the specified menu and frees all associated resources. Any menu that was not assigned to a window by using the SetMenu function must be destroyed by using the DestroyMenu function. Menus assigned to a window are automatically destroyed when the function terminates, and do not need to be explicitly destroyed.

Parameters

hMenu: A handle to the menu to be destroyed.

Return Value

If the function succeeds, it returns TRUE; otherwise it returns FALSE. To get extended error information, call the GetLastError function.

See Also

CreateMenu, CreatePopupMenu, DeleteMenu, RemoveMenu

Example

Please see Listing 12-3 under CreateMenu.

EnableMenuItem *Windows.Pas*

Syntax

```
EnableMenuItem(
hMenu: HMENU;             {a handle to a menu}
uIDEnableItem: UINT;      {a menu item identifier or position}
uEnable: UINT             {menu item flags}
```

): BOOL;   {returns TRUE or FALSE}

Description

This function enables, disables, or grays the specified menu item in the specified menu.

Parameters

hMenu: A handle to the menu containing the menu item to be enabled, disabled, or grayed.

uIDEnableItem: Specifies the menu item to be enabled, disabled, or grayed. This parameter contains either a menu item identifier or a zero-based position, as determined by the contents of the uEnable parameter.

uEnable: A combination of flags that determine how the uIDEnableItem parameter is interpreted and if the menu item is enabled, disabled, or grayed. This parameter can contain either the MF_BYCOMMAND or the MF_BYPOSITION flags combined with one of the following flags: MF_DISABLED, MF_ENABLED, or MF_GRAYED. These flags are described in Table 12-4. Note that if this parameter contains the MF_BYCOMMAND flag, all submenus opened by items in the menu identified by the hMenu parameter are searched for the specified menu item identifier. Thus, using the MF_BYCOMMAND flag and assuming that there are no duplicate menu identifiers, only the main menu handle needs to be specified.

Return Value

If the function succeeds, it returns TRUE; otherwise it returns FALSE.

See Also

AppendMenu, CreateMenu, CreatePopupMenu, GetMenuItemID, GetMenuItemInfo, InsertMenu, InsertMenuItem, ModifyMenu, SetMenuItemInfo

Example

Listing 12-5: Enabling and Disabling the Close System Menu Item

```
procedure TForm1.Button1Click(Sender: TObject);
var
  SysMenu: HMENU;    // holds a handle to the system menu
begin
  {retrieve a handle to the system menu}
  SysMenu := GetSystemMenu(Form1.Handle, FALSE);

  {if the Close menu item is disabled...}
  if (GetMenuState(SysMenu, 6, MF_BYPOSITION) and MF_GRAYED)=MF_GRAYED then
  begin
    {...enable it...}
    EnableMenuItem(SysMenu, 6, MF_BYPOSITION or MF_ENABLED);
    Button1.Caption := 'Disable Close menu item'
  end
  else
  begin
    {...otherwise disable and gray it}
```

```
        EnableMenuItem(SysMenu, 6, MF_BYPOSITION or MF_GRAYED);
        Button1.Caption := 'Enable Close menu item';
    end;
end;
```

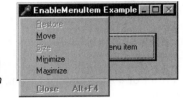

*Figure 12-5:
The disabled
Close System
Menu item*

Table 12-4: EnableMenuItem uEnable Values

Value	Description
MF_BYCOMMAND	Indicates that the uIDEnableItem parameter contains a menu item identifier. This flag is used by default if none are specified, and cannot be combined with the MF_BYPOSITION flag.
MF_BYPOSITION	Indicates that the uIDEnableItem parameter contains a zero-based position. This flag cannot be combined with the MF_BYCOMMAND flag.
MF_DISABLED	Disables the menu item so it cannot be selected, but does not gray it. This flag cannot be combined with the MF_ENABLED or MF_GRAYED flags.
MF_ENABLED	Enables the menu item so it can be selected, and restores it if it was grayed. This flag cannot be combined with the MF_DISABLED or MF_GRAYED flags.
MF_GRAYED	Disables the menu item so it cannot be selected, and draws the menu item in gray. This flag cannot be combined with the MF_ENABLED or MF_DISABLED flags.

GetMenu Windows.Pas

Syntax

```
GetMenu(
hWnd: HWND            {a handle to a window whose menu is to be retrieved}
): HMENU;             {returns a menu handle}
```

Description

This function returns a handle to the menu assigned to the specified window.

Parameters

hWnd: A handle to the window whose menu handle is retrieved.

Return Value

If the function succeeds, it returns a handle to the window's assigned menu. If the window has no menu or the function fails, it returns zero. If the specified window is a child window, the return value is undefined.

See Also

CreateMenu, GetSubMenu, GetSystemMenu, SetMenu

Example

Listing 12-6: Controlling Delphi Through Its Menus

```
var
  Form1: TForm1;
  DelphiWindow: HWND;         // holds a handle to Delphi's main window
  ReopenMenu: HMENU;          // holds a handle to a Delphi submenu

implementation

{$R *.DFM}

procedure TForm1.FormCreate(Sender: TObject);
var
  DelphiMainMenu,            // holds a handle to Delphi's main menu
  DelphiFileMenu: HMENU;     // holds a handle to Delphi's File drop-down menu
begin
  {retrieve a handle to Delphi's main window}
  DelphiWindow := FindWindow('TAppBuilder', NIL);

  {retrieve a handle to Delphi's main menu}
  DelphiMainMenu := GetMenu(DelphiWindow);

  {retrieve a handle to Delphi's File drop-down menu}
  DelphiFileMenu := GetSubMenu(DelphiMainMenu, 0);

  {retrieve a handle to Delphi's Reopen submenu}
  ReopenMenu := GetSubMenu(DelphiFileMenu, 5);
end;

procedure TForm1.FormMouseDown(Sender: TObject; Button: TMouseButton;
  Shift: TShiftState; X, Y: Integer);
var
  MenuPos: TPoint;  // holds converted mouse coordinates
begin
  {if the right mouse button was pressed...}
  if Button = mbRight then
  begin
    {convert the mouse coordinates to screen coordinates}
    MenuPos.X := X;
    MenuPos.Y := Y;
    MenuPos := ClientToScreen(MenuPos);

    {display Delphi's Reopen menu as a pop-up menu}
```

```
        TrackPopupMenu(ReopenMenu, TPM_RIGHTALIGN, MenuPos.X, MenuPos.Y, 0,
                    Form1.Handle, NIL);
  end;
end;

{the overridden WM_COMMAND message handler}
procedure TForm1.WMCommand(var Msg: TMessage);
begin
  {by redirecting the message from the pop-up menu back to Delphi, we can
   control Delphi from our copy of the menu just as if we clicked on the
   menu option in the Delphi IDE}
  PostMessage(DelphiWindow, Msg.Msg, Msg.WParam, Msg.LParam);
  inherited;
end;
```

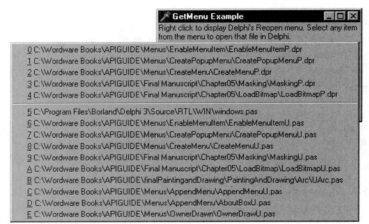

Figure 12-6: Delphi's Reopen menu

GetMenuDefaultItem   Windows.Pas

Syntax

GetMenuDefaultItem(
hMenu: HMENU;   {a menu handle}
fByPos: UINT;   {identifier or position flag}
gmdiFlags: UINT   {search options}
): UINT;   {returns either a menu item identifier or position}

Description

This function retrieves the position or identifier of the default menu item for the specified menu. By default, it will not return the default menu item if it is disabled.

Parameters

hMenu: A handle to the menu whose default menu item is to be retrieved.

fByPos: Indicates if the menu item identifier or its position is to be returned. If this parameter is set to zero, the function returns the default menu item identifier. If it is set to 1, it returns the default menu item's zero-based position.

gmdiFlags: A series of flags that determine how the function searches the specified menu to find the default menu item. This parameter can be zero or a combination of one or more flags from Table 12-5.

Return Value

If the function succeeds, it returns either the default menu item identifier or position; otherwise it returns -1.

See Also

GetMenuItemInfo, SetMenuDefaultItem, SetMenuItemInfo

Example

Please see Listing 12-10 under SetMenuDefaultItem.

Table 12-5: GetMenuDefaultItem gmdiFlags Values

Value	Description
GMDI_GOINTOPOPUPS	Indicates that if the default item in the specified menu opens a submenu, the function will search the submenu for a default item. If the submenu does not contain a default item, the default item that opened the submenu is returned. If the default item in a submenu opens a submenu, this search behavior continues recursively until a final default menu item is found.
GMDI_USEDISABLED	Indicates that the function is to return the default menu item even if it is disabled.

GetMenuItemCount   Windows.Pas

Syntax

```
GetMenuItemCount(
hMenu: HMENU          {a handle to a menu}
): Integer;           {returns the number of menu items in the menu}
```

Description

This function returns the number of menu items contained in the specified menu.

Parameters

hMenu: A handle to the menu whose menu item count is to be retrieved.

12

Chapter

Return Value

If the function succeeds, it returns the number of menu items contained in the specified menu; otherwise it returns -1. To get extended error information, call the GetLastError function.

See Also

GetMenu, GetMenuItemID, GetSubMenu, GetMenuItemInfo, GetMenuString

Example

Please see Listing 12-10 under SetMenuDefaultItem.

GetMenuItemID   Windows.Pas

Syntax

```
GetMenuItemID(
hMenu: HMENU;          {a handle to a menu}
nPos: Integer          {a menu item position}
): UINT;               {returns a menu item identifier}
```

Description

This function returns the menu item identifier of the menu at the indicated position in the specified menu.

Parameters

hMenu: A handle to the menu containing the menu item whose identifier is to be retrieved.

nPos: Specifies the zero-based position of the menu item in the specified menu whose identifier is to be retrieved.

Return Value

If the function succeeds, it returns the specified menu item's identifier. If the function fails, the specified menu item's identifier is null, the specified menu item doesn't exist, or the menu item opens a submenu, the function returns $FFFFFFFF.

See Also

GetMenuItemCount, GetMenuItemID, GetMenuItemInfo, GetMenuString

Example

Please see Listing 12-10 under SetMenuDefaultItem.

GetMenuItemInfo

Windows.Pas

Syntax

```
GetMenuItemInfo(
p1: HMENU;              {a handle to a menu}
p2: UINT;               {a menu item identifier or position}
p3: BOOL;               {identifier or position flag}
var p4: TMenuItemInfo   {a pointer to a TMenuItemInfo structure}
): BOOL;                {returns TRUE or FALSE}
```

Description

This function retrieves specific information about the indicated menu item contained in the specified menu.

Parameters

p1: A handle to the menu containing the menu item whose information is retrieved.

p2: Specifies either the menu item identifier or zero-based position of the menu item whose information is to be retrieved. The value of the p3 parameter indicates how the function interprets the value of this parameter.

p3: Indicates how the function interprets the value of the p2 parameter. If this parameter is set to TRUE, the value of the p2 parameter indicates a zero-based menu item position. If this parameter is set to FALSE, p2 contains a menu item identifier.

p4: A pointer to a TMenuItemInfo data structure containing values that specify the information to retrieve. This data structure receives the requested information when the function returns. The TMenuItemInfo data structure is defined as:

```
TMenuItemInfo = packed record
    cbSize: UINT;              {the size of the data structure}
    fMask: UINT;               {member set or retrieval flags}
    fType: UINT;               {menu item type flags}
    fState: UINT;              {menu item state flags}
    wID: UINT;                 {the menu item identifier}
    hSubMenu: HMENU;           {a handle to a drop-down menu or submenu}
    hbmpChecked: HBITMAP;      {a handle to the checked state bitmap}
    hbmpUnchecked: HBITMAP;    {a handle to the unchecked state bitmap}
    dwItemData: DWORD;         {application-defined value}
    dwTypeData: PAnsiChar;     {menu item content}
    cch: UINT;                 {menu item text length}
end;
```

cbSize: Specifies the size of the data structure, in bytes. This member should be set to SizeOf(TMenuItemInfo).

fMask: A series of flags indicating which members of the structure to retrieve or set. This member can contain a combination of one or more values from Table 12-6.

fType: A series of flags indicating the menu item type. This member can contain a combination of one or more values from Table 12-7.

fState: A series of flags indicating the menu item state. This member can contain a combination of one or more values from Table 12-8.

wID: The menu item identifier.

hSubMenu: A handle to the drop-down menu or submenu activated when the menu item is selected. If the menu item does not activate a submenu or drop-down menu, this member will be set to zero.

hbmpChecked: A handle to the bitmap displayed when the menu item is checked. If this member is set to zero, the default check mark bitmap will be used. If the MFT_RADIOCHECK flag is set in the fType member, the check mark will appear as a bullet.

hbmpUnchecked: A handle to the bitmap displayed when the menu item is not checked. If this member is set to zero, no bitmap is used.

dwItemData: A 32-bit application-defined value associated with the specified menu item. If the fType member contains the MFT_OWNERDRAW flag, this value will be contained in the itemData member of the data structures pointed to by the WM_MEASUREITEM and WM_DRAWITEM messages. The window owning the menu receives these messages when the menu is created or drawn.

dwTypeData: A pointer to extra data associated with the menu item. The contents of this parameter are dependent upon the flags specified in the fType member. If the fType member contains the MFT_BITMAP flag, this member contains a handle to a bitmap. If the fType member contains the MFT_STRING flag, this member points to a null-terminated string. If the fType member contains the MFT_OWNERDRAW flag, this member contains an application-defined 32-bit value.

cch: The length of the menu item text, if the fType member contains the MFT_STRING flag and information is being retrieved. This member is ignored when setting the text of the menu item.

Return Value

If the function succeeds, it returns TRUE; otherwise it returns FALSE. To get extended error information, call the GetLastError function.

See Also

EnableMenuItem, GetMenuItemCount, GetMenuItemID, GetMenuItemRect, GetMenuState, GetMenuString, HiliteMenuItem, InsertMenuItem, ModifyMenu, SetMenuItemBitmaps, SetMenuItemInfo

Example

Please see Listing 12-1 under the owner-drawn menu example in the chapter introduction.

Table 12-6: GetMenuItemInfo p4.fMask Values

Value	Description
MIIM_CHECK MARKS	Retrieves or sets the value of the hbmpChecked and hbmpUnchecked members.
MIIM_DATA	Retrieves or sets the value of the dwItemData member.
MIIM_ID	Retrieves or sets the value of the wID member.
MIIM_STATE	Retrieves or sets the value of the fState member.
MIIM_SUBMENU	Retrieves or sets the value of the hSubMenu member.
MIIM_TYPE	Retrieves or sets the value of the fType and dwTypeData members.

Table 12-7: GetMenuItemInfo p4.fType Values

Value	Description
MFT_BITMAP	Indicates that a bitmap is used to represent the menu item. The handle to the bitmap is specified in the dwTypeData member. This flag cannot be combined with the MFT_STRING or MFT_OWNERDRAW flags.
MFT_MENUBARBREAK	Places the menu item on a new line for menu bars. For submenus and drop-down menus, the menu item is placed in a new column, and the columns are separated by a vertical line. This flag cannot be combined with the MFT_MENUBREAK flag.
MFT_MENUBREAK	Places the menu item on a new line for menu bars. For submenus and drop-down menus, the menu item is placed in a new column. There is no visual indication of column separation. This flag cannot be combined with the MFT_MENUBARBREAK flag.
MFT_OWNERDRAW	Indicates an owner-drawn menu item. When the menu item is displayed for the first time, the owning window receives a WM_MEASUREITEM message, allowing the application to specify the menu item's width and height. The owning window receives a WM_DRAWITEM message when the menu item is to be drawn, allowing the application to draw the menu item in any appearance desired. This flag cannot be combined with the MFT_BITMAP or MFT_STRING flags.
MFT_RADIOCHECK	Indicates that the check mark image used for checked menu items is a bullet, if the hbmpChecked member contains zero.

Value	Description
MFT_RIGHTJUSTIFY	Right justifies the menu item and any subsequent menu items. This flag is valid only for menu items located in a menu bar.
MFT_SEPARATOR	Indicates a menu separator. This menu item is drawn as a horizontal line, and is valid only when used with drop-down menus, pop-up menus, or submenus. This menu item cannot be highlighted, grayed, or disabled, and the dwTypeData and cch members are ignored.
MFT_STRING	Indicates that a string is used to represent the menu item. A pointer to the null-terminated string displayed in the menu item is specified in the dwTypeData member. This flag cannot be combined with the MFT_BITMAP or MFT_OWNERDRAW flags.

Table 12-8: GetMenuItemInfo p4.fState Values

Value	Description
MFS_CHECKED	Places the menu's check mark bitmap next to the menu item. By default, this is an image of a check mark. This flag cannot be combined with the MFS_UNCHECKED flag.
MFS_DEFAULT	Indicates that the menu item is the default menu item. There can be only one default item per menu.
MFS_DISABLED	Disables the menu item so it cannot be selected, but does not gray it. This flag cannot be combined with the MFS_ENABLED or MFS_GRAYED flags.
MFS_ENABLED	Enables the menu item so it can be selected, and restores it if it was grayed. This flag cannot be combined with the MFS_DISABLED or MFS_GRAYED flags. This is the default state of a new menu item.
MFS_GRAYED	Disables the menu item so it cannot be selected, and draws the menu item in gray. This flag cannot be combined with the MFS_ENABLED or MFS_DISABLED flags.
MFS_HILITE	Highlights a menu item.
MFS_UNCHECKED	Places the menu's unchecked check mark bitmap next to the menu item. By default, this is a blank image. This flag cannot be combined with the MFS_CHECKED flag.
MFS_UNHILITE	Unhighlights a menu item. New menu items are not highlighted, and will contain this state flag by default.

GetMenuItemRect   *Windows.Pas*

Syntax

GetMenuItemRect(
hWnd: HWND;   {a handle to the window containing the menu}
hMenu: HMENU;   {a handle to a menu}
uItem: UINT;   {a zero-based menu item position}
var lprcItem: TRect   {a pointer to a TRect structure}
): BOOL;   {returns TRUE or FALSE}

Description

This function retrieves the bounding rectangle, in screen coordinates, of the specified menu item.

Parameters

hWnd: A handle to the window owning the menu whose menu item bounding rectangle is to be retrieved.

hMenu: A handle to the menu containing the menu item whose bounding rectangle is to be retrieved.

uItem: The zero-based position of the menu item.

lprcItem: A pointer to a TRect structure that receives the coordinates of the menu item's bounding rectangle, in screen coordinates.

Return Value

If this function succeeds, it returns TRUE; otherwise it returns FALSE. To get extended error information, call the GetLastError function.

See Also

GetMenu, GetMenuItemCount, GetMenuItemID, GetMenuItemInfo, GetMenuState, GetMenuString, GetSubMenu, GetSystemMenu

Example

Please see Listing 12-10 under SetMenuDefaultItem.

GetMenuState   *Windows.Pas*

Syntax

GetMenuState(
hMenu: HMENU;   {a handle to a menu}
uId: UINT;   {a menu item identifier or position}
uFlags: UINT   {identifier or position flag}
): UINT;   {returns the menu item state flags}

12

Chapter

Description

This function retrieves a series of flags indicating the state of the specified menu item. If the menu item opens a submenu, the function also returns the number of menu items in the opened submenu.

Parameters

hMenu: A handle to the menu containing the menu item whose state is to be retrieved.

uId: Specifies either the menu item identifier or zero-based position of the menu item whose state is to be retrieved. The value of the uFlags parameter indicates how the function interprets the value of this parameter.

uFlags: Indicates how the function interprets the value of the uId parameter. If this parameter is set to MF_BYPOSITION, the value of the uId parameter indicates a zero-based menu item position. If this parameter is set to MF_BYCOMMAND, uId contains a menu item identifier.

Return Value

If the function succeeds, it returns a combination of flags from Table 12-9. The return value can be combined with one of these flags using the AND Boolean operator to determine if the flag is present in the return value (i.e., if (GetMenuState(SysMenu, 6, MF_BYPOSITION) and MF_GRAYED)=MF_GRAYED then...). If the menu item opens a submenu, the low-order word of the return value contains the state flags for the indicated menu item, and the high-order word contains the number of menu items in the opened submenu. If the function fails, it returns $FFFFFFFF.

See Also

GetMenu, GetMenuDefaultItem, GetMenuItemCount, GetMenuItemID, GetMenuItemInfo, GetMenuItemRect, GetMenuString, GetSubMenu

Example

Please see Listing 12-3 under CreateMenu and Listing 12-5 under EnableMenuItem.

Table 12-9: GetMenuState Return Values

Value	Description
MF_CHECKED	Indicates that the menu item is checked.
MF_DISABLED	Indicates that the menu item is disabled.
MF_GRAYED	Indicates that the menu item is disabled and grayed.
MF_HILITE	Indicates that the menu item is highlighted.
MF_MENUBARBREAK	Indicates that the menu item identifies a menu break. For submenus or drop-down menus, the columns will be separated by a vertical bar.

Value	Description
MF_MENUBREAK	Indicates that the menu item identifies a menu break. There will be no visual indication of column separation for drop-down menus or submenus.
MF_SEPARATOR	Indicates that the menu item is a menu separator. This menu item is drawn as a horizontal line, and is valid only for drop-down menus, pop-up menus, or submenus.

GetMenuString   Windows.Pas

Syntax

```
GetMenuString(
hMenu: HMENU;          {a handle to a menu}
uIDItem: UINT;         {a menu item identifier or position}
lpString: PChar;       {a pointer to a null-terminated string buffer}
nMaxCount: Integer;    {the length of the string to be retrieved}
uFlag: UINT            {identifier or position flag}
): Integer;            {returns the number of characters copied to the buffer}
```

Description

This function retrieves the string associated with the specified menu item, storing it in the null-terminated string buffer pointed to by the lpString parameter.

Parameters

hMenu: A handle to the menu containing the menu item whose string is to be retrieved.

uIDItem: Specifies either the menu item identifier or zero-based position of the menu item whose string is to be retrieved. The value of the uFlag parameter indicates how the function interprets the value of this parameter.

lpString: A pointer to a null-terminated string buffer, allocated by the calling application, that will receive the string. This buffer must be large enough to hold the number of characters indicated by the nMaxCount parameter. If this parameter is set to NIL, the function returns the size of buffer required to receive the entire menu item string, in characters.

nMaxCount: Specifies the maximum number of characters to copy into the buffer pointed to by the lpString parameter. If the menu item string is longer than the indicated value, the string is truncated. If this parameter is set to zero, the function returns the length of the menu item string.

uFlag: Indicates how the function interprets the value of the uIDItem parameter. If this parameter is set to MF_BYPOSITION, the value of the uIDItem parameter indicates a zero-based menu item position. If this parameter is set to MF_BYCOMMAND, uIDItem contains a menu item identifier.

Return Value

If the function succeeds, it returns the number of characters copied to the string buffer pointed to by the lpString parameter, not including the null terminator. If the function fails, it returns zero.

See Also

GetMenuItemID, GetMenuItemInfo, GetMenuState, SetMenuItemInfo

Example

Please see Listing 12-10 under SetMenuDefaultItem.

GetSubMenu   *Windows.Pas*

Syntax

```
GetSubMenu(
hMenu: HMENU;          {a handle to a menu}
nPos: Integer          {a zero-based menu item position}
): HMENU;              {returns a handle to a menu}
```

Description

This function retrieves a handle to the drop-down menu or submenu activated by the specified menu item.

Parameters

hMenu: A handle to the menu containing the menu item whose activated drop-down menu or submenu handle is to be retrieved.

nPos: Specifies the zero-based position of the menu item that activates a drop-down menu or submenu.

Return Value

If the function succeeds, it returns the handle to the drop-down menu or submenu activated by the indicated menu item. If the function fails or the indicated menu item does not activate a drop-down menu or submenu, the function returns zero.

See Also

CreatePopupMenu, GetMenu, GetMenuItemInfo, SetMenuItemInfo

Example

Please see Listing 12-6 under GetMenu.

GetSystemMenu   Windows.Pas

Syntax

```
GetSystemMenu(
hWnd: HWND;              {a handle to a window}
bRevert: BOOL            {window menu reset flag}
): HMENU;                {returns a handle to the system menu}
```

Description

This function retrieves a handle to the system menu of the specified window (the menu displayed when the icon in the upper left-hand corner of the window is clicked). An application can modify this menu using any of the commands in this chapter. Menu items added to this menu will send the owning window a WM_SYSCOMMAND when clicked. Note that all predefined menu items in the system menu have identifiers greater than $F000. Any menu items added to the system menu should have identifiers less than $F000.

Parameters

hWnd: A handle to the window whose system menu handle is to be retrieved.

bRevert: Indicates if the system menu should be restored to its default state. If this parameter is set to FALSE, the function returns a handle to the current system menu. If this parameter is set to TRUE, the system menu is reset to its default state and the previous system menu is destroyed.

Return Value

If the function succeeds and the bRevert parameter is set to FALSE, it returns a handle to the current system menu. If the function fails or the bRevert parameter is set to TRUE, the function returns zero.

See Also

AppendMenu, GetMenu, GetSubMenu, InsertMenu, InsertMenuItem, ModifyMenu

Example

Please see Listing 12-4 under CreatePopupMenu.

HiliteMenuItem   Windows.Pas

Syntax

```
HiliteMenuItem(
hWnd: HWND;              {a handle to a window}
hMenu: HMENU;            {a handle to a menu}
uIDHiliteItem: UINT;     {a menu item identifier or position}
uHilite: UINT            {menu item flags}
): BOOL;                 {returns TRUE or FALSE}
```

12

Chapter

Description

This function highlights or unhighlights a menu item in a menu bar.

Parameters

hWnd: A handle to the window owning the menu whose menu item is to be highlighted.

hMenu: A handle to the menu containing the menu item to be highlighted. Note that this must be a handle to a menu bar, not a pop-up menu, drop-down menu, or submenu.

uIDHiliteItem: Specifies the menu item to be highlighted. This parameter contains either a menu item identifier or a zero-based position, as determined by the contents of the uHilite parameter.

uHilite: A combination of flags that determine how the uIDHiliteItem parameter is interpreted and if the menu item is highlighted or unhighlighted. This parameter can contain either the MF_BYCOMMAND or the MF_BYPOSITION flags combined with either the MF_HILITE or MF_UNHILITE flags. These flags are described in Table 12-10.

Return Value

If the function succeeds, it returns TRUE; otherwise it returns FALSE.

See Also

GetMenuItemInfo, GetMenuState, SetMenuItemInfo

Example

Please see Listing 12-3 under CreateMenu.

Table 12-10: HiliteMenuItem uHilite Values

Value	Description
MF_BYCOMMAND	Indicates that the uIDHiliteItem parameter contains a menu item identifier. This flag is used by default if none are specified, and cannot be combined with the MF_BYPOSITION flag.
MF_BYPOSITION	Indicates that the uIDHiliteItem parameter contains a zero-based position. This flag cannot be combined with the MF_BYCOMMAND flag.
MF_HILITE	Highlights the menu item.
MF_UNHILITE	Unhighlights the menu item.

InsertMenu   Windows.Pas

Syntax

```
InsertMenu(
hMenu: HMENU;          {a handle to a menu}
uPosition: UINT;       {a menu item identifier or position}
uFlags: UINT;          {menu item flags}
uIDNewItem: UINT;      {the menu item identifier or submenu handle}
lpNewItem: PChar       {menu item data}
): BOOL;               {returns TRUE or FALSE}
```

Description

This function inserts a new menu item before the indicated menu item in the specified menu. All following menu items are moved downward.

Parameters

hMenu: A handle to the menu into which a new menu item is being inserted.

uPosition: Specifies the menu item before which the new menu item is inserted. This parameter contains either a menu item identifier or a zero-based position, as determined by the contents of the uFlags parameter.

uFlags: A combination of flags that determine how the uPosition parameter is interpreted and how the new menu item will appear and behave. This parameter can contain either the MF_BYCOMMAND or the MF_BYPOSITION flags combined with one or more of the other flags from Table 12-11.

uIDNewItem: Specifies the identifier of the new menu item. If the uFlags parameter contains the MF_POPUP flag, this parameter is set to the handle of the drop-down menu or submenu.

lpNewItem: A pointer to extra data associated with the new menu item. The contents of this parameter are dependent upon the flags specified in the uFlags parameter. If the uFlags parameter contains the MF_BITMAP flag, this parameter contains a handle to a bitmap. If the uFlags parameter contains the MF_STRING flag, this parameter points to a null-terminated string. If the uFlags parameter contains the MF_OWNERDRAW flag, this parameter contains an application-defined 32-bit value. This value will be contained in the itemData member of the data structures pointed to by the WM_MEASUREITEM and WM_DRAWITEM messages that the window receives when the menu is created or drawn.

Return Value

If the function succeeds, it returns TRUE; otherwise it returns FALSE. To get extended error information, call the GetLastError function.

12

Chapter

See Also

AppendMenu, CreateMenu, CreatePopupMenu, DeleteMenu, DestroyMenu, Insert-MenuItem, ModifyMenu, RemoveMenu

Example

Please see Listing 12-4 under CreatePopupMenu.

Table 12-11: InsertMenu uFlags Values

Value	Description
MF_BITMAP	Indicates that a bitmap is used to represent the menu item. The handle to the bitmap is specified in the lpNewItem parameter. This flag cannot be combined with the MF_STRING or MF_OWNERDRAW flags.
MF_BYCOMMAND	Indicates that the uPosition parameter contains a menu item identifier. This flag is used by default if none are specified, and cannot be combined with the MF_BYPOSITION flag.
MF_BYPOSITION	Indicates that the uPosition parameter contains a zero-based position. This flag cannot be combined with the MF_BYCOMMAND flag. Note that if the uPosition parameter is set to $FFFFFFFF, the menu item is appended to the end of the menu.
MF_CHECKED	Places the menu's check mark bitmap next to the menu item. By default, this is an image of a check mark. This flag cannot be combined with the MF_UNCHECKED flag.
MF_DISABLED	Disables the menu item so it cannot be selected, but does not gray it. This flag cannot be combined with the MF_ENABLED or MF_GRAYED flags.
MF_ENABLED	Enables the menu item so it can be selected, and restores it if it was grayed. This flag cannot be combined with the MF_DISABLED or MF_GRAYED flags.
MF_GRAYED	Disables the menu item so it cannot be selected, and draws the menu item in gray. This flag cannot be combined with the MF_ENABLED or MF_DISABLED flags.
MF_MENUBARBREAK	Places the menu item on a new line for menu bars. For submenus and drop-down menus, the menu item is placed in a new column, and the columns are separated by a vertical line. This flag cannot be combined with the MF_MENUBREAK flag.
MF_MENUBREAK	Places the menu item on a new line for menu bars. For submenus and drop-down menus, the menu item is placed in a new column. There is no visual indication of column separation. This flag cannot be combined with the MF_MENUBARBREAK flag.

Value	Description
MF_OWNERDRAW	Indicates an owner-drawn menu item. When the menu item is displayed for the first time, the owning window receives a WM_MEASUREITEM message, allowing the application to specify the menu item's width and height. The owning window receives a WM_DRAWITEM message when the menu item is to be drawn, allowing the application to draw the menu item in any appearance desired. This flag cannot be combined with the MF_BITMAP or MF_STRING flags.
MF_POPUP	Indicates that the menu item opens a drop-down menu or submenu. The handle to the drop-down menu or submenu is specified in the uIDNewItem parameter.
MF_SEPARATOR	Indicates a menu separator. This menu item is drawn as a horizontal line, and is valid only when used with drop-down menus, pop-up menus, or submenus. This menu item cannot be highlighted, grayed, or disabled, and the uIDNewItem and lpNewItem parameters are ignored.
MF_STRING	Indicates that a string is used to represent the menu item. A pointer to the null-terminated string displayed in the menu item is specified in the lpNewItem parameter. This flag cannot be combined with the MF_BITMAP or MF_OWNERDRAW flags.
MF_UNCHECKED	Places the menu's unchecked check mark bitmap next to the menu item. By default, this is a blank image. This flag cannot be combined with the MF_CHECKED flag.

InsertMenuItem   Windows.Pas

Syntax

```
InsertMenuItem(
p1: HMENU;                {a handle to a menu}
p2: UINT;                 {a menu item identifier or position}
p3: BOOL;                 {identifier or position flag}
const p4: TMenuItemInfo   {a pointer to a TMenuItemInfo structure}
): BOOL;                  {returns TRUE or FALSE}
```

Description

This function inserts a new menu item before the specified menu item in the indicated menu. All following menu items are moved downward.

Parameters

p1: A handle to the menu into which the new menu item is to be inserted.

p2: Specifies either the menu item identifier or zero-based position of the menu item before which the new menu item is to be inserted. The value of the p3 parameter indicates how the function interprets the value of this parameter.

p3: Indicates how the function interprets the value of the p2 parameter. If this parameter is set to TRUE, the value of the p2 parameter indicates a zero-based menu item position. If this parameter is set to FALSE, p2 contains a menu item identifier.

p4: A pointer to a TMenuItemInfo data structure containing information about the new menu item. The TMenuItemInfo data structure is defined as:

```
TMenuItemInfo = packed record
        cbSize: UINT;                {the size of the data structure}
        fMask: UINT;                 {member set or retrieval flags}
        fType: UINT;                 {menu item type flags}
        fState: UINT;                {menu item state flags}
        wID: UINT;                   {the menu item identifier}
        hSubMenu: HMENU;             {a handle to a drop-down menu or submenu}
        hbmpChecked: HBITMAP;        {a handle to the checked state bitmap}
        hbmpUnchecked: HBITMAP;      {a handle to the unchecked state bitmap}
        dwItemData: DWORD;           {application-defined value}
        dwTypeData: PAnsiChar;       {menu item content}
        cch: UINT;                   {menu item text length}
end;
```

Please see the GetMenuItemInfo function for a complete description of this data structure.

Return Value

If the function succeeds, it returns TRUE; otherwise it returns FALSE. To get extended error information, call the GetLastError function.

See Also

AppendMenu, CreateMenu, CreatePopupMenu, DeleteMenu, DestroyMenu, Insert-Menu, ModifyMenu, RemoveMenu

Example

Please see Listing 12-3 under CreateMenu.

IsMenu   Windows.Pas

Syntax

```
IsMenu(
hMenu: HMENU              {a handle to a menu}
): BOOL;                  {returns TRUE or FALSE}
```

Description

This function indicates if the specified handle is a handle to a menu.

Parameters

hMenu: Specifies the handle to test.

Return Value

If the function succeeds and the handle identifies a menu, the function returns TRUE. If the function fails or the handle does not identify a menu, the function returns FALSE.

See Also

GetMenu, GetSubMenu, IsWindow

Example

Listing 12-7: Testing Handle Validity

```
procedure TForm1.TestHandle(Value: THandle);
begin
  if IsMenu(Value) then
    ShowMessage('This handle is a menu')
  else
    ShowMessage('This handle is not a menu');
end;
```

ModifyMenu   Windows.Pas

Syntax

```
ModifyMenu(
hMnu: HMENU;              {a handle to a menu}
uPosition: UINT;          {a menu item identifier or position}
uFlags: UINT;             {menu item flags}
uIDNewItem: UINT;         {the menu item identifier or submenu handle}
lpNewItem: PChar          {menu item data}
): BOOL;                  {returns TRUE or FALSE}
```

Description

This function changes the appearance and behavior of the indicated menu item in the specified menu.

Parameters

hMnu: A handle to the menu containing the menu item to be modified.

uPosition: Specifies the menu item to modify. This parameter contains either a menu item identifier or a zero-based position, as determined by the contents of the uFlags parameter.

12

Chapter

uFlags: A combination of flags that determine how the uPosition parameter is interpreted and how the specified menu item is to be modified. This parameter can contain either the MF_BYCOMMAND or the MF_BYPOSITION flags combined with one or more of the other flags from Table 12-12.

uIDNewItem: Specifies the identifier of the new menu item. If the uFlags parameter contains the MF_POPUP flag, this parameter is set to the handle of the drop-down menu or submenu.

lpNewItem: A pointer to extra data associated with the new menu item. The contents of this parameter are dependent upon the flags specified in the uFlags parameter. If the uFlags parameter contains the MF_BITMAP flag, this parameter contains a handle to a bitmap. If the uFlags parameter contains the MF_STRING flag, this parameter points to a null-terminated string. If the uFlags parameter contains the MF_OWNERDRAW flag, this parameter contains an application-defined 32-bit value. This value will be contained in the itemData member of the data structures pointed to by the WM_MEASUREITEM and WM_DRAWITEM messages that the window receives when the menu is created or drawn.

Return Value

If the function succeeds, it returns TRUE; otherwise it returns FALSE. To get extended error information, call the GetLastError function.

See Also

AppendMenu, CreateMenu, CreatePopupMenu, DeleteMenu, DestroyMenu, InsertMenu, InsertMenuItem, RemoveMenu

Example

Listing 12-8: Creating a Tool Palette in a Menu

```
procedure TForm1.FormCreate(Sender: TObject);
begin
  {change the existing menu items in the drop-down menu.  this will give
   the menu the appearance of a toolbar or tool palette}
  ModifyMenu(Palette1.Handle, 0, MF_BYPOSITION or MF_BITMAP,
             GetMenuItemID(Palette1.Handle, 0),
             Pointer(Image1.Picture.Bitmap.Handle));
  ModifyMenu(Palette1.Handle, 1, MF_BYPOSITION or MF_BITMAP,
             GetMenuItemID(Palette1.Handle, 1),
             Pointer(Image2.Picture.Bitmap.Handle));
  ModifyMenu(Palette1.Handle, 2, MF_BYPOSITION or MF_BITMAP,
             GetMenuItemID(Palette1.Handle, 2),
             Pointer(Image3.Picture.Bitmap.Handle));

  {we want to start a new column here}
  ModifyMenu(Palette1.Handle, 3, MF_BYPOSITION or MF_BITMAP or MF_MENUBREAK,
             GetMenuItemID(Palette1.Handle, 3),
             Pointer(Image4.Picture.Bitmap.Handle));
  ModifyMenu(Palette1.Handle, 4, MF_BYPOSITION or MF_BITMAP,
```

```
            GetMenuItemID(Palette1.Handle, 4),
            Pointer(Image5.Picture.Bitmap.Handle));
  ModifyMenu(Palette1.Handle, 5, MF_BYPOSITION or MF_BITMAP,
            GetMenuItemID(Palette1.Handle, 5),
            Pointer(Image6.Picture.Bitmap.Handle));
end;

procedure TForm1.Item11Click(Sender: TObject);
begin
  {display which item was clicked}
  Label2.Caption := TMenuItem(Sender).Caption;
end;
```

Figure 12-7:
The menu tool
palette

Table 12-12: ModifyMenu uFlags Values

Value	Description
MF_BITMAP	Indicates that a bitmap is used to represent the menu item. The handle to the bitmap is specified in the lpNewItem parameter. This flag cannot be combined with the MF_STRING or MF_OWNERDRAW flags.
MF_BYCOMMAND	Indicates that the uPosition parameter contains a menu item identifier. This flag is used by default if none are specified, and cannot be combined with the MF_BYPOSITION flag.
MF_BYPOSITION	Indicates that the uPosition parameter contains a zero-based position. This flag cannot be combined with the MF_BYCOMMAND flag. Note that if the uPosition parameter is set to $FFFFFFFF, the menu item is appended to the end of the menu.
MF_CHECKED	Places the menu's check mark bitmap next to the menu item. By default, this is an image of a check mark. This flag cannot be combined with the MF_UNCHECKED flag.
MF_DISABLED	Disables the menu item so it cannot be selected, but does not gray it. This flag cannot be combined with the MF_ENABLED or MF_GRAYED flags.
MF_ENABLED	Enables the menu item so it can be selected, and restores it if it was grayed. This flag cannot be combined with the MF_DISABLED or MF_GRAYED flags.
MF_GRAYED	Disables the menu item so it cannot be selected, and draws the menu item in gray. This flag cannot be combined with the MF_ENABLED or MF_DISABLED flags.

12

Chapter

Value	Description
MF_MENUBARBREAK	Places the menu item on a new line for menu bars. For submenus and drop-down menus, the menu item is placed in a new column, and the columns are separated by a vertical line. This flag cannot be combined with the MF_MENUBREAK flag.
MF_MENUBREAK	Places the menu item on a new line for menu bars. For submenus and drop-down menus, the menu item is placed in a new column. There is no visual indication of column separation. This flag cannot be combined with the MF_MENUBARBREAK flag.
MF_OWNERDRAW	Indicates an owner-drawn menu item. When the menu item is displayed for the first time, the owning window receives a WM_MEASUREITEM message, allowing the application to specify the menu item's width and height. The owning window receives a WM_DRAWITEM message when the menu item is to be drawn, allowing the application to draw the menu item in any appearance desired. This flag cannot be combined with the MF_BITMAP or MF_STRING flags.
MF_POPUP	Indicates that the menu item opens a drop-down menu or submenu. The handle to the drop-down menu or submenu is specified in the uIDNewItem parameter.
MF_SEPARATOR	Indicates a menu separator. This menu item is drawn as a horizontal line, and is valid only when used with drop-down menus, pop-up menus, or submenus. This menu item cannot be highlighted, grayed, or disabled, and the uIDNewItem and lpNewItem parameters are ignored.
MF_STRING	Indicates that a string is used to represent the menu item. A pointer to the null-terminated string displayed in the menu item is specified in the lpNewItem parameter. This flag cannot be combined with the MF_BITMAP or MF_OWNERDRAW flags.
MF_UNCHECKED	Places the menu's unchecked check mark bitmap next to the menu item. By default, this is a blank image. This flag cannot be combined with the MF_CHECKED flag.

RemoveMenu   Windows.Pas

Syntax

```
RemoveMenu(
hMenu: HMENU;          {a handle to a menu}
uPosition: UINT;       {a menu item identifier or position}
uFlags: UINT           {identifier or position flag}
): BOOL;               {returns TRUE or FALSE}
```

Description

This function removes the indicated menu item from the specified menu, moving all subsequent menu items up. If the menu item opens a submenu or drop-down menu, the submenu or drop-down menu is not destroyed. An application should call the GetSubMenu function to retrieve a handle to the submenu before removing its activating menu item. An application can use the DeleteMenu function to delete a menu item and free its associated submenu or drop-down menu.

Parameters

hMenu: A handle to a menu from which the specified menu item is to be removed.

uPosition: Specifies either the menu item identifier or zero-based position of the menu item to be deleted. The value of the uFlags parameter indicates how the function interprets the value of this parameter.

uFlags: Indicates how the function interprets the value of the uPosition parameter. If this parameter is set to MF_BYPOSITION, the value of the uPosition parameter indicates a zero-based menu item position. If this parameter is set to MF_BYCOMMAND, uPosition contains a menu item identifier.

Return Value

If the function succeeds, it returns TRUE; otherwise it returns FALSE. To get extended error information, call the GetLastError function.

See Also

CreatePopupMenu, DeleteMenu, DestroyMenu, GetMenu, GetSubMenu

Example

Listing 12-9: Removing Items from the System Menu

```
procedure TForm1.FormCreate(Sender: TObject);
begin
  {remove the Maximize, Minimize, and Restore commands from the system menu}
  RemoveMenu(GetSystemMenu(Form1.Handle, FALSE), 4, MF_BYPOSITION);
  RemoveMenu(GetSystemMenu(Form1.Handle, FALSE), 3, MF_BYPOSITION);
  RemoveMenu(GetSystemMenu(Form1.Handle, FALSE), 0, MF_BYPOSITION);
end;
```

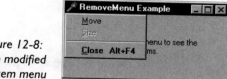

Figure 12-8: The modified system menu

12

Chapter

SetMenu   Windows.Pas

Syntax

```
SetMenu(
hWnd: HWND;              {a handle to a window}
hMenu: HMENU             {a handle to a menu}
): BOOL;                 {returns TRUE or FALSE}
```

Description

This function assigns the specified menu to the specified window. The previous menu, if any, is replaced but not destroyed. An application should call the destroy menu function to delete the previous menu and free its associated resources.

Parameters

hWnd: A handle to the window to which the new menu is assigned.

hMenu: A handle to the menu that is to be assigned to the specified window. This menu creates a menu bar in the window. If this parameter is set to zero, the function simply removes the current menu.

Return Value

If the function succeeds, it returns TRUE; otherwise it returns FALSE. To get extended error information, call the GetLastError function.

See Also

CreateMenu DeleteMenu, DestroyMenu, GetMenu

Example

Please see Listing 12-3 under CreateMenu.

SetMenuDefaultItem   Windows.Pas

Syntax

```
SetMenuDefaultItem(
hMenu: HMENU;            {a handle to a menu}
uItem: UINT;            {a menu item identifier or position}
fByPos: UINT            {identifier or position flag}
): BOOL;                 {returns TRUE or FALSE}
```

Description

This function sets the indicated menu item as the default item for the specified menu. A menu can have only one default item, and the menu item must be located in a drop-down menu, submenu, or pop-up menu.

Parameters

hMenu: A handle to the menu whose default item is to be set.

uItem: Specifies either the menu item identifier or zero-based position of the menu item to be set as the default item. The value of the fByPos parameter indicates how the function interprets the value of this parameter. If this parameter is set to -1, the function removes the default item status from the current default item, leaving the specified menu with no default menu item set.

fByPos: Indicates how the function interprets the value of the uItem parameter. If this parameter is set to MF_BYPOSITION, the value of the uItem parameter indicates a zero-based menu item position. If this parameter is set to MF_BYCOMMAND, uItem contains a menu item identifier.

Return Value

If this function succeeds, it returns TRUE; otherwise it returns FALSE. To get extended error information, call the GetLastError function.

See Also

GetMenuDefaultItem, GetMenuItemID, GetMenuItemInfo, HiliteMenuItem

Example

Listing 12-10: Retrieving Default Menu Item Information

```
procedure TForm1.FormCreate(Sender: TObject);
begin
  {set the maximum value of the spin edit to the number of menu items}
  SpinEdit1.MaxValue := GetMenuItemCount(MainMenu2.Handle)-1;
end;

procedure TForm1.SpinEdit1Change(Sender: TObject);
var
  DefaultItem: Integer;                    // the default menu item position
  DefaultItemRect: TRect;                  // the default menu item coordinates
  DefaultMenuString: array[0..255] of char; // the default menu item string
begin
  {set the default menu item to that specified by the spin edit}
  SetMenuDefaultItem(MainMenu2.Handle, SpinEdit1.Value, 1);

  {retrieve the newly set default item}
  DefaultItem := GetMenuDefaultItem(MainMenu2.Handle, 1, 0);

  {retrieve the default item's coordinates}
  GetMenuItemRect(Form1.Handle, MainMenu2.Handle, DefaultItem, DefaultItemRect);

  {retrieve the text of the default menu item}
  GetMenuString(MainMenu2.Handle, DefaultItem, @DefaultMenuString, 255,
               MF_BYPOSITION);

  {display the position of the default menu item}
```

12

Chapter

```
    Label2.Caption := 'Default Item Position: '+IntToStr(DefaultItem);

    {display the default menu item's identifier}
    Label3.Caption := 'Default Item ID: '+IntToStr(GetMenuItemID(MainMenu2.Handle,
                                          DefaultItem));

    {display the coordinates of the default menu item}
    Label4.Caption := 'Default Item Rect - L: '+IntToStr(DefaultItemRect.Left)+
                  ' T: '+IntToStr(DefaultItemRect.Top)+
                  ' R: '+IntToStr(DefaultItemRect.Right)+
                  ' B: '+IntToStr(DefaultItemRect.Bottom);

    {display the default menu item's text}
    Label5.Caption := 'Default Item String: '+DefaultMenuString;
  end;

  procedure TForm1.Item11Click(Sender: TObject);
  begin
    {display the text of the selected menu item}
    Caption := 'SetMenuDefaultItem Example - '+TMenuItem(Sender).Caption+
            ' selected';
  end;
```

Figure 12-9: The Default menu item attributes

SetMenuItemBitmaps   Windows.Pas

Syntax

```
SetMenuItemBitmaps(
hMenu: HMENU;                  {a handle to a menu}
uPosition: UINT;              {a menu item identifier or position}
uFlags: UINT;                 {identifier or position flag}
hBitmapUnchecked: HBITMAP;    {a handle to the unchecked status bitmap}
hBitmapChecked: HBITMAP       {a handle to the checked status bitmap}
): BOOL;                      {returns TRUE or FALSE}
```

Description

This function specifies the bitmaps to be displayed when the indicated menu item contained in the specified menu is checked or unchecked. The application must manage these bitmaps as they are not destroyed when the menu or menu item is removed or destroyed. Note that if both the hBitmapUnchecked and hBitmapChecked parameters are set to zero, Windows will display a check mark image when the menu item is checked, and no image when the menu item is not checked. The application should use the GetSystemMetrics function with the CX_MENUCHECK and the CY_MENUCHECK flags to determine the appropriate dimensions for the check mark bitmaps.

Parameters

hMenu: A handle to the menu containing the menu item whose checked and unchecked bitmaps are to be set.

uPosition: Specifies either the menu item identifier or zero-based position of the menu item whose checked and unchecked bitmaps are to be set. The value of the uFlags parameter indicates how the function interprets the value of this parameter.

uFlags: Indicates how the function interprets the value of the uPosition parameter. If this parameter is set to MF_BYPOSITION, the value of the uPosition parameter indicates a zero-based menu item position. If this parameter is set to MF_BYCOMMAND, uPosition contains a menu item identifier.

hBitmapUnchecked: A handle to the bitmap that is displayed when the menu item is not checked. If this parameter is set to zero, no image will be displayed when the menu item is not checked.

hBitmapChecked: A handle to the bitmap that is displayed when the menu item is checked. If this parameter is set to zero, no image will be displayed when the menu item is checked.

Return Value

If the function succeeds, it returns TRUE; otherwise it returns FALSE. To get extended error information, call the GetLastError function

See Also

GetMenu, GetMenuItemInfo, GetSubMenu, GetSystemMetrics, SetMenuItemInfo

Example

Listing 12-11: Specifying Custom Check Mark Bitmaps

```
procedure TForm1.FormCreate(Sender: TObject);
begin
  {specify new check mark bitmaps for all menu items}
  SetMenuItemBitmaps(TheMainMenu1.Handle, 0, MF_BYPOSITION,
                     Image2.Picture.Bitmap.Handle,
                     Image1.Picture.Bitmap.Handle);
  SetMenuItemBitmaps(TheMainMenu1.Handle, 1, MF_BYPOSITION,
                     Image2.Picture.Bitmap.Handle,
                     Image1.Picture.Bitmap.Handle);
  SetMenuItemBitmaps(TheMainMenu1.Handle, 2, MF_BYPOSITION,
                     Image2.Picture.Bitmap.Handle,
                     Image1.Picture.Bitmap.Handle);
```

12

Chapter

```
end;

procedure TForm1.ItemOne1Click(Sender: TObject);

  procedure DisplayChecked(Item: TMenuItem; TheLabel: TLabel);
  begin
    {indicate if the item is checked or not}
    if Item.Checked then
      TheLabel.Caption := Item.Caption+' checked'
    else
      TheLabel.Caption := Item.Caption+' not checked'
  end;

begin
  {check the selected menu item}
  TMenuItem(Sender).Checked := not TMenuItem(Sender).Checked;

  {display which menu items are checked}
  DisplayChecked(TheMainMenu1.Items[0], Label1);
  DisplayChecked(TheMainMenu1.Items[1], Label2);
  DisplayChecked(TheMainMenu1.Items[2], Label3);
end;
```

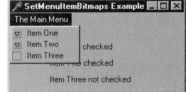

Figure 12-10: The new menu item check marks

SetMenuItemInfo   Windows.Pas

Syntax

```
SetMenuItemInfo(
p1: HMENU;                {a handle to a menu}
p2: UINT;                 {a menu item identifier or position}
p3: BOOL;                 {identifier or position flag}
const p4: TMenuItemInfo   {a pointer to a TMenuItemInfo structure}
): BOOL;                  {returns TRUE or FALSE}
```

Description

This function sets specific information about the indicated menu item contained in the specified menu.

Parameters

p1: A handle to the menu containing the menu item whose information is set.

p2: Specifies either the menu item identifier or zero-based position of the menu item whose information is to be set. The value of the p3 parameter indicates how the function interprets the value of this parameter.

p3: Indicates how the function interprets the value of the p2 parameter. If this parameter is set to TRUE, the value of the p2 parameter indicates a zero-based menu item position. If this parameter is set to FALSE, p2 contains a menu item identifier.

p4: A pointer to a TMenuItemInfo data structure containing values that specify the information to set. The TMenuItemInfo data structure is defined as:

```
TMenuItemInfo = packed record
        cbSize: UINT;              {the size of the data structure}
        fMask: UINT;               {member set or retrieval flags}
        fType: UINT;               {menu item type flags}
        fState: UINT;              {menu item state flags}
        wID: UINT;                 {the menu item identifier}
        hSubMenu: HMENU;           {a handle to a drop-down menu or submenu}
        hbmpChecked: HBITMAP;      {a handle to the checked state bitmap}
        hbmpUnchecked: HBITMAP;    {a handle to the unchecked state bitmap}
        dwItemData: DWORD;         {application-defined value}
        dwTypeData: PAnsiChar;     {menu item content}
        cch: UINT;                 {menu item text length}
end;
```

Please see the GetMenuItemInfo function for a description of this data structure.

Return Value

If the function succeeds, it returns TRUE; otherwise it returns FALSE. To get extended error information, call the GetLastError function.

See Also

EnableMenuItem, GetMenuItemCount, GetMenuItemID, GetMenuItemInfo, GetMenuItemRect, GetMenuState, GetMenuString, HiliteMenuItem, InsertMenuItem, ModifyMenu, SetMenuItemBitmaps

Example

Please see Listing 12-1 under the owner-drawn menu example in the chapter introduction.

TrackPopupMenu   Windows.Pas

Syntax

```
TrackPopupMenu(
hMenu: HMENU;              {a handle to a pop-up menu}
uFlags: UINT;              {position and tracking flags}
```

12

Chapter

x: Integer;	{horizontal screen coordinates}
y: Integer;	{vertical screen coordinates}
nReserved: Integer;	{this parameter is reserved}
hWnd: HWND;	{a handle to the owning window}
prcRect: PRect	{a pointer to a TRect structure}
): BOOL;	{returns TRUE or FALSE}

Description

This function displays a pop-up menu at the specified coordinates on the screen, sending a WM_COMMAND message back to the specified window when the user selects a menu item.

Parameters

hMenu: A handle to the pop-up menu to be displayed. This handle is returned from the CreatePopupMenu function when creating a new pop-up menu, or from the GetSubMenu function when retrieving a submenu or drop-down menu.

uFlags: A combination of flags that indicate the alignment of the pop-up menu in relation to its coordinates and which mouse button indicates a selection. This parameter can be zero or a combination of one item from Table 12-13 and one item from Table 12-14.

x: The horizontal coordinate at which to display the pop-up menu, relative to the screen.

y: The vertical coordinate at which to display the pop-up menu, relative to the screen.

nReserved: This parameter is reserved and must be set to zero.

hWnd: A handle to the window owning the displayed pop-up menu. This window will receive a WM_COMMAND message when the user selects a menu item. The window does not receive the message until after the TrackPopupMenu function returns.

prcRect: A pointer to a TRect structure containing coordinates, relative to the screen, in which the user can click without causing the pop-up menu to disappear. If this parameter is set to NIL, the pop-up menu disappears whenever the user clicks outside of the pop-up menu boundaries.

Return Value

If the function succeeds, it returns TRUE; otherwise it returns FALSE. To get extended error information, call the GetLastError function.

See Also

CreatePopupMenu, GetSubMenu, TrackPopupMenuEx

Example

Please see Listing 12-4 under CreatePopupMenu.

Table 12-13: TrackPopupMenu uFlags Alignment Values

Value	Description
TPM_CENTERALIGN	Centers the pop-up menu relative to the horizontal coordinate.
TPM_LEFTALIGN	Aligns the left side of the pop-up menu relative to the horizontal coordinate.
TPM_RIGHTALIGN	Aligns the right side of the pop-up menu relative to the horizontal coordinate.

Table 12-14: TrackPopupMenu uFlags Mouse Button Values

Value	Description
TPM_LEFTBUTTON	A menu item is selected when it is clicked with the left mouse button.
TPM_RIGHTBUTTON	A menu item is selected when it is clicked with the right mouse button.

TrackPopupMenuEx *Windows.Pas*

Syntax

```
TrackPopupMenuEx(
hMenu: HMENU;                {a handle to a pop-up menu}
Flags: UINT;                 {position and tracking flags}
x: Integer;                  {horizontal screen coordinates}
y: Integer;                  {vertical screen coordinates}
Wnd: HWND;                   {a handle to the owning window}
TPMParams: PTPMParams        {a pointer to a TPMParams structure}
): BOOL;                     {returns TRUE or FALSE}
```

Description

This function is equivalent to the TrackPopupMenu function, in that it displays a pop-up menu at the specified coordinates on the screen, sending a WM_COMMAND message back to the specified window when the user selects a menu item. However, it can additionally specify a rectangular area in which the pop-up menu cannot be displayed. If the pop-up menu would be displayed in this rectangular area, it is moved so as to not fall into this area. This is useful if a control on the form contains information that should not be obscured by the pop-up menu.

Parameters

hMenu: A handle to the pop-up menu to be displayed. This handle is returned from the CreatePopupMenu function when creating a new pop-up menu, or from the GetSub-Menu function when retrieving a submenu or drop-down menu.

Flags: A combination of flags that indicate the alignment of the pop-up menu in relation to its coordinates and which mouse button indicates a selection. This parameter can be zero or a combination of one item from Table 12-15, one item from Table 12-16, and one item from Table 12-17 (if desired).

x: The horizontal coordinate at which to display the pop-up menu, relative to the screen.

y: The vertical coordinate at which to display the pop-up menu, relative to the screen.

Wnd: A handle to the window owning the displayed pop-up menu. This window will receive a WM_COMMAND message when the user selects a menu item. The window does not receive the message until after the TrackPopupMenuEx function returns.

TPMParams: A pointer to a TPMParams structure containing a rectangular area, in screen coordinates, in which the pop-up menu will not appear. If this rectangular area is not needed, this parameter can be set to NIL. The TPMParams structure is defined as:

```
TTPMParams = packed record
     cbSize: UINT;              {the size of the structure}
     rcExclude: TRect;          {the rectangular coordinates}
end;
```

> *cbSize*: Specifies the size of the structure, in bytes. This member should be set to SizeOf(TPMParams).
>
> *rcExclude*: A TRect structure containing the coordinates, relative to the screen, of the rectangular area in which the pop-up menu should not appear.

Return Value

If the function succeeds, it returns TRUE; otherwise it returns FALSE. To get extended error information, call the GetLastError function.

See Also

CreatePopupMenu, GetSubMenu, TrackPopupMenu

Example

Listing 12-12: Displaying a Pop-up menu Without Obscuring a Control

```
procedure TForm1.FormMouseDown(Sender: TObject; Button: TMouseButton;
  Shift: TShiftState; X, Y: Integer);
var
  MenuPos: TPoint;         // holds the menu position in screen coordinates
  ExtraInfo: TTPMParams;   // holds the excluded rectangular area
begin
  {if the right mouse button was pressed, display the pop-up menu}
  if Button = mbRight then
  begin
    {translate the client coordinates into screen coordinates}
    MenuPos.X := X;
    MenuPos.Y := Y;
```

```
        MenuPos := ClientToScreen(MenuPos);

        {initialize the TTPMParams structure, setting the excluded rectangular area
         to that occupied by the list box}
        ExtraInfo.cbSize := SizeOf(TTPMParams);
        ExtraInfo.rcExclude.TopLeft := ClientToScreen(ListBox1.BoundsRect.TopLeft);
        ExtraInfo.rcExclude.BottomRight := ClientToScreen(ListBox1.BoundsRect.
                                           BottomRight);

        {display the pop-up menu}
        TrackPopupMenuEx(PopupMenu1.Handle, 0, MenuPos.X, MenuPos.Y, Form1.Handle,
                         @ExtraInfo);
      end;
  end;


{the overridden WM_COMMAND message}
procedure TForm1.WMCommand(var Msg: TMessage);
begin
  {this is required so that the Delphi pop-up menu control receives the
   correct messages and the functionality is not altered}
  PopupMenu1.DispatchCommand(Msg.wParam);
  inherited;
end;


procedure TForm1.Item11Click(Sender: TObject);
begin
  {display which menu item was selected}
  Label2.Caption := TMenuItem(Sender).Caption;
end;
```

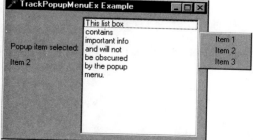

Figure 12-11:
The displayed
pop-up menu

Table 12-15: TrackPopupMenuEx uFlags Alignment Values

Value	Description
TPM_CENTERALIGN	Centers the pop-up menu relative to the horizontal coordinate.
TPM_LEFTALIGN	Aligns the left side of the pop-up menu relative to the horizontal coordinate.
TPM_RIGHTALIGN	Aligns the right side of the pop-up menu relative to the horizontal coordinate.

12

Chapter

Table 12-16: TrackPopupMenuEx uFlags Mouse Button Values

Value	Description
TPM_LEFTBUTTON	A menu item is selected when it is clicked with the left mouse button.
TPM_RIGHTBUTTON	A menu item is selected when it is clicked with the right mouse button.

Table 12-17: TrackPopupMenuEx uFlags Alignment Priority Values

Value	Description
TPM_HORIZONTAL	If the menu will overlap the excluded rectangular region and must be moved, the horizontal alignment has priority over the vertical alignment.
TPM_VERTICAL	If the menu will overlap the excluded rectangular region and must be moved, the vertical alignment has priority over the horizontal alignment.

Appendix A

Messages

If message functions like GetMessage, TranslateMessage, and DispatchMessage are the capillaries and arteries of Windows, messages are the individual blood cells. Even the simplest action usually results in a dozen or more messages being passed between the application and the system. Although it is possible to write very complex Delphi applications without ever being concerned with messages, sometimes handling or sending a message results in a much easier or elegant solution to a problem.

This appendix does not cover every Windows message available. Indeed, such coverage would result in a manual the size of this book or larger. This chapter covers the data structures for which Delphi has defined a large number of messages. These data structures help the developer deal with messages in an efficient manner, as they are more intuitive and informative than dealing with the raw wParam and lParam members of a traditional message.

WM_ACTIVATE

Syntax

```
TWMActivate = record
        Msg: Cardinal;              {the message identifier}
        Active: Word;               {the activation flag}
        Minimized: WordBool;        {the minimized state}
        ActiveWindow: HWND;         {a window handle}
        Result: Longint;            {returns a zero if handled}
    end;
```

Description

A window receives this message when it is being activated or deactivated. This message is sent first to the window being deactivated, and then to the window being activated. If the window being activated is not minimized, it receives the keyboard focus. If the window was activated by a mouse click, it also receives the WM_MOUSEACTIVATE message.

Members

Msg: The message identifier. This member is set to the message identifier constant WM_ACTIVATE.

Active: Indicates if the window is being activated or deactivated, and can be one value from Table A-1.

Minimized: Indicates the minimized state of the window being activated or deactivated. If the window is not minimized, this member will be FALSE.

ActiveWindow: Contains a handle to the window being activated or deactivated. This value is dependent on the value of the Active member. If the Active member contains WA_INACTIVE, this member contains a handle to the window being activated. If the Active member contains WA_ACTIVE or WA_CLICKACTIVE, this member contains a handle to the window being deactivated. This member can contain zero.

Result: If the application handles this message, set this member to zero.

See Also

SetActiveWindow, WM_MOUSEACTIVATE, WM_NCACTIVATE

Table A-I: TWMActivate.Active Values

Value	Description
WA_ACTIVE	The window was activated by some means other than a mouse click, either programmatically or through keyboard commands.
WA_CLICKACTIVE	The window was activated by a mouse click.
WA_INACTIVE	The window is being deactivated.

WM_ACTIVATEAPP

Syntax

```
TWMActivateApp = record
      Msg: Cardinal;          {the message identifier}
      Active: BOOL;           {the activation flag}
      ThreadId: Longint;      {a thread ID}
      Result: Longint;        {returns a zero if handled}
end;
```

Description

This message is sent when a window that does not belong to the current application is being activated. It is sent to both the application owning the window being activated and the application owning the window being deactivated.

Members

Msg: The message identifier. This member is set to the message identifier constant WM_ACTIVATEAPP.

Active: Indicates if the window is being activated or deactivated. If the window is being activated, this member is set to TRUE; otherwise it is set to FALSE.

ThreadId: A thread identifier for the window being activated or deactivated. If the Active member is set to TRUE, this member contains the thread identifier that owns the window being deactivated. If Active is FALSE, this member contains the thread identifier that owns the window being activated.

Result: If the application handles this message, set this member to zero.

See Also

WM_ACTIVATE

WM_ASKCBFORMATNAME

Syntax

```
TWMAskCBFormatName = record
    Msg: Cardinal;          {the message identifier}
    NameLen: Word;          {buffer size in bytes}
    Unused: Word;           {not used}
    FormatName: PChar;      {output buffer}
    Result: Longint;        {returns a zero if handled}
end;
```

Description

A clipboard viewer sends the WM_ASKCBFORMATNAME message to a clipboard owner to get the name of a CF_OWNERDISPLAY clipboard format. As a response, the clipboard owner places the format name in the output buffer provided by the viewer.

Members

Msg: The message identifier. This member is set to the message identifier constant WM_ASKCBFORMATNAME.

NameLen: Specifies the size of the output buffer pointed to by the FormatName member, in bytes.

Unused: This member is not used by this message.

FormatName: A pointer to a null-terminated string buffer that will hold the clipboard format name.

Result: If the application handles this message, set this member to zero.

See Also

WM_DRAWCLIPBOARD

WM_CANCELMODE

Syntax

```
TWMCancelMode = record
      Msg: Cardinal;                    {the message identifier}
      Unused: array[0..3] of Word;      {not used}
      Result: Longint;                  {returns a zero if handled}
  end;
```

Description

A window with the input focus receives a WM_CANCELMODE message when a dialog box or message box is displayed. The window that had focus can then cancel modes such as a mouse capture mode. Upon receiving the message, the DefWindowProc function will cancel internal processing, menu processing, and mouse capture.

Members

Msg: The message identifier. This member is set to the message identifier constant WM_CANCELMODE.

Unused: This member is not used by this message.

Result: If the application handles this message, set this member to zero.

See Also

DefWindowProc, ReleaseCapture

WM_CHANGECBCHAIN

Syntax

```
TWMChangeCBChain = record
      Msg: Cardinal;          {the message identifier}
      Remove: HWND;           {the window being removed}
      Next: HWND;             {the next window in the chain}
      Result: Longint;        {returns a zero if handled}
  end;
```

Description

When a window is being removed from a chain of clipboard viewer windows, a WM_CHANGECBCHAIN message is sent to the first window in that chain. Each window has the handle of the next window in the clipboard viewer chain. When a new clipboard viewer window is created, it becomes the first window in the clipboard viewer chain. Upon receiving this message, each clipboard viewer window should call the SendMessage function to send the message to the next window in the chain, unless the next window is the one being removed. In this case, the window should save the window handle identified by the Next member, as this will be the following window in the chain.

Members

Msg: The message identifier. This member is set to the message identifier constant WM_CHANGECBCHAIN.

Remove: The handle of the window to be removed from the clipboard viewer window chain.

Next: The handle of the next window in the clipboard viewer window chain. This member will contain zero if there are no more windows in the clipboard viewer chain.

Result: If the application handles this message, set this member to zero.

See Also

SendMessage, SetClipboardViewer

WM_CHAR

Syntax

```
TWMChar = record
    Msg: Cardinal;          {the message identifier}
    CharCode: Word;         {character code}
    Unused: Word;           {not used}
    KeyData: Longint;       {contains various information}
    Result: Longint;        {returns a zero if handled}
end;
```

Description

When a key is pressed, a WM_CHAR message is posted to the window that currently has the keyboard focus. This WM_CHAR message is the result of a WM_KEYDOWN message being translated by the TranslateMessage function.

The extended keys on a 101- or 102-key keyboard are:

In the main section of the keyboard, the right Alt and Ctrl keys.

To the left of the keypad, the Ins, Del, Home, End, Page Up, Page Down, and the four arrow keys.

On the numeric keypad, the Num Lock, divide (/), and Enter keys.

The PrintScrn and Break keys.

Members

Msg: The message identifier. This member is set to the message identifier constant WM_CHAR.

CharCode: The character code of the key that was pressed.

Unused: This member is not used by this message.

KeyData: Specifies the repeat count, scan code, extended key flag, context code, previous key state flag, and the transition state flag. Table A-2 shows which information is in which bit position within the 32-bit value of the KeyData member. The high-order word, bits 16 to 31, pertains to the immediately preceding WM_KEYDOWN message which generated the WM_CHAR message through the TranslateMessage function.

Result: If the application handles this message, set this member to zero.

See Also

TranslateMessage, WM_KEYDOWN

Table A-2: TWMChar.KeyData Values

Value	Description
0-15	The repeat count resulting from the user holding down the key.
16-23	The scan code, whose value depends on the OEM maker of the keyboard.
24	The extended key flag. If the key is an extended key (the right-hand Alt and Ctrl keys), this bit is set (1); otherwise it is not set (0).
25-28	Unused.
29	The context code. If the Alt key was held down while the key was pressed, this bit is set (1); otherwise it is not set (0).
30	The previous key state. If the key was held down before the message is sent, this bit is set (1); otherwise it is not set (0).
31	The transition state. If the key is being released, this bit is set (1); otherwise it is not set (0).

WM_CHARTOITEM

Syntax

```
TWMCharToItem = record
      Msg: Cardinal;          {the message identifier}
      Key: Word;              {the value of the key}
      CaretPos: Word;         {the caret position}
      ListBox: HWND;          {the list box handle}
      Result: Longint;        {returns a -1 or -2 if handled}
end;
```

Description

When a list box with the LBS_WANTKEYBOARDINPUT style receives a WM_CHAR message, it sends a WM_CHARTOITEM message to its owner.

Members

Msg: The message identifier. This member is set to the message identifier constant WM_CHARTOITEM.

Key: The value of the key sent by the WM_CHAR message.

CaretPos: The position of the caret in the list box.

ListBox: The handle of the list box.

Result: If the application handles this message, set this member to -1 or -2. If the list box should perform its default action in addition to any application specific message handling, set this member to the zero-based index of the given item in the list box.

See Also

DefWindowProc, WM_CHAR

WM_CHILDACTIVATE

Syntax

```
TWMChildActivate = record
      Msg: Cardinal;                    {the message identifier}
      Unused: array[0..3] of Word;      {not used}
      Result: Longint;                  {returns a zero if handled}
   end;
```

Description

The WM_CHILDACTIVATE message is sent to a multiple document interface (MDI) child window when it is activated.

Members

Msg: The message identifier. This member is set to the message identifier constant WM_CHILDACTIVATE.

Unused: This member is not used by this message.

Result: If the application handles this message, set this member to zero.

See Also

MoveWindow, SetWindowPos

WM_CLEAR

Syntax

```
TWMClear = record
      Msg: Cardinal;                    {the message identifier}
      Unused: array[0..3] of Word;      {not used}
```

Result: Longint;   {not used}
    end;

Description

The WM_CLEAR message is sent to a combo box or an edit control whenever the current selection is to be deleted or cleared.

Members

Msg: The message identifier. This member is set to the message identifier constant WM_CLEAR.

Unused: This member is not used by this message.

Result: This member is not used by this message.

See Also

WM_COPY, WM_CUT, WM_PASTE

WM_CLOSE

Syntax

TWMClose = record
        Msg: Cardinal;   {the message identifier}
        Unused: array[0..3] of Word;   {not used}
        Result: Longint;   {returns a zero if handled}
    end;

Description

When a window or application is to be closed or terminated, it receives a WM_CLOSE message.

Members

Msg: The message identifier. This member is set to the message identifier constant WM_CLOSE.

Unused: This member is not used by this message.

Result: If the application handles this message, set this member to zero.

See Also

DefWindowProc, DestroyWindow

WM_COMMAND

Syntax

TWMCommand = record
        Msg: Cardinal;   {the message identifier}

```
        ItemID: Word;              {an item identifier}
        NotifyCode: Word;          {the notification code}
        Ctl: HWND;                 {the control handle}
        Result: Longint;           {returns a zero if handled}
    end;
```

Description

The WM_COMMAND message is sent when the user presses an accelerator key, a control sends a notification message to a parent window, or the user makes a menu selection. This message is not sent when a user makes a selection from a system menu. Selecting a system menu item sends a WM_SYSCOMMAND message. The system menu is the menu presented when clicking on the icon in the upper left corner of a window. If the window is minimized and an accelerator key is pressed, the WM_COMMAND message will be sent only if the key does not correspond to any menu items in that window's menu or in the system menu.

Members

Msg: The message identifier. This member is set to the message identifier constant WM_COMMAND.

ItemID: The identifier of the menu item, control, or accelerator. This member is set to zero if the user selects a menu separator item.

NotifyCode: Indicates if the message originated from a control, menu item, or accelerator. This member will be set to zero if the message is from a menu item or one if the message is from an accelerator. Any other value indicates a specific notification code from a control.

Ctl: The handle of the control sending the message. This member is set to zero if the message was sent as a result of accelerator key or menu selection.

Result: If the application handles this message, set this member to zero.

See Also

WM_SYSCOMMAND

WM_COMPACTING

Syntax

```
    TWMCompacting = record
        Msg: Cardinal;             {the message identifier}
        CompactRatio: Longint;     {CPU time ratio}
        Unused: Longint;           {not used}
        Result: Longint;           {returns a zero if handled}
    end;
```

Description

The WM_COMPACTING message indicates a low-memory situation. It is sent to all top-level windows when more than one-eighth of the system time in a 30- to 60-second interval is being used for compacting memory. The application should respond by freeing any unused or unneeded memory.

Members

Msg: The message identifier. This member is set to the message identifier constant WM_COMPACTING.

CompactRatio: The ratio of CPU time spent compacting memory to CPU time spent performing all other operations.

Unused: This member is not used by this message.

Result: If the application handles this message, set this member to zero.

See Also

WM_CLOSE, WM_DESTROY, WM_QUIT

WM_COMPAREITEM

Syntax

```
TWMCompareItem = record                              {the message identifier}
    Msg: Cardinal;                                   {the handle of the control}
    Ctl: HWnd;                                       {a pointer to the compare
    CompareItemStruct: PCompareItemStruct;            structure}
                                                     {returns the comparison result}
    Result: Longint;
end;
```

Description

The WM_COMPAREITEM message is sent to the owner of a list box or combo box object when an application adds an item to the object, if it was created with a style of LBS_SORT or CBS_SORT, respectively. It identifies two items whose relative position in the list of items is to be determined. The return value indicates the result of that comparison. For a list with several existing items, Windows will send several WM_COMPAREITEM messages until the exact position of the new item is determined.

Members

Msg: The message identifier. This member is set to the message identifier constant WM_COMPAREITEM.

Ctl: The handle of the control that sent the message.

CompareItemStruct: A pointer to a TCompareItemStruct structure containing information about the two items whose list position is being determined. The TCompareItemStruct structure is defined as:

```
TCompareItemStruct = packed record
     CtlType: UINT;              {the type of control}
     CtlID: UINT;                {the control identifier}
     hwndItem: HWND;             {a handle to the control}
     itemID1: UINT;              {the index of the first item}
     itemData1: DWORD;           {the data being compared}
     itemID2: UINT;              {the index of the second item}
     itemData2: DWORD;           {the data being compared}
     dwLocaleId: DWORD;          {the locale identifier}
end;
```

CtlType: Identifies the type of control that generated the message, and can contain ODT_LISTBOX if the items are in an owner-drawn list box or ODT_COMBOBOX for an owner-drawn combo box.

CtlID: The identifier of the list box or combo box.

hwndItem: The handle of the control sending the message.

itemID1: The index of the first item in the list being compared.

itemData1: The data to be compared. This is the lParam parameter of the message sent by the application that added the item being compared.

itemID2: The index of the second item in the list being compared.

itemData2: The data to be compared. This is the lParam parameter of the message sent by the application that added the item being compared.

dwLocaleId: The locale identifier that can be used as the basis for the comparison.

Result: The message returns a value indicating the relative order of the two items being compared. The message should return -1 if the item identified by the itemData1 member should precede the item identified by itemData2 in the list, it should return 0 if the two items are considered equal, and it should return 1 if itemData2 should precede itemData1 in the list.

See Also

WM_DELETEITEM

WM_COPY

Syntax

```
TWMCopy = record
     Msg: Cardinal;              {the message identifier}
     Unused: array[0..3] of Word;  {not used}
```

```
        Result: Longint;                    {not used}
end;
```

Description

The WM_COPY message is sent to an edit control or combo box when the application or user invokes a copy method (such as Ctrl+C) that will place selected text into the clipboard. The control receiving the message should place its selected text onto the clipboard in the CF_TEXT format.

Members

Msg: The message identifier. This member is set to the message identifier constant WM_COPY.

Unused: This member is not used by this message.

Result: This member is not used by this message.

See Also

WM_CLEAR, WM_CUT, WM_PASTE

WM_COPYDATA

Syntax

```
TWMCopyData = record
    Msg: Cardinal;                          {the message identifier}
    From: HWND;                             {the handle of the sender}
    CopyDataStruct: PCopyDataStruct;        {a pointer to the data being sent}
    Result: Longint;                        {returns a one if handled}
end;
```

Description

The WM_COPYDATA message allows an application to send data to any other application. This message may only be sent with the SendMessage function, and the data identified by the CopyDataStruct member must not contain any pointers or other references to objects or memory that will not be available to the receiving process. During processing, the receiving application should consider the data read only. If it must modify the data, it should copy the data to a local buffer.

Members

Msg: The message identifier. This member is set to the message identifier constant WM_COPYDATA.

From: The handle of the window sending the message.

CopyDataStruct: A pointer to a TCopyDataStruct structure containing the data to be sent to the other application. The TCopyDataStruct structure is defined as:

```
TCopyDataStruct = packed record
     dwData: DWORD;           {a 32-bit data value}
     cbData: DWORD;           {the size of the lpData buffer}
     lpData: Pointer;         {a pointer to additional data}
end;
```

> *dwData*: A 32-bit data value to be passed to the other application.
>
> *cbData*: Specifies the size of the data buffer pointed to by the lpData member.
>
> *lpData*: A pointer to additional data.

Result: If the application handles this message, set this member to one.

See Also

PostMessage, SendMessage

WM_CREATE

Syntax

```
TWMCreate = record
     Msg: Cardinal;              {the message identifier}
     Unused: Integer;            {not used}
     CreateStruct: PCreateStruct; {a pointer to the create structure}
     Result: Longint;            {returns a window creation code}
end;
```

Description

When an application creates a new window by calling the CreateWindow or CreateWindowEx functions, Windows sends a WM_CREATE message to the window procedure of the new window after it is created but before it becomes visible, and before the CreateWindow or CreateWindowEx functions return. The structure carried by the message contains specifications for the new window, and is identical to the information passed to the CreateWindowEx function.

Members

Msg: The message identifier. This member is set to the message identifier constant WM_CREATE.

Unused: This member is not used by this message.

CreateStruct: A pointer to a TCreateStruct structure that contains information about the new window. The TCreateStruct structure is defined as:

```
TCreateStruct = packed record
     lpCreateParams: Pointer;    {a pointer to application-defined data}
     hInstance: HINST;           {a handle to the module instance}
     hMenu: HMENU;               {a handle to the menu, or a child window identifier}
     hwndParent: HWND;           {a handle to the parent window}
```

cy: Integer;	{initial height of the window}
cx: Integer;	{initial width of the window}
y: Integer;	{initial vertical position}
x: Integer;	{initial horizontal position}
style: Longint;	{window style flags}
lpszName: PAnsiChar;	{a pointer to the window name string}
lpszClass: PAnsiChar;	{a pointer to the class name string}
dwExStyle: DWORD;	{extended window style flags}

end;

The lpCreateParams member is a pointer to application-defined data. The other members of this structure contain the information passed in the parameters to the CreateWindow or CreateWindowEx function.

Result: If the application handles this message, it should return a zero to indicate that the window can be created. If the application returns -1, the new window will be destroyed and the CreateWindow or CreateWindowEx function that generated the message will return a zero for the window handle.

See Also

CreateWindow, CreateWindowEx, WM_NCCREATE

WM_CTLCOLORBTN

Syntax

TWMCtlColorBtn = record	
Msg: Cardinal;	{the message identifier}
ChildDC: HDC;	{the device context of the button}
ChildWnd: HWND;	{the window handle of the button}
Result: Longint;	{returns a brush handle}

end;

Description

The WM_CTLCOLORBTN message is sent to a button's parent window whenever the button is about to be drawn. The parent window can respond by setting the button's text and background colors. This message is sent only within a single thread, and cannot be sent between threads.

Members

Msg: The message identifier. This member is set to the message identifier constant WM_CTLCOLORBTN.

ChildDC: A handle to the device context of the button that is to be drawn.

ChildWnd: The window handle of the button that is to be drawn.

Result: If the application handles this message, it should return a handle to a brush that Windows uses to paint the background of the button.

See Also

DefWindowProc, RealizePalette, SelectPalette, WM_CTLCOLOREDIT, WM_CTLCOLORLISTBOX, WM_CTLCOLORMSGBOX, WM_CTLCOLORSCROLLBAR, WM_CTLCOLORSTATIC

WM_CTLCOLOREDIT

Syntax

```
TWMCtlColorEdit = record
    Msg: Cardinal;              {the message identifier}
    ChildDC: HDC;               {the device context of the edit box}
    ChildWnd: HWND;             {the window handle of the edit box}
    Result: Longint;            {returns a brush handle}
end;
```

Description

The WM_CTLCOLOREDIT message is sent to an edit control's parent window whenever the edit control is about to be drawn. The parent window can respond by setting the edit control's text and background colors. This message is sent only within a single thread, and cannot be sent between threads.

Members

Msg: The message identifier. This member is set to the message identifier constant WM_CTLCOLOREDIT.

ChildDC: A handle to the device context of the edit control that is to be drawn.

ChildWnd: The window handle of the edit control that is to be drawn.

Result: If the application handles this message, it should return a handle to a brush that Windows uses to paint the background of the edit control.

See Also

DefWindowProc, RealizePalette, SelectPalette, WM_CTLCOLORBTN, WM_CTLCOLORLISTBOX, WM_CTLCOLORMSGBOX, WM_CTLCOLORSCROLLBAR, WM_CTLCOLORSTATIC

WM_CTLCOLORLISTBOX

Syntax

```
TWMCtlColorListbox = record
    Msg: Cardinal;              {the message identifier}
    ChildDC: HDC;               {the device context of the list box}
    ChildWnd: HWND;             {the window handle of the list box}
    Result: Longint;            {returns a brush handle}
end;
```

Description

The WM_CTLCOLORLISTBOX message is sent to a list box's parent window whenever the list box is about to be drawn. The parent window can respond by setting the list box's text and background colors. This message is sent only within a single thread, and cannot be sent between threads.

Members

Msg: The message identifier. This member is set to the message identifier constant WM_CTLCOLORLISTBOX.

ChildDC: A handle to the device context of the list box that is to be drawn.

ChildWnd: The window handle of the list box that is to be drawn.

Result: If the application handles this message, it should return a handle to a brush that Windows uses to paint the background of the list box.

See Also

DefWindowProc, RealizePalette, SelectPalette, WM_CTLCOLORBTN, WM_CTLCOLOREDIT, WM_CTLCOLORMSGBOX, WM_CTLCOLORSCROLLBAR, WM_CTLCOLORSTATIC

WM_CTLCOLORMSGBOX

Syntax

```
TWMCtlColorMsgbox = record
      Msg: Cardinal;          {the message identifier}
      ChildDC: HDC;           {the device context of the message box}
      ChildWnd: HWND;         {the window handle of the message box}
      Result: Longint;        {returns a brush handle}
end;
```

Description

The WM_CTLCOLORMSGBOX message is sent to a message box's parent window whenever the message box is about to be drawn. The parent window can respond by setting the message box's text and background colors. This message is sent only within a single thread, and cannot be sent between threads.

Members

Msg: The message identifier. This member is set to the message identifier constant WM_CTLCOLORMSGBOX.

ChildDC: A handle to the device context of the message box to be drawn.

ChildWnd: The window handle of the message box to be drawn.

Result: If the application handles this message, it should return a handle to a brush that Windows uses to paint the background of the message box.

See Also

DefWindowProc, RealizePalette, SelectPalette, WM_CTLCOLORBTN, WM_CTLCOLOREDIT, WM_CTLCOLORLISTBOX, WM_CTLCOLORSCROLLBAR, WM_CTLCOLORSTATIC

WM_CTLCOLORSCROLLBAR

Syntax

```
TWMCtlColorScrollbar = record
     Msg: Cardinal;              {the message identifier}
     ChildDC: HDC;               {the device context of the scroll bar}
     ChildWnd: HWND;             {the window handle of the scroll bar}
     Result: Longint;            {returns a brush handle}
end;
```

Description

The WM_CTLCOLORSCROLLBAR message is sent to a scroll bar's parent window whenever the scroll bar is about to be drawn. The parent window can respond by setting the scroll bar's text and background colors. This message is sent only within a single thread, and cannot be sent between threads.

Members

Msg: The message identifier. This member is set to the message identifier constant WM_CTLCOLORSCROLLBAR.

ChildDC: A handle to the device context of the scroll bar to be drawn.

ChildWnd: The window handle of the scroll bar to be drawn.

Result: If the application handles this message, it should return a handle to a brush that Windows uses to paint the background of the scroll bar.

See Also

DefWindowProc, RealizePalette, SelectPalette, WM_CTLCOLORBTN, WM_CTLCOLOREDIT, WM_CTLCOLORLISTBOX, WM_CTLCOLORMSGBOX, WM_CTLCOLORSTATIC

WM_CTLCOLORSTATIC

Syntax

```
TWMCtlColorStatic = record
     Msg: Cardinal;              {the message identifier}
     ChildDC: HDC;               {the device context of the static control}
     ChildWnd: HWND;             {the window handle of the static control}
     Result: Longint;            {returns a brush handle}
end;
```

Description

The WM_CTLCOLORSTATIC message is sent to a static control's parent window whenever the static control is about to be drawn. The parent window can respond by setting the static control's text and background colors. This message is sent only within a single thread, and cannot be sent between threads.

Members

Msg: The message identifier. This member is set to the message identifier constant WM_CTLCOLORSTATIC.

ChildDC: A handle to the device context of the static control to be drawn.

ChildWnd: The window handle of the static control to be drawn.

Result: If the application handles this message, it should return a handle to a brush that Windows uses to paint the background of the static control.

See Also

DefWindowProc, RealizePalette, SelectPalette, WM_CTLCOLORBTN, WM_CTLCOLOREDIT, WM_CTLCOLORLISTBOX, WM_CTLCOLORMSGBOX, WM_CTLCOLORSCROLLBAR

WM_CUT

Syntax

```
TWMCut = record
      Msg: Cardinal;                {the message identifier}
      Unused: array[0..3] of Word;  {not used}
      Result: Longint;              {not used}
   end;
```

Description

The WM_CUT message is sent to an edit control or combo box when the application or user invokes a cut method (such as Ctrl+X) that will place selected text into the clipboard. The control receiving the message should delete the selected text and place it onto the clipboard in the CF_TEXT format.

Members

Msg: The message identifier. This member is set to the message identifier constant WM_CUT.

Unused: This member is not used by this message.

Result: This member is not used by this message.

See Also

WM_CLEAR, WM_COPY, WM_PASTE

WM_DEADCHAR

Syntax

```
TWMDeadChar = record
    Msg: Cardinal;              {the message identifier}
    CharCode: Word;            {the character code}
    Unused: Word;              {not used}
    KeyData: Longint;          {contains various information}
    Result: Longint;           {returns a zero if handled}
end;
```

Description

When a WM_KEYDOWN message is translated by a call to the TranslateMessage function, a WM_DEADCHAR message is sent to the window with the keyboard focus. This message is generated as a result of pressing a dead key. A dead key is a key that generates an additional character to be used in combination with another key to create a combined, or "composite," character. This is typically a character with an accent or diacritical mark. The dead key identifying the accent or diacritical mark is entered first, followed by the key identifying the character that will have the mark applied to it.

Members

Msg: The message identifier. This member is set to the message identifier constant WM_DEADCHAR.

CharCode: The character code of the key that was pressed.

Unused: This member is not used by this message.

KeyData: Specifies the repeat count, scan code, extended key flag, context code, previous key state flag, and the transition state flag. Table A-3 shows which information is in which bit position within the 32-bit value of the KeyData member. The high-order word, bits 16 to 31, pertains to the immediately preceding WM_KEYDOWN message which generated the WM_DEADCHAR message through the TranslateMessage function.

Result: If the application handles this message, set this member to zero.

See Also

TranslateMessage, WM_KEYDOWN, WM_KEYUP, WM_SYSDEADCHAR, WM_SYSKEYDOWN

Table A-3: TWMDeadChar.KeyData Values

Value	Description
0-15	The repeat count resulting from the user holding down the key.
16-23	The scan code, whose value depends on the OEM maker of the keyboard.

Value	Description
24	The extended key flag. If the key is an extended key (the right-hand Alt and Ctrl keys), this bit is set (1); otherwise it is not set (0).
25-28	Unused.
29	The context code. If the Alt key was held down while the key was pressed, this bit is set (1); otherwise it is not set (0).
30	The previous key state. If the key was held down before the message is sent, this bit is set (1); otherwise it is not set (0).
31	The transition state. If the key is being released, this bit is set (1); otherwise it is not set (0).

WM_DELETEITEM

Syntax

```
TWMDeleteItem = record
      Msg: Cardinal;                          {the message identifier}
      Ctl: HWND;                              {the handle of the control}
      DeleteItemStruct: PDeleteItemStruct;    {a pointer to a deleted item data
                                               structure}
      Result: Longint;                        {returns a one if handled}
end;
```

Description

The owner of a list box or combo box receives a WM_DELETEITEM message whenever the control is destroyed or when an item is to be removed from the control as a result of a LB_DELETESTRING, LB_RESETCONTENT, CB_DELETESTRING, or CB_RESETCONTENT message. When deleting items, a WM_DELETEITEM message is sent for each item deleted. Under Windows NT, this message is sent only when deleting items from an owner-drawn combo box or list box.

Members

Msg: The message identifier. This member is set to the message identifier constant WM_DELETEITEM.

Ctl: The handle of the list box or combo box sending the message.

DeleteItemStruct: A pointer to a TDeleteItemStruct structure containing information about the item to be deleted. The TDeleteItemStruct structure is defined as:

```
TDeleteItemStruct = packed record
      CtlType: UINT;        {the type of control}
      CtlID: UINT;          {the control identifier}
      itemID: UINT;         {the index of the item within the control}
      hwndItem: HWND;       {a handle to the control}
```

```
    itemData: UINT;              {the item data}
end;
```

CtlType: Contains a flag specifying the type of control from which the item was deleted. This member will contain either ODT_LISTBOX, indicating a list box, or ODT_COMBOBOX, indicating a combo box.

CtlID: The identifier of the list box or combo box.

itemID: The index of the item in the control to be removed.

hwndItem: The handle of the control requesting the deletion.

itemData: The application-defined data for the specified item.

Result: If the application handles this message, set this member to one.

See Also

WM_COMPAREITEM

WM_DESTROY

Syntax

```
TWMDestroy = record
    Msg: Cardinal;              {the message identifier}
    Unused: array[0..3] of Word;  {not used}
    Result: Longint;            {returns a zero if handled}
end;
```

Description

The WM_DESTROY message is sent to a window that is being destroyed, after it is removed from the display but before the window handle is invalidated. During the destruction process, the WM_DESTROY message is passed on to all child windows. If the window is part of a clipboard viewer chain, it must remove itself from the chain by calling the ChangeClipboardChain function before returning from the WM_DESTROY message.

Members

Msg: The message identifier. This member is set to the message identifier constant WM_DESTROY.

Unused: This member is not used by this message.

Result: If the application handles this message, set this member to zero.

See Also

ChangeClipboardChain, DestroyWindow, PostQuitMessage, SetClipboardViewer, WM_CLOSE

WM_DESTROYCLIPBOARD

Syntax

```
TWMDestroyClipboard = record
      Msg: Cardinal;                    {the message identifier}
      Unused: array[0..3] of Word;      {not used}

      Result: Longint;                  {returns a zero if handled}
end;
```

Description

When the EmptyClipboard function is called to empty the clipboard, the WM_DESTROYCLIPBOARD message is sent to the clipboard owner.

Members

Msg: The message identifier. This member is set to the message identifier constant WM_DESTROYCLIPBOARD.

Unused: This member is not used by this message.

Result: If the application handles this message, set this member to zero.

See Also

EmptyClipboard

WM_DEVMODECHANGE

Syntax

```
TWMDevModeChange = record
      Msg: Cardinal;         {the message identifier}
      Unused: Integer;       {not used}
      Device: PChar;         {the device name}
      Result: Longint;       {returns a zero if handled}
end;
```

Description

All top-level windows receive a WM_DEVMODECHANGE message when the device-mode settings are changed by the user.

Members

Msg: The message identifier. This member is set to the message identifier constant WM_DEVMODECHANGE.

Unused: This member is not used by this message.

Device: A pointer to a null-terminated string containing the name of the device being changed, as stored in the Win.ini file or the registry.

Result: If the application handles this message, set this member to zero.

See Also

RegSetValue, RegSetValueEx

WM_DISPLAYCHANGE

Syntax

```
TWMDisplayChange = record
      Msg: Cardinal;              {the message identifier}
      BitsPerPixel: Integer;      {the color depth}
      Width: Word;                {the horizontal screen size}
      Height: Word;               {the vertical screen size}
end;
```

Description

The WM_DISPLAYCHANGE message is sent to all top-level windows when the display resolution changes.

Members

Msg: The message identifier. This member is set to the message identifier constant WM_DISPLAYCHANGE.

BitsPerPixel: The color depth of the display, in bits per pixel.

Width: The horizontal screen size, in pixels.

Height: The vertical screen size, in pixels.

See Also

ChangeDisplaySettings

WM_DRAWCLIPBOARD

Syntax

```
TWMDrawClipboard = record
      Msg: Cardinal;              {the message identifier}
      Unused: array[0..3] of Word; {not used}
      Result: Longint;            {not used}
end;
```

Description

The WM_DRAWCLIPBOARD message is sent to the first window in the clipboard viewer chain when the contents of the clipboard change, indicating that the viewer window should redisplay its contents to reflect the new contents of the clipboard. Only windows added to the clipboard viewer chain by a call to the SetClipboardViewer function will receive this message. Each window in the clipboard viewer chain must pass this message to the next window in the chain via the SendMessage function so that all viewer windows are notified.

Members

Msg: The message identifier. This member is set to the message identifier constant WM_DRAWCLIPBOARD.

Unused: This member is not used by this message.

Result: This member is not used by this message.

See Also

SendMessage, SetClipboardViewer, WM_CHANGECBCHAIN

WM_DRAWITEM

Syntax

```
TWMDrawItem = record
        Msg: Cardinal;                    {the message identifier}
        Ctl: HWND;                        {the handle of the control sending the
                                           message}
        DrawItemStruct: PDrawItemStruct;  {a pointer to a DrawItemStruct data
                                           structure}
        Result: Longint;                  {returns a one if handled}
    end;
```

Description

The owner of an owner-drawn list box, combo box, menu item, or button receives a WM_DRAWITEM message when some visual aspect of the control changes, such as focus, enabled status, etc. To create an owner-drawn menu item, use the Insert-MenuItem or SetMenuItemInfo functions.

Members

Msg: The message identifier. This member is set to the message identifier constant WM_DRAWITEM.

Ctl: The handle of the window that is sending the WM_DRAWITEM message.

DrawItemStruct: A pointer to a TDrawItemStruct structure that contains information about the control needed by the owner for painting. The TDrawItemStruct structure is defined as:

```
TDrawItemStruct = packed record
        CtlType: UINT;        {the control type flag}
        CtlID: UINT;          {the control identifier}
```

```
    itemID: UINT;                    {a menu identifier or item index}
    itemAction: UINT;                {drawing action flags}
    itemState: UINT;                 {the visual state of the item}
    hwndItem: HWND;                  {the handle of the control}
    hDC: HDC;                        {the device context}
    rcItem: TRect;                   {the item rectangle}
    itemData: DWORD;                 {the 32-bit item data}
  end;
```

CtlType: A flag specifying the type of control. This member can contain one value from Table A-4.

CtlID: Specifies the identifier of the control. This member is ignored if the control is a menu item.

itemID: This member contains the menu item identifier for menu items or the index of a selected item for list boxes and combo boxes. A value of -1 indicates an empty list box or combo box. This allows the owner of the control to redraw only the portion of the control specified in the rcItem member, and is useful for drawing the focus rectangle.

itemAction: Flags indicating what actions should be taken when drawing the item. This member can be one or more values from Table A-5.

itemState: Indicates the new visual state of the control. This member can contain one or more values from Table A-6.

hwndItem: The window handle for combo boxes, list boxes, buttons, and static controls. For menu items, this member contains the window handle of the menu containing the item.

hDC: The device context in which the drawing is to be performed.

rcItem: The rectangle inside the specified device context where the drawing is to be performed. For all controls except menu items, drawing functions are clipped to this rectangular area.

itemData: Specifies the 32-bit data value that was supplied as the lParam parameter of the CB_ADDSTRING, CB_INSERTSTRING, LB_ADDSTRING, or LB_INSERTSTRING messages, or the value last assigned to the control by the LB_SETITEMDATA or CB_SETITEMDATA messages. For a list box or combo box with LBS_HASSTRINGS or CBS_HASSTRINGS, this member is initially zero. If the ctlType member contains the ODT_BUTTON or ODT_STATIC flags, this member is zero.

Result: If the application handles this message, set this member to one.

See Also

WM_MEASUREITEM

Table A-4: TWMDrawItem.TDrawItemStruct.CtlType Values

Value	Description
ODT_BUTTON	Indicates an owner-drawn button.
ODT_COMBOBOX	Indicates an owner-drawn combo box.
ODT_LISTBOX	Indicates an owner-drawn list box.
ODT_LISTVIEW	Indicates an owner-drawn list view.
ODT_MENU	Indicates an owner-drawn menu item.
ODT_STATIC	Indicates an owner-drawn static control.
ODT_TAB	Indicates an owner-drawn tab control.

Table A-5: TWMDrawItem.TDrawItemStruct.itemAction Values

Value	Description
ODA_DRAWENTIRE	The entire control should be drawn.
ODA_FOCUS	The keyboard focus has changed. Check the itemState member for focus status.
ODA_SELECT	The selection status has changed. Check the itemState member for selection status.

Table A-6: TWMDrawItem.TDrawItemStruct.ItemState Values

Value	Description
ODS_CHECKED	The menu item is checked.
ODS_COMBOBOXEDIT	The drawing action is in the edit box of a combo box.
ODS_DEFAULT	Indicates the default item.
ODS_DISABLED	The item should be drawn disabled.
ODS_FOCUS	The item has keyboard focus.
ODS_GRAYED	The menu item is grayed out.
ODS_SELECTED	The menu item is selected.

WM_DROPFILES

Syntax

```
TWMDropFiles = record
        Msg: Cardinal;              {the message identifier}
        Drop: THANDLE;              {the drop structure handle}
        Unused: Longint;            {not used}
        Result: Longint;            {returns a zero if handled}
end;
```

A

Description

If a window is registered to receive files dragged and dropped from the Explorer or File Manager, the WM_DROPFILES message is sent when the user releases the left mouse button on the window to complete the file drag and drop operation. Use the DragAcceptFiles function to register a window as a dropped file recipient.

Members

Msg: The message identifier. This member is set to the message identifier constant WM_DROPFILES.

Drop: The handle of the internal structure that tracks the files being dragged and dropped.

Unused: This member is not used by this message.

Result: If the application handles this message, set this member to zero.

See Also

DragAcceptFiles, DragFinish, DragQueryFile, DragQueryPoint

WM_ENABLE

Syntax

```
TWMEnable = record
      Msg: Cardinal;              {the message identifier}
      Enabled: LongBool;          {the enabled flag}
      Unused: Longint;            {not used}
      Result: Longint;            {returns a zero if handled}
end;
```

Description

When an application changes the enabled status of a window, a WM_ENABLE message is sent to the window whose enabled status is changing. It is sent after the enabled status has changed, but before the EnableWindow function returns.

Members

Msg: The message identifier. This member is set to the message identifier constant WM_ENABLE.

Enabled: This member is set to TRUE if the window is now enabled, or FALSE if it is disabled.

Unused: This member is not used by this message.

Result: If the application handles this message, set this member to zero.

See Also

EnableWindow

WM_ENDSESSION

Syntax

```
TWMEndSession = record
       Msg: Cardinal;            {the message identifier}
       EndSession: LongBool;     {the end session flag}
       Unused: Longint;          {the logoff flag}
       Result: Longint;          {returns a zero if handled}
   end;
```

Description

After the WM_QUERYENDSESSION message is sent to all windows and the results are processed, Windows sends a WM_ENDSESSION message to every application, indicating if the Windows session is ending.

Members

Msg: The message identifier. This member is set to the message identifier constant WM_ENDSESSION.

EndSession: Indicates if the Windows session is ending. If this member is set to TRUE, the session is ending; otherwise it will be set to FALSE.

Unused: Indicates if the user is simply logging off from the current session or is shutting the entire system down. If the user is logging off, this member will be set to ENDSESSION_LOGOFF. If the user is shutting down the system, this member will be set to zero.

Result: If the application handles this message, set this member to zero.

See Also

DestroyWindow, PostQuitMessage, WM_QUERYENDSESSION

WM_ENTERIDLE

Syntax

```
TWMEnterIdle = record
       Msg: Cardinal;            {the message identifier}
       Source: Longint;          {the control type}
       IdleWnd: HWND;            {the handle of the control}
       Result: Longint;          {returns a zero if handled}
   end;
```

Description

If a modal dialog box or a menu is being displayed, and all messages have been processed from its message queue, the menu or modal dialog box enters an idle state and the WM_ENTERIDLE message is sent to the menu or dialog box's owner.

Members

Msg: The message identifier. This member is set to the message identifier constant WM_ENTERIDLE.

Source: Indicates whether a dialog box or a menu is being displayed. This member can be one value from Table A-7.

IdleWnd: The handle of the dialog box or the handle of the window containing the menu.

Result: If the application handles this message, set this member to zero.

See Also

DefWindowProc, WM_ACTIVATE, WM_MOUSEACTIVATE

Table A-7: TWMEnterIdle.Source Values

Value	Descriptions
MSGF_DIALOGBOX	Indicates that a dialog box is displayed.
MSGF_MENU	Indicates that a menu is displayed.

WM_ENTERMENULOOP

Syntax

```
TWMEnterMenuLoop = record
      Msg: Cardinal;                      {the message identifier}
      IsTrackPopupMenu: LongBool;   {shortcut menu flag}
      Unused: Longint;                    {not used}
      Result: Longint;                    {returns a zero if handled}
end;
```

Description

The WM_ENTERMENULOOP message is sent to the main window of an application when a menu is being displayed and the menu modal loop has been entered.

Members

Msg: The message identifier. This member is set to the message identifier constant WM_ENTERMENULOOP.

IsTrackPopupMenu: Indicates if the menu is a pop-up menu or a regular menu. If this member is set to TRUE, the menu is a pop-up menu; otherwise it is a regular menu.

Unused: This member is not used by this message.

Result: If the application handles this message, set this member to zero.

See Also

DefWindowProc, WM_EXITMENULOOP

WM_ERASEBKGND

Syntax

```
TWMEraseBkgnd = record
        Msg: Cardinal;                {the message identifier}
        DC: HDC;                      {device context}
        Unused: Longint;             {not used}
        Result: Longint;             {returns a one if handled}
    end;
```

Description

This message is sent to a window whose background has been invalidated, by actions such as resizing, and needs to be erased. Typically, the window background is erased by redrawing the invalid region using the window class's background brush.

Members

Msg: The message identifier. This member is set to the message identifier constant WM_ERASEBKGND.

DC: The device context of the window whose background is to be erased.

Unused: This member is not used by this message.

Result: If the application handles this message, set this member to one.

See Also

BeginPaint, DefWindowProc, WM_ICONERASEBKGND

WM_EXITMENULOOP

Syntax

```
TWMExitMenuLoop = record
        Msg: Cardinal;                        {the message identifier}
        IsTrackPopupMenu: LongBool;           {shortcut menu flag}
        Unused: Longint;                      {not used}
        Result: Longint;                      {returns a zero if handled}
    end;
```

Description

The WM_EXITMENULOOP message is sent to the main window of an application when a menu is closed and the menu modal loop has been exited.

A

Appendix

Members

Msg: The message identifier. This member is set to the message identifier constant WM_EXITMENULOOP.

IsTrackPopupMenu: Indicates if the menu is a pop-up menu or a regular menu. If this member is set to TRUE, the menu is a pop-up menu; otherwise it is a regular menu.

Unused: This member is not used by this message.

Result: If the application handles this message, set this member to zero.

See Also

DefWindowProc, WM_ENTERMENULOOP

WM_FONTCHANGE

Syntax

```
TWMFontChange = record
    Msg: Cardinal;                    {the message identifier}
    Unused: array[0..3] of Word;      {not used}
    Result: Longint;                  {not used}
end;
```

Description

If an application changes the systemwide font resources through the use of the AddFontResource or RemoveFontResource functions, it should send a WM_FONTCHANGE message to all top-level windows in the system. This message can be sent to all top-level windows by using the SendMessage function with the hWnd parameter set to HWND_BROADCAST.

Members

Msg: The message identifier. This member is set to the message identifier constant WM_FONTCHANGE.

Unused: This member is not used by this message.

Result: This member is not used by this message.

See Also

AddFontResource, RemoveFontResource, SendMessage

WM_GETFONT

Syntax

```
TWMGetFont = record
    Msg: Cardinal;                    {the message identifier}
    Unused: array[0..3] of Word;      {not used}
```

Result: Longint;   {returns a font handle}
   end;

Description

An application can retrieve the font a control is currently using to draw text by sending that control a WM_GETFONT message.

Members

Msg: The message identifier. This member is set to the message identifier constant WM_GETFONT.

Unused: This member is not used by this message

Result: This message returns zero if the system font is being used. Otherwise, the message returns the handle of the currently selected font.

See Also

WM_SETFONT

WM_GETHOTKEY

Syntax

```
TWMGetHotKey = record
    Msg: Cardinal;                      {the message identifier}
    Unused: array[0..3] of Word;        {not used}
    Result: Longint;                    {returns the hot key information}
end;
```

Description

The WM_GETHOTKEY message is sent to a window to retrieve the window's associated hot key.

Members

Msg: The message identifier. This member is set to the message identifier constant WM_GETHOTKEY.

Unused: This member is not used by this message.

Result: This message returns zero if there is no hot key associated with the window. If the window does have an associated hot key, the virtual key code for the hot key is in the low-order byte of the result value, and the hot key modifiers are in the high-order byte. The hot key modifiers may be any combination of values from Table A-8.

See Also

WM_SETHOTKEY, WM_SYSCOMMAND

A

Table A-8: TWMGetHotKey.Result Hot Key Modifier Values

Value	Description
HOTKEYF_ALT	The Alt key.
HOTKEYF_CONTROL	The Ctrl key.
HOTKEYF_EXT	An extended key.
HOTKEYF_SHIFT	The Shift key.

WM_GETICON

Syntax

```
TWMGetIcon = record
    Msg: Cardinal;              {the message identifier}
    BigIcon: Longbool;          {the icon type}
    Unused: Longint;            {not used}
    Result: Longint;            {returns an icon handle}
end;
```

Description

The WM_GETICON message is sent to a window to retrieve its associated large or small icon.

Members

Msg: The message identifier. This member is set to the message identifier constant WM_GETICON.

BigIcon: A flag indicating the type of icon to retrieve. This member can contain ICON_BIG to retrieve the large icon or ICON_SMALL to retrieve the small icon.

Unused: This member is not used by this message.

Result: If the message succeeds, it returns a handle to the large or small icon.

See Also

DefWindowProc, WM_SETICON

WM_GETMINMAXINFO

Syntax

```
TWMGetMinMaxInfo = record
    Msg: Cardinal;              {the message identifier}
    Unused: Integer;            {not used}
    MinMaxInfo: PMinMaxInfo;    {pointer to data structure}
    Result: Longint;            {returns a zero if handled}
end;
```

Description

When a window's size or position is about to be changed, the WM_GETMINMAXINFO message is sent to the window. This can be used to override the default maximized size, maximized position, minimum tracking size, or maximum tracking size.

Members

Msg: The message identifier. This member is set to the message identifier constant WM_GETMINMAXINFO.

Unused: This member is not used by this message.

MinMaxInfo: A pointer to a TMinMaxInfo structure describing the maximum and minimum sizes and position. The TMinMaxInfo structure is defined as:

```
TMinMaxInfo = packed record
      ptReserved: TPoint;          {reserved}
      ptMaxSize: TPoint;           {the maximum size of the window}
      ptMaxPosition: TPoint;       {the location of a maximized window}
      ptMinTrackSize: TPoint;      {the minimum tracking size}
      ptMaxTrackSize: TPoint;      {the maximum tracking size}
end;
```

ptReserved: This member is reserved for future use, and must be set to zero.

ptMaxSize: The new maximized width and height of the window, in pixels.

ptMaxPosition: The new maximized location of the window, in pixels, relative to the upper left corner of the screen.

ptMinTrackSize: The new minimum tracking size of the window, in pixels.

ptMaxTrackSize: The new maximum tracking size of the window, in pixels.

Result: If the application handles this message, set this member to zero.

See Also

MoveWindow, SetWindowPos

WM_GETTEXT

Syntax

```
TWMGetText = record
      Msg: Cardinal;        {the message identifier}
      TextMax: Integer;     {the number of characters to copy}
      Text: PChar;          {a pointer to the output buffer}
      Result: Longint;      {returns the number of characters copied}
end;
```

Description

The WM_GETTEXT message is sent to retrieve the text or caption of a window. The text or caption is stored in the user allocated buffer pointed to by the Text member. For an edit control, the text retrieved is the entire textual content of the edit control. For a combo box, it is the contents of its edit control. For a button, it is the caption displayed by the button. For other windows, it is the window caption. To retrieve the text from a list box item, use the LB_GETTEXT message instead. For a rich edit control with more than 64K of text, use the EM_STREAMOUT or EM_GETSELTEXT messages. When a static control has the SS_ICON style, and the icon was set by a previous WM_SETTEXT message, the WM_GETTEXT message will return the handle of the icon in the first four bytes of the output buffer.

Members

Msg: The message identifier. This member is set to the message identifier constant WM_GETTEXT.

TextMax: Specifies the maximum number of characters to copy, including the null terminator.

Text: A pointer to the output buffer receiving the text.

Result: If the message succeeds, it returns the number of characters copied to the output buffer.

See Also

DefWindowProc, GetWindowText, GetWindowTextLength, WM_GETTEXTLENGTH, WM_SETTEXT

WM_GETTEXTLENGTH

Syntax

```
TWMGetTextLength = record
      Msg: Cardinal;                    {the message identifier}
      Unused: array[0..3] of Word;      {not used}
      Result: Longint;                  {returns the text length in characters}
   end;
```

Description

The WM_GETTEXTLENGTH message is sent to a window to determine the length of the text associated with that window, excluding the null terminator. This message can be used to determine the length of the output buffer required by the WM_GETTEXT message. When the system contains a mixture of ANSI and Unicode strings, the result might be larger than the actual number of bytes required, but will never be smaller than the number of bytes required for the output buffer used by the WM_GETTEXT message. See the WM_GETTEXT message for a description of text associated with various types of controls.

Members

Msg: The message identifier. This member is set to the message identifier constant WM_GETTEXTLENGTH.

Unused: This member is not used by this message.

Result: If the message succeeds, it returns the length of the text associated with the window to which the message was sent, in characters.

See Also

DefWindowProc, GetWindowText, GetWindowTextLength, WM_GETTEXT

WM_HELP

Syntax

```
TWMHelp = record
     Msg: Cardinal;          {the message identifier}
     Unused: Integer;        {not used}
     HelpInfo: PHelpInfo;    {a pointer to a THelpInfo structure}
     Result: Longint;        {always returns a one}
end;
```

Description

The WM_HELP message is sent when the user presses the F1 key for help. If a menu item is open, the message is sent to the window associated with the menu; otherwise the message is sent to the window with the keyboard focus or the currently active window if no window has the keyboard focus.

Members

Msg: The message identifier. This member is set to the message identifier constant WM_HELP.

Unused: This member is not used by this message.

HelpInfo: A pointer to a THelpInfo structure containing information on the window or control for which help was requested. The THelpInfo structure is defined as:

```
THelpInfo = packed record
     cbSize: UINT;               {the size of the THelpInfo structure}
     iContextType: Integer;      {the type of help}
     iCtrlId: Integer;           {the control or menu item identifier}
     hItemHandle: THandle;       {the handle of the control or menu}
     dwContextId: DWORD;         {the help context identifier}
     MousePos: TPoint;           {the mouse screen coordinates}
end;
```

cbSize: Specifies the size of the THelpInfo structure in bytes.

iContextType: Identifies the type of control for which help was requested, and can contain one value from Table A-9.

iCtrlId: Specifies the identifier of the menu item, control, or window.

hItemHandle: Identifies the window handle or menu handle of the window, control, or menu item.

dwContextId: Specifies the help context identifier for the window, control, or menu. The Windows help system retrieves the help topic associated with the help context identifier from the associated help file.

MousePos: Specifies the location of the mouse at the time of the help request, in screen coordinates.

Result: This message always returns a one.

See Also

DefWindowProc, WM_SYSCOMMAND

Table A-9: TWMHelp.THelpInfo.iContextType Values

Value	Description
HELPINFO_MENUITEM	Identifies a help request for a menu item.
HELPINFO_WINDOW	Identifies a help request for a window or control.

WM_HSCROLL

Syntax

```
TWMHScroll = record
     Msg: Cardinal;                {the message identifier}

     ScrollCode: Smallint;         {the scroll request code}
     Pos: Smallint;                {the scroll bar thumb position}
     Scroll bar: HWND;             {the scroll bar handle}
     Result: Longint;              {returns a zero if handled}
end;
```

Description

The WM_HSCROLL message is sent to a window when a horizontal scrolling event occurs, if the window has a standard horizontal scroll bar. It is also sent when a scroll event occurs in a horizontal scroll bar control. If the application changes the position of data in a window as a result of a horizontal scrolling event, it should reset the position of the scroll bar's thumb by calling the SetScrollPos function. The WM_VSCROLL and WM_HSCROLL messages have 16-bit values for scroll positions, restricting the maximum position to 65,535.

Members

Msg: The message identifier. This member is set to the message identifier constant WM_HSCROLL.

ScrollCode: Specifies the type of scrolling request as a result of the scrolling event. This member can contain one value from Table A-10.

Pos: If the ScrollCode member contains SB_THUMBPOSITION or SB_THUMBTRACK, this member specifies the current position of the scroll bar's thumb. Otherwise, this member is not used.

Scroll bar: Specifies the handle of a scroll bar control if it is a scroll bar control that is sending the WM_HSCROLL message. Otherwise, this member is not used.

Result: If the application handles this message, set this member to zero.

See Also

WM_VSCROLL

Table A-10: TWMHScroll.ScrollCode Values

Value	Description
SB_BOTTOM	Indicates a scroll to the lower right.
SB_ENDSCROLL	Indicates an end to the scrolling operation.
SB_LINELEFT	Indicates a scroll left by one unit.
SB_LINERIGHT	Indicates a scroll right by one unit.
SB_PAGELEFT	Indicates a scroll left by one window width.
SB_PAGERIGHT	Indicates a scroll right by one window width.
SB_THUMBPOSITION	Indicates a scroll to the absolute position as specified by the Pos member.
SB_THUMBTRACK	Drags the scroll bar thumb to the position as indicated by the Pos member. This is normally used to provide feedback.
SB_TOP	Indicates a scroll to the upper left.

WM_HSCROLLCLIPBOARD

Syntax

```
TWMHScrollClipboard = record
    Msg: Cardinal;          {the message identifier}
    Viewer: HWND;           {the handle of the clipboard viewer}
    ScrollCode: Word;       {the scroll request code}
    ThumbPos: Word;         {the scroll bar thumb position}
    Result: Longint;        {returns a zero if handled}
end;
```

Description

The WM_HSCROLLCLIPBOARD message is sent by a clipboard viewer window to the clipboard owner when there is an event in the viewer's horizontal scroll bar and the clipboard contains data in the CF_OWNERDISPLAY format. The clipboard owner must scroll the image and then reset the horizontal scroll bar value.

Members

Msg: The message identifier. This member is set to the message identifier constant WM_HSCROLLCLIPBOARD.

Viewer: Specifies the handle of the clipboard viewer window.

ScrollCode: Specifies the type of scrolling request as a result of the scrolling event. This member can contain one value from Table A-11.

ThumbPos: If the ScrollCode member contains SB_THUMBPOSITION, this member specifies the current position of the scroll bar's thumb. Otherwise, this member is not used.

Result: If the application handles this message, set this member to zero.

See Also

WM_VSCROLLCLIPBOARD

Table A-II: TWMHScrollClipboard.ScrollCode Values

Value	Description
SB_BOTTOM	Indicates a scroll to the lower right.
SB_ENDSCROLL	Indicates an end to the scrolling operation.
SB_LINELEFT	Indicates a scroll left by one unit.
SB_LINERIGHT	Indicates a scroll right by one unit.
SB_PAGELEFT	Indicates a scroll left by one window width.
SB_PAGERIGHT	Indicates a scroll right by one window width.
SB_THUMBPOSITION	Indicates a scroll to the absolute position as specified by the Pos member.
SB_TOP	Indicates a scroll to the upper left.

WM_ICONERASEBKGND

Syntax

```
TWMIconEraseBkgnd = record
    Msg: Cardinal;          {the message identifier}
    DC: HDC;                {the device context}
    Unused: Longint;        {not used}
```

Result: Longint;   {returns a one if handled}
    end;

Description

A window that has been minimized receives a WM_ICONERASEBKGND message when the background of the icon must be filled before the icon is painted. This message is sent only if a class icon has been defined for the window; otherwise, the WM_ERASEBKGND message is sent.

Members

Msg: The message identifier. This member is set to the message identifier constant WM_ICONERASEBKGND.

DC: The device context upon which the icon is drawn.

Unused: This member is not used by this message.

Result: If the application handles this message, set this member to one.

See Also

DefWindowProc, WM_ERASEBKGND

WM_INITMENU

Syntax

```
TWMInitMenu = record
    Msg: Cardinal;          {the message identifier}
    Menu: HMENU;            {the menu handle}
    Unused: Longint;        {not used}
    Result: Longint;        {returns a zero if handled}
end;
```

Description

When a menu is about to become active, such as when the user clicks on a menu item or presses a menu shortcut key, a WM_INITMENU message is sent to the window that owns the menu. This enables the application to modify the menu before displaying it. This message is sent only when a menu is first accessed, and only one message is sent for each access. Moving the mouse across several menu items while holding down the button does not generate new messages.

Members

Msg: The message identifier. This member is set to the message identifier constant WM_INITMENU.

Menu: Identifies the handle of the menu.

Unused: This member is not used by this message.

Result: If the application handles this message, set this member to zero.

See Also

WM_ENTERMENULOOP, WM_EXITMENULOOP, WM_INITMENUPOPUP

WM_INITMENUPOPUP

Syntax

```
TWMInitMenuPopup = record
      Msg: Cardinal;              {the message identifier}
      MenuPopup: HMENU;           {the menu handle}
      Pos: Smallint;              {the submenu item position}
      SystemMenu: WordBool;       {the system menu flag}
      Result: Longint;            {returns a zero if handled}
   end;
```

Description

When a drop-down menu or submenu is about to become active, such as when the user clicks on a menu item containing a submenu, a WM_INITMENUPOPUP message is sent to the window that owns the menu. This enables the application to modify the menu before displaying it.

Members

Msg: The message identifier. This member is set to the message identifier constant WM_INITMENUPOPUP.

MenuPopup: Identifies the handle of the drop-down menu or submenu.

Pos: Specifies the zero-based index of the menu item that opened the drop-down menu or submenu.

SystemMenu: Indicates if the activated drop-down menu is the system, or window, menu. If this member is set to TRUE, the activating drop-down menu is the system menu; otherwise it is a regular drop-down menu or submenu.

Result: If the application handles this message, set this member to zero.

See Also

WM_ENTERMENULOOP, WM_EXITMENULOOP, WM_INITMENU

WM_KEYDOWN

Syntax

```
TWMKeyDown = record
      Msg: Cardinal;              {the message identifier}
      CharCode: Word;             {the virtual key code}
      Unused: Word;               {not used}
```

> KeyData: Longint;   {contains various information}
> Result: Longint;   {returns a zero if handled}
> end;

Description

When the user presses a nonsystem key, a WM_KEYDOWN message is sent to the window that has keyboard focus. A nonsystem key is any keystroke combination that does not include the Alt key. If the pressed key is F10, DefWindowProc sets an internal flag. When the WM_KEYUP message is received, DefWindowProc checks this internal flag, and if it is set, sends a WM_SYSCOMMAND message to the top-level window with the CmdType member of the message set to SC_KEYMENU.

Members

Msg: The message identifier. This member is set to the message identifier constant WM_KEYDOWN.

CharCode: Specifies the virtual key code for the key that was pressed.

Unused: This member is not used by this message.

KeyData: Specifies the repeat count, scan code, extended key flag, context code, previous key state flag, and the transition state flag. Table A-12 shows which information is in which bit position within the 32-bit value of the KeyData member.

Result: If the application handles this message, set this member to zero.

See Also

DefWindowProc, WM_CHAR, WM_KEYUP, WM_SYSCOMMAND

Table A-12: TWMKeyDown.KeyData Values

Value	Description
0-15	The repeat count resulting from the user holding down the key.
16-23	The scan code, whose value depends on the OEM maker of the keyboard.
24	The extended key flag. If the key is an extended key (the right-hand Alt and Ctrl keys), this bit is set (1); otherwise it is not set (0).
25-28	Unused.
29	The context code. This bit is always zero.
30	The previous key state. If the key was held down before the message is sent, this bit is set (1); otherwise it is not set (0).
31	The transition state. This bit is always zero.

WM_KEYUP

Syntax

```
TWMKeyUp = record
      Msg: Cardinal;              {the message identifier}
      CharCode: Word;            {the virtual key code}
      Unused: Word;              {not used}
      KeyData: Longint;          {contains various information}
      Result: Longint;           {returns a zero if handled}
end;
```

Description

When the user releases a nonsystem key, a WM_KEYUP message is sent to the window that has keyboard focus. A nonsystem key is any keystroke combination that does not include the Alt key. If the released key is F10, DefWindowProc sends a WM_SYSCOMMAND message to the top-level window with the CmdType member of the message set to SC_KEYMENU.

Members

Msg: The message identifier. This member is set to the message identifier constant WM_KEYUP.

CharCode: Specifies the virtual key code for the key that was released.

Unused: This member is not used by this message.

KeyData: Specifies the repeat count, scan code, extended key flag, context code, previous key state flag, and the transition state flag. Table A-13 shows which information is in which bit position within the 32-bit value of the KeyData member.

Result: If the application handles this message, set this member to zero.

See Also

DefWindowProc, WM_CHAR, WM_KEYDOWN, WM_SYSCOMMAND

Table A-13: TWMKeyUp.KeyData Values

Value	Description
0-15	The repeat count resulting from the user holding down the key.
16-23	The scan code, whose value depends on the OEM maker of the keyboard.
24	The extended key flag. If the key is an extended key (the right-hand Alt and Ctrl keys), this bit is set (1); otherwise it is not set (0).
25-28	Unused.
29	The context code. This bit is always zero.
30	The previous key state. This bit is always one.
31	The transition state. This bit is always one.

WM_KILLFOCUS

Syntax

```
TWMKillFocus = record
      Msg: Cardinal;              {the message identifier}
      FocusedWnd: HWND;           {the handle of the window receiving focus}
      Unused: Longint;            {not used}
      Result: Longint;            {returns a zero if handled}
end;
```

Description

The WM_KILLFOCUS message is sent to a window when it is losing keyboard focus. The window will receive the message before keyboard focus has changed.

Members

Msg: The message identifier. This member is set to the message identifier constant WM_KILLFOCUS.

FocusedWnd: Specifies the handle of the window receiving the keyboard focus.

Unused: This member is not used by this message.

Result: If the application handles this message, set this member to zero.

See Also

SetFocus, WM_SETFOCUS

WM_LBUTTONDBLCLK

Syntax

```
TWMLButtonDblClk = record
      Msg: Cardinal;              {the message identifier}
      Keys: Longint;              {virtual key flags}
      case Integer of
      0: (
      XPos: Smallint;             {the horizontal cursor coordinate}
      YPos: Smallint);            {the vertical cursor coordinate}
      1: (
      Pos: TSmallPoint;           {a TSmallPoint structure containing cursor coordinates}
      Result: Longint);           {returns a zero if handled}
end;
```

Description

If the mouse cursor is in the client area of a window and the left mouse button is double-clicked, a WM_LBUTTONDBLCLK message is sent to the window under the cursor. However, if another window has captured mouse input by calling the

SetCapture function, the message is sent to the capturing window. A double click is generated when the user presses the mouse button, releases it, and presses it again at the same coordinates within the system's double-click time interval. This process generates a series of four messages, in the following order: WM_LBUTTONDOWN, WM_LBUTTONUP, WM_LBUTTONDBLCLK, and WM_LBUTTONUP. Only windows whose class style contains the CS_DBLCLKS flag will receive the WM_LBUTTONDBLCLK message.

Members

Msg: The message identifier. This member is set to the message identifier constant WM_LBUTTONDBLCLK.

Keys: Indicates if specific virtual keys are held down at the time of the double click. This member can contain one or more values from Table A-14.

XPos: Specifies the horizontal coordinate of the mouse cursor, relative to the client area.

YPos: Specifies the vertical coordinate of the mouse cursor, relative to the client area.

Pos: A TSmallPoint structure that contains the current mouse coordinates relative to the client area.

Result: If the application handles this message, set this member to zero.

See Also

GetCapture, GetDoubleClickTime, SetCapture, SetDoubleClickTime, WM_LBUTTONDOWN, WM_LBUTTONUP

Table A-14: TWMLButtonDblClk.Keys Values

Value	Description
MK_CONTROL	Indicates that the Ctrl key is held down.
MK_LBUTTON	Indicates that the left mouse button is down.
MK_MBUTTON	Indicates that the middle mouse button is down.
MK_RBUTTON	Indicates that the right mouse button is down.
MK_SHIFT	Indicates that the Shift key is held down.

WM_LBUTTONDOWN

Syntax

```
TWMLButtonDown = record
        Msg: Cardinal;          {the message identifier}
        Keys: Longint;          {virtual key flags}
        case Integer of
        0: (
```

```
        XPos: Smallint;        {the horizontal cursor coordinate}
        YPos: Smallint);       {the vertical cursor coordinate}
        1: (
        Pos: TSmallPoint;      {a TSmallPoint structure containing cursor coordinates}
        Result: Longint);      {returns a zero if handled}
    end;
```

Description

If the mouse cursor is in the client area of a window and the left button is pressed, a WM_LBUTTONDOWN message is sent to the window under the cursor. However, if another window has captured mouse input by calling the SetCapture function, the message is sent to the capturing window.

Members

Msg: The message identifier. This member is set to the message identifier constant WM_LBUTTONDOWN.

Keys: Indicates if specific virtual keys are held down at the time of the button click. This member can contain one or more values from Table A-15.

XPos: Specifies the horizontal coordinate of the mouse cursor, relative to the client area.

YPos: Specifies the vertical coordinate of the mouse cursor, relative to the client area.

Pos: A TSmallPoint structure that contains the current mouse coordinates relative to the client area.

Result: If the application handles this message, set this member to zero.

See Also

GetCapture, SetCapture, WM_LBUTTONDBLCLK, WM_LBUTTONUP

Table A-15: TWMLButtonDown.Keys Values

Value	Description
MK_CONTROL	Indicates that the Ctrl key is held down.
MK_LBUTTON	Indicates that the left mouse button is down.
MK_MBUTTON	Indicates that the middle mouse button is down.
MK_RBUTTON	Indicates that the right mouse button is down.
MK_SHIFT	Indicates that the Shift key is held down.

WM_LBUTTONUP

Syntax

TWMLButtonUp = record

```
        Msg: Cardinal;              {the message identifier}
        Keys: Longint;             {virtual key flags}
        case Integer of
        0: (
        XPos: Smallint;            {the horizontal cursor coordinate}
        YPos: Smallint);           {the vertical cursor coordinate}
        1: (
        Pos: TSmallPoint;          {a TSmallPoint structure containing cursor coordinates}
        Result: Longint);          {returns a zero if handled}
end;
```

Description

If the mouse cursor is in the client area of a window and the left button is released, a WM_LBUTTONUP message is sent to the window under the cursor. However, if another window has captured mouse input by calling the SetCapture function, the message is sent to the capturing window.

Members

Msg: The message identifier. This member is set to the message identifier constant WM_LBUTTONUP.

Keys: Indicates if specific virtual keys are held down at the time of the button release. This member can contain one or more values from Table A-16.

XPos: Specifies the horizontal coordinate of the mouse cursor, relative to the client area.

YPos: Specifies the vertical coordinate of the mouse cursor, relative to the client area.

Pos: A TSmallPoint structure that contains the current mouse coordinates relative to the client area.

Result: If the application handles this message, set this member to zero.

See Also

GetCapture, SetCapture, WM_LBUTTONDBLCLK, WM_LBUTTONDOWN

Table A-16: TWMLButtonUp.Keys Values

Value	Description
MK_CONTROL	Indicates that the Ctrl key is held down.
MK_MBUTTON	Indicates that the middle mouse button is down.
MK_RBUTTON	Indicates that the right mouse button is down.
MK_SHIFT	Indicates that the Shift key is held down.

WM_MBUTTONDBLCLK

Syntax

```
TWMMButtonDblClk = record
      Msg: Cardinal;          {the message identifier}
      Keys: Longint;          {virtual key flags}
      case Integer of
      0: (
      XPos: Smallint;         {the horizontal cursor coordinate}
      YPos: Smallint);        {the vertical cursor coordinate}
      1: (
      Pos: TSmallPoint;       {a TSmallPoint structure containing cursor coordinates}
      Result: Longint);       {returns a zero if handled}
   end;
```

Description

If the mouse cursor is in the client area of a window and the middle mouse button is double-clicked, a WM_MBUTTONDBLCLK message is sent to the window under the cursor. However, if another window has captured mouse input by calling the SetCapture function, the message is sent to the capturing window. A double click is generated when the user presses the mouse button, releases it, and presses it again at the same coordinates within the system's double-click time interval. This process generates a series of four messages, in the following order: WM_MBUTTONDOWN, WM_MBUTTONUP, WM_MBUTTONDBLCLK, and WM_MBUTTONUP. Only windows whose class style contains the CS_DBLCLKS flag will receive the WM_MBUTTONDBLCLK message.

Members

Msg: The message identifier. This member is set to the message identifier constant WM_MBUTTONDBLCLK.

Keys: Indicates if specific virtual keys are held down at the time of the double click. This member can contain one or more values from Table A-17.

XPos: Specifies the horizontal coordinate of the mouse cursor, relative to the client area.

YPos: Specifies the vertical coordinate of the mouse cursor, relative to the client area.

Pos: A TSmallPoint structure that contains the current mouse coordinates.

Result: If the application handles this message, set this member to zero.

See Also

GetCapture, GetDoubleClickTime, SetCapture, SetDoubleClickTime, WM_MBUTTONDOWN, WM_MBUTTONUP

Table A-17: TWMMButtonDblClk.Keys Values

Value	Description
MK_CONTROL	Indicates that the Ctrl key is held down.
MK_LBUTTON	Indicates that the left mouse button is down.
MK_MBUTTON	Indicates that the middle mouse button is down.
MK_RBUTTON	Indicates that the right mouse button is down.
MK_SHIFT	Indicates that the Shift key is held down.

WM_MBUTTONDOWN

Syntax

```
TWMMButtonDown = record
        Msg: Cardinal;        {the message identifier}
        Keys: Longint;        {virtual key flags}
        case Integer of
        0: (
        XPos: Smallint;       {the horizontal cursor coordinate}
        YPos: Smallint);      {the vertical cursor coordinate}
        1: (
        Pos: TSmallPoint;     {a TSmallPoint structure containing cursor coordinates}
        Result: Longint);     {returns a zero if handled}
end;
```

Description

If the mouse cursor is in the client area of a window and the middle button is pressed, a WM_MBUTTONDOWN message is sent to the window under the cursor. However, if another window has captured mouse input by calling the SetCapture function, the message is sent to the capturing window.

Members

Msg: The message identifier. This member is set to the message identifier constant WM_MBUTTONDOWN.

Keys: Indicates if specific virtual keys are held down at the time of the button click. This member can contain one or more values from Table A-18.

XPos: Specifies the horizontal coordinate of the mouse cursor, relative to the client area.

YPos: Specifies the vertical coordinate of the mouse cursor, relative to the client area.

Pos: A TSmallPoint structure that contains the current mouse coordinates.

Result: If the application handles this message, set this member to zero.

See Also

GetCapture, SetCapture, WM_MBUTTONDBLCLK, WM_MBUTTONUP

Table A-18: TWMMButtonDown.Keys Values

Value	Description
MK_CONTROL	Indicates that the Ctrl key is held down.
MK_LBUTTON	Indicates that the left mouse button is down.
MK_MBUTTON	Indicates that the middle mouse button is down.
MK_RBUTTON	Indicates that the right mouse button is down.
MK_SHIFT	Indicates that the Shift key is held down.

WM_MBUTTONUP

Syntax

```
TWMMButtonUp = record
      Msg: Cardinal;            {the message identifier}
      Keys: Longint;            {virtual key flags}
      case Integer of
      0: (
      XPos: Smallint;           {the horizontal cursor coordinate}
      YPos: Smallint);          {the vertical cursor coordinate}
      1: (
      Pos: TSmallPoint;         {a TSmallPoint structure containing cursor coordinates}
      Result: Longint);         {returns a zero if handled}
end;
```

Description

If the mouse cursor is in the client area of a window and the middle button is released, a WM_MBUTTONUP message is sent to the window under the cursor. However, if another window has captured mouse input by calling the SetCapture function, the message is sent to the capturing window.

Members

Msg: The message identifier. This member is set to the message identifier constant WM_MBUTTONUP.

Keys: Indicates if specific virtual keys are held down at the time of the button release. This member can contain one or more values from Table A-19.

XPos: Specifies the horizontal coordinate of the mouse cursor, relative to the client area.

YPos: Specifies the vertical coordinate of the mouse cursor, relative to the client area.

Pos: A TSmallPoint structure that contains the current mouse coordinates.

Result: If the application handles this message, set this member to zero.

See Also

GetCapture, SetCapture, WM_MBUTTONDBLCLK, WM_MBUTTONDOWN

Table A-19: TWMMButtonUp.Keys Values

Value	Description
MK_CONTROL	Indicates that the Ctrl key is held down.
MK_LBUTTON	Indicates that the left mouse button is down.
MK_RBUTTON	Indicates that the right mouse button is down.
MK_SHIFT	Indicates that the Shift key is held down.

WM_MDIACTIVATE

Syntax

```
TWMMDIActivate = record
      Msg: Cardinal;                {the message identifier}
      case Integer of
      0: (
      ChildWnd: HWND);             {the handle of the child window to activate}
      1: (
      DeactiveWnd: HWND;           {the handle of the child to deactivate}
      ActiveWnd: HWND;             {the handle of the child to activate}
      Result: Longint);            {returns a zero if handled}
   end;
```

Description

An MDI application's client window receives the WM_MDIACTIVATE message when it should activate a new child window. The MDI client window will pass the message on to both the window being deactivated and the window being activated. MDI child windows are activated independently of the MDI frame window. When the frame window becomes active, the last MDI child that was activated by the WM_MDIACTIVATE message receives a WM_NCACTIVATE message, but will not receive another WM_MDIACTIVATE message.

Members

Msg: The message identifier. This member is set to the message identifier constant WM_MDIACTIVATE.

ChildWnd: The handle of the child window being activated. This member is valid only when the message is received by an MDI client window.

DeactiveWnd: The handle of the child window being deactivated. This member is valid only when the message is received by an MDI child window.

ActiveWnd: The handle of the child window being activated. This member is valid only when the message is received by an MDI child window.

Result: If the application handles this message, set this member to zero.

See Also

WM_MDIGETACTIVE, WM_MDINEXT, WM_NCACTIVATE

WM_MDICASCADE

Syntax

```
TWMMDICascade = record
    Msg: Cardinal;          {the message identifier}
    Cascade: Longint;       {the cascade behavior flag}
    Unused: Longint;        {not used}
    Result: Longint;        {returns a one if successful}
end;
```

Description

The WM_MDICASCADE message is sent to the client window of an MDI application to instruct it to cascade all open child windows.

Members

Msg: The message identifier. This member is set to the message identifier constant WM_MDICASCADE.

Cascade: Specifies an alternate behavior for the cascade. If this member is set to MDITILE_SKIPDISABLED, all disabled MDI child windows will be excluded from the cascade. If this member is set to zero, all MDI child windows are cascaded.

Unused: This member is not used by this message.

Result: The MDI client window returns one if the message succeeds; otherwise it returns zero.

See Also

WM_MDIICONARRANGE, WM_MDITILE

WM_MDICREATE

Syntax

```
TWMMDICreate = record
    Msg: Cardinal;          {the message identifier}
    Unused: Integer;        {not used}
```

MDICreateStruct: PMDICreateStruct;	{a pointer to a TMDICreateStruct structure}
Result: Longint;	{returns the handle of the new child window}
end;	

Description

The WM_MDICREATE message is sent to an MDI client window when an application wants to create a child window. The information for the new window is specified by the structure pointed to by the MDICreateStruct member. The child window is created with the window styles of WS_CHILD, WS_CLIPSIBLINGS, WS_CLIPCHILDREN, WS_SYSMENU, WS_CAPTION, WS_THICKFRAME, WS_MINIMIZEBOX, WS_MAXIMIZEBOX, plus whatever is specified in the TMDICreateStruct structure. An application should finish processing the current WM_MDICREATE message before another WM_MDICREATE message is sent. When the MDI client window receives the message, it sends a WM_CREATE message to the child window. The lpCreateParams member of the TCreateStruct structure referenced in the WM_CREATE message will contain a pointer to the TMDICreateStruct structure.

Members

Msg: The message identifier. This member is set to the message identifier constant WM_MDICREATE.

Unused: This member is not used by this message.

MDICreateStruct: A pointer to a TMDICreateStruct structure defining the new child window attributes. The TMDICreateStruct structure is defined as:

```
TMDICreateStruct = packed record
```

szClass: PAnsiChar;	{the window class}
szTitle: PAnsiChar;	{the window title}
hOwner: THandle;	{the owner instance}
x: Integer;	{the horizontal position of the window}
y: Integer;	{the vertical position of the window}
cx: Integer;	{the width of the window}
cy: Integer;	{the height of the window}
style: DWORD;	{the window styles}
lParam: LPARAM;	{an application-defined value}

```
end;
```

szClass: A pointer to a null-terminated, case-sensitive string specifying the window class for the MDI child window. This class is registered by calling the RegisterClass function.

szTitle: A pointer to a null-terminated string. This string is displayed in the title bar of the MDI child window.

hOwner: A handle to the application instance that owns the MDI client window.

x: The horizontal coordinate of child window, relative to the client area.

y: The vertical coordinate of the child window, relative to the client area.

cx: The width of the child window in pixels.

cy: The height of the child window in pixels.

style: A 32-bit number that specifies what styles this window uses. If the MDI client window is using the MDIS_ALLCHILDSTYLES window style flag, this member can be any combination of the styles from the window style table in the CreateWindow function. (This function is detailed in *The Tomes of Delphi 3: Win32 Core API* from Wordware Publishing.) Otherwise, it can be any combination of styles from Table A-20. Two or more styles are specified by using the Boolean OR operator, i.e., WS_MINIMIZE OR WS_HSCROLL.

lParam: A 32-bit application-defined value.

Result: If the message succeeds, the client window returns a handle to the newly created child window; otherwise it returns zero.

See Also

CreateMDIWindow, WM_CREATE, WM_MDIDESTROY

Table A-20: TWMMDICreate.TMDICreateStruct.style Values

Value	Description
WS_MINIMIZE	The MDI child window is initially minimized.
WS_MAXIMIZE	The MDI child window is initially maximized.
WS_HSCROLL	The MDI child window has a horizontal scroll bar.
WS_VSCROLL	The MDI child window has a vertical scroll bar.

WM_MDIDESTROY

Syntax

```
TWMMDIDestroy = record
      Msg: Cardinal;          {the message identifier}
      Child: HWND;            {a handle of a child window}
      Unused: Longint;        {not used}
      Result: Longint;        {returns zero}
end;
```

Description

This message is sent to a multiple document interface (MDI) client window to close a child window. The title of the child window is removed from the MDI frame window and the child window is deactivated.

A

Members

Msg: The message identifier. This member is set to the message identifier constant WM_MDIDESTROY.

Child: Specifies the handle of the MDI child window that is to be closed.

Unused: This member is not used by this message.

Result: This message always returns zero.

See Also

WM_MDICREATE

WM_MDIGETACTIVE

Syntax

```
TWMMDIGetActive = record
      Msg: Cardinal;                {the message identifier}
      Unused: array[0..3] of Word;  {unused}
      Result: Longint;              {returns a handle to a child window}
   end;
```

Description

This message retrieves the handle of the active MDI child window.

Members

Msg: The message identifier. This member is set to the message identifier constant WM_MDIGETACTIVE.

Unused: This member is not used by this message.

Result: If the message succeeds, it returns the handle of the active MDI child window; otherwise it returns zero.

See Also

WM_MDIACTIVATE, WM_MDICREATE, WM_MDIDESTROY

WM_MDIICONARRANGE

Syntax

```
TWMMDIIconArrange = record
      Msg: Cardinal;                {the message identifier}
      Unused: array[0..3] of Word;  {not used}
      Result: Longint;              {not used}
   end;
```

Description

This message is sent to a multiple document interface (MDI) client window to line up all iconic child windows. It has no effect on child windows that are not minimized.

Members

Msg: The message identifier. This member is set to the message identifier constant WM_MDIICONARRANGE.

Unused: This member is not used by this message.

Result: This member is not used by this message.

See Also

WM_MDICASCADE, WM_MDITILE

WM_MDIMAXIMIZE

Syntax

```
TWMMDIMaximize = record
      Msg: Cardinal;              {the message identifier}
      Maximize: HWND;            {a handle to a child window}
      Unused: Longint;           {not used}
      Result: Longint;           {returns zero}
   end;
```

Description

The WM_MDIMAXIMIZE message is sent to a multiple document interface (MDI) client window to maximize a child window. Windows resizes the child window to make its client area fill the client window. The child window's caption is appended to the frame window's caption, and the child window's system menu icon and window buttons are placed on the frame window's menu bar. If the currently active child window is maximized and another child window becomes active, Windows restores the active child window and maximizes the newly activated child window.

Members

Msg: The message identifier. This member is set to the message identifier constant WM_MDIMAXIMIZE.

Maximize: Specifies the handle of the MDI child window to be maximized.

Unused: This member is not used by this message.

Result: This message always returns zero.

See Also

SM_MDIICONARRANGE, WM_MDIRESTORE

WM_MDINEXT

Syntax

```
TWMMDINext = record
      Msg: Cardinal;              {the message identifier}
      Child: HWND;                {a handle to a child window}
      Next: Longint;              {next or previous flag}
      Result: Longint;            {returns zero}
end;
```

Description

The WM_MDINEXT message activates the next or previous child window in an MDI client window. If the currently active child window is maximized and another child window becomes active, Windows restores the active child window and maximizes the newly activated child window.

Members

Msg: The message identifier. This member is set to the message identifier constant WM_MDINEXT.

Child: Specifies a handle of a child window. The next or previous child window relative to this window is activated, depending on the value of the Next member. If this member is zero, the next or previous child window relative to the currently active child window is activated.

Next: The next window or previous window flag. If this member is set to zero, the next child window is activated. If this member is set to one, the previous child window is activated.

Result: This message always returns zero.

See Also

WM_MDIACTIVATE, WM_MDIGETACTIVE

WM_MDIREFRESHMENU

Syntax

```
TWMMDIRefreshMenu = record
      Msg: Cardinal;              {the message identifier}
      Unused: array[0..3] of Word;  {not used}
      Result: Longint;            {returns a menu handle}
end;
```

Description

This message is sent to the MDI frame window to refresh the frame window's menu.

Members

Msg: The message identifier. This member is set to the message identifier constant WM_MDIREFRESHMENU.

Unused: This member is not used by this message.

Result: If this message succeeds, it returns a handle to the menu of the frame window; otherwise it returns zero.

See Also

WM_MDISETMENU

WM_MDIRESTORE

Syntax

```
TWMMDIRestore = record
    Msg: Cardinal;              {the message identifier}
    IDChild: HWND;              {the handle of a child window}
    Unused: Longint;            {not used}
    Result: Longint;            {returns zero}
end;
```

Description

This message restores an MDI child window from a maximized or minimized state.

Members

Msg: The message identifier. This member is set to the message identifier constant WM_MDIRESTORE.

IDChild: Specifies the handle of the MDI child window to be restored.

Unused: This member is not used by this message.

Result: This message always returns zero.

See Also

WM_MDIMAXIMIZE

WM_MDISETMENU

Syntax

```
TWMMDISetMenu = record
    Msg: Cardinal;              {the message identifier}
    MenuFrame: HMENU;           {the handle of the frame window menu}
    MenuWindow: HMENU;          {the handle of the child window menu}
    Result: Longint;            {returns a menu handle}
end;
```

Description

This message is used to replace the entire menu, or just the window menu, of an MDI frame window. The MDI child window menu items are removed from the previous Window menu and added to the new Window menu if this message replaces the Window menu. The system menu icon and window buttons are removed from the previous frame window menu and added to the new frame window menu, if an MDI child window is maximized and this message replaces the MDI frame window menu.

Members

Msg: The message identifier. This member is set to the message identifier constant WM_MDISETMENU.

MenuFrame: Specifies the handle of the new frame window menu. If this member is zero, the frame window menu is unaffected.

MenuWindow: Specifies the handle of the new window menu. If this member is zero, the window menu is unaffected.

Result: If the message succeeds, it returns the handle of the old frame window menu; otherwise it returns zero.

See Also

WM_MDIREFRESHMENU

WM_MDITILE

Syntax

```
TWMMDITile = record
      Msg: Cardinal;          {the message identifier}
      Tile: Longint;          {tile flags}
      Unused: Longint;        {not used}
      Result: Longint;        {returns a one if successful}
end;
```

Description

This message instructs an MDI client window to arrange its child windows in a tiled format.

Members

Msg: The message identifier. This member is set to the message identifier constant WM_MDITILE.

Tile: A flag specifying how the child windows are to be tiled. This member may be set to one value from Table A-21.

Unused: This member is not used by this message.

Result: If the function succeeds, it returns one; otherwise it returns zero.

See Also

WM_MDICASCADE, WM_MDIICONARRANGE

Table A-21: TWMDITile.Tile Values

Value	Description
MDITILE_HORIZONTAL	The windows are tiled horizontally.
MDITILE_SKIPDISABLED	Any disabled windows are not tiled.
MDITILE_VERTICAL	The windows are tiled vertically.

WM_MEASUREITEM

Syntax

```
TWMMeasureItem = record
      Msg: Cardinal;                           {the message identifier}
      IDCtl: HWnd;                             {control ID}
      MeasureItemStruct: PMeasureItemStruct;   {pointer to data structure}
      Result: Longint;                         {returns a one if handled}
   end;
```

Description

The WM_MEASUREITEM structure is sent to the owning window of an owner-drawn button, combo box, list box, list view, or menu item when that control or menu item is created. This allows the application to specify the size of the control. The TWMMeasureItem structure pointed to by the MeasureItemStruct member contains information identifying the control sending the message. The application should fill in the item-Width and itemHeight members of this structure before returning. If a list box or combo box is created with the LBS_OWNERDRAWVARIABLE or CBS_OWNERDRAWVARIABLE style, the message is sent to each item in that control.

Members

Msg: The message identifier. This member is set to the message identifier constant WM_MEASUREITEM.

IDCtl: Specifies the identifier of the control to be measured, and will match the CtlID member of the structure pointed to by the MeasureItemStruct member. If this member is zero, the message was sent by a menu; otherwise it was sent by a button, combo box, list view, or list box. If this member is nonzero and the itemID member of the structure pointed to by the MeasureItemStruct member is set to -1, the message was sent by the edit control of a drop-down combo box.

MeasureItemStruct: A pointer to a TMeasureItemStruct structure containing information on the control sending the message. The application must fill in the itemWidth and itemHeight members of this structure before returning. The TMeasureItemStruct structure is defined as:

```
TMeasureItemStruct = packed record
      CtlType: UINT;              {a control type flag}
      CtlID: UINT;               {the sending control identifier}
      itemID: UINT;              {the item identifier}
      itemWidth: UINT;           {the item width}
      itemHeight: UINT;          {the item height}
      itemData: DWORD;           {associated data}
end;
```

CtlType: A flag specifying the type of control to be measured. This member may contain one value from Table A-22.

CtlID: Specifies the identifier if the sending control is a combo box, list box, or button.

itemID: Specifies the item identifier of the item being measured if the sending control is a menu item, list box, or combo box.

itemWidth: Specifies the width of a menu item, in pixels.

itemHeight: Specifies the height of a menu item or an item in a combo box or list box, in pixels.

itemData: Specifies the 32-bit data value that was supplied as the lParam parameter of the CB_ADDSTRING, CB_INSERTSTRING, LB_ADDSTRING, or LB_INSERTSTRING messages, or the value last assigned to the control by the LB_SETITEMDATA or CB_SETITEMDATA messages. For a list box or combo box with LBS_HASSTRINGS or CBS_HASSTRINGS, this member is initially zero. If the ctlType member contains the ODT_BUTTON or ODT_STATIC flags, this member is zero.

Result: If the application handles this message, set this member to one.

See Also

WM_DRAWITEM

Table A-22: TWMMeasureItem.TMeasureItemStruct.CtlType Values

Value	Description
ODT_BUTTON	Indicates an owner-drawn button.
ODT_COMBOBOX	Indicates an owner-drawn combo box.
ODT_LISTBOX	Indicates an owner-drawn list box.
ODT_LISTVIEW	Indicates an owner-drawn list view.
ODT_MENU	Indicates an owner-drawn menu item.
ODT_STATIC	Indicates an owner-drawn static control.
ODT_TAB	Indicates an owner-drawn tab control.

WM_MENUCHAR

Syntax

```
TWMMenuChar = record
      Msg: Cardinal;            {the message identifier}
      User: Char;               {the ASCII value of the character}
      Unused: Byte;             {not used}
      MenuFlag: Word;           {a menu type flag}
      Menu: HMENU;              {a menu handle}
      Result: Longint;          {returns an action code}
end;
```

Description

This message is sent when a menu is active and the user presses a key that is not an accelerator or shortcut key for any item in the menu.

Members

Msg: The message identifier. This member is set to the message identifier constant WM_MENUCHAR.

User: Specifies the ASCII value of the character that was pressed.

Unused: The member is not used by this message.

MenuFlag: Specifies a flag indicating the type of active menu. If this member is set to MF_POPUP, a drop-down menu, submenu, or pop-up menu is currently active. If this member is set to MF_SYSMENU, the system menu is currently active.

Menu: Specifies the handle of the active menu.

Result: If the application handles this message, it should return one value from Table A-23 in the high-order word of this member.

See Also

WM_CHAR, WM_MENUSELECT

Table A-23: TWMMenuChar.Result Values

Value	Description
0	Discards the character and sends a beep to the system speaker.
1	Closes the active menu.
2	Specifies that the low-order word of the return value contains the zero-based index of the menu item to select.

A

Appendix

WM_MENUSELECT

Syntax

```
TWMMenuSelect = record
       Msg: Cardinal;              {the message identifier}
       IDItem: Word;               {the menu item identifier}
       MenuFlag: Word;             {menu item flags}
       Menu: HMENU;                {a menu handle}
       Result: Longint;            {returns a zero if handled}
end;
```

Description

When the user makes a selection from a menu, a WM_MENUSELECT message is sent to the window that owns the menu.

Members

Msg: The message identifier. This member is set to the message identifier constant WM_MENUSELECT.

IDItem: Specifies the identifier of the selected menu item. If the selected menu item opens a submenu, this member will contain the zero-based index of the menu item opening the submenu.

MenuFlag: A series of flags containing information about the menu item selected. This member may contain one or more flags from Table A-24.

Menu: Specifies the handle of the menu that was clicked.

Result: If the application handles this message, set this member to zero.

See Also

GetSubMenu, WM_ENTERMENULOOP, WM_EXITMENULOOP

Table A-24: TWMMenuSelect.MenuFlag Values

Value	Description
MF_BITMAP	Menu item displays a bitmap.
MF_CHECKED	Menu item is checked.
MF_DISABLED	Menu item is disabled.
MF_GRAYED	Menu item is grayed out.
MF_HILITE	Menu item is highlighted.
MF_MOUSESELECT	Menu item is selected with the mouse.
MF_OWNERDRAW	Menu item is an owner-drawn item.
MF_POPUP	Menu item opens a drop-down menu or submenu.
MF_SYSMENU	Menu item is contained in the system menu.

WM_MOUSEACTIVATE

Syntax

```
TWMMouseActivate = record
        Msg: Cardinal;            {the message identifier}
        TopLevel: HWND;           {a handle to a parent window}
        HitTestCode: Word;        {the hit test value}
        MouseMsg: Word;           {the mouse message}
        Result: Longint;          {returns an action code}
end;
```

Description

The WM_MOUSEACTIVATE message is sent when the user clicks on an inactive window. If the clicked window is a child window, its parent window will receive the message only if the child window passes it to the DefWindowProc function. The DefWindowProc function will pass the message to the child window's parent window before processing the message, allowing the parent window to determine if the child window should be activated.

Members

Msg: The message identifier. This member is set to the message identifier constant WM_MOUSEACTIVATE.

TopLevel: A handle to the top-level parent window of the window to be activated.

HitTestCode: Specifies a flag indicating the area of the window that was clicked. This member may contain one value from Table A-30. Please see the WM_NCHITTEST message for a list of available flags.

MouseMsg: The mouse message that was generated as a result of the mouse button click. This is either processed or discarded according to the return value.

Result: This message returns a result indicating if the window should be activated and if the mouse message should be processed. This may be one value from Table A-25.

See Also

DefWindowProc, WM_ACTIVATE, WM_NCHITTEST

Table A-25: TWMMouseActivate.Result Values

Value	Description
MA_ACTIVATE	Activate the window, post the message
MA_ACTIVATEANDEAT	Activate the window, discard the message
MA_NOACTIVATE	Window not activated, post the message
MA_NOACTIVATEANDEAT	Window not activated, discard the message

WM_MOUSEMOVE

Syntax

TWMMouseMove = record
    Msg: Cardinal;   {the message identifier}
    Keys: Longint;   {virtual key flags}
    case Integer of
    0: (
    XPos: Smallint;   {the horizontal cursor coordinate}
    YPos: Smallint);   {the vertical cursor coordinate}
    1: (
    Pos: TSmallPoint;   {a TSmallPoint structure containing cursor coordinates}
    Result: Longint);   {returns a zero if handled}
end;

Description

This message is posted to a window when the user moves the mouse cursor within the client area of the window. However, if another window captured the mouse, then the message is sent to that window.

Members

Msg: The message identifier. This member is set to the message identifier constant WM_MOUSEMOVE.

Keys: Indicates if specific virtual keys are held down at the time of the mouse move. This member can contain one or more values from Table A-26.

XPos: The horizontal coordinate of the mouse cursor, relative to the client area.

YPos: The vertical coordinate of the mouse cursor, relative to the client area.

Pos: A TSmallPoint structure that contains the current mouse coordinates.

Result: If the application handles this message, set this member to zero.

See Also

GetCapture, SetCapture, WM_NCMOUSEMOVE

Table A-26: TWMMouseMove.Keys Values

Value	Description
MK_CONTROL	Indicates that the Ctrl key is held down.
MK_LBUTTON	Indicates that the left mouse button is down.
MK_MBUTTON	Indicates that the middle mouse button is down.
MK_RBUTTON	Indicates that the right mouse button is down.
MK_SHIFT	Indicates that the Shift key is held down.

WM_MOVE

Syntax

```
TWMMove = record
      Msg: Cardinal;          {the message identifier}
      Unused: Longint;        {not used}
      case Integer of
      0: (
      XPos: Smallint;         {the horizontal cursor coordinate}
      YPos: Smallint);        {the vertical cursor coordinate}
      1: (
      Pos: TSmallPoint;       {a TSmallPoint structure containing cursor coordinates}
      Result: Longint);       {returns a zero if handled}
end;
```

Description

This message is sent when a window is moved. Coordinates are relative to the screen if the window is a top-level window; they are relative to the parent window's client area if the window is a child window.

Members

Msg: The message identifier. This member is set to the message identifier constant WM_MOVE.

Unused: The member is not used by this message.

XPos: The horizontal coordinate of the upper left corner of the client area of the moved window.

YPos: The vertical coordinate of the upper left corner of the client area of the moved window.

Pos: A TSmallPoint structure that contains the coordinates of the upper left corner of the client area of the moved window.

Result: If the application handles this message, set this member to zero.

See Also

WM_GETMINMAXINFO

WM_NCACTIVATE

```
TWMNCActivate = record
      Msg: Cardinal;          {the message identifier}
      Active: BOOL;           {activation state}
      Unused: Longint;        {not used}
      Result: Longint;        {returns one or zero}
end;
```

Description

When a window's nonclient area needs to be changed to indicate an active or inactive state, the WM_NCACTIVATE message is sent.

Members

Msg: The message identifier. This member is set to the message identifier constant WM_NCACTIVATE.

Active: Indicates when a title bar or icon needs to be changed to indicate an active or inactive state. This member is set to TRUE when the title bar and icon are to be drawn as active; it is FALSE when the title bar and icon are to be drawn as inactive.

Unused: This member is not used by this message.

Result: If the Active member is set to TRUE, the return value is ignored. When the Active member is set to FALSE, the application should return a one if the message is to be processed normally; it should return zero to prevent the title bar and icon from being deactivated.

See Also

WM_ACTIVATE

WM_NCCALCSIZE

Syntax

```
TWMNCCalcSize = record
      Msg: Cardinal;                      {the message identifier}
      CalcValidRects: BOOL;               {valid info flag}
      CalcSize_Params: PNCCalcSizeParams; {a pointer to sizing information}
      Result: Longint;                    {returns an action code}
end;
```

Description

This message is sent when the size and position of a window's client area are calculated.

Members

Msg: The message identifier. This member is set to the message identifier constant WM_NCCALCSIZE.

CalcValidRects: Indicates if the application should specify where valid information exists in the client area. If this member is set to TRUE, the CalcSize_Params member will contain a pointer to a TNCCalcSizeParams structure containing data on the size, position, and valid portions of the client area. If this member is set to FALSE, the application does not need to specify the valid portions of the client area and the Calc-Size_Params member will point to a TRect structure.

CalcSize_Params: If the CalcValidRects member is set to FALSE, this member will point to a TRect structure containing the new coordinates of the window. Otherwise, this member points to a TNCCalcSizeParams structure containing information used to calculate the new size and position of the client window. The TNCCalcSizeParams structure is defined as:

```
TNCCalcSizeParams = packed record
      rgrc: array[0..2] of TRect;          {rectangle array}
      lppos: PWindowPos;                   {a pointer to window position data}
end;
```

rgrc: Points to an array of TRect structures that contains window position coordinates. The first entry contains the new coordinates of the window. The second entry contains the original coordinates of the window before it was moved or sized. The third entry contains the original coordinates of the window's client area before it was moved or resized. If the window is a top-level window, these coordinates are relative to the screen. If it is a child window, the coordinates are relative to its parent window's client area.

lppos: A pointer to a TWindowPos structure containing the size and position values specified when the window was moved or sized. The TWindowPos structure is defined as:

```
TWindowPos = packed record
      hwnd: HWND;                      {a handle to a window}
      hwndInsertAfter: HWND;           {a window handle or positioning flag}
      x: Integer;                      {the horizontal position}
      y: Integer;                      {the vertical position}
      cx: Integer;                     {the width of the window}
      cy: Integer;                     {the height of the window}
      flags: UINT                      {size and positioning flags}
end;
```

hwnd: The handle of the window to be moved or resized.

hwndInsertAfter: Identifies the window that will precede the repositioned window in the Z-order. This is either a window handle or one value from Table A-27. This member is ignored if the SWP_NOZORDER flag is set in the flags member. If this member is set to zero, the window will be placed at the top of the Z-order. If a window's Z-order position is placed above all other topmost windows, that window becomes a topmost window. This has the same effect as specifying the HWND_TOPMOST flag for this member.

x: The horizontal coordinate of the window's upper left corner. If this is a child window, the coordinates are relative to the parent window's client area.

y: The vertical coordinate of the window's upper left corner. If this is a child window, the coordinates are relative to the parent window's client area.

cx: The window's new width, in pixels.

cy: The window's new height, in pixels.

flags: Specifies a combination of values from Table A-28 that will affect the size and position of the window. Two or more values can be specified by using the Boolean OR operator.

Result: If the CalcValidRects member is set to FALSE, the application should return zero. If the CalcValidRects member is set to TRUE, the application can return a zero or a combination of values from Table A-29.

See Also

DefWindowProc, MoveWindow, SetWindowPos

Table A-27: TWMNCCalcSize.CalcSize_Params.lppos.hwndInsertAfter Values

Value	Description
HWND_BOTTOM	Places the window at the bottom of the Z-order. If this window was a topmost window, it loses its topmost status and is placed below all other windows.
HWND_NOTOPMOST	Places the window above all non-topmost windows, but behind all topmost windows. If the window is already a non-topmost window, this flag has no effect.
HWND_TOP	Places the window at the top of the Z-order.
HWND_TOPMOST	Places the window above all non-topmost windows; it will retain its topmost position even when deactivated.

Table A-28: TWMNCCalcSize.CalcSize_Params.lppos.flags Values

Value	Description
SWP_DRAWFRAME	Draws the frame defined in the window's class description around the window.
SWP_FRAMECHANGED	Causes a WM_NCCALCSIZE message to be sent to the window, even if the window size is not changing.
SWP_HIDEWINDOW	Hides the window.
SWP_NOACTIVATE	Does not activate the window. If this flag is not set, the window is activated and moved to the top of the topmost or non-topmost group depending on the hwndInsertAfter member.
SWP_NOCOPYBITS	Discards the entire client area. If this flag is not set, the valid area of the client area is saved and copied back into the client area after all movement and positioning is completed.
SWP_NOMOVE	Retains the current position, ignoring the X and Y members.

Value	Description
SWP_NOOWNERZORDER	Does not change the owner window's position in the Z-order.
SWP_NOREDRAW	When this flag is set, no repainting occurs, and the application must explicitly invalidate or redraw any parts of the window that need to be redrawn, including the nonclient area and scroll bars.
SWP_NOREPOSITION	The same as the SWP_NOOWNERZORDER flag.
SWP_NOSENDCHANGING	The window will not receive WM_WINDOWPOSCHANGING messages.
SWP_NOSIZE	Retains the current size, ignoring the CX and CY members.
SWP_NOZORDER	Retains the current Z-order, effectively causing the hwndInsertAfter member to be ignored.
SWP_SHOWWINDOW	Displays the window.

Table A-29: TWMNCCalcSize.Result Values

Value	Description
WVR_ALIGNBOTTOM	Aligns the client area to the bottom of the window.
WVR_ALIGNLEFT	Aligns the client area to the left of the window.
WVR_ALIGNRIGHT	Aligns the client area to the right of the window.
WVR_ALIGNTOP	Aligns the client area to the top of the window.
WVR_HREDRAW	Redraws the entire window if the client area is sized horizontally.
WVR_VREDRAW	Redraws the entire window if the client area is sized vertically.
WVR_REDRAW	Redraws the entire window if the client area is sized vertically or horizontally.
WVR_VALIDRECTS	Indicates that the rectangles specified in rgrc[1] and rgrc[2] are valid source and destination rectangles. These determine which part of the client area is to be preserved. The source rectangle is copied, and any part that is in the destination rectangle gets clipped.

WM_NCCREATE

Syntax

```
TWMNCCreate = record
    Msg: Cardinal;                      {the message identifier}
    Unused: Integer;                    {not used}
    CreateStruct: PCreateStruct;        {a pointer to a TCreateStruct structure}
    Result: Longint;                    {returns zero or one}
```

end;

Description

The WM_NCCREATE message is sent to a window right before the WM_CREATE message is sent when a window is created.

Members

Msg: The message identifier. This member is set to the message identifier constant WM_NCCREATE.

Unused: This member is not used by this message.

CreateStruct: A pointer to a TCreateStruct structure that contains data for initializing the window. The TCreateStruct structure is defined as:

```
TCreateStruct = packed record
    lpCreateParams: Pointer;      {a pointer to application-defined data}
    hInstance: HINST;             {a handle to the module instance}
    hMenu: HMENU;                 {a handle to the menu, or a child window identifier}
    hwndParent: HWND;             {a handle to the parent window}
    cy: Integer;                  {initial height of the window}
    cx: Integer;                  {initial width of the window}
    y: Integer;                   {initial vertical position}
    x: Integer;                   {initial horizontal position}
    style: Longint;               {window style flags}
    lpszName: PAnsiChar;          {a pointer to the window name string}
    lpszClass: PAnsiChar;         {a pointer to the class name string}
    dwExStyle: DWORD;             {extended window style flags}
end;
```

Please see WM_CREATE for a description of this data structure.

Result: If the application processes this message, it should return a one to indicate that the window can be created. Otherwise; it can return zero, blocking the creation of the window and causing the CreateWindow or CreateWindowEx function that was called to create the window to return a zero.

See Also

CreateWindow, CreateWindowEx, DefWindowProc, WM_CREATE

WM_NCDESTROY

Syntax

```
TWMNCDestroy = record
    Msg: Cardinal;                {the message identifier}
    Unused: array[0..3] of Word;  {not used}
    Result: Longint;              {returns a zero if handled}
end;
```

Description

The WM_NCDESTROY message is sent to a window by the DestroyWindow function. It is received following the WM_DESTROY message, and it informs the window that its nonclient area is being destroyed. This message causes any internal memory allocated for the window to be freed.

Members

Msg: The message identifier. This member is set to the message identifier constant WM_NCDESTROY.

Unused: This member is not used by this message.

Result: If the application handles this message, set this member to zero.

See Also

DestroyWindow, WM_CREATE, WM_DESTROY, WM_NCCREATE

WM_NCHITTEST

Syntax

```
TWMNCHitTest = record
      Msg: Cardinal;          {the message identifier}
      Unused: Longint;        {not used}
      case Integer of
      0: (
      XPos: Smallint;         {the horizontal mouse cursor coordinate}
      YPos: Smallint);        {the vertical mouse cursor coordinate}
      1: (
      Pos: TSmallPoint;       {a TSmallPoint structure containing cursor coordinates}
      Result: Longint);       {returns a hit location}
   end;
```

Description

The WM_NCHITTEST message is sent to a window when the mouse cursor moves over the window or a mouse button is clicked. If the mouse has been captured, the message is sent to the capturing window.

Members

Msg: The message identifier. This member is set to the message identifier constant WM_NCHITTEST.

Unused: This member is not used by this message.

XPos: The x coordinate of the mouse cursor relative to the screen.

YPos: The y coordinate of the mouse cursor relative to the screen.

Pos: A TSmallPoint structure containing the coordinates of the mouse cursor relative to the screen.

Result: This message returns a flag indicating the position of the mouse cursor within the window, and may be one value from Table A-30.

See Also

DefWindowProc, WM_MOUSEACTIVATE, WM_MOUSEMOVE, WM_NCMOUSEMOVE

Table A-30: TWMNCHitTest.Result Values

Value	Description
HTBORDER	The border of a window without a sizing border.
HTBOTTOM	The lower horizontal border.
HTBOTTOMLEFT	The lower left corner of a window border.
HTBOTTOMRIGHT	The lower right corner of a window border.
HTCAPTION	The title bar.
HTCLIENT	The client area.
HTERROR	The screen background or a dividing line between windows. This flag is the same as HTNOWHERE, except that it is treated as an error, and the DefWindowProc function produces a system beep.
HTGROWBOX	The size box. This is the same as the HTSIZE flag.
HTHSCROLL	The horizontal scroll bar.
HTLEFT	The left border.
HTMENU	The menu.
HTNOWHERE	The screen background or a dividing line between windows.
HTREDUCE	The Minimize button.
HTRIGHT	The right border.
HTSIZE	The size box.
HTSYSMENU	The system menu or in the Close button in a child window.
HTTOP	The upper horizontal border.
HTTOPLEFT	The upper left corner of a window border.
HTTOPRIGHT	The upper right corner of a window border.
HTTRANSPARENT	In a window currently covered by another window.
HTVSCROLL	The vertical scroll bar.
HTZOOM	The Maximize button.

A

Appendix

WM_NCLBUTTONDBLCLK

Syntax

```
TWMNCLButtonDblClk = record
    Msg: Cardinal;              {the message identifier}
    HitTest: Longint;           {a hit test flag}
    XCursor: Smallint;          {the horizontal cursor coordinate}
    YCursor: Smallint;          {the vertical cursor coordinate}
    Result: Longint;            {returns a zero if handled}
end;
```

Description

If the mouse cursor is in the nonclient area of a window, and the left mouse button is double-clicked, a WM_NCLBUTTONDBLCLK message is sent to the window under the cursor. However, if another window captured mouse input by calling the SetCapture function, the message is not posted. The double click is generated when the user presses the button, releases it, and presses it again at the same coordinates within the system's double-click time interval. This process generates a series of four messages, in the following order: WM_NCLBUTTONDOWN, WM_NCLBUTTONUP, WM_NCLBUTTONDBLCLK, and WM_NCLBUTTONUP. A window does not have to have the CS_DBLCLKS class style to receive the WM_NCLBUTTONDBLCLK message.

Members

Msg: The message identifier. This member is set to the message identifier constant WM_NCLBUTTONDBLCLK.

HitTest: A flag indicating the area in the window where the double click occurred. This can be one value from Table A-30 under the WM_NCHITTEST message.

XCursor: Specifies the horizontal coordinate of the mouse cursor, relative to the screen.

YCursor: Specifies the vertical coordinate of the mouse cursor, relative to the screen.

Result: If the application handles this message, set this member to zero.

See Also

DefWindowProc, WM_NCHITTEST, WM_NCLBUTTONDOWN, WM_NCLBUTTONUP, WM_SYSCOMMAND

WM_NCLBUTTONDOWN

Syntax

```
TWMNCLButtonDown = record
    Msg: Cardinal;              {the message identifier}
    HitTest: Longint;           {a hit test flag}
    XCursor: Smallint;          {the horizontal cursor coordinate}
```

```
            YCursor: Smallint;          {the vertical cursor coordinate}
            Result: Longint;            {returns a zero if handled}
    end;
```

Description

If the mouse cursor is in the nonclient area of a window and the left mouse button is pressed, a WM_NCLBUTTONDOWN message is sent to the window under the cursor. However, if another window has captured mouse input by calling the SetCapture function, the message is not posted.

Members

Msg: The message identifier. This member is set to the message identifier constant WM_NCLBUTTONDOWN.

HitTest: A flag indicating the area in the window where the button press occurred. This can be one value from Table A-30 under the WM_NCHITTEST message.

XCursor: Specifies the horizontal coordinate of the mouse cursor, relative to the screen.

YCursor: Specifies the vertical coordinate of the mouse cursor, relative to the screen.

Result: If the application handles this message, set this member to zero.

See Also

DefWindowProc, WM_NCHITTEST, WM_NCLBUTTONDBLCLK, WM_NCLBUTTONUP, WM_SYSCOMMAND

WM_NCLBUTTONUP

Syntax

```
TWMNCLButtonUp = record
        Msg: Cardinal;             {the message identifier}
        HitTest: Longint;          {a hit test flag}
        XCursor: Smallint;         {the horizontal cursor coordinate}
        YCursor: Smallint;         {the vertical cursor coordinate}
        Result: Longint;           {returns a zero if handled}
    end;
```

Description

If the mouse cursor is in the nonclient area of a window and the left mouse button is released, a WM_NCLBUTTONUP message is sent to the window under the cursor. However, if another window has captured mouse input by calling the SetCapture function, the message is not posted.

Members

Msg: The message identifier. This member is set to the message identifier constant WM_NCLBUTTONUP.

HitTest: A flag indicating the area in the window where the button release occurred. This can be one value from Table A-30 under the WM_NCHITTEST message.

XCursor: Specifies the horizontal coordinate of the mouse cursor, relative to the screen.

YCursor: Specifies the vertical coordinate of the mouse cursor, relative to the screen.

Result: If the application handles this message, set this member to zero.

See Also

DefWindowProc, WM_NCHITTEST, WM_NCLBUTTONDBLCLK, WM_NCLBUTTONDOWN, WM_SYSCOMMAND

WM_NCMBUTTONDBLCLK

Syntax

```
TWMNCMButtonDblClk = record
    Msg: Cardinal;              {the message identifier}
    HitTest: Longint;          {a hit test flag}
    XCursor: Smallint;         {the horizontal cursor coordinate}
    YCursor: Smallint;         {the vertical cursor coordinate}
    Result: Longint;           {returns a zero if handled}
end;
```

Description

If the mouse cursor is in the nonclient area of a window, and the middle mouse button is double-clicked, a WM_NCMBUTTONDBLCLK message is sent to the window under the cursor. However, if another window captured mouse input by calling the Set-Capture function, the message is not posted. The double click is generated when the user presses the button, releases it, and presses it again at the same coordinates within the system's double-click time interval. This process generates a series of four messages, in the following order: WM_NCMBUTTONDOWN, WM_NCMBUTTONUP, WM_NCMBUTTONDBLCLK, and WM_NCMBUTTONUP. A window does not have to have the CS_DBLCLKS class style to receive the WM_NCMBUTTONDBLCLK message.

Members

Msg: The message identifier. This member is set to the message identifier constant WM_NCMBUTTONDBLCLK.

HitTest: A flag indicating the area in the window where the double click occurred. This can be one value from Table A-30 under the WM_NCHITTEST message.

XCursor: Specifies the horizontal coordinate of the mouse cursor, relative to the screen.

YCursor: Specifies the vertical coordinate of the mouse cursor, relative to the screen.

Result: If the application handles this message, set this member to zero.

See Also

DefWindowProc, WM_NCHITTEST, WM_NCMBUTTONDOWN, WM_NCMBUTTONUP, WM_SYSCOMMAND

WM_NCMBUTTONDOWN

Syntax

```
TWMNCMButtonDown = record
    Msg: Cardinal;          {the message identifier}
    HitTest: Longint;       {a hit test flag}
    XCursor: Smallint;      {the horizontal cursor coordinate}
    YCursor: Smallint;      {the vertical cursor coordinate}
    Result: Longint;        {returns a zero if handled}
end;
```

Description

If the mouse cursor is in the nonclient area of a window and the middle mouse button is pressed, a WM_NCMBUTTONDOWN message is sent to the window under the cursor. However, if another window has captured mouse input by calling the SetCapture function, the message is not posted.

Members

Msg: The message identifier. This member is set to the message identifier constant WM_NCMBUTTONDOWN.

HitTest: A flag indicating the area in the window where the button press occurred. This can be one value from Table A-30 under the WM_NCHITTEST message.

XCursor: Specifies the horizontal coordinate of the mouse cursor, relative to the screen.

YCursor: Specifies the vertical coordinate of the mouse cursor, relative to the screen.

Result: If the application handles this message, set this member to zero.

See Also

DefWindowProc, WM_NCHITTEST, WM_NCMBUTTONDBLCLK, WM_NCMBUTTONUP, WM_SYSCOMMAND

WM_NCMBUTTONUP

Syntax

```
TWMNCMButtonUp = record
    Msg: Cardinal;          {the message identifier}
    HitTest: Longint;       {a hit test flag}
    XCursor: Smallint;      {the horizontal cursor coordinate}
    YCursor: Smallint;      {the vertical cursor coordinate}
```

Result: Longint;   {returns a zero if handled}
end;

Description

If the mouse cursor is in the nonclient area of a window and the middle mouse button is released, a WM_NCMBUTTONUP message is sent to the window under the cursor. However, if another window has captured mouse input by calling the SetCapture function, the message is not posted.

Members

Msg: The message identifier. This member is set to the message identifier constant WM_NCMBUTTONUP.

HitTest: A flag indicating the area in the window where the button release occurred. This can be one value from Table A-30 under the WM_NCHITTEST message.

XCursor: Specifies the horizontal coordinate of the mouse cursor, relative to the screen.

YCursor: Specifies the vertical coordinate of the mouse cursor, relative to the screen.

Result: If the application handles this message, set this member to zero.

See Also

DefWindowProc, WM_NCHITTEST, WM_NCMBUTTONDBLCLK, WM_NCMBUTTONDOWN, WM_SYSCOMMAND

WM_NCMOUSEMOVE

Syntax

```
TWMNCMouseMove = record
      Msg: Cardinal;              {the message identifier}
      HitTest: Longint;           {a hit test flag}
      XCursor: Smallint;          {the horizontal cursor coordinate}
      YCursor: Smallint;          {the vertical cursor coordinate}
      Result: Longint;            {returns a zero if handled}
end;
```

Description

This message is posted to a window when the user moves the mouse cursor within the nonclient area of the window. However, if another window captured the mouse, then the message is not posted.

Members

Msg: The message identifier. This member is set to the message identifier constant WM_NCMOUSEMOVE.

HitTest: A flag indicating the area in the window where the movement occurred. This can be one value from Table A-30 under the WM_NCHITTEST message.

XCursor: Specifies the horizontal coordinate of the mouse cursor, relative to the screen.

YCursor: Specifies the vertical coordinate of the mouse cursor, relative to the screen.

Result: If the application handles this message, set this member to zero.

See Also

DefWindowProc, WM_NCHITTEST, WM_SYSCOMMAND

WM_NCPAINT

Syntax

```
TWMNCPaint = record
      Msg: Cardinal;                    {the message identifier}
      Unused: array[0..3] of Word;      {not used}

      Result: Longint;                  {returns a zero if handled}
end;
```

Description

This message is sent to a window when the window's nonclient areas, such as its title bar and frame, need to be drawn.

Members

Msg: The message identifier. This member is set to the message identifier constant WM_NCPAINT.

Unused: The member is not used by this message.

Result: If the application handles this message, set this member to zero.

See Also

DefWindowProc, GetWindowDC, WM_PAINT

WM_NCRBUTTONDBLCLK

Syntax

```
TWMNCRButtonDblClk = record
      Msg: Cardinal;         {the message identifier}
      HitTest: Longint;      {a hit test flag}
      XCursor: Smallint;     {the horizontal cursor coordinate}
      YCursor: Smallint;     {the vertical cursor coordinate}
      Result: Longint;       {returns a zero if handled}
end;
```

Description

If the mouse cursor is in the nonclient area of a window, and the right mouse button is double-clicked, a WM_NCRBUTTONDBLCLK message is sent to the window under the cursor. However, if another window captured mouse input by calling the SetCapture function, the message is not posted. The double click is generated when the user presses the button, releases it, and presses it again at the same coordinates within the system's double-click time interval. This process generates a series of four messages, in the following order: WM_NCRBUTTONDOWN, WM_NCRBUTTONUP, WM_NCRBUTTONDBLCLK, and WM_NCRBUTTONUP. A window does not have to have the CS_DBLCLKS class style to receive the WM_NCRBUTTONDBLCLK message.

Members

Msg: The message identifier. This member is set to the message identifier constant WM_NCRBUTTONDBLCLK.

HitTest: A flag indicating the area in the window where the double click occurred. This can be one value from Table A-30 under the WM_NCHITTEST message.

XCursor: Specifies the horizontal coordinate of the mouse cursor, relative to the screen.

YCursor: Specifies the vertical coordinate of the mouse cursor, relative to the screen.

Result: If the application handles this message, set this member to zero.

See Also

DefWindowProc, WM_NCHITTEST, WM_NCRBUTTONDOWN, WM_NCRBUTTONUP, WM_SYSCOMMAND

WM_NCRBUTTONDOWN

Syntax

```
TWMNCRButtonDown = record
      Msg: Cardinal;              {the message identifier}
      HitTest: Longint;          {a hit test flag}
      XCursor: Smallint;         {the horizontal cursor coordinate}
      YCursor: Smallint;         {the vertical cursor coordinate}
      Result: Longint;           {returns a zero if handled}
end;
```

Description

If the mouse cursor is in the nonclient area of a window and the right mouse button is pressed, a WM_NCRBUTTONDOWN message is sent to the window under the cursor. However, if another window has captured mouse input by calling the SetCapture function, the message is not posted.

Members

Msg: The message identifier. This member is set to the message identifier constant WM_NCRBUTTONDOWN.

HitTest: A flag indicating the area in the window where the button press occurred. This can be one value from Table A-30 under the WM_NCHITTEST message.

XCursor: Specifies the horizontal coordinate of the mouse cursor, relative to the screen.

YCursor: Specifies the vertical coordinate of the mouse cursor, relative to the screen.

Result: If the application handles this message, set this member to zero.

See Also

DefWindowProc, WM_NCHITTEST, WM_NCRBUTTONDBLCLK, WM_NCRBUTTONUP, WM_SYSCOMMAND

WM_NCRBUTTONUP

Syntax

```
TWMNCRButtonUp = record
        Msg: Cardinal;            {the message identifier}
        HitTest: Longint;         {a hit test flag}
        XCursor: Smallint;        {the horizontal cursor coordinate}
        YCursor: Smallint;        {the vertical cursor coordinate}
        Result: Longint;          {returns a zero if handled}
end;
```

Description

If the mouse cursor is in the nonclient area of a window, and the right mouse button is released by the user, a WM_NCRBUTTONUP message is sent to the window under the cursor. However, if another window captured the mouse, then the message is not posted.

Members

Msg: The message identifier. This member is set to the message identifier constant WM_NCRBUTTONUP.

HitTest: A flag indicating the area in the window where the button release occurred. This can be one value from Table A-30 under the WM_NCHITTEST message.

XCursor: Specifies the horizontal coordinate of the mouse cursor, relative to the screen.

YCursor: Specifies the vertical coordinate of the mouse cursor, relative to the screen.

Result: If the application handles this message, set this member to zero.

See Also

DefWindowProc, WM_NCHITTEST, WM_NCRBUTTONDBLCLK, WM_NCRBUTTONDOWN, WM_SYSCOMMAND

WM_NEXTDLGCTRL

Syntax

```
TWMNextDlgCtrl = record
    Msg: Cardinal;              {the message identifier}
    CtlFocus: Longint;          {control handle or direction flag}
    Handle: WordBool;           {the focus flag}
    Unused: Word;               {not used}
    Result: Longint;            {returns a zero if handled}
end;
```

Description

This message instructs the window to move the keyboard focus to the next or previous control.

Members

Msg: The message identifier. This member is set to the message identifier constant WM_NEXTDLGCTRL.

CtlFocus: Specifies the handle of the control to receive the keyboard focus, or a flag indicating the direction that the keyboard focus should move, depending on the value of the Handle member. If the Handle member is set to TRUE, this member contains the handle of the window that should receive keyboard focus. If the Handle member is set to FALSE, this member contains a flag that indicates whether the previous or next control in the tab sequence is to receive keyboard focus. In this instance, if this member is set to zero, the next control receives focus; otherwise the previous control receives focus.

Handle: Indicates if the CtlFocus member contains a handle to a window to receive focus or a flag indicating the focus movement direction. If this member is set to TRUE, the CtlFocus member contains a handle to the control to receive the keyboard focus. If this member is set to FALSE, the CtlFocus member contains a flag indicating the direction in which the keyboard focus should move.

Unused: This member is not used by this message.

Result: If the application handles this message, set this member to zero.

See Also

PostMessage, SendMessage, SetFocus

WM_NOTIFY

Syntax

```
TWMNotify = record
      Msg: Cardinal;          {the message identifier}
      IDCtrl: Longint;        {the control identifier}
      NMHdr: PNMHdr;          {a pointer to a data structure}
      Result: Longint;        {not used}
end;
```

Description

The WM_NOTIFY message alerts a parent window that an event has occurred in the control sending the message.

Members

Msg: The message identifier. This member is set to the message identifier constant WM_NOTIFY.

IDCtrl: The identifier of the control sending the message.

NMHdr: A pointer to a TNMHdr data structure containing information about the control sending the message and the event occurring within the control. The TNMHdr structure is defined as:

```
TNMHdr = packed record
      hwndFrom: HWND;         {the handle of the control}
      idFrom: UINT;           {the control identifier}
      code: Integer;          {the notification code}
end;
```

hwndFrom: Specifies the handle of the control sending the message.

idFrom: Specifies the identifier of the control sending the message.

code: A flag indicating the type of notification. This member can be set to either a control specific notification code or it can contain one value from Table A-31.

Result: This member is not used by this message.

See Also

WM_KILLFOCUS, WM_LBUTTONDOWN, WM_LBUTTONDBLCLK, WM_SETFOCUS, WM_RBUTTONDOWN, WM_RBUTTONDBLCLK

Table A-31: TWMNotify.NMHdr.code Values

Value	Description
NM_CLICK	Indicates a left mouse button click.
NM_DBLCLK	Indicates a left mouse button double click.
NM_KILLFOCUS	Indicates that the control has lost input focus.

Value	Description
NM_OUTOFMEMORY	Indicates an out of memory error.
NM_RCLICK	Indicates a right mouse button click.
NM_RDBLCLK	Indicates a right mouse button double click.
NM_RETURN	Indicates that the control has input focus and the Enter key was pressed.
NM_SETFOCUS	Indicates that the control has received input focus.

WM_NOTIFYFORMAT

Syntax

```
TWMNotifyFormat = record
      Msg: Cardinal;            {the message identifier}
      From: HWND;               {a window handle}
      Command: Longint;         {a command flag}
      Result: Longint;          {returns a format code}
end;
```

Description

The WM_NOTIFYFORMAT message is sent between parent and child windows to determine if an ANSI or Unicode structure should be used in the WM_NOTIFY message.

Members

Msg: The message identifier. This member is set to the message identifier constant WM_NOTIFYFORMAT.

From: Specifies the handle of the control sending the message.

Command: A flag specifying a query status. This member can contain one value from Table A-32.

Result: This message returns a flag indicating the format of the data structure used in the WM_NOTIFY message, and can be one value from Table A-33.

See Also

DefWindowProc, WM_NOTIFY

Table A-32: TWMNotifyFormat.Command Values

Value	Description
NF_QUERY	Used by a control when sending this message to its parent to determine whether to use ANSI or Unicode data structure format. This is used in the creation of a control as a response to an NF_REQUERY message.

Value	Description
NF_REQUERY	Used to request an NF_QUERY message. In this case, the message is sent from a window to a control that it owns.

Table A-33: TWMNotifyFormat.Result Values

Value	Description
NFR_ANSI	WM_NOTIFY should use ANSI data structures.
NFR_UNICODE	WM_NOTIFY should use Unicode data structures.
0	An error has occurred.

WM_PAINT

Syntax

```
TWMPaint = record
      Msg: Cardinal;          {the message identifier}
      DC: HDC;                {a handle to a device context}
      Unused: Longint;        {not used}
      Result: Longint;        {returns zero if handled}
end;
```

Description

The WM_PAINT message is sent to request that an application repaint its window. The request can be made by the system or by another application. It can also be generated when a call is made to the UpdateWindow or RedrawWindow functions. The WM_PAINT message is sent when a window has an invalidated region and there are no other messages in the application's message queue. The DefWindowProc function will validate the invalid regions after the redraw takes place. The DefWindowProc function can also send a WM_NCPAINT message if the frame of the window needs to be repainted, or a WM_ERASEBKGND message if the background needs to be repainted. Note that the WM_PAINT message is sent only one time for each system event that requires a redraw.

If the application calls the RedrawWindow function using the RDW_INTERNALPAINT flag, an application will receive an internal paint message. In this instance, the GetUpdateRect function should be called to determine if there is an invalid region to be updated. If there is no invalid region, the application should not call the BeginPaint or EndPaint functions.

Members

Msg: The message identifier. This member is set to the message identifier constant WM_PAINT.

DC: Specifies the device context upon which the painting should occur. This member may be set to zero if painting is to be done on the window's default device context.

Unused: This member is not used by this message.

Result: If the application handles this message, set this member to zero.

See Also

BeginPaint, DefWindowProc, DispatchMessage, EndPaint, GetMessage, GetUpdateRect, PeekMessage, RedrawWindow, UpdateWindow, WM_ERASEBKGND, WM_NCPAINT

WM_PAINTCLIPBOARD

Syntax

```
TWMPaintClipboard = record
        Msg: Cardinal;                {the message identifier}
        Viewer: HWND;                 {a handle to the clipboard viewer}
        PaintStruct: THandle;         {a handle to a TPaintStruct structure}
        Result: Longint;              {returns a zero if handled}
    end;
```

Description

A clipboard viewer sends the WM_PAINTCLIPBOARD message to a clipboard owner when the clipboard has data of the type CF_OWNERDISPLAY and the viewer's client area needs to be repainted. The clipboard owner should compare the rcPaint member of the PaintStruct object with the dimensions specified in the most recently received WM_SIZECLIPBOARD message to determine which portion of the client area needs to be repainted. The clipboard owner must call the GlobalLock function to access the PaintStruct structure, unlocking it with a call to the GlobalUnlock function before returning.

Members

Msg: The message identifier. This member is set to the message identifier constant WM_PAINTCLIPBOARD.

Viewer: Specifies the handle of the clipboard viewer window.

PaintStruct: Specifies a handle to a global DDESHARE object that contains a TPaint-Struct structure. This structure defines which part of the client area needs to be repainted. The TPaintStruct structure is defined as:

```
TPaintStruct = packed record
        hdc: HDC;                     {a handle to a device context}
        fErase: BOOL;                 {erase background flag}
        rcPaint: TRect;               {the area to be painted}
        fRestore: BOOL;               {reserved}
        fIncUpdate: BOOL;             {reserved}
```

rgbReserved: array[0..31] of Byte; {reserved}
end;

hdc: A handle to the device context in need of repainting.

fErase: A flag indicating if the background of the device context should be erased. If this member is set to TRUE, the background should be erased. This would be used if an application creates a window class that does not have a background brush. This information is specified in the hbrBackground member of the TWndClass structure.

rcPaint: A TRect defining the rectangular coordinates of the region to be repainted.

fRestore: This member is used internally by Windows and should be ignored.

fIncUpdate: This member is used internally by Windows and should be ignored.

rgbReserved: This member is used internally by Windows and should be ignored.

Result: If the application handles this message, set this member to zero.

See Also

GlobalLock, GlobalUnlock, WM_SIZECLIPBOARD

WM_PALETTECHANGED

Syntax

```
TWMPaletteChanged = record
      Msg: Cardinal;              {the message identifier}
      PalChg: HWND;              {a handle to a window}
      Unused: Longint;           {not used}
      Result: Longint;           {not used}
end;
```

Description

The WM_PALETTECHANGED message is sent to all top-level and overlapped windows when the currently focused window changes the system palette by realizing a logical palette. This allows other windows to realize a logical palette as a background palette. This message must be sent to all top-level and overlapped windows, including the one that changed the system palette, and all child windows that use a palette. To avoid creating an infinite loop, a window that receives this message must not realize its palette if the handle identified by the PalChg member matches its own window handle.

Members

Msg: The message identifier. This member is set to the message identifier constant WM_PALETTECHANGED.

PalChg: Specifies the handle of the window that changed the system palette.

Unused: This member is not used by this message.

Result: This member is not used by this message.

See Also

WM_PALETTEISCHANGING, WM_QUERYNEWPALETTE

WM_PALETTEISCHANGING

Syntax

```
TWMPaletteIsChanging = record
      Msg: Cardinal;          {the message identifier}
      Realize: HWND;          {a handle to a window}
      Unused: Longint;        {not used}
      Result: Longint;        {returns a zero if handled}
   end;
```

Description

The WM_PALETTEISCHANGING message is sent when an application is about to realize a logical palette. When the WM_PALETTECHANGED message is sent, the application realizing the logical palette does not wait for other applications to process this message. Therefore, the system palette may already contain new colors by the time an application receives this message.

Members

Msg: The message identifier. This member is set to the message identifier constant WM_PALETTEISCHANGING.

Realize: Specifies the handle of the window that is going to realize its logical palette.

Unused: This member is not used by this message.

Result: If the application handles this message, set this member to zero.

See Also

WM_PALETTECHANGED, WM_QUERYNEWPALETTE

WM_PARENTNOTIFY

Syntax

```
TWMParentNotify = record
      Msg: Cardinal;          {the message identifier}
      case Event: Word of     {an event type flag}
      WM_CREATE, WM_DESTROY: (
      ChildID: Word;          {a child window identifier}
      ChildWnd: HWnd);        {a child window handle}
      WM_LBUTTONDOWN, WM_MBUTTONDOWN, WM_RBUTTONDOWN: (
      Value: Word;            {an event type flag}
      XPos: Smallint;         {the horizontal mouse cursor position}
```

YPos: Smallint);	{the vertical mouse cursor position}
0: (	
Value1: Word;	{an event type flag}
Value2: Longint;	{a child window identifier or mouse cursor position}
Result: Longint);	{returns a zero if handled}
end;	

Description

When a child window is created or destroyed, or when a mouse button is clicked within a child window, a WM_PARENTNOTIFY message is sent to the child window's parent window and all ancestor windows. If a child window is being created, the WM_PARENTNOTIFY message is sent before the CreateWindow or CreateWindowEx function returns to the caller. If a child window is being destroyed, the message is sent before any action has taken place to destroy the window. However, child windows which have the WS_EX_NOPARENTNOTIFY extended style will not send this message to their parent windows.

Members

Msg: The message identifier. This member is set to the message identifier constant WM_PARENTNOTIFY.

Event: A flag indicating the type of event that has occurred. This member can contain one value from Table A-34.

ChildID: Specifies the identifier of the child window.

ChildWnd: Specifies the handle of the child window.

Value: A flag indicating the type of event that has occurred. This member can contain one value from Table A-34.

XPos: Specifies the horizontal position of the mouse cursor. This member is valid only when the Value member identifies the WM_LBUTTONDOWN, WM_MBUTTONDOWN, or WM_RBUTTONDOWN events.

YPos: Specifies the horizontal position of the mouse cursor. This member is valid only when the Value member identifies the WM_LBUTTONDOWN, WM_MBUTTONDOWN, or WM_RBUTTONDOWN events.

Value1: A flag indicating the type of event that has occurred. This member can contain one value from Table A-34.

Value2: If the Value1 member identifies the WM_CREATE or WM_DESTROY events, this member will contain a handle to the child window being created or destroyed. If the Value1 member identifies the WM_LBUTTONDOWN, WM_MBUTTONDOWN, or WM_RBUTTONDOWN events, this member contains the coordinates of the mouse cursor, with the horizontal coordinate in the low-order word and the vertical coordinate in the high-order word.

Result: If the application handles this message, set this member to zero.

See Also

CreateWindow, CreateWindowEx, WM_CREATE, WM_DESTROY,
WM_LBUTTONDOWN, WM_MBUTTONDOWN, WM_RBUTTONDOWN

Table A-34: TWMParentNotify.Event Values

Value	Description
WM_CREATE	Indicates that a child window is being created.
WM_DESTROY	Indicates that a child window is about to be destroyed.
WM_LBUTTONDOWN	Indicates that the mouse cursor is over the child window and the left button has been clicked.
WM_MBUTTONDOWN	Indicates that the mouse cursor is over the child window and the middle button has been clicked.
WM_RBUTTONDOWN	Indicates that the mouse cursor is over the child window and the right button has been clicked.

WM_PASTE

Syntax

```
TWMPaste = record
     Msg: Cardinal;                  {the message identifier}
     Unused: array[0..3] of Word;    {not used}
     Result: Longint;                {not used}
end;
```

Description

This message is sent to an edit control or combo box to copy the text located on the clipboard into the control at the current caret location. Text will be copied into the control only if the clipboard currently has data in the CF_TEXT format. This message will fail if sent to a combo box with the CBS_DROPDOWNLIST style.

Members

Msg: The message identifier. This member is set to the message identifier constant WM_PASTE.

Unused: This member is not used by this message.

Result: This member is not used by this message.

See Also

WM_CLEAR, WM_COPY, WM_CUT

WM_QUERYDRAGICON

Syntax

```
TWMQueryDragIcon = record
      Msg: Cardinal;                    {the message identifier}
      Unused: array[0..3] of Word;      {not used}
      Result: Longint;                  {returns a cursor or icon handle}
end;
```

Description

When a minimized window is about to be dragged and there is no icon defined for that window's class, the WM_QUERYDRAGICON message is sent to the window to determine what image to display when dragging. The application should return the handle of either an icon or a cursor that is compatible with the system's current display driver. If the application does not return a handle to a compatible icon or cursor, the system will use a default cursor. If the icon returned by the application is a color icon, it will be converted to black and white.

Members

Msg: The message identifier. This member is set to the message identifier constant WM_QUERYDRAGICON.

Unused: This member is not used by this message.

Result: If the application handles this message it should return the handle of the cursor or icon to be displayed when dragging the window.

See Also

DefWindowProc, LoadCursor, LoadIcon

WM_QUERYENDSESSION

Syntax

```
TWMQueryEndSession = record
      Msg: Cardinal;        {the message identifier}
      Source: Longint;      {a handle to the terminating window}
      Unused: Longint;      {not used}
      Result: Longint;      {returns a termination code}
end;
```

Description

This message is sent to every active process when Windows is being terminated or an application has called the ExitWindows function. This allows an application to override the session termination request. If any application returns zero, Windows will not be terminated and will stop sending WM_QUERYENDSESSION messages. After processing this message, the system will send the WM_ENDSESSION message to every active process, with the EndSession member of this message set to the results of the WM_QUERYENDSESSION message. By default, the DefWindowProc function returns a value of one for this message. Under Windows NT, when an application returns a value of one for this message, it receives the WM_ENDSESSION message and is terminated, regardless of how other applications respond to the WM_QUERYENDSESSION message. Under Windows 95, applications will receive the WM_ENDSESSION message only after all applications have returned a value of one in the WM_QUERYENDSESSION message.

Members

Msg: The message identifier. This member is set to the message identifier constant WM_QUERYENDSESSION.

Source: Specifies the handle of the window requesting termination.

Unused: This member is not used by this message.

Result: An application should return a value of one if it wishes to terminate; otherwise it should return zero.

See Also

DefWindowProc, ExitWindows, WM_ENDSESSION

WM_QUERYNEWPALETTE

Syntax

```
TWMQueryNewPalette = record
      Msg: Cardinal;              {the message identifier}
      Unused: array[0..3] of Word;   {not used}
      Result: Longint;           {returns a palette realization code}
end;
```

Description

A window receives the WM_QUERYNEWPALETTE message when it is receiving the keyboard focus, indicating that it should realize its logical palette.

Members

Msg: The message identifier. This member is set to the message identifier constant WM_QUERYNEWPALETTE.

Unused: This member is not used by this message.

Result: If the window realizes its logical palette it should return a value of one; otherwise it should return zero.

See Also

WM_PALETTECHANGED, WM_PALETTEISCHANGING

WM_QUERYOPEN

Syntax

```
TWMQueryOpen = record
      Msg: Cardinal;                      {the message identifier}
      Unused: array[0..3] of Word;        {not used}
      Result: Longint;                    {returns a restore code}
end;
```

Description

This message is sent to an iconized window when it is being restored. The application should not perform any action that would cause a focus change while processing this message.

Members

Msg: The message identifier. This member is set to the message identifier constant WM_QUERYOPEN.

Unused: This member is not used by this message.

Result: The application should return a value of one to allow the window to be restored. Returning a value of zero prevents the window from being restored.

See Also

DefWindowProc, WM_SHOWWINDOW, WM_SIZE

WM_QUIT

Syntax

```
TWMQuit = record
      Msg: Cardinal;          {the message identifier}
      ExitCode: Longint;      {an exit code}
      Unused: Longint;        {not used}
      Result: Longint;        {not used}
end;
```

Description

This message is sent as a result of a call to the PostQuitMessage function. It causes the GetMessage function to return zero, thereby exiting the message loop and terminating the application.

Members

Msg: The message identifier. This member is set to the message identifier constant WM_QUIT.

ExitCode: Specifies the exit code. Please see the PostQuitMessage function for a description of this member. (This function is detailed in *The Tomes of Delphi 3: Win32 Core API.*)

Unused: This member is not used by this message.

Result: This member is not used by this message.

See Also

GetMessage, PostQuitMessage

WM_RBUTTONDBLCLK

Syntax

```
TWMRButtonDblClk = record
        Msg: Cardinal;            {the message identifier}
        Keys: Longint;            {virtual key flags}
        case Integer of
        0: (
        XPos: Smallint;           {the horizontal cursor coordinate}
        YPos: Smallint);          {the vertical cursor coordinate}
        1: (
        Pos: TSmallPoint;         {a TSmallPoint structure containing cursor coordinates}
        Result: Longint);         {returns a zero if handled}
    end;
```

Description

If the mouse cursor is in the client area of a window and the right mouse button is double-clicked, a WM_RBUTTONDBLCLK message is sent to the window under the cursor. However, if another window has captured mouse input by calling the SetCapture function, the message is sent to the capturing window. A double click is generated when the user presses the mouse button, releases it, and presses it again at the same coordinates within the system's double-click time interval. This process generates a series of four messages, in the following order: WM_RBUTTONDOWN, WM_RBUTTONUP, WM_RBUTTONDBLCLK, and WM_RBUTTONUP. Only windows whose class style contains the CS_DBLCLKS flag will receive the WM_RBUTTONDBLCLK message.

Members

Msg: The message identifier. This member is set to the message identifier constant WM_RBUTTONDBLCLK.

Keys: Indicates if specific virtual keys are held down at the time of the double click. This member can contain one or more values from Table A-35.

XPos: Specifies the horizontal coordinate of the mouse cursor, relative to the client area.

YPos: Specifies the vertical coordinate of the mouse cursor, relative to the client area.

Pos: A TSmallPoint structure that contains the current mouse coordinates relative to the client area.

Result: If the application handles this message, set this member to zero.

See Also

GetCapture, GetDoubleClickTime, SetCapture, SetDoubleClickTime, WM_RBUTTONDOWN, WM_RBUTTONUP

Table A-35: TWRButtonDblClk.Keys Values

Value	Description
MK_CONTROL	Indicates that the Ctrl key is held down.
MK_LBUTTON	Indicates that the left mouse button is down.
MK_MBUTTON	Indicates that the middle mouse button is down.
MK_RBUTTON	Indicates that the right mouse button is down.
MK_SHIFT	Indicates that the Shift key is held down.

WM_RBUTTONDOWN

Syntax

```
TWMRButtonDown = record
        Msg: Cardinal;          {the message identifier}
        Keys: Longint;          {virtual key flags}
        case Integer of
        0: (
        XPos: Smallint;         {the horizontal cursor coordinate}
        YPos: Smallint);        {the vertical cursor coordinate}
        1: (
        Pos: TSmallPoint;       {a TSmallPoint structure containing cursor coordinates}
        Result: Longint);       {returns a zero if handled}
    end;
```

Description

If the mouse cursor is in the client area of a window and the right button is pressed, a WM_RBUTTONDOWN message is sent to the window under the cursor. However, if another window has captured mouse input by calling the SetCapture function, the message is sent to the capturing window.

Members

Msg: The message identifier. This member is set to the message identifier constant WM_RBUTTONDOWN.

Keys: Indicates if specific virtual keys are held down at the time of the button click. This member can contain one or more values from Table A-36.

XPos: Specifies the horizontal coordinate of the mouse cursor, relative to the client area.

YPos: Specifies the vertical coordinate of the mouse cursor, relative to the client area.

Pos: A TSmallPoint structure that contains the current mouse coordinates relative to the client area.

Result: If the application handles this message, set this member to zero.

See Also

GetCapture, SetCapture, WM_RBUTTONDBLCLK, WM_RBUTTONUP

Table A-36: TWMRButtonDown.Keys Values

Value	Description
MK_CONTROL	Indicates that the Ctrl key is held down.
MK_LBUTTON	Indicates that the left mouse button is down.
MK_MBUTTON	Indicates that the middle mouse button is down.
MK_RBUTTON	Indicates that the right mouse button is down.
MK_SHIFT	Indicates that the Shift key is held down.

WM_RBUTTONUP

Syntax

```
TWMRButtonUp = record
     Msg: Cardinal;              {the message identifier}
     Keys: Longint;             {virtual key flags}
     case Integer of
     0: (
     XPos: Smallint;            {the horizontal cursor coordinate}
     YPos: Smallint);           {the vertical cursor coordinate}
     1: (
     Pos: TSmallPoint;          {a TSmallPoint structure containing cursor coordinates}
     Result: Longint);          {returns a zero if handled}
  end;
```

Description

If the mouse cursor is in the client area of a window and the right button is released, a WM_RBUTTONUP message is sent to the window under the cursor. However, if another window has captured mouse input by calling the SetCapture function, the message is sent to the capturing window.

Members

Msg: The message identifier. This member is set to the message identifier constant WM_RBUTTONUP.

Keys: Indicates if specific virtual keys are held down at the time of the button release. This member can contain one or more values from Table A-37.

XPos: Specifies the horizontal coordinate of the mouse cursor, relative to the client area.

YPos: Specifies the vertical coordinate of the mouse cursor, relative to the client area.

Pos: A TSmallPoint structure that contains the current mouse coordinates relative to the client area.

Result: If the application handles this message, set this member to zero.

See Also

GetCapture, SetCapture, WM_RBUTTONDBLCLK, WM_RBUTTONDOWN

Table A-37: TWMRButtonUp.Keys Values

Value	Description
MK_CONTROL	Indicates that the Ctrl key is held down.
MK_LBUTTON	Indicates that the left mouse button is down.
MK_MBUTTON	Indicates that the middle mouse button is down.
MK_SHIFT	Indicates that the Shift key is held down.

WM_RENDERALLFORMATS

Syntax

```
TWMRenderAllFormats = record
      Msg: Cardinal;                    {the message identifier}
      Unused: array[0..3] of Word;      {not used}
      Result: Longint;                  {returns a zero if handled}
end;
```

Description

This message is sent to the clipboard owner if it is being destroyed and has delayed rendering of one or more clipboard formats. In order for data to remain available to other applications, the clipboard owner must place its data on the clipboard in all formats for which it is capable of rendering. Any nonrendered clipboard formats are removed from the clipboard's list of available formats before the message returns.

Members

Msg: The message identifier. This member is set to the message identifier constant WM_RENDERALLFORMATS.

Unused: This member is not used by this message.

Result: If the application handles this message, set this member to zero.

See Also

EmptyClipboard, OpenClipboard, SetClipboardData, WM_RENDERFORMAT

WM_RENDERFORMAT

Syntax

```
TWMRenderFormat = record
      Msg: Cardinal;          {the message identifier}
      Format: Longint;        {a clipboard format}
      Unused: Longint;        {not used}
      Result: Longint;        {returns a zero if handled}
end;
```

Description

This message is sent to the clipboard owner if it is using delayed rendering for a specific format and an application has requested data from the clipboard in this format. The clipboard owner must not open the clipboard before calling the SetClipboardData function to place the requested data on the clipboard.

Members

Msg: The message identifier. This member is set to the message identifier constant WM_RENDERFORMAT.

Format: Indicates which clipboard data format is to be rendered.

Unused: This member is not used by this message.

Result: If the application handles this message, set this member to zero.

See Also

SetClipboardData, WM_RENDERALLFORMATS

WM_SETCURSOR

Syntax

```
TWMSetCursor = record
      Msg: Cardinal;          {the message identifier}
      CursorWnd: HWND;        {a handle to the window containing the cursor}
      HitTest: Word;          {a hit test flag}
```

MouseMsg: Word;	{a mouse message identifier}
Result: Longint;	{returns a message processing code}
end;	

Description

If the mouse cursor moves in a window and the mouse is not captured, the WM_SETCURSOR message is sent to that window. Before this message is sent to a window, the DefWindowProc function sends it to the window's parent. If the parent window returns a value of one, this message is not sent to the target window. The DefWindowProc function processes this message by changing the cursor to an arrow if it is not in the client area, or to the registered cursor if it is in the client area. If the Hit-Test member contains the HTERROR flag and the MouseMsg member contains an identifier for a button click message, the MessageBeep function is called. If a menu has been activated, the MouseMsg member will be zero.

Members

Msg: The message identifier. This member is set to the message identifier constant WM_SETCURSOR.

CursorWnd: Specifies the handle of the window containing the mouse cursor.

HitTest: A flag indicating the area in the window where the mouse cursor is located. This can be one value from Table A-30 under the WM_NCHITTEST message.

MouseMsg: The identifier of the mouse message that generated the WM_SETCURSOR message.

Result: This message returns the result returned by message processing within the parent window.

See Also

DefWindowProc, MessageBeep, WM_MOUSEMOVE, WM_NCHITTEST

WM_SETFOCUS

Syntax

TWMSetFocus = record	
Msg: Cardinal;	{the message identifier}
FocusedWnd: HWND;	{a handle to a window}
Unused: Longint;	{not used}
Result: Longint;	{returns a zero if handled}
end;	

Description

This message is sent to a window after receiving keyboard focus.

Members

Msg: The message identifier. This member is set to the message identifier constant WM_SETFOCUS.

FocusedWnd: Specifies the handle of the window that has lost keyboard focus. This member may be set to zero if no window previously had keyboard focus.

Unused: This member is not used by this message.

Result: If the application handles this message, set this member to zero.

See Also

SetFocus, WM_KILLFOCUS

WM_SETFONT

Syntax

```
TWMSetFont = record
        Msg: Cardinal;          {the message identifier}
        Font: HFONT;            {a handle to a font}
        Redraw: WordBool;       {control redraw flag}
        Unused: Word;           {not used}
        Result: Longint;        {not used}
    end;
```

Description

The WM_SETFONT message is sent to a control to specify which font to use when drawing text. This message will not alter the size of the control. A control should make any necessary changes to its size before changing the font.

Members

Msg: The message identifier. This member is set to the message identifier constant WM_SETFONT.

Font: Specifies the handle of the font to be used in the control. If this member is set to zero, the control will use the system default font.

Redraw: A flag indicating if the control should be redrawn after setting the font. If this member is set to TRUE, the control will be redrawn.

Unused: This member is not used by this message.

Result: This member is not used by this message.

See Also

CreateFont, CreateFontIndirect, WM_GETFONT

WM_SETHOTKEY

Syntax

```
TWMSetHotKey = record
      Msg: Cardinal;         {the message identifier}
      Key: Longint;          {a virtual key code and modifier}
      Unused: Longint;       {not used}
      Result: Longint;       {returns a success code}
end;
```

Description

The WM_SETHOTKEY message is sent to a window to associate the window with a hot key. When this hot key combination is pressed, the system activates the window and sends it a WM_SYSCOMMAND message with the CmdType member set to SC_HOTKEY. A window can only have one hot key associated with it at a time. If this message is sent to a window that already has a hot key associated with it, the new hot key replaces the old one. However, the same hot key combination can be associated with more than one window. In this instance, a random window will be activated when the hot key is pressed.

The WM_SETHOTKEY message is not related to the operation of the RegisterHotKey function.

Members

Msg: The message identifier. This member is set to the message identifier constant WM_SETHOTKEY.

Key: Specifies the virtual key code and modifier flags for the hot key that will be associated with the window to which the message was sent. Setting this member to zero will remove any hot key associated with the window. The low-order byte of this member should be set to the virtual key code, and the high-order byte should be set to the modifier flags, which can be any combination of values from Table A-38. Note that the VK_ESCAPE, VK_SPACE, and VK_TAB virtual key codes cannot be used in a hot key.

Unused: This member is not used by this message.

Result: This message returns one success code from Table A-39.

See Also

WM_GETHOTKEY, WM_SYSCOMMAND

Table A-38: TWMSetHotKey.Key Values

Value	Description
HOTKEYF_ALT	The Alt key.
HOTKEYF_CONTROL	The Ctrl key.

Value	Description
HOTKEYF_EXT	An extended key.
HOTKEYF_SHIFT	The Shift key.

Table A-39: TWMSetHotKey.Result Values

Value	Description
-1	An error has occurred due to an invalid hot key.
0	An error has occurred due to an invalid window.
1	The hot key was set.
2	The hot key was set, but more than one window is set to the same hot key.

WM_SETICON

Syntax

```
TWMSetIcon = record
      Msg: Cardinal;              {the message identifier}
      BigIcon: Longbool;          {an icon size indicator}
      Icon: HICON;                {the icon handle}
      Result: Longint;            {returns the previous icon handle}
end;
```

Description

The WM_SETICON message associates a new big icon or a small icon with the targeted window.

Members

Msg: The message identifier. This member is set to the message identifier constant WM_SETICON.

BigIcon: A flag indicating if the icon is large or small. This member is set to TRUE if the icon to be associated with the window is a big icon; it is set to FALSE for small icons.

Icon: Specifies the handle of the icon to be associated with the targeted window.

Result: This message returns the handle of the icon that was previously associated with the window, depending on the value of the BigIcon member. It returns zero if the window had no previous associated icon of the indicated size.

See Also

DefWindowProc, WM_GETICON

WM_SETREDRAW

Syntax

```
TWMSetRedraw = record
    Msg: Cardinal;          {the message identifier}
    Redraw: Longint;        {the redraw flag state}
    Unused: Longint;        {not used}
    Result: Longint;        {returns a zero if handled}
end;
```

Description

The WM_SETREDRAW message is sent to a window to set the state of its redraw flag. If the redraw flag is cleared, the window will not be repainted after any drawing functions, behaving similar to the LockWindowUpdate function. The redraw flag must be set before any window painting will occur.

Members

Msg: The message identifier. This member is set to the message identifier constant WM_SETREDRAW.

Redraw: Specifies the state of the redraw flag. If this member is set to one, the redraw flag will be set and painting can occur. If this member is set to zero, the redraw flag will be cleared and the window will not be updated until the redraw flag is set.

Unused: This member is not used by this message.

Result: If the application handles this message, set this member to zero.

See Also

InvalidateRect, LockWindowUpdate

WM_SETTEXT

Syntax

```
TWMSetText = record
    Msg: Cardinal;          {the message identifier}
    Unused: Longint;        {not used}
    Text: PChar;            {a pointer to a null-terminated string}
    Result: Longint;        {returns a success code}
end;
```

Description

This message is sent to a window to change its text.

Members

Msg: The message identifier. This member is set to the message identifier constant WM_SETTEXT.

Unused: This member is not used by this message.

Text: A pointer to a null-terminated string containing the text to be associated with the window.

Result: This message returns one value from Table A-40.

See Also

DefWindowProc, WM_GETTEXT

Table A-40: TWMSetText.Result Values

Value	Description
I	The text was successfully set.
0 (edit controls only)	The text was not set due to insufficient space.
LB_ERRSPACE (list box controls only)	The text was not set due to insufficient space.
CB_ERRSPACE (combo box controls only)	The text was not set due to insufficient space.
CB_ERR (combo box controls only)	The text was not set because the combo box does not have an edit control.

WM_SHOWWINDOW

Syntax

```
TWMShowWindow = record
      Msg: Cardinal;        {the message identifier}
      Show: BOOL;           {the show/hide flag}
      Status: Longint;      {a status code}
      Result: Longint;      {returns zero if handled}
   end;
```

Description

A window will receive a WM_SHOWWINDOW message when it is about to be shown or hidden. If the window has the WS_VISIBLE style set when created, the WM_SHOWWINDOW message is sent after the window is created but before it is displayed. Calling the ShowWindow and ShowOwnedPopups functions will also generate this message. This message is not sent when a top-level overlapped window is created with either the WS_MAXIMIZE or the WS_MINIMIZE styles, or if the SW_SHOWNORMAL flag is specified in a call to the ShowWindow function.

A

Appendix

Members

Msg: The message identifier. This member is set to the message identifier constant WM_SHOWWINDOW.

Show: A flag indicating if the window is being shown or hidden. This member is set to FALSE if the window is being hidden or TRUE if the window is being shown.

Status: A flag indicating the status of the window being shown. This member is set to zero if the message was sent as a result of a call to the ShowWindow function. Otherwise, this member is set to one value from Table A-41.

Result: If the application handles this message, set this member to zero.

See Also

DefWindowProc, ShowOwnedPopups, ShowWindow

Table A-41: TWMShowWindow.Status Values

Value	Description
SW_OTHERUNZOOM	The window is being uncovered because a previously maximized window is being restored or minimized.
SW_OTHERZOOM	The window is being covered because another window is being maximized.
SW_PARENTCLOSING	The window's owner has been minimized.
SW_PARENTOPENING	The window's owner has been restored

WM_SIZE

Syntax

```
TWMSize = record
      Msg: Cardinal;          {the message identifier}
      SizeType: Longint;      {a size type flag}
      Width: Word;            {the new client width in pixels}
      Height: Word;           {the new client height in pixels}
      Result: Longint;        {returns a zero if handled}
end;
```

Description

The WM_SIZE message is sent to a window after its size has changed. If the WM_SIZE message causes the SetScrollPos or MoveWindow functions to be called, the redraw parameter of these functions should be set to TRUE to force the window to be redrawn.

Members

Msg: The message identifier. This member is set to the message identifier constant WM_SIZE.

SizeType: A flag indicating the type of resize operation that has occurred. This member can contain one value from Table A-42.

Width: Specifies the new width of the client area, in pixels.

Height: Specifies the new height of the client area, in pixels.

Result: If the application handles this message, set this member to zero.

See Also

MoveWindow

Table A-42: TWMSize.SizeType Values

Value	Description
SIZE_MAXHIDE	Indicates that another window has been maximized.
SIZE_MAXIMIZED	Indicates that the window has been maximized.
SIZE_MAXSHOW	Indicates that another window has been restored.
SIZE_MINIMIZED	Indicates that the window has been minimized.
SIZE_RESTORED	The window has been resized, but was not minimized or maximized.

WM_SIZECLIPBOARD

Syntax

```
TWMSizeClipboard = record
      Msg: Cardinal;        {the message identifier}
      Viewer: HWND;         {the handle of the clipboard viewer window}
      RC: THandle;          {the handle of a rectangle object}
      Result: Longint;      {not used}
end;
```

Description

The WM_SIZECLIPBOARD message is sent by a clipboard viewer window to the clipboard owner when the size of the client area in the clipboard viewer window has changed. This message will only be sent if the clipboard contains data in the CF_OWNERDISPLAY format. When the clipboard viewer window is about to be destroyed or resized, it will send this message to the clipboard owner, specifying an empty rectangle. The clipboard owner must use the GlobalLock and GlobalUnlock functions to retrieve the rectangle identified by the DDESHARE handle in the RC member.

Members

Msg: The message identifier. This member is set to the message identifier constant WM_SIZECLIPBOARD.

Viewer: Specifies the handle to the clipboard viewer window.

RC: Specifies a handle to a DDESHARE object containing a TRect structure. This TRect structure contains the new coordinates of the clipboard viewer window client area.

Result: This member is not used by this message.

See Also

GlobalLock, GlobalUnlock, WM_RENDERALLFORMATS, WM_RENDERFORMAT

WM_SPOOLERSTATUS

Syntax

```
TWMSpoolerStatus = record
        Msg: Cardinal;            {the message identifier}
        JobStatus: Longint;       {contains the PR_JOBSTATUS constant}
        JobsLeft: Word;           {the number of remaining print jobs}
        Unused: Word;             {not used}
        Result: Longint;          {returns a zero if handled}
end;
```

Description

The WM_SPOOLERSTATUS message is sent from the print manager when a print job is added to or removed from the print queue.

Members

Msg: The message identifier. This member is set to the message identifier constant WM_SPOOLERSTATUS.

JobStatus: This member will be set to the constant PR_JOBSTATUS.

JobsLeft: Specifies the number of print jobs remaining in the print spooler handled by the print manager.

Unused: This member is not used by this message.

Result: If the application handles this message, set this member to zero.

See Also

WM_NOTIFY, WM_NOTIFYFORMAT

WM_STYLECHANGED

Syntax

```
TWMStyleChanged = record
        Msg: Cardinal;                {the message identifier}
        StyleType: Longint;           {style type flag}
        StyleStruct: PStyleStruct;    {a pointer to a TStyleStruct structure}
        Result: Longint;              {returns a zero if handled}
end;
```

Description

The WM_STYLECHANGED message is sent to a window when its styles have been changed as a result of a call to the SetWindowLong function.

Members

Msg: The message identifier. This member is set to the message identifier constant WM_STYLECHANGED.

StyleType: A series of flags specifying whether the window's extended or regular styles have been changed. This member can contain one or more values from Table A-43.

StyleStruct: Specifies a pointer to a TStyleStruct structure. This structure contains the style flags for the window before and after the SetWindowLong function was called. The TStyleStruct structure is defined as:

```
TStyleStruct = packed record
        styleOld: DWORD;              {previous window styles}
        styleNew: DWORD;              {new window styles}
end;
```

    styleOld: Specifies the style flags present before the SetWindowLong function was called.

    styleNew: Specifies the style flags set by the call to the SetWindowLong function.

Please see the CreateWindow and CreateWindowEx functions for a list of available window style flags. These functions are discussed in detail in *The Tomes of Delphi 3: Win32 Core API.*

Result: If the application handles this message, set this member to zero.

See Also

CreateWindow, CreateWindowEx, SetWindowLong, WM_STYLECHANGING

Table A-43: TWMStyleChanged.StyleType Values

Value	Description
GWL_EXSTYLE	Indicates that the window's extended styles were changed.
GWL_STYLE	Indicates that the window's normal styles were changed.

WM_STYLECHANGING

Syntax

```
TWMStyleChanging = record
        Msg: Cardinal;              {the message identifier}
        StyleType: Longint;         {style type flag}
        StyleStruct: PStyleStruct;  {a pointer to a TStyleStruct structure}
        Result: Longint;            {returns a zero if handled}
end;
```

Description

The WM_STYLECHANGING message is sent to a window when its styles are about to be changed as a result of a call to the SetWindowLong function.

Members

Msg: The message identifier. This member is set to the message identifier constant WM_STYLECHANGING.

StyleType: A series of flags specifying whether the window's extended or regular styles are about to be changed. This member can contain one or more values from Table A-44.

StyleStruct: Specifies a pointer to a TStyleStruct structure. This structure contains the existing style flags for the window and the style flags about to be set by the SetWindowLong function. The TStyleStruct structure is defined as:

```
TStyleStruct = packed record
        styleOld: DWORD;        {previous window styles}
        styleNew: DWORD;        {new window styles}
end;
```

Please see the WM_STYLECHANGED message for a description of this data structure.

Result: If the application handles this message, set this member to zero.

See Also

CreateWindow, CreateWindowEx, SetWindowLong, WM_STYLECHANGED

Table A-44: TWMStyleChanging.StyleType Values

Value	Description
GWL_EXSTYLE	Indicates that the window's extended styles were changed.
GWL_STYLE	Indicates that the window's normal styles were changed.

WM_SYSCHAR

Syntax

```
TWMSysChar = record
      Msg: Cardinal;            {the message identifier}
      CharCode: Word;           {character code}
      Unused: Word;             {not used}
      KeyData: Longint;         {contains various information}
      Result: Longint;          {returns a zero if handled}
end;
```

Description

When a key is pressed while the Alt key is held down (indicating a system key), a WM_SYSCHAR message is posted to the window that currently has the keyboard focus. This WM_SYSCHAR message is the result of a WM_SYSKEYDOWN message being translated by the TranslateMessage function.

The extended keys on a 101- or 102-key keyboard are:

In the main section of the keyboard, the right Alt and Ctrl keys.

To the left of the keypad, the Ins, Del, Home, End, Page Up, Page Down, and the four arrow keys.

On the numeric keypad, the Num Lock, divide (/), and Enter keys.

The PrintScrn and Break keys.

Members

Msg: The message identifier. This member is set to the message identifier constant WM_SYSCHAR.

CharCode: The character code of the window menu key.

Unused: This member is not used by this message.

KeyData: Specifies the repeat count, scan code, extended key flag, context code, previous key state flag, and the transition state flag. Table A-45 shows which information is in which bit position within the 32-bit value of the KeyData member. The high-order word, bits 16 to 31, pertains to the immediately preceding WM_SYSKEYDOWN message which generated the WM_SYSCHAR message through the TranslateMessage function.

Result: If the application handles this message, set this member to zero.

See Also

TranslateMessage, WM_SYSKEYDOWN

Table A-45: TWMSysChar.KeyData Values

Value	Description
0-15	The repeat count resulting from the user holding down the key.
16-23	The scan code, whose value depends on the OEM maker of the keyboard.
24	The extended key flag. If the key is an extended key (the right-hand Alt and Ctrl keys), this bit is set (1); otherwise it is not set (0).
25-28	Unused.
29	The context code. If the Alt key was held down while the key was pressed, this bit is set (1); otherwise it is not set (0).
30	The previous key state. If the key was held down before the message is sent, this bit is set (1); otherwise it is not set (0).
31	The transition state. If the key is being released, this bit is set (1); otherwise it is not set (0).

WM_SYSCOLORCHANGE

Syntax

```
TWMSysColorChange = record
      Msg: Cardinal;                    {the message identifier}
      Unused: array[0..3] of Word;      {not used}
      Result: Longint;                  {not used}
end;
```

Description

When a system color setting is changed, the WM_SYSCOLORCHANGE message is sent to all top-level windows. A WM_PAINT message will be sent to any window that will be affected by the color change. This message must be forwarded to any common controls used by the window.

Members

Msg: The message identifier. This member is set to the message identifier constant WM_SYSCOLORCHANGE.

Unused: This member is not used by this message.

Result: This member is not used by this message.

See Also

SetSysColors, WM_PAINT

WM_SYSCOMMAND

Syntax

```
TWMSysCommand = record
      Msg: Cardinal;                    {the message identifier}
      case CmdType: Longint of  {command type flag}
      SC_HOTKEY: (
      ActivateWnd: HWND);               {a handle to a window}
      SC_KEYMENU: (
      Key: Word);                       {a character code}
      SC_CLOSE, SC_HSCROLL, SC_MAXIMIZE, SC_MINIMIZE,
        SC_MOUSEMENU,
      SC_MOVE, SC_NEXTWINDOW, SC_PREVWINDOW, SC_RESTORE,
      SC_SCREENSAVE, SC_SIZE, SC_TASKLIST, SC_VSCROLL: (
      XPos: Smallint;                   {the horizontal mouse cursor position}
      YPos: Smallint;                   {the vertical mouse cursor position}
      Result: Longint);                 {returns a zero if handled}
   end;
```

Description

This message is sent to a window when a system menu item is chosen or the minimize or maximize buttons are clicked. This message can also be sent to the DefWindowProc function to perform any actions identified by the values in Table A-46. Note that if the system menu is modified by the AppendMenu, InsertMenu, ModifyMenu, Insert-MenuItem, or SetMenuItemInfo functions, a user-defined system command value must be specified for the new item. In this instance, the application must handle the WM_SYSCOMMAND message to provide processing for any new menu items.

Members

Msg: The message identifier. This member is set to the message identifier constant WM_SYSCOMMAND.

CmdType: A flag indicating the type of system command. This member can contain a user-defined system command value (used when adding menu items to a window's system menu), or it can contain one value from Table A-46. Note that the four lowest order bits of this value are used internally. If an application is testing for a user-defined system command value, it must combine the value of this member with $FFF0 using the Boolean AND operator.

ActivateWnd: If a hot key associated with a window was pressed, this member will contain the handle of the window to be activated by the hot key.

Key: Contains the character code of the system key that was pressed, if any. This will be the ASCII value of any key pressed while the Alt key is held down. By default, the Alt+Spacebar combination will activate the system menu.

XPos: Specifies the horizontal position of the mouse cursor, in screen coordinates, when a system menu item is selected with the mouse.

YPos: Specifies the vertical position of the mouse cursor, in screen coordinates, when a system menu item is selected with the mouse.

Result: If the application handles this message, set this member to zero.

See Also

AppendMenu, DefWindowProc, GetSystemMenu, InsertMenu, ModifyMenu, WM_COMMAND, WM_SETHOTKEY

Table A-46: TWMSysCommand.CmdType Values

Value	Description
SC_CLOSE	Closes the window.
SC_CONTEXTHELP	The mouse cursor is changed to a pointer with a question mark. Any control clicked on with this mouse cursor will receive a WM_HELP message.
SC_DEFAULT	The menu's default item is selected.
SC_HOTKEY	Indicates that a window's hot key was pressed.
SC_HSCROLL	Scrolls the window horizontally.
SC_KEYMENU	Indicates the system menu was activated by a keystroke.
SC_MAXIMIZE	Maximizes the window.
SC_MINIMIZE	Minimizes the window.
SC_MONITORPOWER	Windows 95 only: Sets the state of the display for devices supporting power saving features.
SC_MOUSEMENU	Indicates the system menu was activated by a mouse click.
SC_MOVE	Moves the window.
SC_NEXTWINDOW	Activates the next window.
SC_PREVWINDOW	Activates the previous window.
SC_RESTORE	Restores the window.
SC_SCREENSAVE	Executes the screen saver.
SC_SIZE	Resizes the window.
SC_TASKLIST	Activates and displays the system task list.
SC_VSCROLL	Scrolls the window vertically.

WM_SYSDEADCHAR

Syntax

```
TWMSysDeadChar = record
     Msg: Cardinal;        {the message identifier}
     CharCode: Word;       {the character code}
     Unused: Word;         {not used}
```

```
         KeyData: Longint;          {contains various information}
         Result: Longint;           {returns a zero if handled}
end;
```

Description

When a WM_SYSKEYDOWN message is translated by a call to the TranslateMessage function, a WM_SYSDEADCHAR message is sent to the window with the keyboard focus. This message is generated as a result of pressing a dead key while holding down the Alt key. A dead key is a key that generates an additional character to be used in combination with another key to create a combined or "composite" character. This is typically a character with an accent or diacritical mark. The dead key identifying the accent or diacritical mark is entered first, followed by the key identifying the character that will have the mark applied to it.

Members

Msg: The message identifier. This member is set to the message identifier constant WM_SYSDEADCHAR.

CharCode: The character code of the key that was pressed.

Unused: This member is not used by this message.

KeyData: Specifies the repeat count, scan code, extended key flag, context code, previous key state flag, and the transition state flag. Table A-47 shows which information is in which bit position within the 32-bit value of the KeyData member. The high-order word, bits 16 to 31, pertains to the immediately preceding WM_SYSKEYDOWN message which generated the WM_SYSDEADCHAR message through the TranslateMessage function.

Result: If the application handles this message, set this member to zero.

See Also

TranslateMessage, WM_DEADCHAR, WM_KEYDOWN, WM_SYSKEYDOWN, WM_SYSKEYUP

Table A-47: TWMSysDeadChar.KeyData Values

Value	Description
0-15	The repeat count resulting from the user holding down the key.
16-23	The scan code, whose value depends on the OEM maker of the keyboard.
24	The extended key flag. If the key is an extended key (the right-hand Alt and Ctrl keys), this bit is set (1); otherwise it is not set (0).
25-28	Unused.
29	The context code. If the Alt key was held down while the key was pressed, this bit is set (1); otherwise it is not set (0).

Value	Description
30	The previous key state. If the key was held down before the message is sent, this bit is set (1); otherwise it is not set (0).
31	The transition state. If the key is being released, this bit is set (1); otherwise it is not set (0).

WM_SYSKEYDOWN

Syntax

```
TWMSysKeyDown = record
        Msg: Cardinal;          {the message identifier}
        CharCode: Word;         {the virtual key code}
        Unused: Word;           {not used}
        KeyData: Longint;       {contains various information}
        Result: Longint;        {returns a zero if handled}
end;
```

Description

The WM_SYSKEYDOWN message is sent whenever the user presses a key with the Alt key held down. It will be sent to the window with the keyboard focus or to the currently active window if no window has the keyboard focus. The context flag in the KeyData member distinguishes between these two events.

Members

Msg: The message identifier. This member is set to the message identifier constant WM_SYSKEYDOWN.

CharCode: Specifies the virtual key code for the key that was pressed.

Unused: This member is not used by this message.

KeyData: Specifies the repeat count, scan code, extended key flag, context code, previous key state flag, and the transition state flag. Table A-48 shows which information is in which bit position within the 32-bit value of the KeyData member.

Result: If the application handles this message, set this member to zero.

See Also

DefWindowProc, WM_SYSCHAR, WM_SYSCOMMAND, WM_SYSKEYUP

Table A-48: TWMSysKeyDown.KeyData Values

Value	Description
0-15	The repeat count resulting from the user holding down the key.
16-23	The scan code, whose value depends on the OEM maker of the keyboard.

Value	Description
24	The extended key flag. If the key is an extended key (the right-hand Alt and Ctrl keys), this bit is set (1); otherwise it is not set (0).
25-28	Unused.
29	The context code. If the Alt key was held down while the key was pressed, this bit is set (1). This bit will not be set if the WM_SYSKEYDOWN message was posted to the active window because no window has the keyboard focus.
30	The previous key state. If the key was held down before the message is sent, this bit is set (1); otherwise it is not set (0).
31	The transition state. This bit will always be zero.

WM_SYSKEYUP

Syntax

```
TWMSysKeyUp = record
        Msg: Cardinal;            {the message identifier}
        CharCode: Word;           {the virtual key code}
        Unused: Word;             {not used}
        KeyData: Longint;         {contains various information}
        Result: Longint;          {returns a zero if handled}
end;
```

Description

The WM_SYSKEYUP message is sent whenever the user releases a key that was pressed with the Alt key held down. It will be sent to the window with the keyboard focus or to the currently active window if no window has the keyboard focus. The context flag in the KeyData member distinguishes between these two events.

On non-U.S. enhanced 102-key keyboards, the right Alt key is interpreted as a Ctrl+Alt combination. When this key is pressed, it produces the following messages in order: WM_KEYDOWN (with a virtual key code of VK_CONTROL), WM_KEYDOWN (with a virtual key code of VK_MENU), WM_KEYUP (with a virtual key code of VK_CONTROL), and WM_SYSKEYUP (with a virtual key code of VK_MENU).

Members

Msg: The message identifier. This member is set to the message identifier constant WM_SYSKEYUP.

CharCode: Specifies the virtual key code for the key that was released.

Unused: This member is not used by this message.

KeyData: Specifies the repeat count, scan code, extended key flag, context code, previous key state flag, and the transition state flag. Table A-49 shows which information is in which bit position within the 32-bit value of the KeyData member.

Result: If the application handles this message, set this member to zero.

See Also

DefWindowProc, WM_SYSCHAR, WM_SYSCOMMAND, WM_SYSKEYDOWN

Table A-49: TWMSysKeyUP.KeyData Values

Value	Description
0-15	The repeat count resulting from the user holding down the key.
16-23	The scan code, whose value depends on the OEM maker of the keyboard.
24	The extended key flag. If the key is an extended key (the right-hand Alt and Ctrl keys), this bit is set (1); otherwise it is not set (0).
25-28	Unused.
29	The context code. If the Alt key was held down while the key was pressed, this bit is set (1). This bit will not be set if the WM_SYSKEYDOWN message was posted to the active window because no window has the keyboard focus.
30	The previous key state. This bit is always one.
31	The transition state. This bit is always one.

WM_TIMECHANGE

Syntax

```
TWMTimeChange = record
     Msg: Cardinal;                    {the message identifier}
     Unused: array[0..3] of Word;      {not used}
     Result: Longint;                  {returns a zero if handled}
end;
```

Description

Any application that modifies the system time should send this message to all top-level windows by using the SendMessage function and setting the hwnd parameter to HWND_TOPMOST.

Members

Msg: The message identifier. This member is set to the message identifier constant WM_TIMECHANGE.

Unused: This member is not used by this message.

Result: If the application handles this message, set this member to zero.

See Also

SendMessage

WM_TIMER

Syntax

```
TWMTimer = record
      Msg: Cardinal;              {the message identifier}
      TimerID: Longint;           {the timer identifier}
      TimerProc: TFarProc;        {the address of the optional callback function}
      Result: Longint;            {returns a zero if handled}
   end;
```

Description

This message is posted to the message queue of the thread that installed a timer when the timer's timeout period has elapsed. If a callback function was specified in the call to the SetTimer function, this message will be passed to the callback function instead of the installing thread's message queue.

Members

Msg: The message identifier. This member is set to the message identifier constant WM_TIMER.

TimerID: The identifier of the timer that is created when the SetTimer function was called.

TimerProc: Specifies the address of the optional callback function. When this member is not NIL, the WM_TIMER message is sent to the callback function; otherwise it is posted to the message queue of the thread that installed the timer.

Result: If the application handles this message, set this member to zero.

See Also

DispatchMessage, SetTimer

WM_UNDO

Syntax

```
TWMUndo = record
      Msg: Cardinal;              {the message identifier}
      Unused: array[0..3] of Word;  {not used}
      Result: Longint;            {returns a one if successful}
   end;
```

Description

The WM_UNDO message is sent to an edit control as a command to undo the last operation. New text is deleted and previously deleted text is restored.

Members

Msg: The message identifier. This member is set to the message identifier constant WM_UNDO.

Unused: This member is not used by this message.

Result: This message will return a value of one if successful; otherwise it returns zero.

See Also

WM_CLEAR, WM_COPY, WM_CUT, WM_PASTE

WM_VKEYTOITEM

Syntax

```
TWMVKeyToItem = record
        Msg: Cardinal;          {the message identifier}
        Key: Word;              {the virtual key code}
        CaretPos: Word;         {the caret position}
        ListBox: HWND;          {the list box handle}
        Result: Longint;        {returns a -1 or -2 if handled}
end;
```

Description

A list box with the LBS_WANTKEYBOARDINPUT style sends a WM_VKEYTOITEM message to its owner in response to a WM_KEYDOWN message.

Members

Msg: The message identifier. This member is set to the message identifier constant WM_VKEYTOITEM.

Key: The virtual key code of the key that generated the WM_KEYDOWN message.

CaretPos: The position of the caret in the list box.

ListBox: The handle of the list box.

Result: This message should return -2 to indicate that the message was handled and no further processing by the list box is necessary. A return value of -1 indicates that the list box should perform its default action for the indicated keystroke. A return value of zero or greater specifies the zero-based index of an item in the list box, and instructs the list box to perform its default action for the indicated keystroke on the specified item.

See Also

DefWindowProc, WM_CHARTOITEM, WM_KEYDOWN

WM_VSCROLL

Syntax

```
TWMVScroll = record
        Msg: Cardinal;              {the message identifier}
        ScrollCode: Smallint;       {the scroll request code}
        Pos: Smallint;              {the scroll bar thumb position}
        Scroll bar: HWND;           {the scroll bar handle}
        Result: Longint;            {returns a zero if handled}
   end;
```

Description

The WM_VSCROLL message is sent to a window when a vertical scrolling event occurs, if the window has a standard vertical scroll bar. It is also sent when a scroll event occurs in a vertical scroll bar control. If the application changes the position of data in a window as a result of a vertical scrolling event, it should reset the position of the scroll bar's thumb by calling the SetScrollPos function. The WM_VSCROLL and WM_HSCROLL messages have 16-bit values for scroll positions, restricting the maximum position to 65,535.

Members

Msg: The message identifier. This member is set to the message identifier constant WM_VSCROLL.

ScrollCode: Specifies the type of scrolling request as a result of the scrolling event. This member can contain one value from Table A-50.

Pos: If the ScrollCode member contains SB_THUMBPOSITION or SB_THUMBTRACK, this member specifies the current position of the scroll bar's thumb. Otherwise, this member is not used.

Scroll bar: Specifies the handle of a scroll bar control if it is a scroll bar control that is sending the WM_HSCROLL message. Otherwise, this member is not used.

Result: If the application handles this message, set this member to zero.

See Also

WM_HSCROLL

Table A-50: TWMVScroll.ScrollCode Values

Value	Description
SB_BOTTOM	Indicates a scroll to the lower right.
SB_ENDSCROLL	Indicates an end to the scrolling operation.

Value	Description
SB_LINEDOWN	Indicates a scroll down by one unit.
SB_LINEUP	Indicates a scroll up by one unit.
SB_PAGEDOWN	Indicates a scroll down by one window width.
SB_PAGEUP	Indicates a scroll up by one window width.
SB_THUMBPOSITION	Indicates a scroll to the absolute position as specified by the Pos member.
SB_THUMBTRACK	Drags the scroll bar thumb to the position as indicated by the Pos member. This is normally used to provide feedback.
SB_TOP	Indicates a scroll to the upper left.

WM_VSCROLLCLIPBOARD

Syntax

```
TWMVScrollClipboard = record
      Msg: Cardinal;              {the message identifier}
      Viewer: HWND;               {the handle of the clipboard viewer}
      ScrollCode: Word;           {the scroll request code}
      ThumbPos: Word;             {the scroll bar thumb position}
      Result: Longint;            {returns a zero if handled}
end;
```

Description

The WM_VSCROLLCLIPBOARD message is sent by a clipboard viewer window to the clipboard owner when there is an event in the viewer's vertical scroll bar and the clipboard contains data in the CF_OWNERDISPLAY format. The clipboard owner must scroll the image and then reset the vertical scroll bar value.

Members

Msg: The message identifier. This member is set to the message identifier constant WM_VSCROLLCLIPBOARD.

Viewer: Specifies the handle of the clipboard viewer window.

ScrollCode: Specifies the type of scrolling request as a result of the scrolling event. This member can contain one value from Table A-51.

ThumbPos: If the ScrollCode member contains SB_THUMBPOSITION, this member specifies the current position of the scroll bar's thumb. Otherwise, this member is not used.

Result: If the application handles this message, set this member to zero.

See Also

WM_HSCROLLCLIPBOARD

Table A-51: TWMVScrollClipboard.ScrollCode Values

Value	Description
SB_BOTTOM	Indicates a scroll to the lower right.
SB_ENDSCROLL	Indicates an end to the scrolling operation.
SB_LINEDOWN	Indicates a scroll down by one unit.
SB_LINEUP	Indicates a scroll up by one unit.
SB_PAGEDOWN	Indicates a scroll down by one window width.
SB_PAGEUP	Indicates a scroll up by one window width.
SB_THUMBPOSITION	Indicates a scroll to the absolute position as specified by the Pos member.
SB_TOP	Indicates a scroll to the upper left.

WM_WINDOWPOSCHANGED

Syntax

```
TWMWindowPosChanged = record
      Msg: Cardinal;              {the message identifier}
      Unused: Integer;            {not used}
      WindowPos: PWindowPos;      {a pointer to a TWindowPos structure}
      Result: Longint;            {returns a zero if handled}
end;
```

Description

This message is sent when a window's size, position, or Z-order is adjusted as a result of calling a window movement or positioning function, such as SetWindowPos or End-DeferWindowPos. The WM_SIZE and WM_MOVE messages will not be sent if the DefWindowProc function is not called by a window in response to this message.

Members

Msg: The message identifier. This member is set to the message identifier constant WM_WINDOWPOSCHANGED.

Unused: This member is not used by this message.

WindowPos: Specifies a pointer to a TWindowPos structure containing the new information about the size and position of the window. The TWindowPos structure is defined as:

```
TWindowPos = packed record
      hwnd: HWND;                 {a handle to a window}
```

hwndInsertAfter: HWND;	{a window handle or positioning flag}
x: Integer;	{the horizontal position}
y: Integer;	{the vertical position}
cx: Integer;	{the width of the window}
cy: Integer;	{the height of the window}
flags: UINT	{size and positioning flags}

end;

Please see the WM_NCCALCSIZE for a description of this data structure.

Result: If the application handles this message, set this member to zero.

See Also

DefWindowProc, EndDeferWindowPos, SetWindowPos, WM_MOVE, WM_NCCALCSIZE, WM_SIZE, WM_WINDOWPOSCHANGING

WM_WINDOWPOSCHANGING

Syntax

TWMWindowPosChanging = record

Msg: Cardinal;	{the message identifier}
Unused: Integer;	{not used}
WindowPos: PWindowPos;	{a pointer to a TWindowPos structure}
Result: Longint;	{returns a zero if handled}

end;

Description

This message is sent when a window's size, position, or Z-order is about to be adjusted as a result of calling a window movement or positioning function, such as SetWindow-Pos or EndDeferWindowPos. If the window has the WS_OVERLAPPED or WS_THICKFRAME styles and sends this message to the DefWindowProc function, a WM_GETMINMAXINFO message will be sent to the window. This validates the new size and position of the window so that the CS_BYTEALIGNCLIENT and CS_BYTEALIGNWINDOW window class styles can be enforced.

Members

Msg: The message identifier. This member is set to the message identifier constant WM_WINDOWPOSCHANGED.

Unused: This member is not used by this message.

WindowPos: Specifies a pointer to a TWindowPos structure containing the new information about the size and position of the window. The TWindowPos structure is defined as:

TWindowPos = packed record

hwnd: HWND;	{a handle to a window}
hwndInsertAfter: HWND;	{a window handle or positioning flag}

x: Integer;	{the horizontal position}
y: Integer;	{the vertical position}
cx: Integer;	{the width of the window}
cy: Integer;	{the height of the window}
flags: UINT	{size and positioning flags}

end;

Please see the WM_NCCALCSIZE for a description of this data structure.

Result: If the application handles this message, set this member to zero.

See Also

DefWindowProc, EndDeferWindowPos, SetWindowPos, WM_GETMINMAXINFO, WM_MOVE, WM_NCCALCSIZE, WM_SIZE, WM_WINDOWPOSCHANGING

Appendix B

Tertiary Raster Operation Codes

ROP Code	Boolean Operation
$00000042	Result is all black
$00010289	NOT (brush OR source OR destination)
$00020C89	NOT (brush OR source) AND destination
$000300AA	NOT (brush OR source)
$00040C88	NOT (brush OR destination) AND source
$000500A9	NOT (brush OR destination)
$00060865	NOT (brush OR NOT(source XOR destination))
$000702C5	NOT (brush OR (source AND destination))
$00080F08	NOT brush AND source AND destination
$00090245	NOT (brush OR (source XOR destination))
$000A0329	NOT brush AND destination
$000B0B2A	NOT (brush OR (source AND NOT destination))
$000C0324	NOT brush AND source
$000D0B25	NOT (brush OR (NOT source AND destination))
$000E08A5	NOT (brush OR NOT (source OR destination))
$000F0001	NOT brush
$00100C85	brush AND NOT (source OR destination)
$001100A6	NOT (source OR destination)
$00120868	NOT (source OR NOT (brush XOR destination))
$001302C8	NOT (source OR (brush AND destination))
$00140869	NOT (destination OR NOT (brush XOR source))
$001502C9	NOT (destination OR (brush AND source))
$00165CCA	brush XOR (source XOR (destination AND NOT (brush AND source)))
$00171D54	NOT (source XOR ((source XOR brush) AND (source XOR destination)))
$00180D59	(brush XOR source) AND (brush XOR destination)
$00191CC8	NOT (source XOR (destination AND NOT (brush AND source)))

ROP Code	Boolean Operation
$001A06C5	brush XOR (destination OR (source AND brush))
$001B0768	NOT (source XOR (destination AND (brush XOR source)))
$001C06CA	brush XOR (source OR (brush AND destination))
$001D0766	NOT (destination XOR (source AND (brush XOR destination)))
$001E01A5	brush XOR (source OR destination)
$001F0385	NOT (brush AND (source OR destination))
$00200F09	brush AND NOT source AND destination
$00210248	NOT (source OR (brush XOR destination))
$00220326	NOT source AND destination
$00230B24	NOT (source OR (brush AND NOT destination))
$00240D55	(source XOR brush) AND (source XOR destination)
$00251CC5	NOT (brush XOR (destination AND NOT (source AND brush)))
$002606C8	source XOR (destination OR (brush AND source))
$00271868	source XOR (destination OR NOT (brush XOR source))
$00280369	destination AND (brush XOR source)
$002916CA	NOT (brush XOR (source XOR (destination OR (brush AND source))))
$002A0CC9	destination AND NOT (brush AND source)
$002B1D58	NOT (source XOR ((source XOR brush) AND (brush AND destination)))
$002C0784	source XOR (brush AND (source OR destination))
$002D060A	brush XOR (source OR NOT destination)
$002E064A	brush XOR (source OR (brush XOR destination))
$002F0E2A	NOT (brush AND (source OR NOT destination))
$0030032A	brush AND NOT source
$00310B28	NOT (source OR (NOT brush AND destination))
$00320688	source XOR (brush OR source OR destination)
$00330008	NOT source
$003406C4	source XOR (brush OR (source AND destination))
$00351864	source XOR (brush OR NOT (source XOR destination))
$003601A8	source XOR (brush OR destination)
$00370388	NOT (source AND (brush OR destination))
$0038078A	brush XOR (source AND (brush OR destination))
$00390604	source XOR (brush OR NOT destination)
$003A0644	source XOR (brush XOR (source XOR destination))
$003B0E24	NOT (source AND (brush OR NOT destination))
$003C004A	brush XOR source
$003D18A4	source XOR (brush OR NOT (source OR destination))
$003E1B24	source XOR (brush OR (NOT source AND destination))
$003F00EA	NOT (brush AND source)

ROP Code	Boolean Operation
$00400F0A	brush AND source AND NOT destination
$00410249	NOT (destination OR (brush XOR source))
$00420D5D	(source XOR destination) AND (brush XOR destination)
$00431CC4	NOT (source XOR (brush AND NOT (source AND destination)))
$00440328	source AND NOT destination
$00450B29	NOT (destination OR (brush AND NOT source))
$004606C6	destination XOR (source OR (brush AND destination))
$0047076A	NOT (brush XOR (source AND (brush XOR destination)))
$00480368	source AND (brush XOR destination)
$004916C5	NOT (brush XOR (destination XOR (source OR (brush AND destination))))
$004A0789	destination XOR (brush AND (source OR destination))
$004B0605	brush XOR (NOT source OR destination)
$004C0CC8	source AND NOT (brush AND destination)
$004D1954	NOT (source XOR ((brush XOR source) OR (source XOR destination)))
$004E0645	brush XOR (destination OR (brush XOR source))
$004F0E25	NOT (brush AND (NOT source OR destination))
$00500325	brush AND NOT destination
$00510B26	NOT (destination OR (NOT brush AND source))
$005206C9	destination XOR (brush OR (source AND destination))
$00530764	NOT (source XOR (brush AND (source XOR destination)))
$005408A9	NOT (destination OR NOT (brush OR source))
$00550009	NOT destination
$005601A9	destination XOR (brush OR source)
$00570389	NOT (destination AND (brush OR source))
$00580785	brush XOR (destination AND (brush OR source))
$00590609	destination XOR (brush OR NOT source)
$005A0049	brush XOR destination
$005B18A9	destination XOR (brush OR NOT (source OR destination))
$005C0649	destination XOR (brush OR (source XOR destination))
$005D0E29	NOT (destination AND (brush OR NOT source))
$005E1B29	destination XOR (brush OR (source AND NOT destination))
$005F00E9	NOT (brush AND destination)
$00600365	brush AND (source XOR destination)
$006116C6	NOT (destination XOR (source XOR (brush OR (source AND destination))))
$00620786	destination XOR (source AND (brush OR destination))
$00630608	source XOR (NOT brush OR destination)

ROP Code	Boolean Operation
$00640788	source XOR (destination AND (brush OR source))
$00650606	destination XOR (NOT brush OR source)
$00660046	source XOR destination
$006718A8	source XOR (destination OR NOT (brush OR source))
$006858A6	NOT (destination XOR (source XOR (brush OR NOT (source OR destination))))
$00690145	NOT (brush XOR (source XOR destination))
$006A01E9	destination XOR (brush AND source)
$006B178A	NOT (brush XOR (source XOR (destination AND (source OR brush))))
$006C01E8	source XOR (brush AND destination)
$006D1785	NOT (brush XOR (destination XOR (source AND (brush OR destination))))
$006E1E28	source XOR (destination AND (brush OR NOT source))
$006F0C65	NOT (brush AND NOT (source XOR destination))
$00700CC5	brush AND NOT (source AND destination)
$00711D5C	NOT (source XOR ((source XOR destination) AND (brush XOR destination)))
$00720648	source XOR (destination OR (brush XOR source))
$00730E28	NOT (source AND (NOT brush OR destination))
$00740646	destination XOR (source OR (brush XOR destination))
$00750E26	NOT (destination AND (NOT brush OR source))
$00761B28	source XOR (destination OR (brush AND NOT source))
$007700E6	NOT (source AND destination)
$007801E5	brush XOR (source AND destination)
$00791786	NOT (destination XOR (source XOR (brush AND (source OR destination))))
$007A1E29	destination XOR (brush AND (source OR NOT destination))
$007B0C68	NOT (source AND NOT (brush XOR destination))
$007C1E24	source XOR (brush AND (NOT source OR destination))
$007D0C69	NOT(destination AND NOT (source XOR brush))
$007E0955	(brush XOR source) OR (source XOR destination)
$007F03C9	NOT (brush AND source AND destination)
$008003E9	brush AND source AND destination
$00810975	NOT ((brush XOR source) OR (source XOR destination))
$00820C49	NOT (brush XOR source) AND destination
$00831E04	NOT (source XOR (brush AND (NOT source OR destination)))
$00840C48	source AND NOT (brush XOR destination)
$00851E05	NOT (brush XOR (destination AND (NOT brush OR source)))

ROP Code	Boolean Operation
$008617A6	destination XOR (source XOR (brush AND (source OR destination)))
$008701C5	NOT (brush XOR (source and destination))
$00800C6	source AND destination
$008911B08	NOT (source XOR (destination OR (brush AND NOT source)))
$008A0E06	(NOT brush OR source) AND destination
$008B0666	NOT (destination XOR (source OR (brush OR destination)))
$008C0E08	source AND (NOT brush OR destination)
$008D0668	NOT (source XOR (destination OR (brush XOR source)))
$008E1D7C	source XOR (source XOR destination AND (brush XOR destination))
$008F0CE5	NOT (brush AND NOT (source AND destination))
$00900C45	brush AND NOT (source XOR destination)
$00911E08	NOT (source XOR (destination AND (brush OR NOT source)))
$009217A9	destination XOR (brush XOR (source AND (brush OR destination)))
$009301C4	NOT (source XOR (brush AND destination))
$009417AA	brush XOR (source XOR (destination AND (brush OR source)))
$009501C9	NOT (destination XOR (brush AND source))
$00960169	brush XOR source XOR destination
$0097588A	brush XOR (source XOR (destination OR NOT (brush OR source)))
$00981888	NOT (source XOR (destination OR NOT (brush OR source)))
$00990066	NOT (source XOR destination)
$009A0709	(brush AND NOT source) XOR destination
$009B07A8	NOT (source XOR (destination AND (brush OR source)))
$009C0704	source XOR (brush AND NOT destination)
$009D07A6	NOT (destination XOR (source AND (brush OR destination)))
$009E16E6	(source XOR (brush OR (source AND destination))) XOR destination
$009F0345	NOT (brush AND (source XOR destination))
$00A000C9	brush AND destination
$00A11B05	NOT (brush XOR (destination OR (NOT brush AND source)))
$00A20E09	(brush OR NOT source) AND destination
$00A30699	NOT (destination XOR (brush OR (source XOR destination)))
$00A41885	NOT (brush XOR (destination OR NOT (brush OR source)))
$00A50065	NOT (brush XOR destination)
$00A60706	(NOT brush AND source) XOR destination
$00A707A5	NOT (brush XOR (destination AND (brush OR source)))
$00A803A9	(brush OR source) AND destination

ROP Code	Boolean Operation
$00A90189	NOT ((brush OR source) XOR destination)
$00AA0029	destination
$00AB0889	NOT (brush OR source) OR destination
$00AC0744	source XOR (brush AND (source XOR destination))
$00AD06E9	NOT (destination XOR (brush OR (source AND destination)))
$00AE0B06	(NOT brush AND source) OR destination
$00AF0229	NOT brush OR destination
$00B00E05	brush AND (NOT source OR destination)
$00B10665	NOT (brush OR (destination OR (brush XOR source)))
$00B12974	source XOR ((brush XOR source) OR (source XOR destination))
$00B03CE8	NOT (source AND NOT (brush AND destination))
$00B4070A	brush XOR (source AND NOT destination)
$00B507A9	NOT (destination XOR (brush AND (source OR destination)))
$00B616E9	destination XOR (brush XOR (source OR (brush AND destination)))
$00B70348	NOT (source AND (brush XOR destination))
$00B8074A	brush XOR (source AND (brush XOR destination))
$00B906E6	NOT (destination XOR (source OR (brush AND destination)))
$00BA0B09	(brush AND NOT source) OR destination
$00BB0226	NOT source OR destination
$00BC1CE4	source XOR (brush AND NOT (source AND destination))
$00BD0D7D	NOT ((brush XOR destination) AND (source XOR destination))
$00BE0269	(brush XOR source) OR destination
$00BF08C9	NOT (brush AND source) OR destination
$00C000CA	brush AND source
$00C11B04	NOT (source XOR (brush OR (NOT source AND destination)))
$00C21884	NOT (source XOR (brush OR NOT(source OR destination)))
$00C3006A	NOT (brush XOR source)
$00C40E04	source AND (brush OR NOT destination)
$00C50664	NOT (source XOR (brush OR (source XOR destination)))
$00C60708	source XOR (NOT brush AND destination)
$00C707AA	NOT (brush XOR (source AND (brush OR destination)))
$00C803A8	source AND (brush OR destination)
$00C90184	NOT (source XOR (brush OR destination))
$00CA0749	destination XOR (brush AND (source XOR destination))
$00CB06E4	NOT (source XOR (brush OR (source AND destination)))
$00CC0020	source
$00CD0888	source OR NOT (brush OR destination)
$00CE0B08	source OR (NOT brush AND destination)

ROP Code	Boolean Operation
$00CF0224	source OR NOT brush
$00D00E0A	brush AND (source OR NOT destination)
$00D1066A	NOT (brush XOR (source OR (brush XOR destination)))
$00D20705	brush XOR (NOT source AND destination)
$00D307A4	NOT (source XOR (brush AND (source OR destination)))
$00D41D78	source XOR (brush XOR source AND (brush XOR destination))
$00D50CE9	NOT (destination AND NOT (brush AND source))
$00D616EA	brush XOR (source XOR (destination OR (brush AND source)))
$00D70349	NOT (destination AND (brush XOR source))
$00D80745	brush XOR (destination AND (brush XOR source))
$00D906E8	NOT (source XOR (destination OR (brush AND source)))
$00DA1CE9	destination XOR (brush AND NOT (source XOR destination))
$00DB0D75	NOT ((brush XOR source) AND (source XOR destination))
$00DC0B04	source OR (brush AND NOT destination)
$00DD0228	source OR NOT destination
$00DE0268	source OR (brush XOR destination)
$00DF08C8	source OR NOT (brush AND destination)
$00E003A5	brush AND (destination OR source)
$00E10185	NOT (brush XOR (source OR destination))
$00E20746	destination XOR (source AND (brush XOR destination))
$00E306EA	NOT (brush XOR (source OR (brush AND destination)))
$00E40748	source XOR (destination AND (brush XOR source))
$00E506E5	NOT (brush XOR (destination OR (brush AND source)))
$00E61CE8	source XOR (destination AND NOT (brush AND source))
$00E70D79	NOT ((brush XOR source) AND (brush XOR destination))
$00E81D74	source XOR ((brush XOR source) AND (source XOR destination))
$00E95CE6	NOT (destination XOR (source XOR (brush AND NOT (source AND destination))))
$00EA02E9	(brush AND source) OR destination
$00EB0849	NOT (brush XOR source) OR destination
$00EC02E8	source OR (brush AND destination)
$00ED0848	source OR NOT (brush XOR destination)
$00EE0086	source OR destination
$00EF0A08	NOT brush OR source OR destination
$00F00021	brush
$00F10885	brush OR NOT (source OR destination)
$00F20B05	brush OR (NOT source AND destination)
$00F3022A	brush OR NOT source
$00F40B0A	brush OR (source AND NOT destination)

ROP Code	Boolean Operation
$00F50225	brush OR NOT destination
$00F60265	brush OR (source XOR destination)
$00F708C5	brush OR NOT (source AND destination)
$00F802E5	brush OR (source AND destination)
$00F90845	brush OR NOT (source XOR destination)
$00FA0089	brush OR destination
$00FB0A09	brush OR NOT source OR destination
$00FC008A	brush OR source
$00FD0A0A	brush OR source OR NOT destination
$00FE02A9	brush OR source OR destination
$00FF0062	Result is all white

Appendix C

ASCII Character Set

Dec	Hex	Char	Description
0	00	NULL	Null
1	01	☺	Start of heading
2	02	☻	Start of text
3	03	♥	End of text
4	04	♦	End of transmission
5	05	♣	Inquiry
6	06	♠	Acknowledge
7	07	•	Bell
8	08	◘	Backspace
9	09	○	Horizontal tab
10	0A	◙	Line feed
11	0B	♂	Vertical tab
12	0C	♀	Form feed
13	0D	♪	Carriage return
14	0E	♫	Shift out
15	0F	☼	Shift in
16	10	►	Data link escape
17	11	◄	Device control 1
18	12	↕	Device control 2
19	13	‼	Device control 3
20	14	¶	Device control 4
21	15	§	Negative acknowledge
22	16	▬	Synchronous idle
23	17	↨	End transmission block
24	18	↑	Cancel
25	19	↓	End of medium
26	1A	→	Substitute
27	1B	←	Escape

Dec	Hex	Char	Description
28	1C	∟	File separator
29	1D	↔	Group separator
30	1E	▲	Record separator
31	1F	▼	Unit separator

Dec	Hex	Char	Dec	Hex	Char	Dec	Hex	Char
32	20	SPACE	65	41	A	98	62	b
33	21	!	66	42	B	99	63	c
34	22	"	67	43	C	100	64	d
35	23	#	68	44	D	101	65	e
36	24	$	69	45	E	102	66	f
37	25	%	70	46	F	103	67	g
38	26	&	71	47	G	104	68	h
39	27	'	72	48	H	105	69	i
40	28	(	73	49	I	106	6A	j
41	29	)	74	4A	J	107	6B	k
42	2A	*	75	4B	K	108	6C	l
43	2B	+	76	4C	L	109	6D	m
44	2C	,	77	4D	M	110	6E	n
45	2D	–	78	4E	N	111	6F	o
46	2E	.	79	4F	O	112	70	p
47	2F	/	80	50	P	113	71	q
48	30	0	81	51	Q	114	72	r
49	31	1	82	52	R	115	73	s
50	32	2	83	53	S	116	74	t
51	33	3	84	54	T	117	75	u
52	34	4	85	55	U	118	76	v
53	35	5	86	56	V	119	77	w
54	36	6	87	57	W	120	78	x
55	37	7	88	58	X	121	79	y
56	38	8	89	59	Y	122	7A	z
57	39	9	90	5A	Z	123	7B	{
58	3A	:	91	5B	[	124	7C	|
59	3B	;	92	5C	\	125	7D	}
60	3C	<	93	5D	]	126	7E	~
61	3D	=	94	5E	^	127	7F	⌂
62	3E	>	95	5F	_	128	80	Ç
63	3F	?	96	60	`	129	81	ü
64	40	@	97	61	a	130	82	é

Dec	Hex	Char	Dec	Hex	Char	Dec	Hex	Char
131	83	â	170	AA	¬	209	D1	╤
132	84	ä	171	AB	½	210	D2	╥
133	85	à	172	AC	¼	211	D3	╙
134	86	å	173	AD	¡	212	D4	╘
135	87	ç	174	AE	«	213	D5	╒
136	88	ê	175	AF	»	214	D6	╓
137	89	ë	176	B0	░	215	D7	╫
138	8A	è	177	B1	▒	216	D8	╪
139	8B	ï	178	B2	▓	217	D9	┘
140	8C	î	179	B3	│	218	DA	┌
141	8D	ì	180	B4	┤	219	DB	█
142	8E	Ä	181	B5	╡	220	DC	▄
143	8F	Å	182	B6	╢	221	DD	▌
144	90	É	183	B7	╖	222	DE	▐
145	91	æ	184	B8	╕	223	DF	▀
146	92	Æ	185	B9	╣	224	E0	α
147	93	ô	186	BA	║	225	E1	ß
148	94	ö	187	BB	╗	226	E2	Γ
149	95	ò	188	BC	╝	227	E3	π
150	96	û	189	BD	╜	228	E4	Σ
151	97	ù	190	BE	╛	229	E5	σ
152	98	ÿ	191	BF	┐	230	E6	µ
153	99	Ö	192	C0	└	231	E7	τ
154	9A	Ü	193	C1	┴	232	E8	Φ
155	9B	¢	194	C2	┬	233	E9	Θ
156	9C	£	195	C3	├	234	EA	Ω
157	9D	¥	196	C4	─	235	EB	δ
158	9E	₧	197	C5	┼	236	EC	∞
159	9F	ƒ	198	C6	╞	237	ED	φ
160	A0	á	199	C7	╟	238	EE	ε
161	A1	í	200	C8	╚	239	EF	∩
162	A2	ó	201	C9	╔	240	F0	≡
163	A3	ú	202	CA	╩	241	F1	±
164	A4	ñ	203	CB	╦	242	F2	≥
165	A5	Ñ	204	CC	╠	243	F3	≤
166	A6	ª	205	CD	═	244	F4	⌠
167	A7	º	206	CE	╬	245	F5	⌡
168	A8	¿	207	CF	╧	246	F6	÷
169	A9	⌐	208	D0	╨	247	F7	≈

C

Appendix

Dec	Hex	Char	Dec	Hex	Char	Dec	Hex	Char
248	F8	°	251	FB	√	254	FE	■
249	F9	·	252	FC	^{n}	255	FF	
250	FA	·	253	FD	^{2}			

Appendix D

Virtual Key Code Chart

Virtual Key Code	Decimal Value	Hex Value	Description
VK_LBUTTON	1	$1	Left mouse button
VK_RBUTTON	2	$2	Right mouse button
VK_CANCEL	3	$3	Ctrl+Break key combination
VK_MBUTTON	4	$4	Middle mouse button
VK_BACK	8	$8	Backspace
VK_TAB	9	$9	Tab
VK_CLEAR	12	$C	Numeric keypad 5, Num Lock off
VK_RETURN	13	$D	Enter
VK_SHIFT	16	$10	Shift
VK_CONTROL	17	$11	Ctrl
VK_MENU	18	$12	Alt
VK_PAUSE	19	$13	Pause
VK_CAPITAL	20	$14	Caps Lock
VK_ESCAPE	27	$1B	Esc
VK_SPACE	32	$20	Space bar
VK_PRIOR	33	$21	Page Up
VK_NEXT	34	$22	Page Down
VK_END	35	$23	End
VK_HOME	36	$24	Home
VK_LEFT	37	$25	Left cursor key
VK_UP	38	$26	Up cursor key
VK_RIGHT	39	$27	Right cursor key
VK_DOWN	40	$28	Down cursor key
VK_SNAPSHOT	44	$2C	Print Screen
VK_INSERT	45	$2D	Insert
VK_DELETE	46	$2E	Delete

D

Appendix

Virtual Key Code	Decimal Value	Hex Value	Description
VK_LWIN	91	$5B	Left Windows key on a Windows 95 compatible keyboard
VK_RWIN	92	$5C	Right Windows key on a Windows 95 compatible keyboard
VK_APPS	93	$5D	Menu key on a Windows 95 compatible keyboard
VK_NUMPAD0	96	$60	Numeric keypad 0
VK_NUMPAD1	97	$61	Numeric keypad 1
VK_NUMPAD2	98	$62	Numeric keypad 2
VK_NUMPAD3	99	$63	Numeric keypad 3
VK_NUMPAD4	100	$64	Numeric keypad 4
VK_NUMPAD5	101	$65	Numeric keypad 5
VK_NUMPAD6	102	$66	Numeric keypad 6
VK_NUMPAD7	103	$67	Numeric keypad 7
VK_NUMPAD8	104	$68	Numeric keypad 8
VK_NUMPAD9	105	$69	Numeric keypad 9
VK_MULTIPLY	106	$6A	Numeric keypad multiply (*)
VK_ADD	107	$6B	Numeric keypad add (+)
VK_SUBTRACT	109	$6D	Numeric keypad subtract (-)
VK_DECIMAL	110	$6E	Numeric keypad decimal (.)
VK_DIVIDE	111	$6F	Numeric keypad divide (/)
VK_F1	112	$70	F1
VK_F2	113	$71	F2
VK_F3	114	$72	F3
VK_F4	115	$73	F4
VK_F5	116	$74	F5
VK_F6	117	$75	F6
VK_F7	118	$76	F7
VK_F8	119	$77	F8
VK_F9	120	$78	F9
VK_F10	121	$79	F10
VK_F11	122	$7A	F11
VK_F12	123	$7B	F12
VK_F13	124	$7C	F13
VK_F14	125	$7D	F14
VK_F15	126	$7E	F15
VK_F16	127	$7F	F16
VK_F17	128	$80	F17

Virtual Key Code	Decimal Value	Hex Value	Description
VK_F18	129	$81	F18
VK_F19	130	$82	F19
VK_F20	131	$83	F20
VK_F21	132	$84	F21
VK_F22	133	$85	F22
VK_F23	134	$86	F23
VK_F24	135	$87	F24
VK_NUMLOCK	144	$90	Num Lock
VK_SCROLL	145	$91	Scroll Lock
VK_LSHIFT	160	$A0	Left shift key
VK_RSHIFT	161	$A1	Right shift key
VK_LCONTROL	162	$A2	Left Ctrl key
VK_RCONTROL	163	$A3	Right Ctrl key
VK_LMENU	164	$A4	Left Alt key
VK_RMENU	165	$A5	Right Alt key

D

Appendix

Appendix E

Bibliography

There exists quite a large knowledge base on Windows programming in general and Delphi programming in particular. The information for this book is based in part on research and knowledge gleaned from the following books:

Miller, Powell, et. al., *Special Edition Using Delphi 3* [QUE, 1997]

Jarol, Haygood, and Coppola, *Delphi 2 Multimedia Adventure Set* [Coriolis Group Books, 1996]

Lischner, Ray, *Secrets of Delphi 2* [Waite Group Press, 1996]

Cooke and Telles, *Windows 95 How-To* [Waite Group Press, 1996]

Simon, Gouker, and Barnes, *Windows 95 Win32 Programming API Bible* [Waite Group Press, 1996]

Swan and Cogswell, *Delphi 32-Bit Programming Secrets* [IDG Books, 1996]

Pacheco and Teixeira, *Delphi 2 Developers Guide* [Sams Publishing, 1996]

Calvert, Charles, *Delphi 2 Unleashed* [Sams Publishing, 1996]

Wallace and Tendon, *Delphi 2 Developer's Solutions* [Waite Group Press, 1996]

Frerking, Wallace, and Niddery, *Borland Delphi How-To* [Waite Group Press, 1995]

Pietrek, Matt, *Windows 95 System Programming Secrets* [IDG Books, 1995]

Rector and Newcomer, *Win32 Programming* [Addison-Wesley Developers Press, 1997]

Petzold and Yao, *Programming Windows 95* [Microsoft Press, 1996]

Cluts, Nancy, *Programming the Windows 95 User Interface* [Microsoft Press, 1995]

Thorpe, Danny, *Delphi Component Design* [Addison-Wesley Developers Press, 1997]

Konopka, Ray, *Developing Custom Delphi 3 Components* [Coriolis Group Books, 1997]

Beveridge and Wiener, *Multithreading Applications in Win32*, [Addison-Wesley Developers Press, 1997]

Richter, Jeffrey, *Advanced Windows*, [Microsoft Press, 1997]

Other Books from Wordware Publishing, Inc.

Popular Applications Series
Build Your Own Computer (2nd Ed.)
Creating Help for Windows Applications
Developing Utilities in Assembly Language
Developing Utilities in Visual Basic 4.0
HP LaserJet Handbook
Learn AutoCAD in a Day
Learn AutoCAD 12 in a Day
Learn AutoCAD LT for Windows in a Day
Learn C in Three Days
Learn CompuServe for Windows in a Day
Learn DOS 6.2 in a Day
Learn Generic CADD 6.0 in a Day
Learn Lotus 1-2-3 Rel. 4 for DOS in a Day
Learn Lotus 1-2-3 Rel. 4 for Windows in a Day
Learn Lotus 1-2-3 Rel. 5 for Windows in a Day
Learn MS Access 2.0 for Windows in a Day
Learn MS Access 7.0 for Windows 95 in a Day
Learn Microsoft Assembler in a Day
Learn MS Excel 7.0 for Windows 95 in a Day
Learn MS PowerPoint 7.0 for Win 95 in a Day
Learn MS Publisher 2.0 for Windows in a Day
Learn MS Word 6.0 for Windows in a Day
Learn MS Word 7.0 for Windows 95 in a Day
Learn Microsoft Works 3.0 in a Day
Learn Microsoft Works 3.0 for Windows in a Day
Learn PageMaker 5.0 in a Day
Learn PAL 4.5 in a Day
Learn PROCOMM PLUS 2.0 for Widows in a Day
Learn Quattro Pro 5.0 in a Day
Learn To Use Your Modem in a Day
Learn Turbo Assembler in a Day
Learn Visual dBASE 5.5 for Windows in a Day
Learn Windows 95 in a Day
Learn WordPerfect 5.2 for Windows in a Day
Learn WordPerfect 6.0 for Windows in a Day
Learn WordPerfect Presentations in a Day
Moving from WP DOS to WP Windows
Networks for Small Businesses
Write TSRs Now
Write Your Own Prog Lang Using C++ (2nd Ed.)

Programmer's Example Series
Nathan Wallace's Delphi 3 Example Book
The HTML Example Book
The Visual Basic 4.0 Example Book
The WordBasic Example Book

At A Glance Series
ACT! 2.0 for Windows at a Glance
CorelDRAW 5.0 for Windows at a Glance
Lotus 1-2-3 Rel. 4 for Windows at a Glance
Microsoft Word 6.0 for Windows at a Glance
Paradox 5.0 for Windows at a Glance
Quattro Pro 5.0 for Windows at a Glance
WordPerfect 6.0 for Windows at a Glance

Hands-On Windows Programming Series
1: Intro To Window Programming
2: Child Windows
3: Painting the Screen
4: Transferring Data To and From Windows
5: Mouse, Timer, and Keyboard Inputs
6: Text and Special Fonts, Menus, and Printing
7: AppStudio Graphics Editor
8: C to C++ Conversion
9: Special Topics, Index for Books 1-9

General and Advanced Computer Books
Adv. CGI Tech. for Info. Processing
Collaborative Computing with Delphi 3
The Complete Communication Hndbk (2nd Ed.)
Demystifying ATM/ADSL
Demystifying ISDN
Demystifying TCP/IP (2nd Ed.)
Developer's Guide to HP Printers
Dev. Enterprise App. w/PowerBuilder 6.0
Developing Internet Information Services
Digital Imaging in C and the WWW
Illustrated UNIX System V
Innovation, Inc.
Internet Pub. with Microsoft Word 98
Learn ACT! 1998 for the Adv. User
Learn ACT! 3.0 for Windows 95

Other Books from Wordware Publishing, Inc.

General and Advanced Computer Books
Learn ActiveX Dev. Using Visual Basic 5.0
Learn ActiveX Dev. Using Visual C++ 98
Learn ActiveX Scripting w/Explorer 4.0
Learn Advanced HTML 4.0
Learn Advanced Internet Relay Chat
Learn Advanced JavaScript Prog.
Learn Advanced MFC Prog. Visual C++ 98
Learn Archiving & File Compr. Visual C++ 98
Learn AutoCAD LT 97
Learn AutoCAD LT for Windows 95
Learn Computers in a Day
Learn Encryption Tech. Visual Basic 98
Learn Graphics File Programming with Delphi 3
Learn Internet Publishing w/MS Publisher 97
Learn Internet Relay Chat
Learn Internet Relay Chat (2nd Ed.)
Learn Lotus Domino
Learn the MFC C++ Classes
Learn the MFC C++ Classes for Visual C++ 98
Learn MS Access 98 Prog. for the Adv. User
Learn MS Active Dsktop Prog. Visual C++ 98
Learn Microsoft Exchange Server 5.0
Learn Microsoft FrontPage 97
Learn Microsoft Office 95
Learn Microsoft Office 97
Learn MS Transact Serv. Dev. Visual C++ 98
Learn P-CAD Master Designer
Learn Pascal in Three Days (2nd Ed.)
Learn Pearl 5 in Three Days
Learn Visio 5.0
Learn Visio 5.0 for the Advanced User
Learn Visual Basic 5.0 in 3 Days
Lotus Notes Developer's Guide
Networking with Windows NT
Object-Oriented Software Project Mgmnt.
Practical Guide to Intranet Client-Server App.
   Using the Web
Practical Guide to SGML Filters
Practical Guide to SGML/XML Filters
The Ultimate Computer Buyer's Guide
Tomes of Delphi 3: Win 32 Core API
Tomes of Delphi 3: Win 32 Graphical API
Visio 4 for Everyone

Games and Entertainment
Alliances Revealed: A Review of the Magic: The
   Gathering Alliances Edition
The Art of Limited Formats for Magic: The
   Gathering
Baxter on Magic: A Guide to Proper Playing
   Techniques for Magic: The Gathering
Deep Magic: Advanced Strategies for Experienced
   Players of Magic: The Gathering
Dominating Dominia: A Type II Tournament
   Player's Guide for Magic: The Gathering
Dominating Dominia II
Magic Cards Simplified: For Player Parents and
   Beginners of Magic: The Gathering
Mastering Legend of the Five Rings
Mastering Middle-earth: Strategies for
   Middle-earth: The Wizards
Mastering Netrunner
Mastering Portal
Mirage Revealed: A Review of the Mirage Edition
   of Magic: The Gathering
Pro Magic: The Art of Professional Deck
   Construction
Single Card Strategies for Magic: The Gathering
Stronghold Revealed: A Review of the Stronghold
   Edition of Magic: The Gathering
The Tables of Magic: The Ultimate Reference
   Guide to Magic: The Gathering
Tempest Revealed: A Review of the Tempest
   Edition of Magic: The Gathering
Tournament Reports for Magic: The Gathering
Visions Revealed: A Review of the Visions Edition
   of Magic: The Gathering
Weatherlight Revealed: A Review of the
   Weatherlight Edition of Magic: The Gathering

CD Usage License Agreement

Please read the following CD usage license agreement before opening the CD and using the contents therein:

1. By opening the accompanying software package, you are indicating that you have read and agree to be bound by all terms and conditions of this CD usage license agreement.

2. The compilation of code and utilities contained on the CD are copyrighted and protected by both U.S. copyright law and international copyright treaties, and is owned by Wordware Publishing. Individual source code, example programs, help files, freeware, shareware, utilities, and evaluation packages, including their copyrights, are owned by the respective authors.

3. No part of the enclosed CD, including all source code, help files, shareware, freeware, utilities, example programs, or evaluation programs, may be made available on a public forum (such as a World Wide Web page, FTP site, bulletin board, or Internet news group) without the express written permission of Wordware Publishing or the author of the respective source code, help files, shareware, freeware, utilities, example programs, or evaluation programs.

4. You may not decompile, reverse engineer, disassemble, create a derivative work, or otherwise use the enclosed programs, help files, freeware, shareware, utilities, or evaluation programs except as stated in this agreement.

5. The software contained on the CD is sold without warranty of any kind. Wordware Publishing and the authors specifically disclaim all other warranties, express or implied, including but not limited to implied warranties of merchantability and fitness for a particular purpose with respect to defects in the disk, the program, source code, sample files, help files, freeware, shareware, utilities, and evaluation programs contained therein, and/or the techniques described in the book and implemented in the example programs. In no event shall Wordware Publishing, its dealers, its distributors, or the authors be liable or held responsible for any loss of profit or any other alleged or actual private or commercial damage, including but not limited to special, incidental, consequential, or other damages.

6. One (1) copy of the CD or any source code therein may be created for backup purposes. The CD and all accompanying source code, sample files, help files, freeware, shareware, utilities, and evaluation programs may be copied to your hard drive. With the exception of freeware and shareware programs, at no time can any part of the contents of this CD reside on more than one computer at one time. The contents of the CD can be copied to another computer, as long as the contents of the CD contained on the original computer are deleted.

7. You may not include any part of the CD contents, including all source code, example programs, shareware, freeware, help files, utilities, or evaluation programs in any compilation of source code, utilities, help files, example programs, freeware, shareware, or evaluation programs on any media, including but not limited to CD, disk, or Internet distribution, without the express written permission of Wordware Publishing or the owner of the individual source code, utilities, help files, example programs, freeware, shareware, or evaluation programs.

8. You may use the source code, techniques, and example programs in your own commercial or private applications unless otherwise noted by additional usage agreements as found on the CD.

On the CD-ROM

The companion CD-ROM that accompanies this book is a multimedia experience containing all of the source code from the book, a complete Delphi syntax compliant help file, shareware, freeware, and an assortment of third-party development and evaluation tools. Using the CD browser you can navigate through the CD and choose which applications and chapter code to install with a single mouse click. Using the CD browser is simple; on a Windows 95 or Windows NT system, simply insert the CD and the browser will begin automatically.

Install Software allows you to install software included on the CD-ROM. Chapter Code allows you to install Delphi code included on the CD-ROM. API-Help Launch allows you to install the API Help file included on the CD-ROM. The help provides a nice companion to Delphi's help files, however, it is not a direct replacement for the Win32 SDK help file that ships with Delphi. In many cases, the Win32 help file will contain additional information that was impractical to include in the book or the help file.

NOTE: The CD browser requires a minimum of 256-color operation and a screen resolution of at least 640x480. Higher resolutions are recommended but not required for optimum viewing. Please review the system requirements for each individual application before installing the software. A description is provided along with system requirements for each application. All evaluation versions are capable of creating actual products, but in a limited form.

782055